Learning to Understand Remote Sensing Images

Learning to Understand Remote Sensing Images

Special Issue Editor

Qi Wang

MDPI • Basel • Beijing • Wuhan • Barcelona • Belgrade

Special Issue Editor
Qi Wang
Northwestern Polytechnical University
China

Editorial Office
MDPI
St. Alban-Anlage 66
4052 Basel, Switzerland

This is a reprint of articles from the Special Issue published online in the open access journal *Remote Sensing* (ISSN 2072-4292) from 2017 to 2018 (available at: https://www.mdpi.com/journal/remotesensing/special_issues/rsimages)

For citation purposes, cite each article independently as indicated on the article page online and as indicated below:

LastName, A.A.; LastName, B.B.; LastName, C.C. Article Title. *Journal Name* **Year**, *Article Number, Page Range*.

Volume 1
ISBN 978-3-03897-684-4 (Pbk)
ISBN 978-3-03897-685-1 (PDF)

Volume 1-2
ISBN 978-3-03897-700-1 (Pbk)
ISBN 978-3-03897-701-8 (PDF)

Contents

About the Special Issue Editor

Qi Wang, Professor, received his B.E. degree in automation and the Ph.D. degree in pattern recognition and intelligent systems from the University of Science and Technology of China, Hefei, China, in 2005 and 2010, respectively. He is currently a Professor with the School of Computer Science and the Center for OPTical IMagery Analysis and Learning (OPTIMAL), Northwestern Polytechnical University, Xi'an, China. His research interests include computer vision and pattern recognition.

Preface to "Learning to Understand Remote Sensing Images"

Accurate and efficient understanding of remote sensing data is an increasingly important issue which can make significant contributions to global environmental analysis and economic development. In this book, we introduce the challenges and advanced techniques in the field of remote sensing image understanding. This area has attracted a lot of research interest, and significant progress has been made during the past years, particularly in the optical, hyperspectral, and microwave remote sensing communities.

Our topic mainly focuses on learning to understand remote sensing images. We discuss some critical problems in major practical applications including image classification, object detection, image segmentation, image correction, hyperspectral unmixing, change detection, etc. We report the state-of-the-art of machine learning techniques and statistical computing methods to analyze remote sensing data, such as deep learning, graphical models, sparse coding, and kernel machines.

Throughout this book, it is assumed that the readers have a basic background in machine learning and remote sensing. We believe the reported advanced techniques can provide considerable value for researchers in teaching and scientific research.

This book is published with the tireless efforts of countless contributors. We thank each author for sharing their research findings with us. We thank the editors and the publishers for their time and support. We hope that through our efforts, more people can contribute to the development of remote sensing.

Qi Wang
Special Issue Editor

Article

Deep Salient Feature Based Anti-Noise Transfer Network for Scene Classification of Remote Sensing Imagery

Xi Gong [1,2], **Zhong Xie** [1,2], **Yuanyuan Liu** [1,*], **Xuguo Shi** [1] **and Zhuo Zheng** [1]

1   Department of Information Engineering, China University of Geosciences, Wuhan 430075, China; gongxi_cug@126.com (X.G.); xiezhong@cug.edu.cn (Z.X.); shixg@cug.edu.cn (X.S.); zhuozheng_2017@163.com (Z.Z.)
2   National Engineering Research Center of Geographic Information System, Wuhan 430075, China
*   Correspondence: liuyy@cug.edu.cn; Tel.: +86-133-4983-0890

Received: 16 January 2018; Accepted: 1 March 2018; Published: 6 March 2018

Abstract: Remote sensing (RS) scene classification is important for RS imagery semantic interpretation. Although tremendous strides have been made in RS scene classification, one of the remaining open challenges is recognizing RS scenes in low quality variance (e.g., various scales and noises). This paper proposes a deep salient feature based anti-noise transfer network (DSFATN) method that effectively enhances and explores the high-level features for RS scene classification in different scales and noise conditions. In DSFATN, a novel discriminative deep salient feature (DSF) is introduced by saliency-guided DSF extraction, which conducts a patch-based visual saliency (PBVS) algorithm using "visual attention" mechanisms to guide pre-trained CNNs for producing the discriminative high-level features. Then, an anti-noise network is proposed to learn and enhance the robust and anti-noise structure information of RS scene by directly propagating the label information to fully-connected layers. A joint loss is used to minimize the anti-noise network by integrating anti-noise constraint and a softmax classification loss. The proposed network architecture can be easily trained with a limited amount of training data. The experiments conducted on three different scale RS scene datasets show that the DSFATN method has achieved excellent performance and great robustness in different scales and noise conditions. It obtains classification accuracy of 98.25%, 98.46%, and 98.80%, respectively, on the UC Merced Land Use Dataset (UCM), the Google image dataset of SIRI-WHU, and the SAT-6 dataset, advancing the state-of-the-art substantially.

Keywords: scene classification; saliency detection; deep salient feature; anti-noise transfer network; DSFATN

1. Introduction

Many RS images have been accumulated due to the rapid development of Remote Sensing (RS) sensors and imaging techniques. The interpretation of such huge amount of RS imagery is a challenging task of significant sense for disaster monitoring, urban planning, traffic controlling and so on [1–5]. RS scene classification, which aims at automatically classifying extracted sub-regions of the scenes into a set of semantic categories, is an effective method for RS image interpreting [6,7]. However, the complex spatial arrangement and the variety of surface objects in RS scenes make the classification quite challenging, especially for scenes in low quality (e.g., various scales and noises), since their within-class differences are more indistinct and between-class similarity are more distinct. How to automatically recognize and represent the RS scene from these different scale and quality RS image data effectively has become a critical task. To deal with such a challenge, this paper proposes a deep salient feature based anti-noise transfer network (DSFATN) approach that effectively enhances and explores the high-layer features for RS scene classification in different scales and noise conditions with great efficiency and robustness.

Many attempts have been made for RS scene classification. Among various previous approach, the bag-of-visual-words (BoVW) based models have drawn much attention for their good performance [1,8–10]. The BoVW based models encode local invariant features of an image and represent the image as a histogram of visual word occurrences. However, the BoVW based models utilize a collection of local features, which may not fully exploit the spatial layouts information thus result in information loss [11]. To solve the problem, the spatial pyramid matching kernel (SPMK) [12] introduced the spatial layout to form improved local features. Even though SPMK shows inspiring results, it only considers the absolute spatial arrangement of visual words. Thus, the improved version of SPMK, spatial co-occurrence kernel (SCK) [1], and its pyramidal version spatial pyramid co-occurrence kernel (SPCK) [13], were proposed to capture both absolute and relative spatial arrangements. Other alternative models, e.g., latent Dirichlet allocation (LDA) model [14–16] and the probabilistic latent semantic analysis (pLSA) model [17,18], represent the image scene as a finite random mixture of topics and obtain competitive performance. In general, these approaches have made some achievements in RS scene classification but demand prior knowledge in handcrafted feature extraction, which is still opening challenging task in scene classification.

Recently, deep learning (DL) methods have achieved dramatic improvements and state-of–the-art performance in many fields (e.g., image recognition [19], object detection [20,21], and image synthesis [22]) due to automatic high-level feature representations from images and powerful ability of abstraction. DL methods also draw much attention in RS image classification [23,24]. For example, Lu et al. [25] proposed a discriminative representation for high spatial resolution remote sensing image by utilizing a shallow weighted deconvolution network and spatial pyramid model (SPM), and classified the representation vector by support vector machine (SVM). Chen et al. [26] utilized the single-layer restricted Boltzmann machine (RBM) and multilayer deep belief network (DBN) based model to learn the shallow and deep features of hyperspectral data, the learnt features can be used in logistic regression to achieve the hyperspectral data classification. As one of the most popular DL approaches, convolutional neural networks (CNNs) show incomparable superiority on several benchmark datasets such as Imagenet [27], and have been widely used in the recognition, detection tasks and obtained impressive results [28–30]. However, training a powerful CNN is complicated since many labeled training samples and techniques are needed, while the available labeled RS scene datasets are not comparable to any natural scene dataset. For example, compared with the dataset ImageNet containing 15 million labeled images in 22,000 classes, the most famous and widely used UC Merced Land Use (UCM) [1] RS scene dataset only contains 21 classes and 2100 label images.

To address the data limitation, an effective strategy is data augmentation. It generates more training image samples by adding rotated, flipped versions and random cropped, stretched patches of the training images [31,32], or patches sampled by some optimized strategy [11,33]. Another effective strategy is transfer learning based on a pre-trained CNN model. Castelluccio et al. [34] fine-tuned the pre-trained CNNs on the UCM dataset. The best result reached 97.10% when fine-tuning the GoogLeNet [35] while training a GoogLeNet from scratch just reached 91.2%. Penatti et al. [36] and Hu et al. [37] investigated the deep features extracted from different pre-trained CNNs for RS scene representation and classification, and proved the effectiveness and superiority of the features from the 1st full-connected layer of CNNs. The features extracted from pre-trained CNNs also have some invariance to small-scale deformations, larger-scale and so on [38,39]. Compared with training a new CNN, transfer learning methods are faster and the classification results are much promising without large amount of training data. It is known that most of the pre-trained CNNs have been trained in dataset with large number of natural images such as ImageNet. In natural image scenes, the objects are almost centrally focused, and the center pixels have more influence on the image semantic labels [11], while, in RS image scenes, the surface objects are usually distributed randomly, and the central parts may not relate closely with the semantic label. Hence, due to the objects distributions difference between natural scenes and RS scenes, the pre-trained CNNs based on transfer learning method is applicable for a limit amount of training date but lacks robustness to low quality variance (e.g., various scales and noises) in RS scene classification.

To address the challenging task, we propose a deep salient feature based anti-noise transfer network (DSFATN) for classification of RS scenes with different scales and various noises. Our method aims at improving both feature representation of RS scene and classification accuracy. In DSFATN, a novel deep salient feature (DSF) and an anti-noise transfer network are introduced to suppress the influences of different scales and noise variances. The saliency-guided DSF extraction conducts a patch-based visual saliency (PBVS) algorithm to guide pre-trained CNNs for producing the discriminative high-level DSF. It compensates the affect caused by objects distribution difference between natural scenes and RS scenes, thus makes the DSF extracted exactly from the most relevant, informative and representative patches of the RS scene related to its category. The anti-noise transfer network is trained to learn and enhance the robust and anti-noise structure information of RS scene by minimizing a joint loss. DSFATN performs excellent with RS scenes in different scales and qualities, even with noise.

The major contributions of this paper are as follows:

- We propose a novel DSF representation using "visual attention" mechanisms. DSF can achieve discriminative high-level feature representation learnt from pre-trained CNN for the RS scenes.
- An anti-noise transfer network is improved to learn and enhance the robust and anti-noise structure information of RS scene, where a joint loss is used to minimize the network by considering anti-noise constraint and softmax classification loss. The simple architecture of the anti-noise transfer network makes it easier to be trained with the limited availability of training data.
- The proposed DSFATN is evaluated on several public RS scene classification benchmarks. The significant performance demonstrated our method is of great robustness and efficiency in various scales, occlusions, and noise conditions and advanced the state-of-the-arts methods.

This paper is organized as follows. In Section 2, we illustrate the proposed DSFATN method in detail. In Section 3, we introduce the experimental data and protocol, provide the performance of the proposed DSFATN and discuss the influence of serval factors. Section 4 concludes the paper with a summary of our method.

2. The Proposed DSFATN Method

2.1. Framework of DSFATN

DSFATN consists of two main steps, as shown in Figure 1.

1. **Saliency-guided DSF extraction**: To achieve discriminative high-level feature representation for RS scenes, we introduce saliency-guided DSF extraction. Instead of using the whole RS scene for feature extraction, saliency-guided DSF extraction produces a novel DSF representation based on saliency-guided RS scene patches using "visual attention" mechanisms. First, we conduct an improved patch-based visual saliency (PBVS) method to detect salient region and sample multi-scales salient patches in an image. Next, the multi-scales salient patches are fed to a pre-trained CNN model to extract the DSF. The saliency-guided DSF extraction ensures the most informative and representative parts are definitely centrally focused in the salient patches. Compared with randomly or densely sampling methods, the saliency-guided sampling is also more targeted and effective. The different scales of the salient patches also help to improve the scale invariance of DSF in the anti-noise transfer network training process.

2. **Anti-noise transfer network based classification**: To suppress the influences of various scales and noises of RS scenes, an anti-noise transfer network is trained as the classifier successively. It introduces an anti-noise layer to tackle with DSFs extracted from RS scene patches in low quality

even with various noises. Except for the anti-noise layer, the anti-noise transfer network only has a fully-connected (FC) layer and a softmax layer, which is a simple CNN architecture and can be trained easily. Different from the traditional CNN model, we optimize a new objective function to train the anti-noise transfer network by imposing an anti-noise constraint, which enforces the training samples before and after adding noises to share the similar features. Meanwhile, for anti-noise transfer network learning, the input scenes contain origin scenes and scenes with various noises, such as: (1) salt and pepper noise; (2) partial occlusions; and (3) their mixed noise. The whole framework works perfectly on three different scale RS scene datasets and even outperforms the state-of-the-art methods.

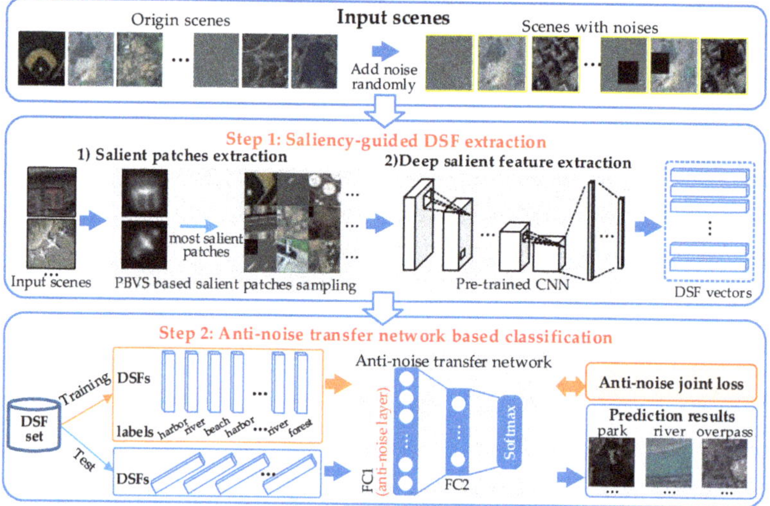

Figure 1. The framework of deep salient feature based anti-noise transfer network (DSFATN) contains two main steps: saliency-guided deep salient feature (DSF) extraction and anti-noise transfer network based classification. The saliency-guided DSF extraction conducts a patch-based visual saliency (PBVS) to guide pre-trained convolutional neural networks (CNNs) for producing the discriminative high-level DSF for remote sensing (RS) scene with different scale and various noises. Then, the anti-noise transfer network is trained to learn and enhance the robust and anti-noise structure information of RS scene by minimizing a joint loss. For anti-noise learning, the input scenes include origin scenes and scenes with various noises (e.g., salt and pepper, occlusions and mixtures).

2.2. Saliency-Guided DSF Extraction

The saliency-guided DSF extraction provides the effective and discriminative high-level features from the most relevant scene patches using "visual attention" mechanisms. This extraction is inspired by the human visual system which interprets complex scenes in real time to get most relevant features of the scenes and reduce the complexity of scene analysis [40]. It also can be divided into two steps (Figure 1): (1) salient patch extraction; and (2) DSF extraction. The first step provides the scene patches sampled from the salient regions of input RS scenes. Inspired by graph-based visual saliency (GBVS) [41,42] method, we introduce a patch-based visual saliency (PBVS) algorithm to support the salient patch extractor. The second step is mainly accomplished by a pre-trained CNN, i.e., VGG-19 [19], where the 4096-dimensional activations of the first FC layer are used as the final DSFs.

2.2.1. Salient Patch Extraction

We improved the PBVS method for salient patch extraction. Different from traditional GBVS algorithm which can only detect the salient region from an image, our PBVS can provide multi-scales salient patches of the image. PBVS can be organized into the following procedures: (1) salient region detection; and (2) salient patch extraction. Figure 2 shows the flowchart of the PBVS based salient patch extraction. The details are described in the following section.

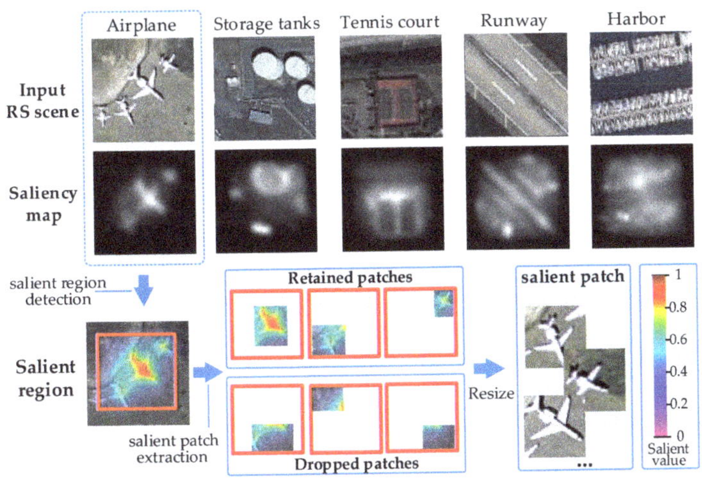

Figure 2. The flowchart of PBVS based salient patch extraction. The brightness in the saliency map indicates the salient level of the corresponding parts in the input RS scenes: brighter in saliency map, more salient in RS scene. The overlay of RS scene and saliency map make the salient level reflected in the input RS scene, the bigger salient value corresponds higher salient level. The red rectangle is the salient region of the scene.

(1) **Salient region detection.** Given a set of n scenes $S = \{s_1, s_2, \cdots, s_n\}$. For expository simplicity, suppose arbitrarily RS scene $s \in S$ is a square image of size $n \times n$. At first step, PBVS extracts feature vectors at locations over s to form the feature map of $M^s_{Fea} : n \times n \to \mathbb{R}$, $M^s_{Fea}(i,j)(1 \leq i \leq n, 1 \leq j \leq n)$ is the value of locations (i,j) in M^s_{Fea}. The dissimilarity between $M^s_{Fea}(i,j)$ and $M^s_{Fea}(p,q)$ is defined as

$$d((i,j)||(p,q)) := \left| \log \frac{M^s_{Fea}(i,j)}{M^s_{Fea}(p,q)} \right| \tag{1}$$

Then, the activation map M^s_{Act} of s needs to be formed. By connecting every node of the feature map M^s_{Fea}, the fully connected directed graph $graph_{Act}$ is obtained. The directed edge from node (i,j) to node (p,q) of $graph_{Act}$ is assigned a weight, as shown in Equation (2). σ is a free parameter that is set to approximately 1/10 to 1/5 of the map width because it has been proven the results were not very sensitive to perturbations around these values. Then, the $graph_{Act}$ is treated as a Markov chain to compute the equilibrium distribution namely get the activation map M^s_{Act}. More details can be found in [41].

$$w_{Act}((i,j)||(p,q)) := d((i,j)||(p,q)) \cdot \exp\left(-\frac{(i-p)^2 + (j-q)^2}{2\sigma^2} \right) \tag{2}$$

Then, activation map M^s_{Act} will be normalized to get the normalization map M^s_{Nor}. Similar to the process of forming M^s_{Act}, another graph $graph_{Nor}$ can be constructed based on activation map M^s_{Act}, but the weight assigned to the edges is defined as Equation (3). Again, a Markov chain on $graph_{Nor}$ is obtained to help obtain the normalization map namely the final saliency map M^s_{Sal}. If multiple activations were generated, these maps will be combined into one saliency map M^s_{Sal} after normalization.

$$w_{\text{Nor}}\big((i,j)\|(p,q)\big) := M^I_{\text{Act}}(p,q)\cdot\exp\left(-\frac{(i-p)^2+(j-q)^2}{2\sigma^2}\right) \tag{3}$$

(2) **Salient patch extraction**. The Salient patch extraction provides multi-scales salient patches from the salient region. As shown in Figure 2, if an object is salient in the image, the corresponding location of its saliency map is high-lighted with bigger salient values. In an image, the salient values of its saliency map range from [0, 1], where 1 indicates the current location in the corresponding RS scene is the most salient, and 0 corresponds to the most non-salient. By finding the minimum bounding rectangle (MBR) [43] of the nonzero salient values in the saliency map M^s_{Sal}, we primarily determine a salient region r_s of RS scene s. Then, α patches will be sampled from r_s by an iterative sampling procedure, where α is the threshold of patches' number. The size of the patch can be scaled as the random rate from 30% to 80% of the salient region. The iterative sampling procedure prefers to sample the patches with bigger salient values in their central boxes, where the central box is defined as the central rectangle region of the sampled patch with its half width and height. In this work, we regard [0.8, 1] as the preferred salient value range γ to conduct the sampling process. Algorithm 1 shows the iterative sampling procedure for RS image scene s. At each iteration, a patch is randomly sampled in the salient region. If its salient values in the central box are all within the preferred salient value range γ, this patch should be considered as the salient patch and be kept, otherwise it should be dropped. The iteration will be continued until α patches with different scales are sampled. In our work, we set $\alpha = 9$, and the influence of α will be discussed in Section 3.5.4.

Algorithm 1. The iterative sampling procedure.

Input: Salient region r_s of RS image scene s
Output: P $= \{p_1, p_2, \ldots, p_\alpha\}$

  1:    Initialization:
  2:        set salient patch set P $= \{\varnothing\}$
  3:        set salient patches' number $n_{\text{patch}} = 0$
  4:    **Iterations:**
  5:    **while** $(n < \alpha)$
  6:        randomly sampled a patch p_{tmp} in r_s
  7:    if (each salient value $v \in \gamma$ in central box)
  8:        put p_{tmp} to P and note p_{tmp} as $p_{n_{\text{patch}}+1}$ in P
  9:        $n_{\text{patch}} = n_{\text{patch}} + 1$
10:    **Return P** $= \{p_1, p_2, \ldots, p_\alpha\}$

2.2.2. DSF Extraction

After selecting the training patches, we employed the VGG-19 architecture [19] (Figure 3) pre-trained with the ImageNet dataset to derive DSF representation. Additionally, we have compared different pre-trained CNN models in the Experimental Section and showed that VGG-19 performed the best. VGG-19 is one of the very deep CNN models proposed by Simonyan et al. [19]. Hu et al. [37] compared the performance of the activation vectors from different layers of the model, and found the activation vectors from the 1st FC layer are more capable to represent the image feature. Hence, the 4096-dimensional activation vector from the 1st FC layer of VGG-19 is adopted for deep salient feature representation in the case.

The pre-trained VGG-19 model includes 16 convolutional layers, five maxpool layers and three FC layers. When the multi-scales salient patches are fed to VGG-19 and preprocessed to the size of 224×224, the DSF can be extracted on the 1st FC layer. Supposing a set of n scenes $S = \{s_1, s_2, \cdots, s_n\}$, the t-th DSF vector can be described as:

$$d_t = f\big(h_j(\phi_k(s_t), \alpha)\big)\, (\, k \in \{0, 1, 2, 3\},\, j \leq \alpha\,), \tag{4}$$

where $\phi_k(s_t)$ returns scene s_t added with the k-th kind of noises (see Figure 1) and $k = 0$ means none noise is added. PBVS function $h_j(\cdot)$ returns the j-th salient patch of the corresponding scene. α is the threshold of sampled salient patches, as described in Section 2.2.1. f defines the deep feature extraction from the 1-st FC layer from VGG-19.

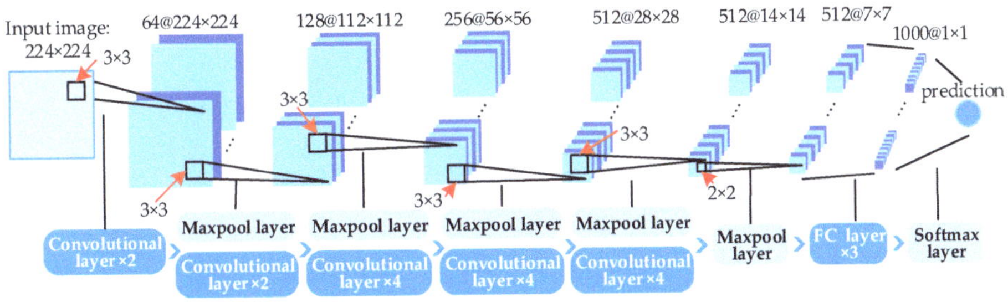

Figure 3. The architecture of the very deep CNN with 19 layers (VGG-19)

2.3. Anti-Noise Transfer Network Based Classification

Different from the traditional CNN models, an anti-noise transfer network is introduced to deal with the 4096-dimensional DSF vectors, as shown in Figure 4. The anti-noise transfer network is designed with simple architecture that can be trained easily with limited availability of the training data. It works well for DSFs of different RS scenes even with lower quality due to the anti-noise layer. The anti-noise layer imposes an anti-noise constraint to enforce the training samples before and after adding noises to share the similar output features. Thus, it can produce more robust and discriminative scene features to make the classification easier. Combining the anti-noise constraint to the softmax classification loss function, the anti-noise transfer network is learned by minimizing a joint loss, which is very different from the training of the traditional CNN models. The architecture and loss function of the anti-noise transfer network is described in detail below.

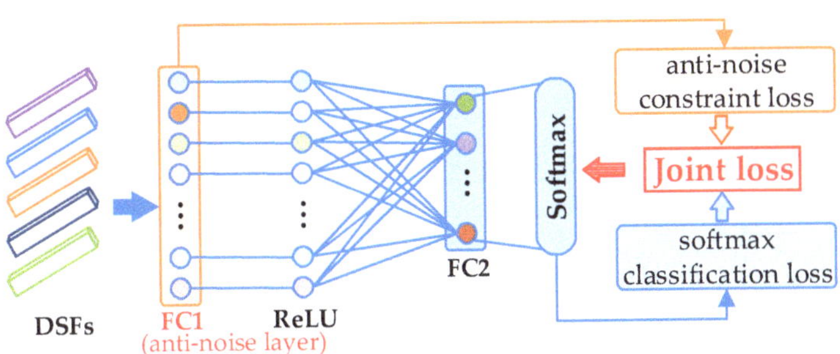

Figure 4. The anti-noise transfer network.

2.3.1. DSF Based Anti-Noise Transfer Network Architecture

As Figure 4 demonstrates, the anti-noise transfer network consists of two FC layers named FC1 and FC2 and a softmax layer, where rectified linear units (ReLU) [44] function is adopted to activate the output of FC1. FC1 and FC2 generate 4096-dimensional and N-dimensional vectors, respectively. N is the category number of the dataset. FC2 transfers the output vector of FC1 into N-dimensional vector thus it can be processed by softmax to produce the final classification results. The 4096-dimensional input DSF vector d_t will be fed to anti-noise layer FC1 and activated by ReLU as:

$$o_{FC1}(d_t) = \sigma(\mathbf{W}_{FC1}d_t + b_{FC1}), \tag{5}$$

where $\sigma(x) = (0, x)$ is the ReLU function, $\boldsymbol{b}_{FC1}$ is the bias. Since the output of FC1 is 4096-dimensional, the weights $\mathbf{W}_{FC1} \in \boldsymbol{R}^{4096 \times 4096}$. Analogously, $\boldsymbol{o}_{FC1}(\boldsymbol{d}_t)$ will be processed by FC2 and the last softmax layer as follows:

$$\boldsymbol{o}_{FC2}(\boldsymbol{d}_t) = \varphi(\mathbf{W}_{FC2}\boldsymbol{d}_t + \boldsymbol{b}_{FC2}), \tag{6}$$

where $\varphi(x) = e^x / \sum e^x$ is the softmax function, $\boldsymbol{b}_{FC2}$ is the bias. $\boldsymbol{o}_{FC2}(\boldsymbol{d}_t)$ is N-dimensional, N equals the category number of scene categories, thus the weights $\mathbf{W}_{FC2} \in \boldsymbol{R}^{4096 \times N}$. $\boldsymbol{o}_{FC2}(\boldsymbol{d}_t)$ is also the final output of the transfer network T_{net}. Setting $y_i = \boldsymbol{o}_{FC2}(\boldsymbol{d}_t, i)$, where $\boldsymbol{o}_{FC2}(\boldsymbol{d}_t, i)$ is the i-th element of $\boldsymbol{o}_{FC2}(\boldsymbol{d}_t)$, the final prediction vector of $\boldsymbol{d}_t$ can be represented as $T_{net}(\boldsymbol{d}_t) = \{y_1, y_2, \ldots, y_N\}$, which indicates the probabilities of the corresponding DSF $\boldsymbol{d}_t$ belongs to each category. In the test phase, i-th category is the prediction label of $\boldsymbol{d}_t$ when y_i is the maximum element of $T_{net}(\boldsymbol{d}_t)$.

2.3.2. Joint Loss Function Learning

To suppress the influence of noises, we propose a joint loss function to improve the anti-noise capability of the transfer network, where an anti-noise constraint is imposed to enforce the training samples before and after adding noise to share similar features. More specifically, for each training RS scene s_t and its corresponding scene with the l-th noise $\phi_l(s_t) (l \in \{1, 2, 3\})$, their DSFs $\boldsymbol{d}_t^0$ and $\boldsymbol{d}_t^l$ are enforced to generate similar output features in the transfer network by the anti-noise layer FC1. To achieve this goal, the novel joint loss function is proposed to learn parameters. Given the training RS scene set $S_{tr} = \{s_t, \phi_l(s_t) | s_t \in S\}$, their DSF set can be obtained as $D_{tr} = \left\{ \boldsymbol{d}_t \middle| \boldsymbol{d}_t \in D^0 \cup D^l \right\}$, where D^0 is the DSF set of origin scenes (e.g., s_t) and D^l is the DSF set of corresponding scenes with the l-th ($l \in \{1, 2, 3\}$) noise (e.g., $\phi_2(s_t)$). Y_{tr} is the true label set of D_{tr}. The joint loss value L can be computed by:

$$L = loss(D_{tr}, Y_{tr}) + dis\left(D^0, D^l\right), \tag{7}$$

where the first term $loss(D_{tr}, Y_{tr})$ is the softmax classification loss function and the second term $dis\left(D^0, D^l\right)$ is the anti-noise constraint. The joint loss L is feedback for backpropagation update. Stochastic Gradient Descent (SGD) approach is employed here to solve the optimization problem, which is a widely used method for neural work training. By minimizing the joint loss value L, both the softmax classification loss and the distance between features extracted from training samples before and after adding noises are minimized.

The softmax classification loss is defined by Equation (8), where $y_{d_t} \in Y_{tr}$ is the true label of $\boldsymbol{d}_t$, the first term of Equation (8) is the cross-entropy loss of $\boldsymbol{d}_t$, the second term is the L2 regularization to avoid over-fitting for better performance [45], $\mathbf{W}_i = \{\mathbf{W}_{FC1}, \mathbf{W}_{FC2}\}$ is the weights of the anti-noise transfer network, and λ is the regularization coefficient, balance the weight between the two terms to be added, which is determined by the product of the weights decay.

$$loss(D_{tr}, Y_{tr}) = - \sum_{d_t \in D_{tr}} y_{d_t} \log(\boldsymbol{o}_{FC2}(\boldsymbol{d}_t)) + \frac{\lambda}{2}\|\mathbf{W}_i\|^2, \tag{8}$$

The anti-noise constraint is proposed to enforce the training DSFs before and after adding noises to share the similar output features extracted by FC1, which introduced as the anti-noise layer in the transfer network. We define the constraint term by measuring the distance between DSFs before and after adding noises as:

$$dis\left(D^0, D^l\right) = \frac{1}{M} \sum_{d_t^0 \in D^0} \|\boldsymbol{o}_{FC2}\left(\boldsymbol{d}_t^0\right) - \boldsymbol{o}_{FC2}\left(\boldsymbol{d}_t^l\right)\|^2, \tag{9}$$

where $\boldsymbol{d}_t^0 \in D^0$ and $\boldsymbol{d}_t^l \in D^l$ are extracted from one RS scene before and after adding the l-th ($l \in \{1, 2, 3\}$) noises. M is the number of D^0, namely half of the joint number of the training samples.

By incorporating Equations (10) and (11) into Equation (9), the joint loss value L is defined as:

$$L = - \sum_{d_t \in D_{tr}} y_{d_t} \log(o_{FC2}(d_t)) + \frac{\lambda}{2}\|\mathbf{W}_i\|^2 + \frac{1}{M} \sum_{d_t^0 \in D^0} \|o_{FC2}\left(d_t^0\right) - o_{FC2}\left(d_t^l\right)\|^2 \qquad (10)$$

3. Experiments and Analysis

3.1. Dataset and Experimental Protocol

Three different scale datasets are utilized; their specific categories are shown in Figure 5.

1. UC Merced Land Use Dataset [1] (UCM) is collected from the large aerial orthoimagery of USGS National Map Urban Area Imagery collection. There are 100 images for each of 21 classes. Each image measures 256×256 pixels, with a 1-ft spatial resolution.

2. The Google image dataset designed by RS_IDEA Group in Wuhan University (SIRI-WHU) [10] is acquired from Google Earth (Google Inc., Mountain View, CA, USA) and mainly covers urban areas in China. It contains 12 scene categories. Each class consists of 200 images with a size of 200×200 pixels and a spatial resolution of 2 m.

3. SAT-6 dataset [46] is extracted from the National Agriculture Imagery Program and consists of a total of 405,000 image patches of size 28×28 and covering six classes. We choose 200 images from each class for our experiments.

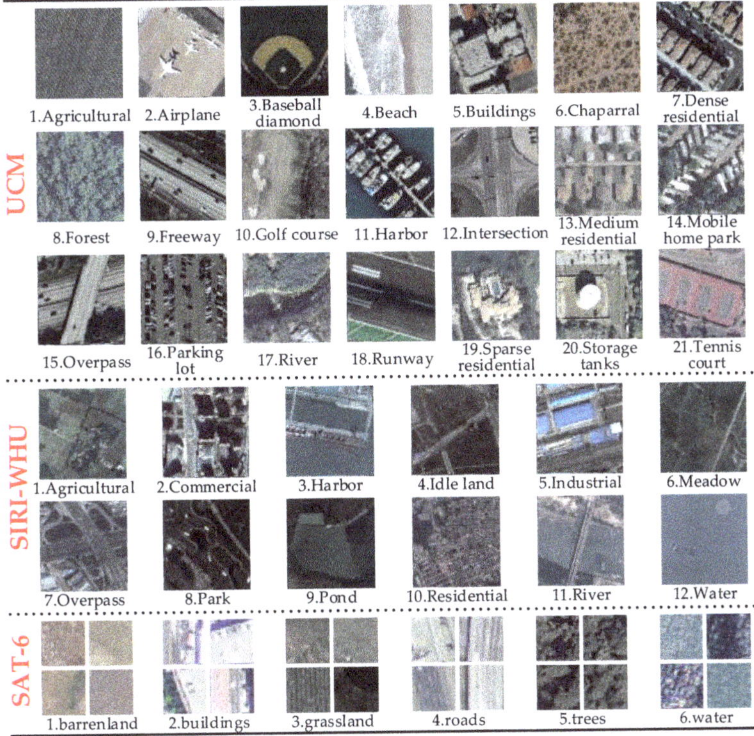

Figure 5. The categories sequences of the UC Merced Land Use Dataset (UCM), The Google image dataset designed by RS_IDEA Group in Wuhan University (SIRI-WHU) and the SAT-6 dataset: the numbers before the category names will be used to represent the corresponding categories in the experiments.

All experiments are implemented with a 4.0 GHz Intel Core i7-6700K CPU, and two 8 GB GeFore GTX 1080 GPUs. We carried out experiments with five-fold cross-validation protocol on each RS scene dataset. The training set contained 80% of the RS scenes for each class, and the remaining scenes were used for testing. The numbers of training and test images of each RS scene dataset are listed in Table 1. Moreover, in this paper, three kinds of noise-adding strategies are applied: (1) salt and pepper noise with fixed noise density 0.1; (2) partial occlusion at random position that covers 20–30% of the image; and (3) their mixed noise. In the mixed noise strategy, origin scenes, scenes with salt and pepper noise and scenes with partial occlusion account 1/3 of the total scenes, respectively. Although much fewer images are utilized in this work than benchmark datasets such as ImageNet, DSFATN performs in different scales and noise conditions with great efficiency and robustness.

Table 1. Training and test images' numbers of the three RS scene datasets.

	UCM	**SIRI-WHU**	**SAT-6**
Training	1680	1920	960
Test	420	480	240
Total	2100	2400	1200

We mainly analyze the performance of DSFATN by the following aspects: (a) the effectiveness and applicability of DSFATN on the three different datasets; (b) the representation ability of DSF; (c) the robustness of the model by the anti-noise layer learning; and (d) the influence factors including patches' number and pre-training models. Comparisons with the state-of-the-arts also demonstrate the superiority of our method.

3.2. Performance on Different Datasets

RS scenes from the three datasets employed in our experiments have a tremendous difference in image resolution and size. The UCM and SIRI-WHU datasets can provide different high-resolution RS scene images with proper image size, while the RS scenes from SAT-6 are really blurry with a quite small size. The diversity of the datasets can test DSFATN to the utmost.

(1) **UCM dataset.** We compared DSFATN with the state-of-the-arts such as the second extended spatial pyramid co-occurrence kernel (SPCK++) [13], pyramid-of-spatial-relations (PSR) [47], saliency-guided unsupervised feature learning (SG+UFL) [33] on the UCM dataset as shown in Table 2. Although most CNN methods can obtain results higher than 90%, especially the fine-tuning on GoogLeNet [34] get the second highest accuracy in the table, it is still 1.15% lower than the result of DSFATN. The CNN (including six convolutional layers and two FC layers) derived from [48] performs badly with the limited amount of data, while DSFATN deals with it well and obtains the highest accuracy, topping the accuracy of random forest (RF) [49] by almost 55%.

Table 2. Accuracy comparison of state-of-the-art methods and DSFATN on UCM dataset.

Rank	Methods	Accuracy (%)
1	RF [49]	44.77
2	CNN(6conv+2fc)	76.40
3	SPCK++ [13]	77.38
4	LDA [15]	81.92 ± 1.12
5	SG + UFL [33]	82.72 ± 1.18
6	PSR [47]	89.10
7	OverFeat [36]	90.91 ± 1.19
8	Caffe-Net [36]	93.42 ± 1.00
9	GoogLeNet [34]	97.10
10	**DSFATN**	**2**

Figure 6 displays the confusion matrix of DSFATN on the UCM dataset. Most scenes can be classified into the right category, especially, the 6th class chaparral whose accuracy equals 1. While the 20th class storage tanks, as the lowest accuracy owner, are mistaken for several other classes, particularly the 5th category buildings and 14th category mobile home park, which is reasonable since some storage tanks are located on the roofs of buildings. The accuracy of storage tanks is higher than 96%, and the whole classification accuracy of DSFATN on the UCM dataset is quite satisfactory.

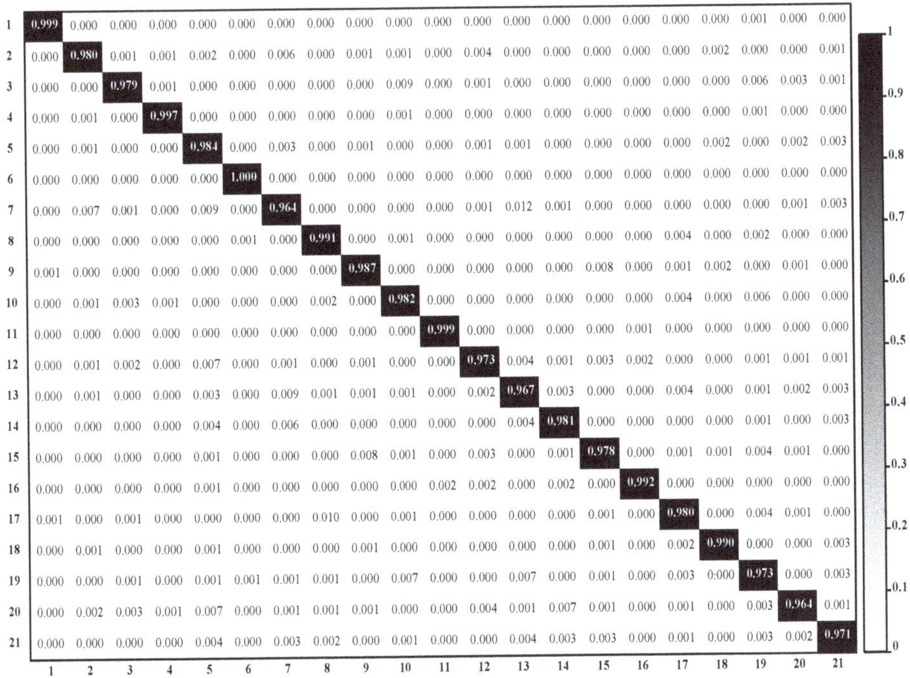

Figure 6. Confusion matrix of DSFATN on the UCM dataset: the horizontal and vertical axes represent the predict labels and true labels respectively. All categories obtain accuracy higher than 0.96.

(2) **SIRI-WHU dataset**. Table 3 shows the results of DSFATN and several compared methods such Spatial Pyramid Matching (SPM) [12] on the SIRI-WHU dataset. Similar to the results on the UCM dataset, DSFATN obtains a high classification result of over 98%. RF and CNN(6conv+2fc) obtain the higher results than the UCM dataset because the SIRI-WHU dataset has fewer categories and more images in each category. It is obvious that DSFATN outperforms the other methods. Moreover, Figure 7a is the confusion matrix of DSFATN on the SIRI-WHU dataset. The accuracy of each category is higher than 97%. The worst misclassification probability is resulted by the 3rd class harbor: 0.9% of the harbor scenes are mistaken for 12th class water. The reason is that these two classes both consist of ship and water. For the same reason, the majority of the confusion occurs among categories that have the same component parts. For example, both the 2nd class commercial and 10th class residential consist of buildings and roads, while both the 9th class pond and the 11th class river are mainly made up of water. All categories achieve accuracies of over 97%.

Table 3. Classification results on the SIRI-WHU dataset.

Methods	RF [49]	LDA [15]	CNN(6conv+2fc)	SPM [12]	DSFATN
Accuracy (%)	0	60.32 ± 1.20	78.20	77.69 ± 1.01	**98.46**

(a)

	1	2	3	4	5	6	7	8	9	10	11	12
1	0.996	0.000	0.000	0.000	0.000	0.003	0.000	0.000	0.001	0.000	0.000	0.000
2	0.000	0.988	0.001	0.002	0.002	0.000	0.001	0.003	0.001	0.004	0.000	0.000
3	0.000	0.003	0.975	0.001	0.003	0.001	0.001	0.000	0.000	0.001	0.006	0.009
4	0.002	0.002	0.001	0.979	0.006	0.004	0.001	0.001	0.001	0.002	0.001	0.000
5	0.000	0.001	0.000	0.003	0.993	0.001	0.001	0.001	0.000	0.001	0.000	0.000
6	0.000	0.000	0.002	0.003	0.000	0.983	0.001	0.006	0.004	0.000	0.001	0.001
7	0.000	0.000	0.002	0.001	0.000	0.001	0.993	0.002	0.000	0.002	0.000	0.000
8	0.003	0.002	0.000	0.002	0.000	0.004	0.002	0.981	0.006	0.001	0.000	0.000
9	0.002	0.000	0.002	0.002	0.001	0.004	0.001	0.003	0.977	0.000	0.008	0.000
10	0.000	0.008	0.001	0.002	0.003	0.001	0.002	0.002	0.000	0.980	0.001	0.000
11	0.000	0.001	0.008	0.004	0.001	0.001	0.001	0.003	0.006	0.000	0.974	0.002
12	0.000	0.000	0.002	0.000	0.000	0.000	0.000	0.000	0.001	0.000	0.001	0.996

(b)

	1	2	3	4	5	6
1	0.980	0.001	0.018	0.000	0.001	0.000
2	0.000	0.988	0.000	0.012	0.000	0.000
3	0.013	0.000	0.982	0.001	0.005	0.000
4	0.000	0.014	0.001	0.984	0.001	0.000
5	0.001	0.000	0.006	0.000	0.994	0.000
6	0.000	0.000	0.000	0.000	0.000	1.000

Figure 7. Confusion matrix of DSFATN on: (**a**) the SIRI-WHU dataset; and (**b**) the SAT-6 dataset. The horizontal and vertical axes represent the predict labels and true labels respectively.

(3) **SAT-6 dataset.** Note that the image scenes in the SAT-6 dataset are already salient patches with the dimension of 28 × 28 from RS imageries. Even though the image resolution and scale in the SAT-6 dataset are identically low, DSFATN obtains the average accuracy of 98.80%, as shown in Table 4. The experiments show the impressive representation ability of DSFATN for small scale image scenes. Figure 7b is the confusion matrix of DSFATN on the SAT-6 dataset. Compared with results of the UCM and SIRI-WHU datasets, the misclassification probabilities of the SAT-6 dataset are much higher due to the high similarity between the scenes in smaller scale. The majority of the confusion occurs between the 1st class barren-land and the 3rd class grassland, and the 2nd class buildings and the 4th class roads, because these two pairs of categories have similar color and texture distribution, e.g., the former pair of categories both consist of green grass and brown earth.

Table 4. Classification results on SIRI-WHU dataset.

Methods	RF [49]	CNN(6conv+2fc)	DeepSat [46]	DSFATN
Accuracy (%)	89.29	92.67	93.92	**91.96**

3.3. Representative Ability Comparison of Different Features

In this section, to demonstrate the discriminative ability of DSF, we compared the DSF with several different features including histogram of oriented gradients (HOG) [50], scale invariant feature transform (SIFT) [51], and local binary patterns (LBP) [52], as shown in Table 5. For CNN(6conv+2fc), we extract its activations from the 1st FC layer as the representation features. After obtaining these features, we simply implement scene classification by training a linear support vector machine (SVM) classifier with each kind of features.

Table 5. Classification results on three datasets with different features.

Features	UCM		SIRI-WHU		SAT-6	
	Accuracy (%)	Kappa	Accuracy (%)	Kappa	Accuracy (%)	Kappa
Raw image	33.10	0.3361	35.83	0.3469	87.08	0.8116
HOG [50]	52.14	0.4975	44.79	0.3977	57.92	0.4950
SIFT [51]	58.33	0.5625	53.96	0.4977	45.00	0.3400
LBP [52]	31.43	0.2800	46.25	0.4136	77.08	0.7250
CNN(6conv+2fc)	63.10	0.6424	60.42	0.5523	94.58	0.9188
DSF	98.07	0.9801	88.96	0.8766	96.25	0.9437

As Table 5 shows, no matter the accuracy or kappa coefficient, DSF obtained much higher results than other features on the three datasets. The high kappa values indicate the almost perfect coherence of DSF. On the UCM and SIRI-WHU datasets, the classification results of raw images are worse than the classification results of low-level features (e.g., HOG and LBP), and as expected both are worse than the classification results of high-level features extracted from CNNs including the CNN(6conv+2fc) feature and DSF. The raw images of SAT-6 perform much better than those low-level features owing to the characteristics of the SAT-6 dataset. The distinctive colors of the raw image in the SAT-6 dataset help a lot in the raw image classification but does not help in the low-level features extraction. Instead, the small image size and blurry image quality of SAT-6 image scenes make the low-level features extracted from raw images more unrepresentative. However, the features extracted from CNNs are discriminated, both the CNN(6conv+2fc) feature and DSF obtain accuracies over 90%. Especially the CNN(6conv+2fc) feature, although it does not perform well on the more complex UCM and SIRI-WHU datasets, it works quite well on the SAT-6 dataset due to the fewer categories and small RS scene image size of the SAT-6 dataset. The DSF performs more efficient and robust than the others in all three datasets.

Moreover, we embed the high-dimensional features to 2-D space by t-SNE [53], thus to visualize and compare the features extracted from these datasets. As shown in Figure 8, subfigures from top to bottom are the 2-D feature visualization images of HOG, LBP, SIFT, CNN(6conv+2fc) feature and DSF in order, and from left to right are the 2-D feature visualization images of the UCM, SIRI-WHU and SAT-6 datasets respectively. Each color in the images represents a category in the corresponding dataset. Obviously, the 2-D features of HOG, SIFT, and LBP are distributed disordered and only form very few clusters. In contrast, the 2-D features of DSF form clusters separated much clearly. Moreover, the 2-D features of CNN(6conv+2fc) also form more clusters than HOG, SIFT and LBP since the high-level features that contain more abstract semantic information than the low-level features. Notice that CNN(6conv+2fc) feature performs very well in the SAT-6 dataset, obtaining a high result of 94.58%, which very close to the result 96.25% obtained by DSF; this is also reflected in the 2-D feature visualization images, both kinds of features can form the main six clusters. Barren-land class, grassland class and trees class are very close to each other and have some overlap, since in the small scale and resolution SAT-6 dataset, these three categories all consist of soils and vegetation with different vegetation cover rate. The grassland has a middle vegetation plant cover rate; therefore, its features locate between features of barrenland and trees. The buildings class and the roads class have similar situations because the roof of the buildings and the roads are both mainly made up of cement concrete. Particularly, the water class is not similar to the five other categories, and the overlap between the grassland class and the water class in the CNN (6conv+2fc) situation turns out to be unreasonable. While the DSFATN discriminates the difference since the pink area that represents the water features locates far away from the five other categories. Moreover, compared with DSFATN, the CNN(6conv+2fc) feature generates more points that do not locate in the clusters they belong to. In general, DSF learns to be more discriminative.

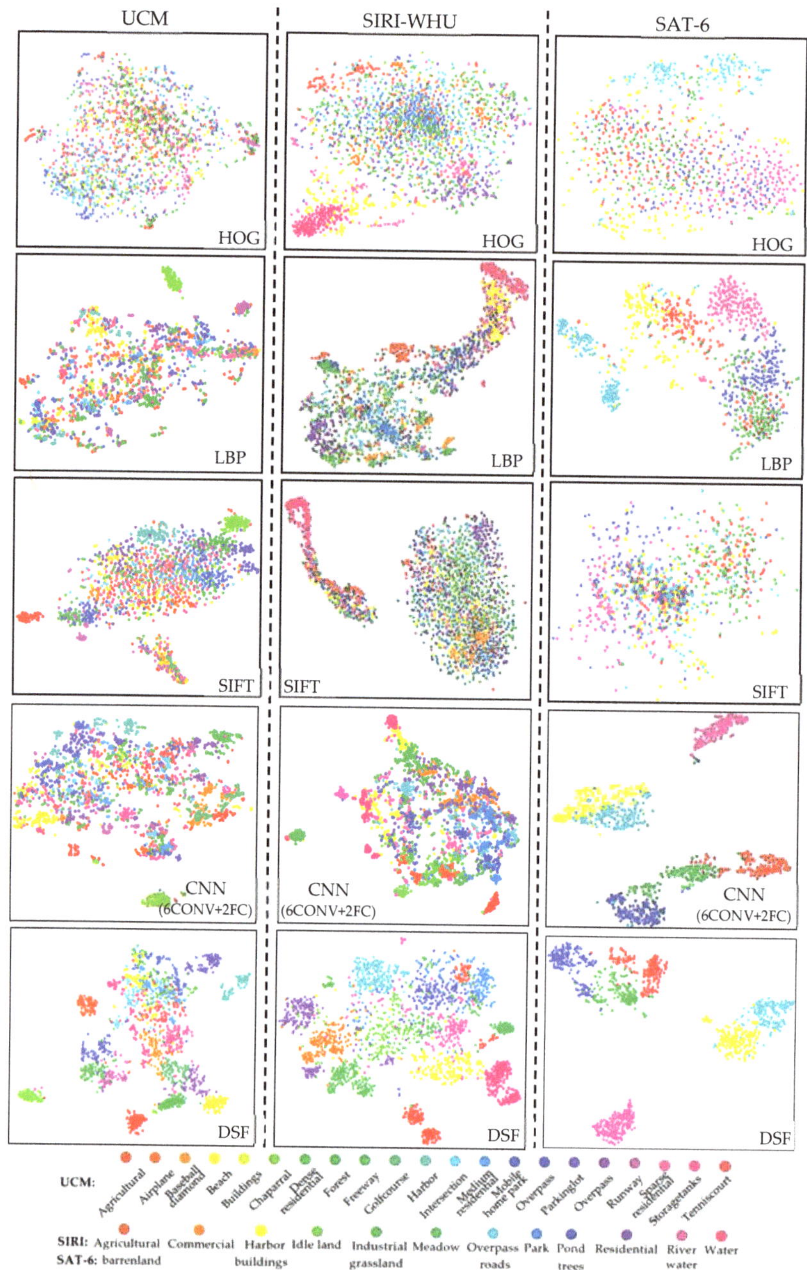

Figure 8. The comparison of different features on the three datasets by per-class two-dimensional feature visualization. From left to right: the UCM dataset, the SIRI-WHU dataset and the SAT-6 dataset. From top to bottom: histogram of oriented gradients (HOG), local binary patterns (LBP), scale invariant feature transform (SIFT), CNN(6conv+2fc) feature, and DSF. It is obvious that DSF (the last row) has more clearly separated clusters.

3.4. Evaluation of Image Distortion

In this section, we validate the robustness of DSFATN for two kinds image distortion conditions: (1) images with noises; and (2) images in different scales. In Section 3.2, we have already proven DSFATN worked well on the SAT-6 dataset which contains RS scenes in small scale and low resolution, thus, in this section, we perform the anti-noise tests on the UCM and SIRI-WHU datasets.

3.4.1. Evaluation of Noises

To validate the anti-noise ability of DSFATN, we compared DSFATN with several different methods under three kinds of noise. Particularly, to prove the indispensability and effectiveness of multi-scales salient patches and anti-noise layer, two variant models derived from DSFATN are introduced. Table 6 lists their difference with the proposed DSFATN. TN-1 refers to DSFATN without multi-scales salient patches sampling and anti-noise layer training. TN-2 refers to DSFATN without multi-scales salient patches sampling but with anti-noise layer training. The absence of anti-noise layer training is simply achieved by learning the joint loss without the anti-noise constraint.

Table 6. Difference between DSFATN and its variant compared models.

Model	Multi-Scales Salient Patch Sampling	Anti-Noise Layer Training
TN-1	×	×
TN-2	×	√
DSFATN	√	√

Table 7 compares the models on the UCM dataset and the SIRI-WHU dataset. Obviously, RF and CNN(6conv+2fc) have a very weak anti-noise property for obtaining accuracies less than 50% with all three kinds of noises, while the classification results of DSFATN are all above 95%. In particular, the result difference between TN-2 and DSFATN almost reaches 10%, which indicates the great importance of saliency patches sampling. Analogously, TN-1 has much worse results compared with TN-2, where the result difference even reaches 47.66% on the SIRI-WHU dataset with salt and pepper noise. The averaged result difference between TN-1 and TN-2 on the UCM and SIRI-WHU datasets with the three kinds of noises reaches 19.92%, which shows the effectiveness of anti-noise layer. As expected, on both the UCM and SIRI-WHU datasets, the results with the three kinds of noises rank in the order: TN-1 < TN-2 < DSFATN. This reflects the important role played by salient patches and the anti-noise layer.

Table 7. Classification results on the UCM dataset and SIRI-WHU dataset with three kinds of noises.

Model	Classification Accuracy (%)					
	UCM			SIRI-WHU		
	Salt and Pepper Noise	Partial Occlusion	Mixed Noise	Salt and Pepper Noise	Partial Occlusion	Mixed Noise
RF		0.0	0.0	0.0	0.0	0.0
CNN(6conv+2fc)	1.60	0.32.00	0.380	0.460	0.5520	0.66240
TN-1	-0.2	-0.04	-0.05	-0.06	-0.07	-0.08
TN-2	-0.4	88.76	88.33	83.83	52.1	84.79
DSFATN	**0.0**	**0.0**	**0.0**	**0.0**	**0.0**	**0.0**

Figure 9 shows the per-class accuracies of TN-1, TN-2, and DSFATN on the UCM and SIRI-WHU datasets with the three kinds of noises. Similar to the trend of the whole results, in most cases, the accuracies are in the following order: DSFATN > TN-2 > TN-1. It is interesting to find that TN-1 and TN-2 perform well in several classes with accuracies over 90%, which even equal or exceed the results of DSFATN, such as the 1st class agricultural, the 11th class harbor, the 16th class overpass, the 18th class runway of the UCM dataset and the 12th class water of the SIRI-WHU dataset. These scenes including duplicate texture information (e.g., ships, water, roads, and roads) make saliency detection confusing. Moreover, irrelevant objects (e.g., a ship in the water class scene) occasionally appearing misled the saliency detection results. Nevertheless, TN-1 and TN-2 behave poor in the other categories, and the corresponding accuracies dropped in different degrees. In general, on both the UCM and SIRI-WHU datasets, TN-2 obtains mediocre performance, better than TN-1 and worse than DSFATN, while TN-1 obtains quite uneven results—most of its results are below 80%. In sharp contrast to this is the stable performance of the DSFATN, which ensures most results are higher than 90%.

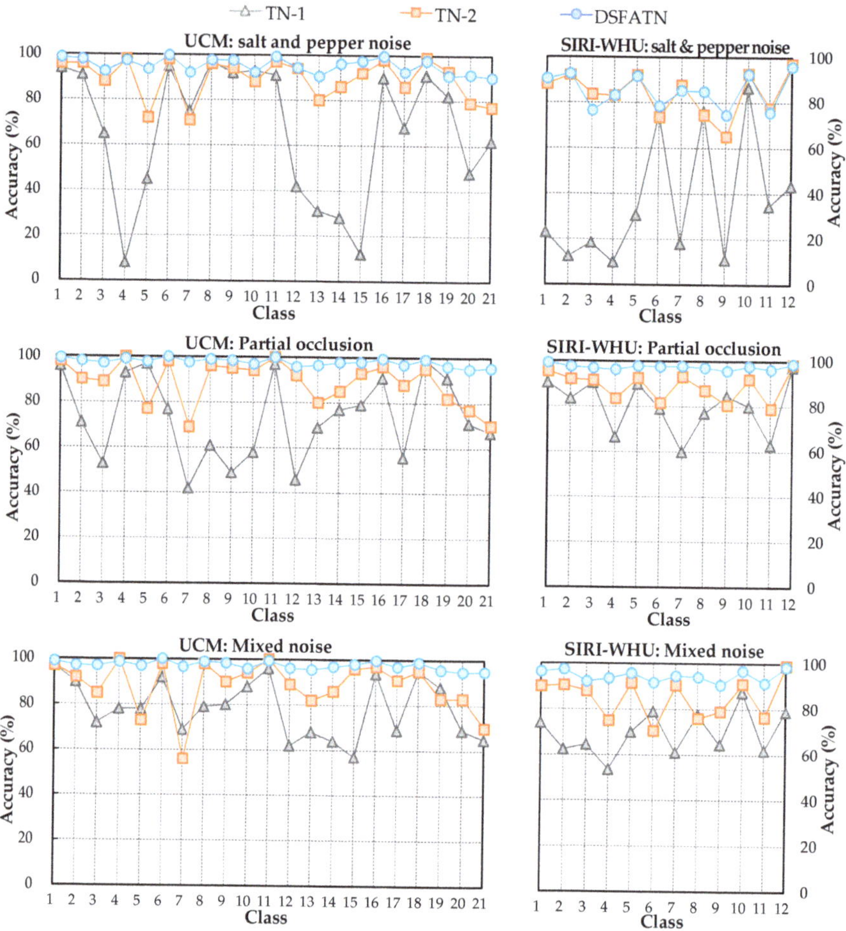

Figure 9. The per-class accuracy comparisons on: the UCM dataset with salt and pepper noise (**top left**); the SIRI-WHU dataset with salt and pepper noise (**top right**); the UCM dataset with partial occlusion (**middle left**); the SIRI-WHU dataset with partial occlusion (**middle right**); the UCM dataset with mixed noise (**bottom left**); and the SIRI-WHU dataset with mixed noise (**bottom right**). In most cases, the accuracies rank in the following order: DSFATN > TN-2 > TN-1.

To further confirm the ability of the anti-noise layer FC1 in the anti-noise transfer network, we compare the FC1 layer's output feature $O_{FC1}(\mathbf{DSF})$ with different features under the three kinds of noises (see Table 8), similar to in Section 3.3. Compared with the accuracies in Table 5, the results of corresponding features in Table 8 have declined in different degrees due to the influence of the noises.

CNN(6con+2fc) feature and DSF show some superiority compared with the low-level features in this anti-noise experiments, obtaining accuracies even higher than the results obtained by the low-level features extracted from origin RS scene images without any noise (see Table 5). However, it is not robust enough to represent the images with noises. The last row of Table 8 shows the accuracies obtained by features extracted from the FC1 layer; most of them are higher than 0.90, and all the results are significantly enhanced compared to the results classified by DSF. The great difference between DSF and $O_{FC1}(\mathbf{DSF})$ indicates introducing the FC1 layer to the anti-noise transfer network is indeed very important.

Table 8. Anti-noise analysis on the UCM and SIRI-WHU datasets with different features.

Features	Classification Accuracy (%)					
	UCM			SIRI-WHU		
	Salt and Pepper Noise	Partial Occlusion	Mixed Noise	Salt and Pepper Noise	Partial Occlusion	Mixed Noise
HOG [50]	41.19	34.76	25.47	40.21	40.63	31.46
SIFT [51]	62.62	41.43	44.05	51.25	46.46	46.46
LBP [52]	25.00	18.10	10.48	37.92	39.38	25.42
CNN(6conv+2fc)	56.19	38.57	47.62	52.92	65.63	53.96
DSF	89.76	83.10	82.62	79.58	87.29	83.54
$O_{FC1}(\mathbf{DSF})$	**96.61**	**98.04**	**97.70**	**86.39**	**97.52**	**94.56**

3.4.2. Evaluation of Multiple Scales

To evaluate the impact of image scale, we resized the RS scene images from the UCM and SIRI-WHU datasets to five different scales, i.e., a quarter of original image size (height and width dimensions), half of original image size, three quarters of original image size, original image size and one and a quarter size.

We compared DSFATN with CNN(6conv+2fc) and the TN-2 model. As the results in Tables 9 and 10 show, DSFTAN performs the best on the UCM and SIRI-WHU datasets at all five scales. Almost all the accuracies are over 98%, and the results of DSFATN are quite stable for obtaining the lowest STD value. The results of CNN(6conv+2fc) are very unstable with the image scale variances. Particularly, TN-2, which does not conduct multi-scales patches sampling, compared with DSTATN, also obtained high accuracies around 90% on the two datasets. However, the STD values of TN-2 are much higher. Moreover, the UCM, SIRI-WHU and SAT-6 datasets also have different scales and resolutions, especially the SAT-6 dataset. Our method demonstrated robustness across the three datasets.

Table 9. Classification results on the UCM dataset with five kinds of scales.

Models	25%	50%	75%	100%	125%	STD
CNN(6conv+2fc)	76.60	80.00	77.80	76.40	80.00	1.58
TN-2	92.20	91.40	91.60	92.60	91.20	0.52
DSFATN	97.87	98.53	98.46	98.25	98.22	0.23

Table 10. Classification results on the SIRI-WHU dataset with five kinds of scales.

Models	25%	50%	75%	100%	125%	STD
CNN(6conv+2fc)	77.00	77.40	77.00	78.20	75.40	0.91
TN-2	87.60	89.20	89.60	90.00	90.60	1.01
DSFATN	98.30	98.39	98.73	98.46	98.92	0.23

3.5. The Analysis of Influence Factors

In this section, we analyze several influence factors in DSFATN: (a) the threshold of salient patches' number α; (b) the regularization coefficient λ; (c) the pre-trained CNN models; and (d) the noise level. For simplicity and equity, all comparison experiments were conducted on the UCM dataset.

3.5.1. Influence of Salient Patches' Number α

Figure 10 shows the influence of salient patches' number α. Time consumption refers to the time for obtaining all the DSF of the RS image scenes utilized in the corresponding experiments. $\alpha = 0$ means salient regions are not detected thus the DSF are directly extracted from the origin image scenes. As α increases from 0 to 9, the time consumption increases slowly while the accuracy rises sharply. When $\alpha \in [9, 36]$, the accuracy keeps a flat level of growth while the time consumption steepens. Only when $\alpha = 9$, a high classification accuracy can be gained without much time consumption. Hence, $\alpha = 9$ is selected in our method.

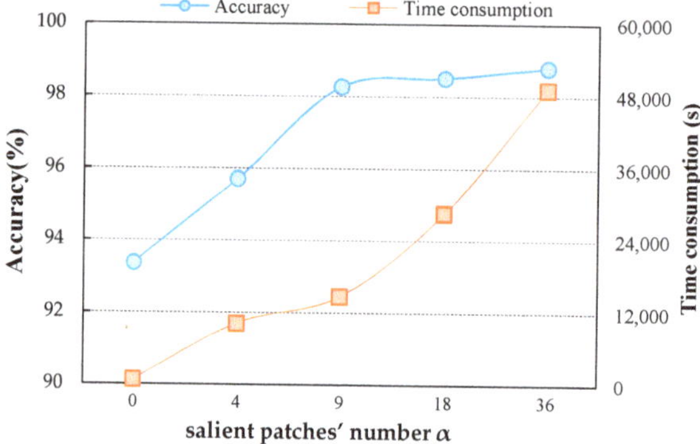

Figure 10. The influence of salient patches' number α in DSFATN on UCM dataset.

3.5.2. Influence of the Regularization Coefficient λ

Figure 11 shows the classification results of DSFATN in different regularization coefficient λ. When λ is very small (i.e., $\lambda \in [1 \times 10^{-7}, 1 \times 10^{-1}]$), DSFATN performs quite good, and the accuracy levels out at around 98%. When λ is assigned bigger values (i.e., $\lambda > 1 \times 10^{-1}$), the accuracy declines fast. When $\lambda = 1 \times 10^{-4}$, DSFATN achieves the highest result.

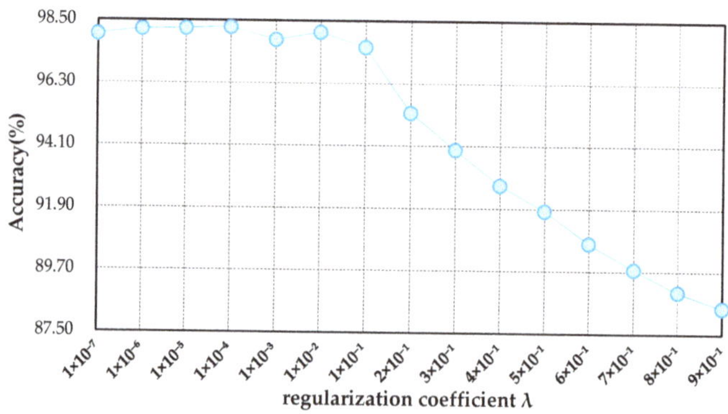

Figure 11. The influence of the regularization coefficient λ.

3.5.3. Influence of Pre-Trained CNNs

We changed the pre-trained CNN in DSFATN from VGG-19 to several other kinds of CNNs, while keeping the rest of the structure of DSFATN unchanged. Table 11 presents the classification results of different pre-trained CNNs. Note that, for the pre-trained CNN models which contain three FC layers (Rows 1–7), we extracted the features from the 1st FC layer as the feature presentation. For the other per-trained CNNs (Rows 8–15), we regarded the output of the layer that generate one-dimensional vectors (e.g., logits layer in InceptionV3) as the representation. All extracted representations have the same anti-noise transfer network architecture but are trained separately. As shown in Table 11, compared with VGG-19, most pre-trained CNNs can achieve comparable results over 96% (e.g., Rows 1–6 and 11–12). Although the inception models perform well too, they are not so competitive with other models for deep feature extraction, since they are not deep enough compared with Resnetv1_50 and Resnetv1_101. The fully connected layers, which appear in each traditional CNNs (e.g., Rows 1–7), play a great role for deep feature extraction. Nevertheless, the results of inceptions are still higher than 90%. One can see that our DSFATN with VGG-19 outperforms the others.

Table 11. Result comparison with different pre-trained CNNs.

No.	Pre-Trained CNNs	Classification Accuracy (%)
1	Alexnet [48]	96.85
2	Caffenet [54]	97.35
3	VGG -F [55]	97.54
4	VGG -M [55]	97.57
5	VGG -S [55]	97.12
6	VGG-16 [19]	97.91
7	VGG-19 [19]	1.4
8	Inceptionv1 [35]	91.25
9	Inceptionv2 [56]	90.54
10	Inceptionv3 [57]	91.82
11	Resnetv1_50 [58]	97.89
12	Resnetv1_101 [58]	97.94

3.5.4. Influence of Noise Levels

We investigate the robustness sensitivity of DSFATN at five different levels of noises. Table 12 shows the parameters of the salt and pepper noise and partial occlusion at these five levels of noise conditions; the mixed noise is still the mixture of the former two kinds noise and original image scenes with the same proportion. Note that Level 2 noise condition has been adopted as the setting in the preceding experiment part (see Section 3). Figure 12 demonstrates these five noise levels of an example tennis court scene. Obviously, when the noise level becomes higher, the scenes with salt and pepper noise are blurrier with more noise pixels, and the scenes with partial occlusion are covered with larger black region. At Levels 3–5, the tennis court cannot be seen in the image scene.

Table 12. The parameters of the salt and pepper noise and partial occlusion at five levels.

Level	Salt and Pepper Noise Density	Partial Occlusion Covering Scale
1	0.05	10–20%
2	0.1	20–30%
3	0.15	30–40%
4	0.2	40–50%
5	0.25	50–60%

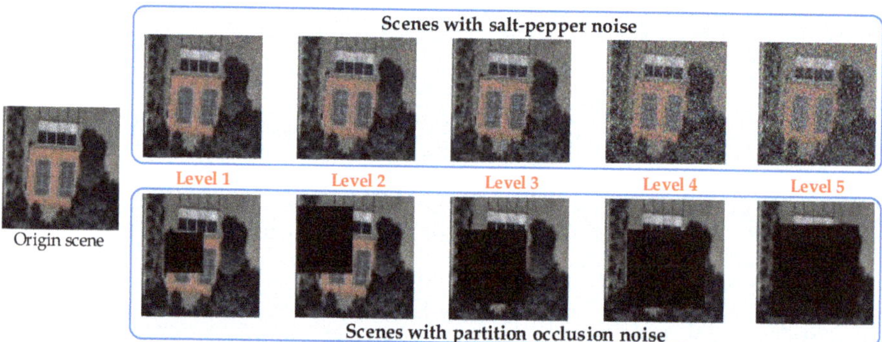

Figure 12. The example scenes of an example tennis court scene at five levels of noise conditions.

The average accuracies of DSFATN at these five noise levels are shown in Figure 13. As expected, the higher the noise level is, the lower the classification accuracy is. In salt and pepper noise condition, the salt and pepper noise with higher noise level brings more noise pixels to the scene, which makes the performance of saliency detection degenerate. In partial occlusion condition, the higher partial occlusion level leads to the semantic information loss. When the noise level is higher than 2, the results of salt and pepper noise and partial collusion conditions declines more sharply than the result of mixed noise condition. The origin scenes in the mixed noise condition, which supplement the information loss caused by the salt and pepper noise and partial occlusion to some extent. In general, although the accuracies have a declining trend, all results are higher than 80%, even for partial occlusion covering almost half scale of the scenes. The results are also higher than the accuracies obtained by some traditional methods in the origin scenes without any noises (see Table 2).

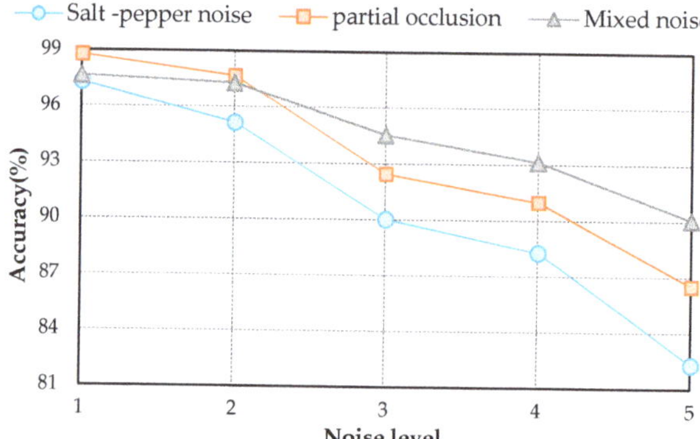

Figure 13. The results of DSFATN at five levels of noise conditions: the classification accuracies decrease when the noise level increases.

4. Conclusions

This paper proposes a deep salient feature based anti-noise transfer network (DSFATN) method for RS scene classification with different scales and various noises. In DSFATN, the saliency-guided DSF extraction extracts the discriminative high-level DSF from the most relevant, informative and representative patches of the RS scene sampled by the Patch-Based Visual Saliency (PBVS) method. The VGG-19 is selected as the pre-trained CNN to extract DSF among various candidate CNNs for its better performance. DSF achieves discriminative high-level feature representation learned from pre-trained VGG-19 for the RS scenes. Meanwhile, an anti-noise transfer network is introduced to learn and enhance the robust and anti-noise structure information of RS scene by directly propagating the label information to fully-connected layers. By minimizing the joint loss concerning anti-noise constraint and softmax classification loss simultaneously, the anti-noise transfer network can be trained easily with limited amount of data and without accuracy loss. DSFATN performs excellent with RS scenes in different quality, even with noise.

The results on three different scale datasets with limited data are encouraging: the classification results are all above 98%, which outperforms the results of state-of-the-art methods. DSFATN also obtains satisfactory results under various noises. For example, the results on the widespread UCM with noises are higher than 95%, which is even better than the best results of some state-of-the-art methods on UCM without noise. The remarkable results indicate the effectiveness and wide applicability of DSFATN and prove the robustness of DSFATN.

However, the strong anti-noise property of DSFATN is dependent on different datasets; for example, under salt and pepper noise, the accuracy of DSFATN reaches 95.12% on the UCM dataset while it dropped to 84.98% on the SIRI-WHU dataset. In the future, we will conduct an end-to-end multi-scale and multi-channel network to jointly extract more adaptive representation for RS scene with limited availability of training data for complex scene understanding.

Acknowledgments: This study was financially supported by the National Natural Science Foundation of China (No. 41671400, No. 41701446 and No. 61602429); National key R & D program of China (No. 2017YFC0602204); Hubei Natural Science Foundation of China (2015CFA012).

Author Contributions: Yuanyuan Liu and Zhong Xie conceived and designed the experiments. Xi Gong and Zhuo Zheng performed the experiments. Yuanyuan Liu and Xi Gong contributed to the analysis. The manuscript was written by Xi Gong with contributions from Yuanyuan Liu, Xuguo Shi.

Conflicts of Interest: The authors declare no conflict of interest.

References

1. Yang, Y.; Newsam, S. Bag-of-visual-words and spatial extensions for land-use classification. In Proceedings of the 18th SIGSPATIAL International Conference on Advances in Geographic Information Systems, San Jose, CA, USA, 3–5 November 2010; pp. 270–279.
2. Cheriyadat, A.M. Unsupervised feature learning for aerial scene classification. *IEEE Trans. Geosci. Remote Sens.* **2014**, *52*, 439–451. [CrossRef]
3. Yang, W.; Yin, X.; Xia, G.S. Learning high-level features for satellite image classification with limited labeled samples. *IEEE Trans. Geosci. Remote Sens.* **2015**, *53*, 4472–4482. [CrossRef]
4. Shao, W.; Yang, W.; Xia, G.S. Extreme value theory-based calibration for the fusion of multiple features in high-resolution satellite scene classification. *Int. J. Remote Sens.* **2013**, *34*, 8588–8602. [CrossRef]
5. Wang, Q.; Meng, Z.; Li, X. Locality Adaptive Discriminant Analysis for Spectral–Spatial Classification of Hyperspectral Images. *IEEE Geosci. Remote Sens. Lett.* **2017**, *14*, 2077–2081. [CrossRef]
6. Bosch, A.; Muñoz, X.; Martí, R. Which is the best way to organize/classify images by content? *Image Vis. Comput.* **2007**, *25*, 778–791. [CrossRef]
7. Zhong, Y.; Zhu, Q.; Zhang, L. Scene classification based on the multifeature fusion probabilistic topic model for high spatial resolution remote sensing imagery. *IEEE Trans. Geosci. Remote Sens.* **2015**, *53*, 6207–6222. [CrossRef]
8. Zhou, L.; Zhou, Z.; Hu, D. Scene classification using a multi-resolution bag-of-features model. *Pattern Recognit.* **2013**, *46*, 424–433. [CrossRef]
9. Zhao, B.; Zhong, Y.; Zhang, L.; Huang, B. The fisher kernel coding framework for high spatial resolution scene classification. *Remote Sens.* **2016**, *8*, 157. [CrossRef]
10. Zhao, B.; Zhong, Y.; Xia, G.-S.; Zhang, L. Dirichlet-derived multiple topic scene classification model fusing heterogeneous features for high spatial resolution remote sensing imagery. *IEEE Trans. Geosci. Remote Sens.* **2016**, *54*, 2108–2123. [CrossRef]
11. Zhong, Y.; Fei, F.; Zhang, L. Large patch convolutional neural networks for the scene classification of high spatial resolution imagery. *J. Appl. Remote Sens.* **2016**, *10*, 025006. [CrossRef]

12. Lazebnik, S.; Schmid, C.; Ponce, J. Beyond bags of features: Spatial pyramid matching for recognizing natural scene categories. In Proceedings of the IEEE Conference on Computer Vision and Pattern Recognition, New York, NY, USA, 17–22 June 2006; Volume 2, pp. 2169–2178.

13. Yang, Y.; Newsam, S. Spatial pyramid co-occurrence for image classification. In Proceedings of the IEEE International Conference on Computer Vision, Barcelona, Spain, 6–13 November 2011; pp. 1465–1472.

14. Blei, D.M.; Ng, A.Y.; Jordan, M.I. Latent dirichlet allocation. *J. Mach. Learn. Res.* **2003**, *3*, 993–1022.

15. Lienou, M.; Maitre, H.; Datcu, M. Semantic annotation of satellite images using latent dirichlet allocation. *IEEE Geosci. Remote Sens. Lett.* **2010**, *7*, 28–32. [CrossRef]

16. Vaduva, C.; Gavat, I.; Datcu, M. Latent dirichlet allocation for spatial analysis of satellite images. *IEEE Trans. Geosci. Remote Sens.* **2013**, *51*, 2770–2786. [CrossRef]

17. Bosch, A.; Zisserman, A.; Muñoz, X. Scene classification using a hybrid generative/discriminative approach. *IEEE Trans. Pattern Anal. Mach. Intell.* **2008**, *30*, 712–727. [CrossRef] [PubMed]

18. Cheng, G.; Guo, L.; Zhao, T.; Han, J.; Li, H.; Fang, J. Automatic landslide detection from remote-sensing imagery using a scene classification method based on BoVW and pLSA. *Int. J. Remote Sens.* **2013**, *34*, 45–59. [CrossRef]

19. Simonyan, K.; Zisserman, A. Very deep convolutional networks for large-scale image recognition. In Proceedings of the International Conference on Learning Representations, San Diego, CA, USA, 7–9 May 2015.

20. Zou, Z.; Shi, Z. Ship detection in spaceborne optical image with SVD networks. *IEEE Trans. Geosci. Remote Sens.* **2016**, *54*, 5832–5845. [CrossRef]

21. Gao, J.; Wang, Q.; Yuan, Y. Embedding structured contour and location prior in siamesed fully convolutional networks for road detection. In Proceedings of the IEEE International Conference on Robotics and Automation, Singapore, 29 May–3 June 2017; pp. 219–224.

22. Li, C.; Wand, M. Combining markov random fields and convolutional neural networks for image synthesis. *arXiv*, **2016**.

23. Zhang, L.; Zhang, L.; Du, B. Deep Learning for Remote Sensing Data: A Technical Tutorial on the State of the Art. *IEEE Geosci. Remote Sens. Mag.* **2016**, *4*, 22–40. [CrossRef]

24. Zhu, X.X.; Tuia, D.; Mou, L.; Xia, G.S.; Zhang, L.; Xu, F. Deep Learning in Remote Sensing: A Comprehensive Review and List of Resources. *IEEE Geosci. Remote Sens. Mag.* **2017**, *5*, 8–36. [CrossRef]

25. Lu, X.; Zheng, X.; Yuan, Y. Remote sensing scene classification by unsupervised representation learning. *IEEE Trans. Geosci. Remote Sens.* **2017**, *55*, 5148–5157. [CrossRef]

26. Chen, Y.; Zhao, X.; Jia, X. Spectral–spatial classification of hyperspectral data based on deep belief network. *IEEE J. Sel. Top. Appl. Earth Obs. Remote Sens.* **2015**, *8*, 2381–2392. [CrossRef]

27. Deng, J.; Dong, W.; Socher, R.; Li, L.J.; Li, K.; Fei-Fei, L. Imagenet: A large-scale hierarchical image database. In Proceedings of the IEEE Conference on Computer Vision and Pattern Recognition, Miami, FL, USA, 20–25 June 2009; pp. 248–255.

28. Li, H.; Fu, K.; Yan, M.; Sun, X.; Sun, H.; Diao, W. Vehicle detection in remote sensing images using denoising-based convolutional neural networks. *Remote Sens. Lett.* **2017**, *8*, 262–270. [CrossRef]

29. Yang, Y.; Zhuang, Y.; Bi, F.; Shi, H.; Xie, Y. M-FCN: Effective fully convolutional network-based airplane detection framework. *IEEE Geosci. Remote Sens. Lett.* **2017**, *14*, 1293–1297. [CrossRef]

30. Chen, X.; Xiang, S.; Liu, C.L.; Pan, C.H. Vehicle detection in satellite images by hybrid deep convolutional neural networks. *IEEE Geosci. Remote Sens. Lett.* **2017**, *11*, 1797–1801. [CrossRef]

31. Simard, P.Y.; Steinkraus, D.; Platt, J.C. Best practices for convolutional neural networks applied to visual document analysis. In Proceedings of the Seventh International Conference on Document Analysis and Recognition, Edinburgh, UK, 3–6 August 2003; pp. 958–962.

32. Dieleman, S.; Willett, K.W.; Dambre, J. Rotation-invariant convolutional neural networks for galaxy morphology prediction. *Mon. Not. R. Astron. Soc.* **2015**, *450*, 1441–1459. [CrossRef]

33. Zhang, F.; Du, B.; Zhang, L. Saliency-guided unsupervised feature learning for scene classification. *IEEE Trans. Geosci. Remote Sens.* **2015**, *53*, 2175–2184. [CrossRef]

34. Castelluccio, M.; Poggi, G.; Sansone, C.; Verdoliva, L. Land use classification in remote sensing images by convolutional neural networks. *arXiv*, 2015.

35. Szegedy, C.; Liu, W.; Jia, Y.; Sermanet, P.; Reed, S.; Anguelov, D. Going deeper with convolutions. In Proceedings of the IEEE Conference on Computer Vision and Pattern Recognition, Boston, MA, USA, 11–12 June 2015; pp. 1–9.

36. Penatti, O.A.; Nogueira, K.; dos Santos, J.A. Do deep features generalize from everyday objects to remote sensing and aerial scenes domains? In Proceedings of the IEEE Conference on Computer Vision and Pattern Recognition Workshops, Boston, MA, USA, 12 June 2015; pp. 44–51.

37. Hu, F.; Xia, G.S.; Hu, J.; Zhang, L. Transferring deep convolutional neural networks for the scene classification of high-resolution remote sensing imagery. *Remote Sens.* **2015**, *7*, 14680–14707. [CrossRef]

38. Gong, Y.; Wang, L.; Guo, R.; Lazebnik, S. Multi-scale orderless pooling of deep convolutional activation features. In *The European Conference on Computer Vision (ECCV)*; Springer: Cham, Swizerland, 2014; pp. 392–407.

39. Lee, H.; Grosse, R.; Ranganath, R.; Ng, A.Y. Convolutional deep belief networks for scalable unsupervised learning of hierarchical representations. In Proceedings of the 26th annual international conference on machine learning, Montreal, QC, Canada, 14–18 June 2009; pp. 609–616.

40. Itti, L.; Koch, C.; Niebur, E. A model of saliency-based visual attention for rapid scene analysis. *IEEE Trans. Pattern Anal. Mach. Intell.* **1998**, *20*, 1254–1259. [CrossRef]

41. Harel, J.; Koch, C.; Perona, P. Graph-based visual saliency. In Proceedings of the Advances in Neural Information Processing Systems, Vancouver, BC, Canada, 3 December 2007; pp. 545–552.

42. Harel, J. A Saliency Implementation in MATLAB. Available online: http://www.vision.caltech.edu/~harel/share/gbvs.php (accessed on 10 January 2018).

43. Caldwell, D.R. Unlocking the mysteries of the bounding box. *Coord. Online J. Map Geogr. Round Tab. Am. Libr. Assoc.* **2005**. Available online: http://www.stonybrook.edu/libmap/coordinates/seriesa/no2/a2.pdf (accessed on 10 January 2018).

44. Glorot, X.; Bordes, A.; Bengio, Y. Deep sparse rectifier neural networks. In Proceedings of the Fourteenth International Conference on Artificial Intelligence and Statistics, Lauderdale, FL, USA, 11–13 April 2011; pp. 315–323.

45. Peng, X.; Lu, C.; Yi, Z.; Tang, H. Connections between Nuclear Norm and Frobenius-Norm-Based Representations. *IEEE Trans. Neural Netw. Learn. Syst.* **2016**. [CrossRef] [PubMed]

46. Basu, S.; Ganguly, S.; Mukhopadhyay, S.; Dibiano, R.; Karki, M.; Nemani, R. Deepsat: A learning framework for satellite imagery. In Proceedings of the 23rd ACM SIGSPATIAL International Conference on Advances in Geographic Information Systems, Seattle, WA, USA, 3–6 November 2015; p. 37.

47. Chen, S.; Tian, Y. Pyramid of spatial relatons for scene-level land use classification. *IEEE Trans. Geosci. Remote Sens.* **2015**, *53*, 1947–1957. [CrossRef]

48. Krizhevsky, A.; Sutskever, I.; Hinton, G.E. ImageNet classification with deep convolutional neural networks. In Proceedings of the Twenty-Sixth International Conference on Neural Information Processing Systems, Lake Tahoe, NY, USA, 3–8 December 2012; pp. 1097–1105.

49. Breiman, L. Random forests. *Mach. Learn.* **2001**, *45*, 5–32. [CrossRef]

50. Dalal, N.; Triggs, B. Histograms of oriented gradients for human detection. In Proceedings of the IEEE Computer Society Conference on Computer Vision and Pattern Recognition, San Diego, CA, USA, 20–26 June 2005; pp. 886–893. [CrossRef]

51. Lowe, D.G. Distinctive image features from scale-invariant keypoints. *Int. J. Comput. Vis.* **2004**, *60*, 91–110. [CrossRef]

52. Ojala, T.; Pietikainen, M.; Maenpaa, T. Multiresolution gray-scale and rotation invariant texture classification with local binary patterns. *IEEE Trans. Pattern Anal. Mach. Intell.* **2002**, *24*, 971–987. [CrossRef]

53. Van der Maaten, L.; Hinton, G. Visualizing data using t-SNE. *J. Mach. Learn. Res.* **2008**, *9*, 2579–2605.

54. Jia, Y.; Shelhamer, E.; Donahue, J.; Karayev, S.; Long, J.; Girshick, R.; Guadarrama, S.; Darrell, T. Caffe: Convolutional architecture for fast feature embedding. In Proceedings of the ACM International Conference on Multimedia, Orlando, FL, USA, 3–7 November 2014.

55. Chatfield, K.; Simonyan, K.; Vedaldi, A.; Zisserman, A. Return of the devil in the details: Delving deep into convolutional nets. In Proceedings of the British Machine Vision Conference, Nottingham, UK, 1–5 September 2014.

56. Ioffe, S.; Szegedy, C. Batch normalization: Accelerating deep network training by reducing internal covariate shift. In Proceedings of the International Conference on Machine Learning, Lille, France, 6–11 July 2015; pp. 448–456.
57. Szegedy, C.; Vanhoucke, V.; Ioffe, S.; Shlens, J.; Wojna, Z. Rethinking the inception architecture for computer vision. In Proceedings of the IEEE Conference on Computer Vision and Pattern Recognition, Las Vegas, NV, USA, 26 June–1 July 2016; pp. 2818–2826.
58. He, K.; Zhang, X.; Ren, S.; Sun, J. Deep residual learning for image recognition. In Proceedings of the IEEE conference on computer vision and pattern recognition, Las Vegas, NV, USA, 26 June–1 July 2016; pp. 770–778.

 *remote sensing*

Article

Topic Modelling for Object-Based Unsupervised Classification of VHR Panchromatic Satellite Images Based on Multiscale Image Segmentation

Li Shen [1,2,*], Linmei Wu [1,2], Yanshuai Dai [1,2], Wenfan Qiao [1,2] and Ying Wang [1,2]

1 State-Province Joint Engineering Laboratory of Spatial Information Technology for High-Speed Railway Safety, Southwest Jiaotong University, Chengdu 611756, China; linmay23@yeah.net (L.W.); 15708455802@163.com (Y.D.); swjtu_qiaowenfan@163.com (W.Q.); elaine.wy@foxmail.com (Y.W.)
2 Faculty of Geosciences and Environmental Engineering, Southwest Jiaotong University, Chengdu 611756, China
* Correspondence: lishen@swjtu.edu.cn; Tel.: +86-28-66-367-439

Academic Editor: Qi Wang
Received: 31 May 2017; Accepted: 10 August 2017; Published: 14 August 2017

Abstract: Image segmentation is a key prerequisite for object-based classification. However, it is often difficult, or even impossible, to determine a unique optimal segmentation scale due to the fact that various geo-objects, and even an identical geo-object, present at multiple scales in very high resolution (VHR) satellite images. To address this problem, this paper presents a novel unsupervised object-based classification for VHR panchromatic satellite images using multiple segmentations via the latent Dirichlet allocation (LDA) model. Firstly, multiple segmentation maps of the original satellite image are produced by means of a common multiscale segmentation technique. Then, the LDA model is utilized to learn the grayscale histogram distribution for each geo-object and the mixture distribution of geo-objects within each segment. Thirdly, the histogram distribution of each segment is compared with that of each geo-object using the Kullback-Leibler (KL) divergence measure, which is weighted with a constraint specified by the mixture distribution of geo-objects. Each segment is allocated a geo-object category label with the minimum KL divergence. Finally, the final classification map is achieved by integrating the multiple classification results at different scales. Extensive experimental evaluations are designed to compare the performance of our method with those of some state-of-the-art methods for three different types of images. The experimental results over three different types of VHR panchromatic satellite images demonstrate the proposed method is able to achieve scale-adaptive classification results, and improve the ability to differentiate the geo-objects with spectral overlap, such as water and grass, and water and shadow, in terms of both spatial consistency and semantic consistency.

Keywords: very high resolution (VHR) satellite image; topic modelling; object-based image analysis; image segmentation; unsupervised classification; multiscale representation

---

1. Introduction

Recent advances in remote sensing technology, particularly those relating to spatial resolution, are helping to make detailed observations of the Earth's surface possible. However, the resulting vast amounts of very high resolution (VHR) satellite images pose a challenge for automatic classification, due to the large amount of information and with-class variance characteristics of this kind of images [1].

It is widely acknowledged that, compared to their pixel-based counterparts, object-based classification methods, which can take advantage of both spectral and spatial information, are probably more appropriate for VHR satellite images [2–4]. In a typical object-based classification framework, image segmentation is usually an initial and vital step. The goal of segmentation is to partition an original image into a set of non-overlapping homogeneous segments, which are regarded as higher-level units that are more meaningful and efficient for subsequent processing. Thus, the classification accuracy of object-based classification is dependent, to a large extent, on the quality of image segmentation [5]. In order to characterize image structures at different scales, multiscale segmentation (MS) is often used to conduct a series of segmentation maps at multiple scales from fine to coarse ones, sequentially, by varying the scale parameter (SP) [6]. As pointed out by Dragut et al. [6], the SP controls the average segment size, i.e., a smaller value of the SP produces segmentations with small regions and detailed structures, and a larger value allows for more merges, thus preserving only large segments and coarse features. Therefore, the SP needs to be appropriately determined in order to create segments that can match the actual boundaries of landscape features of various sizes as much as possible [7]. However, there exist several problems in practical applications: (1) the determination of the optimal SP, in many cases, still relies on a trial-and-error optimization, which is time-consuming when it applies to complex image scenes [8]; (2) it is often impossible to determine a unique optimal SP for a whole scene or each geo-object, due to the fact that different geo-objects and even an identical geo-object may appear at different scales in the same image. Any specific SP is likely to cause over-segmentation of some parts of the image, but under-segmentation of other parts.

To overcome these shortcomings, many approaches that attempt to directly model multiple segmentations have been proposed instead of seeking and using an optimal one from multiple candidate segmentation maps [9–12]. In this direction, Russel et al. [10] used multiple segmentations to discover objects in natural image collections. The authors assumed while none of the SP settings can achieve the optimal image segmentation, some segments in some of the segmentations appear to be correct. Therefore, instead of selecting any particular optimal SP, they utilized multiple segmentation results to identify objects of various sizes by the learning machine. In a similar framework, Akcay et al. [13] proposed automatic detection of geospatial objects using multiple hierarchical segmentations. Afterwards, Santos et al. [14] presented a kind of boost-classifier adapted to MS for supervised classification, in which a sequential strategy of training for weak classifiers was adopted based on a hierarchy of image segmentations from fine to coarse. However, both [13] and [14] are built on hierarchical image segmentation [15], which cannot be directly obtained in many cases due to the reason that most image segmentation methods do not consider the hierarchical structures. These observations motive us to develop a novel object-based unsupervised classification based on MS, in which multiple segmentation maps are jointly utilized by means of topic modelling. In the proposed framework, the original image does not require to be hierarchically partitioned to form multiple segmentation maps.

Attracted by the success of topic models, e.g., latent Dirichlet allocation (LDA) [16] and its relatives [17,18], in text analysis community, there has been an increasing interest in applying such models for semantically-driven understanding of satellite images, such as image annotation [19–21], object detection [13,22], scene classification [23–25], and image classification or clustering [26–29]. Among various advantages provided by topic models is their ability to deal with polysemy [16]. For example, the word "bachelor" could refer to a kind of degree or an unmarried man. Based on co-occurrence of words in the context, topic models are able to capture the polysemous use of words. This characteristic offers a potential solution to cope with the perplexing, but so common, phenomenon in VHR satellite image classification, i.e., different geo-objects with nearly identical spectra. For image classification or clustering, the square image blocks with fixed-size or segments with arbitrary shape are viewed as the documents [27,29], and the pixels or local patches extracted from the images are regarded as the words in topic modeling. Using the probabilistic latent semantic analysis (pLSA) model, Yi et al. [26] presented a novel semantic clustering algorithm for VHR satellite images. The experiment results confirmed the advantage of topic modelling. However, in the proposed framework, a pre-processing step was required to partition the original satellite image into image documents, and an accompanying post-processing step was required to combine the allocated multiple labels of a pixel into a unique one using a certain voting rule. To address this problem, Tang et al. [27] developed a msLDA model, which built an automatic framework that combined a latent Dirichlet allocation with a multiscale image representation of a panchromatic satellite image. The msLDA archived an adaptive smoothing on clustering results. Nevertheless, its application usually introduces a computational bottleneck, due to the manner in which image documents are generated, where each pixel and its surrounding pixels within the square neighborhood constitute a document. Shu et al. [30] presented a nonparametric Bayesian hierarchical model to conduct unsupervised classification of VHR panchromatic satellite images by considering over-segments as documents. However, it also suffers from the same problems as the traditional object-based methods mentioned previously, i.e., it is modelled based on single-scale segmentation.

In this paper, a novel object-based unsupervised classification for VHR panchromatic satellite images using multiple image segmentation maps via the LDA model is presented. The proposed approach consists of four components: (1) a multiscale image segmentation component that allows characterizing of image structures at different scales; (2) a topic model component that learns the grayscale histogram distribution for each geo-object and the mixture distribution of geo-objects in each segment in an unsupervised manner; (3) a category label allocation component that classifies each segment by the ranking of probability-based similarities; and (4) an automatic application framework component that integrates multiple classification results at different scales into a unique one. It should be noted that while the proposed method still needs to determine the range of scales for creating a multiscale segmentation representation, the work has been greatly simplified compared to searching for the optimal image segmentation. The main contribution of the proposed method is an automatic framework of combining a topic model with a multiscale image segmentation representation to model both the co-occurrence of various geo-objects and multiscale structures.

This paper extends and improves on a preliminary work [31], which presents our initial ideas and results. In this paper: (1) a novel strategy of integrating multiple classification results at different scales into a unique one is added, which can ensure an adaptive smoothing classification result can be achieved; (2) a constraint specified by the mixture distribution of geo-objects, which can characterize the co-occurrence relationships of various geo-objects, is incorporated to correct the KL similarity between the histogram distribution of each segment and that of each geo-object; and (3) a more thorough presentation of introduction, methodology, experimental analysis, and discussion is conducted.

The remainder of this paper is organized as follows. In Section 2, the proposed methodology is presented in detail. Experimental results and related discussion are given in Section 3. Finally, the conclusion is drawn in Section 4.

2. Methodology

In this section, we present our approach for performing the object-based unsupervised classification of panchromatic satellite images, using the LDA model.

For the proposed method, a key prerequisite is to create a MS representation of the original satellite image with varied scales. Since the goal of MS is to produce enough segmentation maps of the image so as to have a high probability of acquiring better segments that can correspond to potential geo-objects, we do not need image segmentation at each scale to be exactly correct. Any method that can create a reasonable MS of a satellite image may meet the requirement.

Given the MS representation, the proposed method is composed of the following three steps: Firstly, the LDA model is utilized to learn the grayscale histogram distribution for each geo-object and the mixture distribution of geo-objects within each segment in an unsupervised manner. Then, the histogram distribution of each segment is compared with that of each geo-object using the Kullback-Leibler (KL) divergence measure [10], which is further weighted with a constraint specified by the mixture distribution of geo-objects. Each segment is allocated a geo-object category label with the minimum KL divergence. Finally, the scale-adaptive unsupervised classification map is achieved by integrating the multiple classification results at different scales. The general scheme is shown in Figure 1.

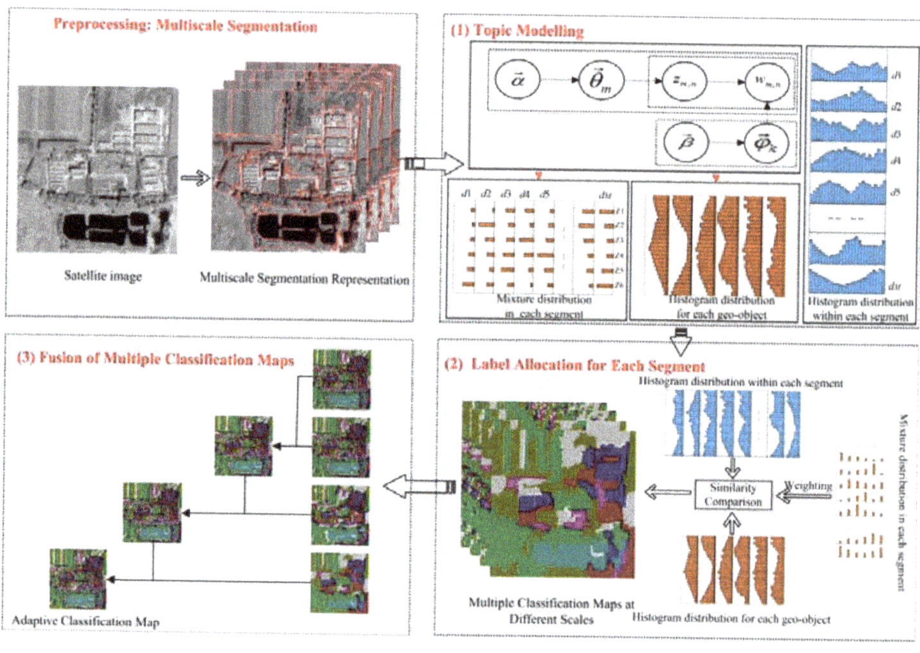

Figure 1. Flowchart of the proposed method.

2.1. Topic Modelling

2.1.1. Latent Dirichlet Allocation

The LDA is a generative hierarchical Bayesian probabilistic model, which is originally proposed to model collections of discrete data, such as text documents and natural images [32]. In this model, each document is viewed as a finite mixture of various latent topics. Each topic, in turn, is a probability distribution over words. For a corpus of M documents, the LDA assumes the following generative process for the m-th document of length N:

- For the k-th element of K topics, sample the topic-specific term distribution $\vec{\phi}_k$ according to the Dirichlet distribution, i.e., $\vec{\phi}_k \sim \mathrm{Dirchlet}(\vec{\beta})$, where $\vec{\beta}$ is the hyperparameter.
- Sample the topic mixture $\vec{\theta}_m$ according to the Dirichlet distribution, i.e., $\vec{\theta}_m \sim \mathrm{Dirchlet}(\vec{\alpha})$, where $\vec{\alpha}$ is the hyperparameter.
- For each word $w_{mn} \in \{w_{m1}, w_{m2}, \ldots, w_{mN}\}$, sample a topic z_{mn} according to the multinomial distribution, i.e., $z_{mn} \sim \mathrm{Multinomial}(\vec{\theta}_m)$, and sample a word w_{mn} according to the multinomial distribution, i.e., $w_{mn} \sim \mathrm{Multinomial}(\vec{\phi}_{z_{mn}})$.

Both variational inference and Gibbs sampling have been used to infer and estimate the parameters of the LDA. To solve the inferential problem, we need to calculate the posterior probability of the hidden variables given a corpus, i.e., $P(\vec{z}|\vec{w}, \vec{\alpha}, \vec{\beta})$. The general formulation of a Gibbs sampler for such latent-variable models becomes:

$$P(z_i|\vec{z}_{-i}, \vec{w}, \vec{\alpha}, \vec{\beta}) = \frac{P(\vec{z}, \vec{w}|\vec{\alpha}, \vec{\beta})}{\int_Z P(\vec{z}, \vec{w}|\vec{\alpha}, \vec{\beta}) dz_i}, \tag{1}$$

which can be approximated by interactively sampling each of the K topics using the chain rule and noting that $\vec{w} = \left\{\vec{w}_{-i}, w_i = v\right\}$ and $\vec{z} = \left\{\vec{z}_{-i}, z_i = k\right\}$:

$$\begin{aligned} P(z_i|\vec{z}_{-i}, \vec{w}, \vec{\alpha}, \vec{\beta}) &= \frac{P(\vec{z}, \vec{w}|\vec{\alpha}, \vec{\beta})}{P(\vec{z}_{-i}, \vec{w}|\vec{\alpha}, \vec{\beta})} \\ &\propto \frac{n_{k,-i}^{(v)} + \beta_t}{\sum\limits_{v'=1}^{V}(n_k^{(v')} + \beta_{v'}) - 1} * \frac{n_{m,-i}^{(k)} + \alpha_k}{\sum\limits_{k'=1}^{K}(n_m^{(k')} + \alpha_{k'})}, \end{aligned} \tag{2}$$

where the counts $n_{\cdot,-i}^{(\cdot)}$ represents the number of the words or topics with exception of index i.

For a new topic-word pair $(\tilde{z} = k, \tilde{w} = v)$ that is observed in a document $d(\tilde{w}) = d(\tilde{z}) = m$, given the state $(\tilde{z}, \tilde{w})$, the multinomial parameters can be determined by:

$$\phi_{k,v} = \frac{n_k^{(v)} + \beta_v}{\sum\limits_{v'=1}^{V}(n_k^{(v')} + \beta_{v'})}, \tag{3}$$

$$\theta_{m,k} = \frac{n_m^{(k)} + \alpha_k}{\sum\limits_{k'=1}^{K}(n_m^{(k')} + \alpha_{k'})}, \tag{4}$$

where V is the number of words in the vocabulary, α_k and β_v stand for the k-th element and v-th element of hyperparameter $\vec{\alpha}$ and $\vec{\beta}$, respectively. For details regarding the derivation, please refer to [33].

2.1.2. Build an Analogue of Text-Related Terms in the Image Domain

To borrow techniques used in the text domain to satellite images, the first issue that needs to be addressed is how to build an analogue of text terms in the image domain. For the proposed method, we follow the definition in [27,29]

- Word: a unique grayscale value of a pixel is defined as a word;
- Vocabulary: the unique grayscale values of the satellite image form the vocabulary;
- Document: each segment is regarded as a document, thus, all segments of multiple segmentation maps at different scales constitute the corpus;
- Topic: each topic corresponds to a specific geo-object category.

Given multiple segmentation maps at different scales, we can use the LDA model to learn K grayscale histogram distributions for K geo-objects, i.e., $\{\vec{\phi}_k\}_{k=1}^{K}$, and M mixture distributions of geo-objects within M segments, i.e., $\{\vec{\theta}_m\}_{m=1}^{M}$. Furthermore, M grayscale histogram distributions within M segments, i.e., $\{\vec{\pi}_m\}_{m=1}^{M}$, can also be easily obtained just by counting the frequencies of different grayscale values.

2.2. Label Allocation for Each Segment

Although there may be some differences in size due to the scale effect, the segments that correspond to the identical geo-object should have similar grayscale histogram distributions. As a consequence, the category label allocation for each segment is determined according to the following rule: the histogram distribution of each segment is compared with those of K geo-objects, respectively. The similarity between two types of distributions is measured using the KL divergence, which has been proved to be effective in measuring the probability-based similarity. The category label of the geo-object, which has the minimum KL divergence with the segment, is allocated as the label of the segment. Given the segment d_m, its category label c_{d_m} is mathematically given by:

$$c_{d_m} = \arg\min_{1 \leq k \leq K} KL(\vec{\pi}_m, \vec{\phi}_k), \tag{5}$$

where $KL(\vec{\pi}_m, \vec{\phi}_k)$ denotes the symmetrical KL divergence between two discrete distributions, i.e., $\vec{\pi}_m$ and $\vec{\phi}_k$. To be specific, the symmetrical KL divergence in the discrete form can be represented as the following:

$$KL(\vec{\pi}_m, \vec{\phi}_k) = \frac{\sum_{v=1}^{V} \{\pi_m^v In(\frac{\pi_m^v}{\phi_k^v}) + \phi_k^v In(\frac{\phi_k^v}{\pi_m^v})\}}{2}, \tag{6}$$

where π_m^v refers to the v-th element of $\vec{\pi}_m$, which describes the histogram distribution within the segment m. Likewise, ϕ_k^v refers to the v-th element of $\vec{\phi}_k$, which describes the histogram distribution for the geo-object k.

Furthermore, it is easy to understand: with the increase of the mixture proportion of a certain geo-object within the segment, the probability of classifying the segment as the corresponding geo-object should be improved accordingly. The mixture distribution of geo-objects within each segment, i.e., $\{\vec{\theta}_m\}_{m=1}^{M}$, learned by topic modelling, exactly provides the mixture proportion features. Thus, Equation (5) can be further weighted with a constraint specified by the mixture distribution of geo-objects:

$$c_{d_m} = \arg\min_{1 \leq k \leq K} KL(\vec{\pi}_m, \vec{\phi}_k) \cdot u_m^k, \tag{7}$$

where $\vec{u}_m$ is empirically set to $-In(\vec{\theta}_m)$, and u_m^k denotes the weight with the geo-object k.

Overall, by means of Equation (7), the category label of each segment is determined jointly by both the grayscale distribution and mixture distribution of geo-objects, which can characterize the co-occurrence relationships of various geo-objects.

2.3. Fusion of Multiple Classification Maps

After finishing step 2.2, multiple unsupervised classification maps at different scales are achieved. However, due to the existence of multiscale effects in VHR satellite images, any classification map based the single-scale segmentation cannot take into account the various granularities of the geo-objects, e.g., the narrow roads may be suitable to be extracted at a fine scale, while the large-area field should be classified at a coarse scale. Therefore, the final classification map is achieved by integrating the multiple classification maps at different scales, in order to achieve a scale-adaptive unsupervised classification.

Given the scale range $\{1, 2, \ldots, S\}$, S classification maps at multiple scales can be obtained by the means of topic modelling presented above. In other words, each pixel i in the original satellite image will be allocated S category labels. Let $d_{i,s}(s \in \{1, 2, \ldots S\})$ denote the segment covering the pixel i at the scale s, and $k(d_{i,s})$ denote the category label of the segment $d_{i,s}$, the category label of the pixel i is given by:

$$\begin{cases} s^* = \arg\min_{1 \leq s \leq S} KL(\vec{\pi}_{d_{i,s}}, \vec{\phi}_{k(d_{i,s})}), \\ c_i = k(d_{i,s^*}). \end{cases} \qquad (8)$$

where $\vec{\pi}_{d_{i,s}}$ denotes the grayscale histogram distribution within the segment $d_{i,s}$, $\vec{\phi}_{k(d_{i,s})}$ denotes the grayscale histogram distribution for the geo-object $k(d_{i,s})$, and s^* denotes the optimal scale for the pixel i.

3. Results and Discussion

In this section, we firstly describe the experimental images. Then, we introduce the quantitative evaluation methods for the experimental results and the state-of-art methods for comparison, and the parameter settings are also given in detail. Thirdly, we compare the performance of different approaches for three typical of geographical scenes in terms of both qualitative and quantitative aspects. The computational efficiency for different approaches is also discussed. Finally, we analyze the effects of scale setting in the proposed method on the classification results.

3.1. Experiment Data

In order to assess the effectiveness of the proposed approach, three panchromatic satellite images with different scenes and spatial resolutions are used. The first data is a panchromatic Mapping Satellite-1 image with 1600×1600 pixels and 2 m spatial resolution, which was acquired on 13 August 2012 and covers an area of Miyun District, Beijing, China. As shown in Figure 2a, five major types of geo-objects, i.e., building, road, water, grass, and ground, occur in this image. The second data is a panchromatic QuickBird image with 900×900 pixels and 0.6 m spatial resolution, as shown in Figure 2c. It was acquired on 22 April 2006 and located in Tong Zhou district of Beijing, China. There are six major types of geo-objects distributed in the image, including building, road, water, shadow, tree, and field. The third data is a panchromatic ZiYuan-3 (ZY-3) image that was acquired over an area of Tanggu District, Tianjin, China, on 15 August 2015. The image size is 3500×3500 pixels, and the spatial resolution is 2.1 m. As shown in Figure 2e, the image is made up of five major types of geo-objects, including building, road, water, grass, and field. We manually annotated all the original images at the pixel level as ground truth label data through visual interpretation. The corresponding ground truth maps for three satellite images are shown in Figure 2b,d,f, respectively.

3.2. Experiment Setup

3.2.1. Methods for Comparison with the Proposed Approach

To evaluate the effectiveness on three aspects of classification accuracy, spatial smoothness, and semantic consistency, the performance of the proposed approach is compared with that of four state-of-the-art unsupervised classification methods based on image segmentation: (1) the spectral-spatial ISODATA, where the pixel-based ISODATA classification is followed by a majority voting within the adaptive neighborhoods defined by the over-segmentation (termed as O_ISODATA) [34]; (2) the spectral-spatial LDA, similar to O_ISODATA, where the same over-segmentation is applied to the classification result of the LDA model using just the single-scale image segmentation map as corpus [30] (termed as O_LDA); (3) the msLDA proposed in [27]; and (4) the HDP_IBP proposed in [30].

For convenience, the proposed approach is referred to as the mSegLDA.

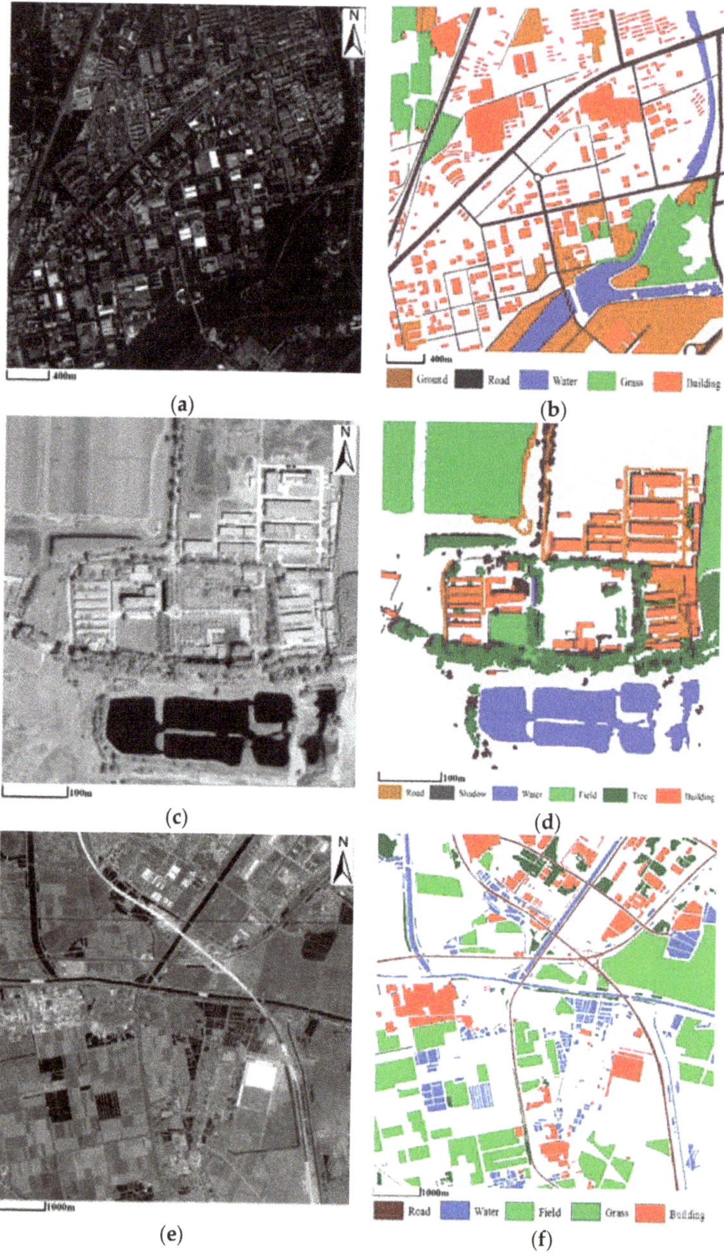

Figure 2. Experimental datasets. (**a**) Mapping Satellite-1 panchromatic image; (**b**) ground truth map of the Mapping Satellite-1 image; (**c**) QuickBird panchromatic image; (**d**) ground truth map of the QuickBird image; (**e**) ZY-3 panchromatic image; and (**f**) ground truth map of the ZY-3 panchromatic image.

3.2.2. Evaluation Criteria

In our experiments, two quantitative criteria, as well as visual inspection, are utilized to evaluate the unsupervised classification results, i.e., overall accuracy (OA) and overall entropy (OE).

- Overall accuracy (OA): OA, which serves as a quantitative measurement of the agreement between the classification result and the ground truth map, is one of the most widely used statistics for evaluating the classification accuracy. OA can be calculated by dividing the total correctly-classified pixels by the total number of pixels checked by the ground truth map, and is given as $OA = N_{correct}/N_{total}$, where $N_{correct}$ is the total number of correct pixels, and N_{total} is total number of pixels.
- Overall entropy (OE): entropy is an information theoretical criterion that is able to measure the homogeneity of the classification results. OE is defined as a linear combination of the class entropy, which describes how the pixels of the same geo-object are presented by the various clusters created, and the cluster entropy, which reflects the quality of the individual clusters in terms of the homogeneity of the pixels in a cluster. Generally speaking, a smaller overall entropy value corresponds to the classification map with a higher homogeneity. For details regarding, please refer to [27,35].

3.2.3. Parameter Setting

In order to produce multiple segmentation maps at different scales, this paper uses the entropy rate superpixel segmentation (ERSS) algorithm [36], which has been proven to be both effective and efficient. It should be noted that any method that can create a reasonable MS of satellite image may meet the requirement of the proposed approach. The ERSS algorithm utilizes the number of segments to control the scale size of image segmentation, i.e., a large number of segments may result in fine-scale segmentation, and conversely, a small number of segments will generate coarse-scale segmentation. For the Mapping Satellite-1 image, the QuickBird image and the ZY-3 image, the number of scales S is set to 6, 9, and 11, respectively, and the corresponding numbers of segments include {100, 200, 500, 800, 1000, 1500}, {100, 200, 500, 800, 1000, 1500, 2000, 2500, 3000}, and {2000, 3500, 5000, 6500, 8000, 9500, 11,000, 12,500, 14,000, 15,500, 17,000}.The range of scales, reflected by the numbers of segments, should be able to characterize multiscale structures in the images as much as possible. For both O_ISODATA and O_LDA, the over-segmentation map with 1500 segments, 2500 segments, and 17,000 segments are used in the three images.

Furthermore, topic model based methods initializes the Dirichlet priors as symmetric priors empirically, i.e., $\alpha = 0.1$, $\beta = 0.01$ for the Mapping Satellite-1 image, $\alpha = 0.01$, $\beta = 0.8$ for the QuickBird image, and $\alpha = 50/K$, $\beta = 0.01$ for the ZY-3 image. The number of geo-objects K is set to 6, 7, and 6 according to the distributions of geo-object classes, respectively.

3.3. Comparison of Classification Results

The classification results of various methods for three satellite images are shown in Figures 3–5, where each geo-object is represented by a different color.

3.3.1. Mapping Satellite-1 and QuickBird Images

From visual inspection, all the unsupervised classification results seem to be compact. The obvious speckle noise or the isolated pixel patches which are often found in the results of pixel-based classification approaches are greatly eliminated. Thus, the advantages of enforcing spatial consistency over the classification by means of performing image segmentation are confirmed. On the other hand, obvious misclassification between water and grass in Figure 3b,g, and water and shadow in Figure 4b,g can be observed in the classification results of the ISODATA. Two types of geo-objects, i.e., grass and shadow, are entirely incorrectly identified as water. This phenomenon can be explained by the fact that there exist obvious spectral overlaps between water and grass in Figure 2a, and water and shadow in Figure 2c. For this reason, the ISODATA which groups image pixels merely according to their grayscale values and, thus, are not able to differentiate various geo-objects with similar spectra well. While the O_ISODATA that conducts pixel-based ISODATA classification, followed by spatial regularization using the segmentation map can ensure spatial continuity within segments, it does not change the essential mechanism of the ISODATA.

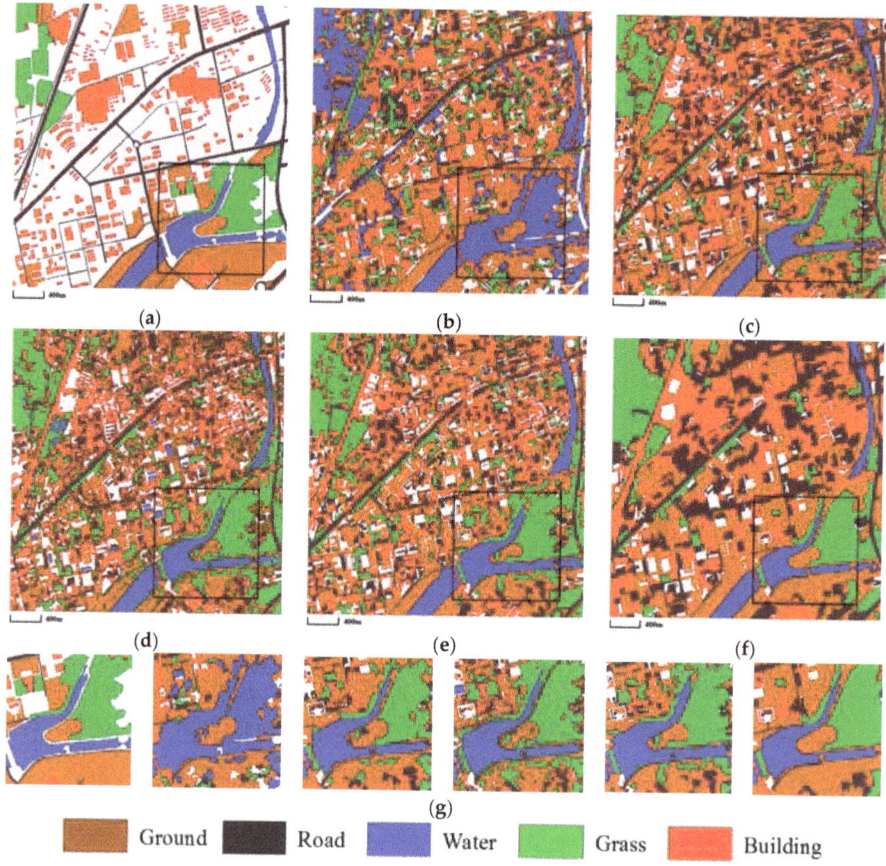

Figure 3. Classification results of various methods for the Mapping Satellite-1 image. (**a**) Ground truth map; (**b**) O_ISODATA; (**c**) O_LDA; (**d**) msLDA; (**e**) HDP_IBP; (**f**) mSegLDA; and (**g**) Details of (**a–f**).

However, benefitting from topic modelling, for the topic model-based approaches, the co-occurrence information, characterized by the mixture distribution of various geo-objects within each segment, can be utilized to correctly recognize different objects with similar spectra. As illustrated in Figures 3c–g and 4c–g, two types of geo-objects, i.e., grass and shadow, are well separated from water in the classification results of the topic model based approaches.

Furthermore, because the O_LDA is built on a single-scale over-segmentation map, it lacks a mechanism to model multiscale features of various-objects and, thus, cannot realize an adaptive smoothing on classification results. As shown in Figure 4c, the smoothing effect on the fine-scale road is proper, but is not sufficient for the large-scale field. Additionally, the majority voting scheme adopted by the O_LDA within the adaptive neighborhoods defined by the over-segmentation also results in the relatively fragmented classification map. In order to encode the scale-adaptive classification ability, the msLDA combines the topic model with a multiscale image representation derived by convoluting a given image with a variable-scale Gaussian into an automatic framework by embedding both image block and scale selections, and the HDP_IBP introduces the hierarchical spatial information, particularly the high-level scene cues, into the classification. As shown in Figures 3d–e and 4d–e, both the HDP_IBP and msLDA improve the adaptive smoothing effect on the classification results to a certain extent compared with the O_LDA. However, the improvement is still limited. As a contrast, as shown in Figure 3f,g and Figure 4f,g the proposed mSegLDA could realized a more significant self-adaptive spatial regularization on classification results according to various geo-object types at different scales, i.e., the large-scale geo-object (e.g., field) is heavily smoothed, resulting in a more homogenous classification, and the fine-scale geo-object (e.g., road) accepts a slight smoothing, thus preserving detailed structures and edge patterns.

From quantitative evaluation, both OA and OE in different classification results for two experiment images are calculated, as shown in Tables 1 and 2, respectively. The mSegLDA approach yields the best classification accuracies and the lowest values of OE, compared to other methods, indicating the proposed method can achieve a better classification performance on the whole.

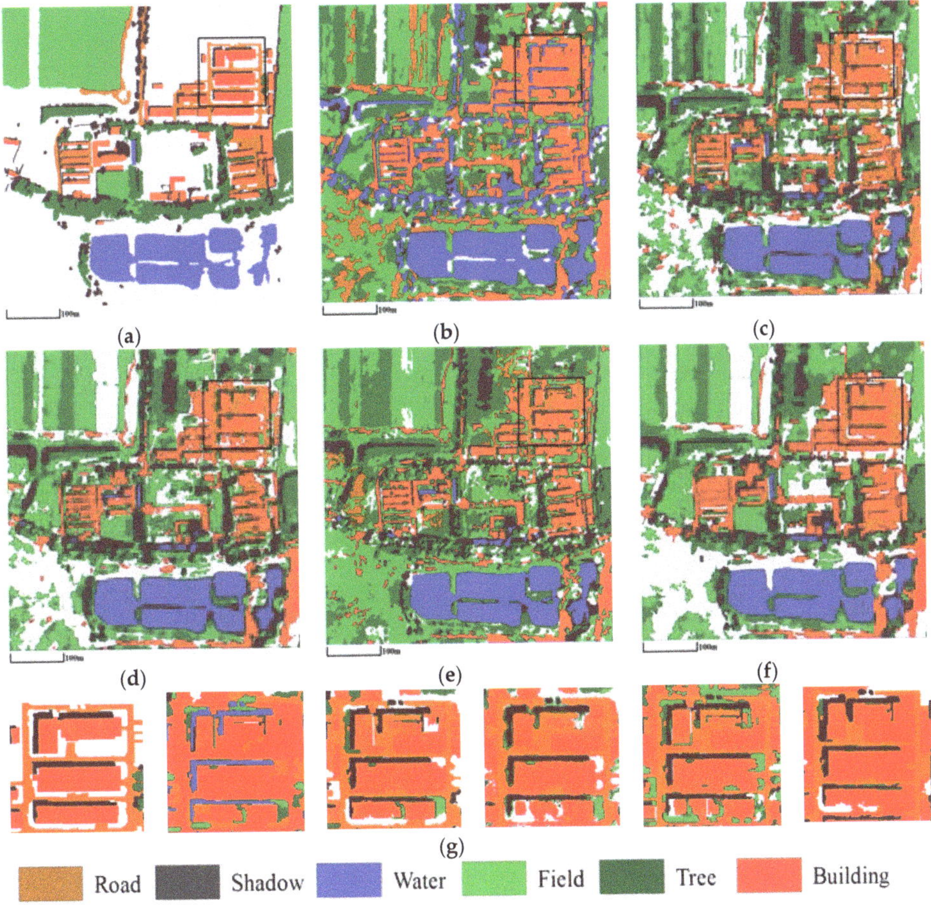

Figure 4. Classification results of various methods for the QuickBird image. (**a**) Ground truth map; (**b**) O_ISODATA; (**c**) O_LDA; (**d**) msLDA; (**e**) HDP_IBP; (**f**) mSegLDA; and (**g**) Details of (**a**–**f**).

Table 1. OA and OE of various methods for the Mapping Satellite-1 image.

	O_ISODATA	O_LDA	msLDA	HDP_IBP	mSegLDA
OA	48.6	69.3	68.4	70.1	72.0
OE	0.89	0.79	0.84	0.76	0.72

Table 2. OA and OE of various methods for the QuickBird image.

	O_ISODATA	O_LDA	msLDA	HDP_IBP	mSegLDA
OA	49.8	65.1	68.2	65.5	74.3
OE	0.96	0.84	0.80	0.84	0.71

3.3.2. ZY-3 Image

In this subsection, a ZY-3 satellite image of a large scene covering over 50 km^2 is used to evaluate the effectiveness of the proposed mSegLDA. As shown in Figure 5, the complexity of the scene significantly increases. For example, various geo-objects, and even an identical geo-object (e.g., building or field), are present at different sizes in the image. However, the proposed mSegLDA is still able to realize a more significant self-adaptive spatial regularization on classification maps according to various geo-object types at different scales, compared to other methods. As shown in Table 3, the largest value of OA and the lowest value OE are also obtained by the mSegLDA.

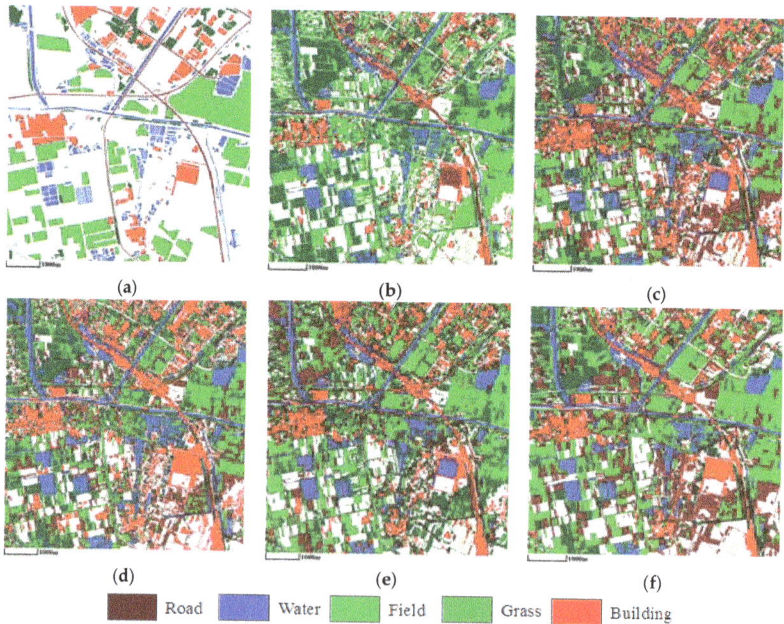

Figure 5. Classification results of various methods for the ZY-3 image. (**a**) Ground truth map; (**b**) O_ISODATA; (**c**) O_LDA; (**d**) msLDA; (**e**) HDP_IBP; and (**f**) mSegLDA.

Table 3. OA and OE of various methods for the ZY-3 image.

	O_ISODATA	O_LDA	msLDA	HDP_IBP	mSegLDA
OA	63.0	58.9	61.6	59.2	65.7
OE	0.78	0.93	0.85	0.87	0.74

3.4. Analysis of Computational Efficiency

The computational efficiency of the mSegLDA is also compared with that of other three topic model-based methods using the QuickBird image as an example, i.e., the O_LDA, the msLDA and the HDP_IBP. All the methods are coded using MATLAB R2013b (The MathWorks, Inc., Natick, MA, USA), and have been performed on a PC with an Intel (R) Core (TM) i7-4710MQ 2.50 GHz CPU and 8.00 GB RAM. As can be seen in Table 4, the O_LDA and the HDP_IBP spend a relatively less amount of running time compared to the msLDA and the mSegLDA due to their modelling mechanism, i.e., utilizing only a single-scale segmentation map as a corpus. Instead, since the mSegLDA needs to use multiple segmentation maps for the topic model inference and calculate a large number of KL divergences between segments, it is less efficient than the O_LDA and the HDP_IBP. However, the computation efficiency of the mSegLDA is better than that of the msLDA, because each pixel and its surrounding pixels within the square neighborhood represent a document in the msLDA, resulting in the significant increase in the number of documents and accompanying extensive computation.

Table 4. Running time of various methods for the QuickBird image.

Methods	Running Time (in Seconds)
O_LDA	797
msLDA	5056
HDP_IBP	766
mSegLDA	2413

In order to speed up the execution of the proposed mSegLDA, the Gibbs sampling component of the mSegLDA, which is computationally expensive, has been written using C++ MEX code. The running time of the mSegLDA for the QuickBird image is approximately 65 s.

3.5. Analysis of Scale Setting

3.5.1. Influence of Different Settings on the Range of Scales

As the number of scales S may influence the classification results, we, therefore, analyze how the performance of the proposed mSegLDA behaves with different settings on the range of scales using the Mapping Satellite-1 and QuickBird images. Since the ERSS algorithm utilizes the number of segments to control the scale size of image segmentation, the number of segments could be equivalent to the size of scales. Given the candidate scale set {100, 200, 500, 800, 1000, 1500, 2000, 2500, 3000, 3500, 4000}, for both the Mapping Satellite-1 and QuickBird images, a set of experiments for two images with different settings on the range of scales by adding one scale every time, i.e., {100, 200}, {100, 200, 500}, {100, 200, 500, 800} . . . , {100, 200, 500, 800, 1000, 1500, 2000, 2500, 3000, 3500, 4000}, are modelled using the mSegLDA.

Figures 6 and 7 show the values of OA and OE against the different settings on the range of scales. As can be seen, as the number of scales S increases, there is an approximately monotonic increase in OA and decrease in OE, and the classification performance remains relatively stable when S is larger than 6 for the Mapping Satellite-1 and 9 for the QuickBird image. This is due to the reason that, the mSegLDA approach needs to create a series of segmentation maps at multiple scales from fine to coarse ones for modelling, and the ideal multiscale image segmentation representation is expected to be able to represent all structural patterns at different scales as much as possible. Hence, a too small S, e.g., {100, 200}, means that only large-scale structure information can be characterized. As the increase of S, e.g., {100, 200, 500, 800, 1000, 1500} and {100, 200, 500, 800, 1000, 1500, 2000, 2500, 3000}, the fine to coarse range of scales makes it possible to characterize multiscale features of various geo-objects. On the other hand, although it can also ensure all structural patterns at different scales are presented, a larger value of S increases the computational efficiency.

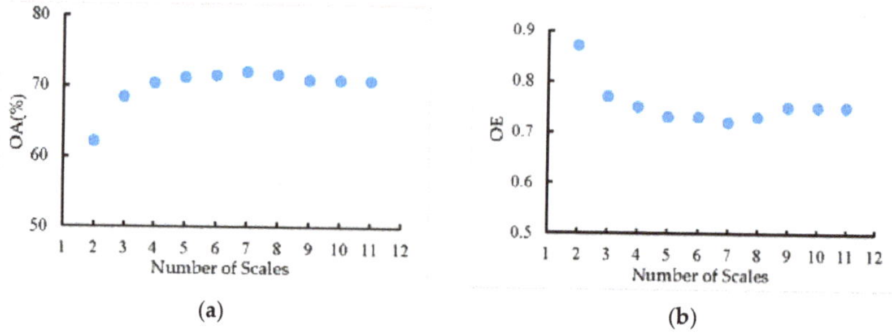

Figure 6. OA and OE versus the number of scales for the Mapping Satellite-1 image. (**a**) Influence on OA; and (**b**) influence on OE.

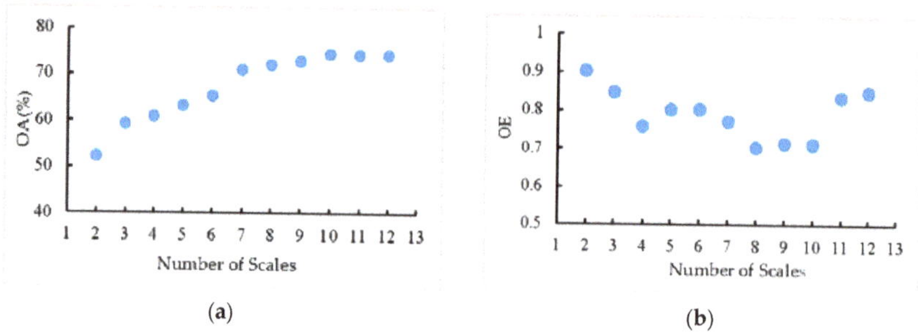

Figure 7. OA and OE versus the number of scales for the QuickBird image. (**a**) Influence on OA; and (**b**) influence on OE.

Following the above rules, the range of scales for three experiment images are set to {100, 200, 500, 800, 1000, 1500}, {100, 200, 500, 800, 1000, 1500, 2000, 2500, 3000}, and {2000, 3500, 5000, 6500, 8000, 9500, 11,000, 12,500, 14,000, 15,500, 17,000}, respectively.

3.5.2. Special Cases of the mSegLDA

In this subsection, we analyze several special cases of the mSegLDA for the Mapping Satellite-1 and QuickBird images qualitatively and quantitatively to evaluate the effectiveness of modelling multiple segmentations by setting the number of scales to 1, i.e.,

- Case #1: the mSegLDA based on a single-segmentation map with 100 segments;
- Case #2: the mSegLDA based on a single-segmentation map with 200 segments;
- Case #3: the mSegLDA based on a single-segmentation map with 500 segments;
- Case #4: the mSegLDA based on a single-segmentation map with 800 segments;
- Case #5: the mSegLDA based on a single-segmentation map with 1000 segments;
- Case #6: the mSegLDA based on a single-segmentation map with 1500 segments;
- Case #7: the mSegLDA based on a single-segmentation map with 2000 segments;
- Case #8: the mSegLDA based on a single-segmentation map with 2500 segments; and
- Case #9: the mSegLDA based on a single-segmentation map with 3000 segments.

As shown in Figures 8 and 9, a smaller number of segments results in a more heavily smoothed classification result. However, it also filters the detailed patterns of certain geo-objects. On the contrary, a larger number of segments produces a relatively fragmented result. The advantage of integrating multiscale segmentation maps for modelling is further confirmed, as shown Tables 5 and 6.

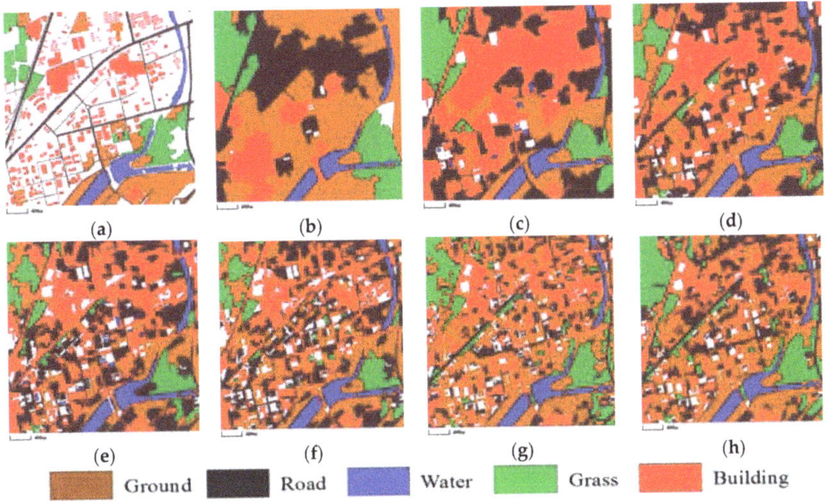

Figure 8. Classification results of six special cases of the mSegLDA for the Mapping Satellite-1 image. (**a**) Ground truth map; (**b**) Case #1; (**c**) Case #2; (**d**) Case #3; (**e**) Case #4; (**f**) Case #5; (**g**) Case #6; and (**h**) mSegLDA.

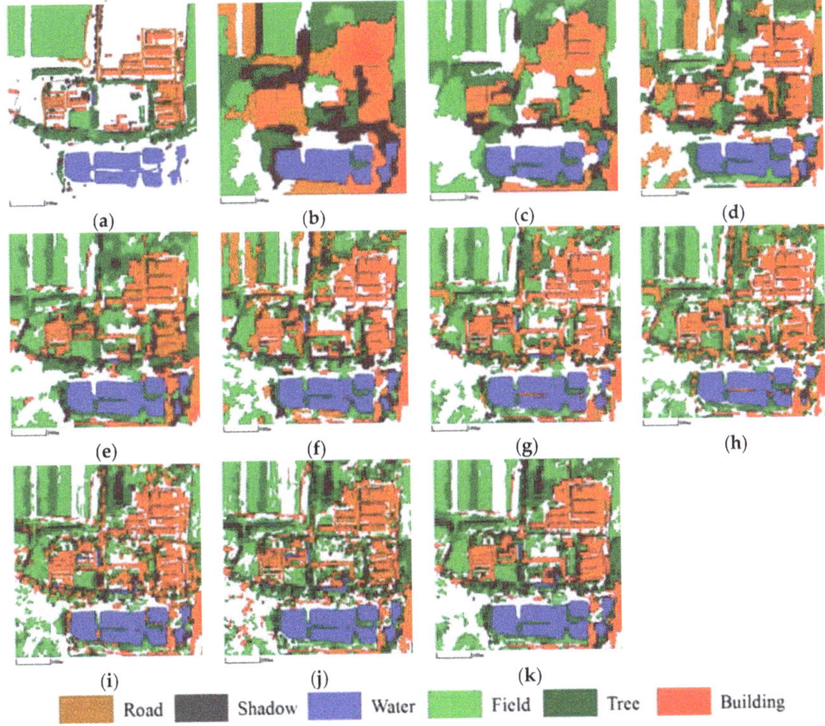

Figure 9. Classification results of nine special cases of the mSegLDA for the QuickBird image. (**a**) Ground truth map; (**b**) Case #1; (**c**) Case #2; (**d**) Case #3; (**e**) Case #4; (**f**) Case #5; (**g**) Case #6; (**h**) Case #7; (**i**) Case #8; (**j**) Case #9; and (**k**) mSegLDA.

Table 5. OA and OE of six special cases of the mSegLDA for the Mapping Satellite-1 image.

	Case #1	Case #2	Case #3	Case #4	Case #5	Case #6	mSegLDA
OA	64.1	62.6	66.2	66.1	68.1	66.0	72.0
OE	0.87	0.89	0.83	0.83	0.81	0.81	0.72

Table 6. OA and OE of nine special cases of the mSegLDA for the QuickBird image.

	Case #1	Case #2	Case #3	Case #4	Case #5	Case #6	Case #7	Case #8	Case #9	mSegLDA
OA	57.8	67.7	59.7	60.1	65.4	67.1	63.7	66.5	0.71	74.3
OE	0.87	0.87	0.76	0.75	0.85	0.74	0.74	0.79	0.78	0.72

4. Conclusions

This paper has presented a novel unsupervised object-based approach named mSegLDA for the classification of VHR panchromatic satellite images. The approach addresses the issues that: (1) various structural patterns at different scales are usually presented simultaneously in the same scene of a VHR image; and (2) different geo-objects may have nearly identical spectra. Our major contribution is to propose an automatic framework that combines the latent Dirichlet allocation with a multiscale image segmentation representation to model both the co-occurrence of various geo-objects and multiscale structures. Experimental results using VHR panchromatic satellite images with different scenes and spatial resolutions indicate that the proposed approach can achieve scale-adaptive classification results, and improve the ability to differentiate the geo-objects with spectral overlap, such as water and grass, and water and shadow.

Furthermore, the proposed framework still needs to determine the range of scales for creating multiscale segmentation empirically. In the future, we will develop an automatic strategy to obtain the appropriate range.

Acknowledgments: This work is supported in part by the National Key Research and Development Program of China under grant 2016YFB0501403, in part by the National Natural Science Foundation of China under grant 41401374, in part by the National Basic Research Program (973 program) of China under grant 2012CB719901, and in part by the Fundamental Research Funds for the Central Universities under grant 2682016CX079.

Author Contributions: Li Shen and Linmei Wu conceived and designed the experiments; Linmei and Yanshuai Dai performed the experiments; Yanshuai Dai, Wenfan Qiao and Ying Wang analyzed the data, and Li Shen wrote the manuscript.

Conflicts of Interest: The authors declare no conflict of interest.

References

1. Benediktsson, J.A.; Chanussot, J.; Moon, W.M. Advances in very-high-resolution remote sensing. *Proc. IEEE* **2013**, *101*, 566–569. [CrossRef]
2. Blaschke, T. Object based image analysis for remote sensing. *ISPRS J. Photogramm. Remote Sens.* **2010**, *65*, 2–16. [CrossRef]
3. Myint, S.W.; Gober, P.; Brazel, A.; Grossman-Clarke, S.; Weng, Q. Per-pixel vs. Object-based classification of urban land cover extraction using high spatial resolution imagery. *Remote Sens. Environ.* **2011**, *115*, 1145–1161. [CrossRef]
4. Blaschke, T.; Hay, G.J.; Kelly, M.; Lang, S.; Hofmann, P.; Addink, E.; Feitosa, R.Q.; van der Meer, F.; van der Werff, H.; van Coillie, F.; et al. Geographic object-based image analysis-towards a new paradigm. *ISPRS J. Photogramm. Remote Sens.* **2014**, *87*, 180–191. [CrossRef] [PubMed]
5. Judah, A.; Hu, B.; Wang, J. An algorithm for boundary adjustment toward multi-scale adaptive segmentation of remotely sensed imagery. *Remote Sens.* **2014**, *6*, 3583–3610. [CrossRef]
6. Dragut, L.; Csillik, O.; Eisank, C.; Tiede, D. Automated parametrisation for multi-scale image segmentation on multiple layers. *ISPRS J. Photogramm. Remote Sens.* **2014**, *88*, 119–127. [CrossRef] [PubMed]

7. Yang, J.; He, Y.; Weng, Q. An automated method to parameterize segmentation scale by enhancing intrasegment homogeneity and intersegment heterogeneity. *IEEE Geosci. Remote Sens. Lett.* **2015**, *12*, 1282–1286. [CrossRef]

8. Zhang, L.; Jia, K.; Li, X.; Yuan, Q.; Zhao, X. Multi-scale segmentation appoach for object-based land-cover classification using high-resolution imagery. *Remote Sens. Lett.* **2014**, *5*, 73–82. [CrossRef]

9. Malisiewicz, T.; Efros, A.A. Improving spatial support for objects via multiple segmentations. In Proceedings of the 18th British Machine Vision Conference, Warwick, UK, 10–13 September 2007.

10. Russell, B.C.; Freeman, W.T.; Efros, A.A.; Sivic, J.; Zisserman, A. Using multiple segmentations to discover objects and their extent in image collections. In Proceedings of the 2006 IEEE Computer Society Conference on Computer Vision and Pattern Recognition, New York, NY, USA, 17–22 June 2006.

11. Pantofaru, C.; Schmid, C.; Hebert, M. Object recognition by integrating multiple image segmentations. In Proceedings of the 10th European Conference on Computer Vision, Marseille, France, 12–28 October 2008; pp. 481–494.

12. Karadağ, Ö.Ö.; Senaras, C.; Vural, F.T.Y. Segmentation fusion for building detection using domain-specific information. *IEEE J. Sel. Top. Appl. Earth Obs. Remote Sens.* **2015**, *8*, 3305–3315. [CrossRef]

13. Akcay, H.G.; Aksoy, S. Automatic detection of geospatial objects using multiple hierarchical segmentations. *IEEE Trans. Geosci. Remote Sens.* **2008**, *46*, 2097–2111. [CrossRef]

14. Santos, J.A.d.; Gosselin, P.-H.; Philipp-Foliguet, S.; Torres, R.d.S.; Falao, A.X. Multiscale classification of remote sensing images. *IEEE Trans. Geosci. Remote Sens.* **2012**, *50*, 3764–3775. [CrossRef]

15. Syu, J.-H.; Wang, S.-J.; Wang, L.-C. Hierarchical image segmentation based on iterative contraction and merging. *IEEE Trans. Image Process.* **2017**, *26*, 2246–2260. [CrossRef] [PubMed]

16. Blei, D.M.; Ng, A.Y.; Jordan, M.I. Latent dirichlet allocation. *J. Mach. Learn. Res.* **2003**, *3*, 993–1022.

17. Hofmann, T. Probabilistic latent semantic indexing. In Proceedings of the 22nd Annual International SIGIR Conference on Research and Development in Information, Retrieval Berkeley, CA, USA, 15–19 August 1999; pp. 50–57.

18. Teh, Y.W.; Jordan, M.I.; Beal, M.J.; Blei, D.M. Hierarchical dirichlet processes. *J. Am. Stat. Assoc.* **2006**, *101*, 1566–1581. [CrossRef]

19. Lienou, M.; Maitre, H.; Datcu, M. Semantic annotation of satellite images using latent dirichlet allocation. *IEEE Geosci. Remote Sens. Lett.* **2010**, *7*, 28–32. [CrossRef]

20. Bratasanu, D.; Nedelcu, I.; Datcu, M. Bridging the semantic gap for satellite image annotation and automatic mapping applications. *IEEE J. Sel. Top. Appl. Earth Obs. Remote Sens.* **2011**, *4*, 193–204. [CrossRef]

21. Luo, W.; Li, H.; Liu, G.; Zeng, L. Semantic annotation of satellite images using author-genre-topic model. *IEEE Trans. Geosci. Remote Sens.* **2013**, *52*, 1356–1368. [CrossRef]

22. Li, S.; Tang, H.; He, S.; Shu, Y.; Mao, T.; Li, J.; Xu, Z. Unsupervised detection of earthquake-triggered roof-holes from uav images using joint color and shape features. *IEEE Geosci. Remote Sens. Lett.* **2015**, *12*, 1823–1827.

23. Zhao, B.; Zhong, Y.; Zhang, L. Scene classification via latent dirichlet allocation using a hybrid generative/discriminative strategy for high spatial resolution remote sensing imagery. *Remote Sens. Lett.* **2013**, *4*, 1204–1213. [CrossRef]

24. Zhong, Y.; Zhu, Q.; Zhang, L. Scene classification based on the multifeature fusion probabilistic topic model for high spatial resolution remote sensing imagery. *IEEE Trans. Geosci. Remote Sens.* **2015**, *53*, 6207–6222. [CrossRef]

25. Zhao, B.; Zhong, Y.; Xia, G.-S.; Zhang, L. Dirichlet-derived multiple topic scene classification model for high spatial resolution remote sensing imagery. *IEEE Trans. Geosci. Remote Sens.* **2016**, *54*, 2108–2123. [CrossRef]

26. Yi, W.; Tang, H.; Chen, Y. An object-oriented semantic clustering algorithm for high-resolution remote sensing images using the aspect model. *IEEE Geosci. Remote Sens. Lett.* **2011**, *8*, 522–526. [CrossRef]

27. Tang, H.; Shen, L.; Qi, Y.; Chen, Y.; Shu, Y.; Li, J.; Clausi, D.A. A multiscale latent dirichlet allocation model for object-oriented clustering of vhr panchromatic satellite images. *IEEE Trans. Geosci. Remote Sens.* **2013**, *51*, 1680–1692. [CrossRef]

28. Xu, K.; Yang, W.; Liu, G.; Sun, H. Unsupervised satellite image classification using markov field topic model. *IEEE Geosci. Remote Sens. Lett.* **2013**, *10*, 130–134. [CrossRef]

29. Shen, L.; Tang, H.; Chen, Y.; Gong, A.; Li, J.; Yi, W. A semisupervised latent dirichlet allocation model for object-based classification of vhr panchromatic satellite images. *IEEE Geosci. Remote Sens. Lett.* **2014**, *11*, 863–867. [CrossRef]

30. Shu, Y.; Tang, H.; Li, J.; Mao, T.; He, S.; Gong, A.; Chen, Y.; Du, H. Object-based unsupervised classification of vhr panchromatic satellite images by combining the hdp and ibp on multiple scenes. *IEEE Trans. Geosci. Remote Sens.* **2015**, *53*, 6148–6162. [CrossRef]

31. Shen, L.; Wu, L.; Li, Z. Topic modelling for object-based classification of VHR satellite images based on multiscale segmentations. *Int. Arch. Photogramm. Remote Sens. Spat. Inf. Sci.* **2016**, *41*, 359–363. [CrossRef]

32. Barnard, K.; Duygulu, P.; Forsyth, D.; de Freitas, N.; Blei, D.M.; Jordan, M.I. Matching words and pictures. *J. Mach. Learn. Res.* **2003**, *3*, 1107–1135.

33. Heinrich, G. *Parameter Estimation for Text Analysis*; Technical Note; Vsonix GmbH: Darmstadt, Germany; University of Leipzig: Leipzig, Germany, 2008.

34. Tarabalka, Y.; Benediktsson, J.A.; Chanussot, J. Spectral-spatial classification of hyperspectral imagery based on partitional clustering techniques. *IEEE Trans. Geosci. Remote Sens.* **2009**, *47*, 2973–2987. [CrossRef]

35. Halkidi, M.; Batistakis, Y.; Vazirgiannis, M. On clustering validation techniques. *J. Intell. Inf. Syst.* **2001**, *17*, 107–145. [CrossRef]

36. Liu, M.-Y.; Tuzel, O.; Ramalingam, S.; Chellappa, R. Entropy rate superpixel segmentation. In Proceedings of the 13rd IEEE Conference on Computer Vision and Pattern Recognition, Colorado Springs, CO, USA, 20–25 June 2011; pp. 2097–2104.

 *remote sensing*

Article

Nonlinear Classification of Multispectral Imagery Using Representation-Based Classifiers

Yan Xu [1], Qian Du [1,*], Wei Li [2], Chen Chen [3] and Nicolas H. Younan [1]

[1] Department of Electrical and Computer Engineering, Mississippi State University, Starkville, MS 39762, USA; yx131@msstate.edu (Y.X.); younan@ece.msstate.edu (N.H.Y.)
[2] College of Information Science and Technology, Beijing University of Chemical Technology, Beijing 100029, China; liwei089@ieee.org
[3] Center for Research in Computer Vision, University of Central Florida, Orlando, FL 32816, USA; chenchen870713@gmail.com
* Correspondence: du@ece.msstate.edu; Tel.: +1-662-325-2035

Received: 10 May 2017; Accepted: 25 June 2017; Published: 28 June 2017

Abstract: This paper investigates representation-based classification for multispectral imagery. Due to small spectral dimension, the performance of classification may be limited, and, in general, it is difficult to discriminate different classes with multispectral imagery. Nonlinear band generation method with explicit functions is proposed to use which can provide additional spectral information for multispectral image classification. Specifically, we propose the simple band ratio function, which can yield better performance than the nonlinear kernel method with implicit mapping function. Two representation-based classifiers—i.e., sparse representation classifier (SRC) and nearest regularized subspace (NRS) method—are evaluated on the nonlinearly generated datasets. Experimental results demonstrate that this dimensionality-expansion approach can outperform the traditional kernel method in terms of high classification accuracy and low computational cost when classifying multispectral imagery.

Keywords: multispectral imagery; nonlinear classification; kernel method; dimensionality expansion

1. Introduction

Airborne and spaceborne optical remote sensors collect useful information from the Earth's surface based on the radiance reflected by different materials. Hyperspectral sensors acquire images at contiguous spectral ranges with high spectral resolution. On the contrary, multispectral sensors acquire only several wide bands with high spatial resolution. The high spectral resolution of hyperspectral imagery provides major advantages for classification and detection. However, due to the high dimensionality, its vast data volume can cause issues in data transmission, storage, and analysis [1,2]. Although multispectral imagery has low spectral resolution and it may be difficult to distinguish materials with similar spectral signatures, its high spatial resolution and wide coverage make it still popular in practical applications.

Recently, sparse representation classifier (SRC) [3] and collaborative representation classifier (CRC) [4] have gained much attention for hyperspectral imagery classification. Different from the traditional classifiers, such as support vector machine (SVM), these representation-based classifiers do not use the training-testing fashion. Instead, in these methods, a testing pixel is classified based on representation residual using labeled samples. The nearest regularized subspace (NRS) [5] is an improved version of CRC, where samples similar to the testing pixels are allowed to have high weights in the representation. Other variants of SRC or CRC have been proposed for hyperspectral imagery. For example, in [6], a local sparse representation-based nearest neighbor is proposed to increase the performance by utilizing class-specific sparse coefficients. A weighted joint collaborative representation based classifier is presented in [7], which adopts more appropriate weights by considering the similarity between the centered pixel and its surrounding pixels. Bian et al. proposed a multi-layer spatial-spectral representation framework for hyperspectral classification [8]. NRS is implemented as a class-specific version by using samples of each class separately in [9], and it is performed on Gabor features in [10], yielding improved classification accuracy. Representation-based approaches for hyperspectral classification and detection are summarized in [11]. However, the performance of such representation-based classifiers in multispectral image classification is limited, because the low-dimensional pixel vectors cannot offer significant discrepancy in representation residual when using training samples of different classes, producing ambiguity in label assignment.

As a classical feature expansion approach, the kernel method has been successfully applied to hyperspectral and multispectral classification. Using the kernel trick, it maps the original data to a high dimensional feature space without the need of knowing the actual mapping function. Kernel SVM (KSVM) is applied for hyperspectral image classification, which has been considered as a standard classifier [12]. Bernabe et al. employed kernel principal component analysis to extend the original principal component analysis to a nonlinear version [13]. Kernel collaborative representation with Tikhonov regularization (denoted as KNRS) is presented in [14], and Kernel sparse representation classifier (KSRC) is developed in [15]. The difficulties of the traditional kernel methods include high computational cost in the computation of Gram matrix and exhaustive searching in parameter tuning.

In this paper, we propose to use a simple strategy to generate artificial bands for multispectral imagery classification. The goal of this approach is to use explicit nonlinear functions to contrast the dissimilarity between original spectral measurements, which can provide additional spectral information for classification problems [16]. By generating new artificial bands, the spectral contrast between different classes can be increased. Our major contribution is to use the simple band ratio as the explicit nonlinear function for dimensionality expansion, which can offer better performance than the traditional kernel method in terms of high classification accuracy and low computational cost. Here, we limit the discussion in representation-based classifiers, although the discussed band expansion can be applicable to any other classifier.

The rest of this paper is organized as follows. Section 2 introduces the two representation-based classifiers, i.e., SRC and NRS. Section 3 presents the simple nonlinear band generation method. Section 4 discusses experimental result. The conclusion is drawn in Section 5.

2. Representation-Based Algorithms

Let the dataset with n labeled samples in c classes be $\mathbf{X} = \{\mathbf{X}_{1_i}, \mathbf{X}_2, \ldots, \mathbf{X}_c\} \in \Re^{d \times n}$, where d is the number of bands and $\mathbf{X}_i$ includes labeled samples for the i-th class.

2.1. SRC

In SRC [3], a testing sample $\mathbf{y}$ is linearly represented by all the training samples. The objective is to find a sparse weight vector $\mathbf{a}$ that minimizes the term $\|\mathbf{y} - \mathbf{Xa}\|_2^2$, i.e.,

$$\arg \min_{\mathbf{a}} \|\mathbf{y} - \mathbf{Xa}\|_2^2 + \lambda \|\mathbf{a}\|_1 \tag{1}$$

where λ is the regularization term. In this research, Equation (1) is solved by mexLassoWeighted.m in MATLAB [17].

After the sparse weight vector $\mathbf{a}$ is estimated, the residual error for each class i is calculated as

$$r_i(\mathbf{y}) = \|\mathbf{y} - \mathbf{X}_i \mathbf{a}_i\|_2^2 \tag{2}$$

where $\mathbf{a}_i$ denotes the entries of sparse weight vector $\mathbf{a}$ associated with the i-th class. The testing sample is assigned as

$$\text{class}(\mathbf{y}) = \arg \min_{i=1,2,\ldots,C} (r_i(\mathbf{y})) \tag{3}$$

2.2. NRS

It has been argued that it is the collaborative representation instead of the l_1 norm that actually improves the classification accuracy [4]. The NRS [5,9,10] can adaptively adjust the regularization term per sample such that only samples similar to the testing sample can actually participate in collaborative representation. Its objective function is expressed as

$$\arg\min_{\mathbf{a}} \|\mathbf{y} - \mathbf{Xa}\|_2^2 + \lambda \mathbf{\Gamma} \|\mathbf{a}\|_2^2 \tag{4}$$

where $\mathbf{\Gamma}$ is a diagonal matrix, which is defined as

$$\mathbf{\Gamma} = \begin{bmatrix} \|(\mathbf{y} - \mathbf{x}^{(1)})\|_2^2 & & 0 \\ & \ddots & \\ 0 & & \|(\mathbf{y} - \mathbf{x}^{(n)})\|_2^2 \end{bmatrix} \tag{5}$$

where $\mathbf{x}^{(i)}$ is the i-th column of the dictionary $\mathbf{X}$. The coefficient $\mathbf{a}$ has a closed-form solution as

$$\mathbf{a} = \left(\mathbf{X}^T\mathbf{X} + \lambda\mathbf{\Gamma}\right)^{-1}\mathbf{X}^T\mathbf{y} \tag{6}$$

Similarly, the residual error is used to determine the class label as Equation (3).

In SRC and NRS, the regularization parameter λ needs to be tuned, which can be the optimal value for the training samples.

3. Nonlinear Band Generation Method

A simple way for band generation is to adopt some explicit nonlinear functions to create artificial images that serve as additional linearly independent spectral measurements [16,18]. Although any nonlinear functions may be used, in our paper, we limit our discussion on multiplication and division. Band multiplication is related to their correlation, while band ratio is often used to remove the illumination factor [19]. Three new datasets can be generated by these two methods. The first dataset uses pixel-wise multiplication, and the second dataset is generated by division, i.e., band ratio. If we combine the original dataset with the artificial bands by both division and multiplication, we have the third dataset with a total number of N^2 bands.

Note that, in the traditional kernel method, the kernel trick is to avoid to explicitly identify the nonlinear functions to use. We will show that simple multiplication and division can offer better classification than the kernel trick, and band ratio (division) is the best choice for the nonlinear function while keeping the data dimensionality manageable.

3.1. Multiplication

Suppose two images $\mathbf{B}_i$ and $\mathbf{B}_j$ (pixels at the same locations) are multiplied together, then a new image $\{\mathbf{B}_i\mathbf{B}_j\}_{i=1,j=i+1}^{N-1}$ is produced, where N is the total number of bands of the original multispectral imagery. Although multiplication can be used for a single band, we only apply multiplication to each pair of bands in order to compare with the division method yielding the same number of bands, i.e., $\{\mathbf{B}_i/\mathbf{B}_j\}_{i=1,j=i+1}^{N-1}$. Combining the original multispectral dataset with the generated artificial bands with multiplication, there are a total of $N^2/2 + N/2$ bands.

3.2. Division

New bands can be created as $\{\mathbf{B}_i/\mathbf{B}_j\}_{i=1,j=i+1}^{N-1}$ by dividing the pixels at the same locations in the original bands in the multispectral dataset. If we only combine the original dataset with the bands generated by division, we get the second dataset. The total number of bands after combining the original bands is $N^2/2 + N/2$ in the second dataset. If we combine the original dataset with the artificial bands by both division and multiplication, we have the third dataset with a total number of N^2 bands.

The proposed framework is shown in Figure 1, which includes the comparison of four cases: original bands, original bands and bands generated with multiplication (original + multiplication), original bands and bands generated with division (original + division), original bands and bands generated with both multiplication and division (original + multiplication + division).

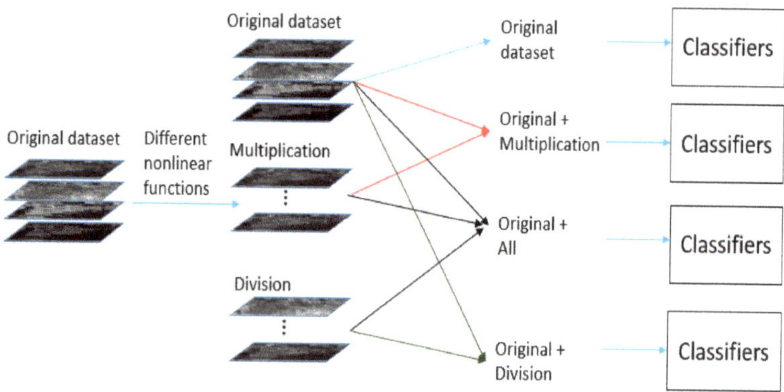

Figure 1. Framework of the band generation method.

3.3. Practical Consideration

In order for the generated bands to have similar dynamic ranges as the original bands, data is normalized by dividing the maximum value; in other words, after normalization, the maximum value of all the data points becomes 1. In division, the band with the larger local maximum value is chosen as the divider, or the band with non-zero minimum value is the divider.

In practice, the value of 0 often occurs at the same pixel locations, such as shadow pixels in all the bands. Then the band ratio is set to be 0. However, for pixels with very small non-zero values, such as water pixels, it may be needed to introduce a small constant in both denominator and numerator as [20]: $\left\{ (\mathbf{B}_i + K)/(\mathbf{B}_j + K) \right\}_{i=1, j=i+1}^{N-1}$. Note that due to spectral correlation, the materials (e.g., water, shadow) consistently have low or zero reflectance values without sudden change.

4. Experiment Results

4.1. Data Description and Experimental Setup

Due to lack of multispectral images with pixel level ground truth, data used in the experiments are simulated from hyperspectral images through band grouping.

The first multispectral dataset is simulated from hyperspectral Indian Pines dataset acquired by the Airborne Visible and Infrared Imaging Spectrometer (AVIRIS) over the Indiana's Indian Pines in June 1992. The spatial size is 145 $\times$ 145 with the spatial resolution 20 m/pixel, and the 220 spectral bands are from 0.4 to 2.5 um. We generate six bands from this dataset since it has wider spectral range. The generated six bands are to simulate blue, green, red, near infrared, short wave infrared channels by grouping band range 6~12, 13~21, 24~33, 40~54, 123~143, and 177~220 of the Indian Pines dataset [21]. Using the technique in Section 3, 15 bands are generated with multiplication, and another 15 bands are generated with division. There are, in total, 16 different classes from the original ground truth; however, we select eight classes from the original dataset from a statistic viewpoint [5]. The eight classes we used in the experiments are *Corn-no-till, Corn-min-till, Grass-pasture, Hay-windowed,*

Soybean-no-till, Soybean-min-till, Soybean-clean, and woods. The number of labeled samples are tabulated in Table 1. The false color-infrared image of this dataset is shown in Figure 2a.

Table 1. Number of samples per class for Indian Pines Dataset (the eight classes studied are bolded).

Class No.	Class Name	Number of Samples
C1	Alfalfa	46
C2	**Corn-no-till**	1460
C3	**Corn-min-till**	834
C4	Corn	237
C5	**Grass-pasture**	483
C6	Grass-trees	730
C7	Grass-pasture-mowed	28
C8	**Hay-windowed**	478
C9	Oats	20
C10	**Soybean-no-till**	972
C11	**Soybean-min-till**	2455
C12	**Soybean-clean**	593
C13	Wheat	205
C14	**Woods**	1265
C15	Building-grass-trees-drives	386
C16	Stone-steel-towers	93
Total		10,249

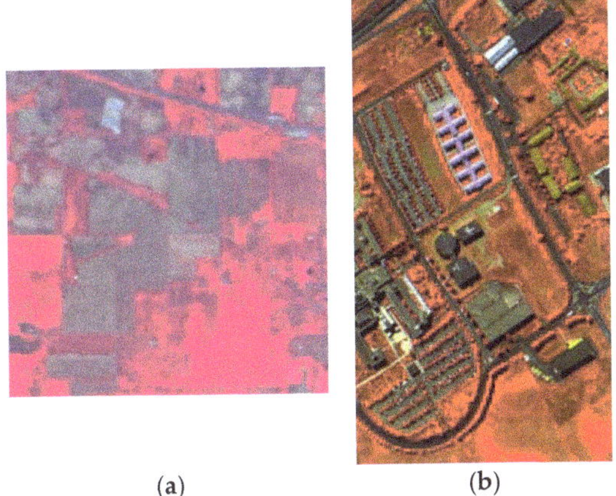

(a)   (b)

Figure 2. Color-infrared composites for (**a**) Indian Pines Dataset; (**b**) University of Pavia dataset.

The second multispectral dataset is generated from a hyperspectral image acquired by the reflective optics system imaging spectrometer (ROSIS) sensor. The image scene, covering the University of Pavia, has 115 spectral bands ranging from 0.43 to 0.86 um with the spatial size of 610 × 340 pixels, and the spatial resolution is 1.3 m per pixel. This dataset consists of 102 spectral bands after removing the 12 noisy bands. We generate four bands from this dataset according to [22]. Four bands—i.e., blue, green, red, near infrared channels—are simulated by grouping band range 6~24, 25~45, 54~69, and 89~103 in the original hyperspectral dataset. Based on these four bands, six bands are generated with multiplication, and another six with division. The number of labeled samples of nine classes are shown in Table 2. The false color-infrared image of this dataset is shown in Figure 2b.

Table 2. Number of samples per class for University of Pavia Dataset.

Class No.	Class Name	Number of Samples
C1	Asphalt	6631
C2	Meadows	18,649
C3	Gravel	2099
C4	Trees	3064
C5	Painted metal sheets	1345
C6	Bare Soil	5029
C7	Bitumen	1330
C8	Self-Blocking Bricks	3682
C9	Shadows	947
	Total	42,776

4.2. Classification Results

The datasets using nonlinear band generation method are evaluated on SRC, NRS, their kernel versions with kernel trick (i.e., KSRC, KNRS), and KSVM. Each experiment is conducted 10 times to avoid any bias in sampling, and average performance of overall accuracy (OA) is reported. The number of training samples are set to 10, 30, 50, 70, 90, and 110, which are randomly selected. The regularization parameter λ is critical to the performance of the two classifiers, and we adopt 10-fold cross validation to choose the λ. Figures 3 and 4 show the thematic maps from the NRS for Indian Pines and University of Pavia datasets, respectively. Obviously, there are many misclassified pixels. However, it can be observed that the maps using the original bands only are worse than others.

Figure 5 shows the results for the datasets generated by Indian Pines. We conclude the division method provides the best performance among other band generation methods. The OA using the division method for both classifiers increases approximately 7%, compared to using the original data only. Combining multiplication and division can provide approximately the same performance as using the division only. The KSRC performs slightly better than the original SRC. When the number of training samples is large, the KNRS outperforms the original NRS. However, when the number of training samples becomes small, the KNRS may be even worse than the linear NRS. The KSVM using the original multispectral imagery is inferior to SRC or NRS on the generated bands. The advantage of using generated bands is more obvious when the number of training samples is small, which may be because the dimensionality is expanded to a reasonable level.

Figure 6 presents the SRC and NRS results for the University of Pavia dataset. For SRC, using nonlinear bands outperforms KSRC with the change of training samples. The three datasets containing nonlinearly generated bands provide comparable performance. When the number of training samples is small, the KSRC offers similar performance as the SRC on the original dataset. However, when the number of training sample increases, the KSRC provides much better accuracy than the linear SRC. For the case of NRS, with a small number of training samples, the KNRS produces approximately the same performance as its linear version. When the training size is small, using nonlinear bands can outperform the KSVM; using nonlinear bands can provide an approximately similar performance as KSVM when the training size is large.

Tables 3 and 4 provide the computation cost of different algorithms in MATLAB when the training sample is 110 per class. The computer has 3.40 GHz CPU and 16.0 GB RAM. We conclude that the KSRC is computationally expensive compared to the original SRC. If bands are nonlinearly generated for the SRC, then the computational cost is only slightly higher than using the original bands. The discrepancy on computational cost between NRS and KNRS is less significant. However, KNRS costs more time than the method using NRS on the generated datasets. The KSVM is the most time consuming approach. Compared with the NRS and SRC approaches, the KSVM is more computationally expensive.

Table 3. Computing time (in seconds) in multispectral Indian Pines dataset using 110 samples per class.

Datasets	SRC	KSRC	NRS	KNRS	KSVM
Original	50.49	311.89	122.70	152.81	1572.29
Original + Multiplication	54.84	—	131.27	—	—
Original + Division	56.78	—	135.90	—	—
Original + Multiplication + Division	57.88	—	137.05	—	—

Table 4. Computing time (in seconds) the multispectral University of Pavia dataset using 110 samples per class.

Datasets	SRC	KSRC	NRS	KNRS	KSVM
Original	228.54	2046.9	592.97	794.09	2122.59
Original + Multiplication	240.34	—	611.35	—	—
Original + Division	245.34	—	604.75	—	—
Original + Multiplication + Division	251.48	—	620.75	—	—

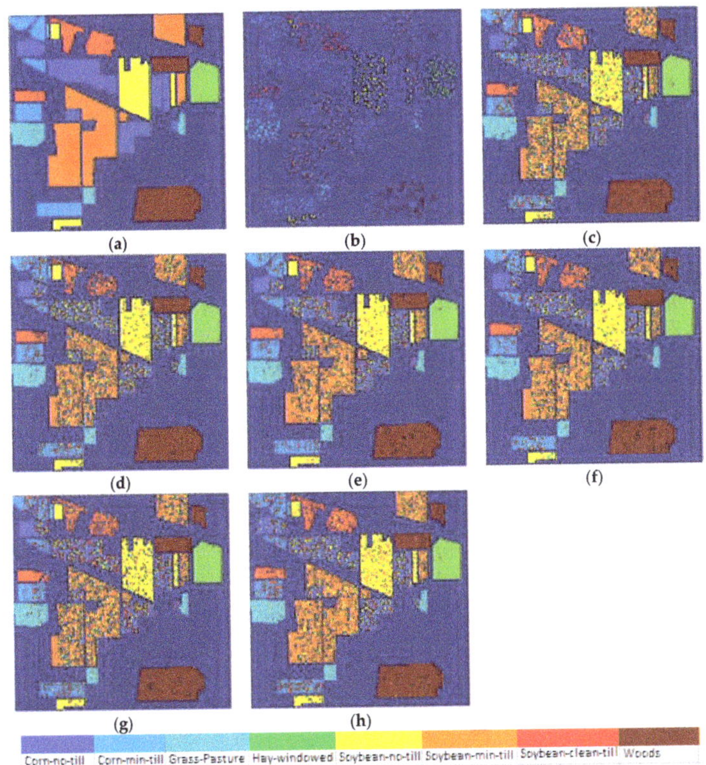

Figure 3. Thematic maps using 110 samples per class for the multispectral Indian Pines dataset with eight classes (and OA values). (**a**) Ground truth; (**b**) Training; (**c**) Original + NRS (0.7492); (**d**) Original + Multiplication + NRS (0.7781); (**e**) Original + Division + NRS (0.8159); (**f**) Original + Multiplication + Division + NRS (0.8124); (**g**) Original + KNRS (0.7852); (**h**) Original + KSVM (0.8193).

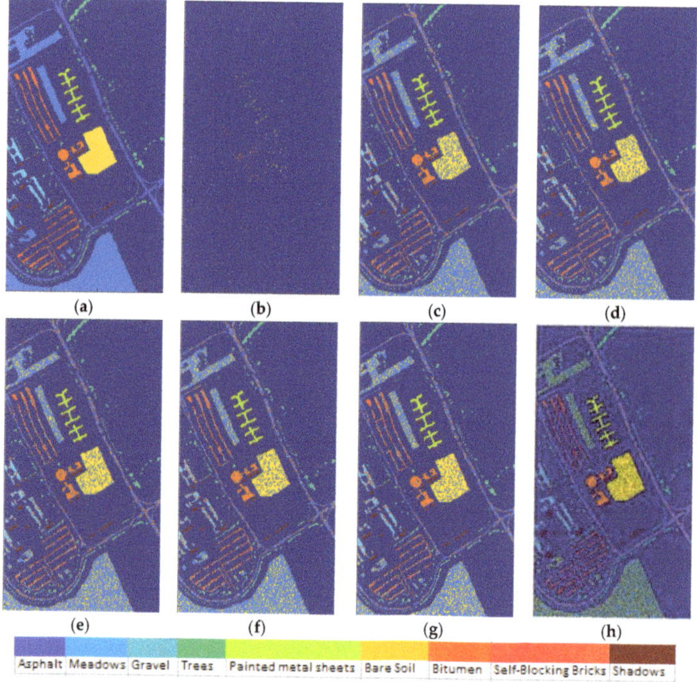

Figure 4. Thematic maps using 110 samples per class for the multispectral University of Pavia dataset with nine classes (and OA values). (**a**) Ground truth; (**b**) Training; (**c**) Original + NRS (0.7698); (**d**) Original + Multiplication + NRS (0.7820); (**e**) Original + Division + NRS (0.7896); (**f**) Original + Multiplication + Division + NRS (0.7880); (**g**) Original + KNRS (0.7736); (**h**) Original + KSVM (0.7981).

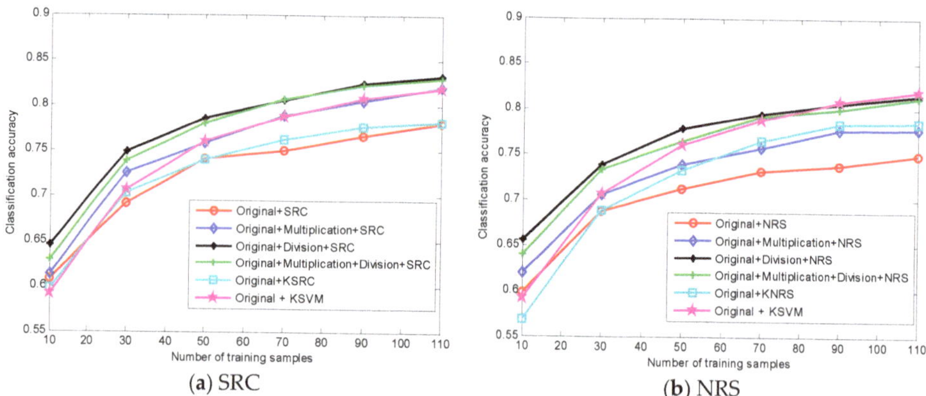

Figure 5. Classification on the multispectral dataset generated from the hyperspectral Indian Pines dataset.

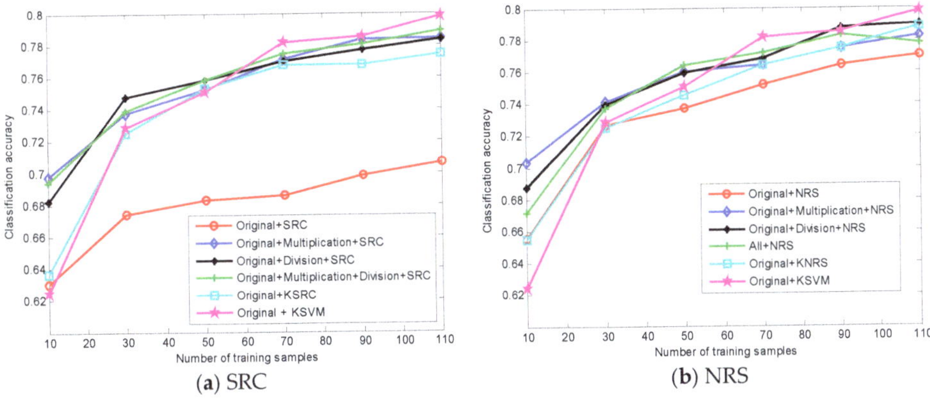

(a) SRC   **(b)** NRS

Figure 6. Classification on the multispectral dataset generated from the hyperspectral University of Pavia dataset.

4.3. Parameter Tuning

The parameter λ is important to the representation-based classifiers. In this session, we present the effects of different λ on both Indian Pines and the University of Pavia datasets using NRS and SRC. Figure 7a,b show the classification accuracy changes with λ in Indian Pines and Pavia University datasets, respectively. The training samples are set to be 90 per class, and each experiment is conducted 10 times to estimate the average results. Since the Original + Division provides better performance with less computational cost, we test the effects of different λ on its generated dataset. We can conclude a relatively small λ, e.g., 10^{-2}, can guarantee satisfactory performance for both NRS and SRC. Obviously, NRS is less sensitive to λ due to the fact that the Γ matrix can adaptively adjust the penalty according to the similarity between the training and testing pixels.

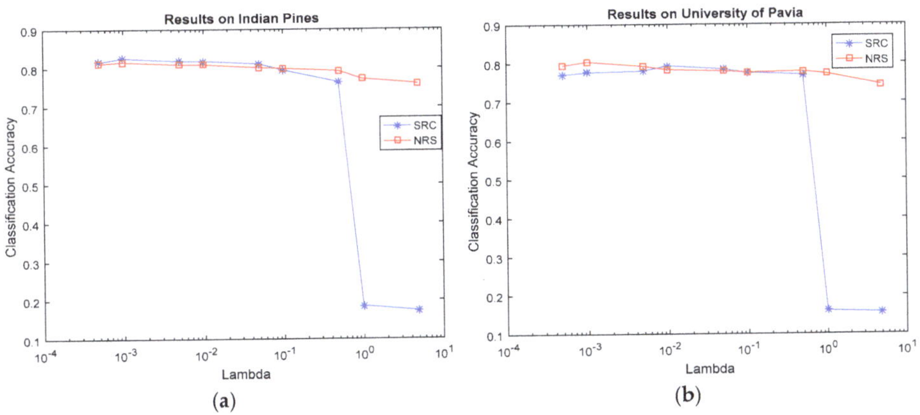

(a)   **(b)**

Figure 7. Classification Accuracy with different λ using NRS and SRC for: **(a)** multispectral Indian Pines; and **(b)** multispectral University of Pavia datasets.

In KSRC and KCRC, the radial basis function (RBF) is chosen as the kernel function. According to [12], the parameter γ of the kernel function is set as the median value of $1/(||\mathbf{x}_i - \bar{\mathbf{x}}||_2^2)$, $i = 1, 2, \ldots, n$, where $\bar{\mathbf{x}} = (1/n)\sum_{i=1}^{n} \mathbf{x}_i)$ is the mean of all available training samples. This simple strategy offers a similar performance as using the parameter tuned by cross-validation. For the RBF kernel in the KSVM, we choose the parameter γ and regularization parameter C with cross-validation.

4.4. Modified Band Ratio

To avoid a very small divider when calculating band ratio, a constant value of K can be added to both numerator and denominator. Figures 8 and 9 show the results for the Indian Pines and University of Pavia datasets. Since the minimum value of the Indian Pines data is about 0.12 (after normalization), the original version of band ratio with $K = 0$ may be sufficient. In the University of Pavia dataset with many close-to-zero values, this strategy can improve the performance. Overall, a small value of K, such as $K = 0.01$, is an appropriate choice for both SRC and NRS.

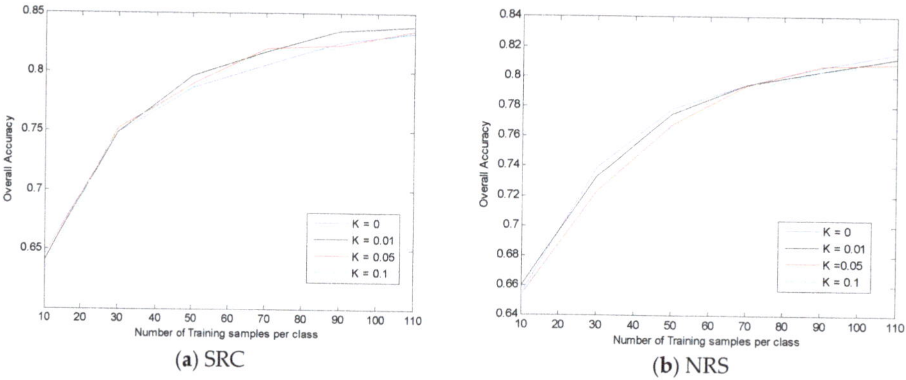

(a) SRC   (b) NRS

Figure 8. Classification on the multispectral Indian Pines dataset using the original plus division-generated bands (original + division) with different adjustment parameter K.

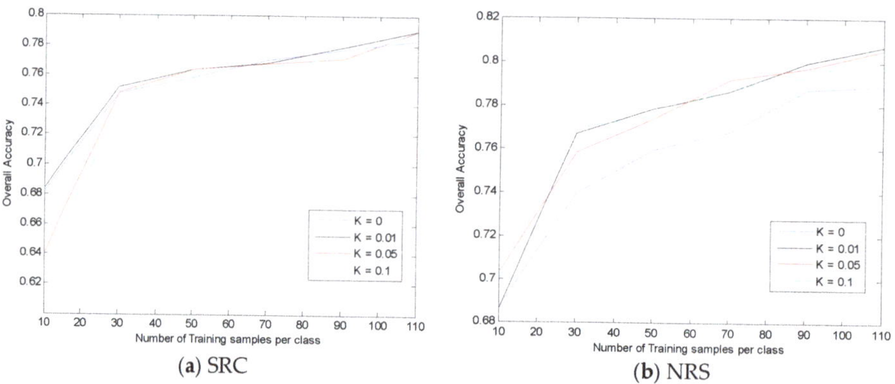

(a) SRC   (b) NRS

Figure 9. Classification on the multispectral University of Pavia dataset using the original plus division-generated bands (original + division) with different adjustment parameter K.

5. Conclusions

This paper proposes to use nonlinear band generation method with explicit functions for multispectral classification. Two classifiers, i.e., SRC and NRS, and their kernel versions are evaluated on the new datasets. The experimental results show that this method performs better than the traditional kernel methods with higher classification accuracy and much lower computational cost. In particular, it can outperform when the number of training samples is small.

The difficulty of nonlinear band generation is choosing an appropriate nonlinear function for different datasets collected by various sensors covering all kinds of image scenes. In our experiments, it turns out that the band ratio offers the best performance. Considering its role in removing illumination factor [19], it would be a reasonable choice. Modified band ratio with a small adjustment parameter may further improve the performance when an image scene contains materials with very low reflectance.

Author Contributions: Yan Xu and Qian Du designed the experiments, prepared the first draft, and edited the manuscript. Wei Li, Chen Chen, and Nicolas H. Younan reviewed and edited the manuscript.

References

1. Xu, Y.; Du, Q.; Younan, N. Particle swarm optimization-based band selection for hyperspectral target detection. *IEEE Geosci. Remote Sens. Lett.* **2017**, *14*, 554–558. [CrossRef]
2. Su, H.; Yang, H.; Du, Q.; Sheng, Y. Semi-supervised band clustering for dimensionality reduction of hyperspectral imagery. *IEEE Geosci. Remote Sens. Lett.* **2011**, *8*, 1135–1139. [CrossRef]
3. Wright, J.; Yang, A.Y.; Ganesh, A.; Sastry, S.S.; Ma, Y. Robust face recognition via sparse representation. *IEEE PAMI* **2009**, *31*, 210–227. [CrossRef] [PubMed]
4. Zhang, L.; Yang, M.; Feng, X. Sparse Representation or Collaborative Representation: Which Helps faCe Recognition? In Proceedings of the 2011 International Conference on Computer Vision, Barcelona, Spain, 6–13 November 2011; pp. 471–478.
5. Li, W.; Tramel, E.W.; Prasad, S.; Fowler, J.E. Nearest regularized subspace for hyperspectral classification. *IEEE Trans. Geosci. Remote Sens.* **2014**, *52*, 477–489. [CrossRef]
6. Zou, J.; Li, W.; Du, Q. Sparse representation-based nearest neighbor classifiers for hyperspectral imagery. *IEEE Geosci. Remote Sens. Lett.* **2015**, *12*, 2418–2422.
7. Xiong, M.; Ran, Q.; Li, W.; Zou, J.; Du, Q. Hyperspectral image classification using weighted joint collaborative representation. *IEEE Geosci. Remote Sens. Lett.* **2015**, *12*, 1209–1213. [CrossRef]
8. Bian, X.; Chen, C.; Xu, Y.; Du, Q. Robust hyperspectral image classification by multi-layer spatial-spectral sparse representations. *Remote Sens.* **2016**, *8*, 985. [CrossRef]
9. Li, W.; Du, Q. Joint within-class collaborative representation for hyperspectral image classification. *IEEE J. Sel. Top. Appl. Earth Obs. Remote Sens.* **2014**, *7*, 2200–2208. [CrossRef]
10. Li, W.; Du, Q. Gabor-filtering based nearest regularized subspace for hyperspectral image classification. *IEEE J. Sel. Top. Appl. Earth Obs. Remote Sens.* **2014**, *7*, 1012–1022. [CrossRef]
11. Li, W.; Du, Q. A survey on representation-based classification and detection in hyperspectral imagery. *Pattern Recognit. Lett.* **2016**, *83*, 115–123. [CrossRef]
12. Melgani, F.; Bruzzone, L. Classification of hyperspectral remote sensing images with support vector machines. *IEEE Trans. Geosci. Remote Sens.* **2004**, *42*, 1778–1790. [CrossRef]
13. Bernabe, S.; Marpu, P.R.; Plaza, A.; Mura, M.D.; Benediktsson, J.A. Spectral–spatial classification of multispectral images using kernel feature space representation. *IEEE Geosci. Remote Sens. Lett.* **2014**, *11*, 288–292. [CrossRef]
14. Li, W.; Du, Q.; Xiong, M. Kernel collaborative representation with Tikhonov regularization for hyperspectral image classification. *IEEE Geosci. Remote Sens. Lett.* **2015**, *12*, 48–52.
15. Chen, Y.; Nasrabadi, N.M.; Tran, T.D. Hyperspectral image classification via kernel sparse representation. *IEEE Trans. Geosci. Remote Sens.* **2013**, *51*, 217–231. [CrossRef]

16. Ren, H.; Chang, C.-I. A generalized orthogonal subspace projection approach to unsupervised multispectral image classification. *IEEE Trans. Geosci. Remote Sens.* **2000**, *38*, 2515–2528.
17. SPArse Modeling Software. Available online: http://spams-devel.gforge.inria.fr/ (accessed on 15 October 2016).
18. Du, Q.; Kopriva, I.; Szu, H. Independent component analysis for classifying multispectral images with dimensionality limitation. *Int. J. Inf. Acquis.* **2004**, *1*, 201–216. [CrossRef]
19. Lillesand, T.; Kiefer, R.W. *Remote Sensing and Image Interpretation*; Wiley: Hoboken, NJ, USA, 2015.
20. Wang, Z.; Bovik, A.C.; Sheikh, H.R.; Simoncelli, E.P. Image quality assessment: from error visibility to structural similarity. *IEEE Trans. Image Proc.* **2004**, *13*, 600–612. [CrossRef]
21. Platt, R.V.; Goetz, A.F.H. A comparison of AVIRIS and Landsat for land use classification at the urban fringe. *Photogram. Eng. Remote Sens.* **2004**, *70*, 813–819. [CrossRef]
22. Kramer, H.J. *Observations of the Earth and Its Environment*; Springer: Berlin, Germany, 2002.

 *remote sensing*

Article

One-Dimensional Convolutional Neural Network Land-Cover Classification of Multi-Seasonal Hyperspectral Imagery in the San Francisco Bay Area, California

Daniel Guidici [1] and Matthew L. Clark [2,*]

[1]   Department of Engineering Science, Sonoma State University, 1801 E Cotati Ave, Rohnert Park, CA 94928, USA; daniel.giudici@gmail.com
[2]   Center for Interdisciplinary Geospatial Analysis (CIGA), Department of Geography, Environment and Planning, Sonoma State University, 1801 E Cotati Ave, Rohnert Park, CA 94928, USA
*   Correspondence: mateolclark@gmail.com; Tel.: +1-707-664-2558

Academic Editors: Qi Wang, Nicolas H. Younan, Carlos López-Martínez and Prasad S. Thenkabail
Received: 10 May 2017; Accepted: 14 June 2017; Published: 20 June 2017

Abstract: In this study, a 1-D Convolutional Neural Network (CNN) architecture was developed, trained and utilized to classify single (summer) and three seasons (spring, summer, fall) of hyperspectral imagery over the San Francisco Bay Area, California for the year 2015. For comparison, the Random Forests (RF) and Support Vector Machine (SVM) classifiers were trained and tested with the same data. In order to support space-based hyperspectral applications, all analyses were performed with simulated Hyperspectral Infrared Imager (HyspIRI) imagery. Three-season data improved classifier overall accuracy by 2.0% (SVM), 1.9% (CNN) to 3.5% (RF) over single-season data. The three-season CNN provided an overall classification accuracy of 89.9%, which was comparable to overall accuracy of 89.5% for SVM. Both three-season CNN and SVM outperformed RF by over 7% overall accuracy. Analysis and visualization of the inner products for the CNN provided insight to distinctive features within the spectral-temporal domain. A method for CNN kernel tuning was presented to assess the importance of learned features. We concluded that CNN is a promising candidate for hyperspectral remote sensing applications because of the high classification accuracy and interpretability of its inner products.

Keywords: hyperspectral imagery; 1-dimensional (1-D); Convolutional Neural Network (CNN); Support Vector Machine (SVM); Random Forests (RF); machine learning; deep learning; TensorFlow; multi-seasonal; regional land cover

---

1. Introduction

Land-cover maps provide information for natural resource and ecosystem service management, conservation planning, urban planning, agricultural monitoring, and the assessment of long-term land change. The automated classification of land cover from satellite imagery is a challenging task due to spectral mixing, intra-class spectral variability, and low spectral contrast among classes. Hyperspectral, or imaging spectroscopy, data consist of hundreds of spectral bands, and capture more spectral detail and variability relative to conventional multispectral sensors used for mapping land cover. Terrestrial hyperspectral applications have shown success in mapping composition, physiology, and biochemistry of vegetation, ecosystem disturbance, and built-up environments [1]. The analysis of hyperspectral data presents issues in classification, due to large data volumes, and increased spectral variability as recorded by hundreds of correlated bands [2]. Additionally, the classification task becomes more difficult when presented with the larger spatial extents and temporally detailed data collected by spaceborne hyperspectral sensors with repeat measurements.

A traditional classification method for hyperspectral imagery involves Multiple Endmember Spectral Mixture Analysis (MESMA), which consists of unmixing image spectra with pure spectral profiles (endmembers), and assigning the class through endmembers selected in the unmixing solution [3]. This family of methods typically requires regionally specific libraries of pure spectral profiles that are from field spectra, synthetically generated, or selected from large libraries of image spectra [4]. This type of classification is the most closed form solution available currently, analytically processing an exhaustive combination of endmembers that most closely match the data to be classified [3]. Further, MESMA assumes linear mixing, which is often violated by the interaction of photons with components within an individual pixel and from nearby pixels.

Machine learning is an alternative domain of classification techniques that can accurately distinguish land cover in hyperspectral and multi-seasonal imagery [5]. In contrast to MESMA, these classifiers can learn non-linear decision spaces and do not require training data optimization steps to select spectrally pure endmembers. There are many different varieties of machine learning algorithms implemented on different platforms. Picking the classifier to analyze a dataset at times falls to the user's familiarity with the computational platform and/or algorithm for a specific field. Random Forests (RF) and Support Vector Machines (SVM) are widely adopted machine learning classifiers in the remote sensing community [6,7]. These algorithms have provided robust results across many platforms and datasets, surpassing many other families and implementations of classifiers [8].

Convolutional Neural Network (CNN) is a leading machine learning classifier for image recognition tasks that use 2-dimensional (2-D) image data [9,10], such as identifying faces in photographs of people. Applications of CNN have extended into the classification of other contiguous data types, like speech recognition utilizing 1-dimensional (1-D) data [11]. In remote sensing, there have been several recent applications of CNNs and other similar "deep" network topologies [12–18]. The form in which CNNs are applied to remote sensing data can vary significantly depending on the data available, as there is no universal deep network classification architecture. The application of a CNN to classify land cover from 2-D visual images has been performed with good results in their respective applications. For example, Kussel et al. [15] achieved a 95% overall accuracy with land-cover classification and Li et al. [19] had a 96% correct detection of plants within a scene. In some applications, segmentation and previously learned features can be transferred and leveraged as part of the CNN classification task [12,20–22]. The method within [18,23,24] applies down-selected spectra to a 2-D CNN architecture, thereby mainly exploiting the spatial extent of the data. The spectral dimension is reduced because large number of features present with hyperspectral imagery typically poses a problem for some classifiers, and many studies use dimensionality reduction (DR) to aid in the classification process [13,18,23–26]. In [23–25] the spectral dimension was reduced, for example by applying principal component analysis [23,24], comparing salient band vectors in a manifold ranking space to consider hyperspectral data structure [25], or clustering similar bands and extracting features [26]. All these methods reduce the number of spectral bands before subjecting the data to the classifier. The method provided in [6] pre-calculates features based on physical and chemical composition. All these DR methods have shown an increase in classification accuracy as compared to using the full hyperspectral data. In contrast, some studies have shown increased classification accuracy when utilizing the full spectra, invalidating the need for complex DR preprocessing. For example, the work done in [13] shows the comparison between a 3-dimensional (3-D) CNN, which utilizes the full spectral dimension, and other methods that do not utilize the full spectral dimension. The 3-D CNN spanning the full spectral dimension increased accuracy by up to 3%. In this case, the CNN classifier determines what are the distinctive features from the initial data, without a DR pre-processing step. As another example, Hu et al. [17] utilized single-season hyperspectral data and 1-D CNN across the full spectral dimension to classify land cover with 90 to 93% overall accuracy, and CNN outperformed SVM by 1 to 3%. A distinction between the extraction of key spectra by using DR and spectral feature generation from the CNN is that the CNN approach extracts features based on spectral characteristics directly driven from reducing classification error. This makes CNN a promising method for the exploitation of the distinctive aspects of the spectral dimension of the data and warrants further investigation with hyperspectral land-cover mapping applications at various spatial and temporal scales.

A broad goal of this study is to assess the accuracy of a 1-D CNN for classifying land cover from multi-seasonal hyperspectral imagery. Accuracy from this CNN is compared to those from the two leading machine learning classification methods in remote sensing, RF and SVM. These methods were utilized as a control group due to their high accuracy rates, high prevalence within the field and the robust libraries available for their implementation. In order to support applications based on spaceborne hyperspectral imagery, our analyses were performed with simulated Hyperspectral Infrared Imager (HyspIRI) imagery, a satellite mission currently being considered by NASA. Our analyses are regional in scale, covering the San Francisco Bay Area, California, and land-cover classes followed the global Land-Cover Classification System (LCCS) [27].

A CNN architecture requires the data to be in a contiguous format as convolutional layers of the network distinguish, or filter, local features or patterns from neighboring regions throughout the data. The neural network then performs the subsequent classification based on these learned features. A potentially useful feature of CNN architectures is that the inner resulting data products, such as properties of convolutional filters, can provide some insight into what the classifier has learned to make its classification. The inner data products of CNN architectures as applied to 1-D hyperspectral data have not been discussed in the literature. Thus, another goal of this study is to show how the inner data products of CNN can provide insight into the classification task and the features extracted from the spectra through the training of the network. With the analysis of feature maps that the convolutional layer of this network creates, local regions within the spectral dimension of the data that are excited by the convolutional layer of the network can be shown to have an impact on the classification accuracy. The importance of these learned features can be then traced back to how important they are to the classification task, by zeroing them from the network and re-computing the accuracy. Additional processing of the feature maps extracted from the CNN enables an illustrative visual that reveals which spectral areas assist in separating the classes. By standardizing, scaling and capturing only the magnitude of the convolutional kernel feature maps, the spectral-temporal band importance can be visually explored.

2. Materials and Methods

2.1. Study Area

The study area was the San Francisco Bay Area in northern California, USA (Figure 1) and is described in Clark and Kilham [6]. Natural vegetation in the study area includes evergreen needleleaf forests (conifer), evergreen broadleaf forests, deciduous broadleaf forests, mixed forests, shrublands and grasslands. Anthropomorphic land cover includes dense urban areas around the San Francisco Bay and perennial crops (e.g., vineyards, fruit orchards) and annual crops (e.g., strawberries, cotton, rice).

2.2. Simulated HyspIRI Imagery

Hyperspectral imagery for the ~30,000 km^2 study area was from NASA's Airborne Visible Infrared Imaging Spectrometer (AVIRIS) "Classic" sensor, flown in spring, summer and fall of year 2015 [1]. The AVIRIS-C sensor images spectral radiance in 224 bands from 370 nm (visible) to 2500 nm (shortwave infrared, SWIR) with 10 nm sampling and SNR of >1000:1 at 600 nm and >400:1 at 2200 nm [28,29]. There were twelve, ~12 km swath flight runs per season that provided 20% image overlap among runs. Complete spring and fall runs were used while different dates were used to make a complete, cloud-free summer dataset (Table 1, Figure 1).

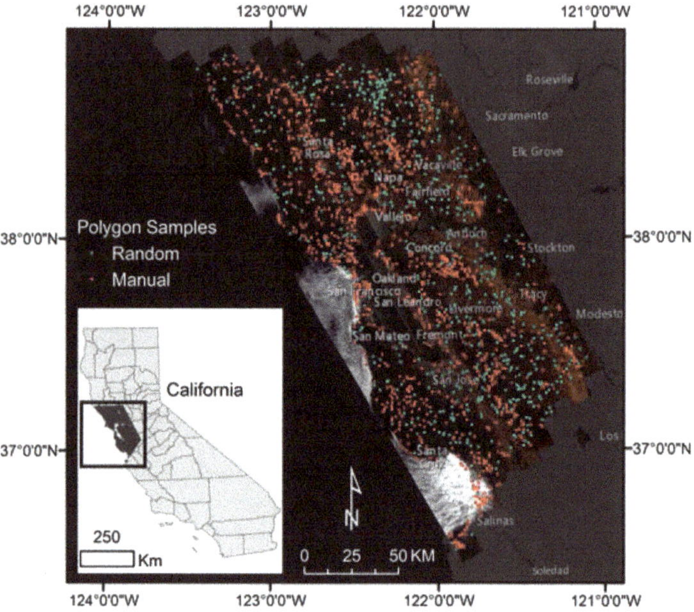

Figure 1. Study area overview with an AVIRIS-C, 11 June 2015 RGB mosaic of 12 individual flight runs. Reference data are red and cyan points. Inset shows the multi-seasonal image extent with water and cloud mask applied.

Table 1. Summary of San Francisco Bay Area AVIRIS-C images for the year 2015.

Season	Image Collection Dates (UTC)	Runs Used	Average Solar Zenith	Average Solar Azimuth
Spring	30 April (16:48–21:25)	Runs 06–17	26.7°	147.0°
Summer	11 June (18:30–23:42)	Runs 09–20	20.1°	227.2°
	15 June (21:32–22:51)	Runs 12, 15	33.3°	254.5°
Fall	2 October (17:19–22:32)	Runs 06–13; Runs 16–20	42.2°	191.9°

Hyperspectral images from AVIRIC-C were used to simulate HyspIRI as part of a preparatory science campaign [1,6]. The current configuration of HyspIRI is a satellite sensor with 30-m spatial resolution, 185 km swath width, and 16-day repeat global coverage [1]. The measurements would cover 380 to 2510 nm in ≤10-nm contiguous bands (~214 bands). The AVIRIS-C radiance data were processed by NASA's Jet Propulsion Laboratory into HyspIRI Precursor Data Products (Figure 1) and can be downloaded at http://aviris.jpl.nasa.gov. The 30-m simulated HyspIRI products include, in order: orthrorectification and 90 × 90-m Gaussian-weighted resampling of at-sensor radiance to 30 m pixels, addition of noise approximating a HyspIRI visible-SWIR Noise Equivalent Delta Radiance (NEdL) function, and ATREM-based per-pixel atmospheric correction and apparent surface reflectance retrieval [6,30]. Bands in the shortwave infrared with strong atmospheric water vapor absorption and poor signal-to-noise were removed, leaving 186 bands for analysis per season. Clouds and water in simulated images were masked prior to image classification using a Random Forests classifier developed in Clark and Kilham [6]. The analysis of multi-season data was performed on an image cube of seasonal spectral data stacked in temporal sequence (spring, summer, fall), resulting in an input vector of 558 bands; $N_d = 186\ (bands) \times 3\ (seasons)$.

2.3. Land-Cover Reference Data

Reference data for training and testing were collected using visual interpretation of high-resolution imagery in Google Earth. Detailed methods are found in Clark and Kilham [6] and summarized below. Data were percent cover of the following twelve "land-cover components" within a polygon: evergreen needleleaf trees (ENT); evergreen broadleaf trees (EBT); deciduous broadleaf trees (DBT); shrubs; herbaceous; dune vegetation; tidal marsh; annual crops; perennial crops; impervious surfaces; urban landscape; and, bare non-vegetated (beaches, dunes, rocks, bare soil). Percent cover data were visually estimated in 10% intervals using high-resolution Google Earth imagery in 100-, 250- or 500-m square polygons. Different polygon sizes were chosen depending on patch size in order to maximize pixels collected in large patches (e.g., 500-m square chosen), while minimizing mixed pixels in relatively small patches (e.g., 100-m square chosen). Polygons were located over areas of well-mixed land-cover components, with most centers further than 1000 m to a neighboring sample. Initially, a simple random method was used to locate samples, which led to under-represented samples of some classes. This necessitated manual placement to ensure an adequate sample of class types (Figure 1). Each polygon was classified into one of twelve discrete Land-Cover Classification System [27] classes using a decision-tree of rules applied to a polygon's percent cover data (Table A1; [6]). Open-canopy trees (woodlands) and shrubs (shrublands) have >10–65% tree or shrub cover, respectively; closed-canopy trees (forests) and shrubs (thickets) have >65% tree or shrub cover, respectively. In this study, we focus on mapping closed-canopy tree and shrub classes.

There were 1495 total reference polygons for the twelve LCCS classes. Reference reflectance spectra were extracted from polygons overlaid on the three-season image cube for each run (Figure 2). To exclude potentially mixed pixels at edges and minimize geolocation error, polygons were buffered inward using a half-pixel buffer, and only pixels that were 100% contained by the buffered polygon were selected. Due to scene overlap, there were some polygons that were located in two images. In these cases, all available pixels were extracted. Reference data were split at the polygon level into training and testing sets using the same polygon designations found in Clark & Kilham [6], except polygons in areas of fires between years 2013 and 2015 were removed from the analysis. Training spectra were then filtered at the polygon level to remove outliers following methods in Clark & Kilham [6]. Single- and three-season data were processed for outliers separately for each group of variables. There were a total of 71,362 training pixels and 52,510 testing pixels (Figure 3).

2.4. Classifier Architectures and Tuning

Three machine classifiers were assessed in this work: Random Forest (RF), Support Vector Machine (SVM) and Convolutional Neural Network (CNN). We used Python's Scikit-learn machine learning library for training and classification. This library provides access to established data mining and data analysis tools and algorithms for implementing RF and SVM. The adaptations of the respective CNN architectures require a relatively flexible platform for development. A CNN is a deep network topology that can be formed as a computational graph and Google's open-source computational platform, TensorFlow™, is directly suited for this application. In this study, we used TensorFlow™ for the CNN definition, training and classification portion of this work. This platform had the additional advantage of using the GPU to speed data processing, whereas Scikit-learn relied solely on the CPU.

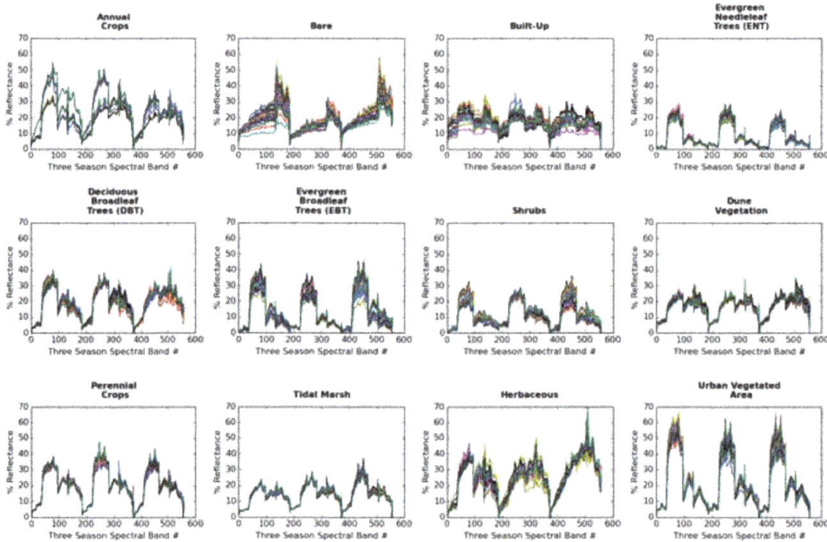

Figure 2. Twenty-five randomly selected three-season reflectance spectra from each of the twelve LCCS classes. Note that the x-axis is the band number (1–558) with seasons in spring- summer-fall sequence. Bad bands have been removed within each season (186 bands per season).

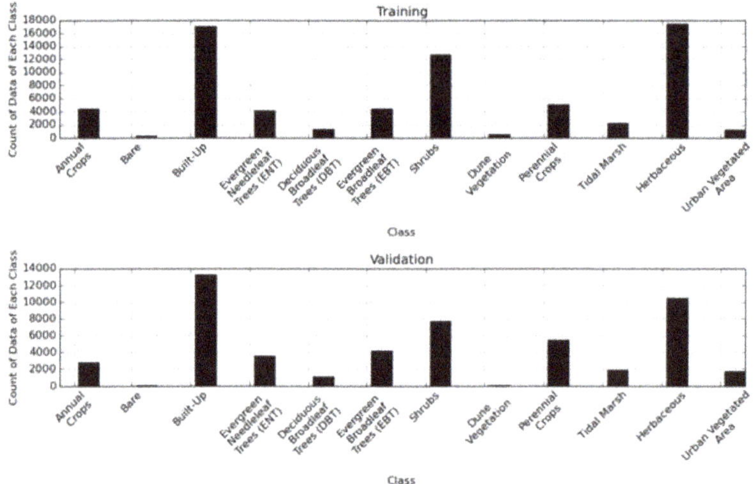

Figure 3. Training and testing reference data distributions.

Below we provide a brief background and explanation of the RF, SVM and CNN classifiers and their respective hyper-parameters. An overview of the method is shown in Figure 4. Training and testing reference data included duplicate pixels from areas of scene overlap, thus providing spectral variation for differences in sensor view and sun angle in the classification process. We did not have a validation dataset due to the limited number of samples of some classes within the data. Training data were thus used to train the classifier, while hyper-parameter tuning was performed by observing training and test data accuracies. The final accuracy assessment was performed by extracting the most trusted classification from each classifier in the areas of scene overlap. This consists of utilizing data classifications that result from classifications that have the highest confidence for RF or highest probability for SVM and CNN (Section 2.6; Figure 4, LCCS-labeled Land-Cover Samples).

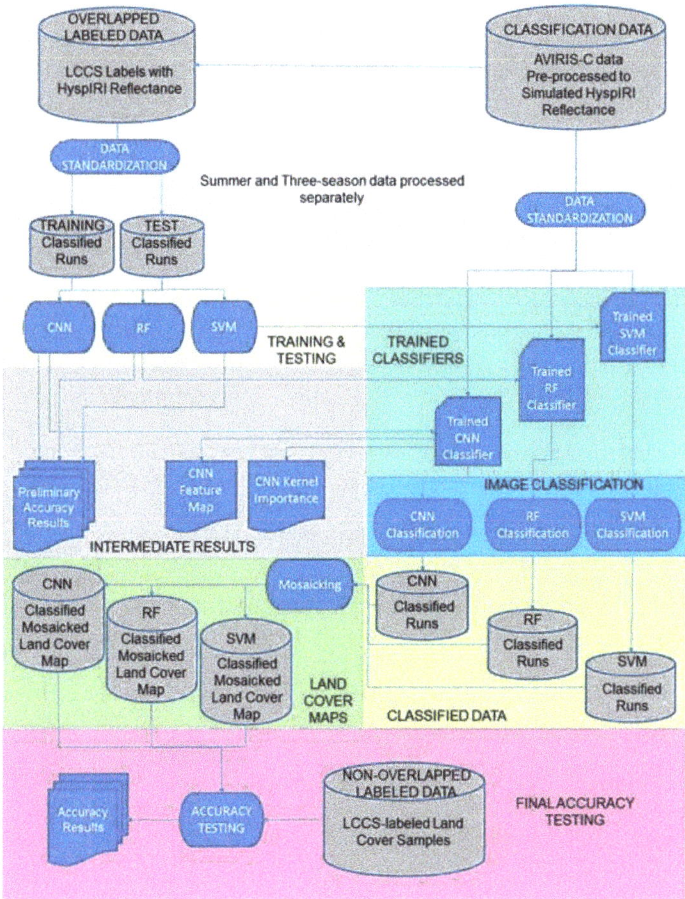

Figure 4. Overview of machine learning classification and accuracy assessment methodology.

2.4.1. Random Forest

The RF classifier is a technique of training an ensemble of decision trees through randomized draws of training data. Once the ensemble of trees is created, data are applied to the classifier and the prediction across the individual trees is captured [31]. The plurality of predictions is the resulting classification of this algorithm.

There are three main parameters when tuning a Random Forest classifier: the number of estimators (or trees), the maximum number of features utilized at each decision point within a tree and the minimum samples at each leaf. As a general rule, the number of features utilized in RF classifiers is $\sqrt{N_f}$, where N_f is the number of features. In hyperspectral imagery, each feature is an individual reflectance band. The number of trees included in the ensemble typically improves classification accuracy until a critical point is reached, beyond which accuracy does not increase further. For the minimum leaf size, smaller values result in RF classifiers that are more prone to capturing noise in the training data. Optimization of these parameters should be considered when training a RF classifier on a particular dataset [32].

For this work the standard *Max Number of Features* $= \sqrt{N_f}$ was utilized. The number of trees was increased until there was not a significant change in prediction accuracy, resulting in a parameter of 1000 trees. A search across the minimum leaf sizes was performed, resulting in a parameter of 1 sample in leaves.

2.4.2. Support Vector Machine

The SVM classifier separates training data by defining a hyperplane(s) through the data to segment the classes. In two dimensions, this can be visualized as a line drawn between two classes that defines the maximum separation in spectral space. For non-linear and high dimensional classification tasks, the data are mapped to an even higher dimensional space and the "line" that is drawn between the classes is, in effect, a plane which creates the most separation between the classes. How this mapping to the higher-dimensional space is performed is dictated by hyper-parameters. A standard linear Support Vector Classifier that utilizes a one-vs.-rest classification scheme was utilized for this work. This implementation simplifies the tuning of the classifier down to one parameter, cost (C). This parameter accounts for the trade-off between misclassification of training examples and simplicity of the decision surface. A low C makes this decision surface smooth, while a high C aims at classifying all training examples by giving the model freedom to select more samples as support vectors [33]. A linear search for this tuning parameter was performed from 1.0×10^{-2} to 1.0×10^{10} and the highest accuracy classifier was chosen; a C value of 0.1 was utilized for this work.

2.4.3. Convolutional Neural Network

At a broad level, a CNN is a deep-network topology that typically combines convolutional filter layers in conjunction with a classification network, which for this work is a fully connected Neural Network (NN). Through the standard back-propagation training process, convolutional filters are trained to capture salient structural feature information from the sequential input data. Hu and colleagues [17] mention these structural features as the "intraclass appearance and shape variation" within spectra. As an extension from this previous literature, here we demonstrate that these structural features actually represent those features present within the data that distinguish the classes from each other. The architecture feeds these features, or filtered input data, into a subsequent classification process.

A flow diagram of our CNN process is shown in Figure 5. For some datasets, like those consisting of 2-D imagery, larger networks are required.

CNN Architecture

The feature generation and feature classification nature of CNN can become complex with multiple layers that extract different levels of features from the data. A few examples of more complex CNN architectures as implemented for image classification tasks can be reviewed in [9,10]. These complex networks required the learning of a large number of features and a high level of neural network complexity. These traditional CNN architectures are implemented in two dimensions (i.e., 2-D, width and a height). The convolutional operation for these networks occurs with multi-dimensional kernels and in various configurations, with the goal to classify the full or subsets of the image. In contrast, hyperspectral data classification can be a pixel-based operation spanning only the spectral dimension (i.e., 1-D), or in the spatial and spectral dimensions (i.e., 3-D). To simplify implementation and compare results to RF and SVM, we chose to apply the CNN across the spectral domain of hyperspectral pixels; and thus, the convolutional operation of the network only needs to operate on this single dimension. This in turn greatly simplifies the architecture of the hyperspectral CNN relative to 2-D or 3-D implementations [9,10,13,15].

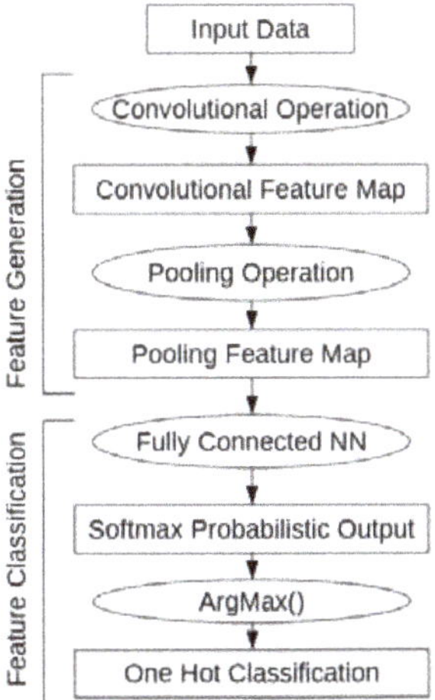

Figure 5. Convolutional Neural Network (CNN) flow diagram.

Our CNN architecture resembles a network that has been recently introduced for hyperspectral data classification in [17]. The network consists of a single convolution layer paired with a pooling layer that feeds a fully connected neural network. Our network was further refined by adding Dropout and Regularization of the fully connected layer [34,35]. Additionally, here we tune the convolutional layers based on a technique that reduces the number of kernels trained within the network by accounting for their impact on the classifier accuracy.

The single convolutional layer accepts the 1-D spectral profile input data and performs the convolutional operation on the input data with each kernel in the architecture (Figure 6). This filtering of input data with each kernel creates the features for classification. In our implementation of CNN, the number of initial kernels to be trained was set at 86, the number of single-season engineered metrics used in our previous research with these hyperspectral data and the RF classifier [6]. In that study, engineered "spectral metrics" targeted vegetation biochemical and structural properties found in reflectance spectra, and perform a similar function as the kernels for this network. Because the learned features within the CNN are not tied to any pre-selected spectral features, rather only spectral properties that best distinguish the classes, the number of kernels in the CNN was drastically reduced by evaluating kernel importance (Section 3.2).

The pooling layer can be thought of as a spectral down-sampling of the convolutional feature map (Figure 6). A Max Pooling operation was utilized here. This layer accepts the convolutional feature map, evaluates pairs of data elements across the spectral dimension of the feature maps and passes the maximum value onto the next layer. This down-samples the data by a factor of two while preserving the maximum excitations from the convolutional feature map. This operation reduces the size of the feature map while preserving the features observed within the convolutional feature map. This provides a level of invariance to the spectral location of feature excitation within the feature generation network and reduces the overall number of connections to the fully connected network; and subsequently, this process will decrease the total number of trainable parameters for the network, thereby reducing overall training time.

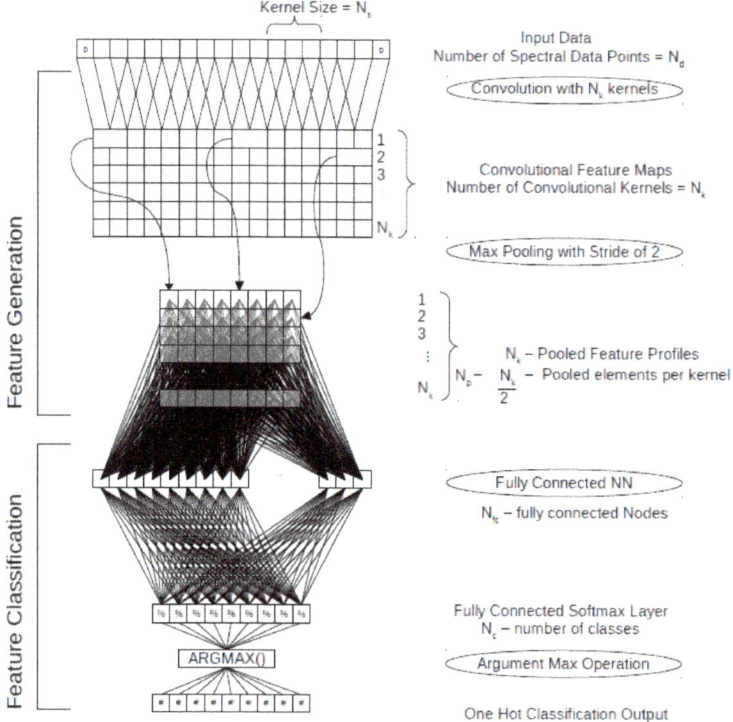

Figure 6. Detailed Convolutional Neural Network (CNN) architecture.

This Pooled Feature map is then provided to the feature classification network (Figure 6). In this architecture the feature classification network consists of a fully connected neural network. This fully connected network layer consists of a hidden layer with 500 nodes. This network's learning is regularized by including standard neural network regularization techniques; specifically, dropout with a 50% dropout level and L2 regularization on the weights connecting the pooled feature map and the fully-connected NN's hidden nodes. These two techniques enable the classification network to learn information throughout the fully connected network and encourage "smaller" weights to be utilized within the classification network. This ensures that individual weights between the two networks (feature generation and feature classification) are not exorbitantly larger than the other weights within the same layer, helping to prevent overfitting of the training data. By applying a penalty for large weights at this layer, the network is encouraged to learn information through all of the kernels and not just a few of them.

The output of the hidden layer is connected to a final Softmax output layer that produces a probabilistic output per class, or a vector of length of the number of classes, with each value representing the probability that the input data belongs to a specific class (Figure 6). This probability or confidence that the Softmax layer calculates is shown in Equation (1).

$$\sigma(z)_j = \frac{e^{z_j}}{\Sigma_{k=1}^{K} e^{z_k}} \; for \; j = 1, \ldots K \tag{1}$$

where Z_j are the inputs from the previous fully-connected layer applied to each Softmax layer node and K is the number of Softmax layer nodes (i.e., the number of classes). Finding the location of the argument with the largest probability value via the Argmax() function provides a one-hot representation of the class (Figure 6).

Stochastic gradient decent was utilized for training of the CNN. During training, this learning method subjects randomized labeled data to the network and calculates a loss function. This loss is then propagated back through the network to modify the network's interconnections, based on the impact the respective weights had on the previous epoch's classification. This is the gradient of the network, and is essentially the degree to which the weights of the network have impacted a given classification and resulted in a respective loss. Modifying the network based on the loss calculated by the classification or misclassification of the labeled data is effectively the back-propagation algorithm. As training progresses, the back-propagation modifies the interconnection of the network to reduce the loss function. This decreasing of the loss function indicates the classified data more closely matches the labeled data. Learning curves are provided in Appendix Figures A2 and A3 for the training and testing data, respectively, and show overfitting is not occurring within the testing data.

The TensorFlow™ platform has built-in implementations for calculating the gradients of the network and the minimization of the loss function to be back-propagated through the network. The Adagrad adaptive learning rate algorithm was utilized from the TensorFlow™ platform. The usage of an adaptive learning rate provided a significant boost to the performance of this architecture on the order of 4% overall classification accuracy. Additionally, the Adagrad adaptive learning rate greatly sped up the training of the network as compared to fixed and the exponential decaying learning rate optimizers. The Adagrad optimizer adjusts the learning rate, the extent the network can be modified, based on the gradient recently seen by the network. As this optimizer is suited for relatively sparse data and the dataset analyzed here is relatively unbalanced (Figure 3), this optimizer seemed to be an appropriate fit for this architecture. Empirical testing proved that this algorithm reached a maximum accuracy with a seed-learning rate of 0.1.

Hyper-Parameter Tuning

Dominant tunable hyper-parameters of this architecture are: K_s the kernel size, N_k the number of kernels, and N_h the number of hidden nodes within the classification network (Figure 6). While other characteristics can be modified within the network, these three hyper-parameters were determined to be the most influential. Other parameters such as dropout level and regularization level on the hidden weights could be adjusted, but our experience was that just having these parameters defined would increase the accuracy of the network. We used values of 50% dropout and 1×10^{-4} for regularization.

The kernel size dictates the size of the feature to capture. It is the size of the local receptive field considered within the spectral dimension for the convolution with the data. A rule of thumb originating from the currently engineered features utilized in [6] is to use local receptive fields that are roughly 10 bands long (10 bands × 10 nm spacing = 100 nm) for a single season. Informal experiments indicated that K_s could change in size as long as the Number of Kernels, N_k, varied inversely with this value. We believe that this is because the modification of these two parameters effectively varies the capacity of the network to learn the data, as long as the network is sufficiently able to learn the parameters equivalent accuracy should be able to be achieved. Due to familiarity with local receptive fields of 10 in prior work this was used as the kernel size in our CNN implementation.

The number of kernels contained within the network represents the number of features able to be learned. As the capacity of the network to learn features is a combination of the number of kernels and the kernel size. If each of those features are very descriptive, and has a large kernel size, then it would be expected that fewer of them would be required to achieve similar results. With the kernel size set, it was determined that the number of kernels can be reduced until zeroing a kernel from the classifier always has negative effect on overall accuracy. This ensures that the feature maps with respect to each kernel are excited and that each kernel is important to increasing overall accuracy.

Evaluating Kernel Importance

A main goal of training deep network topologies is to appropriately load the weights of the network. If a network has too many nodes or has too many layers, it may not effectively learn the appropriate weights for its interconnections, in effect not learning the decision space. As applied to CNNs, too many kernels can produce excess capacity that does not contribute to an increase in overall accuracy of the classification. With that in mind, we developed a way to verify that each kernel contributes to an increase in accuracy. CNNs can be evaluated with a similar method to the Mean Decrease Accuracy utilized in RF to determine feature importance. By zeroing out each convolutional filter or kernel and assessing the effect on the overall accuracy, information on how important that kernel is to the classification task can be determined. Kernels with significant impact on accuracy can be regarded as containing information of distinguishing characteristic(s) of the data.

In our study, the number of kernels trained was reduced to ensure that all the kernels were important to some degree. Each time the number of kernels was reduced the network was retrained with the training data to appropriately learn the new kernels. It was determined that the number of kernels trained within the network could be reduced until the Kernel Importance Table always showed a negative average percent impact on the classification accuracy for all kernels (Section 3.2). Reducing the number of kernels beyond this started to have a negative impact on the overall classification accuracy. While this was determined experimentally, it proved to be useful in reducing the total size of the network. Additionally, as the learned information is more condensed in fewer trainable kernels, the features that each kernel is extracting should be more expressive. With this kernel reduction performed, we expect that the network does not have too much excess capacity and the likelihood of over training is minimized. In this study, we started with 86 kernels and were able to reduce this drastically. Acceptable parameters for a three-season CNN were: $N_k = 7$ and $K_s = 10$. These parameters were also applied to the single-season CNN.

Hidden Layer Nodes

The number of hidden layer nodes within the classification portion of the network determines the capacity of the classification network to make an accurate "combination" of the features learned. It is important that this network has enough capacity with the upper limit being mainly to keep the size of the network only large enough to not limit the classification accuracy of the network. Here we chose 500 hidden layer nodes, N_h.

Convolutional Filter Visualization

Useful visualizations for CNN are the feature maps generated by the network. Feature maps are created by applying individual pieces of data to the network and extracting the resulting convolutional excitations for each class of data. When a single piece of data is applied to the network, every kernel is convolved with this data point. This creates the $N_d \times N_k$ convolutional feature map. Visualizing this convolutional feature map enables the identification of where within the temporal-spectral signature the data is being excited or filtered by a respective kernel. This is the information that is provided to the feature classification network.

As feature maps are connected to the same spectral locations within the hidden layer, if the feature maps from each of the classes all are excited in the same area then those excitations do not provide any distinctive information to the classification network and would have little effect in determining the class of the data. Thus, for visualization purposes the mean across all class feature maps was removed from individual class feature maps. As any deviation from zero within the modified feature map indicates that the kernel learned something in that region, viewing the magnitude of the mean-removed feature map provides a more useful view. Additionally, averaging feature maps from 75 spectra of the same class provides the average excitations from convolution with those data, showing general trends for each class. The resulting visualization feature maps can then shed some light on the distinguishing characteristics of the class, on a class-by-class basis. To provide context for the feature map, a random piece of data from the feature map's class is provided as a silhouette. This was done to illustrate the typical structure of that class's spectral profile across all three seasons. An example is provided in Figure 7 for Annual Crops.

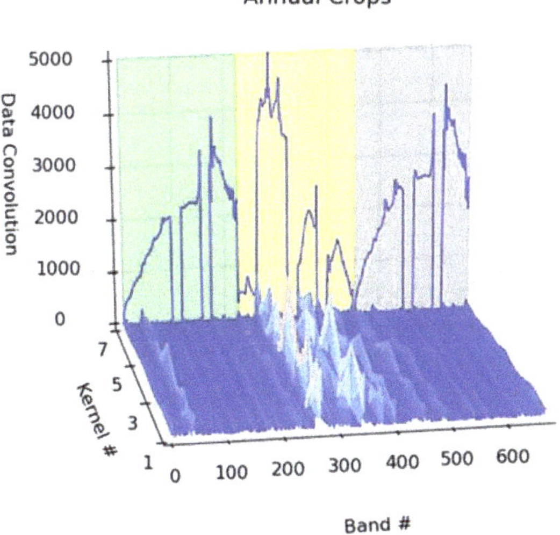

Figure 7. An example convolutional feature map for an Annual Crop three-season spectrum. The example class spectrum is shown in background. Green, yellow and gray background areas represent bands in the spring, summer and fall, respectively. Each season has 186 bands, ordered 370 to 2500 nm. However, in this figure the original 224 bands per season are shown in order to display the bad data gaps (e.g., atmospheric absorption windows).

2.5. Data Pre-Processing

Standardizing data for neural networks is a common practice and enables the network to operate on data that has a similar dynamic range [36]. This frees the network from having to "learn" this dimension or characteristic of the data. The zero mean and standardization of the data with respect to spectra effectively removes common structural content from the data and then scales the data to have an appropriate dynamic range on a per spectra basis. The formula below is the operation performed for this standardization for each spectral band.

$$X_{i\_newspectra} = \frac{x_{i\_rawspectra} - \mu_{i\_rawspectra}}{\sigma_{i\_rawspectra}} \ for \ i = 1, \ldots N_d \tag{2}$$

where N_d is the number of spectra or data, $\mu_{i\_rawspectra}$ and $\sigma_{i\_rawspectra}$ are the mean and standard deviation of all the training at the spectral index i.

This standardization of the data boosted performance of the CNN roughly 1% in classification accuracy and made the training more stable. These same standardized data were applied to RF and SVM but did not make any noticeable impact on accuracy of these classifiers (Figure 4). As per standard practice, the mean and standard deviations for this standardization were developed from the training dataset and then extended to condition the testing and classification image data. This is to prevent standardization knowledge of the testing data to influence the training of the classifier.

2.6. Classification Post-Processing and Accuracy Assessment

The final classified LCCS map products were created from mosaics of classified runs from respective classifiers (Figure 4). In areas of scene overlap, the map class was determined by selecting the pixels with the maximum number of votes (RF) or highest probability (CNN and SVM). An accuracy assessment was conducted using confusion matrices, overall percent accuracy and kappa statistics based on respective classifiers applied to independent test data. In this case, test data did not include duplicate pixels in areas of scene overlap; that is, the class from the respective mosaicked map was chosen as the reference class in areas of overlap.

3. Results

3.1. Accuracy Assessment

With single-season (summer) data, CNN had 0.5% and 9.3% significantly higher overall accuracy (OA) than SVM and RF, respectively ($Z > 3.2$, $p < 0.01$, Table 2). With three-season (spring, summer, fall) data, CNN had 0.3% and 7.3% significantly higher OA than SVM and RF, respectively ($Z > 2.1$, $p < 0.05$, Table 2). Overall accuracy for three-season data was 1.9 to 3.5% significantly higher than single-season data for all three classifiers ($Z > 2.1$, $p < 0.05$). Given their superior performance, remaining results will focus on three-season CNN and SVM classifications.

Table 2. Overall percent accuracy per classifier using single (summer) or three seasons (spring, summer, fall) of data. Kappa statistics are provided in parentheses.

	CNN	SVM	RF
Single Season	88.0 (0.86)	87.5 (0.86)	78.7 (0.75)
Three Season	89.9 (0.88)	89.5 (0.88)	82.2 (0.80)

The three-season CNN map had average producer accuracies (PA) of 76.7%, and that ranged from 0.0 (Dune Vegetation) to 98.3% (Built-up, Table 3). The CNN map user accuracies (UA) averaged 80.0% and ranged from 0.0 (Dune Veg.) to 97.9% (Tidal Marsh). The SVM map had average PA of 73.5%, and that ranged from 0.0 (Dune Vegetation) to 98.8% (Built-up, Table 4). The SVM map UA averaged 80.0% and ranged from 0.0 (Dune Veg.) to 97.9% (Tidal Marsh). The class accuracy for Dune Vegetation was 0.0% due to low class sample size ($n = 132$ pixels) and spectral confusion with Herbaceous, Annual Crops, Bare, and DBT (Tables 3 and 4). Being located along the coast, Dune Vegetation was not prevalent in the study area and was thus underrepresented in reference data. Annual Crops had 12.3% greater PA with CNN over SVM, with confusion in both classifiers spanning Perennial Crops, Herbaceous and Urban Vegetation. Bare had a 35.3% greater PA in CNN over SVM, with greater confusion with Annual Crops and Built-up in SVM. In both classifiers, deciduous broadleaf forests (DBT) tended to be confused with evergreen broadleaf forests (EBT). Evergreen broadleaf forests were confused with conifers (ENT), deciduous forests (DBT), and shrubs.

The mosaicked classified maps created with RF, CNN and SVM are shown in Figure 8. At this scale, it is visible that all classifiers map land cover relatively well, and are relatively consistent throughout their respective classification. In general, the RF map tended to be more speckled than SVM or CNN maps. The RF map had more obvious problems with classifying shrublands in the southeast corner of the map (Figure 8B), with over-mapping of Perennial Crops; RF also had over-mapping of Built-up in the Tidal Marsh areas along the northeast bay. Some class differences toward the coast, such as near San Francisco, are explained by clouds in the imagery that were not fully masked from the analysis.

Table 3. CNN confusion matrix for the three-season classification.

	Annual Crops	Bare	Built	ENT	DBT	EBT	Shrubs	Dune Veg.	Perennial Crops	Tidal Marsh	Herbaceous	Urban Veg.	Total	User
1. Ann. Crops	3513	62	35	0	0	0	0	45	394	110	41	52	4252	83%
2. Bare	3	479	30	0	0	0	0	22	16	5	1	10	566	85%
3. Built-Up	33	106	13,210	4	2	0	5	0	70	77	6	617	14,130	93%
4. ENT	1	0	2	11,101	0	302	9	0	17	3	0	2	11,437	97%
5. DBT	0	0	0	2	1032	431	16	0	2	4	20	3	1510	68%
6. EBT	2	0	2	394	369	5297	100	0	1	2	3	4	6174	86%
7. Shrubs	11	0	5	262	24	350	7066	0	4	29	156	16	7923	89%
8. Dune Veg.	3	0	0	1	0	0	8	0	0	6	0	0	18	0%
9. Per. Crops	631	0	9	0	10	6	8	0	5359	29	3	37	6092	88%
10. Tidal Marsh	2	0	0	0	0	0	3	1	0	4930	98	2	5036	98%
11. Herbaceous	876	73	52	1	3	21	52	64	148	467	9357	66	11,180	84%
12. Urban Veg.	57	0	92	8	1	17	0	0	0	32	0	1772	1979	90%
Total	5132	720	13,437	11,773	1441	6424	7267	132	6011	5694	9685	2581		
Producer	68%	67%	98%	94%	72%	82%	97%	0%	89%	87%	97%	69%		

Table 4. SVM confusion matrix for the three-season classification.

	Annual Crops	Bare	Built	ENT	DBT	EBT	Shrubs	Dune Veg.	Perennial Crops	Tidal Marsh	Herbaceous	Urban Veg.	Total	User
1. Ann. Crops	2881	256	15	0	0	0	0	21	226	115	38	6	3558	81%
2. Bare	0	225	7	0	0	0	0	25	0	0	0	0	257	88%
3. Built-Up	83	223	13,272	151	1	2	2	7	61	78	65	575	14,520	91%
4. ENT	1	0	1	11,438	1	411	3	0	0	5	0	4	11,864	96%
5. DBT	18	0	4	0	1047	230	11	67	0	2	8	0	1387	75%
6. EBT	3	0	0	131	351	5351	59	0	11	0	0	2	5908	91%
7. Shrubs	0	0	1	34	17	389	7145	0	1	22	129	3	7741	92%
8. Dune Veg.	25	0	0	6	0	1	1	0	0	0	2	0	35	0%
9. Per. Crops	678	5	19	0	20	9	1	0	5560	61	19	65	6437	86%
10. Tidal Marsh	10	0	10	0	0	0	2	1	0	4856	74	5	4958	98%
11. Herbaceous	1124	11	16	1	4	28	43	11	152	524	9307	109	11,330	82%
12. Urban Veg.	309	0	92	12	0	3	0	0	0	31	43	1812	2302	79%
Total	5132	720	13,437	11,773	1441	6424	7267	132	6011	5694	9685	2581		
Producer	56%	31%	99%	97%	73%	83%	98%	0%	92%	85%	96%	70%		

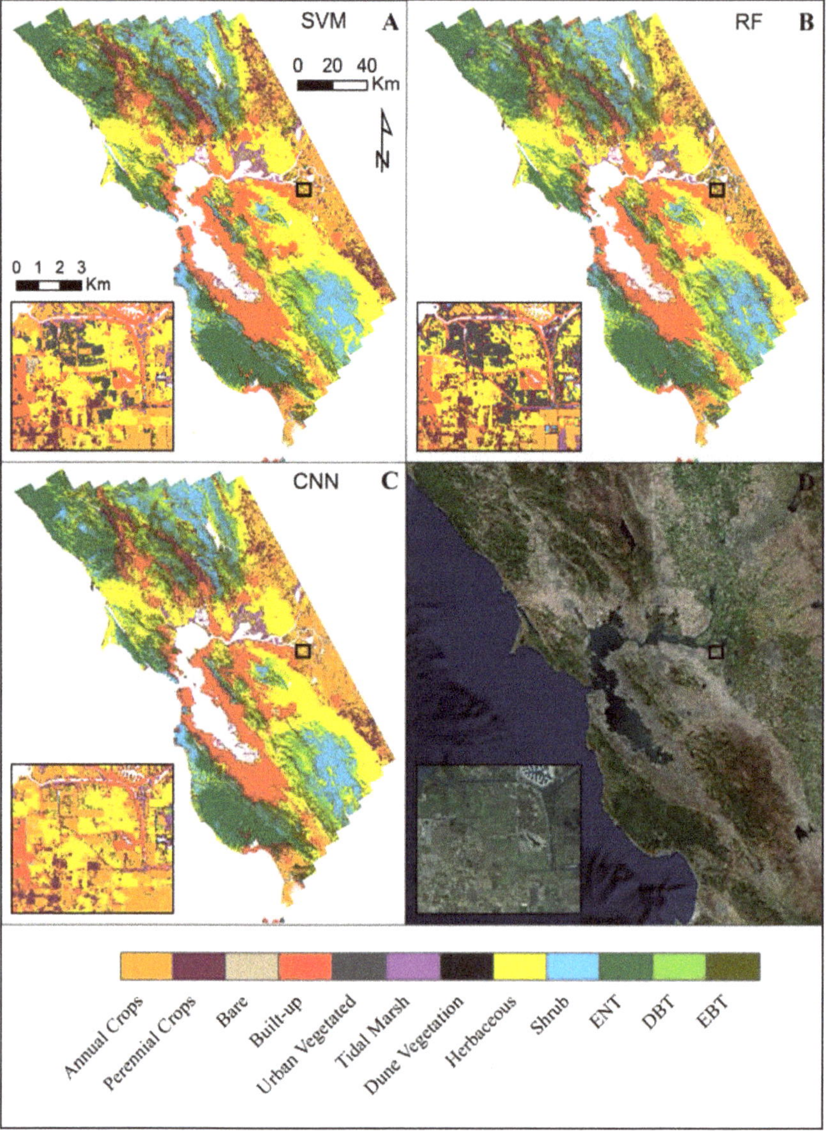

Figure 8. Classified land-cover maps for (**A**) Support Vector Machine; (**B**) Random Forests; and (**C**) Convolutional Neural Networks. White areas indicate pixels that were not classified (e.g., water, clouds, no data); (**D**) Natural color mosaic of imagery from June 2015.

The insets show an example of the classifications in the Bay Area delta agricultural zone. This area is predominantly agricultural land with some urban areas. In this anthropogenic landscape, homogenous geometric shapes are dictated by property lines (Figure 8D). The RF classifier performs the worst with many areas with more speckle (i.e., more heterogeneity) of classes across the landscape. The RF and SVM maps both misclassified several parcels with Urban Vegetated that were mapped as Annual Crops by CNN. This is an area of irrigated sod production, which has temporal and spectral similarities to irrigated golf courses found in the Urban Vegetated class. Despite this spectral similarity, CNN tended to correctly map these areas as agriculture.

3.2. CNN Kernel Importance and Visualization

The three-season CNN kernel importance matrix (Figure 9) shows the impact of zeroing a kernel from the CNN on class producer accuracy. For example, conifer forests (ENT, class index 4) producer accuracy decreases 95.2% if Kernel 7 is removed from the CNN. With Kernel 4 removed, six classes have a 15.9 to 65.31% decrease in accuracy. In contrast, some kernels have a positive impact if removed from the network. For example DBT (class index 5) and Urban Vegetation (class index 12) producer accuracy increases 6% and 10.8% if Kernel 5 is removed from the CNN. On Average, the most important kernel was Kernel 7 while the least important was Kernel 5.

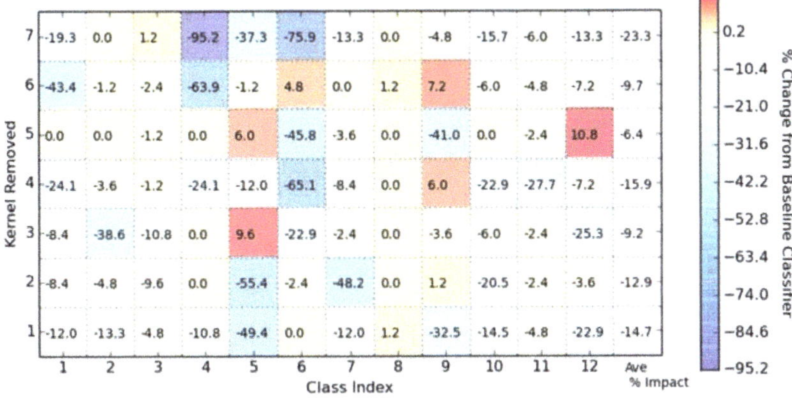

Figure 9. Kernel Importance Matrix. This table shows the percent change in producer accuracy when zeroing a kernel from the CNN. Class index definitions found in Table 3.

3.3. CNN Feature Map Visualization

Convolutional feature maps show, for an example spectrum from each class, kernel excitations subtracted from the average excitation across all classes at a given wavelength (Figure 10). Figure 10 shows the average feature map excitations from 75 randomly selected spectra per class. In general, feature maps show that kernels tend to excite in specific spectral-temporal regions for a given class, forming strips in the feature map. At these regions of activity, the kernels tend to be excited at different magnitudes (e.g., peaks and valleys along a strip).

By observing under which season of the feature map the excitations occur, distinctiveness of phenological spectral variation can be observed within classes. This effectively enables the feature maps to show under which season features are more prominent for respective classes. For example, for the Annual Crop spectrum there is heavy kernel excitation in the summer (Figure 10). The forest spectra (EBT, DBT, ENT) have excitations throughout the seasons. In contrast, Tidal Marsh and Shrubs spectra have relatively low excitation throughout the year.

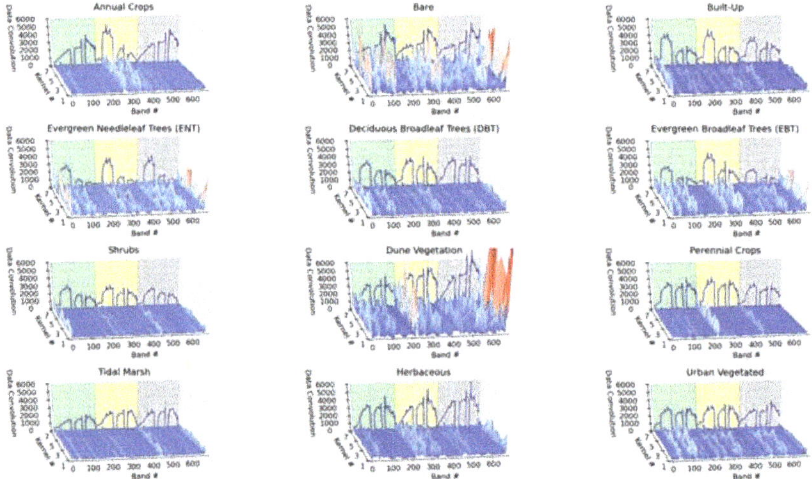

Figure 10. Convolutional feature maps for each class for the three-season CNN. These feature maps are the result of averaging the convolution of the kernels with 75 spectra per class (Section 2.4.3). An example class spectrum is shown in background. Green, yellow and gray background areas represent bands in the spring, summer and fall, respectively. Each season has 186 bands, ordered 370 to 2500 nm. However, in this figure the original 224 bands per season are shown in order to display the bad data gaps (e.g., atmospheric absorption windows).

4. Discussion

4.1. Classified Land-Cover Maps

The classification scheme in this study included twelve classes defined by LCCS rules designed for global-scale applications. Forest classes had closed-canopies of one leaf type (e.g., deciduous or evergreen), and thus excluded more mixed forest or open-canopy classes that have more spectral variability, and subsequent class confusion and decrease in overall accuracy [6]. However, the broad classes include spectral-temporal variability over a large region. This aspect of this study is unique for testing machine-learning classifiers with hyperspectral and multi-seasonal datasets.

We found that the 1-D (per-pixel) SVM and CNN classifiers had over 7% overall accuracy improvement over the RF classifier for these data and a classification scheme. This is similar to a 5% increase in overall accuracy observed for 1-D CNN over RF in a study focused on crop classification in Ukraine with multi-temporal multispectral Landsat and Sentinel-2 images [15]. We found that CNN only had 0.3 (three-season) to 0.5% (summer) greater overall accuracy than the popular SVM classifier. This result is similar to a previous study with 1-D hyperspectral imagery (not multi-temporal) that found CNN to improve overall accuracy by 0.9 to 2.6% relative to SVM [17]. In our study, we found the addition of multi-seasonal data modestly (but significantly) improved classification accuracy by 1.9 to 3.5% over using summer-only data. The Kussal et al. study [15] did not specifically isolate individual seasons for testing multi-temporal data, and to our knowledge there are no studies that compare the relative advantage of temporal data in CNN. However, multi-temporal data have been shown to increase overall accuracy from ~2 to 8% with a variety of classifiers [37]

Our previous research in this study area with 2013 AVIRIS data and the same training and testing reference data was based on the RF classifier [6]. We found reflectance data yielded a 62.9% and 78.8% overall accuracy with single- and three-season data, respectively. The RF classifier in the current study produced 15.8% (single-season) and 3.4% (three-season) higher overall accuracy, respectively. The current study was not designed to replicate our previous research design. Some of the discrepancy in results is explained by a difference in image years, improvements in the atmospheric correction process, and differences in processing code (Python vs. R). Further, our previous work used a RF node size of 10 to avoid overfitting and to train a more generalized classifier, while the current study used a node size of 1. Despite these differences, our results indicate that the CNN and SVM classifiers offer improved performance relative to RF, and both classifiers should be considered in hyperspectral classification applications.

All classifications in our study tended to have class confusion among spectrally similar forest classes, a result in accordance with our previous RF study [6]. Annual Crops were broadly confused with Herbaceous cover, and to lesser extent Urban Vegetated. Not all agriculture in this area is irrigated or plowed, and tends to have similar physiognomy and phenology as grasslands, which are dominated by exotic annual grasses; and thus, spectral-temporal confusion between these two classes is expected.

4.2. CNN Feature Maps and Land Cover

The usage of CNN is promising with respect to classification accuracy as well as visualization of features within the data. From convolutional feature maps, the seasonal and spectral contribution to the CNN for each class is visible as excitations by the kernels (Figure 10). This visualization, paired with the confusion matrices, provide a point of exploration into the distinctive nature of the classes. For example, the example Annual Crop spectrum has heavy kernel excitation within the summer reflectance bands (Figure 7). This indicates that the Annual Crop class contains distinctive features within the summer season as compared to the other classes. This could be due to the lack of chlorophyll absorption features in the spring and fall visible spectrum and presence of these features in summer; the example spectrum appears to be green in the summer. The kernels may thus be sensitive to chemical properties of crops. In contrast, herbaceous cover follows the cycle of precipitation (wet spring, dry summer and fall) and senesces in the early summer and is fully senesced by the fall (Figure 2—note lack of chlorophyll absorption in summer and fall). The Herbaceous example spectrum has convolutional excitations spread more evenly across seasons relative to Annual Crops, with some excitations occurring in fall where annual crops had none (Figure 10). The Bare class by definition has relatively low plant cover and minimal chlorophyll absorption signal, although there is high within-class spectral diversity (Figure 2). With the example spectra, kernels are more uniformly excited across all three seasons of the feature map, indicating that this class is less influenced by seasonal variation than within-season spectral properties. This is visible by the additional excitation around the low-signal area (e.g., low blue, high SWIR) within each season of the class data.

An interesting aspect from feature maps is the kernel activations around areas of low blue, far shortwave infrared and around atmospheric absorption bands. These are spectral regions that tend to have more noise due to lower solar irradiance, atmospheric effects (e.g., scattering, absorption), and spectrometer sensitivity. Engineered metrics used in remote sensing target vegetation chemistry and structure with narrowband ratios (e.g., indices such as NDVI), spectral derivatives, and absorption-feature fitting techniques that span the different spectral ranges with well-known continuous areas [6]. In general, engineered metrics avoid these noise-prone spectral regions. However, because some CNN feature maps are excited in these regions, these results indicate that these regions can be important to classification accuracy and warrant further investigation.

One criticism of neural networks and SVM is that they are relatively "black box"; classification performance may be high, but it is difficult to understand the relative importance of spectral and temporal information in the input vector. The CNN feature maps and kernel importance matrix introduced in this study have potential to provide more insight into the classifier and should be explored further with other datasets. In comparison to RF variable importance, we found these CNN diagnostic tools to be less easy to interpret [6]. With RF variable importance, there is a direct linkage between a predictor variable (e.g., reflectance band) and the impact on class and overall accuracy with its removal. Despite the very different architectures between CNN and RF, we found that RF importance (Figure A1) tended to cluster around some of the same regions as identified by the CNN feature maps, such as blue (spring, summer, fall), high SWIR (spring, summer) and the border of SWIR atmospheric absorption (band index 500, which is 1761 nm from fall imagery).

4.3. Future Work with CNN Hyperspectral Image Classification

The application of CNN to hyperspectral data has only recently been explored and there are thus many avenues for future work. The consideration of the spatial domain is an area of current investigation. The extension of this architecture to include the spatial dimension as in [13] could continue to add more distinctive information that could aid in the classification process. A 3-D convolutional network paired with a respective importance figure (Figure 9) could shed light on to the spatial as well as the spectral features that impact the classification on a per class basis. In a similar manner, the temporal dimension of image data should be investigated. As in this study, this could be done by vertically stacking the temporal season data creating a $N_d \times N_{ns}$ sized input data array, where N_d is the number of bands within a single season of image data and N_{ns} is the number of seasons (rather than horizontally stacked data in temporal sequence, as in our study). This data format would dictate the architecture of networks that could convolve higher dimension kernels across the input data, or perform multiple layered convolutional operations. The additional benefit would be that the kernel's local receptive field could enable the network to capture patterns within the temporal and spectral dimensions in an integrated machine-learning framework. If there is distinctive information within these dimensions, this could increase the accuracy as well as provide more ancillary information about the distinctive aspects of the data through analysis of convolutional feature maps.

It was observed when reviewing the feature maps that the kernels were exciting the convolutional feature maps in similar spectral regions, across all kernels. This appeared as strips of excited kernels. This indicates that the kernels are not capturing unique information. If kernels were "encouraged" to learn information that is "unique" this would enable the feature maps to show different structural features in the data on a per kernel basis. One potential way to do this would be to provide regularization on the kernels during training that would penalize kernels that are not orthogonal. Although this may enhance CNN as a tool for exploring features that discriminate classes, this approach may not improve classification accuracy.

As data from future hyperspectral satellites are more readily available, such as from the Environmental Mapping and Analysis Program (EnMAP) satellite due to launch in 2019, the scalability of classification techniques should be considered. As TensorFlow has been designed to scale from multiple-core, GPU(s), and multiple-computer clustered configurations, the CNN can readily scale for large global and temporal datasets. The Python Scikit-learn library used for RF and SVM in this study does not have this capability, and thus does not offer a direct comparison of GPU processing with CNN and TensorFlow. The computers utilized for this work were an 8 Core Xenon 3.7 Ghz CPU processor with 32 GB ram and a NVIDIA K2200 GPU, as well as a second i7-2640M (2.8 GHz) dual-core CPU with 8 GB of RAM. We tested the CNN architecture with both CPU- and GPU-based configurations. The GPU-based implementation performed all graph computations within the GPU, and was 5 to 8 times faster than CPU-based processing, depending on the learning batch size (larger batch size increased performance within the GPU space). With our data, the GPU-based CNN was slower to train than SVM; however, image classification was 9 times faster with CNN (Table A2). For applications that use large datasets, particularly with the inclusion of spatial and temporal information in the classification design, the CNN with TensorFlow or similar machine learning platform may have a considerable advantage in processing time while offering relatively high classification accuracy.

5. Conclusions

A broad goal of this work was to implement and explain how a Convolutional Neural Network (CNN) with a one-dimensional architecture could be applied to multi-seasonal hyperspectral images. The results show that CNN can be applied to simulated spaceborne hyperspectral reflectance data (HyspIRI) to achieve high classification accuracy rates comparable to that from Support Vector

Machine (SVM), and surpassing the Random Forest (RF) classifier. Highest overall accuracies were with three-season data (spring, summer, fall), with 89.9% for CNN, 89.5% for SVM and 82.2% for RF. Single-season (summer) classifications had overall accuracies that were 1.9 to 3.5% lower than with three-season data. Spectral and temporal information is readily visible through CNN feature map visualizations and their respective importance is traceable back to kernel importance. In summary, the CNN is a promising classifier for future hyperspectral classification tasks and this study identifies future work to increase CNN performance, scalability and incorporation of spatial and temporal information.

Supplementary Materials: The following are available online at www.mdpi.com/2072-4292/9/6/629/s1. The code utilized within this work can be cloned from the following repository: https://ciga_ssu@bitbucket.org/ciga_ssu/hsi-cnn-repo.git.

Acknowledgments: Funding for this project was provided by NASA HyspIRI Preparatory Airborne Activities and Associated Science Research, grant NNX12AP09G. Simulated HyspIRI-like reflectance products were provided by NASA Jet Propulsion Lab (JPL), with key involvement by Bo Cai Gao, David R Thompson, Sarah Lundeen and Robert Green, as well as Philip Dennison of Univ. of Utah for AVIRIS-to-HyspIRI resampling (NASA grant NNX12AP08G). Kelsey Dunn helped prepare maps for this paper. Bala Ravikumar and Farid Farahmand of Sonoma State University provided initial review and input into this study.

Author Contributions: D.G. and M.C. conceived and designed the experiments; D.G. performed the experiments; D.G. and M.C. analyzed the data; M.C. contributed materials and analysis tools; D.G. and M.C. wrote the paper.

Conflicts of Interest: The authors declare no conflict of interest.

Appendix A

Table A1. The Land-Cover Classification System (LCCS) rules applied to percent cover estimates of land cover in reference samples in order to create discrete class labels. Open-canopy (open) trees and shrubs have >10–65% trees or shrubs, respectively. Closed-canopy (closed) trees and shrubs have >65% trees or shrubs, respectively. This study focused on closed-canopy tree and shrub classes only.

Rules Based on Land-Cover Abundance	LCCS Class
1. If >10% Vegetated	
2. If >50% Natural/Semi-natural Vegetation	
3. If >50% tidal salt marsh	**Tidal Marsh**
3. If >10% of cover is woody vegetation (trees + shrubs) and >10% of woody vegetation is trees	
4. If ≥75% of relative tree cover is needleleaf trees	**Evergreen Needleleaved Trees (ENT)**
4. If >75% of relative tree cover is broadleaf trees	
5. ≥75% of tree cover is evergreen	**Evergreen Broadleaved Trees (EBT)**
5. ≥75% of broadleaf tree cover is deciduous	**Deciduous Broadleaved Trees (DBT)**
3. If >10% of cover is woody vegetation (trees + shrubs) and >10% of woody vegetation is shrubs	**Shrubs**
3. Else herbaceous cover	
6. ≥75% of herbaceous cover is upland grasses and forbs	**Herbaceous**
6. ≥75% of herbaceous cover is dune vegetation	**Dune Vegetation**
2. Else Cultivated/Managed Vegetation	
7. >50% perennial crops	**Perennial Crops**
7. >50% annual crops	**Annual Crops**
7. >50% urban landscape	**Urban Vegetated**
1. Else Not Vegetated	
8. >50% impervious surface	**Built-up**
8. >50% non-vegetated	**Bare**

Table A2. Classifier training and classification times in seconds for three season data. For CNN, (1) initial steady-state validation accuracy; and (2) a 4-mil epoch standard training session. The CNN classifier utilized GPU-based processing, while SVM and RF were restricted to CPU-based processing.

	CNN-1 (s)	CNN-2 (s)	SVM (s)	RF (s)
Training Time	1500	21,146	358	3452
Classification Time per GB	65	65	590	768
Classification Time Per Pixel	0.0008	0.0008	0.00773	0.00959

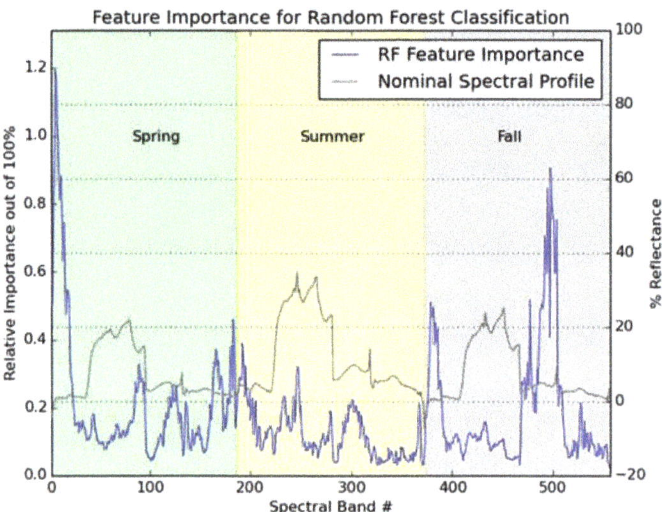

Figure A1. Feature importance for the three-season Random Forests classifier. Nominal spectral profile for ENT shown for context.

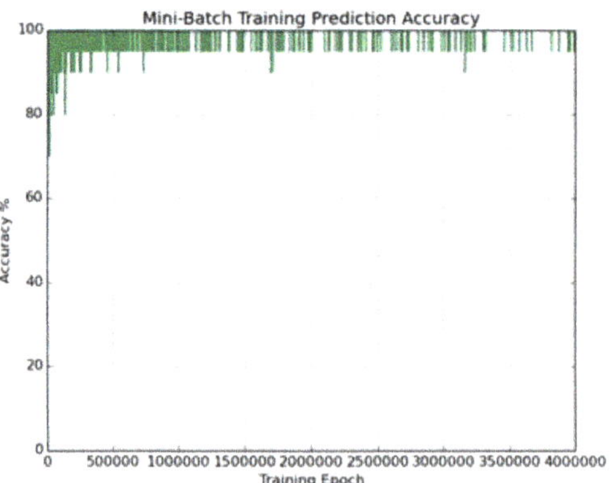

Figure A2. Mini-batch training accuracy curve.

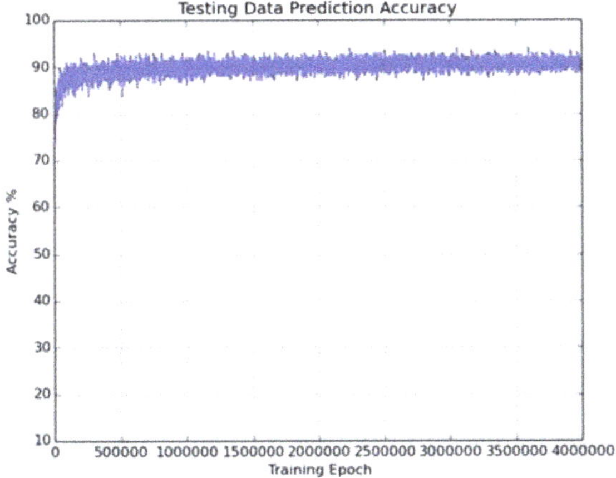

Figure A3. Testing accuracy curve.

References

1. Lee, C.M.; Cable, M.L.; Hook, S.J.; Green, R.O.; Ustin, S.L.; Mandl, D.J.; Middleton, E.M. An Introduction to the NASA Hyperspectral InfraRed Imager (HyspIRI) Mission and Preparatory activities. *Remote Sens. Environ.* **2015**, *167*, 6–19. [CrossRef]
2. Somers, B.; Asner, G.P.; Tits, L.; Coppin, P. Endmember Variability in Spectral Mixture Analysis: A Review. *Remote Sens. Environ.* **2011**, *117*, 1603–1616. [CrossRef]
3. Roberts, D.A.; Gardner, M.; Church, R.; Ustin, S.; Scheer, G.; Green, R.O. Mapping Chaparral in the Santa Monica Mountains Using Multiple Endmember Spectral Mixture Models. *Remote Sens. Environ.* **1998**, *65*, 267–279. [CrossRef]
4. Franke, J.; Roberts, D.A.; Halligan, K.; Menz, G. Hierarchical Multiple Endmember Spectral Mixture Analysis (MESMA) of Hyperspectral Imagery for Urban Environment. *Remote Sens. Environ.* **2008**, *113*, 1712–1723. [CrossRef]
5. Camps-Valls, G. Machine Learning in Remote Sensing Data Processing. Proceedings of IEEE International Workshop on Machine Learning for Signal Processing (MLSP), Grenoble, France, 2–4 September 2009; pp. 1–6.
6. Clark, M.L.; Kilham, N.E. Mapping of Land Cover in Northern California with Simulated HyspIRI imagery. *ISPRS J. Photogramm. Remote Sens.* **2016**, *119*, 228–245. [CrossRef]
7. Mountrakis, G.; Im, J.; Ogole, C. Support Vector Machines in Remote Sensing: A Review. *ISPRS J. Photogramm. Remote Sens.* **2011**, *66*, 247–259. [CrossRef]
8. Fernandex-Delgado, M.; Cernadas, E.; Barro, S.; Amorim, D. Do We Need Hundreds of Classifiers to Solve Real World Classification Problems? *J. Mach. Learn. Res.* **2014**, *15*, 3133–3181.
9. Krizhevsky, A.; Sutskever, I.; Hinton, G. Imagenet Classification with Deep Convolutional Neural Networks. Proceedings of 25th International Conference on Neural Information Processing Systems, Lake Tahoe, NV, USA, 3–6 December 2012; pp. 1097–1105.
10. Szegedy, C.; Liu, W.; Jia, Y.; Sermanet, P.; Reed, S.; Anguelov, D.; Erhan, D.; Vanhoucke, V.; Rabinovich, A. Going Deeper with Convolutions. In Proceedings of the IEEE Conference on Computer Vision and Pattern Recognition, Boston, MA, USA, 7–12 June 2015.
11. Abdel-Hamid, O.; Mohamed, A.; Jiang, H. Convolutional Neural Networks for Speech Recognition. *IEEE/ACM Trans. Audio Speech Lang. Process.* **2014**, *22*, 1533–1545. [CrossRef]
12. Castelluccio, M.; Poggi, G.; Sansone, C.; Verdoliva, L. Land Use Classification in Remote Sensing Images by Convolutional Networks. Available online: http://arxiv.org/abs/1508.00092 (accessed on 8 May 2017).

13. Li, Y.; Zhang, H.; Shen, Q. Spectral-Spatial Classification of Hyperspectral Imagery with 3D Convolutional Neural Network. *Remote Sens.* **2017**, *9*, 67. [CrossRef]
14. Langkvist, M.; Kiselev, A.; Alirezaie, M.; Loutfi, A. Classification and Segmentation of Satellite Orthoimagery Using Convolutional Neural Networks. *Remote Sens.* **2016**, *8*, 329. [CrossRef]
15. Kussul, N.; Lavreniuk, M.; Skakun, S.; Shelestov, A. Deep Learning Classification of Land Cover and Crop Types Using Remote Sensing Data. *IEEE Geosci. Remote Sens. Lett.* **2017**, *14*, 5. [CrossRef]
16. Chen, C.; Li, W.; Su, H.; Liu, K. Spectral-Spatial Classification of Hyperspectral Image Based on Kernel Extreme Learning Machine. *Remote Sens.* **2014**, *6*, 5795–5814. [CrossRef]
17. Hu, W.; Huang, Y.; Wei, L.; Zhang, F.; Li, H. Deep Convolutional Neural Networks for Hyperspectral Image Classification. *J. Sens.* **2015**, *2015*, 258619. [CrossRef]
18. Makantasis, K.; Karantzalos, K.; Doulamis, A.; Doulamis, N. Deep Supervised Learning for Hyperspectral Data Classification through Convolutional Neural Networks. In Proceedings of the 2015 IEEE International Symposium Geoscience and Remote Sensing (IGARSS 2015), Milan, Italy, 26–31 July 2015; pp. 4959–4962.
19. Li, W.; Fu, H.; Yu, L.; Cracknell, A. Deep Learning Based Oil Palm Tree Detection and Counting for High-Resolution Remote Sensing Images. *Remote Sens.* **2017**, *9*, 22. [CrossRef]
20. Wang, J.; Luo, C.; Huang, H.; Zhao, H.; Wang, S. Transferring Pre-Trained Deep CNNs for Remote Scene Classification with General Features Learned from Linear PCA Network. *Remote Sens.* **2017**, *9*, 225. [CrossRef]
21. Hu, F.; Xia, G.-S.; Hu, J.; Zhang, L. Transferring Deep Convolutional Neural Networks for Scene Classification of High-Resolution Remote Sensing Imagery. *Remote Sens.* **2015**, *7*, 14680–14707. [CrossRef]
22. Mesay, B.B.; Zeggada, A.; Nouffidj, A.; Melgani, F.; A Convolutional Neural Network Approach for Assisting Avalanche Search and Rescue Operations with UAV Imagery. *Remote Sens.* **2017**, *9*, 100.
23. Liang, H.; Li, Q. Hyperspectral Imagery Classification using Sparse Representations of Convolutional Neural Network Features. *Remote Sens.* **2016**, *8*, 99. [CrossRef]
24. Zhao, W.; Du, S. Spectral-Spatial Feature Extraction for Hyperspectral Image Classification: A Dimension Reduction and Deep Learning Approach. *IEEE Trans. Geosci. Remote Sens.* **2016**, *54*, 8. [CrossRef]
25. Wang, Q.; Lin, J.; Yuan, Y. Salient Band Selection for Hyperspectral Image Classification via Manifold Ranking. *IEEE Trans. Neural Net. Learn. Syst.* **2016**, *27*, 6. [CrossRef] [PubMed]
26. Yuan, Y.; Lin, J.; Wang, Q. Hyperspectral Image Classification via Multitask Joint Sparse Representation and Stepwise MRF Optimization. *IEEE Trans. Neural Netw. Learn. Syst.* **2016**, *46*, 12. [CrossRef] [PubMed]
27. Di Gregorio, A. *Land Cover Classification System: Classification Concepts and User Manual*; LCCS (No.8); Food and Agriculture Organization: Rome, Italy, 2005.
28. Green, R.O.; Eastwood, M.L.; Sarture, C.M.; Chrien, T.G.; Aronsson, M.; Chippendale, B.J.; Faust, J.A.; Pavri, B.E.; Chovit, C.J.; Solis, M.S.; et al. Imaging Spectroscopy and the Airborne Visible/Infrared Imaging Spectrometer (AVIRIS). *Remote Sens. Environ.* **1998**, *65*, 227–248. [CrossRef]
29. Thorpe, A.K.; Frankenberg, C.; Aubrey, A.D.; McFadden, J.P. Mapping Methane Concentrations from a Controlled Release Experiment using the Next Generation Airborne Visible/Infrared Imaging Spectrometer (AVIRIS-NG). *Remote Sens. Environ.* **2016**, *179*, 104–115. [CrossRef]
30. Thompson, D.R.; Gao, B.C.; Green, R.O.; Roberts, D.A.; Dennison, P.E.; Lundeen, S.R. Atmospheric Correction for Global Mapping Spectroscopy: ATREM advances for the HyspIRI preparatory campaign. *Remote Sens. Environ.* **2015**, *167*, 64–77. [CrossRef]
31. Breiman, L. Random forests. *Mach. Learn.* **2001**, *45*, 5–32. [CrossRef]
32. Ensemble Methods. Available online: http://scikit-learn.org/stable/modules/ensemble.html#forest (accessed on 8 May 2017).
33. RBF SVM Parameters. Available online: www.scikit-learn.org/stable/auto_examples/svm/plot_rbf_parameters.html (accessed on 8 May 2017).
34. Srivastava, N.; Hinton, G.; Krizhevsky, A.; Sutskever, I.; Salakhutdinov, R. Dropout: A Simple Way to Prevent Neural Networks from Overfitting. *J. Mach. Learn. Res.* **2014**, *15*, 1929–1958.
35. Nielsen, M. Chapter 3, Improving the Way Neural Networks Learn, Neural Networks and Deep Learning. Available online: http://neuralnetworksanddeeplearning.com/chap3.html (accessed on 8 May 2017).

36. CS231n Convolutional Neural Networks for Visual Recognition. Available online: http://cs231n.github.io/convolutional-networks/ (accessed on 8 May 2017).
37. Khatami, R.; Mountrakis, G.; Sehman, S. A Meta-analysis of Remote Sensing Research on Supervised Pixel-based Land-cover Image Classification Processes: General guidelines for Practitioners and Future Research. *Remote Sens. Environ.* **2016**, *177*, 89–100. [CrossRef]

Article

Convolutional Neural Networks Based Hyperspectral Image Classification Method with Adaptive Kernels

Chen Ding *, Ying Li, Yong Xia, Wei Wei, Lei Zhang and Yanning Zhang

Shaanxi Key Lab of Speech & Image Information Processing (SAIIP), School of Computer Science and Engineering, Northwestern Polytechnical University, Xi'an 710129, China; lybyp@nwpu.edu.cn (Y.L.); yxia@nwpu.edu.cn (Y.X.); weiweinwpu@nwpu.edu.cn (W.W.); zhanglei211@mail.nwpu.edu.cn (L.Z.); ynzhang@nwpu.edu.cn (Y.Z.)
* Correspondence: dingchen@mail.nwpu.edu.cn; Tel.: +86-159-0299-1949

Academic Editors: Qi Wang, Nicolas H. Younan, Carlos López-Martínez and Prasad S. Thenkabail
Received: 10 May 2017; Accepted: 14 June 2017; Published: 16 June 2017

Abstract: Hyperspectral image (HSI) classification aims at assigning each pixel a pre-defined class label, which underpins lots of vision related applications, such as remote sensing, mineral exploration and ground object identification, etc. Lots of classification methods thus have been proposed for better hyperspectral imagery interpretation. Witnessing the success of convolutional neural networks (CNNs) in the traditional images based classification tasks, plenty of efforts have been made to leverage CNNs to improve HSI classification. An advanced CNNs architecture uses the kernels generated from the clustering method, such as a K-means network uses K-means to generate the kernels. However, the above methods are often obtained heuristically (e.g., the number of kernels should be assigned manually), and how to data-adaptively determine the number of convolutional kernels (i.e., filters), and thus generate the kernels that better represent the data, are seldom studied in existing CNNs based HSI classification methods. In this study, we propose a new CNNs based HSI classification method where the convolutional kernels can be automatically learned from the data through clustering without knowing the cluster number. With those data-adaptive kernels, the proposed CNNs method achieves better classification results. Experimental results from the datasets demonstrate the effectiveness of the proposed method.

Keywords: hyperspectral image classification; automatic cluster number determination; adaptive convolutional kernels

---

1. Introduction

Different from traditional images (e.g., RGB image), hyperspectral image (HSI) contains a continuous spectrum at each pixel, which is beneficial for identifying different imaged land covers. With such abundant spectral information, hyperspectral image (HSI) classification that aims at assigning each pixel a pre-defined class label has facilitated various applications, such as mineral exploration, ground object identification, survey of agriculture and monitoring of geology, etc. Therefore, plenty of efforts have been made in HSI classification. According to the feature utilized, HSI classification methods can be roughly divided into hand-crafted feature based methods and the deep learning feature based methods. A detailed review can be seen from Section 2. For hand-crafted feature based methods, HSI is often represented by the features designed manually [1–7]. However, due to their shallow structure, the representation ability of such features is limited, especially for HSIs which often exhibit high nonlinearity aroused by the high-dimensionality and mixture of pixels. On the contrary, deep learning feature based methods can automatically extract features from training data with deep architectures. It has been proved that those deep features perform well in representing the complicated nonlinearity of data, which has promoted the development of deep learning feature based HSI classification methods in recent years [8–12].

Since the convolutional kernels should be updated through the network training, traditional deep learning based methods exhaust much training time. To address this problem, an advanced CNNs architecture has been proposed recently, which adopts the kernels pre-learned from clustering the training data without updating them in the training process any more. One typical method is the K-means Net proposed in [13], where each CNNs kernel is first learned from a specific cluster obtained by conducting the K-means algorithm on training data. Nevertheless, the cluster number K (i.e., the number of kernels in CNNs) of K-means Net should be assigned empirically, which limits the representational power of CNNs. Specifically, a different number K of kernels designed manually in the convolutional layer will change the structure of CNNs and thus influence the output of CNNs. In addition, the number K is expected to be adaptive to different images and tasks. Therefore, how to data-adaptively choose a proper number of kernels is crucial for representing data characteristics with CNNs. However, most of the existing CNNs based HSI classification methods fail to pay sufficient consideration to this problem.

In this study, we propose a MCFSFDP based CNNs framework for HSI classification. First, inspired by clustering by fast search and find of peaks (CFSFDP) [14], a novel clustering method, named modified clustering by fast search and find of peaks (MCFSFDP), is proposed to data-adaptively learn a specific number of kernels from training data. The convolution kernels can be automatically determined by the center of each cluster and the inter-cluster margin, which guarantees the pre-learned kernels to be suitable for the data structure. Then, the CNNs framework with those pre-learned convolutional kernels is employed to classify each pixel in the HSI. Extensive experimental results demonstrate that the proposed method outperforms several state-of-the-art CNNs based methods in classification accuracy.

In summary, the proposed CNNs framework has two key advantages: (1) a specific number of convolutional kernels can be data-adaptively learned from training data, which can well represent the data characteristics; and (2) the MCFSFDP based CNNs framework is effective for HSI classification.

2. Related Work

Based on the feature adopted in classification of HSI, the HSI classification method can be roughly divided into two categories, including the hand-crafted feature based methods and the deep learning feature based methods.

2.1. Hand-Crafted Feature Based Methods

Linear features extracted by principal component analysis (PCA) [15] and partial least squares (PLS) [16] are applied to classify the HSI data. The kernel methods are further developed to exploit the nonlinear feature of HSI [17]. To depict the spatial texture of image, the wavelet transform (WT) methods [18,19] have been widely used, which often show different scales and perform effectively for classification in the high spatial resolution remotely sensed (HSRRS) data. Considering the complicated spatial correlation, some Gaussian Markov Random Field (GMRF) [20,21] methods are proposed to model such correlation within a graph structure. In [22], a spatial feature index that measured the gray similarity distance in every direction is used to describe the shape feature in local area that is surrounding a pixel in HSI. An adaptive mean-shift (MS) analysis framework [2] is proposed for object extraction and classification of HSI over urban areas, which is able to obtain an object-oriented representations of HSI data. Li et al. [3] integrate the spectral and spatial information in a Bayesian framework, which utilizes a Multinomial Logistic Regression (MLR) algorithm to learn the posterior probability distributions from the spectral information. In addition, this method uses subspace projection to better characterize noise, highly mixed pixels and contextual information. In [4], a mathematical morphology (MM) based method is utilized to process the HSI data. In this approach, opening and closing morphological transforms are used to isolate bright (opening) and dark (closing) structures in images, where bright/dark means brighter/darker than the surrounding features in the images. To model different kinds of structural information, morphological attribute profiles (APs) are adopted to provide a multi-level characterization for an image created by the sequential application of morphological attribute filters [23]. Based on Gray Level Co-occurrence matrix (GLCM), Zortea et al. attempt to extract the contextual information of images by concatenating the spectral features used for classification [1]. To improve the classification result of HSI, the Edge-Aware Filtering (EAF) and Edge-Preserving Filtering (EPF) methods are proposed in [24,25]. Based on the EPF method, a spectral-spatial classification framework was proposed in [25], which can significantly enhance the classification accuracy. Kang et al. propose combining a recursion with image fusion to enhance the image classification accuracy [26]. Recently, the Bag-of-Words (BOW) model has shown a promising way to handle the remote sensing imagery classification problem. In the BOW model, images can be represented by the frequency of visual words that are constructed by quantizing local features with a clustering method, such as K-means and so on [27,28]. Due to the capacity of extracting the handcrafted local features, such as local structural points, color histogram and texture features [29,30], BOW based methods present good performance. Manifold regularized kernel logistic regression (KLR) are proposed to solve multi-view image classification [31]. To integrate different levels of features for saliency detection, Wang et al. [32] propose a multiple-instance learning based framework that fuses the low-level, mid-level, and high-level features into a unified model. While effective, the trepresentation capacity of the manual feature extraction based methods is limited.

2.2. Deep Learning Feature Based Methods

Recently, with the development of deep learning technology, lots of methods based on deep learning have been developed for image classification, such as deep brief network (DBN) and stacked auto-encoder (SAE). The DBN and SAE are unsupervised learning methods that are also used for spectral-spatial classification of hyperspectral data without using the label information [9,33]. The concept of deep learning is introduced into the hyperspectral data classification for the first time [9]. The Canonical Correlation Analysis Network is useful for multi-view image classification [34]. With the development of convolutional neural networks (CNNs) [35], which has been widely applied to the image processing and achieved spectacular effects, more and more deep CNNs frameworks have emerged, such as AlexNet [36], VGGNet [37], GoogLeNet [38] and ResNet [39], which can provide results comparable with human beings in image classification and recognition tasks. Those methods can automatically learn features from the training data, which can replace the manually-engineered features, and have shown significant effects on HSI classification [8–10]. For example, Li et al. [40] applied 3D-CNNs for spectral-spatial feature extraction and classification, where 3D kernels were used to extract the feature from HSI cube without any preprocessing or post-processing. In [41], the transfer learning method for HRRS scene classification is used for transferring features from successfully pre-learned CNNs. Different from the CNNs methods, the convolutional kernels are updated in the training process, and the kernels in PCA-Net [42] and K-means Net are pre-learned before the network training and don't need to be updated in the network training. In addition, the kernels come from data directly. PCA-Net [42] adopts the principle components of training data as multistage filter banks, while K-means Net learns the kernels by clustering the training data. In this study, we mainly focus on the K-means Net. Although K-means Net can be directly applied to the classification and reduces the training time by employing the pre-learned kernels, it is difficult to determine the number of kernels that is crucial for the performance. To address this issue, we attempt to adaptively generate a specific number of kernels from the training data of CNNs framework.

3. MCFSFDP Based CNNs

The traditional CNNs framework contains the convolutional layer, fully connected layer and a classification layer. The convolution layer is updated through the error feedback process, which is different from the pre-learned convolutional kernels based CNNs framework.

The proposed MCFSFDP based CNNs method includes three major modules: (1) data pre-processing module, which extracts patches from block samples; (2) MCFSFDP based kernel learning module, which learns the convolutional kernels from those extracted patches; and (3) classification modules which utilize the learned convolution kernels.

The flowchart of our MCFSFDP based CNNs method is shown in Figure 1.

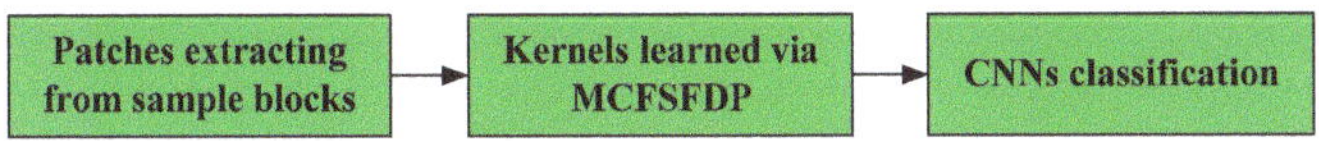

Figure 1. The flowchart of the MCFSFDP based CNNs method.

3.1. Data Pre-Processing

In this study, we follow the standard data pre-processing principle in K-means Net [13]. Specifically, a HSI used in this classification task is denoted by R. Though HSI is 3D data, it also can be seen as a collection of 2D images (i.e., images from different bands). Here, we denote the HSI as 2D form. First, we randomly select M pixels from R, and then extract M corresponding blocks $\{B_i\}_{i=1}^{M}$ with a size of $m \times m$ as samples, where each block is centered at each selected pixel. These extracted M samples are roughly divided into three parts, namely, training samples, validation samples and testing samples. The property of center block pixel is described by all the pixels in the block. Then, $\{B_i\}_{i=1}^{M}$ are put into the network and the center pixel labels of block B_i are used as the ground truth for training.

In addition, we randomly extract N patches $\{P_j\}_{j=1}^{N}$ with a size of $n \times n$ from M_T training samples, M_T denotes the number of training samples, where $M_T < M$ and $n < m$. The extracted N patches $\{P_j\}_{j=1}^{N}$ are used for learning the convolutional kernels with a size of $n \times n$ via MCFSFDP. The producing process of the block (sample) and patch is shown in Figure 2.

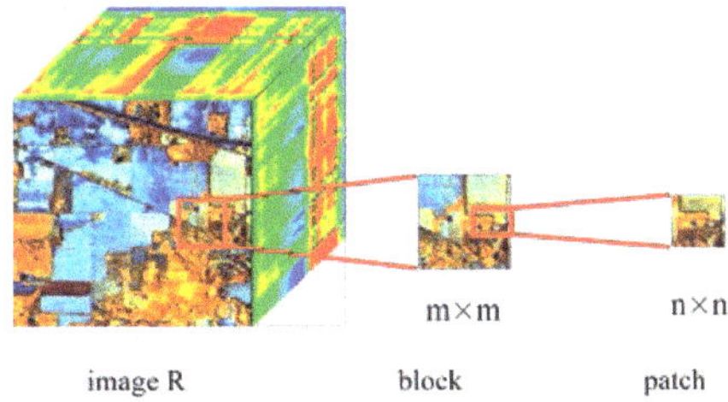

Figure 2. The block (sample) is extracted from image R and the patch is extracted from block, respectively.

3.2. MCFSFDP Based CNNs Kernels Learning

To obtain the kernels with those cropped patches, a suitable clustering method is necessary. Lots of clustering methods have been proposed, among which clustering by fast search and find of peaks (CFSFDP) [14], is a typical state-of-the-art method. The reason for partial success of CFSFDP on clustering is based on the idea that "cluster centers are characterized by a higher density than their neighbors and by a relatively large distance from points with higher densities" and the cluster centers can be determined through two thresholds of distance and density [14].

Though CFSFDP has shown its power for clustering, we find that when we apply it directly to generate the kernels for CNNs, the generated kernels are not always optimal for hyperspectral image classification tasks. This phenomena is observed from the experimental results (a similar conclusion also can be seen from the results in Section 4.3.1). In our opinion, we consider kernels (filters) as the standards for comparing the samples, which also show the evaluation standards for determining which cluster they belong to. Since the inter-cluster points are difficult to classify, we should also select several inter-cluster points with representations as the clusters (kernels). To address this problem, we propose a new clustering method based on CFSFDP, which only uses distance threshold to generate the kernel centers. The proposed method differs from the traditional CFSFDP in two aspects: (1) CFSFDP simultaneously uses the points with a large distance and high density to determine the cluster center, which easily excludes the outlier points into the generation of cluster centers; while the proposed MCFSFDP method only uses distance threshold to generate the cluster center, the cluster centers can be generated from either outlier points (with only large distance) or points of density; (2) the number of clusters via CFSFDP is determined 'semi-automatically', i.e., an extra frame needs to be introduced to help determine the number of clusters, while the number of clusters can be automatically determined through the proposed method. We give the details of the proposed method as follows.

The same as the CFSFDP algorithm in [14], we assume that the cluster centers are characterized by a higher density than their neighbors and by a relatively large distance from points with higher densities.

Following this idea, we firstly reshape each patch P_j into a column vector as a data point j with a size of $1 \times n^2$. For each point j, we compute two values: its local density ρ_j and its distance δ_j from the point with higher density, where, if the point j has the highest density, δ_j denotes the largest distance between j and other points.

Both of these values depend only on the Euclidean distances d_{jk} between any pair of data points j and k. The local density ρ_j of data j is defined as

$$\rho_j = \sum_k \chi(d_{jk} - d_c), \tag{1}$$

where $\chi(x) = 1$ if $x < 0$ and $\chi(x) = 0$ otherwise, and d_c is a cut-off distance. Basically, ρ_j is equal to the number of points that are closer than d_c to point j. δ_j is evaluated through computing the minimum distance between the point j and any other point with higher density in Equation (2):

$$\delta_j = \min_{k:\rho_k > \rho_j} \left(d_{jk}\right). \tag{2}$$

For the point with the highest density, we usually take $\delta_j = \max_k(d_{jk})$. Note that δ_j is much larger than the typical nearest neighbor distance only for points that are local or global maxima in the density. Thus, the cluster centers are recognized as points for which the value of δ_j is anomalously large and the value of ρ_j is higher than a value density at the same time. To show the distance and density of each point intuitively, we give the decision graph of 10,000 patches with a size of 10×10 from the real Indian pines dataset in Figure 3.

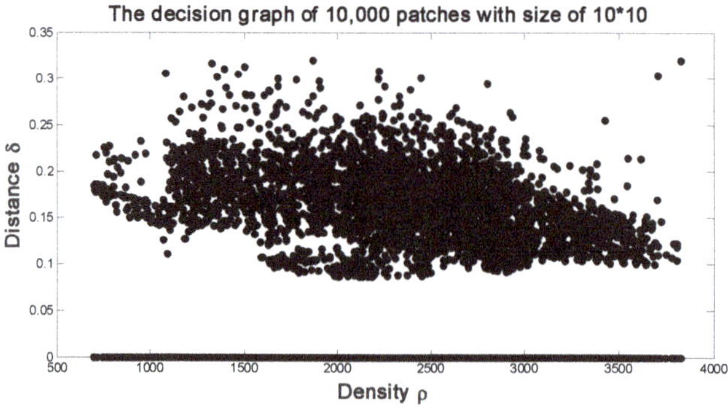

Figure 3. Decision graph of 10,000 patches with a size of 10×10 on the Indian pines dataset.

Different from choosing cluster centers in CFSFDP [14], we use the MCFSFDP algorithm to learn the kernels adaptively. Firstly, we choose the distance δ as the only threshold for choosing kernels from the decision graph in MCFSFDP.

To adapt the kernels and choose the number of kernels, we select the optimal distance threshold value δ_A as the following steps:

$$num_v = f(\delta_v), \tag{3}$$

$$con_v = [f(\delta_{v+1}) - f(\delta_v)]/(\delta_{v+1} - \delta_v), \tag{4}$$

$$quo_v = |con_v/con_{v+1}|. \tag{5}$$

where, in Equation (3), δ_v denotes the value of distance that contains points and $f(\delta_v)$ gives the mapping relationship of the number of points whose distances are equal or larger than δ_v, as shown as Figure 4a. In Equation (4), where $\delta_{v+1} \geq \delta_v$, con_v denotes the differential of $f(\delta_v)$, which is an intermediate result between Equations (3) and (5). Equation (5) denotes the variation quantity of the number of points with δ_v, shown as Figure 4b.

δ_A denotes the adaptive distance threshold, and the points whose distances are larger than δ_A are chosen as CNN kernels. δ_A is a critical point that must satisfy the number num_v and num_{v+1} of points are stable (in other words, they have a similar quantity), at the same time, the value $|con_v/con_{v+1}|$ is larger than the value $|con_{v+1}/con_{v+2}|$. In this time, δ_v is selected as the adaptive distance threshold δ_A.

In other words, to determine the adaptive distance threshold δ_A intuitively, from Figure 4a, we can find the value region δ_v (0.25–0.30) from curve 1 when num_v begins to approach to 0; as can be seen from Figure 4b, con_v with the distance value δ_v in region (0.25–0.30) has a local maxima at $\delta_v = 0.28$. The distance δ_v (0.28) that belongs to the region (0.25–0.30) is confirmed as the adaptive threshold distance as δ_A. In conclusion, by observing Figure 4, the adaptive distance threshold δ_A is determined as 0.28 on the Indian Pines dataset.

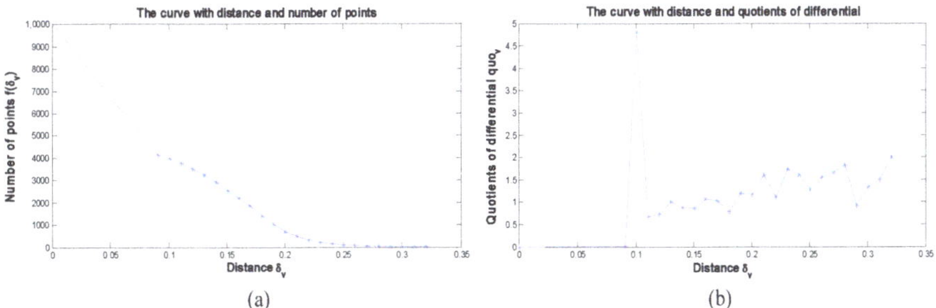

Figure 4. The curve for determining the adaptive distance with patches with a size of 10×10 the on Indian pines dataset. (**a**) shows the curve of point-number over distance δ_v; (**b**) gives the curve of quotients of differential over distance δ_v.

Finally, the points j with the distance value $\delta_j > \delta_A$ are adaptively chosen as the kernels and thus the number of kernels is also adaptively determined through the threshold δ_A. Those chosen points are then reshaped to patches with a size of $n \times n$ as the convolutional kernels in the CNNs framework. The CNNs with the pre-learned adaptive kernels are called MCFSFDP Net. The pre-learned kernels are denoted as w^k in the following sections.

3.3. Convolutional Neural Networks

With the pre-learned kernels w^k, a convolutional neural network such as [13] is designed for per-pixel level HSI classification. This CNNs structure consists of an input layer, a convolutional layer, a pooling layer, a fully connected layer and a soft-max layer, as shown in Figure 5.

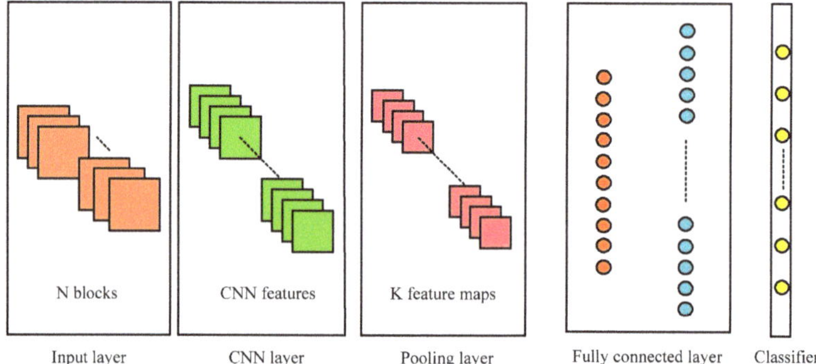

Figure 5. The structure of MCFSFDP based CNNs.

There are k kernels in the convolutional layer. Each feature map is calculated by taking the dot product between the k-th kernel w^k of size $n \times n$, $w \in R^{n \times n \times k}$, and local context area x of size $m \times m$ with c number of channels, $x \in R^{m \times m \times c}$. The feature map corresponding with the k-th filter $f \in R^{(m-n+1) \times (m-n+1)}$ is calculated as:

$$f_{ij}^k = \sigma(\sum_c \sum_{a=0}^{n-1} \sum_{b=0}^{n-1} w_{abc}^k x_{i+a,j+b}^c), \tag{6}$$

where σ is the rectified linear unit (ReLU). The kernels were pre-trained using the MCFSFDP algorithm.

The maximum pooling over a local non-overlapping spatial region is adopted to down-sample the convolutional layer. The pooling layer for the k-th filter, $g \in R^{(m-n+1)/p \times (m-n+1)/p}$, is calculated as:

$$g_{ij}^k = \max(f_{1+p(i-1),1+p(j-1)}^k, \cdots, f_{pi,1+p(j-1)}^k, \cdots, f_{1+p(i-1),pj}^k, \cdots, f_{1+pi,pj}^k). \tag{7}$$

The k feature maps are reshaped to the column vectors and all the column vectors are connected with a fully connected auto-encode unit. The autoencode unit is used to process the connected column vector and represented the feature of the column vector. The output results of the hide layer in the auto-encode unit were used to connect the classification layer.

The last CNNs step is a soft-max layer used for final classification.

4. Experiments and Analysis

Three datasets were utilized to validate the feasibility and effectiveness of the proposed CNNs based MCFSFDP method (named as MCFSFDP Net) in HSI classification. In the following sections, dataset and experimental settings are described firstly, and then the effectiveness and the superiority of the proposed method are tested.

4.1. Datasets

To find images with less categories and obvious discriminations between categories, we firstly select an image dataset with a size of 256 × 256. The image of this dataset has been manually labeled as three categories, including mountains, sky and roads. One hundred samples with a size of 25 × 25 from each category that were extracted from this image. We randomly choose 210 context area samples for training, 30 samples for validation and 60 other samples for testing. The details of selected image samples were given in Table 1.

Table 1. Ground truth classes and their respective sample numbers in Dataset 1.

Class	Samples		
	Training	Validation	Testing
Mountain	70	10	20
Sky	70	10	20
Road	70	10	20

In order to evaluate the proposed method on complex data, Dataset 2 includes the benchmark Indian Pines image, which is HSI data captured by the airborne visible imaging spectrometer (AVIRIS) sensor with a moderate spatial resolution of 20 m over the Indian Pines test site in northwestern Indiana in 1992. As shown in Figure 6, this image contains145 × 145 pixels and 224 spectral bands, whose wavelength ranges from 0.4 to 2.5 um. The number of bands of corrected data was reduced to 200 (extracted the 1–200 bands). In addition, 6476 image context area samples with a size of 19 × 19 were extracted. Among them, 3238, 647 and 2591 samples were used for training, validation and testing, respectively. The details of each category of image samples were given in Table 2.

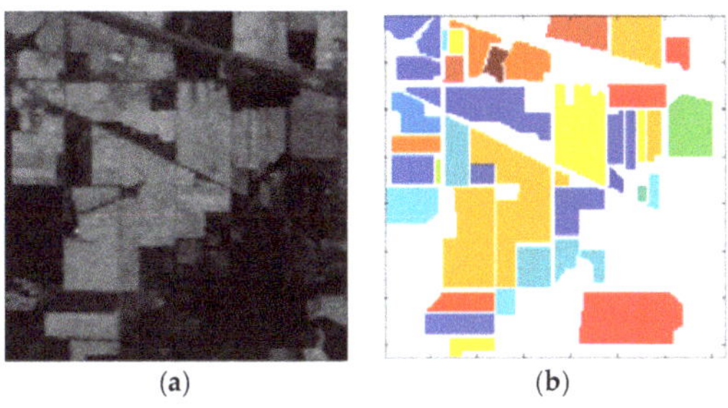

(a)　　　　(b)

Figure 6. The Indian Pines on Dataset 2. (**a**) shows the composite image; (**b**) shows the groundtruth of Indian Pines dataset, where the white area denotes the unlabeled pixels.

Table 2. Groundtruth of classes and their respective sample numbers on Indian Pines scene.

Class		Samples			
Number	Classes	Total	Training	Validation	Testing
1	Alfalfa	46	23	4	19
2	Corn-notill	1288	636	132	520
3	Corn-mintill	63	29	7	27
4	Corn	35	17	3	15
5	Grass-pasture	180	90	14	76
6	Grass-trees	730	342	84	304
7	Grass-pasture-mowed	28	16	1	11
8	Hay-windrowed	94	45	8	41
9	Oats	20	10	2	8
10	Soybean-notill	807	406	71	330
11	Soybean-mintill	2067	1019	215	833
12	Soybean-clean	227	124	22	81
13	Wheat	204	107	28	69
14	Woods	560	307	44	209
15	Buildings-Grass-Trees-Drives	73	38	9	26
16	Stone-Steel-Towers	54	29	3	22
	Total	6476	3238	647	2591

The third Dataset 3 includes the benchmark Pavia University image, which is HSI data captured by a ROSIS sensor with a moderate spatial resolution of 1.3 m over the flight campaign over Pavia, northern Italy. As shown in Figure 7, this image contains 610 × 610 pixels and 103 spectral bands. The number of bands was reduced to 100 (extracted the 1–100 bands). Furthermore, 34,400 image context area samples with a size of 11 × 11 were extracted. Among them, 17,200, 3440 and 13,760 samples were used for training, validation and testing, respectively. The details of each category of samples were given in Table 3.

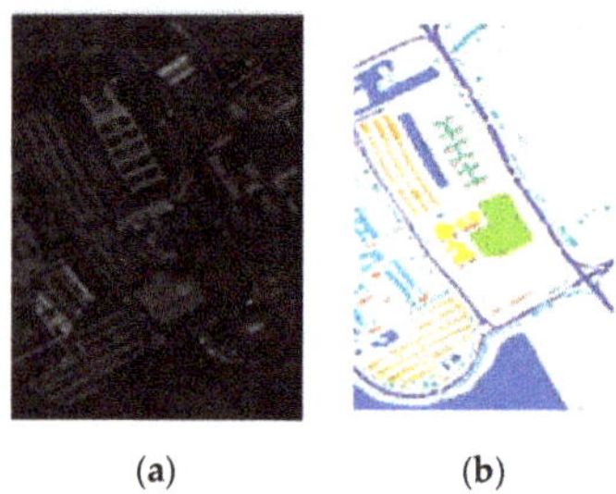

(a)   (b)

Figure 7. The Pavia University in Dataset 3. (**a**) shows the composite image; (**b**) shows the groundtruth of the Pavia University dataset, white area denotes the unlabeled pixels.

Table 3. Groundtruth of classes and their respective sample numbers in the Pavia University scene.

Class		Samples			
Number	Classes	Total	Training	Validation	Testing
1	Asphalt	5446	2718	580	2148
2	Meadows	12,695	6307	1320	5068
3	Gravel	1314	674	126	514
4	Trees	2709	1329	241	1139
5	Painted metal sheets	1345	688	153	504
6	Bare Soil	5029	2517	453	2059
7	Bitumen	1330	686	120	524
8	Self-Blocking Bricks	3630	1810	362	1458
9	Shadows	902	471	85	346
	Total	**34,400**	**17,200**	**3440**	**13,760**

4.2. Experimental Parameter Settings

Ten thousand patches were randomly extracted from the training samples for learning kernels. For each dataset, the sample (blocks) size and the number of patches should be maintained consistently in different pre-learned CNNs frameworks.

The CNNs framework that is shown in Figure 5 uses one convolutional layer, one pooling layer, one auto-encode layer and a classifier. In our algorithm, the pooling layer adopted the non-overlap rule, the number of neurons in the hide layer of auto encode was set to 100 and the maximum iterations for training the classifier was 400. The learning rate is 0.0001 and momentum is 1. The batch sizes on the three datasets are chosen as 10, 50 and 200, respectively.

The codes are running on the computer with Intel Xeon E5-2678 V3 2.50 GHz × 2 (Intel, Santa Clara, CA, USA), NVIDIA Tesla (NVIDIA, Santa Clara, CA, USA) K40c GPU × 2, 128 GB RAM, 120 GB SSD and Matlab 2016a (MathWorks, Natick, MA, USA). The gradient is computed via batch gradient descent, which is not computed by GPU.

The average test accuracy is calculated on 10 independent Monte Carlo runs.

4.3. Experimental Results

4.3.1. Effectiveness of the Kernels Learned by MCFSFDP

The aim of this experiment is to validate the effectiveness of the kernels learned by MCFSFDP. To this end, we compared those kernels with those learned as the cluster center obtained by CFSFDP algorithm. Those two kinds of kernels were then integrated into the same CNNs framework for HSI classification on Dataset 1. To obtain fair comparison results, both of the numbers of kernels in those two methods were fixed at 49. The kernel size was set to 14 × 14 and the pooling size was designed as 4 × 4. The average testing classification accuracy of those two methods was shown in Table 4.

Table 4. The testing accuracy compared with learned 49 kernels via CFSFDP and MCFSFDP-M on Dataset 1.

Methods	CFSFDP Net	MCFSFDP Net
Accuracy (%)	81.67 ± 0.5904	**95.00 ± 0.5887**

It reveals that the kernels learned by the MCFSFDP are more effective than the kernels learned by the CFSFDP.

4.3.2. Effectiveness of the Kernels Number Determined by MCFSFDP

To demonstrate the effectiveness of the kernels number determined by MCFSFDP, we compared MCFSFDP with its variants for classification in each dataset. Those variants shared the same CNNs architecture and the kernel learning scheme excepted choosing the kernels number manually. Dataset 1, Dataset 2 and Dataset 3 were used in the experiment. For each dataset, the kernel size and the pooling size can be found in Table 5.

Table 5. The chosen block size, kernel size and pooling size of each dataset.

Dataset	Dataset 1	Dataset 2	Dataset 3
Block Size	25 × 25	19 × 19	11 × 11
Kernel Size	10 × 10	6 × 6	2 × 2
Pooling Size	4 × 4	7 × 7	2 × 2

We report the testing classification accuracy of all these methods on each dataset in Tables 6–8, respectively. Each variant is denoted as MCFSFDP-M Net followed with a specific number which indicates the kernel number chosen manually. Similarly, the number that followed MCFSFDP Net represents the kernel number automatically determined by the proposed method.

Table 6. The testing accuracy of MCFSFDP-M Net compared with MCFSFDP Net on Dataset 1.

Methods	MCFSFDP-M Net-20	MCFSFDP-M Net-25	MCFSFDP-M Net-41	MCFSFDP-M Net-55	MCFSFDP Net-35
Accuracy (%)	93.33 ± 0.5887	95.00 ± 0.5904	95.00 ± 0.5904	95.00 ± 0.5904	**96.67 ± 0.5887**
Distance threshold	0.19	0.18	0.16	0.15	**0.17**
Number of kernels	20	25	41	55	**35**

Table 7. The testing accuracy of MCFSFDP-M Net compared with MCFSFDP Net on Dataset 2.

Methods	MCFSFDP-M Net-14	MCFSFDP-M Net-24	MCFSFDP-M Net-31	MCFSFDP-M Net-83	MCFSFDP-M Net-151	MCFSFDP Net-50
Accuracy (%)	95.29 ± 0.0870	96.51 ± 0.4146	97.03 ± 0.1940	97.07 ± 0.3434	96.82 ± 0.1457	**97.84 ± 0.2249**
Distance threshold	0.27	0.26	0.25	0.23	0.22	**0.24**
Number of kernels	14	24	31	83	151	**50**

Table 8. The test accuracy of MCFSFDP-M Net compared with MCFSFDP Net on Dataset 3.

Methods	MCFSFDP-M Net-19	MCFSFDP-M Net-42	MCFSFDP-M Net-152	MCFSFDP Net-78
Accuracy (%)	88.98 ± 0.2651	89.32 ± 0.1908	89.54 ± 0.1002	**90.58 ± 0.1477**
Distance threshold	0.08	0.07	0.05	**0.06**
Number of kernels	19	42	152	**78**

In Table 6, the proposed method determines the kernel number as 35. The manually chosen kernel number in other variants are 20, 25, 41 and 55, respectively. The accuracy, distance threshold and the number of kernels for each method are shown in different rows. It can be seen that the proposed method shows the best classification accuracy. Similar phenomenon arises in Tables 7 and 8. Therefore, we can conclude that the proposed method is able to seek a good kernel number for different datasets.

4.3.3. Performance Evaluation of MCFSFDP Net

In this part, the proposed method was compared with three state-of-the-art pre-learned kernels based CNNs methods, including K-means Net [13], PCA-Net [42] and Random Net. For fair comparison, the same CNNs architecture was adopted by all comparison methods. The number of kernels for K-means Net, PCA-Net and Random Net was set to 50, while the proposed method determines the number of kernels automatically. For each dataset, the kernel size and the pooling size can be found in Table 9.

Table 9. The testing accuracy of different CNNs methods compared with MCFSFDP Net on Dataset 1.

Methods	K-Means Net-50	PCA Net-50	Random Net-50	MCFSFDP Net-35
Accuracy (%)	93.33 ± 0.5887	90.00 ± 1.8175	95.00 ± 1.8175	**96.67 ± 0.5887**

It reveals that the proposed algorithm can produce more accuracy for pixel classification than those three types of pre-learned kernels based CNNs methods on this dataset as shown in Table 9. Moreover, the proposed MCFSFDP Net with 35 kernels that has less computational complexity than comparison methods with 50 kernels in the training process.

The average testing classification accuracy of our proposed algorithm, K-means Net, PCA-Net and Random Net on Dataset 2 was given in Table 10. The results obviously show that the proposed MCFSFDP Net obtains better accuracy than those three types of pre-learned kernels based CNNs methods, which is consistent with the results obtained from Dataset 1.

Table 10. The testing accuracy of different CNNs methods compared with MCFSFDP Net on Dataset 2.

Methods	K-Means Net-50	PCA Net-50	Random Net-50	MCFSFDP Net-50
Accuracy (%)	95.02 ± 0.3343	97.30 ± 1.1916	97.12 ± 0.6195	**97.84 ± 0.2249**

The average classification accuracy of our proposed method compared with another three kernels pre-learned based CNNs on the Pavia University image was presented in Table 11. The results show that our proposed CNNs method is more accurate than those three types of pre-learned kernels based CNNs methods. Even if the proposed method needs more kernels number to perform the better classification result.

Table 11. The testing accuracy of different CNNs methods compared with MCFSFDP Net on Dataset 3.

Methods	K-Means Net-50	PCA Net-50	Random Net-50	MCFSFDP Net-78
Accuracy (%)	89.77 ± 0.3399	90.14 ± 0.2652	90.47 ± 0.5113	**90.58 ± 0.1477**

5. Discussion

5.1. Effect of the Number of Kernels

In the MCFSFDP-M Net, the number of kernels influences the pixel-level classification. Figure 8 shows the classification accuracy achieved with different numbers A_k that were manually selected via MCFSFDP on Dataset 1, Dataset 2 and Dataset 3.

Figure 8a shows the classification results with the variation of kernel numbers A_k on each kernel size $n \times n$ on Dataset 1. The accuracy of MCFSFDP-M Net computation cannot be enhanced when the kernel number A_k was increased. Figure 8b shows the highest accuracy on Dataset 2. While the kernel number is manually chosen via MCFSFDP, the accuracy can get a high point in the number range of the kernels, as the adaptive kernels learned through the MCFSFDP method. It demonstrates again that the accuracy cannot be enhanced with the increased kernel number on Dataset 3, as shown in Figure 8c.

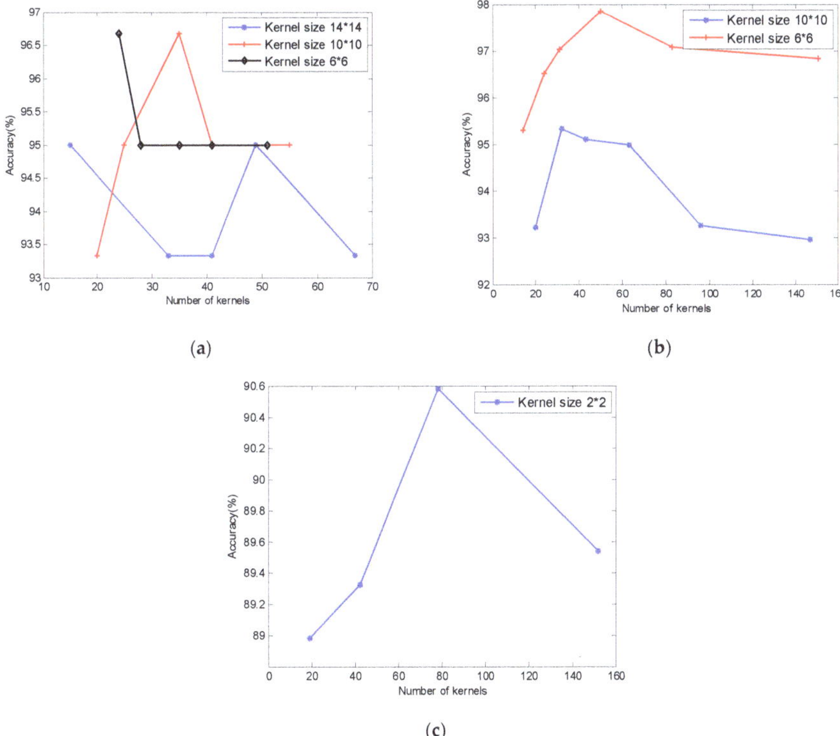

Figure 8. The classification accuracy influence with the number of kernels. (**a**) the classification accuracy with the increased number of kernels with different kernel size on Dataset 1; (**b**) the classification accuracy with the increased number of kernels with different kernel size on Dataset 2; (**c**) the classification accuracy with the increased number of kernels on Dataset 3.

5.2. Effect of the Kernel Size

In our proposed MCFSFSP based CNN method, the kernel size has a major impact on the pixel classification performance. Table 12 gives the average classification accuracy obtained by using different kernel size. It shows that the highest classification accuracy was achieved when kernel size was set to 10×10 and 6×6 on Dataset 1 and 6×6 on Dataset 2.

Table 12. The average classification accuracy obtained by using different kernel size.

Dataset	Dataset 1			Dataset 2	
Pooling Size	4×4	4×4	4×4	5×5	7×7
Kernel Size	14×14	10×10	6×6	10×10	6×6
Number of Kernels	15	35	24	32	50
Distance Value	0.22	0.17	0.17	0.28	0.24
Accuracy (%)	95	**96.67**	**96.67**	95.33	**97.84**

6. Conclusions

In this paper, we propose a novel CNNs classification framework for HSIs, which can data-adaptively learn a specific number of kernels from the training data. In particular, this model adopts the MCFSFDP algorithm to cluster the training data, and then the convolutional kernels can be determined automatically by the cluster center and inter-cluster margin. With those pre-learned kernels, a CNNs framework is developed for classifications. We have compared the proposed CNNs framework against three state-of-the-art deep learning methods with pre-trained kernels on three datasets. The experimental results demonstrate the superiority of the proposed CNNs framework in classification accuracy. Moreover, we validate that the proposed method is able to seek a good kernel number for a specific dataset. These adaptively learned kernels can help us understand the complexity of data and adjust the CNNs architecture for good feature extraction.

In terms of future research, we will exploit a multi-layer architecture via MCSFDP based CNNs to enhance the classification accuracy with less samples.

Acknowledgments: This work was supported by the Key Project of the National Natural Science Foundation of China (Grant No. 61231016), the National Natural Science Foundations of China (Grant No. 61471297, Grant No. 61671385 and Grant No. 61301192) and the China 863 Program (Grant No. 2015AA016402).

Author Contributions: All of the authors made significant contributions to this work. Chen Ding and Yanning Zhang devised the approach and analyzed the data; Yong Xia, Wei Wei, Lei Zhang and Ying Li helped design the remote sensing experiments and provided advice for the preparation and revision of the work; Chen Ding performed the experiments.

References

1. Zortea, M.; Martino, M.D.; Serpico, S. A SVM ensemble approach for spectral-contextual classification of optical high spatial resolution imagery. In Proceedings of the 2007 IEEE International Geoscience and Remote Sensing Symposium, Barcelona, Spain, 23–28 July 2007; pp. 1489–1492.
2. Huang, X.; Zhang, L. An Adaptive Mean-Shift Analysis Approach for Object Extraction and Classification From Urban Hyperspectral Imagery. *IEEE Trans. Geosci. Remote Sens.* **2008**, *46*, 4173–4185. [CrossRef]
3. Li, J.; Bioucas-Dias, J.M.; Plaza, A. Spectral-Spatial Hyperspectral Image Segmentation Using Subspace Multinomial Logistic Regression and Markov Random Fields. *IEEE Trans. Geosci. Remote Sens.* **2012**, *50*, 809–823. [CrossRef]
4. Benediktsson, J.A.; Palmason, J.A.; Sveinsson, J.R. Classification of hyperspectral data from urban areas based on extended morphological profiles. *IEEE Trans. Geosci. Remote Sens.* **2005**, *43*, 480–491. [CrossRef]
5. Wei, W.; Zhang, Y.; Tian, C. Latent subclass learning-based unsupervised ensemble feature extraction method for hyperspectral image classification. *Remote Sens. Lett.* **2015**, *6*, 257–266. [CrossRef]
6. Zhang, L.; Wei, W.; Tian, C.; Li, F.; Zhang, Y. Exploring Structured Sparsity by a Reweighted Laplace Prior for Hyperspectral Compressive Sensing. *IEEE Trans. Image Process.* **2016**, *25*, 4974–4988. [CrossRef]

7. Zhang, L.; Wei, W.; Zhang, Y.; Shen, C.; van den Hengel, A.; Shi, Q. Dictionary learning for promoting structured sparsity in hyperspectral compressive sensing. *IEEE Trans. Geosci. Remote Sens.* **2016**, *54*, 7223–7235. [CrossRef]

8. Zhang, L.; Zhang, L.; Du, B. Deep Learning for Remote Sensing Data: A Technical Tutorial on the State of the Art. *IEEE Geosci. Remote Sens. Mag.* **2016**, *4*, 22–40. [CrossRef]

9. Chen, Y.; Lin, Z.; Zhao, X.; Wang, G.; Gu, Y. Deep Learning-Based Classification of Hyperspectral Data. *IEEE J. Sel. Top. Appl. Earth Obs. Remote Sens.* **2014**, *7*, 2094–2107. [CrossRef]

10. Zhao, W.; Du, S. Spectral-Spatial Feature Extraction for Hyperspectral Image Classification: A Dimension Reduction and Deep Learning Approach. *IEEE Trans. Geosci. Remote Sens.* **2016**, *54*, 4544–4554. [CrossRef]

11. Wang, Q.; Lin, J.; Yuan, Y. Salient Band Selection for Hyperspectral Image Classification via Manifold Ranking. *IEEE Trans. Neural Netw. Learn. Syst.* **2016**, *27*, 1279. [CrossRef] [PubMed]

12. Wang, Q.; Yuan, Y.; Yan, P. Visual Saliency by Selective Contrast. *IEEE Trans. Circuits Syst. Video Technol.* **2013**, *23*, 1150–1155. [CrossRef]

13. Längkvist, M.; Kiselev, A.; Alirezaie, M.; Loutfi, A. Classification and Segmentation of Satellite Orthoimagery Using Convolutional Neural Networks. *Remote Sens.* **2016**, *8*, 329. [CrossRef]

14. Rodriguez, A.; Laio, A. Clustering by fast search and find of density peaks. *Science* **2014**, *344*, 1492–1496. [CrossRef] [PubMed]

15. Timmerman, M.E. Principal Component Analysis (2nd ed.) by I.T. Jolliffe. *J. Am. Stat. Assoc.* **2003**, *98*, 1082–1083. [CrossRef]

16. Rosipal, R.; Krämer, N. Overview and recent advances in partial least squares. In *Subspace, Latent Structure and Feature Selection, Proceedings of the Statistical and Optimization Perspectives Workshop (SLSFS 2005), Bohinj, Slovenia, 23–25 February 2005*; Springer: Berlin/Heidelber, Germany, 2006; pp. 34–51.

17. Camps-Valls, G.; Bruzzone, L. *Kernel Methods for Remote Sensing Data Analysis*; John Wiley & Sons: River Street Hoboken, NJ, USA, 2009.

18. Myint, S.W. Wavelets for Urban Spatial Feature Discrimination: Comparisons with Fractal, Spatial Autocorrelation, and Spatial Co-occurrence Approaches. *Photogramm. Eng. Remote Sens.* **2004**, *70*, 803–812. [CrossRef]

19. Zhu, C.; Yang, X. Study of remote sensing image texture analysis and classification using wavelet. *Int. J. Remote Sens.* **1998**, *19*, 3197–3203. [CrossRef]

20. Dong, Y.; Forester, B.C.; Milne, A.K. Segmentation of radar imagery using the Gaussian Markov random field model. *Int. J. Remote Sens.* **1999**, *20*, 1617–1639. [CrossRef]

21. Dong, Y.; Forster, B.C.; Milne, A.K. Comparison of radar image segmentation by Gaussian-and Gamma-Markov random field models. *Int. J. Remote Sens.* **2003**, *24*, 711–722. [CrossRef]

22. Zhang, L.; Huang, X.; Huang, B.; Li, P. A pixel shape index coupled with spectral information for classification of high spatial resolution remotely sensed imagery. *IEEE Trans. Geosci. Remote Sens.* **2006**, *44*, 2950–2961. [CrossRef]

23. Dalla Mura, M.; Benediktsson, J.A.; Waske, B.; Bruzzone, L. Morphological Attribute Profiles for the Analysis of Very High Resolution Images. *IEEE Trans. Geosci. Remote Sens.* **2010**, *48*, 3747–3762. [CrossRef]

24. He, K.; Sun, J.; Tang, X. Guided image filtering. *IEEE Trans. Pattern Anal. Mach. Intell.* **2011**, *35*, 1397.

25. Kang, X.; Li, S.; Benediktsson, J.A. Spectral-Spatial Hyperspectral Image Classification With Edge-Preserving Filtering. *IEEE Trans. Geosci. Remote Sens.* **2014**, *52*, 2666–2677.

26. Kang, X.; Li, S.; Benediktsson, J.A. Feature Extraction of Hyperspectral Images With Image Fusion and Recursive Filtering. *IEEE Trans. Geosci. Remote Sens.* **2014**, *52*, 3742–3752.

27. Sivic, J.; Zisserman, A. Video Google: A Text Retrieval Approach to Object Matching in Videos. In Proceedings of the Ninth IEEE International Conference on Computer Vision (ICCV), Nice, France, 13–16 October 2003; pp. 1470–1477.

28. Lazebnik, S.; Schmid, C.; Ponce, J. Beyond bags of features: Spatial pyramid matching for recognizing natural scene categories. In Proceedings of the 2006 IEEE Computer Society Conference on Computer Vision and Pattern Recognition, New York, NY, USA, 17–22 June 2006; pp. 2169–2178.

29. Xia, G.S.; Delon, J.; Gousseau, Y. Accurate Junction Detection and Characterization in Natural Images. *Int. J. Comput. Vis.* **2014**, *106*, 31–56.

30. Xia, G.S.; Delon, J.; Gousseau, Y. Shape-based Invariant Texture Indexing. *Int. J. Comput. Vis.* **2010**, *88*, 382–403.

31. Liu, W.; Liu, H.; Tao, D.; Wang, Y.; Lu, K. Manifold regularized kernel logistic regression for web image annotation. *Neurocomputing* **2016**, *172*, 3–8.
32. Wang, Q.; Yuan, Y.; Yan, P.; Li, X. Saliency Detection by Multiple-Instance Learning. *IEEE Trans. Cybern.* **2013**, *43*, 660–672. [PubMed]
33. Chen, Y.; Zhao, X.; Jia, X. Spectral-Spatial Classification of Hyperspectral Data Based on Deep Belief Network. *IEEE J. Sel. Top. Appl. Earth Obs. Remote Sens.* **2015**, *8*, 2381–2392.
34. Yang, X.; Liu, W.; Tao, D.; Cheng, J. Canonical Correlation Analysis Networks for Two-view Image Recognition. *Inf. Sci.* **2017**, *385–386*, 338–352.
35. LeCun, Y.; Bottou, L.; Bengio, Y.; Haffner, P. Gradient-based learning applied to document recognition. *Proc. IEEE* **1998**, *86*, 2278–2324.
36. Krizhevsky, A.; Sutskever, I.; Hinton, G.E. ImageNet classification with deep convolutional neural networks. In *Advances in Neural Information Processing Systems 25, Proceedings of the Neural Information Processing Systems, Stateline, NV, USA, 3–8 December 2012*; Neural Information Processing Systems Foundation, Inc.: La Jolla, CA, USA, 2012; pp. 1097–2013.
37. Simonyan, K.; Zisserman, A. Very Deep Convolutional Networks for Large-Scale Image Recognition. *arXiv*, **2014**, arXiv:1409.1556.
38. Szegedy, C.; Liu, W.; Jia, Y.; Sermanet, P.; Reed, S.; Anguelov, D.; Rabinovich, A. Going deeper with convolutions. In Proceedings of the IEEE Conference on Computer Vision and Pattern Recognition, Boston, MA, USA, 8–10 June 2015; pp. 1–9.
39. He, K.; Zhang, X.; Ren, S.; Sun, J. Deep Residual Learning for Image Recognition. In Proceedings of the IEEE Conference on Computer Vision and Pattern Recognition, Las Vegas, NV, USA, 26 June–1 July 2016; pp. 770–778.
40. Li, Y.; Zhang, H.; Shen, Q. Spectral-Spatial Classification of Hyperspectral Imagery with 3D Convolutional Neural Network. *Remote Sens.* **2017**, *9*, 67. [CrossRef]
41. Hu, F.; Xia, G.S.; Hu, J.; Zhang, L. Transferring Deep Convolutional Neural Networks for the Scene Classification of High-Resolution Remote Sensing Imagery. *Remote Sens.* **2015**, *7*, 14680–14707. [CrossRef]
42. Chan, T.H.; Jia, K.; Gao, S.; Lu, J.; Zeng, Z.; Ma, Y. PCANet: A Simple Deep Learning Baseline for Image Classification? *IEEE Trans. Image Process.* **2015**, *24*, 5017–5032. [CrossRef] [PubMed]

Technical Note

Flood Inundation Mapping from Optical Satellite Images Using Spatiotemporal Context Learning and Modest AdaBoost

Xiaoyi Liu [1,2], Hichem Sahli [3,4], Yu Meng [1,*], Qingqing Huang [1] and Lei Lin [1,2]

[1]   Institute of Remote Sensing and Digital Earth, Chinese Academy of Sciences, Beijing 100101, China; liuxy01@radi.ac.cn (X.L.); huangqq@radi.ac.cn (Q.H.); linlei@radi.ac.cn (L.L.)

[2]   University of Chinese Academy of Sciences, Beijing 100049, China

[3]   Department of Electronics and Informatics, Vrije Universiteit Brussel, 1050 Brussels, Belgium; hsahli@etrovub.be

[4]   Interuniversity Microelectronics Centre (IMEC), 3001 Heverlee, Belgium

*   Correspondence: mengyu@radi.ac.cn; Tel.: +86-10-64847442

Academic Editors: Qi Wang, Nicolas H. Younan, Carlos López-Martínez and Prasad S. Thenkabail
Received: 20 March 2017; Accepted: 10 June 2017; Published: 16 June 2017

Abstract: Due to its capacity for temporal and spatial coverage, remote sensing has emerged as a powerful tool for mapping inundation. Many methods have been applied effectively in remote sensing flood analysis. Generally, supervised methods can achieve better precision than unsupervised. However, human intervention makes its results subjective and difficult to obtain automatically, which is important for disaster response. In this work, we propose a novel procedure combining spatiotemporal context learning method and Modest AdaBoost classifier, which aims to extract inundation in an automatic and accurate way. First, the context model was built with images to calculate the confidence value of each pixel, which represents the probability of the pixel remaining unchanged. Then, the pixels with the highest probabilities, which we define as 'permanent pixels', were used as samples to train the Modest AdaBoost classifier. By applying the strong classifier to the target scene, an inundation map can be obtained. The proposed procedure is validated using two flood cases with different sensors, HJ-1A CCD and GF-4 PMS. Qualitative and quantitative evaluation results showed that the proposed procedure can achieve accurate and robust mapping results.

Keywords: inundation mapping; flood; optical sensors; spatiotemporal context learning; Modest AdaBoost; HJ-1A/B CCD; GF-4 PMS

---

1. Introduction

Natural disasters are common phenomena in all parts of the world. There are many types of natural disasters [1], of which a flood is considered to be one of the most destructive, widespread and frequent disasters [2,3]. Every year, tremendous loss of life and property is caused by flooding [3]. Due to the changes in global climate and land use, floods are becoming more severe and more frequent all around the world [3,4]. Although it is difficult to prevent floods, it is possible to minimise their impact through proper rescue, relief and resource allocation for recovery and reconstruction. Therefore, accurate inundation mapping, especially near real time, is very important for establishing a fast response plan and mitigating the disaster [5–7].

Traditional methods for inundation mapping are based on ground survey and aerial observation. However, when the flood spreads to a large scale, these approaches are time- and resource-consuming, which cannot satisfy the need for a fast response to a disaster. Moreover, aerial observation can be unrealistic in some extreme weather conditions, and the density of gauging stations is not satisfactory in many countries [8]. An alternative choice is provided by satellite remote sensing (RS) techniques [6]. Due to their time availability and cost effectiveness, satellite data has played an important role in understanding inundation [9–13]. The availability of multi-date images makes it possible to monitor the progress of floods.

Satellites used for mapping floods can be divided into those that are optical and those that are microwave. Due to its capacity to penetrate the frequent clouds in a flood event, microwave remote sensing is all-weather and invaluable for flood monitoring. With multispectral images, the flood can be analysed in a more straightforward way with simpler pre-processing [14]. In this study, we mainly focus on methods using multispectral satellite images.

Numerous methods have been proposed for mapping inundation using multispectral remote sensing images. Among them, the one most frequently used is thresholding. Usually, indices are first calculated through different band combinations, such as the normalised difference water index (NDWI) created by McFeeters [15], which has been proven to produce good results for inundated areas [16]. Then a threshold is selected to determine the water range in the image. A manual threshold is accurate, but has difficulty satisfying the need for fast disaster response. Moreover, it is subjective, as different operators may produce different results. To overcome the problems, unsupervised thresholding methods have been proposed. For instance, Xie et al. [17] introduced Otsu's algorithm to implement automatic selection of the water threshold. But due to the common illumination differences and mixed pixels in satellite images, its effectiveness is reduced, especially for some complicated scenes.

The segmentation (semi-supervised) technique [18] has been proposed to minimise the involvement of the user. The user first selects some seed points, with which the connectivity map is generated using fuzzy logic. For example, in [19], a fast flood map and a detailed flood map were obtained using growing strategies with seed points. However, the detailed map result still depended on the correctness of the seed points.

Unsupervised strategies without any human involvement have attracted a lot of attention in recent years. There are several kinds of unsupervised inundation mapping methods. Besides the unsupervised threshold, unsupervised feature extraction methods have been utilised. Chignell et al. [20] combines the pre- and post-flood images and apply the independent component analysis (ICA) to them. Segmentation and threshold are used to extract the flood from the change components. The cloud and crop components help to refine the maximum flood extent. In the work by Rokni et al. [21], the multi-temporal NDWI images are composited into one file. Principal component analysis (PCA) is applied to the composited file. The principle components are classified by the thresholding technique, and the result of the change detection for the lake is obtained. But these methods are only based on spectral information. When they are applied to cases using different sensors, the ability of the method can vary with the changes of spectral characteristics.

Recently, context information, especially spatiotemporal context information, has attracted more attention and proven to bring much improvement in monitoring the water surface. It is combined with other techniques to generate chains of processing for better representation of an event. Chen et al. [22] proposed a water surface monitoring method using contextual information. First, permanent water/non-water pixels were detected by judging the statistical consistency between an image point and its neighbourhood. Then, a distance-based classifier was used to map the other pixels with the obtained permanent pixels. Experiments on Moderate Resolution Imaging Spectroradiometer (MODIS) proved its validity and superiority over other unsupervised methods. However, the proposed definition of the statistical equality depended on simple one-dimensional features, which were the means and mediums of temporally adjacent pixels. A pixel was considered to be permanent if it had more than five spatially adjacent and statistically equal pixels. This simple count strategy can reduce the robustness of the method. Moreover, the low spatial resolution of MODIS data also limited its performance in spatial dimension.

To resolve these issues, in this paper, we introduce a spatiotemporal context learning (STCL) method and propose a novel work flow for flood mapping. The main objective is to delineate the water surface in an accurate and automatic way. First, a statistical model is built for the contextual information of multi-temporal NDWI. Then, permanent pixels are extracted according to their contextual consistency confidence values calculated from the model. Finally, a Modest AdaBoost (MADB) classifier, trained with the permanent pixels and a variety of spectral characteristics, is adopted to map the image into water and non-water categories. Through making full use of the spatiotemporal and spectral information, the proposed approach improves the ability to map inundated surfaces. The uncertainty caused by the sensor and scene differences is also reduced. Two different multispectral datasets with medium resolution, HJ-1A CCD (30 m) and GF-4 PMS (50 m), are employed for the validation.

2. Experimental Set Up

2.1. Datasets

Several kinds of multispectral satellite data have been used for flood mapping, such as Advanced Very High Resolution Radiometer (AVHRR), MODIS, and Landsat TM/ETM+ data. However, most of these data do not have high spatial and temporal resolution at the same time [23]. This has limited their ability to map inundation, which changes complicatedly and rapidly over time. For example, AVHRR and MODIS have a frequent revisiting cycle, which can be even shorter than 1 day. Their high temporal resolution makes them useful for monitoring environmental changes, while the spatial resolution of AVHRR and MODIS is 1 km and 250 m, respectively, which is coarse. Only general extent, not accurate results, can be obtained using these data for flood mapping. On the contrary, Landsat TM/ETM+ data have a middle-to-high spatial resolution of 30 m, but the observation is repeated every 16 days, which cannot satisfy the needs for timely response.

On 6 September 2008, two optical satellites named HJ-1A/B (short for HuanJing-1A/B), also known as the Chinese Environment and Disaster Monitoring and Forecasting Small Satellite Constellation, were launched in China. The data can be downloaded from the website (http://www.cresda.com/) free of charge, and have been successfully applied in several applications such as land mapping, yield prediction, and environment assessment. The two satellites were equipped with CCD cameras, which take multispectral images on the earth surface with a spatial resolution of 30 m. For each satellite, the time interval is 4 days. The constellation of the two satellites theoretically has a higher revisiting frequency of 2 days. With both the advantages of spatial and temporal resolution, HJ-1A/B satellites are regarded as an effective tool for monitoring and post-flood assessment [24].

The recently emerged geostationary satellite GaoFen-4 (GF-4) also has a high application value in rapid assessment and emergency response of floods [25]. Due to its optical geostationary orbit, GF-4 shows a better performance in time resolution over other satellites. It is equipped with a camera for visible, near infrared and middle-wavelength infrared spectra. The spatial resolution is 50 m. To the best of our knowledge, research work using GF-4 imagery is limited, as it was only launched on 29 December 2015, and officially put in use on 13 June 2016. In this work, we also want to explore the potential of the multispectral GF-4 PMS data in flood mapping. The main parameters of the HJ-1A/B CCD data and GF-4 PMS data are listed in Tables 1 and 2. Slightly different from the HJ-1A/B CCD data, the GF-4 PMS data have an additional panchromatic band.

Table 1. Technical parameters of the HJ-1A/B CCD data.

Satellite Sensor	Band No.	Spectral Range (µm)	Spatial Resolution (m)	Revisiting Time
HJ-1A/B CCD	1	0.43–0.52	30	4 days
	2	0.52–0.60		
	3	0.63–0.69		
	4	0.76–0.90		

As can be seen, the HJ-1A/B CCD data and the GF-4 PMS data show balanced abilities in spatial and temporal resolutions. Due to the limitations stated above in other multispectral data, we decide to utilise these two datasets for verifying the methods, and for understanding more about the potential of these two datasets in flood mapping as well, as they are not so commonly used as MODIS or Landsat data. Certainly, another reason why the HJ-1A/B CCD and GF-4 PMS data are chosen is because of their free access.

Table 2. Technical parameters of the GF-4 PMS data.

Satellite Sensor	Band No.	Spectral Range (μm)	Spatial Resolution (m)	Revisiting Time
	1	0.45–0.90		
	2	0.45–0.52		
GF-4 PMS	3	0.52–0.60	50	20 s
	4	0.63–0.69		
	5	0.76–0.90		

2.2. Study Area

The Heilongjiang River is one of the largest rivers in Northeast Asia, flowing through four countries (Mongolia, China, Russia and North Korea). The main stream has a total length of 2821 km, and also forms the boundary between China and Russia. There are abundant water resources in the Heilongjiang River, with a yearly runoff of 346.5 billion cubic meters. The main climate type in that region is monsoon. The precipitation distribution varies with the season. From April to October, the precipitation accounts for 90–93% of the annual precipitation, and the period from June to August accounts for 60–70%. From December, the winter dry season starts and the precipitation mainly falls in the form of snow.

From 12 August 2013, several severe precipitation events continuously hit the northeastern part of Asia, leading to great flood in 39 rivers including part of the Heilongjiang River. Especially for the Tongjiang and Fuyuan Reaches of the Heilongjiang River, the flood had been the most serious one in the past 100 years. On 24 August 2013, more than 5 million people were affected in this disaster. The first case study analyses the event in this region. Two cloud-free scenes of HJ-1A CCD data are utilised. One image was obtained on 12 July 2013, which is around one month before the flood, and the other one was obtained on 27 August 2013 during the peak flow period. The dimension of the study region is 1082 × 1321 pixels (around 1286 square kilometres). Its location and extent are shown in Figure 1.

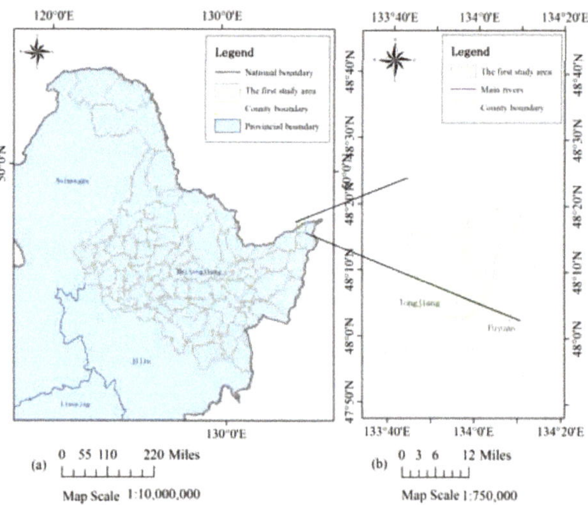

Figure 1. (**a**) Location of the first study site near the border of Russia and China; (**b**) Extent of the HJ-1A CCD data used in this study.

Dongting Lake is one of the most essential lakes in China, and one of the most important wetlands in the world as well. It is located on the southern bank of the Jinjiang section of the middle Yangtze River, and is one of the important dispatching lakes for the Yangtze River because of the strong ability of flood storage. The area of the lake is approximately 2690 square kilometres, across Hunan and Hubei provinces, and is roughly composed of East Dongting Lake, South Dongting Lake and West Dongting Lake. The water of Dongting Lake is clean and this area is one of the main freshwater fishery bases for commercial purposes. Due to its good environment and richness in water, soil and wildlife resources, it is one of the earliest birth places of Chinese rice raising agriculture. The basin area is of 262.8 thousand square kilometres, accounting for 14.6% of the Yangtze River basin area.

In June and July 2016, heavy rains hit the middle and lower reaches of the Yangtze River basin, causing a catastrophic and wide flood in southern China. Eleven provinces and more than 10 million people were affected. On 3 July 2016, the water at the Chenglingji station in Dongting Lake also surpassed the warning level 32.50 m. A regional flood occurred in Dongting Lake. The second case study focuses on this area during this flood. Two cloud-free GF-4 PMS images are selected as the experimental data, which were obtained on 17 June 2016 (before the flood occurred) and 23 July 2016 (during the flood period), with a dimension of 2534 × 2235 pixels (around 14,159 square kilometres). The location and extent of the second study site are shown in Figure 2.

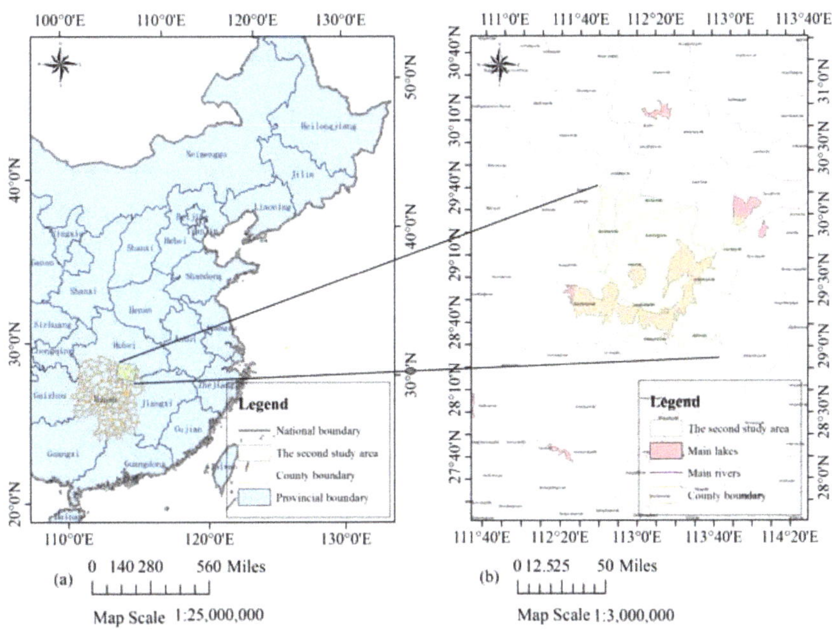

Figure 2. (a) Location of the second study site at the North of Hunan Province in China; (b) Extent of the GF-4 PMS data used in this study.

As can be seen from the figures, these two study sites are located in different geographic positions. The first case study mainly presents a river flood and the second one presents a lake flood. Studies on different kinds of floods can help validate the robustness of the method. Moreover, these two floods took place in 2013 and 2016. Each of them is one of the most severe flood events in that year, bringing about a large amount of damage and wide effects. The areas covered by the first and the second case studies are also areas with high flood risk every year, so it is significant to choose these two areas for study, which can help the government to make better decisions in disaster prevention in these areas.

Before the experiment, these two pairs of data are preprocessed. For HJ-1A/B CCD data, we download the absolute calibration coefficients from the data source website (http://www.cresda.com/), and apply the absolute radiometric corrections to the data. These coefficients are obtained through field experiment and authenticity testing by the China Centre for Resource Satellite Data and Application (CRESDA). For the GF-4 PMS data and the GF-1 WFV data used for validation, a relative radiometric correction is implemented before they are archived. We have not made further modifications to their radiation values. All the satellites images used in this study are geometrically registered using the software ERDAS IMAGEINE AutoSync. Specifically, in either of these two case studies, the experimental data before the flood is considered the reference data. Other images used in the same case are all registered to it. The co-registration technology adopts the cubic polynomial. The mean displacement error is 0.5 pixels. All the data are projected to the WGS 1984 UTM coordinate system.

2.3. Validation

The extent of the water surface during a flood process can have daily changes. It is almost impossible to obtain an accurate map of inundation regions on a particular day. In general, most of the flood products are a rough outline of the main inundated areas. In order to achieve the qualitative and quantitative evaluation, we produce two approximate reference maps for the first and second case studies. Either of them is based on a remote sensing image over the same site and taken on the same date as the corresponding experiment data. The spatial resolution of the data used for generating the reference map is necessarily higher than that of the experiment data. For the first case study using HJ-1A/B CCD data, there is a scene of GF-1 WFV data that can meet the requirements. The technical parameters of the GF-1 WFV data are listed in Table 3. For the second case using GF-4 PMS data, no corresponding GF-1 WFV data could be found. Instead, we find a scene of HJ-1B CCD data that is qualified. The technical parameters of the HJ-1B CCD data can be found in Table 1.

Table 3. Technical parameters of the GF-1 WFV data.

Satellite Sensor	Band No.	Spectral Range (μm)	Spatial Resolution (m)	Width
	1	0.45–0.52		
GF-1 WFV	2	0.52–0.59	16	800 km
	3	0.63–0.69		
	4	0.77–0.89		

For the process of how the reference map is made, we use a traditional water extraction method. We take the first case study as an example. First, the selected GF-1 WFV image is geometrically registered to the experimental HJ-1A CCD data. Then, we calculate the NDWI of the GF-1 WFV image. Compared with the ground information from Google Earth software, we manually select a threshold in NDWI to separate water and non-water pixels. Finally, the binary water mask is resampled to the spatial resolution of HJ-1A CCD data (30 m). Similar processes are applied to the second case study. Given that there is no detailed ground truth available, and that it is not feasible to get one by field investigation, we use the reference map in this study as an approximation of the real inundated extent, helping to evaluate and compare the detection results qualitatively and quantitatively.

3. Methods

3.1. Permanent Pixel Extraction Using Spatiotemporal Context Learning

The images before and after a flood are referred to as image #1 and image #2, respectively. The pixels with a constant land cover type, no matter what the type is, are defined as permanent pixels. The proposed method is divided into two steps. First, the permanent pixels in image #1 and image #2 are extracted based on the STCL strategy. This is a method that models the relative relationship between an object and its context. We introduce it to formulate the relationship between a satellite image pixel and its context. Through comparing the models at different time points, a confidence value for whether a pixel changes or not is calculated to extract the permanent pixels. Second, using these permanent pixels as a training set, a widely adopted machine learning classifier, Modest AdaBoost, is trained and implemented for mapping inundation in image #2. Modest AdaBoost is one of the derivations of the boosting algorithm, like the original AdaBoost algorithm. It combines the performance of a set of weak classifiers, and also proves better than other boosting algorithms for convergence ability. More details about these methods will be given below. In this section, we will first discuss the procedure in the first step.

Due to its capacity for targeting specific land cover type and reducing influence from inconstant band representation, spectral indices are commonly used in diverse remote sensing applications, such as disaster monitoring, land cover mapping and disease prevention [26–28]. For mapping different cover types in different applications, various indices have been proposed, including the normalised difference vegetation index (NDVI), the enhanced vegetation index (EVI), NDWI, and the normalised difference built-up index (NDBI) and so on. Among these indices, the NDWI has been successfully applied to mapping land surface water, and proved more effective than other general feature classification methods [29]. In this study, we calculate the NDWI in the experimental datasets (the HJ-1A CCD data for the first case study and the GF-4 PMS data for the second case study) first. Then, the steps for extracting permanent pixels will be executed on the NDWI data. The NDWI is calculated as:

$$\text{NDWI} = \frac{\text{Green} - \text{NIR}}{\text{Green} + \text{NIR}} \tag{1}$$

where Green and NIR are the reflected green and near infrared radiance, respectively, which are replaced by band 2 and band 4 in the HJ1-A CCD data case, and band 3 and band 5 in the GF-4 PMS data case [15]. NDWI can eliminate the influence from the band value difference, but not the influence caused by the different weather conditions. However, as it is the relative relationship between neighbouring pixels that we use, influences from changes of overall brightness are limited in the proposed procedure.

In the visual tracking field, as the video frames usually change continuously, a strong spatiotemporal correlation is thought to exist between a target and its surroundings. In order to make better use of this relative relationship, Zhang et al. [30] proposed the STCL method. In this method, a rectangular contextual region was first built with the target in the centre. With the low-level features (including the image density and location) of the contextual region, the relative relationship between the target and its surroundings in contextual region was modelled. When a new frame came, it was put into the model to calculate a confidence map, indicating the location that best matched the contextual relationship of previous frames. This location was the inferred location of the target in the new frame. As it depended on a kind of relative relationship, the illumination difference during the frames cannot influence the result. Extensive experiments showed its effectiveness and good degree of precision. This method has also been further employed and extended in other visual trackers [31,32].

A remote sensing image time series shares many similar characteristics with video data, although video sequence images have a higher sampling rate. It can be inferred that there is also a relationship between a target pixel and its spatiotemporal neighbourhoods in a local scene of RS images, if the images are of good quality, without too many clouds and shadows. Due to the constant changes in weather and light conditions, radiation values of the same cover type can vary greatly in different scenes. Furthermore, it is rather difficult to calibrate the radiation of two RS images to absolute consistency. As a result, more false positives can be introduced in mapping the changes. While the relative relationship between unchanged pixels and their nearby pixels is relatively constant, the STCL method, which aims at modelling this kind of relationship, is supposed to be robust also to illumination variation in RS images. What is more, the STCL method provides a fast solution to online problems. In this work, we borrow the concept of STCL to build a procedure for extracting permanent pixels for flood mapping. The proposed flowchart for extracting permanent pixels is shown in Figure 3.

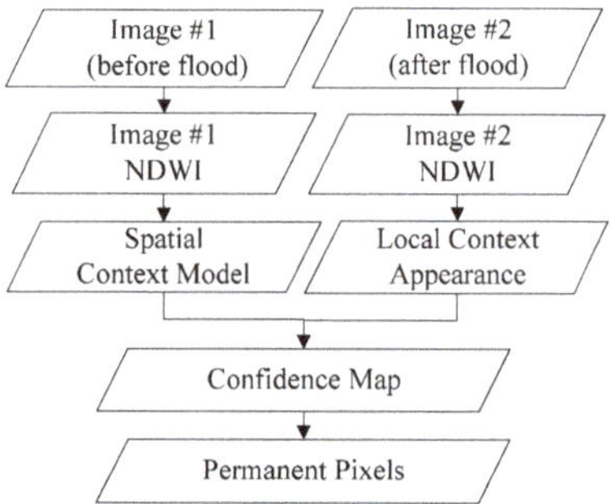

Figure 3. Flowchart of permanent pixel extraction procedure.

One core of the STCL method is its utilisation of the attention focus property in biological visual systems. In the mechanism of biological vision, assume that we are observing a point in a picture. Besides the point itself, which draws most of our attention, other points around the target point are the part we pay the second most attention to in the picture. The further one point is from the target point, the less concern it will get from the visual system. On the contrary, if someone tries to find a known point in an image, the visual mechanism first roughly figures out the background of the target, and then, on the basis of a correlation between the background and the point, the point can be easily targeted. But if only the feature of the target itself is considered, the search will be time and labour intensive. In the visual tracking field, it means the tracker may get lost.

According to this conception, the STCL proposed by Zhang et al. [30] in the visual tracking field uses the distribution of the attention focus, which is formulated as a curved surface function. In the function, the peak is located at the target point and its surroundings gradually decrease. With the weights from this function, the correlation of the target with its local background in image density and location are modelled. If the target location gradually changes, this context model will gradually change as well, and will be updated in each frame. When a new frame comes, although there are illumination variation and occlusion problems, the new location of the target can still be found by comparing the model with that of each pixel in the image. We borrow the concept and the formulation of the spatiotemporal context in STCL, and propose a method based on this context information for extracting permanent pixels. Details of the method are described as follows. The core of this problem is calculating the confidence map $c(x)$ between image #1 and image #2, which is also the probability of that the pixel is permanent. It can be formulated as

$$c(x) = P(x), \tag{2}$$

where $x \in R^2$ is a pixel location, and $P(x)$ is the probability. The higher $P(x)$ is, the more likely x will be permanent. After transformation, $P(x)$ can be given by

$$P(x) = \sum_{f(z) \in X_C} P(x| f(z))P(f(z)) \tag{3}$$

where $X_C = \{f(z) = (I(z), z) | z \in \Omega(x)\}$. $I(z)$ denotes the pixel value, i.e., the NDWI value, at location z, and $\Omega(x)$ is the neighbourhood of location x. $P(f(z))$ is the context prior probability that models the appearance of the local context, and $P(x|f(z))$ represents the relative relationship between x and its neighbourhood, which is defined as the spatial context model

$$g_{SC}(x - z) = P(x| f(z)) \tag{4}$$

In image #1, $x*$ and z are, respectively, the locations of the target pixel and its local context. For context prior probability, when $x*$ is permanent, if the values of $x*$ and z, as well as $I(x*)$ and $I(z)$, are closer, there is a higher probability that the pixel at location z will also be permanent. Different from the original solution for the tracking problem, we model the context prior probability $P(f(z))$ as

$$P(f(z)) = e^{-|I(x*)-I(z)|}\omega_\sigma(z - x*), \tag{5}$$

where $\omega_\sigma(z - x*)$ is a spatial weight function. With regard to the attention focus principle, if the local context pixel z is located closer to the object $x*$, z should make a greater contribution to the contextual characteristics of $x*$ in (5), and a higher weight should be given to it, and vice versa. Given that the weight should decrease smoothly with the increase of the distance to the object, ω_σ is defined as an exponential type as

$$\omega_\sigma(z) = ae^{-\frac{|z|^2}{2\sigma^2}}, \tag{6}$$

where a is a normalising constant that restricts $P(f(z))$ to a range from 0 to 1. $\sigma = 0.5$ is the scale parameter. As there are no changes occurring to $x*$ in image #1, we set its confidence value $c(x*) = 1$. According to the correlation between adjacent pixels, if the context pixel is located closer to the object, it should be more likely to be permanent. Therefore, the confidence function in image #1 can be modelled as

$$c(x) = P(x) = e^{-|\frac{x-x*}{\alpha}|^\beta}, \tag{7}$$

where α is a scale parameter and β is a shape parameter. The confidence value changes monotonically with the values of α and β. Therefore, these two parameters can be neither too large nor too small. For instance, if β is too large, the model can easily get over-fitted. While if β is too small, the smoothing may cause some errors. We empirically set $\alpha = 4.5$ and $\beta = 1$ for all the experiments here. Based on (2)–(5), it can be inferred that

$$c(x) = P(x) = \sum_{f(z)\in X_C} P(x|\,f(z))P(f(z)) = \sum_{z\in\Omega(x')} g_{SC}(x - z)e^{-|I(x*)-I(z)|}\omega_\sigma(z - x*)$$
$$= g_{SC}(x) \otimes (e^{-|I(x*)-I(x)|}\omega_\sigma(x - x*)) \tag{8}$$

where $\otimes$ denotes the convolution operation. According to (7), (8) can be transformed to the frequency domain as:

$$F(c(x)) = F(e^{-|\frac{x-x*}{\alpha}|^\beta}) = F(g_{SC}(x)) \odot F(e^{-|I(x*)-I(x)|}\omega_\sigma(x - x*)), \tag{9}$$

where F donates the Fourier transform function. $\odot$ is the element-wise product. So, for image #1, the spatial context model is

$$g_{SC}(x) = F^{-1}\left(\frac{F(e^{-|\frac{x-x*}{\alpha}|^\beta})}{F(e^{-|I(x*)-I(x)|}\omega_\sigma(x - x*))}\right) \tag{10}$$

With the spatial context model gained from image #1, according to (9), the confidence map of image #2 can be calculated by

$$c'(x) = F^{-1}(F(g_{SC}(x)) \odot F(P'(f'(x)))) = F^{-1}(F(g_{SC}(x)) \odot F(e^{-|I'(x*')-I'(x)|}\omega_\sigma(x - x*'))), \tag{11}$$

where $x*'$ is the location of the target pixel in image #2, and $f'(x)$ and $I'(x)$, respectively, represent the context prior probability and image intensity in image #2 [30]. After the permanence confidence map is calculated for image #2, obtained after a flood, we select the pixels with top $n\%$ confidence values as the final permanent pixels. In this work, we choose $n = 2$. More discussion on how n influences the result will be given later.

3.2. Inundation Mapping Based on Modest AdaBoost

3.2.1. Permanent Pixels Labelling

According to the previous section, we get the set of permanent pixels. In order to utilise the permanent pixels for training the classifier later, we need to label the permanent pixels into water and non-water categories. In keeping the whole process automatic, manual labelling should not be used. In this study, we adopt the openly accessible MODIS 250 m land-water mask, which is called MOD44W for short, to achieve this purpose. MOD44W is a constant product, which is derived from Terra MODIS data MOD44C 250 m 16-day composites. If a pixel is identified as water in more than 50% of the period May to September of years 2000–2002, this pixel is labelled as water in the MOD44W product. This method effectively smooths the short-term water surface changes caused by flood and drought. Therefore, although the MOD44W was produced years before the case study, it is widely accepted as the description of average water distribution [33]. Here, we adopt MOD44W to label the permanent pixels. It is acknowledged that there are most likely some mistakes, caused by small changes in water surface over the years. But, as the general condition changes little, and the permanent pixels have high probability of being unchanged, the labels from MOD44W are generally reliable.

For both the first and second study area, there is only one scene of MOD44W data. We resample the MOD44W data to the same spatial resolution as the experimental image, and then label the permanent pixels into permanent water pixels and permanent non-water pixels according to the MOD44W values. As the labels of the permanent pixels are used for classifier training, the proportion of the permanent pixels of each class will influence the classifier training result. However, as most changes happen inside or around the river regions, it can be inferred that the permanent confidence is generally higher in non-water regions than in water regions. Among the pixels of the highest confidence values, we selected the water and non-water permanent pixels with the same proportion as that in the same scene in MOD44W. The sum of water and non-water permanent pixels remained $n\%$ of the total. With the labelled permanent pixels, the Modest AdaBoost classifier is trained. Then it is applied to the testing set consisting of multiple features of image #2. The final inundation mapping result can be calculated.

3.2.2. Inundation Mapping

Boosting is a technique that combines several weak classifiers to generate a powerful one. The first proposed boosting algorithm, AdaBoost, was created by Freund and Schapire in 1996 [34], which is regarded as the basis for all other kinds of boosting method. Due to its good generalisation ability, low computational complexity and high execution efficiency, boosting has become one of the most popular and effective classification tools in computer vision [35] and pattern recognition [36]. A number of algorithms are derived from the boosting method, such as the Discrete AdaBoost (DADB), Real AdaBoost (RADB) and Gentle AdaBoost (GADB). DADB is a boosting method that mainly employs binary weak classifiers, and RADB is a generalisation version of the basic AdaBoost algorithm [37]. On the basis of RADB, GADB is designed with better performance and higher resistance to outliers [38]. Here, we adopt a different boosting method called Modest AdaBoost, which proves to outperform GADB in generalisation error and overfitting. Its natural stopping criterion is also an advantage, which other boosting techniques lack [36]. The flowchart of mapping inundation using Modest AdaBoost is shown in Figure 4.

Modest AdaBoost is a variant of boosting proposed by A. Vezhnevets et al. [36]. The basic idea of this method is that in every iteration for computing the new distribution, more importance is given to the samples that are misclassified in the previous step (with low margins). In every step, the method is committed to improve the lowest margins of samples. While those training samples that already have high margins may be misclassified with the new distribution and the margins are decreased, this forces the weak classifier to work only in its domain and be 'modest', which is the origin of the name MADB. Through this strategy, some regions of the input space have fewer chances to become overconfident, and the generalisation ability of the method benefits from this. The open source GML AdaBoost Matlab Toolbox [39] is used in the experiments to implement the Modest AdaBoost algorithm. It is a collection of classes and functions of several boosting algorithms. More details about the mapping procedure are presented below.

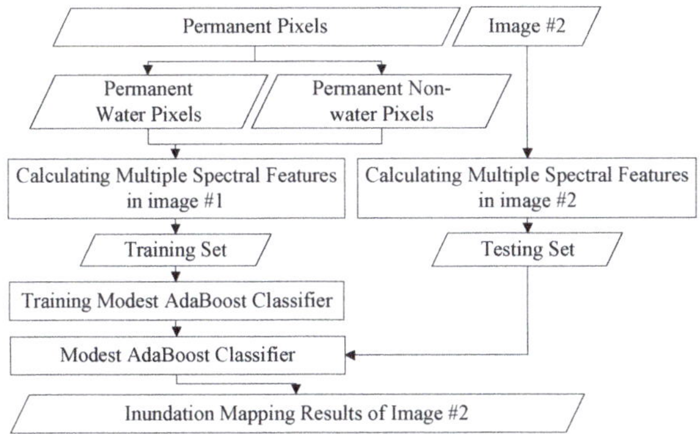

Figure 4. Flowchart of inundation mapping procedure.

First, each permanent pixel is set as a training sample point. Thus, the training dataset $(x_1, y_1),, (x_N, y_N)$ can be obtained. $x_i \in X$ is the input vector, which consists of several feature values of the permanent pixel, and $y_i \in \{-1, +1\}$, which is the corresponding class label of the permanent pixel. Here we define $y = +1$ when the pixel is water, and $y = -1$ when the pixel is non-water. N is the number of permanent pixels. At the beginning, we initialise the weight distribution on the input data as $D_0(i) = 1/N, i = 1, 2, \ldots, N$.

For each iteration $t = 1, \ldots, T$, with the weight distribution $D_t(i)$, the weak classifier $s_t(x) \in S$ can be trained by weighted least squares:

$$s_t = \underset{s}{\mathrm{argmin}} \left(\sum_{i=1}^{N} D_t(i) \cdot (y_i - s(x_i))^2 \right), \tag{12}$$

In addition, the 'inverted' distribution of the data weights is calculated by

$$D_t(i) = (1 - D_t(i))\bar{\alpha}_t, \tag{13}$$

where $\bar{\alpha}_t$ is the normalisation coefficient. Then we compute the probabilities:

$$P_t^{+1}(x) = P_{D_t}(y = +1 \cap s_t(x)), \tag{14}$$

$$\overline{P}_t^{+1}(x) = P_{\overline{D}_t}(y = +1 \cap s_t(x)), \tag{15}$$

$$P_t^{-1}(x) = P_{D_t}(y = -1 \cap s_t(x)), \tag{16}$$

$$\overline{P}_t^{-1}(x) = P_{\overline{D}_t}(y = -1 \cap s_t(x)). \tag{17}$$

Set

$$f_t(x) = (P_t^{+1}(1 - \overline{P}_t^{+1}) - P_t^{-1}(1 - \overline{P}_t^{-1}))(x), \tag{18}$$

and update the distribution by:

$$D_{t+1}(i) = D_t(i) \exp(-y_i f_t(x_i))\alpha_t, \tag{19}$$

where α_t is the normalisation coefficient. After T iterations or $f_t = 0$, the final classifier can be constructed by [36]

$$F(x) = sign[\sum_{t=1}^{T} f_t(s_t(x))] \tag{20}$$

The procedure of training the Modest AdaBoost classifier uses the permanent pixels extracted in previous steps, which contain the typical characteristics of water and non-water. After the strong classifier is obtained, it is applied to image #2 to get the inundation mapping results. Due to the difference in the bands of different satellites, the individual index of fixed band combination cannot always be effective in different flood scenarios. In order to overcome this shortcoming and make the method more robust, we set the components of the training vector using several bands and indices: (1) original bands; (2) NIR − Red; (3) NIR/Red; (4) EVI; (5) NDVI; (6) NDWI. All of these indices can be applied to optical satellite images. The computing method of NDWI is described in (1). For the EVI and the NDVI, the computing methods are as follows [40,41]. The training and classification processes are performed individually on each pixel of the image.

$$\text{EVI} = \frac{2.5 \times (\text{NIR} - \text{Red})}{6 \times \text{Red} + \text{NIR} - 7.5 \times \text{Blue} + 1}, \tag{21}$$

$$\text{NDVI} = \frac{\text{NIR} - \text{Red}}{\text{NIR} + \text{Red}}, \tag{22}$$

For comparison, the commonly used unsupervised classification method K-MEANs, and another two different permanent pixel extraction methods combined with Modest AdaBoost, are also applied to the same experimental datasets. K-MEANs is implemented using the ENVI 5.0 software. The change threshold is set as 5.0%. One permanent pixel extraction method is from [22], which determines the permanent pixels through the means and mediums of the spatial neighbouring pixels. In another permanent pixel extraction method, a similar judgment rule using mediums and means, but extended to spatiotemporal field, is utilised. Specifically, each pixel has 8 spatial neighbouring pixels, and in the spatial neighbourhood-based permanent pixel extraction method (SP) in [22], if more than 5 among the 8 spatial neighbouring pixels are statistically equal (having the same medium or mean) to the target, the target pixel is considered permanent. For the spatiotemporal neighbourhood-based permanent pixel extraction method (STP), not only more than five spatially neighbouring pixels, but also more than five among the nine temporally neighbouring pixels, need to be statistically equal to the target for the target to be considered permanent. These permanent pixels are utilised with MADB in the same way as the proposed method. The inundation mapping results from each comparison method is then obtained. Here we call these two comparison methods utilising different permanent pixel strategies SP-MADB and STP-MADB, for short. All of these comparison methods are applied on the same multiple feature set of the classification step to the proposed method.

4. Results

4.1. Inundation Mapping Using HJ-1A CCD Data

As described above, in the first case study, two images, acquired on 12 July 2013 (before the flood) and 27 August 2013 (after the flood), are selected for the analysis. After pre-processing, the false colour composite images of the study area and the corresponding MOD44W product used for labelling the training data are shown in Figure 5.

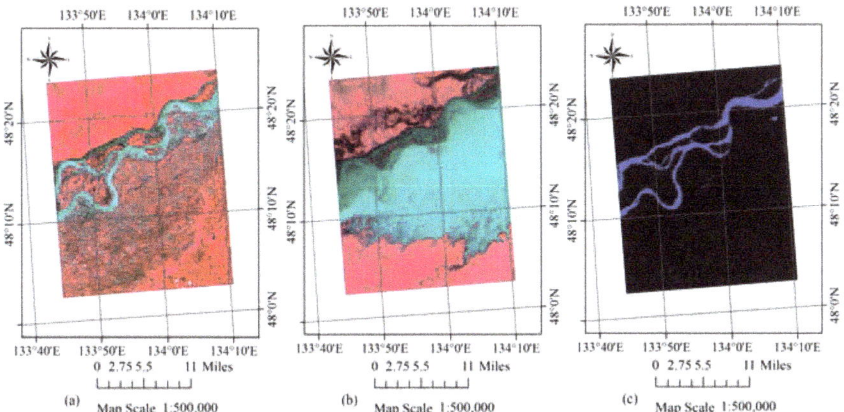

Figure 5. False colour composites (R4G3B2) of HJ-1A CCD images acquired on (**a**) 12 July 2013 (before the flood) and (**b**) 27 August 2013 (after the flood) for the first case study. (**c**) Corresponding MOD44W water mask product with water in blue and land in black.

The proposed spatiotemporal-context-learning-based permanent pixels-MADB (STCLP-MADB) method and three other comparison methods (K-MEANS, SP-MADB and STP-MADB) are each respectively applied to the experimental data. The final inundation mapping result for the individual method is shown in Figure 6. For a better visualization of the obtained results, we select four sub-regions and make a detailed zoom in. The location and size of the four sub-regions are shown in Figure 6e. The enlarged view of the small regions and their corresponding false colour composite, flood extraction result and the reference map are shown in Figure 7. Table 4 lists the number of inundated pixels derived by different methods in the full scene and sub-regions.

Table 4. The first case study in 2013—Number of inundated pixels.

Method	Full Region	Sub-Region A	Sub-Region B	Sub-Region C	Sub-Region D
K-MEANs	528,238	1833	16,236	7778	1442
SP-MADB	710,587	96	8470	5207	0
STP-MADB	843,570	1750	16,060	7009	1345
STCLP-MADB	812,610	1308	13,884	7011	1047
Reference Map	764,470	1176	11,861	6267	873

From the above figures and table, some comments can be made:

(1) The proposed inundation mapping method, based on STCL permanent pixel extraction and MADB, successfully extracts most of the flood regions in the first case study. In each column of the Table 4, the STCLP-MADB method achieves the closest number of inundated pixels to the reference, except in sub-region C. It is the second best among the methods, and has almost the same number of inundated pixels as the best. All of this evidence proves the effectiveness of the HJ-1A CCD data and the proposed procedure for mapping wide inundated areas in a river flood event.

(2) On the whole, it can be seen that the main regions of the flood are mostly well-delineated by each inundation mapping algorithm, except for small tributaries—for example the tributaries near the sub-region A and D—which are omitted by the SP-MADB method, and are shown in yellow. The STCLP-MADB performs better than the three other methods from the visual effect. In these regions, the K-MEANs and STP-MADB results present more false alarms, and the SP-MADB method makes more omissions. The result derived from STCLP-MADB is most consistent with

the reference map. Its effectiveness for precision mapping is significant for inferring the future evolution of the flood.

(3)   From the detailed mapping results, it can be found that the inundated regions are delineated differently by different methods. In the map derived using K-MEANs, many points of false positive can be found in the unflooded regions. However, the SP-MADB method produces more false negatives in some small flood regions and half-submerged regions. More advanced results are obtained by STP-MADB and STCLP-MADB methods. Further comparisons of the details show that the results from STCLP-MADB provide finer outlines and are slightly better.

(4)   Although the results from STCLP-MADB are quite promising, there are still some false positive errors, mainly occurring in the small unflooded areas surrounded by large flooded areas. For example, in Figure 6d, we can find some pixels in blue inside the main region of the flood, which are unflooded areas but determined as flood by the STCLP-MADB method. This is because these areas mostly comprise mixed pixels. Different proportions and locations of water in one mixed pixel influence what class the pixel is distributed to.

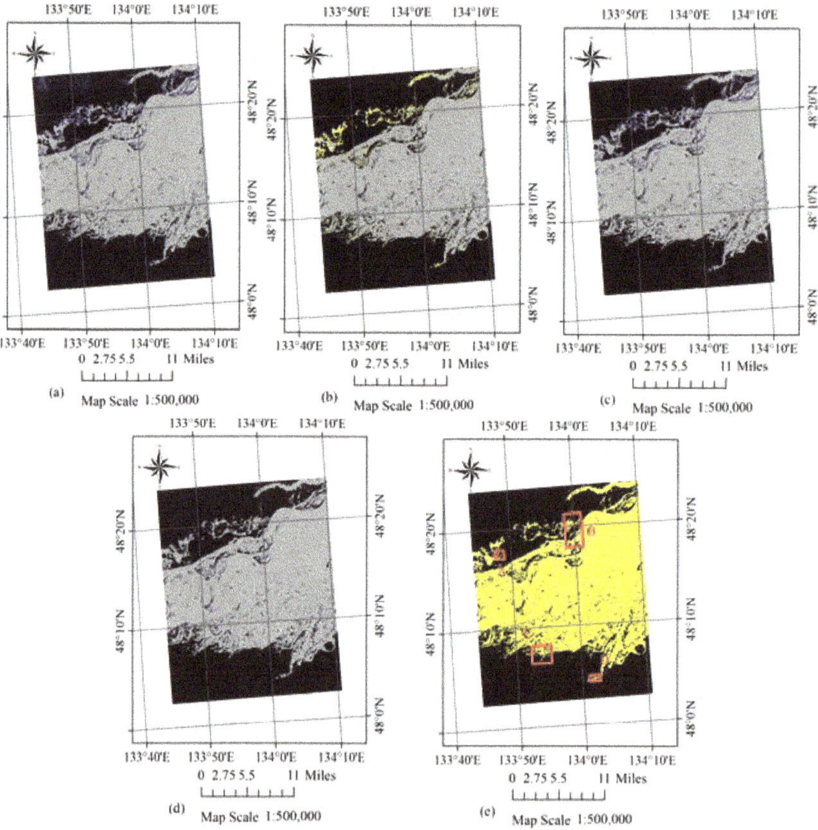

Figure 6. (**a–d**) Flood inundation mapping results for the first case study using K-MEANs, SP-MADB, STP-MADB and STCLP-MADB methods. (Gray: flood pixels in both the detection and reference maps; Blue: flood pixels only in the detection map; Yellow: flood pixels only in the reference map; Black: the background). (**e**) The locations of the four sub-regions in red rectangle, shown on the reference map of inundation derived from the GF-1 WFV data, with the water in yellow and the background in black.

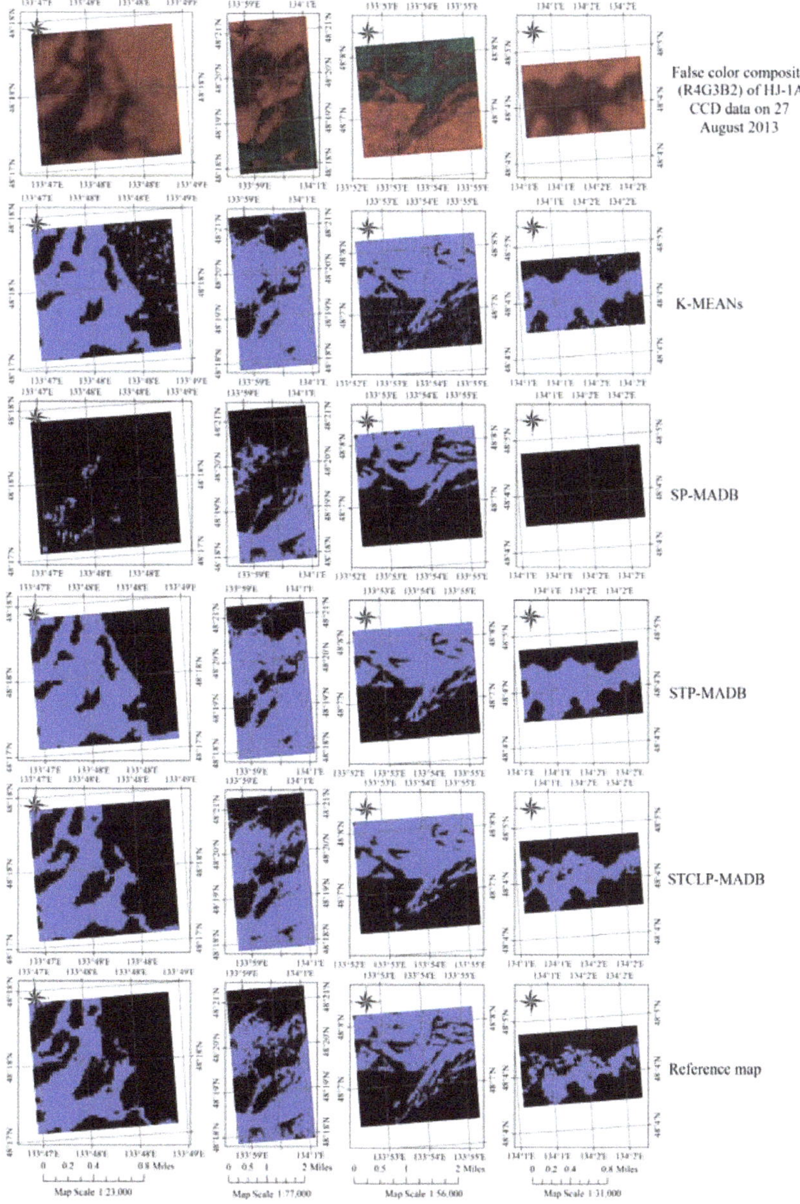

Figure 7. From the left to the right column: the regions of interest A, B, C and D for the first case study. From the second to the fifth row: corresponding detection and reference maps with the flood in blue and the background in black.

Besides the qualitative evaluation, a quantitative evaluation is also made for the test. For classification, the confusion matrix is one of the most commonly used methods for calculating accuracy. In this study, the reference and the detection results are all binary maps with two categories, water and non-water. Then, the confusion matrix can be produced. The accuracies of each method can be calculated, among which the overall accuracy is the rate of correctly classified water and non-water pixels among the total pixels. The values are shown in Table 5.

From the numbers reported in Table 5, a few further conclusions can be summarised:

(1) STCLP-MADB achieves the highest overall accuracy and kappa coefficient among these four methods, which shows that STCLP-MADB performs better than the others in terms of quantitative evaluation. Extending the SP strategy to STP strategy improves mapping accuracy. Furthermore, utilising STCL confidence calculation instead of a simple counting strategy in STP also enhances the mapping results.

(2) With incomplete flood information, different flood detectors produce different commission and omission errors. The best omission and commission rates are achieved by the K-MEANs and SP-MADB methods, respectively. However, there is always a balance between the omission and the commission. A decrease in omission errors usually brings about an increase in commission errors and vice versa. As can be seen from Table 5, the high commission and omission rates limit the ability of K-MEANs and SP-MADB methods in inundation mapping, which is illustrated in Figures 6 and 7, while the STCLP-MADB method achieves a balance between these two rates and provides a more acceptable result.

Table 5. The first case study in 2013—Accuracy.

Method	Overall Accuracy (%)	Kappa	Omission (%)	Commission (%)
K-MEANs	87.48	0.7450	2.77	17.51
SP-MADB	90.73	0.8146	12.18	5.53
STP-MADB	91.22	0.8220	3.03	12.13
STCLP-MADB	92.25	0.8435	4.10	9.78

We also discuss the relation between accuracy of the proposed method and the n in the permanent pixels extraction step, i.e., the influence that the number of selected permanent pixels has over mapping precision. The result is shown in Figure 8 below. In this work, we try $n = 1, 2, \ldots, 9$, for if n is too big, it will cost a lot of computation resources and time for training the classifier, which is impractical and cannot satisfy the need for a quick response to a disaster.

From the figure, it can be seen that more permanent pixels leads to an increase in commission and decrease in omission, but this only happens when $n \leq 2$. When the value of n gets higher, there is no significant change in commission and omission. Similarly, for overall accuracy, there is only a slight decrease (around 0.1%) when n changes from 1 to 2. After that, the overall accuracy remains almost unchanged. Therefore, it can be concluded that for the proposed STCLP-MADB method using HJ-1A CCD data, the number of permanent pixels has a very limited influence on mapping precision. Given the importance of computation efficiency in disaster response, it is quite enough to set n as 1 or 2.

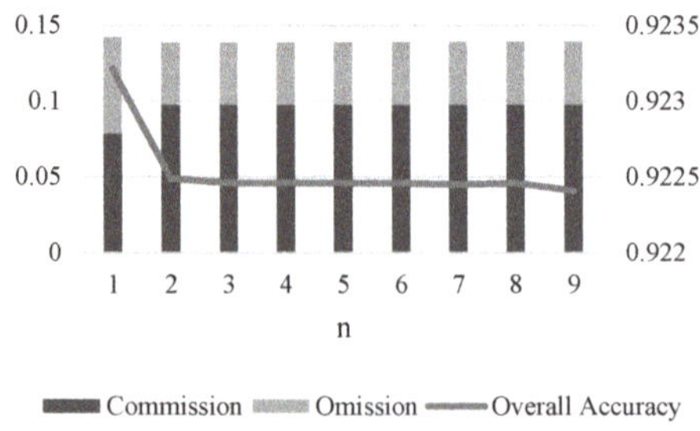

Figure 8. The first case study: commission, omission and overall accuracy in function of n, the percentage of permanent pixels.

4.2. Inundation Mapping Using GF-4 PMS Data

The second case study aims to analyse the GF-4 PMS data for the 2016 flood event at Dongting Lake. Figure 9 shows the two images selected for this case, which were acquired on 17 June 2016 (before the flood) and 23 July 2016 (after the flood). The corresponding MOD44W product used as the ancillary data is also shown in Figure 9.

In the second case study, inundation mapping results using different strategies are shown in Figure 10. Similar to the first case study, four sub-regions located at different positions are selected and shown in Figure 11, which aims to visually compare the results in a more detailed way. With regards to quantitative evaluation, Tables 6 and 7 report the number of inundated pixels and the final accuracy values, respectively. Figure 12 illustrates the relation between the permanent pixel proportion and detection accuracy.

As can be seen from the figures and the table, many similarities exist between the results of the second and the first case studies, and several slight differences as well. They are described as follows:

(1)   In terms of the performance in categorisation, results in the second test are similar to that in the first test. The proposed STCLP-MADB method still achieves the best overall accuracy and kappa coefficient. K-MEANs and STP-MADB methods achieve the best omission and commission, respectively, while STCLP-MADB shows an average performance of these two rates. As the two test datasets are from different sensors, locations and inundation cases, this experiment further proves the good robustness of the proposed method.

(2)   K-MEANs makes use of the statistical properties of the whole image, which causes high commission because the inundated pixels can have a different appearance in different contextual situations. SP-MADB and STP-MADB draw more attention to the local characteristics, but they make the determination of permanent pixels by counting, which lacks a theoretical foundation and can be easily disturbed. This can be found by comparing Figures 6c and 10c. In the first case, using HJ-1A CCD data, the STP-MADB method produces more commission, while in the second case study, using GF-4 PMS data, more omission than commission is introduced in the STP-MADB result. In the proposed method, a spatiotemporal context confidence calculating model is adopted to overcome the limitation of counting. With the formulised combination of local spatiotemporal and spectral information, we achieve a more accurate and robust inundation map than other methods.

(3)   The changing curves of accuracy with n are more unstable than those in the first test. The influence of n on result precision does not change monotonically. It is difficult to find any rules in the curves at all. This could be because the outline of the inundation is more complicated in the second case study than in the first. Moreover, the spatial resolution of the GF-4 PMS data is sparser than that of the HJ-1A CCD data, which brings out more mixed pixels. With the increase in these uncertainties, the variation in accuracy becomes more unpredictable. Nevertheless, the fluctuation is still within a limited range. The effectiveness of the proposed method is rather stable.

(4)   As the GF-4 satellite was officially put into service not long ago (in June 2016), research on GF-4 PMS data is rare. Our work explores the applied value of this new dataset and proves its effectiveness for inundation mapping. More promising research about GF-4 PMS data could be carried out in the future.

Table 6. The second case study in 2016—Number of inundated pixels.

Method	Full Region	Sub-Region A	Sub-Region B	Sub-Region C	Sub-Region D
K-MEANs	2,417,535	74,610	21,785	10,363	13,001
SP-MADB	1,103,408	23,946	1488	5884	6163
STP-MADB	873,738	16,908	1468	5233	3848
STCLP-MADB	1,215,464	30,502	2116	6668	6961
Reference Map	1,357,670	37,529	3654	7963	7510

Table 7. The second case study in 2016—Accuracy.

Method	Overall Accuracy (%)	Kappa	Omission (%)	Commission (%)
K-MEANs	79.73	0.5613	3.24	45.66
SP-MADB	92.88	0.7877	26.43	4.29
STP-MADB	91.01	0.7190	36.58	1.46
STCLP-MADB	93.66	0.8195	18.47	8.93

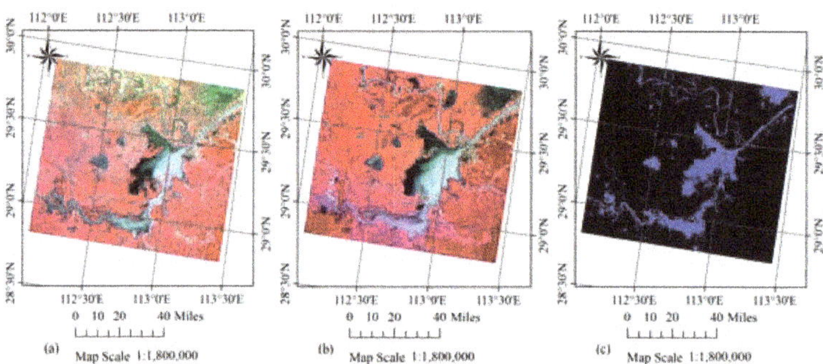

Figure 9. False colour composites (R: 5, G: 4, B: 3) of GF-4 PMS images acquired on (**a**) 17 June 2016 (before the flood) and (**b**) 23 July 2016 (after the flood) for the second test case. (**c**) Corresponding MOD44W water mask product with water in blue and land in black.

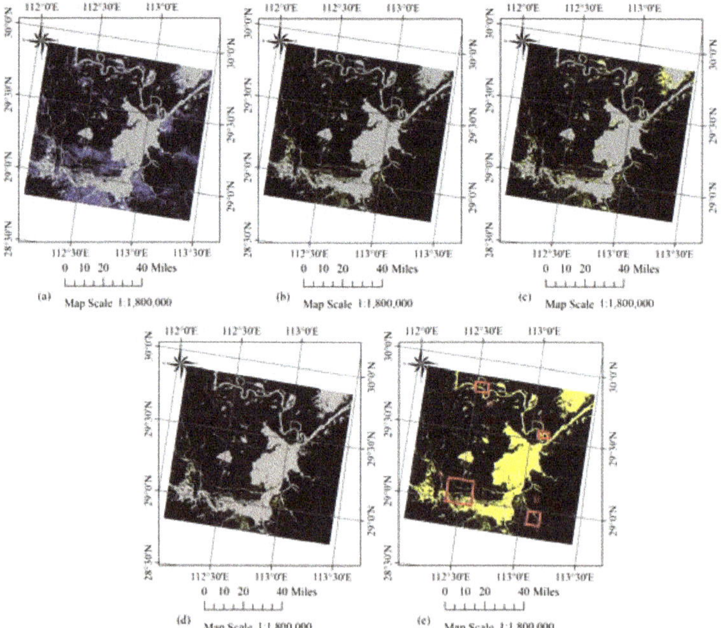

Figure 10. (**a–d**) Flood inundation mapping results for the second test area using K-MEANs, SP-MADB, STP-MADB and STCLP-MADB methods. (Gray: flood pixels in both the detection and reference maps; Blue: flood pixels only in the detection map; Yellow: flood pixels only in the reference map; Black: the background). (**e**) The locations of the four sub-regions in red rectangle, shown on the reference map of inundation derived from the HJ-1B CCD data, with the water in yellow and the background in black.

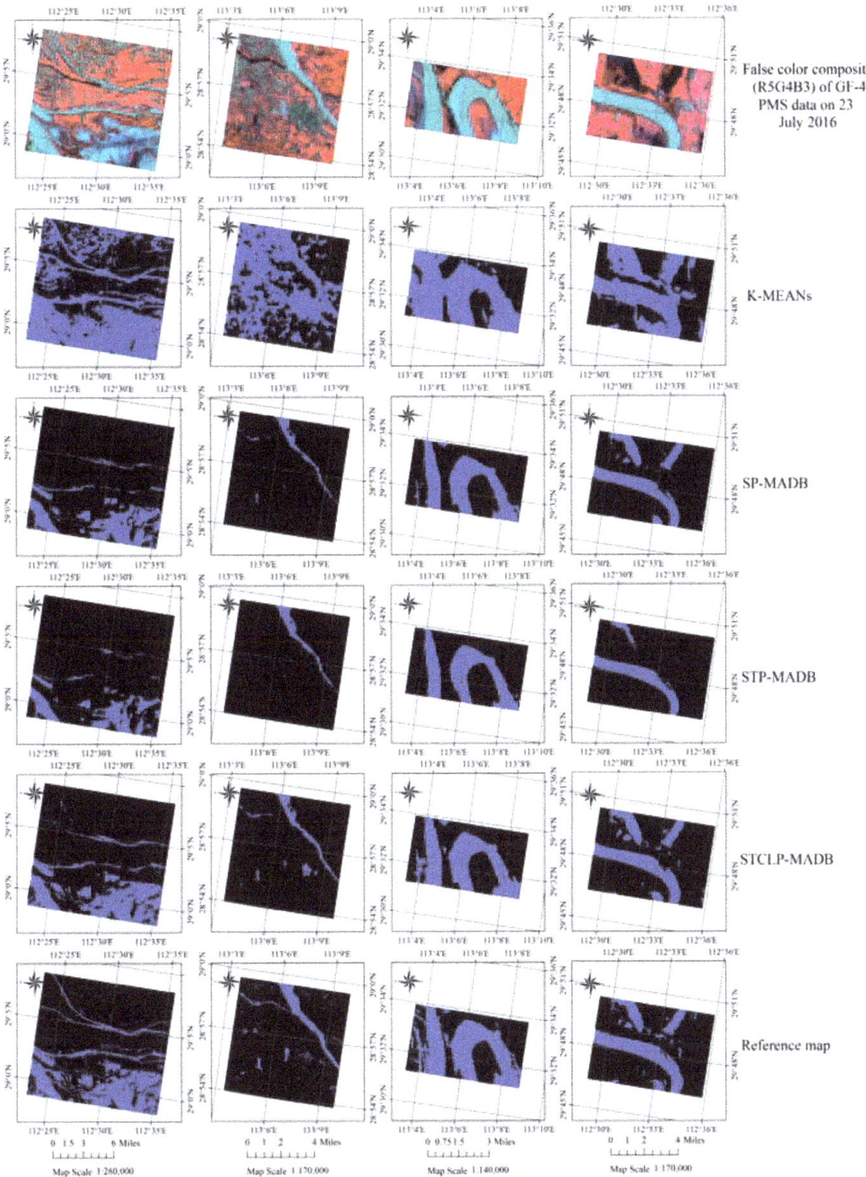

Figure 11. From the left to the right column: the regions of interest A, B, C and D for the second case study. From the second to the fifth row: corresponding detection and reference maps with the flood in blue and the background in black.

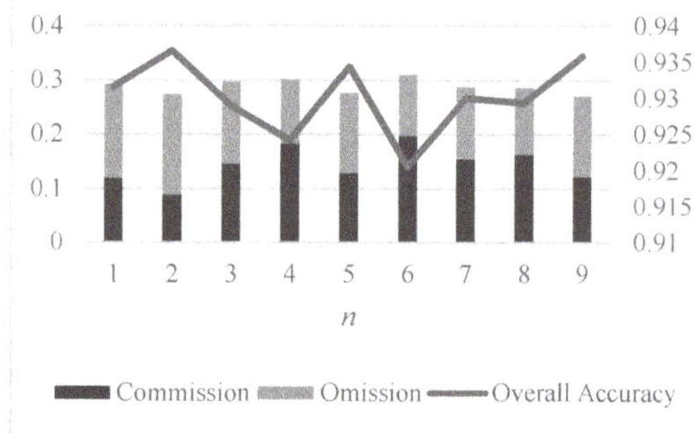

Figure 12. Second test—commission, omission and overall accuracy in function of n, the percentage of permanent pixels.

5. Discussion

In this study, we choose cloud-free images for the experiment. In practice, clouds and their shadows have been a critical issue for flood mapping using multispectral images, especially the as flood is usually accompanied by rainy and cloudy weather. This is because the visible and near infrared spectra cannot penetrate the cloud, so the image quality is frequently affected during flood periods. We put forward some analysis and speculation regarding how this may influence the result of the proposed method. First, the confidence value calculated in the step of STCL will certainly be affected by the clouds. As the STCL method models the correlation of image density and distance, and the cloud has different characteristics with those of the land or the water, the relative relationship will change a lot with the interference of clouds. According to the description in Section 3.1, if there are some clouds present nearby, the confidence value will decrease. However, since we only extract pixels with high confidence values for training the classifier, its impact on the final flood mapping may be limited. On the other hand, the GF-4 is a geostationary satellite. When a disaster happens, it can take images of the same region with a very high time resolution if needed. Through combining the common region of multiple images over a short time, data hidden by clouds and shadows may be recovered. Anyhow, it is a deficiency in our work that no experiment using cloudy data has been carried out. More explorations concerning cloudy data will be made in a future work.

In the proposed process for flood mapping, the MOD44W product plays a role in separating permanent pixels into permanent water pixels and permanent non-water pixels. With the introduction of this water mask, some issues are introduced as well. One is that this product is obtained based on the MODIS data from 2000 to 2002, while our case studies are in 2013 and 2016. There was over a decade between the MOD44W product and the experimental data. The outlines of the water are very likely to have altered. Besides the difference in time, the huge gap between the spatial resolutions of the water mask and the experimental data could also lead to problems. The spatial resolution of the MOD44W product is 250 m, which is much lower than that of the HJ-1A/B CCD and GF-4 PMS data. Many jagged edges can be found in the resampled result of the MOD44W product. Moreover, some small water surfaces are omitted because of the low spatial resolution. Both of these issues will bring about errors in labelling the permanent pixels. Nevertheless, as the labelled permanent pixels serve as the training set for the Modest AdaBoost classifier, not the final detailed classification result, we think a certain number of errors can be tolerated. Figures 5c and 9c also show that, in the experimental areas, from the visual effect, the MOD44W product is able to provide a general outline of the water before the flood comes. From another perspective, for the areas near the edges of the rivers and lakes, where most of the differences between the MOD44W product and the study data exist, the confidence value is generally low because of the changes induced by the flood. Therefore, the pixels at these areas are less likely to be selected as permanent pixels, and their corresponding MOD44W labels would have little influence on the final result.

According to the demand for automation and details in disaster assessment, this study aims to explore a novel solution for flood mapping that can achieve precise results with minimal human intervention. After two experiments on different regions and data, the proposed method shows better performance than other automatic methods. Several important reasons we infer are as follows. The first is the introduction of the machine learning classification method. Extensive literature shows that the precision of supervised classification methods is generally better than that of unsupervised classification methods. Unsupervised flood mapping methods, like K-MEANs, can bring about more errors in scenes of large area or complicated distribution. Because in these situations, the radiation value of water may vary a lot at different locations. Without a learning strategy, some non-water pixels with similar features to the water at other locations could be identified as water, as can be seen in Figure 10a of the Dongting Lake case. With the aid of the samples, the supervised classifier can learn and adapt itself better to different land cover characteristics in different scenes, resulting in higher accuracy. But the samples usually need to be selected manually, which limits their applicability in disaster response. Another essential advantage of the proposed method is that it proposes an automatic sample selection method, and combines it with a learning method. With the advantages of these two methods, both good precision and automation can be achieved.

The utilisation of local information is also a factor bringing improvement to the result. On one hand, it is more robust to utilise both contextual and global information than to utilise global information only. On the other hand, the experiment results show that the proposed method outperforms (qualitatively and quantitatively) the SP-MADB, STP-MADB methods. The only distinction among these three methods is the permanent pixel extraction strategy. All three methods utilise the local relationship between a pixel and its surroundings. The SP-MADB and STP-MADB methods count the number of 8-neighbourhood or 17-neighbourhood pixels with equal mean or medium to the object pixel. Noise and radiation variation, which exist all the time, can easily change the count result. Moreover, if a pixel and its neighbouring pixels simultaneously change from one cover type to another, the mean and medium will still remain the same, leading to errors in the permanent pixel set. From the experiment results we can see that the STP-MADB method obviously makes more commissions than omissions in the first case study, but makes more omissions in the second case, which proves its lack of robustness. Whereas, the proposed method builds a model between the pixel and its neighbouring regions, instead of counting the few adjacent pixels. Even if there are some noise pixels, the general structure of the model will not change. With better selection of the permanent pixels and the training set, the STCLP-MADB method produces a more precise outline of the inundated areas.

This study is proposed for floods, which is a practical problem. Hence it makes sense that this proposed method can be applied operationally, and that it can help when a real flood comes. Here we propose some suggestions for implementation, which may help the STCL-MADB method to be effectively applied in a real application. The whole workflow can be divided into three steps: extracting permanent pixels using STCL, training the classifier and mapping the inundation. The first step, especially the STCL algorithm, accounts for most of the time consumption in the whole process. Not only because the STCL algorithm has higher computation complexity than other steps, but the operations need to be performed pixel by pixel. For example, in the second case study at Dongting Lake, the size of the data is 2534×2235 pixels. The first step takes around 3 days, while the second and third steps take around 15 min and a few dozen seconds, respectively. All these experiments are implemented by MATLAB 2013 on a laptop with an i7-4710HQ CPU and 8 GB RAM. In practice, a library of permanent pixels can be built in advance for regions with high flood risk. With the accumulation of time series data, the library can be updated continuously. Then, the classifier can also be trained and updated with the new library. As soon as the latest scene of remote sensing data arrives, the ready classifier can be directly applied to it. In addition, implementing the process in other programming languages and utilising high-performance processors could also help promote efficiency.

Above all, remote sensing data with middle-high spatial and temporal resolution are recommended in the proposed method, as the spatiotemporal contextual information in the image is important for the method. If the spatial or the temporal resolution is rather low in the data, the correlation between neighbouring pixels could be unremarkable.

6. Conclusions

Due to its vast coverage in spatial and temporal scales, flood is considered to be one of the most complex disasters in the world. A novel inundation mapping approach based on spatiotemporal context learning and Modest AdaBoost is proposed and verified in this paper. The proposed method is implemented and evaluated in two different flooding cases using images from different sensors, HJ-1A CCD and GF-4 PMS. The experimental results show that the proposed approach is effective, and is able to produce more accurate mapping results than other state-of-the-art methods and, more importantly, without any artificial samples and thresholds.

On one hand, compared with the traditional global-based unsupervised flood mapping methods (such as K-MEANs), the SP-MADB, STP-MADB and the proposed method combine an automatic sample selection strategy with a machine learning classifier, leading to higher accuracies in an automatic way. With the samples extracted using local information, each of these three methods achieves an overall accuracy of more than 90% in both of the first and second case studies. By comparing the results of the SP-MADB and STP-MADB methods, it can be seen that only extending the neighbouring region to the temporal domain cannot significantly improve the performance of the SP-MADB method. With a formulised model of the spatiotemporal context information instead of simple counting, the proposed approach achieves a more accurate and robust result than other methods. As a result of mixed pixels, there are still some inaccuracies in the result. Moreover, the effect of the proposed method on cloudy data needs to be explored. Future work will focus on these aspects and validate the proposed method with more kinds of data.

Acknowledgments: This work is supported by the National Natural Science Foundation of China (Grant No. 41401474) and the National Key Research and Development Plan (No. 2016YFB0502502). The HJ-1A/B CCD data, GF-1 WFV data and GF-4 PMS data were provided by the China Centre for Resources Satellite Data and Application (CRESDA, http://www.cresda.com). The MODIS water mask (MOD44W) was obtained through the online Data Pool at the NASA Land Processes Distributed Active Archive Centre (LP DAAC), USGS/Earth Resources Observation and Science (EROS) Centre (https://lpdaac.usgs.gov). We thank the above organisations for providing the data. We thank the University of Chinese Academy of Sciences for scholarship support of Xiaoyi Liu.

Author Contributions: Xiaoyi Liu conceived and designed the experiments, performed the experiments and wrote the paper under the guidance of Hichem Sahli and Yu Meng. Qingqing Huang and Lei Lin analysed the data and contributed analysis tools.

Conflicts of Interest: The authors declare no conflict of interest.

References

1. O'Keefe, P.; Westgate, K.; Wisner, B. Taking the naturalness out of natural disasters. *Nature* **1976**, *260*, 566–567. [CrossRef]
2. Sanyal, J.; Lu, X.X. Application of remote sensing in flood management with special reference to monsoon Asia: A review. *Nat. Hazards* **2004**, *33*, 283–301. [CrossRef]
3. Berz, G.; Kron, W.; Loster, T.; Rauch, E.; Schimetschek, J.; Schmieder, J.; Siebert, A.; Smolka, A.; Wirtz, A. World map of natural hazards—A global view of the distribution and intensity of significant exposures. *Nat. Hazards* **2001**, *23*, 443–465. [CrossRef]
4. Akıncı, H.; Erdoğan, S. Designing a flood forecasting and inundation-mapping system integrated with spatial data infrastructures for Turkey. *Nat. Hazards* **2014**, *71*, 895–911. [CrossRef]
5. Smith, L.C. Satellite remote sensing of river inundation area, stage, and discharge: A review. *Hydrol. Process.* **1997**, *11*, 1427–1439. [CrossRef]
6. Brivio, P.A.; Colombo, R.; Maggi, M.; Tomasoni, R. Integration of remote sensing data and GIS for accurate mapping of flooded areas. *Int. J. Remote Sens.* **2002**, *23*, 429–441. [CrossRef]

7. Wang, Y.; Colby, J.D.; Mulcahy, K.A. An efficient method for mapping flood extent in a coastal floodplain using Landsat TM and DEM data. *Int. J. Remote Sens.* **2002**, *23*, 3681–3696. [CrossRef]

8. Rahman, M.S.; Di, L. The state of the art of spaceborne remote sensing in flood management. *Nat. Hazards* **2017**, *85*, 1223–1248. [CrossRef]

9. Li, L.; Chen, Y.; Yu, X.; Liu, R.; Huang, C. Sub-pixel flood inundation mapping from multispectral remotely sensed images based on discrete particle swarm optimization. *ISPRS J. Photogramm. Remote Sens.* **2015**, *101*, 10–21. [CrossRef]

10. Brakenridge, R.; Anderson, E. MODIS-based flood detection, mapping and measurement: The potential for operational hydrological applications. In *Transboundary Floods: Reducing Risks through Flood Management*; Marsalek, J., Stancalie, G., Balint, G., Eds.; Springer: Dordrecht, The Netherlands, 2006; Volume 72, pp. 1–12.

11. Ticehurst, C.J.; Chen, Y.; Karim, F.; Dutta, D.; Gouweleeuw, B. Using MODIS for mapping flood events for use in hydrological and hydrodynamic models: Experiences so far. In Proceedings of the 20th International Congress on Modelling and Simulation, Adelaide, Australia, 1–6 December 2013; pp. 1–6.

12. Kwak, Y.; Park, J.; Yorozuya, A.; Fukami, K. Estimation of flood volume in Chao Phraya River basin, Thailand, from MODIS images couppled with flood inundation level. In Proceedings of the 2012 IEEE International Geoscience and Remote Sensing Symposium (IGARSS), Munich, Germany, 22–27 July 2012.

13. Khan, S.I.; Hong, Y.; Wang, J.; Yilmaz, K.K.; Gourley, J.J.; Adler, R.F.; Brakenridge, G.R.; Policelli, F.; Habib, S.; Irwin, D. Satellite remote sensing and hydrologic modeling for flood inundation mapping in Lake Victoria basin: Implications for hydrologic prediction in ungauged basins. *IEEE Trans. Geosci. Remote Sens.* **2011**, *49*, 85–95. [CrossRef]

14. Schumann, G. Preface: Remote Sensing in Flood Monitoring and Management. *Remote Sens.* **2015**, *7*, 17013–17015. [CrossRef]

15. McFeeters, S.K. The use of the Normalized Difference Water Index (NDWI) in the delineation of open water features. *Int. J. Remote Sens.* **1996**, *17*, 1425–1432. [CrossRef]

16. Jain, S.K.; Singh, R.D.; Jain, M.K.; Lohani, A.K. Delineation of flood-prone areas using remote sensing techniques. *Water Resour. Manag.* **2005**, *19*, 333–347. [CrossRef]

17. Xie, H.; Luo, X.; Xu, X.; Pan, H.; Tong, X. Evaluation of Landsat 8 OLI imagery for unsupervised inland water extraction. *Int. J. Remote Sens.* **2016**, *37*, 1826–1844. [CrossRef]

18. Giordano, F.; Goccia, M.; Dellepiane, S. Segmentation of coherence maps for flood damage assessment. In Proceedings of the IEEE International Conference on Image Processing, Genova, Italy, 14 September 2005; Volume 2, p. II-233.

19. Dellepiane, S.; Angiati, E.; Vernazza, G. Processing and segmentation of COSMO-SkyMed images for flood monitoring. In Proceedings of the 2010 IEEE International Geoscience and Remote Sensing Symposium, Honolulu, HI, USA, 25–30 July 2010.

20. Chignell, S.M.; Anderson, R.S.; Evangelista, P.H.; Laituri, M.J.; Merritt, D.M. Multi-temporal independent component analysis and Landsat 8 for delineating maximum extent of the 2013 Colorado front range flood. *Remote Sens.* **2015**, *7*, 9822–9843. [CrossRef]

21. Rokni, K.; Ahmad, A.; Selamat, A.; Hazini, S. Water feature extraction and change detection using multitemporal Landsat imagery. *Remote Sens.* **2014**, *6*, 4173–4189. [CrossRef]

22. Chen, X.C.; Khandelwal, A.; Shi, S.; Faghmous, J.H.; Boriah, S.; Kumar, V. Unsupervised method for water surface extent monitoring using remote sensing data. In *Machine Learning and Data Mining Approaches to Climate Science*; Springer International Publishing: Cham, Switzerland, 2015; pp. 51–58.

23. Huang, C.; Chen, Y.; Wu, J. Dem-based modification of pixel-swapping algorithm for enhancing floodplain inundation mapping. *Int. J. Remote Sens.* **2014**, *35*, 365–381. [CrossRef]

24. Lu, S.; Wu, B.; Yan, N.; Wang, H. Water body mapping method with hj-1a/b satellite imagery. *Int. J. Appl. Earth Obs. Geoinf.* **2011**, *13*, 428–434. [CrossRef]

25. Gu, X.; Tong, X. Overview of china earth observation satellite programs. *IEEE Geosci. Remote Sens. Mag.* **2015**, *3*, 113–129.

26. Gu, Y.; Hunt, E.; Wardlow, B.; Basara, J.B.; Brown, J.F.; Verdin, J.P. Evaluation of MODIS NDVI and NDWI for vegetation drought monitoring using oklahoma mesonet soil moisture data. *Geophys. Res. Lett.* **2008**, *35*, 1092–1104. [CrossRef]

27. George, C.; Rowland, C.; Gerard, F.; Balzter, H. Retrospective mapping of burnt areas in central siberia using a modification of the normalised difference water index. *Remote Sens. Environ.* **2006**, *104*, 346–359. [CrossRef]

28. Mcfeeters, S.K. Using the normalized difference water index (NDWI) within a geographic information system to detect swimming pools for mosquito abatement: A practical approach. *Remote Sens.* **2013**, *5*, 3544–3561. [CrossRef]

29. Li, W.; Du, Z.; Ling, F.; Zhou, D.; Wang, H.; Gui, Y.; Sun, B.; Zhang, X. A comparison of land surface water mapping using the normalized difference water index from TM, ETM+ and ALI. *Remote Sens.* **2013**, *5*, 5530–5549. [CrossRef]

30. Zhang, K.; Zhang, L.; Yang, M.H.; Zhang, D. Fast tracking via spatio-temporal context learning. *arXiv*, **2013**, preprint arXiv:1311.1939.

31. Zuo, Z.Y.; Tian, S.; Pei, W.Y.; Yin, X.C. Multi-strategy tracking based text detection in scene videos. In Proceedings of the IEEE 13th International Conference on Document Analysis and Recognition, Tunis, Tunisia, 23–26 August 2015.

32. Xu, J.; Lu, Y.; Liu, J. Robust tracking via weighted spatio-temporal context learning. In Proceedings of the 2014 IEEE International Conference on Image Processing (ICIP), Paris, France, 27–30 October 2014.

33. Muster, S.; Heim, B.; Abnizova, A.; Boike, J. Water body distributions across scales: A remote sensing based comparison of three arctic tundra wetlands. *Remote Sens.* **2013**, *5*, 1498–1523. [CrossRef]

34. Freund, Y.; Schapire, R.E. A desicion-theoretic generalization of on-line learning and an application to boosting. In *European Conference on Computational Learning Theory*; Springer: Berlin/Heidelberg, Germany, 1995; pp. 23–37.

35. Viola, P.; Jones, M. Robust real-time object detection. *Int. J. Comput. Vis.* **2001**, *57*, 34–37.

36. Vezhnevets, A.; Vezhnevets, V. Modest AdaBoost-teaching AdaBoost to generalize better. *Graphicon* **2005**, *12*, 987–997.

37. Sam, K.T.; Tian, X.L. Rapid license plate detection using Modest AdaBoost and template matching. In Proceedings of the 2nd International Conference on Digital Image Processing, Singapore, 26 February 2010.

38. Qahwaji, R.; Al-Omari, M.; Colak, T.; Ipson, S. Using the real, gentle and modest AdaBoost learning algorithms to investigate the computerised associations between coronal mass ejections and filaments. In Proceedings of the 2008 IEEE Communications, Computers and Applications, Amman, Jordan, 8–10 August 2008.

39. MSU Graphics & Media Lab, Computer Vision Group. Available online: http://graphics.cs.msu.ru (accessed on 3 June 2016).

40. Gao, B.C. NDWI—A normalized difference water index for remote sensing of vegetation liquid water from space. *Remote Sens. Environ.* **1996**, *58*, 257–266. [CrossRef]

41. Huete, A.; Didan, K.; Miura, T.; Rodriguez, E.P.; Gao, X.; Ferreira, L.G. Overview of the radiometric and biophysical performance of the MODIS vegetation indices. *Remote Sens. Environ.* **2002**, *83*, 195–213. [CrossRef]

Article

Optimized Kernel Minimum Noise Fraction Transformation for Hyperspectral Image Classification

Lianru Gao [1], Bin Zhao [1,2], Xiuping Jia [3], Wenzhi Liao [4] and Bing Zhang [1,2,*]

[1] Key Laboratory of Digital Earth Science, Institute of Remote Sensing and Digital Earth, Chinese Academy of Sciences, Beijing 100094, China; gaolr@radi.ac.cn (L.G.); zhaobin@radi.ac.cn (B.Z.)
[2] University of Chinese Academy of Sciences, Beijing 100049, China
[3] School of Engineering and Information Technology, The University of New South Wales, Canberra Campus, Bruce ACT 2006, Australia; x.jia@adfa.edu.au
[4] Department of Telecommunications and Information Processing, Ghent University, Ghent 9000, Belgium; wenzhi.liao@telin.ugent.be
*   Correspondence: zb@radi.ac.cn; Tel.: +86-10-8217-8002; Fax: +86-10-8217-8009

Academic Editors: Qi Wang, Nicolas H. Younan, Carlos López-Martínez and Prasad S. Thenkabail
Received: 27 April 2017; Accepted: 26 May 2017; Published: 1 June 2017

Abstract: This paper presents an optimized kernel minimum noise fraction transformation (OKMNF) for feature extraction of hyperspectral imagery. The proposed approach is based on the kernel minimum noise fraction (KMNF) transformation, which is a nonlinear dimensionality reduction method. KMNF can map the original data into a higher dimensional feature space and provide a small number of quality features for classification and some other post processing. Noise estimation is an important component in KMNF. It is often estimated based on a strong relationship between adjacent pixels. However, hyperspectral images have limited spatial resolution and usually have a large number of mixed pixels, which make the spatial information less reliable for noise estimation. It is the main reason that KMNF generally shows unstable performance in feature extraction for classification. To overcome this problem, this paper exploits the use of a more accurate noise estimation method to improve KMNF. We propose two new noise estimation methods accurately. Moreover, we also propose a framework to improve noise estimation, where both spectral and spatial de-correlation are exploited. Experimental results, conducted using a variety of hyperspectral images, indicate that the proposed OKMNF is superior to some other related dimensionality reduction methods in most cases. Compared to the conventional KMNF, the proposed OKMNF benefits significant improvements in overall classification accuracy.

Keywords: hyperspectral image; feature extraction; dimensionality reduction; optimized kernel minimum noise fraction (OKMNF)

1. Introduction

Hyperspectral images provide very rich spectral information of earth objects [1,2]. In general, a hyperspectral image contains hundreds of spectral bands with high spectral resolution. However, the high dimensionality reduces the efficiency of hyperspectral data processing. Moreover, in hyperspectral image classification, another problem is known as the curse of dimensionality or the Hughes phenomenon [3]. Namely, the more spectral bands the image has, the more training samples are needed in order to achieve an acceptable classification accuracy. Obviously, it is not easy to be satisfied to the hyperspectral case [4]. Dimensionality reduction is a very effective technique to solve this problem [5,6]. Dimensionality reduced data should well represent the original data, and can be considered as the extracted features for classification [7–9]. When the data dimensionality is lower, the computing time will be reduced, and the number of training samples required will become less demanding [10–13]. Therefore, dimensionality reduction is a very critical pre-processing step for hyperspectral image classification [14–16]. Typically, several approaches exist for dimensionality reduction in hyperspectral data that can be split into two major groups. The first group includes band selection approaches. Such methods aim at selecting a subset of relevant data from the original information. This group includes not only a supervised method such as Bhattacharyya distance, Jeffries–Matusita distance, divergence, kernel dependence, mutual information, and spectral angle mapper, but also unsupervised methods such as geometric-based representative bands, dissimilar bands based on linear projection, manifold ranking [17] and dual clustering [18,19], which have proven to be valuable to achieve superior classification results. The second group relates to feature extraction approaches. Feature extraction methods transform original hyperspectral data into an optimized feature space by mathematical transformation, and then achieve dimensionality reduction through feature selection. A number of techniques have been developed for feature extraction. These techniques can be categorized as two major classes. The first class includes supervised feature extraction methods such as linear discriminant analysis (LDA) [20], nonparametric weighted feature extraction (NWFE) [21], sparse graph based feature extraction and their extensions [22–24]. The second class relates to unsupervised feature extraction approaches such as principal component analysis (PCA) [25] and minimum noise fraction (MNF) [26], sparse-graph learning-based dimensionality reduction method [27], which do not need priori knowledge on label information. PCA and MNF are two of the widely adopted methods for dimensionality reduction of hyperspectral images. As we all know, the performance of PCA highly relies on noise characteristics [26,28]. When the noise is not uniformly distributed across all of the spectral bands or when the noise variance is larger than the signal variance in one band, PCA cannot guarantee that the first few principal components have the highest image quality [26]. MNF generates new components ordered by image quality and provides better spectral features in the major components than PCA, no matter how the spectral noise is distributed [28]. Original MNF is a linear dimensionality reduction method. It is simple in processing and can be applied in most conditions. However, it is not easy for this method to handle the nonlinear characteristics within the data. The nonlinear characteristics of hyperspectral data is often due to the nonlinear nature of scattering as described in the bidirectional reflectance distribution function, multiple scattering within a pixel, and the heterogeneity of subpixel constituents [29,30]. The Kernel MNF (KMNF) method is developed to overcome this weakness in MNF [31–33]. KMNF is a nonlinear dimensionality reduction method, which introduces the use of kernel functions [34] to model the nonlinear characteristics within the data. The nonlinear transformation based on a kernel function can transform the original data into a higher dimensional feature space, and then a linear analysis can be followed in this space, as the complex nonlinear characteristics in the original input space have become simpler linear characteristics in the new feature space [35–39]. Using a similar theory of the kernel methods such as KMNF, kernel PCA (KPCA) was also proposed for nonlinear dimensionality reduction of hyperspectral images [40].

While MNF is a valuable dimensionality reduction method for hyperspectral image classification, it is found that the traditional version of MNF cannot provide desired results in real applications. From the theoretical and experimental analysis, it has been reported that noise estimation is the key factor leading to this problem [41–43]. In the traditional MNF, it is assumed that spatial neighboring pixels have very high correlation and the differences between these pixels can be considered as the noise. It works when the image has very high spatial resolution. Due to the limitation of hyperspectral sensors, hyperspectral images are often unable to offer high spatial resolution, and mixed pixels are very common in a hyperspectral image [44]. Thus, spatial information adopted in the traditional MNF is less reliable for estimating noise for a hyperspectral image. Obviously, the spectral resolution of hyperspectral images is very high, which means that hyperspectral images have strong spectral correlation between bands [45]. It has been found that the combination of the spatial and the spectral information is much more appropriate to estimate noise in hyperspectral images than only using single spatial information [46,47]. Optimized MNF (OMNF) utilized spectral and spatial de-correlation (SSDC) [48–50] to improve noise estimation [51]. However, existing SSDC combines the spectral information with only one spatial neighbor for noise estimation [48–50], leading to imperfect exploitation of spatial information. KMNF is a kernel version of MNF, and can well treat nonlinear characteristics within the data. However, the classification results using the features extracted by KMNF are often disappointing, and sometimes even worse than using MNF. The fundamental reason of this problem mainly also lies in the fact that the original KMNF adopts only spatial information to estimate noise that has a lot of errors and is not stable.

To overcome the above limitations, we propose a new framework to optimize KMNF (OKMNF) for feature extraction of hyperspectral data. Instead of only relying on single spatial information for noise estimation, the proposed OKNMF estimates noises by taking into account both spectral and spatial correlations through multiple linear regression. We also propose a more general method than SSDC [51–53] for noise estimation, where more spatial neighbors are exploited. Moreover, the proposed OKMNF can well treat nonlinear characteristics within the data, which cannot be effectively processed by linear OMNF and MNF. Therefore, OKMNF is much more stable and accurate than KMNF on the noise estimation, and enables better performances on both dimensionality reduction and its post application to classification. Last but not least, the proposed framework can be extended to a general model, when some other accurate noise estimation methods are available.

The remainder of this paper is organized as follows. In Section 2, the OKMNF method will be introduced in detail. Section 3 validates the proposed approach and reports experimental results, comparing them to several state-of-the-art alternatives. Section 4 discusses the performance of noise estimation algorithms and dimensionality reduction methods. Section 5 states the conclusions.

2. Proposed OKMNF Method

Let us consider a hyperspectral image data set with n pixels and b spectral bands organized as a matrix $\mathbf{X}$ with n rows and b columns. Hyperspectral images inevitably contain noises due to the sensor error and other environmental factors' influence. Normally, we can consider the original hyperspectral image $\mathbf{X}$ as a sum of a signal part and a noise part [26,54–56]:

$$\mathbf{x}(p) = \mathbf{x}_S(p) + \mathbf{x}_N(p),\tag{1}$$

where $\mathbf{x}(p)$ is the pixel vector in position p, $\mathbf{x}_N(p)$ and $\mathbf{x}_S(p)$ are noise and signal contained in $\mathbf{x}(p)$, respectively. In optical images, noises and signals are often considered to be independent. Thus, the covariance matrix $\mathbf{S}$ of image $\mathbf{X}$ could be written as a sum of the noise covariance matrix $\mathbf{S}_N$ and signal covariance matrix $\mathbf{S}_S$,

$$\mathbf{S} = \mathbf{S}_N + \mathbf{S}_S.\tag{2}$$

Let us consider $\widetilde{x}_k$ as the average of the kth band, and we can get the matrix $\mathbf{X}_{mean}$ with n rows b columns:

$$\mathbf{X}_{mean} = \begin{bmatrix} \widetilde{x}_1 & \widetilde{x}_2 & \cdots & \widetilde{x}_b \\ \widetilde{x}_1 & \widetilde{x}_2 & \cdots & \widetilde{x}_b \\ \vdots & \vdots & \vdots & \vdots \\ \widetilde{x}_1 & \widetilde{x}_2 & \cdots & \widetilde{x}_b \end{bmatrix},\tag{3}$$

$\mathbf{Z}$ as the center matrix of $\mathbf{X}$, is given by

$$\mathbf{Z} = \mathbf{X} - \mathbf{X}_{mean}.\tag{4}$$

The covariance matrix $\mathbf{S}$ of images $\mathbf{X}$ could be written as

$$\mathbf{S} = \mathbf{Z}^\mathrm{T}\mathbf{Z}/(n-1).\tag{5}$$

Let us consider $\tilde{x}_{Nk}$ as the average of the noise in kth band, and we can get the matrix $\mathbf{X}_{Nmean}$ with n rows and b columns:

$$\mathbf{X}_{Nmean} = \begin{bmatrix} \tilde{x}_{N1} & \tilde{x}_{N2} & \cdots & \tilde{x}_{Nb} \\ \tilde{x}_{N1} & \tilde{x}_{N2} & \cdots & \tilde{x}_{Nb} \\ \vdots & \vdots & \vdots & \vdots \\ \tilde{x}_{N1} & \tilde{x}_{N2} & \cdots & \tilde{x}_{Nb} \end{bmatrix}. \tag{6}$$

$\mathbf{Z}_N$, as the center matrix of the noise matrix $\mathbf{X}_N$, can be computed as

$$\mathbf{Z}_N = \mathbf{X}_N - \mathbf{X}_{Nmean}. \tag{7}$$

The covariance matrix $\mathbf{S}_N$ of $\mathbf{X}_N$ could be expressed as

$$\mathbf{S}_N = \mathbf{Z}_N^{\mathrm{T}} \mathbf{Z}_N / (n-1). \tag{8}$$

The noise fraction $\mathbf{NF}$ could be defined as the ratio of the noise variance to the total variance, so for a linear combinations, $\mathbf{a}^T \mathbf{z}(p)$ [26,31], we get

$$\mathbf{NF} = \mathbf{a}^T \mathbf{S}_N \mathbf{a} / \mathbf{a}^T \mathbf{S} \mathbf{a} = \mathbf{a}^T \mathbf{Z}_N^T \mathbf{Z}_N \mathbf{a} / \mathbf{a}^T \mathbf{Z}^T \mathbf{Z} \mathbf{a}, \tag{9}$$

where $\mathbf{a}$ is the eigenmatrix of $\mathbf{NF}$. In $\mathbf{NF}$, it is significant that the noise is estimated reliably. The original KMNF method [31] mainly adopts the spatial neighborhood (3 by 3) feature of a hyperspectral image to estimate noise $\mathbf{Z}_N$ [57], as shown below:

$$\begin{aligned} n_{i,j,k} &= z_{i,j,k} - \hat{z}_{i,j,k} \\ &= z_{i,j,k} - (-z_{i-1,j-1,k} + 2z_{i,j-1,k} - z_{i+1,j-1,k} + 2z_{i-1,j,k} + \\ & \quad 5z_{i,j,k} + 2z_{i+1,j,k} - z_{i-1,j+1,k} + 2z_{i,j+1,k} - z_{i+1,j+1,k})/9 \end{aligned} \tag{10}$$

where $z_{i,j,k}$ is the value of pixel located at line i, column j, and band k of the original hyperspectral image $\mathbf{Z}$, $\hat{z}_{i,j,k}$ is the estimated value of this pixel, and $n_{i,j,k}$ is the estimated noise value of $z_{i,j,k}$.

However, noise estimation based on spatial information alone can be unstable and data-selective [25,51,53]. It is because hyperspectral images do not always have very high spatial resolution, and the difference between pixels may contain a significant signal instead of pure noise. In contrast, in hyperspectral images, correlation between bands generally is very high. Therefore, we can incorporate the high correlations between bands for noise estimation, such as SSDC, which is a useful method for hyperspectral image noise estimation. In SSDC, the spatial and spectral correlations are removed through a multiple linear regression model, and the remaining residuals are the estimates of noise [49,50,58]. Recent works show that SSDC can offer reliable results for noise estimation when there are different land cover types in the hyperspectral images [50].

2.1. Noise Estimation

In noise estimation based on spectral and spatial de-correlation, an image is uniformly divided into non-overlapping small sub-blocks $\mathbf{X}_{sub}$ with $w \times h$ pixels, in order to reduce the influence of the variations in ground cover types. In SSDC, a multiple linear regression formula is adopted as follows for each pixel [49,50]:

$$x_{i,j,k} = a + bx_{i,j,k-1} + cx_{i,j,k+1} + dx_{p,k}, \tag{11}$$

$$x_{p,k} = \begin{cases} x_{i-1,j,k}; & i > 1, j = 1 \\ x_{i,j-1,k}; & j > 1 \end{cases}, \tag{12}$$

where $1 \leq i \leq w, 1 \leq j \leq h$, and $(i,j) \neq (1,1)$, a, b, c, and d are the coefficients need to be determined. For each sub-block $\mathbf{X}_{sub}$, the multiple linear regression models could be written as

$$X_{sub} = B\mu + \varepsilon,\tag{13}$$

$$X_{sub} = \begin{bmatrix} x_{1,2,k} \\ x_{1,3,k} \\ \vdots \\ x_{w,h,k} \end{bmatrix}, B = \begin{bmatrix} 1 & x_{1,2,k-1} & x_{1,2,k+1} & x_{1,1,k} \\ 1 & x_{1,3,k-1} & x_{1,3,k+1} & x_{1,2,k} \\ \vdots & \vdots & \vdots & \vdots \\ 1 & x_{w,h,k-1} & x_{w,h,k+1} & x_{w,h-1,k} \end{bmatrix}, \mu = \begin{bmatrix} a \\ b \\ c \\ d \end{bmatrix},\tag{14}$$

where X_{sub} is sub-block matrix, B is the spectral-spatial neighborhoods matrix, μ is the coefficients matrix, and ε is residual value.

However, SSDC integrates spectral information and one spatial neighbor in multiple linear regression for noise estimation. This way the spatial information might not be well exploited to estimate noise. To solve this problem, we propose two methods to improve the SSDC, named $SSDC_1$ and $SSDC_2$, where more spatial neighbors are incorporated into multiple linear regression for noise estimation.

We define $SSDC_1$ in the same multiple linear regression (same as Equation (11)) framework, but adopts the spatial neighbor parts $x_{p,k}$ as follows:

$$x_{p,k} = \begin{cases} (x_{i-1,j,k} + x_{i+1,j,k})/2; & i > 1, j = 1 \\ (x_{i,j-1,k} + x_{i,j+1,k})/2; & j > 1 \end{cases},\tag{15}$$

where X_{sub} and μ are the same as SSDC, but B is different from it, and can be defined as follows:

$$B = \begin{bmatrix} 1 & x_{1,2,k-1} & x_{1,2,k+1} & (x_{1,1,k} + x_{1,3,k})/2 \\ 1 & x_{1,3,k-1} & x_{1,3,k+1} & (x_{1,2,k} + x_{1,4,k})/2 \\ \vdots & \vdots & \vdots & \vdots \\ 1 & x_{w,h,k-1} & x_{w,h,k+1} & (x_{w,h-1,k} + x_{,w,h+1,k})/2 \end{bmatrix}.\tag{16}$$

We can also improve multiple linear regression, which we define as $SSDC_2$:

$$x_{i,j,k} = a + bx_{i,j,k-1} + cx_{i,j,k+1} + dx_{i,j-1,k} + ex_{i,j+1,k},\tag{17}$$

where X_{sub} is the same as SSDC, but B and μ are defined as follows:

$$B = \begin{bmatrix} 1 & x_{1,2,k-1} & x_{1,2,k+1} & x_{1,1,k} & x_{1,3,k} \\ 1 & x_{1,3,k-1} & x_{1,3,k+1} & x_{1,2,k} & x_{1,4,k} \\ \vdots & \vdots & \vdots & \vdots & \vdots \\ 1 & x_{w,h,k-1} & x_{w,h,k+1} & x_{w,h-1,k} & x_{w,h+1,k} \end{bmatrix}, \mu = \begin{bmatrix} a \\ b \\ c \\ d \\ e \end{bmatrix}.\tag{18}$$

μ could be estimated by

$$\hat{\mu} = (B^T B)^{-1} B^T X_{sub}.\tag{19}$$

Signal value could be estimated through

$$\hat{X}_{sub} = B\hat{\mu}.\tag{20}$$

Finally, the noise value N_{sub} can be obtained by

$$N_{sub} = X_{sub} - \hat{X}_{sub}.\tag{21}$$

The procedure of noise estimation is summarized in Algorithm 1.

Algorithm 1. Noise Estimation.

Input: hyperspectral image $\mathbf{X}$, sub-block width $w \times h$.
Step 1: compute the coefficients a, b, c, d and e of the multiple linear regression models for each sub-block using Equation (11) or Equation (17); then:
$x_{i,j,k} = a + bx_{i,j,k-1} + cx_{i,j,k+1} + dx_{p,k}$, or
$x_{i,j,k} = a + bx_{i,j,k-1} + cx_{i,j,k+1} + dx_{i,j-1,k} + ex_{i,j+1,k}$
Step 2: estimate noise: $n_{i,j,k} = x_{i,j,k} - \hat{x}_{i,j,k}$
Output: noise data $\mathbf{N}$.

We analyze the influences of sub-block size by using hyperspectral image as shown in Figure 1a. From the experiments, we found that, when the sub-block size is 4×4, or 5×5, some sub-blocks are homogeneous and have similar DN values in certain bands; thus, it makes the matrix inversion in multiple linear regression infeasible. When the sub-block size is too large, such as 15×15 and 30×30, some sub-blocks contain multiple types of earth surface features, and the results of noise estimation become inaccurate and instable. When the sub-block size is 6×6, as shown in Figures 2 and 3, the results of noise estimation are reliable and stable. Therefore, we set the sub-block size to 6×6 for SSDC, SSDC$_1$ and SSDC$_2$. The width and height of each sub-block are set as $w = 6$, $h = 6$.

2.2. Kernelization and Regularization

After noise is estimated through SSDC, SSDC$_1$ or SSDC$_2$, it will be included in KMNF. In KMNF, in order to get the new components ordered by image quality after dimensionality reduction, we should minimize the **NF**. For the convenience of mathematics, we can maximize the $1/\mathbf{NF}$, which can be presented as

$$1/\mathbf{NF} = \mathbf{a}^T\mathbf{S}\mathbf{a}/\mathbf{a}^T\mathbf{S}_N\mathbf{a} = \mathbf{a}^T\mathbf{Z}^T\mathbf{Z}\mathbf{a}/\mathbf{a}^T\mathbf{Z}_N^T\mathbf{Z}_N\mathbf{a}. \tag{22}$$

We can get to the dual formulation by reparametrizing and setting $\mathbf{a} \propto \mathbf{Z}^T\mathbf{b}$ [31,34]:

$$1/\mathbf{NF} = \mathbf{b}^T\mathbf{Z}\mathbf{Z}^T\mathbf{Z}\mathbf{Z}^T\mathbf{b}/\mathbf{b}^T\mathbf{Z}\mathbf{Z}_N^T\mathbf{Z}_N\mathbf{Z}^T\mathbf{b}. \tag{23}$$

For the kernelization of $1/\mathbf{NF}$, we will consider an embedding map

$$\Phi : x \to \Phi(x), \tag{24}$$

where $x \in R^n$, $\Phi(x) \in R^N$, $N > n$, and nonlinear mapping $\Phi(x)$ can transform the original data x into higher dimensional feature space F [34].

After mapping $\Phi(x)$, the kernelized $1/\mathbf{NF}$ can be expressed as

$$1/\mathbf{NF} = \mathbf{b}^T\Phi(\mathbf{Z})\Phi(\mathbf{Z})^T\Phi(\mathbf{Z})\Phi(\mathbf{Z})^T\mathbf{b}/\mathbf{b}^T\Phi(\mathbf{Z})\Phi(\mathbf{Z}_N)^T\Phi(\mathbf{Z}_N)\Phi(\mathbf{Z})^T\mathbf{b}. \tag{25}$$

Traditionally, the inner products $\langle\Phi(x),\Phi(y)\rangle$ $(x,y \in R^n)$ sometimes can be computed more efficiently as a direct function of the input features, without explicitly computing the mapping $\Phi(x)$ [34]. This function is called the kernel function κ, which can be expressed as

$$\kappa(x,y) = \langle\Phi(x),\Phi(y)\rangle. \tag{26}$$

Therefore, Equation (25) could be written as

$$1/\mathbf{NF} = \mathbf{b}^T\kappa^2\mathbf{b}/\mathbf{b}^T\kappa_N\kappa_N^T\mathbf{b}, \tag{27}$$

where $\kappa = \Phi()\Phi()^T$ with elements $\kappa(z_i,z_j)$, and $\kappa_N = \Phi(\mathbf{Z})\Phi(\mathbf{Z}_N)^T$ with elements $\kappa(z_i,z_{Nj})$. To ensure the uniqueness of the result in Equation (27), we regulate the $1/\mathrm{NF}$ by introducing a regulator

r, similarly to what the other kernel methods (e.g., KMNF, KPCA [28,31]) have done. This way, we get a version which is regulated as

$$1/\mathbf{NF} = \mathbf{b}^T[(1-r)\kappa^2 + r\kappa]\mathbf{b}/\mathbf{b}^T\kappa_N\kappa_N^T\mathbf{b}. \tag{28}$$

2.3. OKMNF Transformation

The regulated version described above is a symmetric generalized eigenvalue problem, which could be solved by maximizing the Rayleigh quotient in Equation (28). Therefore, this problem can be written as

$$[(1-r)\kappa^2 + r\kappa]\mathbf{b} = \lambda\kappa_N\kappa_N^T\mathbf{b}, \tag{29}$$

$$[(1-r)\kappa^2 + r\kappa]\mathbf{b} = \lambda(\kappa_N\kappa_N^T)^{1/2}(\kappa_N\kappa_N^T)^{1/2}\mathbf{b}, \tag{30}$$

$$(\kappa_N\kappa_N^T)^{-1/2}[(1-r)\kappa^2 + r\kappa](\kappa_N\kappa_N^T)^{-1/2}[(\kappa_N\kappa_N^T)^{1/2}\mathbf{b}] = \lambda[(\kappa_N\kappa_N^T)^{1/2}\mathbf{b}], \tag{31}$$

where λ and $(\kappa_N\kappa_N^T)^{1/2}\mathbf{b}$ are eigenvalues and eigenvectors of $(\kappa_N\kappa_N^T)^{-1/2}[(1-r)\kappa^2 + r\kappa](\kappa_N\kappa_N^T)^{-1/2}$, respectively. $\mathbf{a} \propto \mathbf{Z}^T\mathbf{b}$, after mapping $\Phi(x)$, $\mathbf{Z}^T\mathbf{b}$ transforms to $\Phi(\mathbf{Z})^T\mathbf{b}$. Thus, we can get the value of $\mathbf{b}$, and the feature extraction result $\mathbf{Y}$ can be obtained by:

$$\begin{aligned}\mathbf{Y} &= \Phi(\mathbf{Z})\mathbf{a}\\ &= \Phi(\mathbf{Z})\Phi(\mathbf{Z})^T\mathbf{b} \\ &= \kappa\mathbf{b}\end{aligned} \tag{32}$$

From the above analysis, we can see that noise estimation is a very critical step in the OKMNF method. Firstly, in the original data space, based on original hyperspectral data $\mathbf{Z}$, we get the estimated data $\hat{\mathbf{Z}}$ calculated by multiple linear regression models. Then, we transform the original real hyperspectral data $\mathbf{Z}$ and the estimated data $\hat{\mathbf{Z}}$ to the kernel space. In this space, we get the results of noise estimation through calculating the difference of kernel $\mathbf{Z}$ and kernel $\hat{\mathbf{Z}}$. It means that the noise is estimated in the kernel space. Finally, we get the transformation matrix by maximizing regulated $1/\mathbf{NF}$ and achieve the dimensionality reduction. A good noise estimation is important for effective dimensionality reduction.

In many real applications, a hyperspectral image typically has a huge amount of pixels. Then, the kernel matrix could be very large (for example, the matrix sizes of κ and κ_N are n by n, and n is the number of pixels). In this case, even in conventional hyperspectral remote sensing images, the kernel matrix will exceed the memory capacity of an ordinary personal computer. For example, a hyperspectral image of n = 512 × 512 pixels, the size of the kernel matrix is $n \times n$ = (512 × 512) × (512 × 512) elements. To reduce memory cost and computational complexity, we can randomly subsample the image and perform the kernel eigenvalue analysis only on these selected samples (suppose m), which can be used as training samples. We can generate a transformed version of the entire image by mapping all pixels onto the primal eigenvectors obtained from the subset samples. The procedure of OKMNF is summarized in Algorithm 2.

Algorithm 2. The Proposed OKMNF.

Input: hyperspectral image $\mathbf{X}$, and m training samples.
Step 1: compute the residuals (noises) of training samples: $n_{i,j,k} = x_{i,j,k} - \hat{x}_{i,j,k}$.
Step 2: dual transformation, kernelization and regularization of $1/\mathbf{NF}$ using Equation (22).
Step 3: compute the eigenvectors of $(\kappa_N\kappa_N^T)^{-1/2}[(1-r)\kappa^2 + r\kappa](\kappa_N\kappa_N^T)^{-1/2}$.
Step 4: mapping all pixels onto the primal eigenvectors.
Output: feature extraction result $\mathbf{Y}$.

---

3. Experiments and Results

This section designs three experiments to evaluate the performances of a few noise estimation algorithms and dimensionality reduction methods. The first experiment using real images with different land covers is to assess the robustness of noise estimation algorithms adopted in OKMNF, and the results are shown in Figure 4. The other two experiments are to validate the performances of dimensionality reduction methods in terms of maximum likelihood-based classification (ML) on two real hyperspectral images. The experimental results of Indian Pines image (as shown in Figure 5) are shown in Figures 6–9. The experimental results of Minamimaki scene image (as shown in Figure 10) are shown in Figures 11–13.

3.1. Parameter Tuning

In Equation (28), we introduced a parameter r to guarantee the uniqueness of the eigenvectors. Figures 7a and 12a show the sensitivity of kernel dimensionality reduction methods (KPCA, KMNF, and OKMNF) with respect to r. We can see that the values of parameter r have little effect on kernel dimensionality reduction methods, and OKMNF gets overall better or comparable accuracy than KMNF and KPCA. To fairly compare different dimensionality reduction methods, we adopt the optimal value of parameter r within the range of requirements when the classification accuracy of hyperspectral images achieves the maximum value. According to our empirical study, in the Indian Pines scene, r of OKMNF, KMNF, and KPCA are all set to 0.0025, and in the Minamimaki Scene, r of KMNF is set to 0.1, and r of OKMNF and KPCA are both set to 0.005.

Another important parameter is the number of subsamples (pixels), m. They were used to derive eigenvectors for data transformation. Figures 7b and 12b show the sensitivity of kernel dimensionality reduction methods (KPCA, KMNF, and OKMNF) with respect to m. We can see that the values of parameter m have little effect on KPCA. To the Indian Pines scene and the Minamimaki scene, the classification accuracy of OKMNF and KMNF both evidently descend when the value of parameter m is greater than 100. However, OKMNF shows lower sensitivity on parameter m than KMNF, and is even better or comparable to KPCA when the value of parameter m is less than 80. We fix the number of the extracted features to see the impact of subsample size on classification. We see the performance decrease, as the number of subsample increases. The reason is that when m increases, more extracted features are required. To reduce the computational time and memory use, we will adopt a small number of subsamples. It is an important empirical rule that can be considered in the applications of OKMNF. Here, we also adopt the optimal value of parameter m within the range of requirements when the classification accuracy of hyperspectral images achieves the maximum value. According to our empirical study, in the Indian Pines scene, m of OKMNF and KPCA are both set to 63, and m of KMNF is set to 42. In the Minamimaki Scene, m of KMNF and KPCA are both set to 30, and m of OKMNF is set to 25.

In this paper, the employed kernel function is the Gaussian radial basis function, which is the same as KPCA, KMNF, and OKMNF [59] The Gaussian radial basis function is defined as

$$\kappa(\mathbf{x}_i, \mathbf{x}_j) = \exp[-||\mathbf{x}_i - \mathbf{x}_j||^2 / (2\sigma^2)], \tag{33}$$

where $\mathbf{x}_i$ and $\mathbf{x}_j$ are vectors of observations, $\sigma = s\sigma_0$, σ_0 is the mean distance between the observations in feature space and s is a scale factor [33,37]. Figures 7c and 12c show the sensitivity of KPCA, KMNF, and OKMNF with respect to s. We can see that both OKMNF and KPCA show better performance than KMNF. In the Indian Pines scene, OKMNF performs better than KPCA. Just like above, we adopt the optimal value of parameter s within the range of requirements when the classification accuracy of hyperspectral images achieves the maximum value. According to our empirical study, s of KPCA, KMNF, and OKMNF are set to 35, 1, and 15 for the Indian Pines scene, respectively. Then, for the Minamimaki scene, s of OKMNF is set to 25, and s of KPCA and KMNF are both set to 10.

3.2. Experiments on Noise Estimation Algorithms in KMNF and OKMNF

To assess the performance of noise estimation algorithms adopted in KMNF and OKMNF, six real Airborne Visible/Infrared Imaging Spectrometer (AVIRIS) radiance images with very different land cover types were used in this experiment. These images are shown in Figure 1. Each of them contains 300×300 pixels, and covers spectral wavelengths from 400 nm to 2500 nm. Normally, the random noise in AVIRIS sensor images is mainly additive and uncorrelated with the signal [60]. More detailed descriptions are shown in Table 1.

We assess the performance of noise estimation algorithms by computing noise standard deviation, after we get noise data through Algorithm 1. The local standard deviation (LSD) of each sub-block is estimated by

$$LSD = [\frac{1}{w \times h - 4} \sum_{i=1}^{w} \sum_{j=1}^{h} n_{i,j,k}^2]^{\frac{1}{2}} \tag{34}$$

where $w \times h - 4$ means that four parameters are used in the multiple linear regression model and that the degree of freedom is $w \times h - 4$. The LSD of each sub-block is calculated as the noise estimate of that region. The mean value of these LSD is considered as the best estimate of the band noise.

The AVIRIS hyperspectral imageries in Figure 1 were acquired from July 1996 to June 1997. Figure 1a–f are cut from the same image, respectively. Therefore, their noise level should be the same [50].

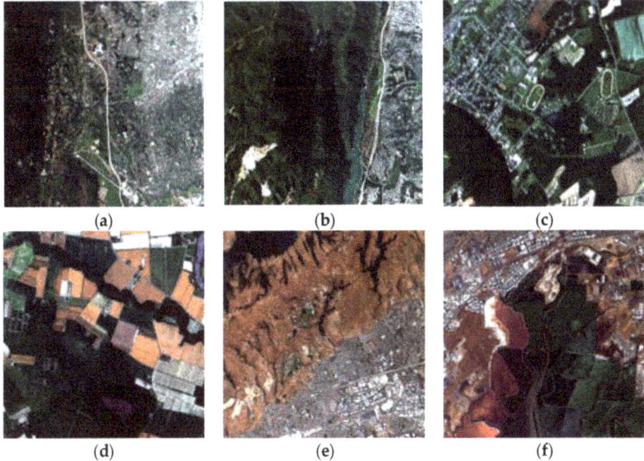

Figure 1. Airborne Visible/Infrared Imaging Spectrometer radiance images used for noise estimation, where (**a**) is the first subimage of Jasper Ridge; (**b**) is the second subimage of Jasper Ridge; (**c**) is the first subimage of Low Altitude; (**d**) is the second subimage of Low Altitude; (**e**) is the first subimage of Moffett Field; and (**f**) is the second subimage of Moffett Field.

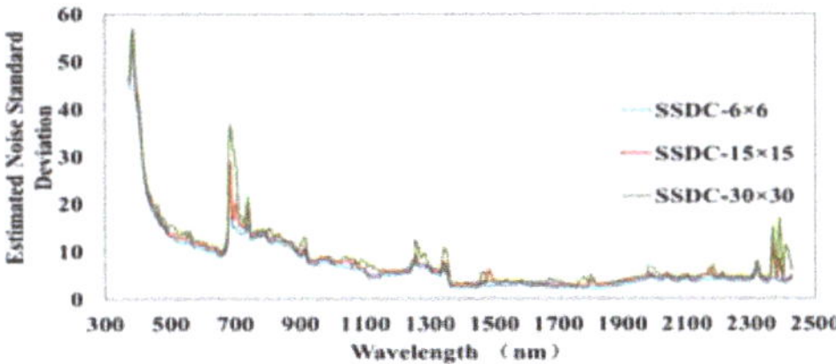

Figure 2. Noise estimation results of spectral and spatial de-correlation (SSDC) of Figure 1a in a different size of sub-block.

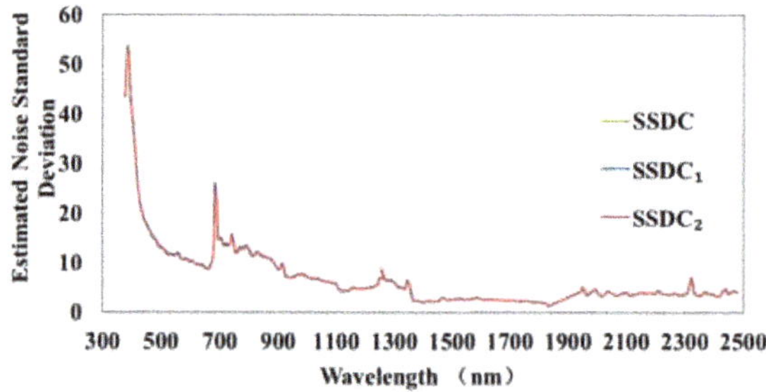

Figure 3. Noise estimation results of SSDC, $SSDC_1$, and $SSDC_2$ of Figure 1a in the 6 × 6 size of sub-block.

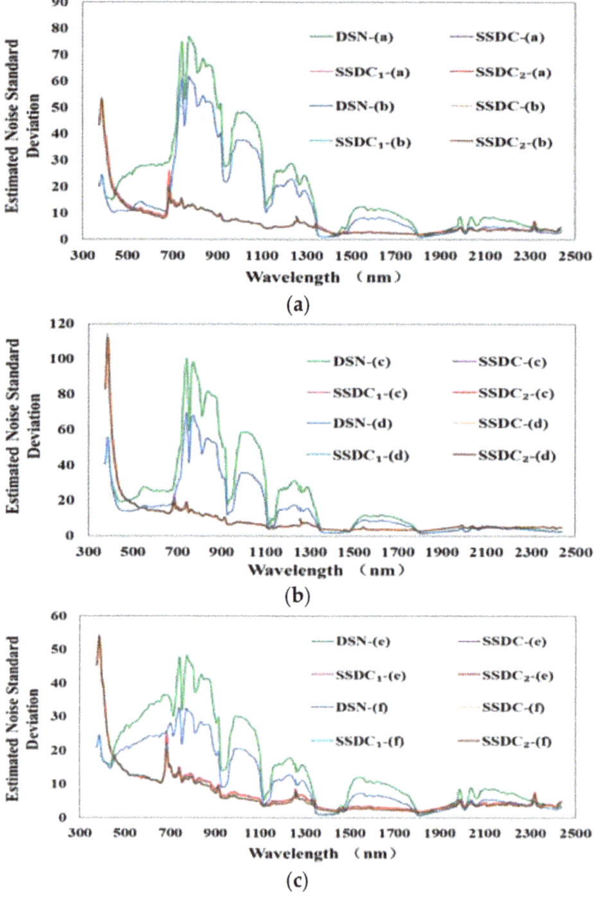

Figure 4. Noise estimation results of (**a**) Figure 1a,b; (**b**) Figure 1c,d; (**c**) Figure 1e,f, through the difference of spatial neighborhood (DSN) used in kernel minimum noise fraction (KMNF), and the SSDC, $SSDC_1$, and $SSDC_2$ used in optimize KMNF (OKMNF).

Table 1. Detailed description of Airborne Visible/Infrared Imaging Spectrometer images shown in Figure 1.

	Spatial Resolution	Acquired Site	Acquired Time	Image Description
(a) (b)	20 m	Jasper Ridge	3 April 1997	Dominated by a heterogeneous city area Dominated by a homogeneous vegetation area
(c) (d)	3.4 m	Low Altitude	5 July 1996	Dominated by a heterogeneous city area Homogeneous farmland
(e) (f)	20 m	Moffett Field	20 June 1997	A mix of a heterogeneous city area and a homogeneous bare soil Dominated by a homogeneous water

3.3. Experiments on Dimensionality Reduction Methods

In these experiments, the dimensionality reduction performance of OKMNF is evaluated in terms of classification results on two real hyperspectral images. Classification accuracies using the features extracted by PCA, KPCA, MNF, KMNF, OMNF, and OKMNF (OKMNF-SSDC, OKMNF-SSDC$_1$, and OKMNF-SSDC$_2$) are compared. Each experiment was run ten times, and the average of these ten experiments was reported for comparisons.

3.3.1. Experiments on the Indian Pines Image

The experimental dataset was collected by the AVIRIS at Indian Pines. The image contains 145 × 145 pixels with spatial resolution of 20 m, and is with 220 spectral bands from 400 nm to 2500 nm. In this experiment, we compare with different dimensionality reduction methods based on original image including all the 220 bands. It is worth observing that 20 bands covering the region of water absorption are really noisy, thus allowing us to analyze the robustness of the different dimensionality reduction methods to real noise. As shown in Figures 5 and 9, large classes are considered in this experiment. In addition, 25% of samples are randomly selected for training and the others 75% are employed for testing [61,62]. The numbers of training and testing samples are listed in Table 2. The first three features extracted by different dimensionality reduction methods are shown in Figure 8. The overall accuracies of ML classification after different dimensionality reduction methods are shown in Table 3 and Figure 6. The results of ML classification after different dimensionality reduction (number of features = 5) methods are shown in Figure 9.

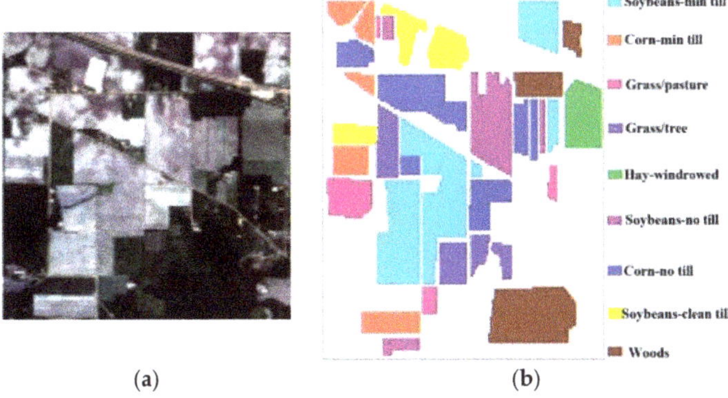

(a)   (b)

Figure 5. (a) original Indian Pines image; (b) ground reference map containing nine land-cover classes.

Table 2. Training and testing samples used in Indian Pines image.

Classes	Training	Testing
Corn-no till	359	1075
Corn-min till	209	625
Grass/Pasture	124	373
Grass/Trees	187	560
Hay-windrowed	122	367
Soybean-no till	242	726
Soybean-min till	617	1851
Soybean-clean till	154	460
Woods	324	970
Total	2338	7007

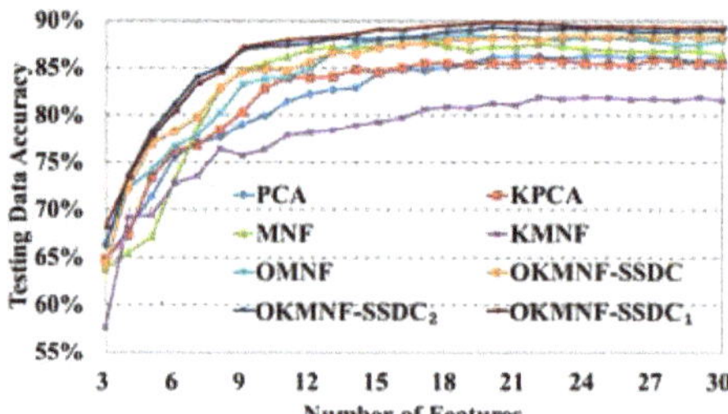

Figure 6. Comparison of accuracies of maximum likelihood-based classification (ML) classification after different dimensionality reduction methods.

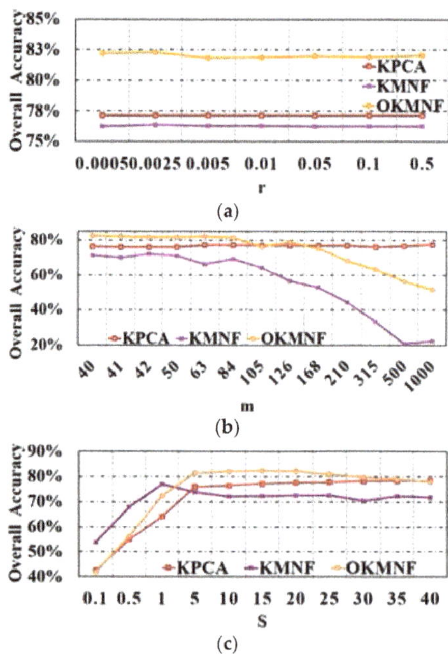

Figure 7. Parameter tuning in the experiments using the Indian Pines dataset for ML classification after different feature extraction methods (number of features = 8), where (**a**) is r versus accuracies; (**b**) is m versus accuracies; (**c**) is s versus accuracies.

Table 3. The overall accuracies of maximum likelihood-based classification (ML) classification after different dimensionality reduction methods.

Number of Features	PCA	KPCA	MNF	KMNF	OMNF	OKMNF-SSDC	OKMNF-SSDC$_1$	OKMNF-SSDC$_2$
3	64.57%	64.84%	63.75%	57.63%	66.50%	64.21%	**68.19%**	66.19%
4	67.90%	67.33%	65.44%	69.14%	72.25%	72.23%	73.34%	**73.60%**
5	71.35%	73.41%	67.14%	69.36%	74.15%	76.93%	77.74%	**78.29%**
6	75.60%	76.23%	73.09%	72.76%	76.69%	78.31%	80.48%	**81.22%**
7	77.08%	76.81%	78.43%	73.53%	77.88%	79.73%	83.35%	**84.07%**
8	77.65%	78.45%	82.76%	76.39%	80.21%	82.86%	84.56%	**85.03%**
9	79.01%	80.32%	84.74%	75.71%	83.27%	84.59%	**87.21%**	86.93%
10	79.92%	82.82%	85.43%	76.35%	83.84%	84.87%	**87.56%**	87.26%
11	81.40%	83.96%	86.16%	77.88%	83.97%	84.69%	**87.94%**	87.44%
12	82.27%	83.96%	86.93%	78.18%	84.96%	85.66%	**88.17%**	87.60%
13	82.67%	84.10%	87.15%	78.42%	86.61%	86.63%	**88.33%**	88.13%
14	82.90%	84.84%	87.08%	78.94%	87.57%	86.50%	**88.63%**	88.04%
15	84.49%	84.54%	87.33%	79.31%	87.95%	87.17%	**89.10%**	88.04%
16	84.87%	85.03%	87.48%	79.72%	88.30%	87.43%	**89.04%**	88.17%
17	84.72%	85.50%	87.55%	80.66%	88.05%	87.64%	**89.37%**	88.41%
18	85.02%	85.50%	87.34%	80.89%	88.28%	87.91%	**89.51%**	88.84%
19	85.50%	85.37%	86.91%	80.78%	88.47%	87.98%	**89.68%**	89.00%
20	86.16%	85.59%	87.27%	81.25%	88.25%	88.20%	**89.82%**	89.30%
21	86.21%	85.41%	87.21%	81.13%	88.37%	88.24%	**89.77%**	89.14%
22	86.23%	85.89%	87.57%	81.88%	88.10%	88.01%	**89.64%**	89.03%
23	86.00%	85.76%	87.28%	81.76%	88.00%	88.30%	**89.55%**	89.15%
24	86.24%	85.49%	86.97%	81.88%	88.17%	88.28%	**89.35%**	89.14%
25	86.27%	85.40%	86.87%	81.82%	88.08%	88.23%	**89.42%**	89.14%
26	86.06%	85.30%	86.74%	81.66%	88.11%	88.34%	**89.34%**	88.89%
27	86.27%	85.84%	86.76%	81.72%	87.85%	88.20%	**89.28%**	88.82%
28	85.96%	85.59%	86.84%	81.60%	87.43%	88.27%	**89.27%**	88.88%
29	85.71%	85.50%	86.80%	81.92%	87.50%	88.25%	**89.28%**	88.91%
30	85.89%	85.39%	86.31%	81.60%	87.87%	88.24%	**89.23%**	88.97%

PCA: principal component analysis; KPCA: kernel PCA; MNF: minimum noise fraction; KMNF: kernel minimum noise fraction; OMNF: optimized MNF; OKMNF: optimized kernel minimum noise fraction.

Figure 8. The first three features (from up to bottom) of kernel PCA (KPCA), KMNF, OKMNF-SSDC, OKMNF-SSDC$_1$, and OKMNF-SSDC$_2$.

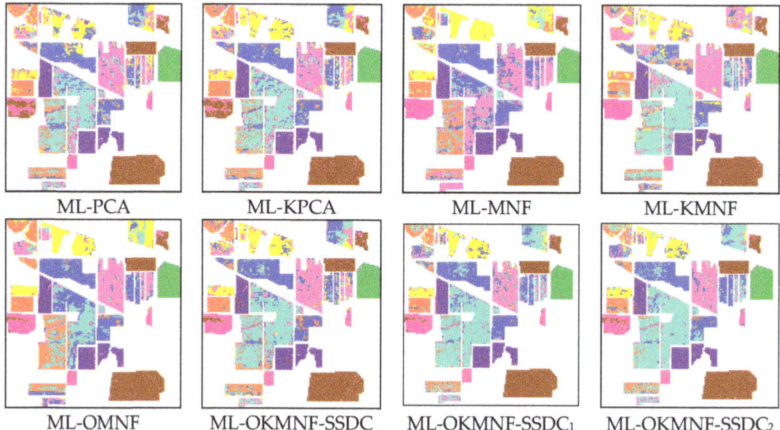

Figure 9. The results of ML classification after different dimensionality reduction methods (number of features = 5).

3.3.2. Experiments on the Minamimaki Scene

This scene was collected by the Pushbroom Hyperspectral Imager (PHI) sensor over Minamimaki, Japan. The PHI sensor was developed by the Shanghai Institute of Technical Physics of the Chinese Academy of Sciences, China. The data has 200 × 200 pixels with a spatial resolution of 3 m and 80 spectral bands from 400 nm to 850 nm. As shown in Figure 10, this image has six classes. About 10% of samples per class were randomly selected for training and the other 90% were employed for testing. The numbers of training and testing samples are listed in Table 4. The overall accuracies of ML classification after different dimensionality reduction methods are shown in Table 5 and Figure 11. The results of ML classification (number of features = 3) are shown in Figure 13.

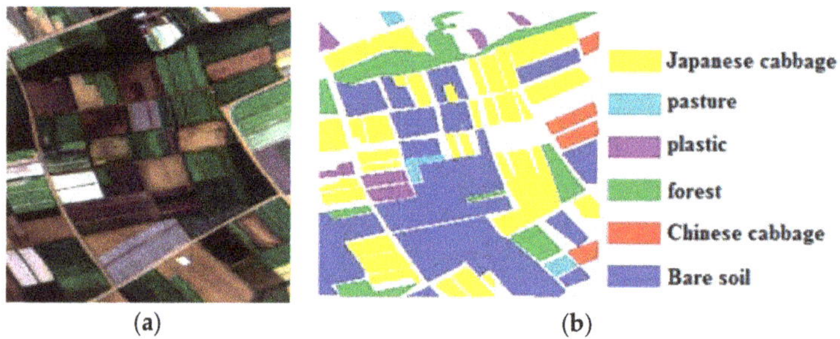

Figure 10. (**a**) true color image of the Minamimaki scene; (**b**) ground reference map with 6 classes.

Table 4. Training and testing samples used in the Minamimaki scene.

Classes	Training	Testing
Bare soil	1238	11,150
plastic	33	300
Chinese cabbage	29	245
forest	111	1000
Japanese cabbage	425	3830
pasture	20	153
Total	1856	16,678

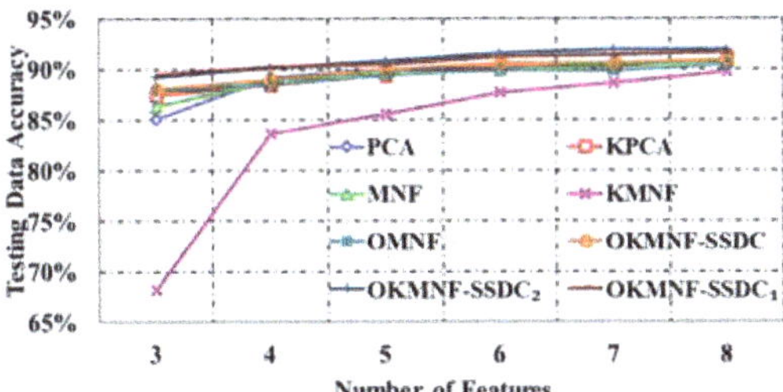

Figure 11. Comparison of accuracies of ML classification after different dimensionality reduction methods.

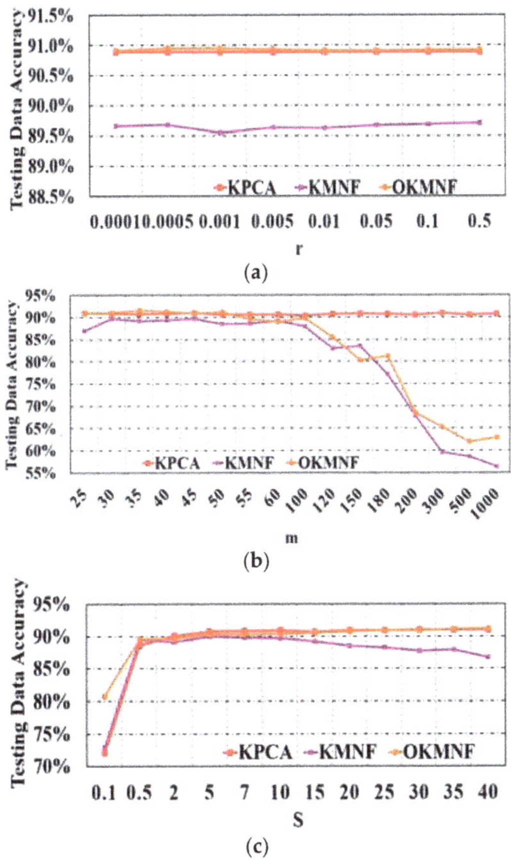

Figure 12. Parameter tuning in experiments using the Minamimaki dataset for ML classification after different dimensionality methods (number of features = 8), where (**a**) is r versus accuracies; (**b**) is m versus accuracies; (**c**) is s versus accuracies.

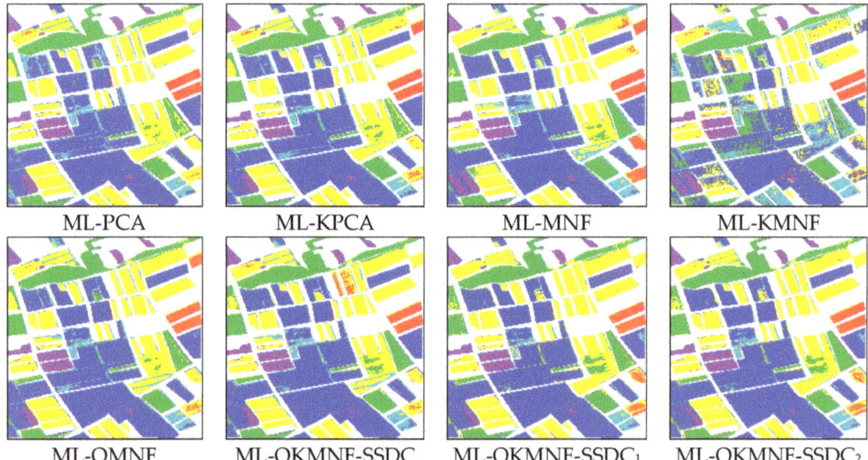

ML-PCA   ML-KPCA   ML-MNF   ML-KMNF

ML-OMNF   ML-OKMNF-SSDC   ML-OKMNF-SSDC$_1$ ML-OKMNF-SSDC$_2$

Figure 13. The results of ML classification after different dimensionality reduction methods (number of features = 3).

Table 5. The overall accuracies of ML classification after different dimensionality reduction methods.

Method	Number of Features					
	3	4	5	6	7	8
PCA	85.14%	89.13%	89.86%	90.17%	90.44%	90.75%
KPCA	87.43%	88.41%	89.46%	90.19%	90.22%	90.87%
MNF	86.34%	88.73%	89.48%	89.69%	90.32%	90.59%
KMNF	68.30%	83.81%	86.02%	87.69%	88.61%	89.66%
OMNF	87.82%	88.51%	89.32%	90.10%	89.88%	90.51%
OKMNF-SSDC	88.10%	88.94%	89.98%	90.60%	90.63%	90.97%
OKMNF-SSDC$_1$	**89.46%**	**90.18%**	90.44%	91.19%	91.39%	91.68%
OKMNF-SSDC$_2$	89.24%	90.17%	**90.78%**	**91.56%**	**91.88%**	**91.89%**

4. Discussion

This section discusses the performances of noise estimation algorithms, and these results are shown in Section 3.2. In addition, the results of the dimensionality reduction methods are shown in Section 3.3.

Based on the experiment of assessing the performance of noise estimation algorithms adopted in KMNF and OKMNF, it can be seen in Figure 4 that the estimated noise curves through the difference of spatial neighborhood used in KMNF show a strong relationship with land cover types in the scene, and the noise levels are not the same for the two subimages from the same image. There are no such problems when the noise is estimated by OKMNF through SSDC, SSDC$_1$ and SSDC$_2$. We can see that SSDC, SSDC$_1$ and SSDC$_2$ are more reliable noise estimation methods than that used in KMNF. Thus, we can adopt SSDC, SSDC$_1$ and SSDC$_2$ to estimate noise for OKMNF.

Based on the experiment of assessing the performance of dimensionality reduction methods from Section 3.3.1, it can be seen in Figure 8 that the feature quality of KMNF is worse than other dimensionality reduction methods. OKMNF, by considering SSDC, SSDC$_1$ or SSDC$_2$ for noise estimation, outperforms the other dimensionality reduction methods. It can be seen in Table 3, and Figures 6 and 9 that the classification results using transformed data by MNF are not always better than those of PCA on low dimension space. KMNF performs worse than KPCA. By considering the spectral and spatial de-correlation for noise estimation, linear OMNF always performs better than PCA and mostly better than MNF. OKMNF, by considering SSDC, $SSDC_1$ or $SSDC_2$ for noise estimation, outperforms the other dimensionality reduction methods (including linear OMNF and kernel MNF), with less sensitivity for parameter settings, as well as better performances for classification. This is because OKMNF not only can treat nonlinear characteristics well within the data but also take into account both spectral and spatial correlations for reliable noise estimation. Moreover, OKMNF-$SSDC_1$ and OKMNF-$SSDC_2$ perform better than OKMNF-SSDC. This indicates that, by incorporating more spatial neighbors, we enable better noise estimation, as well as improve the classification performances.

Based on the experiment of assessing the performance of dimensionality reduction methods from Section 3.3.2, it can be seen in Table 5, and Figures 11 and 13 that the performances of PCA, KPCA, MNF, and OMNF are very similar, and all of them are better than KMNF. When we optimized the KMNF method through SSDC, $SSDC_1$ and $SSDC_2$ noise estimation, the performance of KMNF was greatly improved. OKMNF gets much better results than KMNF, and also performs slightly better than the other four dimensionality reduction methods.

The two experimental results, based on the experiment of assessing the performance of dimensionality reduction methods, show that: (1) the greater the number of features extracted, the higher classification accuracy is; (2) it is better not to use KMNF for dimensionality reduction in many cases, the overall accuracies of ML classification after KMNF are lower than MNF and other dimensionality reduction methods; (3) our proposed OKMNF, OKMNF-SSDC, OKMNF-$SSDC_1$, and OKMNF-$SSDC_2$ perform much better than KMNF and mostly better than OMNF and MNF. These results imply that the dimensionality reduction results of KMNF are not suitable for image classification. By exploiting both spectral and spatial information for noise estimation, the proposed OKMNF benefits both dimensionality reduction and its post applications (e.g., classification). Compared to linear MNF, the proposed OKMNF not only has good performance in dimensionality reduction for classification but also does better in dealing with nonlinear problems.

To compare the efficiency of feature extraction methods, we took Indian Pines data as an example, and the consumed time (by extracting 30 features) of OKMNF-SSDC, OKMNF-$SSDC_1$, OKMNF-$SSDC_2$, KPCA, KMNF, OMNF, MNF, and PCA are 23.07 s, 25.27 s, 22.80 s, 1.03 s, 1.26 s, 22.87 s, 0.52 s and 0.20 s, respectively. We can find that the proposed OKMNF (OKMNF-SSDC, OKMNF-$SSDC_1$, OKMNF-$SSDC_2$) methods consume comparatively longer time but with better dimensionality reduction performances. However, we can use high performance computing techniques such as graphics processing unit to reduce the processing time of OKMNF. In real applications, the number of features kept for classification should be determined for both classification performance and computing cost. Too few features may not provide adequate class separability. On the other hand, more features might not always bring higher classification accuracy, which can be seen from the results listed in Table 3. It is important to use as few features as possible to avoid overfitting and minimise computational load.

5. Conclusions

This paper proposes an optimized KMNF for dimensionality reduction of hyperspectral imagery. The main reason affecting the original KMNF in dimensionality reduction is the larger error and the instability in estimating noise. Here, we conduct a comparative study for noise estimation algorithms using real images with different land cover types. The experimental results show that the combined spatial and spectral correlation information provides better results than the algorithms only using spatial neighborhood information. OKMNF adopts SSDC, $SSDC_1$, and $SSDC_2$ to stably estimate noise from hyperspectral images. Through this optimization, the overall accuracies of ML classification after OKMNF are much higher than those of KMNF, and the dimensionality reduction results of OKMNF are also better than OMNF, MNF, KPCA, and PCA in most situations. It can be concluded that OKMNF solves the problems existing in original KMNF well and improves the quality of dimensionality reduction. Moreover, OKMNF is valuable to reduce the dimensionality of nonlinear data. We can also expect that OKMNF will enhance the separability among endmember classes and improve the quality of spectral unmixing. Our future work will focus on incorporating more validations on other applications (e.g., target detection).

Acknowledgments: This research was supported by the National Natural Science Foundation of China under Grant No. 41571349, No. 91638201 and No. 41325004.

Author Contributions: Lianru Gao contributed to design the theoretical framework for the proposed methods and to the experimental analysis. Bin Zhao was primarily responsible for mathematical modeling and experimental design. Xiuping Jia improved the mathematical model and revised the paper. Wenzhi Liao provided important suggestions for improving technical quality of the paper. Bing Zhang proposed the original idea of the paper.

Conflicts of Interest: The authors declare no conflict of interest.

References

1. Goetz, A.F.H. Three decades of hyperspectral remote sensing of the Earth: A personal view. *Remote Sens. Environ.* **2009**, *113*, S5–S16. [CrossRef]
2. Plaza, A.; Benediktsson, J.A.; Boardman, J.W.; Brazile, J.; Bruzzone, L.; Camps-Valls, G.; Chanussot, J.; Fauvel, M.; Gamba, P.; Gualtieri, A.; et al. Recent advances in techniques for hyperspectral image processing. *Remote Sens. Environ.* **2009**, *113*, S110–S122. [CrossRef]
3. Hughes, G. On the mean accuracy of statistical pattern recognizers. *IEEE Trans. Inf. Theory* **1968**, *14*, 55–63. [CrossRef]
4. Liu, C.H.; Zhou, J.; Liang, J.; Qian, Y.T.; Li, H.X.; Gao, Y.S. Exploring structural consistency in graph regularized joint spectral-spatial sparse coding for hyperspectral image classification. *IEEE J. Sel. Top. Appl. Earth Obs. Remote Sens.* **2016**, *99*, 1–14. [CrossRef]
5. Jia, X.P.; Kuo, B.; Crawford, M.M. Feature mining for hyperspectral image classification. *Proc. IEEE* **2013**, *101*, 676–697.
6. Benediktsson, J.A.; Palmason, J.A.; Sveinsson, J.R. Classification of hyperspectral data from urban areas based on extended morphological profiles. *IEEE Trans. Geosci. Remote Sens.* **2005**, *43*, 480–491. [CrossRef]
7. Qian, Y.T.; Yao, F.T.; Jia, S. Band selection for hyperspectral imagery using affinity propagation. *IET Comput. Vis.* **2010**, *3*, 213–222. [CrossRef]
8. Falco, N.; Benediktsson, J.A.; Bruzzone, L. A study on the effectiveness of different independent component analysis algorithms for hyperspectral image classification. *IEEE J. Sel. Top. Appl. Earth Obs. Remote Sens.* **2014**, *7*, 2183–2199. [CrossRef]
9. Zabalza, J.; Ren, J.C.; Wang, Z.; Zhao, H.M.; Marshall, S. Fast implementation of singular spectrum analysis for effective feature extraction in hyperspectral imaging. *IEEE J. Sel. Top. Appl. Earth Obs. Remote Sens.* **2015**, *8*, 2845–2853. [CrossRef]
10. Xie, J.Y.; Hone, K.; Xie, W.X.; Gao, X.B.; Shi, Y.; Liu, X.H. Extending twin support vector machine classifier for multi-category classification problems. *Intell. Data Anal.* **2013**, *17*, 649–664.
11. Chen, W.S.; Huang, J.; Zou, J.; Fang, B. Wavelet-face based subspace LDA method to solve small sample size problem in face recognition. *Int. J. Wavelets Multiresolut. Inf. Process.* **2009**, *7*, 199–214. [CrossRef]
12. Gu, Y.F.; Feng, K. Optimized laplacian SVM with distance metric learning for hyperspectral image classification. *IEEE J. Sel. Top. Appl. Earth Obs. Remote Sens.* **2013**, *6*, 1109–1117. [CrossRef]
13. Ma, A.L.; Zhong, Y.F.; Zhao, B.; Jiao, H.Z.; Zhang, L.P. Semisupervised subspace-based DNA encoding and matching classifier for hyperspectral remote sensing imagery. *IEEE Trans. Geosci. Remote Sens.* **2016**, *54*, 4402–4418. [CrossRef]
14. Zhang, L.F.; Zhang, L.P.; Tao, D.C.; Huang, X. On combining multiple features for hyperspectral remote sensing image classification. *IEEE Trans. Geosci. Remote Sens.* **2012**, *50*, 879–893. [CrossRef]
15. Melgani, F.; Bruzzone, L. Classification of hyperspectral remote sensing images with support vector machines. *IEEE Trans. Geosci. Remote Sens.* **2004**, *42*, 1778–1790. [CrossRef]
16. Harsanyi, J.; Chang, C. Hyperspectral image classification and dimensionality reduction: An orthogonal subspace projection approach. *IEEE Trans. Geosci. Remote Sens.* **1994**, *32*, 779–785. [CrossRef]
17. Wang, Q.; Lin, J.; Yuan, Y. Salient band selection for hyperspectral image classification via manifold ranking. *IEEE Trans. Neural Netw. Learn. Syst.* **2016**, *27*, 1279–1289. [CrossRef] [PubMed]
18. Yuan, Y.; Lin, J.; Wang, Q. Dual clustering based hyperspectral band selection by contextual analysis. *IEEE Trans. Geosci. Remote Sens.* **2016**, *54*, 1431–1445. [CrossRef]

19. Yuan, Y.; Lin, J.; Wang, Q. Hyperspectral image classification via multi-task joint sparse representation and stepwise MRF optimization. *IEEE Trans. Cybern.* **2016**, *46*, 2966–2977.

20. Fukunaga, K. *Introduction to Statistical Pattern Recognition*; Academic Press: Cambridge, MA, USA, 1990.

21. Kuo, B.C.; Landgrebe, D.A. Nonparametric weighted feature extractionfor classification. *IEEE Trans. Geosci. Remote Sens.* **2004**, *42*, 1096–1105.

22. Ly, N.; Du, Q.; Fowler, J.E. Sparse graph-based discriminant analysis for hyperspectral imagery. *IEEE Trans. Geosci. Remote Sens.* **2014**, *52*, 3872–3884.

23. Ly, N.; Du, Q.; Fowler, J.E. Collaborative graph-based discriminant analysis for hyperspectral imagery. *IEEE J. Sel. Top. Appl. Earth Obs. Remote Sens.* **2014**, *7*, 2688–2696. [CrossRef]

24. Xue, Z.H.; Du, P.J.; Li, J.; Su, H.J. Simultaneous sparse graph embedding for hyperspectral image classification. *IEEE Trans. Geosci. Remote Sens.* **2015**, *53*, 6114–6133. [CrossRef]

25. Roger, E.R. Principal components transform with simple, automatic noise adjustment. *Int. J. Remote Sens.* **1996**, *17*, 2719–2727. [CrossRef]

26. Green, A.A.; Berman, M.; Switzer, P.; Craig, M.D. A transformation for ordering multispectral data in terms of image quality with implications for noise removal. *IEEE Trans. Geosci. Remote Sens.* **1998**, *26*, 65–74. [CrossRef]

27. Chen, P.H.; Jiao, L.C.; Liu, F.; Gou, S.P.; Zhao, J.Q.; Zhao, Z.Q. Dimensionality reduction of hyperspectral imagery using sparse graph learning. *IEEE J. Sel. Top. Appl. Earth Obs. Remote Sens.* **2016**, *99*, 1–17. [CrossRef]

28. Lee, J.B.; Woodyatt, S.; Berman, M. Enhancement of high spectral resolution remote-sensing data by a noise-adjusted principal components transform. *IEEE Trans. Geosci. Remote Sens.* **1990**, *28*, 295–304. [CrossRef]

29. Bachmann, C.M.; Ainsworth, T.L.; Fusina, R.A. Exploiting manifold geometry in hyperspectral imagery. *IEEE Trans. Geosci. Remote Sens.* **2005**, *43*, 441–454.

30. Mohan, A.; Sapiro, G.; Bosch, E. Spatially coherent nonlinear dimensionality reduction and segmentation of hyperspectral images. *IEEE Geosci. Remote Sens. Lett.* **2007**, *4*, 206–210. [CrossRef]

31. Nielsen, A.A. Kernel maximum autocorrelation factor and minimum noise fraction transformations. *IEEE Trans. Image Process.* **2011**, *20*, 612–624. [CrossRef] [PubMed]

32. Gomez-Chova, L.; Nielsen, A.A.; Camps-Valls, G. Explicit signal to noise ratio in reproducing kernel hilbert spaces. In Proceedings of the IEEE International Geoscience and Remote Sensing Symposium (IGARSS), Vancouver, BC, Canada, 24–29 July 2011; pp. 3570–3573.

33. Nielsen, A.A.; Vestergaard, J.S. Parameter optimization in the regularized kernel minimum noise fraction transformation. In Proceedings of the IEEE International Geoscience and Remote Sensing Symposium (IGARSS), Munich, Germany, 22–27 July 2012; pp. 370–373.

34. Shawe-Taylor, J.; Cristianini, N. *Kernel Methods for Pattern Analysis*; Cambridge University Press: New York, NY, USA, 2004.

35. Li, W.; Prasad, S.; Fowler, J.E. Decision fusion in kernel-induced spaces for hyperspectral image classification. *IEEE Trans. Geosci. Remote Sens.* **2014**, *52*, 3399–3411. [CrossRef]

36. Li, W.; Prasad, S.; Fowler, J.E.; Bruce, L.M. Locality preserving dimensionality reduction and classification for hyperspectral image analysis. *IEEE Trans. Geosci. Remote Sens.* **2012**, *50*, 1185–1198. [CrossRef]

37. Li, W.; Prasad, S.; Fowler, J.E.; Bruce, L.M. Locality-preserving discriminant analysis in kernel-induced feature spaces for hyperspectral image classification. *IEEE Geosci. Remote Sens. Lett.* **2011**, *8*, 894–898. [CrossRef]

38. Zhang, Y.H.; Prasad, S. Locality preserving composite kernel feature extraction for multi-source geospatial image analysis. *IEEE J. Sel. Top. Appl. Earth Obs. Remote Sens.* **2015**, *8*, 1385–1392. [CrossRef]

39. Kuo, B.C.; Ho, H.H.; Li, C.H.; Huang, C.C.; Taur, J.S. A kernel-based feature selection method for SVM with RBF kernel for hyperspectral image classification. *IEEE J. Sel. Top. Appl. Earth Obs. Remote Sens.* **2014**, *7*, 317–326.

40. Schölkopf, B.; Smola, A.; Müller, K.-R. Nonlinear component analysis as a kernel eigenvalue problem. *Neural Comput.* **1998**, *10*, 1299–1319. [CrossRef]

41. Gao, L.R.; Zhang, B.; Chen, Z.C.; Lei, L.P. Study on the issue of noise estimation in dimension reduction of hyperspectral images. In Proceedings of the IEEE Workshop on Hyperspectral Image and Signal Processing: Evolution in Remote Sensing (WHISPERS), Lisbon, Portugal, 6–9 June 2011; pp. 1–4.

42. Zhao, B.; Gao, L.R.; Zhang, B. An optimized method of kernel minimum noise fraction for dimensionality reduction of hyperspectral imagery. In Proceedings of the IEEE International Geoscience and Remote Sensing Symposium (IGARSS), Beijing, China, 10–15 July 2016; pp. 48–51.

43. Zhao, B.; Gao, L.R.; Liao, W.Z.; Zhang, B. A new kernel method for hyperspectral image feature extraction. *Geo-Spat. Inf. Sci.* **2017**, *99*, 1–11.

44. Bioucas-Dias, J.M.; Plaza, A.; Dobigeon, N.; Parente, M.; Du, Q.; Gader, P.; Chanussot, J. Hyperspectral unmixing overview: Geometrical, statistical, and sparse regression-based approaches. *IEEE J. Sel. Top. Appl. Earth Obs. Remote Sens.* **2012**, *5*, 354–379. [CrossRef]

45. Jia, S.; Xie, Y.; Tang, G.H.; Zhu, J.S. Spatial-spectral-combined sparse representation-based classification for hyperspectral imagery. *Soft Comput.* **2014**, 1–10. [CrossRef]

46. Chen, C.; Li, W.; Tramel, E.W.; Cui, M.S.; Prasad, S.; Fowler, J.E. Spectral–spatial preprocessing using multihypothesis prediction for noise-robust hyperspectral image classification. *IEEE J. Sel. Top. Appl. Earth Obs. Remote Sens.* **2014**, *7*, 1047–1059. [CrossRef]

47. Ghamisi, P.; Benediktsson, J.A.; Jon, A.; Cavallaro, G.; Plaza, A. automatic framework for spectral–spatial classification based on supervised feature extraction and morphological attribute profiles. *IEEE J. Sel. Top. Appl. Earth Obs. Remote Sens.* **2014**, *7*, 2147–2160. [CrossRef]

48. Gao, L.R.; Du, Q.; Yang, W.; Zhang, B. A comparative study on noise estimation for hyperspectral imagery. In Proceedings of the IEEE Workshop on Hyperspectral Image and Signal Processing: Evolution in Remote Sensing (WHISPERS), Shanghai, China, 4–7 June 2012; pp. 1–4.

49. Roger, E.R.; Arnold, F.J. Reliably estimating the noise in AVIRIS hyperspectral images. *Int. J. Remote Sens.* **1996**, *17*, 1951–1962. [CrossRef]

50. Gao, L.R.; Du, Q.; Zhang, B.; Yang, W.; Wu, Y.F. A comparative study on linear regression-based noise estimation for hyperspectral imagery. *IEEE J. Sel. Top. Appl. Earth Obs. Remote Sens.* **2013**, *6*, 488–498. [CrossRef]

51. Gao, L.R.; Zhang, B.; Sun, X.; Li, S.S.; Du, Q.; Wu, C.S. Optimized maximum noise fraction for dimensionality reduction of Chinese HJ-1A hyperspectral data. *EURASIP J. Adv. Signal Process.* **2013**, *1*, 1–12. [CrossRef]

52. Gao, L.R.; Zhang, B.; Zhang, X.; Zhang, W.J.; Tong, Q.X. A new operational method for estimating noise in hyperspectral images. *IEEE Geosci. Remote Sens. Lett.* **2008**, *5*, 83–87. [CrossRef]

53. Liu, X.; Zhang, B.; Gao, L.R.; Chen, D.M. A maximum noise fraction transform with improved noise estimation for hyperspectral images. *Sci. China Ser. F Inf. Sci.* **2009**, *52*, 1578–1587. [CrossRef]

54. Landgrebe, D.A.; Malaret, E. Noise in remote-sensing systems: The effect on classification error. *IEEE Trans. Geosci. Remote Sens.* **1986**, *24*, 294–299. [CrossRef]

55. Corner, B.R.; Narayanan, R.M.; Reichenbach, S.E. Noise estimation in remote sensing imagery using data masking. *Int. J. Remote Sens.* **2003**, *24*, 689–702. [CrossRef]

56. Gao, B.-C. An operational method for estimating signal to noise ratios from data acquired with imaging spectrometers. *Remote Sens. Environ.* **1993**, *43*, 23–33. [CrossRef]

57. Documentation for Minimum Noise Fraction Transformations. Available online: http://people.compute.dtu.dk/alan/software.html (accessed on 31 March 2017).

58. Wu, Y.F.; Gao, L.R.; Zhang, B.; Zhao, H.N.; Li, J. Real-time implementation of optimized maximum noise fraction transform for feature extraction of hyperspectral images. *J. Appl. Remote Sens.* **2014**, *8*, 1–16. [CrossRef]

59. Camps-Valls, G.; Bruzzone, L. Kernel-based methods for hyperspectral image classification. *IEEE Trans. Geosci. Remote Sens.* **2005**, *43*, 1351–1362. [CrossRef]

60. Acito, N.; Diani, M.; Corsini, G. Signal-dependent noise modeling andmodel parameter estimation in hyperspectral images. *IEEE Trans. Geosci. Remote Sens.* **2011**, *49*, 2957–2971. [CrossRef]

61. Zhang, X.J.; Xu, C.; Li, M.; Sun, X.L. Sparse and low-rank coupling image segmentation model via nonconvex regularization. *Int. J. Pattern Recognit. Artif. Intell.* **2015**, *29*, 1–22. [CrossRef]

62. Zhu, Z.X.; Jia, S.; He, S.; Sun, Y.W.; Ji, Z.; Shen, L.L. Three-dimensional Gabor feature extraction for hyperspectral imagery classification using a memetic framework. *Inf. Sci.* **2015**, *298*, 274–287. [CrossRef]

Article

Hypergraph Embedding for Spatial-Spectral Joint Feature Extraction in Hyperspectral Images

Yubao Sun, Sujuan Wang, Qingshan Liu *, Renlong Hang and Guangcan Liu

Jiangsu Key Laboratory of Big Data Analysis Technology, Jiangsu Collaborative Innovation Center on Atmospheric Environment and Equipment Technology, Nanjing University of Information Science and Technology, Nanjing 210044, China; sunyb@nuist.edu.cn (Y.S.); SuJuanWang_2018@163.com (S.W.); renlong_hang@163.com (R.H.); gcliu@nuist.edu.cn (G.L.)
* Correspondence: qsliu@nuist.edu.cn; Tel.: +86-187-5197-3295

Academic Editors: Qi Wang, Nicolas H. Younan, Carlos López-Martínez, Xiaofeng Li and Prasad S. Thenkabail
Received: 18 March 2017; Accepted: 14 May 2017; Published: 22 May 2017

Abstract: The fusion of spatial and spectral information in hyperspectral images (HSIs) is useful for improving the classification accuracy. However, this approach usually results in features of higher dimension and the curse of the dimensionality problem may arise resulting from the small ratio between the number of training samples and the dimensionality of features. To ease this problem, we propose a novel algorithm for spatial-spectral feature extraction based on hypergraph embedding. Firstly, each HSI pixel is regarded as a vertex and the joint of extended morphological profiles (EMP) and spectral features is adopted as the feature associated with the vertex. A hypergraph is then constructed by the K-Nearest-Neighbor method, in which each pixel and its most *K* relevant pixels are linked as one hyperedge to represent the complex relationships between HSI pixels. Secondly, the hypergraph embedding model is designed to learn a low dimensional feature with the reservation of geometric structure of HSI. An adaptive hyperedge weight estimation scheme is also introduced to preserve the prominent hyperedges by the regularization constraint on the weight. Finally, the learned low-dimensional features are fed to the support vector machine (SVM) for classification. The experimental results on three benchmark hyperspectral databases are presented. They highlight the importance of spatial–spectral joint features embedding for the accurate classification of HSI data. The weight estimation is better for further improving the classification accuracy. These experimental results verify the proposed method.

Keywords: feature extraction; hypergraph learning; morphological profiles; hyperedge weight estimation

1. Introduction

Hyperspectral imaging is an important mode of remote sensing imaging, which has been widely used in a diverse range of applications, including environment monitoring, urban planning, precision agriculture, geological exploration, etc. [1–3]. Most of these applications depend on the key problem of classifying the image pixels within hyperspectral imagery (HSI) into multiple categories, i.e., HSI classification, and extensive research efforts have been focused on this problem [4–9].

In HSI, each pixel contains hundreds of spectral bands from the visible to the infrared range of the electromagnetic spectrum. In general, the spectral signature of each pixel can be directly used as the feature for classification. However, due to the noise corruption and high correlation between spectral bands, the using of the spectral feature alone is often unable to obtain good classification results. It is well accepted that the HSI pixels within a small spatial neighborhood are often made up of the same materials. Thus, spatial contextual information is also useful for classification [10,11]. Landgrebe and Ketting proposed the well-known extraction and classification of homogeneous objects (ECHO) approach that partitioned the HSI pixels into homogeneous object and classified homogeneous object as different categories [12]. Later, Markov random field (MRF) modeling was widely adopted to capture the interpixel dependency through the neighbor system [13,14]. However, the optimization of MRF-based methods is very time-consuming. Due to the high dimensionality of HSI data, the computationally effective algorithm is desirable. In this sense, Pesaresi and Benediktsson [15] proposed the use of morphological transformations to build a morphological profile (MP) for extracting the structural information. Palmason et al. [16] extended the method proposed in [15] to the high-resolution hyperspectral data classification. They first extracted several principal components of the hyperspectral data. Then, the MP is constructed based on each selected principal component. At last, all MPs are jointed as extended MP (EMP), which is input into a neural network for classification. However, EMP was primarily designed for classification of urban structures and it did not fully utilize the spectral information in the data. Regrading this issue, Fauvel et al. [17] proposed fusing the morphological information and the original hyperspectral data, i.e., the two vectors of attributes are concatenated into one feature vector. The final classification is achieved by using a support vector machine classifier. Many other spectral and spatial joint features [18–22], such as 3D wavelet [18], spatial and spectral kernel [19], matrix-based discriminant subspace analysis [20], etc. are used for classification.

These joint features usually have a high dimension. In order to avoid the Hughes phenomenon, feature extraction and dimensionality reduction must be conducted before classification. Principal component analysis (PCA) and Fisher's linear discriminant analysis (LDA) [23] are two simple and effective approaches for dimension reduction. PCA aims at projecting the data along the directions of maximal variance. LDA is designed to generate the optimal linear projection matrix by maximizing the between-class distance while minimizing the within-class distance. Apart from these linear methods, many nonlinear versions have been developed, such as kernel PCA [24] and kernel LDA [25]. Some other feature extraction techniques have also been proposed, e.g., locality preserving projection (LPP) [26], independent component analysis (ICA) [27,28], and locally linear embedding (LLE) [29]. In particular, Yan et al. [30] proposed a general graph embedding (GE) model that seamlessly includes many existing feature extraction techniques. In this GE model, each data point is visualized as a vertex and a pairwise edge is used to represent the association relationship between two data points. They consider each feature extraction algorithm as an undirected weighted graph that describes geometric structures of data. GE algorithms have been widely explored for dimension reduction of HSI. Besides the geometric structures of data, sparsity is also explored to construct the graph embedding model. Luo et al. proposed constructing a graph with the sparse coefficients that reveals the sparse properties of data, and the transformation matrix is obtained for feature reduction [31]. In addition, by regarding different band sets as different views of land covers, multiview graph ensemble-based graph embedding is also utilized to promote the performance of graph embedding for hyperspectral image classification [32].

A hypergraph is a generalization of a pairwise graph. Different from pairwise graphs, each edge in a hypergraph is capable of connecting more than two vertices [33]. Thus, the complex relationships of the dataset can be captured by a hypergraph, and hypergraphs have been gaining more and more attention in recent years. Bu et al. [34] presented a hypergraph learning based music recommendation method with the use of hyperedges to exploit the complex social media information. A hypergraph semi-supervised learning model [35] was also proposed for image classification. Yuan et al. [36] utilized a hypergraph embedding model for HSI feature reduction, in which the spatial hypergraph models (SHs) are construed by selecting the K-nearest neighbors within the spatial region of the centroid pixel. Experimental results demonstrated that SH outperformed many existing feature extract methods for HSI classification, including raw spectral feature (RAW), PCA, LPP, LDA, nonparametric weighted feature extraction (NWFE) [37] and semi-supervised local discriminant analysis (SELD) [38]. However, SH is designed to learn the projection matrix for reducing the spectral feature. The spatial structure is not exploited for hypergraph embedding, which is not capable of simultaneously extracting the spectral-spatial features. Furthermore, the hyperedge weight is computed in advance and fixed in the hypergraph embedding procedure. As the discussion stated in [39,40], all of the hyperedges do not have the same effect on the learning procedure. Some hyperedges are not as informative as others. The hypergraph embedding should be enhanced by estimating the hyperedge weights adaptively.

In order to cope with these issues, we propose a novel algorithm for HSI spatial-spectral joint feature extraction. We combine the EMP and spectral features and adopt the KNN method to construct a hypergraph, where each sample and its K nearest neighbors are enclosed in one hyperedge. Similar to [36], a linear projection matrix $\mathbf{P}$ can be learnt by solving the hypergraph embedding model. However, in [36], the hyperedges' weights in the hypergraph embedded model are fixed. Inspired by [39,40], we introduce a scheme to update the weights adaptively to preserve the prominent hyperedge and further learn the low-dimensional structure. It helps improve the accuracy of the final HSI classification to a certain extent. Finally, the leaned low-dimensional features are fed to the SVM for classification. The flowchart of the proposed method is shown in Figure 1. Experiments conducted on three widely used types of HSI demonstrate that the proposed method achieves superior performance over many other feature extract methods for HSI classification.

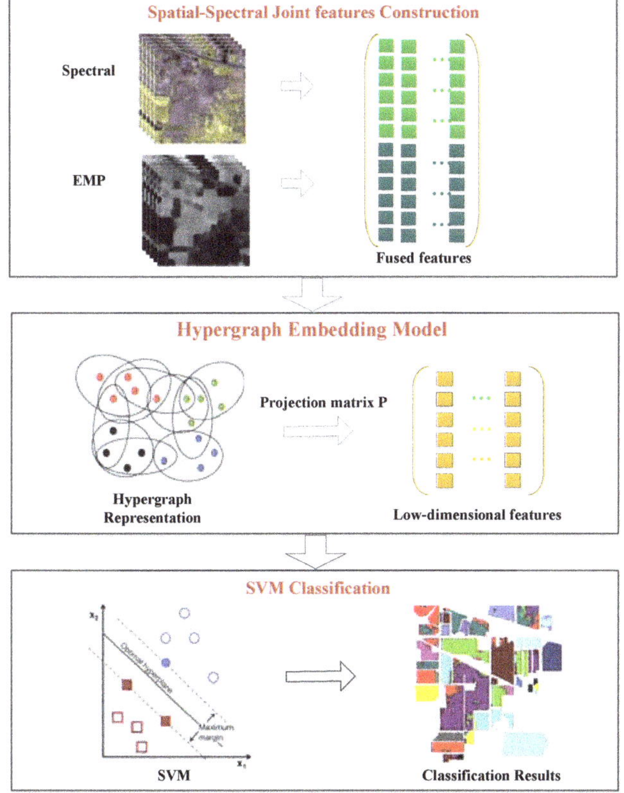

Figure 1. The flowchart of the proposed method.

2. Hypergraph Model

Denote a hypergraph as $\mathbf{G} = (\mathbf{V},\mathbf{E},\mathbf{W})$, which consists of a set of vertices $\mathbf{V}$, a family of hyperedge $\mathbf{E}$ and a weight matrix $\mathbf{W}$ of hyperedges. Different from pairwise graphs (For convenience, we call it a simple graph in the following), every hyperedge e_i can contain multiple vertices and is assigned a weight $w(e_i)$. As shown in Figure 2b, hyperedge e_1 is composed of vertices v_1, v_2 and v_3. e_2 is composed of vertices v_3 and v_4. e_3 is composed of vertices v_4, v_5, v_6 and v_7. $\mathbf{W}$ is a diagonal matrix of the hyperedge weights. The connection relationship of hypergraph **G** can be represented by an incidence matrix $\mathbf{H} \in \mathbf{R}^{|V| \times |E|}$, which can be defined as:

$$H_{ij} = \mathbf{H}(v_i, e_j) = \begin{cases} 1, & \text{if } v_i \in e_j, \\ 0, & \text{if } v_i \notin e_j. \end{cases} \tag{1}$$

The degree of vertex v and hyperedge e can be respectively represented as:

$$d(v_i) = \sum_{e_j \in \mathbf{E}} w(e) \mathbf{H}(v_i, e_j), \tag{2}$$

$$\delta(e_j) = \delta_j = \sum_{v_i \in \mathbf{V}} \mathbf{H}(v_i, e_j). \tag{3}$$

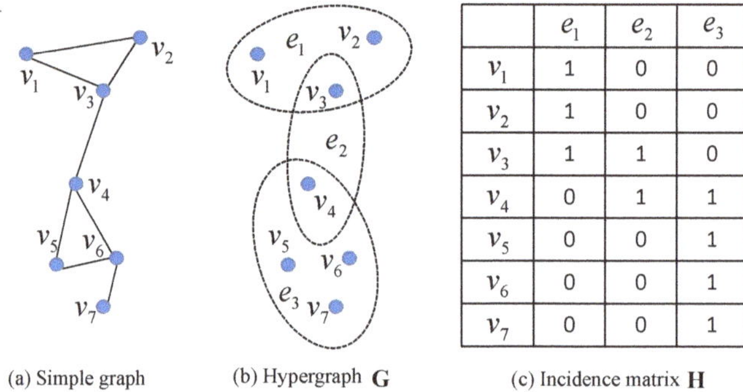

(a) Simple graph   (b) Hypergraph **G**   (c) Incidence matrix **H**

Figure 2. The example of graph and hypergraph (**a**) simple graph, each edge consists of only two data points; (**b**) hypergraph **G**, each hyperedge is marked by an ellipse and consists of at least two data points; (**c**) taking the seven vertices as example, **H** is the incidence matrix of **G**, whose values are usually binary.

According to the above definition, the main difference between hypergraphs and simple graphs is that every hyperedge can link more than two vertexes. Therefore, hypergraph is suitable to represent local group information and the high-order relationship of data. For example, considering seven vertices in Figure 2b, they are attributed to three groups and the corresponding incidence matrix is shown in Figure 2c. In terms of building a simple graph with these seven data points, the complex relations within the group are broken into multiple pairwise links. Some valuable information may be lost in this procedure; therefore, a simple graph can not describe the group structure well.

3. Hypergraph Embedding of Spatial-Spectral Joint Features

As shown in Figure 1, our algorithm mainly consists of three steps: spatial-spectral joint feature construction, hypergraph embedding and SVM classification.

3.1. Spatial-Spectral Joint Feature Construction

Following [16], we first extract several PCs from the original HSI $\mathbf{I}(x)$ and then build an MP from each of the PCs:

$$\mathbf{MP}(x) = \left\{ \mathbf{CP}_n(x), \ldots, \mathbf{I}(x), \ldots, \mathbf{OP}_n(x) \right\}, \tag{4}$$

where n is the number of the circular structural element (SE) with different radius sizes, $\mathbf{OP}_n(x)$ and $\mathbf{CP}_n(x)$ are the opening profile (OP) and the closing profile (CP) at the pixel x with an SE of a size n, respectively. Specifically, we have $\mathbf{CP}_0(x) = \mathbf{OP}_0(x) = \mathbf{I}(x)$. The MP of **I** contains the original image **I**,

n opening profile and n closing profile. Therefore, each MP is a $(2n+1)$-dimensional vector. Finally, all MPs are stacked together in one as EMP:

$$\mathbf{EMP}\,(x) = \left\{ \mathbf{MP}_{\mathrm{PC^1}}\,(x)\,, \mathbf{MP}_{\mathrm{PC^2}}\,(x)\,, \ldots, \mathbf{MP}_{\mathrm{PC^m}}\,(x)\right\}, \tag{5}$$

where m represents the number of PCs. The EMP is defined as an $m(2n+1)$-dimensional vector.

After obtaining the EMP feature, we represent the spatial and spectral joint feature of the i-th HSI pixel as

$$v_i = \begin{bmatrix} x_i \\ \mathrm{EMP}(x_i) \end{bmatrix} \in R^{\mathrm{m}(2\mathrm{n}+1)+d}, \tag{6}$$

where d is the number of the spectral bands. Denote the spectral features matrix of HSI as $\mathbf{X} = [x_1, x_2, \ldots, x_N] \in \mathbf{R}^{d \times N}$, EMP matrix of HSI as $\mathbf{EMP} = [\mathrm{EMP}(x_1), \cdots, \mathrm{EMP}(x_N)]$, where x_i is the i-th pixel, and N is the number of HSI pixels. Then, the joint feature matrix of HSI can be represented as: $\mathbf{V} = \begin{bmatrix} \mathbf{X} \\ \mathbf{EMP} \end{bmatrix} \in R^{(\mathrm{m}(2\mathrm{n}+1)+d) \times N}$.

3.2. Hypergraph Embedding

We take each pixel of HSI as a vertex and construct a hypergraph $\mathbf{G} = (\mathbf{V}, \mathbf{E}, \mathbf{W})$ to represent the correlation between HSI pixels. Each vertex v_i is associated with the spatial and spectral joint feature defined in Equation (6). The hypergraph G is constructed by the K-nearest neighbor method. In detail, each pixel v_i and its K nearest neighbors are enclosed as hyperedge e_i. Thus, hyperedge set $\mathbf{E} = \{e_1, e_2, \ldots, e_N\}$ contains N hyperedges. Meanwhile, the weight $w(e_i)$ of hyperedge e_i is defined as:

$$w\,(e_i) = \sum_{v_i, v_j \in e_i} \exp\left(-\frac{\left\|v_j - v_i\right\|_2^2}{2\sigma^2}\right), \tag{7}$$

where σ is the mean distance between all vertices and can be calculated by $\sigma = \frac{1}{N^2}\sum_i\sum_j d\,(v_i, v_j)$, $d\,(v_i, v_j)$ is the distance between vertex v_i and vertex v_j. The degree of vertex v_i and the degree of hyperedge e_i can be computed by Equations (2) and (3), respectively. Based on this definition, the more "compact" hyperedge (local group) is assigned with a higher weight.

Denote $\mathbf{D}_v$ and $\mathbf{D}_e$ as two diagonal matrices of the vertex degrees and the hyperedge degrees, respectively, and $\mathbf{P} \in \mathbf{R}^{(m(2n+1)+d) \times u}$ (generally, $m\,(2n+1)+d >> u$) as the linear projection matrix. The objective of hypergraph embedding model is to learn the projection matrix $\mathbf{P}$ for reducing the feature dimension with the preservation of geometric property in the original space. The objective function is formulated as:

$$\min_{\mathbf{P}^T \mathbf{VD}_v \mathbf{V}^T \mathbf{P}=1} \frac{1}{2} \sum_{e \in \mathbf{E}} \sum_{v_i, v_j \in e} \frac{w\,(e)\,h\,(v_i, e)\,h\,(v_j, e)}{\delta\,(e)} \left\|\mathbf{P}^T v_i - \mathbf{P}^T v_j\right\|_2^2$$

$$= \frac{1}{2} \sum_{k=1}^{N} \sum_{i,j=1}^{N} \frac{w_k h_{ik} h_{jk}}{\delta_k} \left\|\mathbf{P}^T v_i - \mathbf{P}^T v_j\right\|_2^2 \tag{8}$$

$$= \mathrm{trace}\left(\mathbf{P}^T \mathbf{VLV}^T \mathbf{P}\right),$$

where $\mathbf{L} = \mathbf{D}_v - \mathbf{HWD}_e^{-1}\mathbf{H}^T$ is the hypergraph laplacian matrix. The constraint $\mathbf{P}^T \mathbf{VD}_v \mathbf{V}^T \mathbf{P} = 1$ is used for scale normalization of the low-dimensional representations. This objective function induces the constraint that if v_i and v_j are similar and belong to the same hyperedge, they should also be adjacent in embedded space. In addition, an efficient hypergraph weight estimation scheme is proposed to preserve the prominent hyperedges. Assuming that $w = (w_1, w_2, \ldots, w_N)^T$ is composed of the elements lying in the main diagonal of $\mathbf{W}$, we enforce $\mathbf{1}_N^T w = 1$ and add an l_2 norm regularizer on w. Then, our proposed embedding model is finally defined as:

$$\{\mathbf{P}^*, w^*\} = \arg \min_{\mathbf{P}^T \mathbf{VD}_v \mathbf{V}^T \mathbf{P}=1} \left\{ \mathrm{trace}\left(\mathbf{P}^T \mathbf{VLV}^T \mathbf{P}\right) + \lambda \|w\|^2 \right\} \quad \text{s.t. } \mathbf{1}_N^T w = 1. \tag{9}$$

3.3. Optimization Algorithm

The objective function Equation (9) is a multiple variables optimization problem, and it is non-convex with respect to w and $\mathbf{P}$ jointly. However, it is convex with either of them individually when the other is fixed. Thus, an alternative iteration strategy is adopted to get the solution of Equation (9). We first initialize w according to Equation (7). With w fixed, we optimize $\mathbf{P}$ according to Equation (8). The solution of Equation (8) is to find the eigenvectors corresponding to the first u largest eigenvalues of the matrix $\left(\mathbf{VLV}^T\right)^{-1}\left(\mathbf{VD}_v\mathbf{V}^T\right)$.

Next, fix $\mathbf{P}$ and optimize w:

$$\arg \min_w \left\{ \mathrm{trace}\left(\mathbf{P}^T \mathbf{VLV}^T \mathbf{P}\right) + \lambda \|w\|^2 \right\} \quad \text{s.t. } \mathbf{1}_N^T w = 1. \tag{10}$$

In this paper, we employ the Lagrangian algorithm to optimize the Equation (10). The Lagrangian function of the objective function (10) is defined as:

$$\begin{aligned}
\psi\left(w, c\right) &= \mathrm{trace}\left(\mathbf{P}^T \mathbf{VLV}^T \mathbf{P}\right) + \lambda w^T w + c\left(\mathbf{1}_N^T w - 1\right) \\
&= \frac{1}{2} \sum_{k=1}^{N} \sum_{i,j=1}^{N} \frac{w_k h_{ik} h_{jk}}{\delta_k} \left\| \mathbf{P}^T v_i - \mathbf{P}^T v_j \right\|_2^2 + \lambda w^T w + c\left(\mathbf{1}_N^T w - 1\right).
\end{aligned} \tag{11}$$

The partial derivatives of ψ w.r.t. $w_i, i = 1, 2, \cdots, M$ are given by:

$$\frac{\partial \psi\left(w, c\right)}{\partial w_k} = \frac{1}{2} \sum_{i,j=1}^{N} \frac{h_{ik} h_{jk}}{\delta_k} \left\| \mathbf{P}^T v_i - \mathbf{P}^T v_j \right\|_2^2 + 2\lambda w_k + c = 0. \tag{12}$$

By simplifying Equation (12), w_k can be calculated as:

$$w_k = -\frac{\frac{1}{2} \sum\limits_{i,j=1}^{N} \frac{h_{ik} h_{jk}}{\delta_k} \left\| \mathbf{P}^T v_i - \mathbf{P}^T v_j \right\|_2^2 + c}{2\lambda}. \tag{13}$$

According to the constraint $\mathbf{1}_N^T w = 1$, the Lagrange multiplier can be calculated as:

$$c = -\frac{1}{N}\left[\frac{1}{2} \sum_{k=1}^{N} \sum_{i,j=1}^{N} \frac{h_{ik} h_{jk}}{\delta_k} \left\| \mathbf{P}^T v_i - \mathbf{P}^T v_j \right\|_2^2 + 2\lambda\right]. \tag{14}$$

By substituting Equation (14) into Equation (13), we can obtain w finally.

Following this iteration process, w and $\mathbf{P}$ are alternately optimized until the maximal iteration number is reached or the relative difference of objective function value of Equation (9) is smaller than a given tolerance const ε, i.e.,

$$\frac{|f(t+1) - f(t)|}{|f(t)|} \leqslant \varepsilon, \tag{15}$$

where $f(t+1)$ and $f(t)$ is the function value of Equation (9) at iteration $t+1$ and t, respectively. In addition, we can obtain the final projection matrix $\mathbf{P}^*$. At last, the joint feature set $\mathbf{V}$ is reduced as a low-dimensional feature set $\mathbf{Y} = \left[(\mathbf{P}^*)^T v_1, \ldots, (\mathbf{P}^*)^T v_N\right]$, which is then transmitted into an SVM classifier. Based on the above analysis, the proposed method can be summarized in Algorithm 1.

Algorithm 1: The proposed method (denoted as SSHG*) for HSI classification.

Input: Data matrix $\mathbf{X}$, the reduced dimensionality u, the nearest neighbors number K and regularization parameter λ.

Output: The class-label vector f.

1 Normalize all the features to [0,1].

2 Build the MP from each of the PCs: $\mathbf{MP}(x) = \{\mathbf{CP}_n(x), \ldots, \mathbf{I}(x), \ldots, \mathbf{OP}_n(x)\}$.

3 Obtain the EMP by stacking all MPs: $\mathbf{EMP}(x) = \{\mathbf{MP}_{\mathrm{PC}^1}(x), \mathbf{MP}_{\mathrm{PC}^2}(x), \ldots, \mathbf{MP}_{\mathrm{PC}^m}(x)\}$.

4 Represent the new stacked joint feature set as:

$$\mathbf{V} = [\mathbf{X}; \mathbf{EMP}] = [v_1, v_2, \ldots, v_N] \in \mathbf{R}^{(m(2n+1)+d) \times N}.$$

5 Compute the incidence matrix $\mathbf{H} \in \mathbf{R}^{|\mathbf{V}| \times |\mathbf{E}|}$ by KNN, set $\mathbf{H}(v, e) = 1$, if $v \in e$, otherwise, $\mathbf{H}(v, e) = 0$.

6 Construct the hypergraph G and Calculate the weight of hyperedge e_i:

$$w(e_i) = \sum_{v_j \in e_i} \exp\left(-\frac{\|v_j - v_i\|_2^2}{2\sigma^2}\right), \text{ the vertex degree: } d(v_j) = \sum_{e_i \in \mathbf{E}} w(e_i)\mathbf{H}(v_j, e_i), \text{ and the}$$

hyperedge degree: $\delta(e_i) = \sum_{v_j \in \mathbf{V}} \mathbf{H}(v_j, e_i)$.

7 Obtain the projection matrix $\mathbf{P}$ by optimizing Equation (8)

8 Solve Equation (10) and obtain the hyperedge weights computed as Equation (13).

9 With the new hyperedge weights, update $\mathbf{D}_v$, $\mathbf{L}$ and $\mathbf{W}$.

10 Repeat the steps 7–9 until the convergence criterion 15 is met or the maximal iteration number is reached.

11 Find the final projection matrix $\mathbf{P}^*$.

12 Project the joint feature set into a low-dimensional feature set: $\mathbf{Y} = \left[(\mathbf{P}^*)^T v_1, \ldots, (\mathbf{P}^*)^T v_N\right]$.

13 Feed the learned low-dimensional feature set $\mathbf{Y}$ into the SVM for classification.

14 **return** the class-label vector f.

---

4. Experiments and Discussion

4.1. Data Sets

In order to verify the performance of our proposed method, we conduct the experiments on the following three benchmark datasets.

(1) Indian Pines data set—the first data set was acquired by the AVIRIS sensor over the Indian Pines test site in Northwestern Indiana, USA. The size of the image is 145 pixels $\times$ 145 pixels with a spatial resolution of 20 m per pixel. Twenty water absorption bands (104–108, 150–163, 220) were removed, and the 200-band image is used for experiments. Sixteen classes of interest are considered.

(2) Pavia University data set—the second data set was acquired by the ROSIS sensor during a flight campaign over Pavia, northern Italy. The size of the image is 610 pixels $\times$ 340 pixels with a spatial resolution of 1.3 m per pixel. Twelve channels were removed due to noise. The remaining 103 spectral bands are processed. Nine classes of interest are considered.

(3) Botswana data set—the third data set was acquired by the NASA EO-1 satellite over the Okavango Delta, Botswana, in 2001. The size of the image is 1476 pixels $\times$ 256 pixels with a spatial resolution of 30 m per pixel. Uncalibrated and noisy bands that cover water absorption features were removed, and the remaining 145 bands are used for experiment. Fourteen classes of interest are considered.

4.2. Experimental Setting

In order to demonstrate the effectiveness of adaptive weight estimation, we implement our algorithm as two versions. One is SSHG, which only utilizes the KNN hypergraph model for dimension reduction of the stacked feature set without adaptive weight estimation. The other is SSHG* shown in Algorithm 1. They are compared with the following feature extraction methods: (1) the method by using PCA to extract spectral features (denoted as PCA); (2) the method by using EMP features without dimension reduction (denoted as EMP); (3) the method [17] stacking the EMP and the spectral features as feature without dimension reduction (denoted as EMPSpe); and (4) the spatial hypergraph embedding method proposed in [36] (denoted as SH). In order to facilitate comparisons with these competing feature extraction methods, we adopt the overall accuracy (OA), the average accuracy (AA), the per-class accuracy and Kappa coefficient (κ) to evaluate the classification performance. Furthermore, the SVM classifier with Gaussian kernel is adopted to classify all of the aforementioned feature data of these feature extraction methods. The grid search tool is used to select the parameters of the optimal penalty term and Gaussian kernel variance in SVM within the given sets $\{2^{-10}, ..., 2^{10}\}$ and $\{2^{-10}, ..., 2^{10}\}$, respectively. The one-against-all strategy is adopted for multi-class classification. Regarding the three data sets, we select 15 samples from each class randomly to form a training set and the remaining samples are used as the test set. The training sample selection and the classification process are repeated ten times to reduce the bias induced by random sampling. We retain the average results. The parameters setting of SH is the same as the original paper [36]. With respect to our algorithm, the tolerance const ε is set as 1×10^{-3} and the regularization parameter λ is set as 100. The number of nearest neighbors K is selected as 10, 15, 5 for Indian Pines, Pavia University and Botswana data sets, respectively.

4.3. Experimental Results

The classification results of various methods upon three types of HSI are reported in Tables 1–3, respectively. The best results are highlighted with bold fonts. The number in brackets corresponds to the optimal dimensionality of reduced features. Classification maps of these different approaches are shown in Figures 3–5, respectively. According to the experimental results, our proposed method achieves the highest OA, AA, and κ among all of the competing methods, which shows the effectiveness of our feature extraction algorithm. The effectiveness of our SSHG method owes much to the hypergraph embedding of spatial and spectral joint features.

Table 1. Classification accuracy of various algorithms on the Indian Pines image.

Class	PCA (25)	EMP (27)	EMPSpe (227)	SH (22)	SSHG (44)	SSHG* (44)
1	91.61	98.71	**99.03**	94.87	98.06	98.06
2	47.36	61.46	64.28	**82.59**	72.53	73.96
3	48.60	78.75	77.14	73.50	84.06	**84.85**
4	68.29	95.90	91.76	91.32	96.76	**97.21**
5	75.75	87.78	88.85	**92.12**	89.83	90.32
6	85.37	91.48	92.36	**98.22**	93.93	94.04
7	91.54	99.23	99.23	**100**	**100**	**100**
8	79.52	98.47	98.92	98.31	99.57	**99.63**
9	96.00	**100**	**100**	**100**	**100**	**100**
10	56.22	74.23	71.61	**87.51**	76.81	77.68
11	49.62	69.51	71.02	64.41	**75.65**	75.57
12	45.43	75.67	77.40	84.31	84.33	**84.79**
13	93.47	98.68	99.00	**99.49**	99.37	99.37
14	69.55	93.25	94.83	94.84	97.57	**97.58**
15	46.42	95.96	95.85	75.07	97.74	**97.76**
16	89.62	97.56	98.46	98.75	99.74	**99.87**
OA	58.90	79.14	79.88	82.33	84.36	**84.75**
AA	70.90	88.54	88.73	89.71	91.62	**91.92**
kappa	53.88	76.42	77.24	80.06	82.27	**82.73**

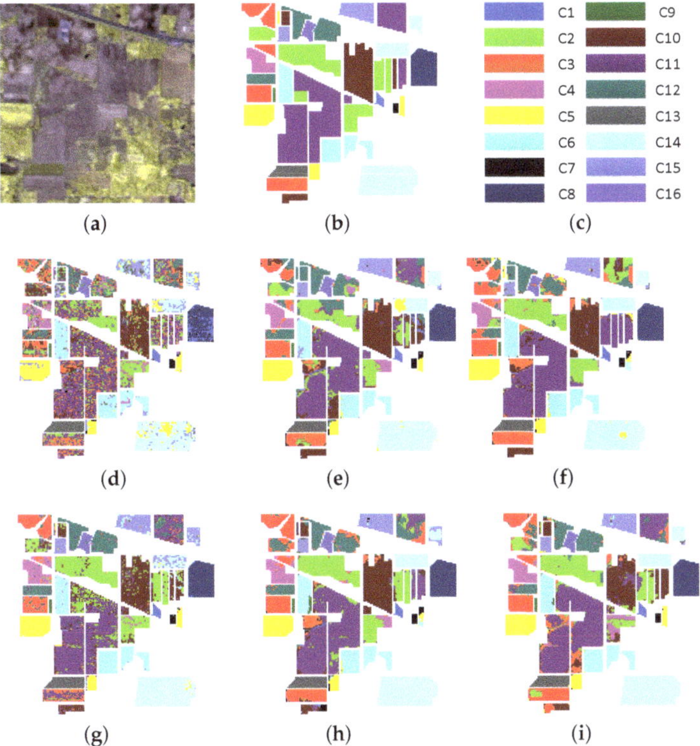

Figure 3. Indian Pines. (**a**) three-channel color composite image with bands 65, 52, 36; (**b,c**) ground-truth map and class labels; (**d–i**) classification maps of PCA, EMP, EMPSpe, SH, SSHG, SSHG*, respectively.

Table 2. Classification accuracy of various algorithms on the Pavia university image.

Class	PCA (10)	EMP (27)	EMPSpe (130)	SH (30)	SSHG (46)	SSHG* (46)
1	66.21	82.40	81.57	70.33	81.67	**82.70**
2	65.14	83.44	84.09	82.13	**92.02**	91.44
3	70.00	77.04	77.79	72.37	**80.47**	80.08
4	85.26	97.42	**97.44**	89.58	93.93	94.90
5	99.37	99.76	99.75	99.61	99.79	**99.80**
6	69.16	78.91	80.16	**91.76**	86.50	89.63
7	90.45	94.07	93.28	92.68	94.16	**94.44**
8	71.34	**86.12**	85.30	72.16	83.07	84.06
9	**99.72**	96.04	97.44	99.51	98.26	98.15
OA	70.59	84.77	85.05	81.88	89.01	**89.43**
AA	79.63	88.35	88.53	85.57	89.99	**90.58**
kappa	63.20	80.38	80.78	76.80	85.64	**86.24**

Comparing the EMP and EMPSpe method, we can find that EMPSpe method is always slightly better than EMP due to the fusion of EMP and spectral features for classification. As mentioned in [17], the stacked EMP and spectral features are transformed to low dimensional features by the decision boundary feature extraction (DBFE) and NWFE methods before classification. However, the DBFE and NWFE did not bring about the effective improvement of algorithm performance. SH utilized the hypergraph embedding model for feature reduction. Compared with PCA, the SH method has much better classification performance, which verifies the capacity of the hypergraph to capture the intrinsic complex relationships between HSI pixels. However, SH utilized only the spectral similarity for finding the nearest neighbors within a given spatial region. The superiority of SSHG over SH demonstrates that the embedding of EMP and spectral features is better for HSI classification. Specifically, our SSHG method can extract the rich spatial structures in the Pavia University data and achieve the maximum improvement upon this data. SSHG* obtains better classification results than SSHG, which demonstrates that adaptive hypergraph weight estimation is also beneficial for improving the classification accuracy.

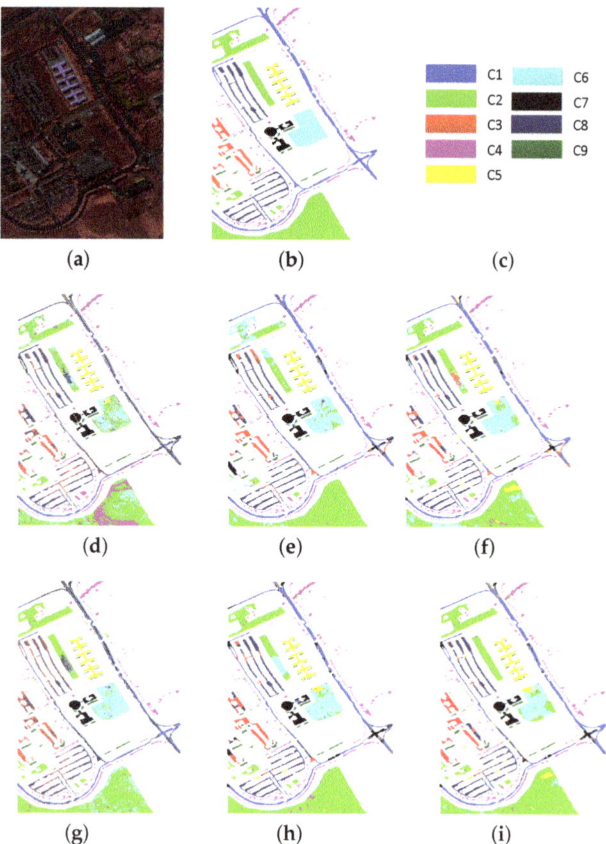

Figure 4. Pavia university. (**a**) three-channel color composite image with bands 102, 56, 31; (**b**,**c**) ground-truth map and class labels; (**d**–**i**) classification maps of PCA, EMP, EMPSpe, SH, SSHG, SSHG*, respectively.

There are two parameters, i.e., K and u, in our proposed method. The parameter K is the number of nearest neighbors, which determines how many pixels are included in the hyperedge. u is the dimensionality of the embedded low-dimensional feature. To evaluate their effects on the classification performance, we conduct the experiments on the above three datasets. We firstly fix the reduced dimensionality as $u = 40$ and evaluate the influence of different K on the OA. As seen in Figure 6, when K is set as 10, 15, 5 for Indian Pines, Pavia University and Botswana data sets, respectively, the OA achieves the highest value. Taken as a whole, $[5, 15]$ is usually a good range for the selection of parameter K. We then fix the K as 10, 15, 5 for the three datasets, respectively, and evaluate the influence of different us on the OA. Figure 7 shows the changes of OA with the reduced dimensions on three types of HSI. We can see that the inflection point of classification results is around the dimensionality 25 for these three HSIs, and there was no significant improvement on the classification results if the dimension continues to grow up.

Table 3. Classification accuracy of various algorithms on the Botswana image.

Class	PCA (22)	EMP (27)	EMPSpe (172)	SH (25)	SSHG (34)	SSHG* (34)
1	**100**	99.92	99.89	**100**	**100**	**100**
2	96.51	**100**	97.99	**100**	99.68	98.05
3	96.19	94.79	95.85	99.15	96.76	**100**
4	99.00	95.85	98.83	**99.50**	98.41	93.27
5	81.10	79.76	82.32	82.86	91.79	**96.38**
6	69.29	81.73	88.34	81.89	96.37	**99.22**
7	96.31	97.70	99.20	98.77	99.72	**99.95**
8	98.40	99.63	99.48	99.47	**100**	97.42
9	79.93	92.34	94.47	96.32	98.86	**99.79**
10	95.28	98.33	97.98	99.57	**99.92**	97.97
11	83.45	97.24	95.19	97.59	94.97	**99.88**
12	93.98	99.94	99.88	88.55	**100**	99.49
13	89.33	99.60	98.37	94.47	**99.92**	99.75
14	98.75	99.25	98.35	**100**	91.36	99.63
OA	89.83	94.69	95.65	95.10	97.79	**98.38**
AA	91.25	95.43	96.15	95.58	97.70	**98.63**
kappa	88.98	94.24	95.36	94.68	97.60	**98.24**

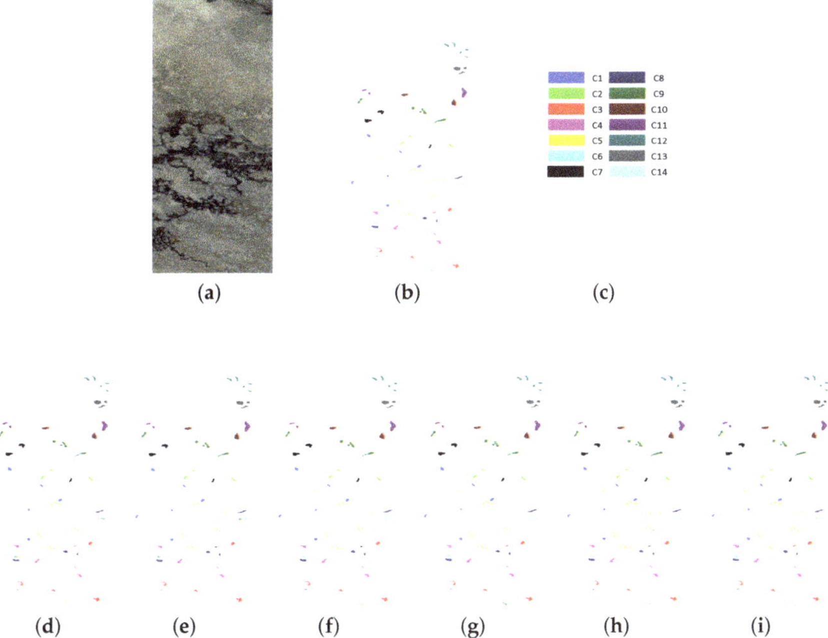

Figure 5. Botswana. (**a**) three-channel color composite image with bands 65, 52, 36; (**b**,**c**) ground-truth map and class labels; (**d–i**) classification maps of PCA, EMP, EMPSpe, SH, SSHG, SSHG*, respectively.

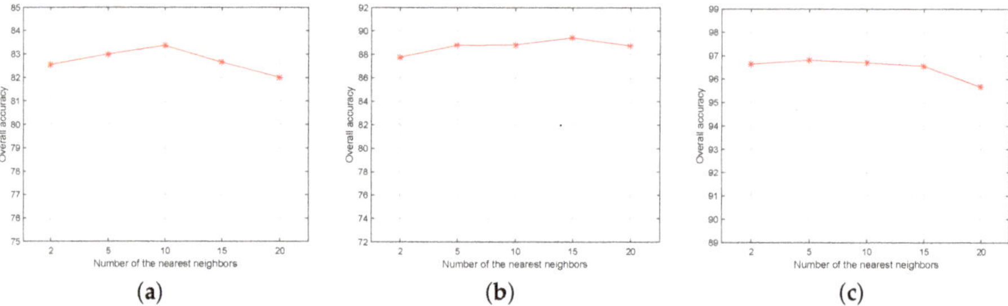

(a) (b) (c)

Figure 6. Effects of the number K of nearest neighbors on OA. (**a**) Indian Pines; (**b**) Pavia University; (**c**) Botswana.

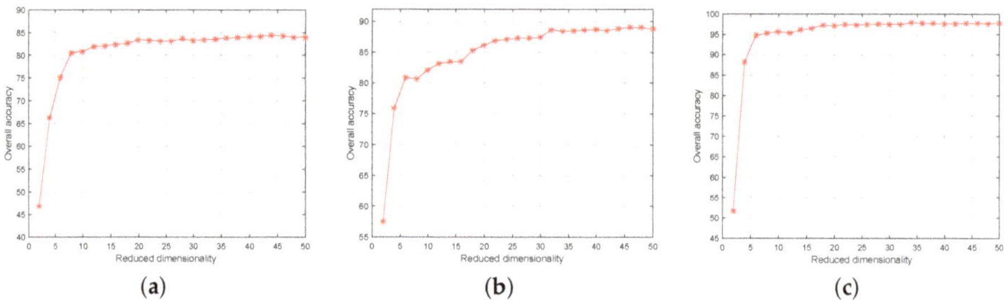

(a) (b) (c)

Figure 7. Effects on the reduced dimensions. (**a**) Indian Pines; (**b**) Pavia University; (**c**) Botswana.

5. Conclusions

In this paper, we propose a novel algorithm for spatial-spectral feature extraction based on hypergraph learning. A hypergraph is constructed by the KNN method and the embedding operation is conducted to transform the joint EMP and spectral features into the low-dimensional representation. Meanwhile, an efficient hypergraph weight estimation scheme is adopted to preserve the prominent hyperedges. Classification is performed with SVM using the embedded features. The experimental results on three benchmark hyperspectral datasets verify that our embedded representation can enhance the classification accuracy effectively. The hypergraph weight estimation can further improve the accuracy of HSI classification.

Acknowledgments: This work was supported in part by the Natural Science Foundation of China under Grant Numbers: 61672292, 61532009, 61622305, 61502238, 61300162 and, in part, by the Six Talent Peaks Project of Jiangsu Province, China, under Grant DZXX-037.

Author Contributions: Yubao Sun and Sujuan Wang contributed equally to this work. They proposed the algorithm and performed the experiments. Qingshan Liu supervised the study, analyzed the results and gave insightful suggestions for the manuscript. Sujuan Wang and Yubao Sun drafted the manuscript. Guangcan Liu and Renlong Hang contributed to the revision of the manuscript. All authors read and approved the submitted manuscript.

Conflicts of Interest: The authors declare no conflict of interest.

References

1. Clement, A. Advances in remote sensing of agriculture: context description, existing operational monitoring systems and major information needs. *Remote Sens.* **2013**, *5*, 949–981, doi:10.3390/rs5020949.
2. Shafri, H. Z. M.; Taherzadeh, E.; Mansor, S.; Ashurov, R. Hyperspectral remote sensing of urban areas: an overview of techniques and applications. *Res. J. Appl. Sci. Eng. Technol.* **2012**, *4*, 1557–1565.

3. Abbate, G.; Fiumi, L.; De Lorenzo, C.; Vintila, R. Avaluation of remote sensing data for urban planning. Applicative examples by means of multispectral and hyperspectral data. In Proceedings of the GRSS/ISPRS Joint Workshop on Remote Sensing and Data Fusion over Urban Areas, Berlin, Germany, 22–23 May 2003; pp. 201–205.

4. Wu, Z.; Wang, Q.; Plaza, A.; Li, J.; Sun, L. Parallel spatial-spectral hyperspectral image classification with sparse representation and markov random fields on GPUs. *IEEE J. Sel. Top. Appl. Earth Obs. Remote Sens.* **2015**, *8*, 2926–2938, doi:10.1109/JSTARS.2015.2413931.

5. Yuan, Y.; Lin, J.; Wang, Q. Hyperspectral image classification via multitask joint sparse representation and stepwise MRF optimization. *IEEE Trans. Cybern.* **2016**, *46*, 2966–2977, doi:10.1109/TCYB.2015.2484324.

6. Wang, Q.; Lin, J.; Yuan, Y. Salient band selection for hyperspectral image classification via manifold ranking. *IEEE IEEE Trans. Neural Netw. Learn. Syst.* **2016**, *27*, 1279–1289, doi:10.1109/TNNLS.2015.2477537.

7. Hang, R.; Liu, Q.; Sun, Y.; Yuan, X.; Pei, H.; Plaza, J.; Plaza, A. Robust matrix discriminative analysis for feature extraction from hyperspectral images. *IEEE J. Sel. Top. Appl. Earth Obs. Remote Sens.* **2017**, *10*, 2002–2011, doi:10.1109/JSTARS.2017.2658948.

8. Wu, Z.; Li, Y.; Plaza, A.; Li, J.; Xiao, F.; Wei, Z. Parallel and distributed dimensionality reduction of hyperspectral data on cloud computing architectures. *IEEE J. Sel. Top. Appl. Earth Obs. Remote Sens.* **2016**, *9*, 2270–2278, doi:10.1109/JSTARS.2016.2542193.

9. Sun, Y.; Hang, R.; Liu, Q.; Zhu, F.; Pei, H. Graph-Regularized low rank representation for aerosol optical depth retrieval. *Int. J. Remote Sens.* **2016**, *37*, 5749–5762, doi:10.1080/01431161.2016.1249302.

10. Fauvel, M.; Tarabalka, Y.; Benediktsson, J.A.; Chanussot, J.; Tilton, J.C. Advances in spectral-spatial classification of hyperspectral images. *Proc. IEEE* **2013**, *101*, 652–675, doi:10.1109/JPROC.2012.2197589.

11. Yuan, Y.; Lin, J.; Wang, Q. Dual-Clustering-Based hyperspectral band selection by contextual analysis. *IEEE Trans. Geosci. Remote Sens.* **2016**, *54*, 1431–1445, doi:10.1109/TGRS.2015.2480866.

12. Kettig, R.L.; Landgrebe, D.A. Classification of multispectral image data by extraction and classification of homogeneous objects. *IEEE Trans. Geosci. Electron.* **1976**, *14*, 19–26, doi:10.1109/TGE.1976.294460.

13. Descombes, X.; Sigelle, M.; Preteu, F. GMRF parameter estimation in a non-stationary framework by a renormalization technique: application to remote sensing imaging. *IEEE Trans. Image Process.* **1999**, *8*, 490–503, doi:10.1109/83.753737.

14. Jackson, Q.; Landgrebe, D.A. Adaptive bayesian contextual classification based on markov random fields. *IEEE Trans. Geosci. Remote Sens.* **2002**, *40*, 2454–2463, doi:10.1109/TGRS.2002.805087.

15. Pesaresi, M.; Benediktsson, J.A. A new approach for the morphological segmentation of high-resolution satellite imagery. *IEEE Trans. Geosci. Remote Sens.* **2001**, *39*, 309–320, doi:10.1109/36.905239.

16. Benediktsson, J.A.; Palmason, J.A.; Sveinsson, J.R. Classification of hyperspectral data from urban areas based on extended morphological profiles. *IEEE Trans. Geosci. Remote Sens.* **2005**, *43*, 480–491, doi:10.1109/TGRS.2004.842478.

17. Fauvel, M.; Benediktsson, J.A.; Chanussot, J.; Sveinsson, J.R. Spectral and spatial classification of hyperspectral data using svms and morphological profiles. *IEEE Trans. Geosci. Remote Sens.* **2008**, *46*, 3804–3814, doi:10.1109/TGRS.2008.922034.

18. Guo, X.; Huang, X.; Zhang, L. Three-Dimensional wavelet texture feature extraction and classification for multi/hyperspectral imagery. *IEEE Geosci. Remote Sens. Lett.* **2014**, *11*, 2183–2187, doi:10.1109/LGRS.2014.2323963.

19. Li, L.; Marpu, P.R.; Plaza, A.; Bioucas-Dias, J.M. Generalized composite kernel framework for hyperspectral image classification. *IEEE Trans. Geosci. Remote Sens.* **2013**, *51*, 4816–4829, doi:10.1109/TGRS.2012.2230268.

20. Hang, R.; Liu, Q.; Song, H.; Sun, Y. Matrix-based discriminant subspace ensemble for hyperspectral image spatial–spectral feature fusion. *IEEE Trans. Geosci. Remote Sens.* **2016**, *54*, 783–794, doi:10.1109/TGRS.2015.2465899.

21. Fang, L.; Li, S.; Kang, X.; Benediktsson, J.A. Spectral-spatial hyperspectral image classification via multiscale adaptive sparse representation. *IEEE Trans. Geosci. Remote Sens.* **2014**, *52*, 7738–7749, doi:10.1109/TGRS.2014.2318058.

22. Chen, Y.; Lin, Z.; Zhao, X.; Wang, G.; Gu, Y. Deep learning-based classification of hyperspectral data. *IEEE J. Sel. Top. Appl. Earth Obs.* **2014**, *7*, 2094–2107, doi:10.1109/JSTARS.2014.2329330.

23. Du, Q. Modified fisher's linear discriminant analysis for hyperspectral imagery. *IEEE Geosci. Remote Sens. Lett.* **2007**, *4*, 503–507, doi:10.1109/LGRS.2007.900751.

24. Fauvel, M.; Chanussot, J.; Benediktsson, J.; Atli, N. Kernel principal component analysis for the classification of hyperspectral remote sensing data over urban areas. *EURASIP J. Adv. Signal Process.* **2009**, *2009*, 1–14, doi:10.1155/2009/783194.

25. Li, W.; Prasad, S.; Fowler, J.E. Decision fusion in kernel-induced spaces for hyperspectral image classification. *IEEE Trans. Geosci. Remote Sens.* **2014**, *52*, 3399–3411, doi:10.1109/TGRS.2013.2272760.

26. He, X.; Niyogi, P. Locality preserving projections. In Proceedings of the Advances in Neural Information Processing Systems (NIPS), Vancouver, BC, Canada, 8–13 December 2003; pp. 186–197.

27. Villa, A.; Benediktsson, J.A.; Chanussot, J.; Jutten, C. Hyperspectral image classification with independent component discriminant analysis. *IEEE Trans. Geosci. Remote Sens.* **2011**, *49*, 4865–4876, doi:10.1109/TGRS.2011.2153861.

28. Mura, M.D.; Villa, A.; Benediktsson, J.A.; Chanussot, J. Classification of hyperspectral images by using extended morphological attribute profiles and independent component analysis. *IEEE Geosci. Remote Sens. Lett.* **2011**, *8*, 542–546, doi:10.1109/LGRS.2010.2091253.

29. Roweis, S.T.; Saul, L.K. Nonlinear dimensionality reduction by locally linear embedding. *Science* **2000**, *290*, 2323–2326, doi:10.1126/science.290.5500.2323.

30. Yan, S.; Xu, D.; Zhang, B.; Zhang, H.J. Graph embedding and extensions: A general framework for dimensionality reduction. *IEEE Trans. Pattern Anal. Mach. Intell.* **2007**, *29*, 40–51, doi:10.1109/TPAMI.2007.250598.

31. Luo, F.; Huang, H.; Liu, J.; Ma, Z. Fusion of graph embedding and sparse representation for feature extraction and classification of hyperspectral imagery. *Photogramm. Eng. Remote Sens.* **2017**, *83*, 37–46, doi:10.14358/PERS.83.1.37.

32. Chen, P.; Jiao, L.; Liu, F.; Zhao, J.; Zhao, Z. Dimensionality reduction for hyperspectral image classification based on multiview graphs ensemble. *J. Appl. Remote Sens.* **2016**, *10*, 030501, doi:10.1117/1.JRS.10.030501.

33. Zhou, D.; Huang, J.; Schölkopf, B. Learning with hypergraphs: clustering, classification, and embedding. In Proceedings of the Advances in Neural Information Processing Systems, Vancouver, BC, Canada, 3–6 December 2007; pp. 1601–1608.

34. Bu, J.; Tan, S.; Chen, C.; Wang, C.; Wu, H.; Zhang, L.; He, X. Music recommendation by unified hypergraph: combining social media information and music content. In Proceedings of the 18th ACM international conference on Multimedia, Firenze, Italy, 25–29 October 2010; pp. 391–400.

35. Liu, Q.; Sun, Y.; Wang, C.; Liu, T.; Tao, D. Elastic net hypergraph learning for image clustering and semi-supervised classification. *IEEE Trans. Image Process.* **2017**, *26*, 452–463, doi:10.1109/TIP.2016.2621671.

36. Yuan, H.; Tang, Y.Y. Learning with hypergraph for hyperspectral image feature extraction. *IEEE Trans. Geosci. Remote Sens. Lett.* **2015**, *12*, 1695–1699, doi:10.1109/LGRS.2015.2419713.

37. Kuo, B.C.; Landgrebe, D.A. Nonparametric weighted feature extraction for classification. *IEEE Trans. Geosci. Remote Sens.* **2004**, *42*, 1096–1105, doi:10.1109/TGRS.2004.825578.

38. Liao, W.; Pizurica, A.; Scheunders, P.; Philips, W.; Pi, Y. Semisupervised local discriminant analysis for feature extraction in hyperspectral images. *IEEE Trans. Geosci. Remote Sens.* **2013**, *51*, 184–198, doi:10.1109/TGRS.2012.2200106.

39. Pliakos, K.; Kotropoulos, C. Weight estimation in hypergraph learning. In Proceedings of the IEEE International Conference on Acoustics, Speech and Signal Processing, South Brisbane, Australia, 19–24 April 2015; pp. 1161–1165.

40. Gao, Y.; Wang, W.; Zha, Z.J.; Shen, J.; Li, X.; Wu, X. Visual-textual joint relevance learning for tag-based social image search. *IEEE Trans. Image Process.* **2013**, *22*, 363–376, doi:10.1109/TIP.2012.2202676.

 *remote sensing*

Article

Classification for High Resolution Remote Sensing Imagery Using a Fully Convolutional Network

Gang Fu [1,2,*], **Changjun Liu** [2], **Rong Zhou** [3], **Tao Sun** [2] and **Qijian Zhang** [4]

[1] Department Of Engineering Physics, Tsinghua University, Beijing 100084, China
[2] China Institute of Water Resources and Hydropower Research (IWHR), Beijing 100038, China; lcj2005@iwhr.com (C.L.); sunt@iwhr.com (T.S.)
[3] Beijing Soil and Water Conservation Center, Beijing 100036, China; zhour@bjwater.gov.cn
[4] Water Resources Information Center of Henan Province, Zhengzhou 450003, China; zqj@hnsl.gov.cn
* Correspondence: gangfu2008@hotmail.com; Tel.: +86-10-6279-4967

Academic Editors: Qi Wang, Nicolas H. Younan, Carlos López-Martínez, Lenio Soares Galvao and Prasad S. Thenkabail
Received: 21 March 2017; Accepted: 16 May 2017; Published: 18 May 2017

Abstract: As a variant of Convolutional Neural Networks (CNNs) in Deep Learning, the Fully Convolutional Network (FCN) model achieved state-of-the-art performance for natural image semantic segmentation. In this paper, an accurate classification approach for high resolution remote sensing imagery based on the improved FCN model is proposed. Firstly, we improve the density of output class maps by introducing Atrous convolution, and secondly, we design a multi-scale network architecture by adding a skip-layer structure to make it capable for multi-resolution image classification. Finally, we further refine the output class map using Conditional Random Fields (CRFs) post-processing. Our classification model is trained on 70 GF-2 true color images, and tested on the other 4 GF-2 images and 3 IKONOS true color images. We also employ object-oriented classification, patch-based CNN classification, and the FCN-8s approach on the same images for comparison. The experiments show that compared with the existing approaches, our approach has an obvious improvement in accuracy. The average precision, recall, and Kappa coefficient of our approach are 0.81, 0.78, and 0.83, respectively. The experiments also prove that our approach has strong applicability for multi-resolution image classification.

Keywords: deep learning; convolutional neural network (CNN); fully convolutional network (FCN); classification; remote sensing; high resolution

---

1. Introduction

Classification is a fundamental task for remote sensing imagery analysis. Applying intelligent methods, such as pattern recognition and statistical learning, is an effective way to obtain class information of ground objects. It is always the main focus of research and commercial development. Early classification was mainly for low spatial resolution (10–30 m) images and pixel-leveled images, including unsupervised classification (also known as clustering, such as K-means [1]) and supervised classification (such as Neural Networks [2,3] and Support Vector Machines [4,5]). These methods often use only spectral information of the images, and have formed general modules in commercial software, and have been successfully applied in land resources, environment, agriculture, and other fields. In recent years, some new approaches have appeared that are much superior to the traditional approaches. For example, Yuan Yuan et al. [6] and Qi Wang et al. [7] applied the latest achievements in the machine learning field, such as Manifold Ranking and Sparse Representation, to hyperspectral image classification.

High resolution (2 m spatial resolution and higher) remote sensing images contain more ground details. Many applications tend to obtain attributes of a ground object (such as a single building) rather than pixels. However, the pixel-level classification methods are sensitive to noise, and lack semantic meaning of the objects, and are difficult for obtaining object-level information. Therefore, object-oriented classification [8] is proposed, and it has made great achievements in high resolution image classification. At present, eCognition [9], ENVI [10], and other commercial software have developed object-oriented classification modules. Most of the object-oriented approaches perform a "segmentation-classification" mode. In the segmentation stage, Multi-Resolution (MR) [11], Full-Lambda Schedule (FLS) [12], Mean-Shift [13], Quadtree-Seg [14], and other image segmentation approaches are used to generate image segments, which we called image objects. In the classification stage, object features (color, texture, and geometric features) are calculated, which are taken as inputs of supervised or unsupervised classification, or a manually designed rule set for feature filtering, to achieve the final class discrimination.

Land-cover has various types, and is affected by noise, illumination, season, and many other factors, and brings great difficulties to classification using high resolution images. Even using the object-oriented approaches, accurate classification is still very difficult. From the pattern recognition perspective, selection/extraction of representative features is the bottleneck to improving accuracy. That is, the use of a specific set of features cannot be achieved on the classification for all kinds of ground objects. Therefore, learning features automatically from a remote sensing data set rather than using manually designed features, and then performing classification on the learned features, is an effective way to improve the accuracy of classification.

Deep learning theory was explicitly proposed by Hinton et al. [15] in 2006. It is a branch of machine learning based on a set of algorithms that attempt to model high level abstractions in data [16]. The basic motivation of deep learning is to establish a deep neural network to simulate the leaning and analysis mechanism of the human brain. Compared with the traditional machine learning theories, the most significant difference of deep learning is emphasizing automatic feature learning from a huge data set through the organization of multi-layer neurons. In recent years, various deep learning architectures such as Deep Belief Networks (DBN) [17], Convolutional Neural Networks (CNN) [18], and Recurrent Neural Networks (RNN) [19] have been applied to fields like computer vision [20,21], speech recognition, natural language processing, audio recognition, and bioinformatics, and they have been shown to produce state-of-the-art results in these domains.

In deep learning techniques, CNN has achieved remarkable results in image classification, recognition, and other vision tasks, and has the highest score on many visual databases such as ImageNet, Pattern Analysis, Statistical Modeling and Computational Learning Visual Object Classes (PASCAL VOC), and Microsoft Common Objects in Context (MS-COCO). For image classification, the basic structure of the standard CNN is stacks of "convolutional-pooling" layers as multi-scale feature extractors, and subsequent numbers of fully connected layers as classifiers. Many works on CNN-based remote sensing image analysis emerged in recent years. Nguyen et al. [22] presented an approach for satellite image classification using a five-layered network and achieved classification accuracy higher than 75%. Wang et al. [23] used a CNN structure with three layers and Finite State Machine (FSM) for road network extraction for long-term path planning. Marco Castelluccio et al. [24] explored the use of CNNs for the semantic classification of remote sensing scenes. Similarly, Hu et al. [25] also classified different scenes from high resolution remote sensing imagery using a pre-trained CNN model. Weixun Zhou et al. [26] employed CNN architecture as a deep feature extractor for high-resolution remote sensing image retrieval (HRRSIR). Volodymyr Mnih [27] proposed a CNN-based architecture to learn large scale contextual features for aerial image labeling. The model produces a dense classification patch, instead of outputting a single value image category. Martin Lagkvist et al. [28] presented a novel remote sensing imagery classification method based on CNNs for five classes (vegetation, ground, road, building, and water), outperforming the existing classification approaches. Besides the CNN family approaches, Yuan Yuan et al. [6] used a Stacked

AutoEncoder classifier for a classification experiment after using the Manifold Ranking based salient band selection.

The standard CNN is in an "image-label" manner and its output is the probability distribution over different classes. However, most of the remote sensing image classification expects a dense class map as the output, which has the same dimensions as the original image. A class map is a 2-D distribution of class labels with pixel correspondence, which is in a "pixel-label" mode. In the study of Martin Lagkvist et al. [28], a "per-pixel" classification is considered using overlapped patches and average post-processing. However, the use of the overlapped patches introduces too much redundant computations, and the averaging processing may easily lose useful edge information. Based on the standard CNN, Jonathan Long et al. [29] proposed the Fully Convolutional Network (FCN) model in 2015. By replacing fully connected (FC) layers in the standard CNN with convolutional layers, the FCN model maintains the 2-D structure of images, and firstly carries out CNN-based image semantic segmentation. In order to obtain a dense class map, Liang-Chieh Chen et al. [30] used the "atrous" convolution instead of the ordinary convolution, increasing the density of the predicted class labels, and then performed the Conditional Random Fields (CRFs) as post-processing to refine the region boundaries. The CRFs-based boundary refinement is also used in the works of Sakrapee et al. [31]. In order to integrate the CRFs procedure into the training stage, Shuai Zheng et al. [32] applied the idea of RNN to image segmentation, implementing an "end-to-end" training procedure. In the remote sensing society, several studies employ FCN-based approaches for dense class map generation. Jamie Sherrah [33] analyzed the down-sampling and up-sampling mechanism in CNNs, and adopted an FCN architecture for aerial image semantic labelling. The down-sampling mechanism of standard FCN is removed by involving deconvolution. D. Marmanis et al. [34] also used FCN and subsequent deconvolution architecture to perform a semantic segmentation for aerial images. Emmanuel Maggiori et al. [35–37] addressed the dense classification problem, and compared the patch-based CNN dense classification using CNN with FCN. With the advantages of FCN, the author proposed an end-to-end framework for large-scale remote sensing classification. A multi-scale mechanism was also considered by designing a specific neuron module that processes its input at multiple scales.

In this paper, we perform a FCN-based classification on high spatial resolution remote sensing imagery with 12 classes (bare land, grass, tree, water, building, cement ground, parking lot, playground, city road, trail, shadow, and others). These classes are typical ground objectives in city areas, and some of them (such as building, cement ground, road, and parking lot) are easily confused in traditional classification tasks. The class configurations were arranged to test the effectiveness of our approach in a complex environment. We fine-tuned the model parameters of the ImageNet-pretrained VGG-16 [37] network using GF-2 satellite images, to adapt it to our remote sensing imagery classification task. The VGG network has a more compact structure of convolutional and pooling layers, and achieved the highest classification accuracy for ImageNet ILSVRC-2014. To overcome the noise caused by pixel-level classification, we refine the region boundaries using fully connected CRFs, following the procedure of Liang-Chieh Chen et al. [30] and Sakrapee et al. [31]. The refined output is more readily applied to an object-oriented analysis.

We compare our approach with the object-oriented approach with MR segmentation [11] and SVM classification, patch-based CNN classification proposed in [27], and the FCN-8s approach proposed in [29], which achieved success for high resolution imagery classification or natural image segmentation. The result shows that our approach achieves higher accuracy in the classification. For those objectives which are difficult to be classified, our approach has lower confusion rates.

2. Methods

Similar to other supervised classification, our approach generally has two stages: the training stage and the classification stage, which is illustrated in Figure 1. In the training stage (the upper part of Figure 1), image-label pairs, with pixel-class correspondence, are input into the FCN network as training samples. The error between predicted class labels and ground truth (GT) labels is calculated and back-propagated through the network using the chain rule, and then the parameters of the FCN network are updated using the gradient descent method. The above iteration will be stopped when the error is less than a given threshold. In the classification stage (the lower part of Figure 1), the trained FCN network is performed on an input image to generate a rough class prediction. The rough class prediction, with the input image, is then input into the CRFs post-processing module to generate the final refined classification. The details of the training stage and classification stage are presented in Sections 2.2 and 2.3, respectively.

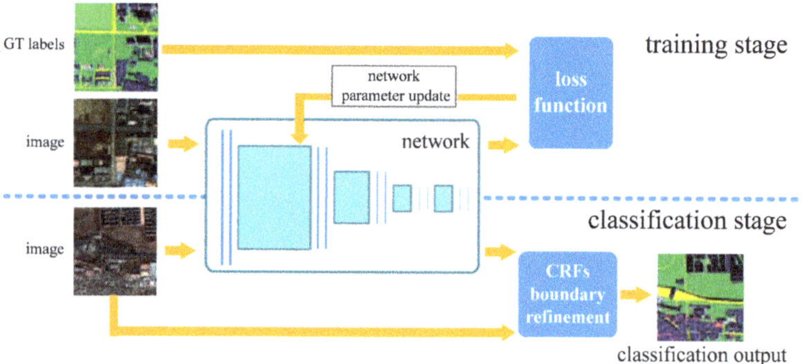

Figure 1. The general pipeline of our approach: The training stage and the classification stage are illustrated in the upper and lower parts, respectively.

2.1. Network Architecture

CNN currently is the state-of-the-art in visual recognition such as classification and detection. Simonyan et al. [38] developed the very deep CNN networks (VGG) by increasing the depth to 16–19 weight layers. To reduce the number of parameters in the networks, small 3×3 filters are used in all the convolutional layers. VGG models won the runner-up in ImageNet ILSVRC-2014. Although the subsequently emerged deeper models, such as ResNet [39] and Inception-V4 [40], achieved a higher score in many vision tasks, VGG networks have clear structures and compact memory requirements, which can be easily extended and applied, so we chose the 16-layered VGG network as our basic network architecture. Based on the VGG network, we constructed the FCN model by replacing the last three fully connected layers (two layers with 4096 neurons and one with 1000 neurons) with convolutional layers. Then following the idea of Liang-Chieh Chen et al. [30], we use "atrous" convolution (also known as "dilation" convolution in other studies) instead of the ordinary convolution to increase the feature density, and build the multi-scale classification model by adding the skip-layer network architecture.

2.1.1. Fully Convolutional Network

In classification tasks, the last structures in standard CNN are always several Fully Connected (FC) layers (see Figure 2a for illustration). These layers play the role of classifier like standard BP neural networks (For example, in Figure 2a, the 3 FC layers are similar to a 3-layered BP network with one hidden layer). From the first FC layer, the 2-D structure of the input image maintained by the convolutional-pooling layers is lost. The output of standard CNN is a 1-D distribution over classes (for a Softmax regression). It works in an "image-label" manner. In other words, given an image, it predicts one class label (a scalar) for it. The "image-label" mode has great advantages in single scene classification. The effectiveness has been presented in studies of Marco Castelluccio et al. [24] and Hu et al. [25].

However, in most remote sensing applications, a 2-D dense class map is required as an output. To maintain the 2-D structure, some approaches were presented based on the common CNN structures. The most typical one is the patch-based CNN approach [27,28]. The basic idea of patch-based CNN is: separate the large image into small patches, and apply the common CNN model on each patch to predict the class label(s) centered at the corresponding patch. Finally, the class labels will be arranged in a 2-D layout as the output. Jonathan Long et al. [29] proposed the FCN model, which is a convolutionalized version of CNN. FCN replaces all the FC layers with convolutional layers. Thus, the important 2-D structure of the image is maintained. Figure 2b is the illustration of the FCN model.

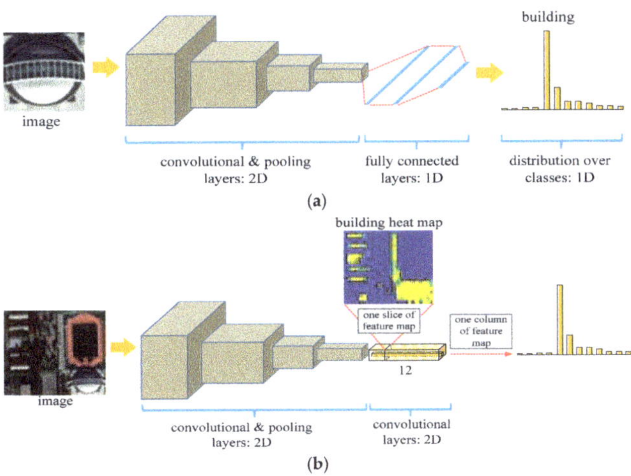

Figure 2. Network architectures for standard Convolutional Neural Network (CNN) and Fully Convolutional Network (FCN). (**a**) Architecture of standard CNN: stacks of convolutional-pooling layers and fully connected (FC) layers. Given an image, the distribution over classes is predicted. The class with the largest distribution value is considered as the class of a given image; (**b**) Architecture of FCN: FC layers are replaced by convolutional layers. FCN maintains the 2-D structure of the image.

Compared with patch-based CNN, the advantages of the FCN model are obvious for

- *Easy implementation*: The FCN architecture is designed brilliantly by replacing the FC layers by convolutional layers, which enables us to take arbitrary sized images as inputs. Additionally, by training entire images at a time instead of patch cropping, FCN does not have to rearrange the output labels together to obtain the label predictions and thus reduces the implementation complexity.
- *Higher accuracy*: Under the patch-based CNN learning framework, only the "intra-patch" context information is taken into account. Nevertheless, correlations among patches are ignored, which might lead to obvious gaps between patches. Unlike the patch-based CNN, FCN performs the classification in a single-loop manner, and considers the context information overall and seamlessly. Please refer to Section 4.2 for more details.
- *Less expensive computation*: In patch-based CNN, when using overlapped patches for dense class label generation, such as the study of Martin Lagkvist et al. [28], it introduces too much redundant computations (especially convolutions) on the overlapped regions. By performing a single loop operation, the FCN model makes remarkable progress and allows the large image classification to be implemented in a more effective way.

We adopt the FCN model for remote sensing imagery classification. The output number (channels) of the last convolutional layer (also called feature maps) is equal to the class number of our task (so in this paper, it is 12 for 12-class classifications). The feature maps can be seen as a stack of heat maps for all classes. A 2-D slice along the channel axis represents the heap map (score distribution) of the corresponding class (For example in Figure 2b and in Figure 3c, we extract the heap map for the building).

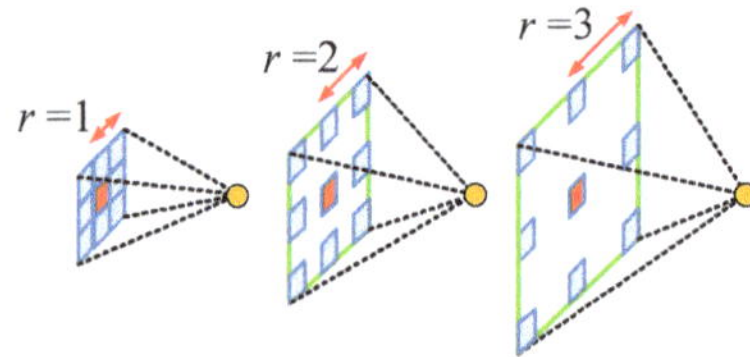

Figure 3. "Atrous" convolutions with $r = 1, 2,$ and 3. The first convolution ($r = 1$) is actually the ordinary convolution.

2.1.2. Atrous Convolution for Dense Feature Extraction

The repeated combination of pooling and striding at consecutive layers significantly reduces the spatial resolution of the resulting feature map. Typically in our VGG-16 model, 5 max-pooling layers with 1/2 down-sampling cause 1/32 total factor reduction in spatial resolution. For high resolution remote sensing image classification tasks, such operations lead to a serious loss of spatial information. Liang-Chieh Chen et al. [30], inspired by the Wavelet Transform, proposed the "atrous" convolution for generating dense feature maps. In the 1-D case, given the input signal $x[i]$, and the convolutional kernel w, the output of "atrous" convolution y$[i]$ is calculated as:

$$y[i] = \sum_{k=1}^{K} x[i + r \cdot k]w[k] \tag{1}$$

where r denotes the *rate* parameter corresponding to the stride. In the 2-D cases, "atrous" convolutions (use 3×3 kernel) with rate $r = 1$, 2, and 3 are demonstrated in Figure 3.

In order to further illustrate the effect of "atrous" convolution, we compare it with standard convolution using a simple example in Figure 4. Firstly, represented by the red route, we take an image patch (300×300) as an input, and perform 1/2 down-sampling and 10×10 standard convolution (horizontal Gaussian derivative kernel) on it, which is used to simulate a pooling-convolution combination in standard CNNs. The receptive field corresponding to the original image is 20×20, and only 1/4 of the image positions are involved in calculating the feature map. The obtained low resolution feature map is then enlarged by an up-sampling operation with a factor of 2. Secondly, as a comparison, we perform "atrous" convolution with rate $r = 2$ on the original image. The size of the receptive field is unchanged, but the density of the feature map is increased by two times, which means half of the image positions are considered for generating the feature map. Compared with the standard convolution, the "atrous" convolution generates a high resolution feature map, while keeping the size of receptive field. Besides, there is no extra parameter involved. The "atrous" convolution for dense feature map generation is illustrated by the blue route in Figure 4.

The "atrous" convolution is generally applicable and allows us to efficiently compute dense CNN feature maps at any target subsampling rate without introducing any approximations and extra parameters. Theoretically, the "atrous" convolution can be applied to each convolutional layer of the network to maintain the resolution, but this ends up being too costly, and the advantage for translation invariant brought by the down-sampling operation could also be weakened. So we modify the basic VGG-16 network to adapt it to our classification task. We take this modified network as our primary architecture (we add multi-scale functionality, which is described in Section 2.1.3).

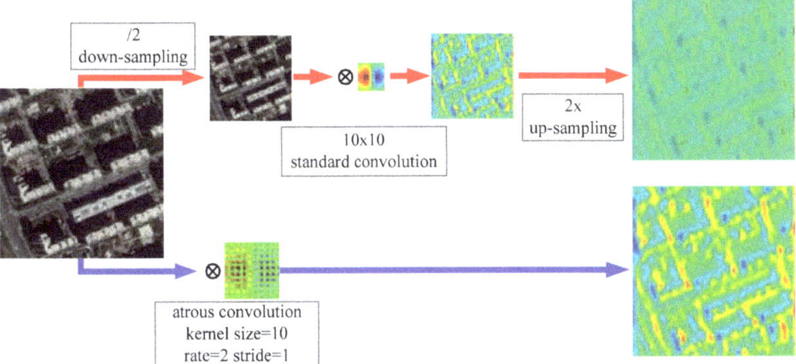

Figure 4. Illustration of atrous convolution for dense feature map generation. Red route: standard convolution performed on a low resolution feature map. Blue route: dense feature map generated using atrous convolution with rate $r = 2$ on a high resolution input feature map.

2.1.3. Network Architecture for Multi-Scale Classification

The variant of resolution will affect the classification accuracy. Single-scale classification has great limitation in its applicability. Therefore, many works considered multi-scale classification in their approaches [29–32]. A simple method for a multi-scale classification is training the model on datasets that contain objects of varying sizes. However, this approach needs the times of sample storage and training time (more iteration to traverse all the samples). A good idea for CNN-based multi-scale segmentation and detection is using the skip-layer network architecture [29,41]. In this architecture, links are added to incorporate the feature responses from different levels of the primary network stream, and these responses are then combined in a shared output layer [42]. Our multi-scale network architecture is illustrated in Figure 5.

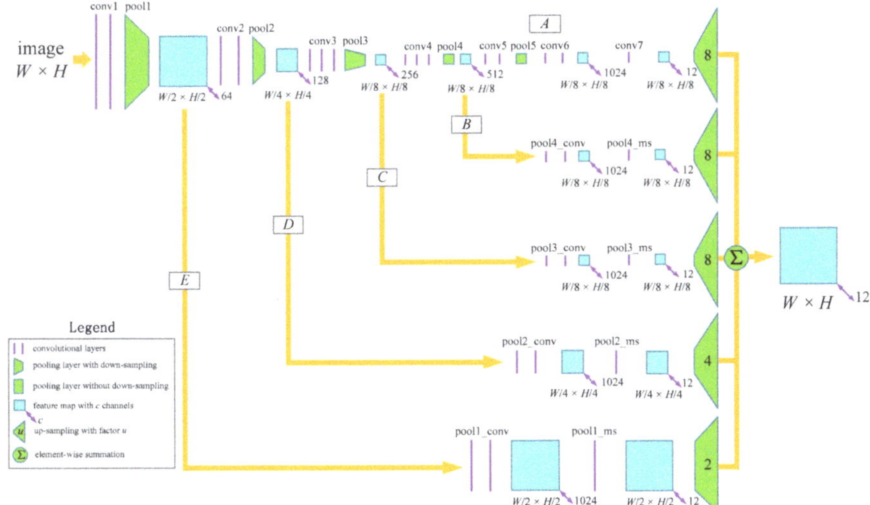

Figure 5. Multi-scale network architecture.

As presented in Figure 5, feature maps are generated along five streams. The stream *A* is our primary network, generating a feature map with dimension $W/8 \times H/8 \times 12$, which is described in Section 2.1.2. Branch streams *B* to *E* are the added skip-layer architecture for the multi-scale classification. These streams begin from the feature map generated by layers pool4 to pool1, respectively. For each branch stream, the subsequent architecture is the layer group with two convolutional layers, generating a feature map with 1024 channels, and then a convolutional layer (kernel $1 \times 1 \times 12$) outputs a 12-channeled feature map. Each stream, including the primary stream and the branch streams, introduce down-sampling effects caused by the max-pooling operation (the factor is $1/8$ for stream *A* to *C*, $1/4$ for stream *D*, and $1/2$ for stream *E*). However, in the applications of remote sensing classification, we need the class map to have the same size with the input image. So we perform the up-sampling operation after the feature maps are generated by these streams to recover the feature maps at the original image resolution. In this paper, we adopt Liang-Chieh Chen et al.'s [30] approach, and use simple bilinear interpolation to increase the resolution by a factor of 8, 4, and 2 at negligible computational cost. The up-sampled feature maps are then combined using summation in an element-wise manner. The output of this network architecture is a feature map with dimension $W \times H \times 12$. Our multi-scale network architecture captures three levels of resolution, represented by stream *A* to *C*, stream *B*, and stream *E*.

2.2. Network Training

Our training dataset is collected from two GF-2 high resolution remote sensing images (true color fusion images with 0.8 meter resolution) of northeastern Beijing, China.

The images were taken in 5 December 2014 and 2 September 2015, respectively. The reason why we chose images with different imaging times is to increase the anti-interference abilities of our model, such as the change of seasons, to enhance its applicability. In our training dataset, there are a total of 74 images (size 1024×1024). We manually labeled all images at the pixel level as ground truth (GT) label data. In other words, for each image, there exists a 1024×1024 label map, having a pixel-class (row-col indexed) correspondence with it. We used 70 images for training, and the remaining 4 images for testing. Three image-GT label pair examples are illustrated in Figure 6.

The general procedure of our training stage is: Image-GT label pairs are input into the multi-scale classification network as training samples. The *Softmax* function is performed on the output feature map generated by the network to predict the class distribution. Then the cross entropy loss is calculated and back-propagated, and finally the network parameters are updated using Stochastic Gradient Descent (SGD) with momentum. The general procedure is shown in Figure 7.

The softmax function is used to *probabilize* the output feature map of our multi-scale network. However, the mode of softmax here is different from that in the standard CNNs: it is performed on each location with row-column coordinate $(i, j), 0 \leq i < H \; and \; 0 \leq j < W$, and it outputs a dense distribution over the classes. Figure 8 illustrates this function.

Figure 8 shows that the output of our multi-scale network is a $H \times W \times 12$ feature map, which has the same width and height as the original image. A "drill hole" along the channel axis at location (i, j) is the feature vector with 12 elements corresponding to the pixel at the same location. The softmax function is adopted on this feature vector to generate a 12-D probabilized vector, which is the discrete distribution over 12 classes at location (i, j). The softmax function will traverse each location to obtain the dense class distribution.

The SGD method with momentum is used for parameter updates in our training, which is described by the following:

$$W^{(n+1)} = W^{(n)} - \Delta W^{(n+1)} \tag{2}$$

where $W^{(n)}$ and $W^{(n+1)}$ denote the old parameters and new parameters, respectively, and $\Delta W^{(n+1)}$ is the increment for the current iteration, which is a combination of old parameters, gradient, and historical increment:

$$\Delta W^{(n+1)} = \eta \cdot \left(d_w \cdot W^{(n)} + \frac{\partial J(W)}{\partial W^{(n)}} \right) + m \cdot \Delta W^{(n)} \tag{3}$$

where $J(W)$ is the loss function, η is the learning rate for step length control, and d_w and m denote the weight decay and momentum, respectively.

We employ the VGG-16 network which has been pre-trained on ImageNet for fast convergence. We use a "step" policy for learning rate adjustment ($gamma = 0.1$, $step\_size = 15,000$) so that closer to the error minimum, the smaller the step length is. The base learning rate is 0.0001. The basic parameters for calculating increments are: $m = 0.9$, and $d_w = 0.0005$. The max iteration in our training is 60,000. In the training procedure, we first randomly shuffle the samples, and then feed them into the network in batches. Each batch contains 10 images. We also crop and rotate samples randomly in each batch to increase the diversity and variability of the samples.

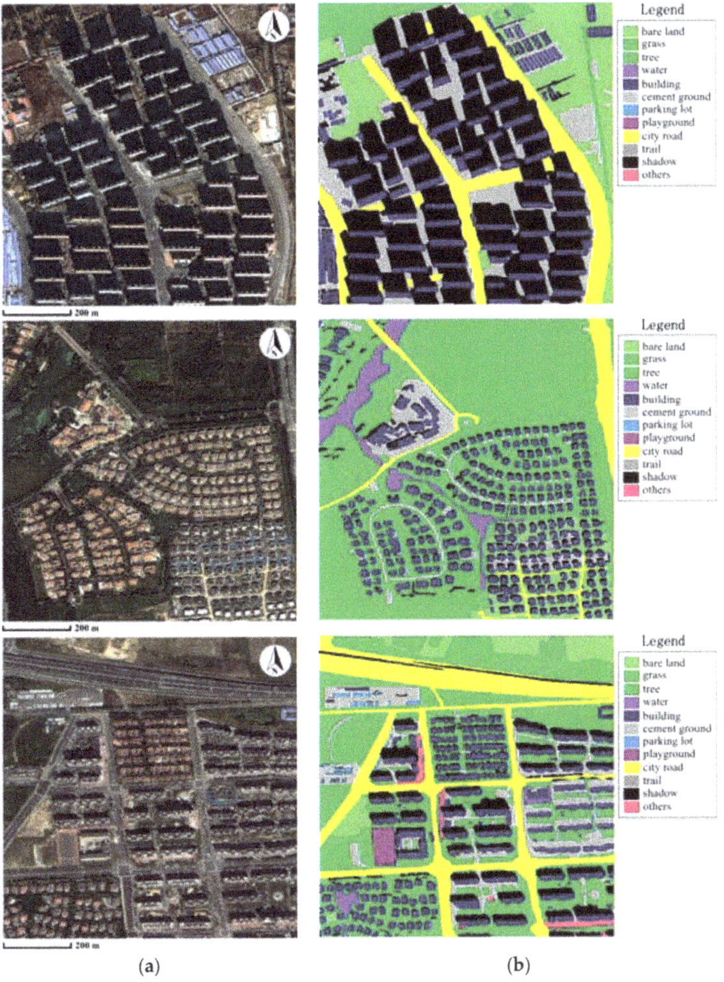

(a) (b)

Figure 6. Three sample examples for our classification training. (a) Original images; (b) Ground truth (GT) labels corresponding to the images in (a).

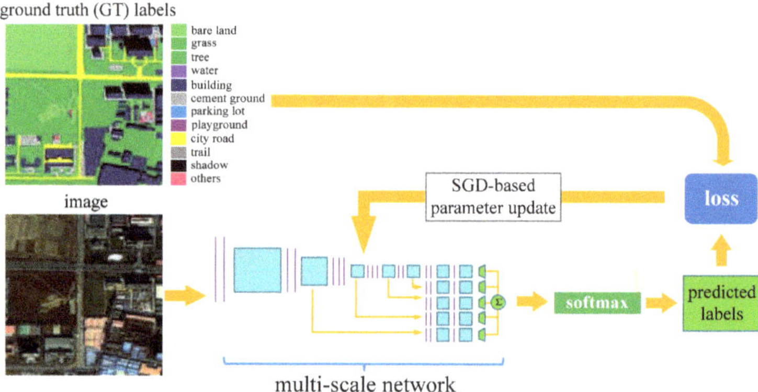

Figure 7. General procedure of network training.

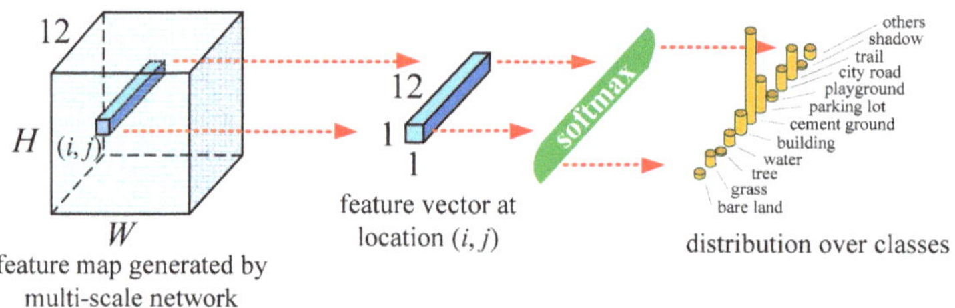

Figure 8. Softmax function performed on the output feature map.

2.3. Classification Using the Trained Network

The trained network is adopted on an image for classification. However, our multi-scale network involves up-sampling operations, leading to the blurring of classification boundaries. Several works [29–32] use CRFs as post-processing to refine the image segmentation results. So following their idea, we adopt the fully connected CRFs for our rough class prediction. The model employs the energy function:

$$E(\mathbf{x}) = \sum_i \theta_i(x_i) + \sum_{ij} \theta_{ij}(x_i, x_j) \tag{4}$$

where x is the label assignment for pixels. $\theta_i(x_i) = -\log P(x_i)$ is the *unary potential*, where $P(x_i)$ is the label assignment probability at pixel i as the output of our multi-scale network after the softmax function. $\theta_{ij}(x_i, x_j)$ is the *pairwise potential* represented by a fully connected graph, connecting all pairs of image pixels i and j. We use the following definition of the pairwise potential [43]

$$\theta_{ij}(x_i, x_j) = \mu(x_i, x_j) \sum_{m=1}^{K} w_m \cdot k^m(f_i, f_j) \tag{5}$$

where $\mu(x_i, x_j)$ is the sign function, and $\mu(x_i, x_j) = 1$ if $x_i \neq x_j$, and is zero otherwise. $\mu(x_i, x_j)$ removes the self-connected links from the graph. k^m is a Gaussian kernel function that takes feature as input (denoted by f_i and f_j extracted for pixel i and j). Each Gaussian kernel is weighted by w_m. In our study, the bilateral position and color terms is adopted as the kernel function

$$w_1 \cdot \exp\left(-\frac{\|p_i - p_j\|^2}{2\sigma_\alpha^2} - \frac{\|I_i - I_j\|^2}{2\sigma_\beta^2}\right) + w_2 \cdot \exp\left(-\frac{\|p_i - p_j\|^2}{2\sigma_\gamma^2}\right) \tag{6}$$

where p_i, p_j denote the locations, and p_i, p_j denote the color of pixel i, j. So the first kernel depends on both pixel positions and color, and the second kernel only depends on pixel positions. σ_α, σ_β, and σ_γ are the hyper parameters that control the scale of the Gaussian kernels. The classification pipeline is illustrated in Figure 9.

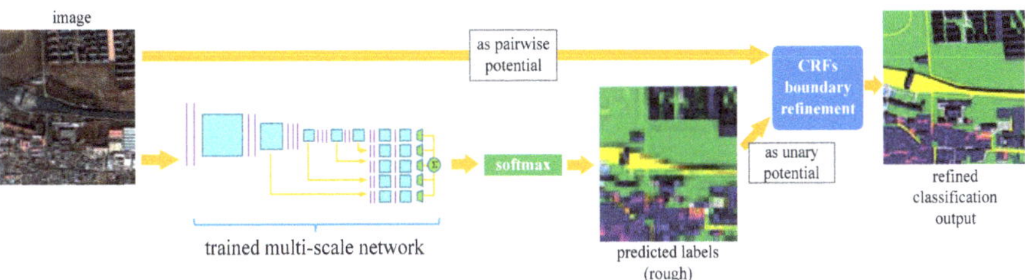

Figure 9. General procedure of image classification using the trained network.

In CRFs post-processing, the rough class distribution predicted by the multi-scale network is input as the unary potential, and the original image provides the pairwise potential with position and color information. The CRFs is solved using mean field approximation [43]. The class labels are adjusted and refined under the position-color constraints. The weight parameters we adopt in this paper are $w_1 = 4, w_2 = 3$, which are the default configuration of [30]. Following the idea of [43], we use $\sigma_\alpha = 54, \sigma_\beta = 5$, and $\sigma_\gamma = 4$ through a cross-validation on the training set. We employ 10 mean field iterations for solving CRFs.

3. Experiment and Comparison

In the following section, the experiment and comparison will be presented to evaluate our classification approach. Our algorithm is implemented using Microsoft Visual C++ 11, and is performed on the Windows 7 operating system installed NVIDIA GeForce GTX980M graphic device with 8G byte graphic memory.

3.1. Comparison Setup

We conduct two groups of experiment (denoted as Experiment A and B) on GF-2 and IKONOS true color images, respectively. We compare our approach with object-oriented classification using MR segmentation [11], SVM classification (MR-SVM), patch-based CNN classification proposed in [27], and the FCN-8s approach proposed in [29].

3.1.1. MR-SVM

For Multi-Resolution and Support Vector Machine (MR-SVM) object-oriented classification, the first step is MR segmentation [11] to generate image objects. The quality of image objects directly affects the classification results. We believe that the high quality image objects are neither over-covered nor over-segmented. Ideally, each image object contains only a single-class ground object. The MR segmentation is controlled by the scale, shape, and compactness parameters. In order to obtain high-quality image objects, we determine the parameters through the times of experiments by different settings, to achieve the ideal segmentation as much as possible. The parameters we used in MR segmentation are listed in Table 1.

Once the image objects are obtained, we construct the initial feature space using 60 common features involving spectral, geometric, and texture aspects:

- *Spectral features*: mean, standard deviation, brightness, and max difference for each band.
- *Geometric features*: area, length, width, length-width ratio, border length, compactness, elliptic fit, rectangular fit, density, shape index, main direction, and symmetry.

- *Texture features*: Features calculated from the Gray Level Co-occurrence Matrix (GLCM) and the Gray Level Difference Vector (GLDV) with all directions, etc.

Table 1. Scale, shape, and compactness parameters used in the Multi-Resolution (MR) segmentation.

Experiment	Scale	Shape	Compact
Exp.A-(1)	115	0.5	0.5
Exp.A-(2)	140	0.3	0.8
Exp.A-(3)	105	0.4	0.5
Exp.A-(4)	100	0.4	0.7
Exp.B-(1)	120	0.3	0.5
Exp.B-(2)	80	0.5	0.4
Exp.B-(3)	85	0.5	0.7

To select the most representative features for the following classification, we seek significant features for optimal class separation using the Separability and Thresholds (SEaTH) method [44]. According to the SEaTH method, we optimize the 60-D initial feature space, and obtain a 10-D sub feature space including: mean value and brightness for each band; density and length-width ratio of the image object; GLCM-mean value for each band; GLDV-mean for the first band. In the classification stage, we select almost 25% of the image objects from each image as training samples, and input their features to the SVM classifier implemented using the LibSVM library [45]. The kernel function we used in SVM is the Radial Basis Function (RBF), and the objective function type is the C-Support Vector Classification (C-SVC). To determine the optimal penalty factor C and kernel function parameter γ, we employ a simple grid search for all training samples on the $C - \gamma$ domain that minimize the classification error. The search range of C and γ are $[0.4, 1.6]$ and $[0.02, 0.14]$ according to the experience [45]. The step lengths are 0.2 and 0.01, respectively. According to the grid search, the optimal parameters we used for the SVM classifier are $C = 1.2$ and $\gamma = 0.08$.

3.1.2. Patch-Based CNN

In the patch-based classification experiment, the general procedure is illustrated in Figure 10.

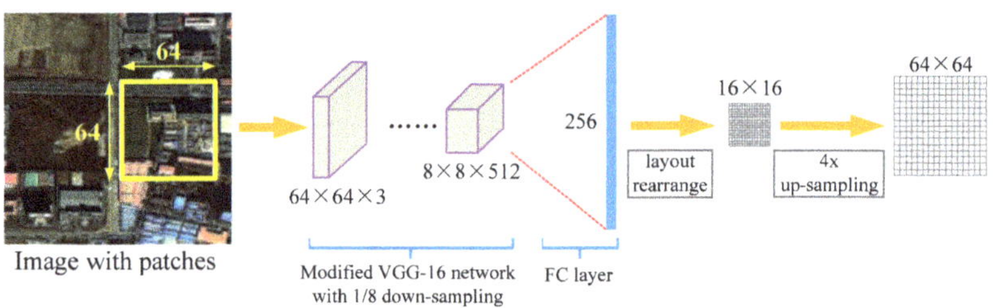

Figure 10. General procedure of our patch-based CNN classification experiment.

Different from the architecture used in [27], we employ the VGG-16 network as the main structure for its high performance in the previous vision tasks. In order to prevent excessive reduction of the resolution, we modified the stride and padding values of the last two pooling layers (the stride and padding values we used are all 1) so that the architecture has a 1/8 down-sampling effect. Following the idea of Volodymyr Mnih [27], the last 3 FC layers are modified to a single FC layer with output number 256 representing a 16 × 16 prediction area. So for 64 × 64 input patches, the overall architecture causes a 1/4 down-sampling. Finally, we perform an up-sampling post-processing with a factor of 2 to increase the resolution.

3.1.3. FCN-8s

For the FCN model, we directly employ the FCN-8s model proposed by Jonathan Long et al. [29]. The architecture of the model is also the VGG-16 network with skip-layer structure. The final prediction is fused from the output of three branches (from the primary network, the pool4 layer, and the pool3 layer, respectively) after the up-sampling operation. In the training phase, by modifying the number of outputs from 21 to 12, we fine-tuned the network based on the ImageNet pre-trained model. The training parameters for FCN-8s in the experiment are the same as ours. In the testing stage, except for the CRF-based post-processing, we use the same classification parameters as our approach. Please refer to [29] for detailed information.

3.2. Experiments and Comparison

In Experiment A, we adopt our trained model on four GF-2 true color images (0.8 m resolution) for the classification (In the following section, they will be abbreviated as Exp.A-(1) to Exp.A-(4)). All the image sizes are 1024×1024. These images are the testing images that are not involved in training. Figure 11 is the illustration of the results and the comparison. In Experiment B, we adopt the same trained model on three IKONOS true color images (1.0 m resolution) for the classification (Abbreviated as Exp.B-(1) and Exp.B-(3) in the following section) to test the applicability. All the image sizes are also 1024×1024. Figure 12 illustrates the classification results and comparison.

We employ precision, recall, and Kappa coefficient as the indicators to evaluate our approach. These indexes are calculated from the confusion matrix C, where the precision is calculated as $\frac{1}{12} \sum_i C_{ii} / \sum_j C_{ij}$ that denotes the average proportion of pixels being classified to one class that are correct, and the recall is computed as $\frac{1}{12} \sum_i C_{ii} / \sum_i C_{ij}$ that represents the average proportion of pixels that are correctly classified, and the Kappa coefficient measures the consistency of the predicted classes with the GT classes. The comparisons are listed in Table 2.

Table 2. Comparison between approaches using MR-SVM, patch-based CNN, FCN-8s, and our approach.

Approach	Index	Exp.A-(1)	Exp.A-(2)	Exp.A-(3)	Exp.A-(4)	Exp.B-(1)	Exp.B-(2)	Exp.B-(3)	Mean
	Precision	0.67	0.72	0.67	0.66	0.65	0.73	0.64	0.68
MR-SVM	Recall	0.52	0.59	0.52	0.63	0.39	0.51	0.74	0.56
	Kappa	0.55	0.66	0.62	0.65	0.54	0.64	0.64	0.61
	Precision	0.68	0.64	0.71	0.55	0.73	0.76	0.70	0.68
Patch-based CNN	Recall	0.61	0.61	0.70	0.73	0.47	0.58	0.74	0.63
	Kappa	0.64	0.69	0.62	0.70	0.63	0.71	0.75	0.68
	Precision	0.83	0.84	0.68	0.66	0.81	0.78	0.83	0.78
FCN-8s	Recall	0.71	0.79	0.80	0.80	0.66	0.66	0.79	0.74
	Kappa	0.73	0.80	0.81	0.80	0.76	0.81	0.82	0.79
	Precision	**0.86**	**0.87**	**0.74**	**0.68**	**0.84**	**0.78**	**0.92**	**0.81**
Ours	Recall	**0.83**	**0.78**	**0.81**	**0.82**	**0.70**	**0.68**	**0.84**	**0.78**
	Kappa	**0.79**	**0.85**	**0.84**	**0.83**	**0.78**	**0.84**	**0.89**	**0.83**

The above statistics show our approach obtains the best performance compared with the others. Approaches using carefully-designed MR-SVM and patch-based CNN achieve similar accuracy levels, and the FCN-8s approach performs much better than those two. Some ground objects such as building, city road, and cement ground, have similar spectral and geometrical features, which are hard to distinguish. For example, in Exp.A-(2), when using MR-SVM, the recall for "cement ground" is 0.41. That means that more than half of the pixels are wrongly classified. The proportions that are incorrectly classified as "building" and "road" are 0.26 and 0.19. It means that in that case, the object-oriented classification has almost no effect on distinguishing these classes.

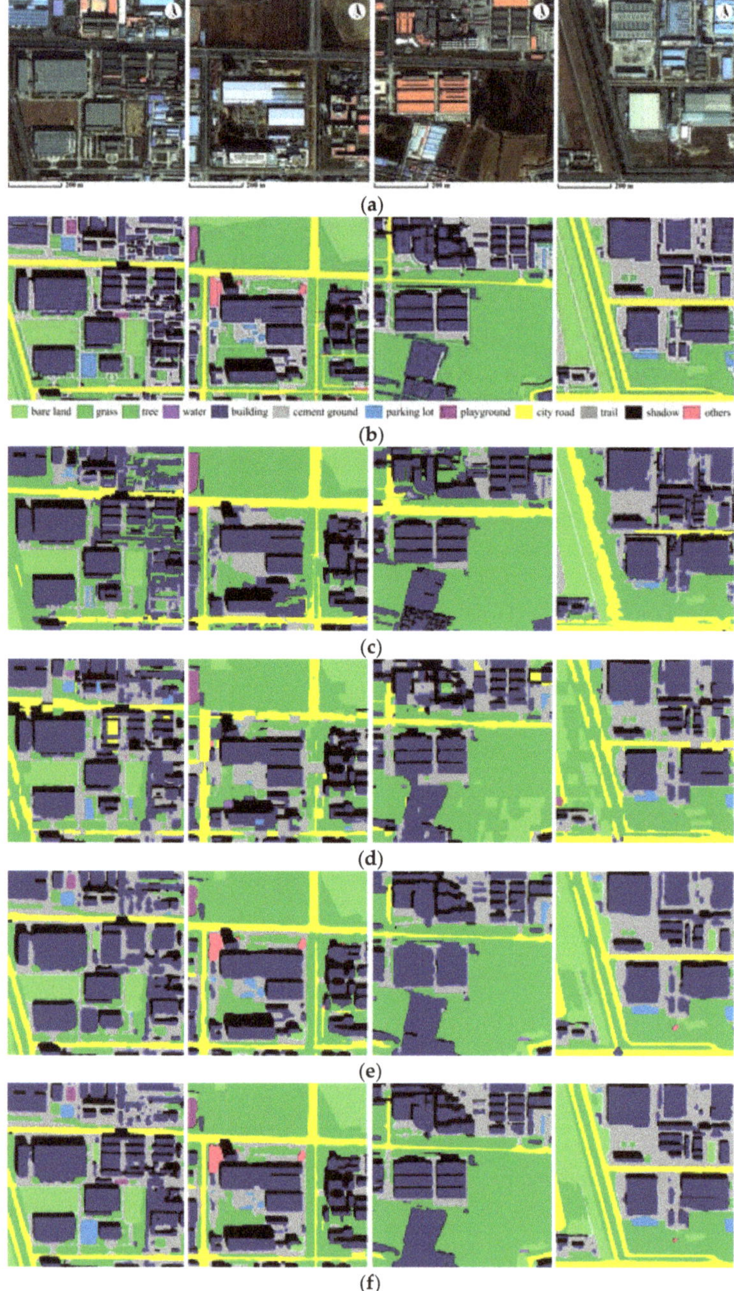

Figure 11. Classification results on GF-2 images (Experiment A). (**a**) Original images; (**b**) GT labels corresponding to the images in (**a**); (**c**–**e**) Results of the MR-SVM object-oriented classification, patch-based CNN classification, and FCN-8s classification corresponding to the images in (**a**), respectively; (**f**) Our classification results corresponding to the images in (**a**).

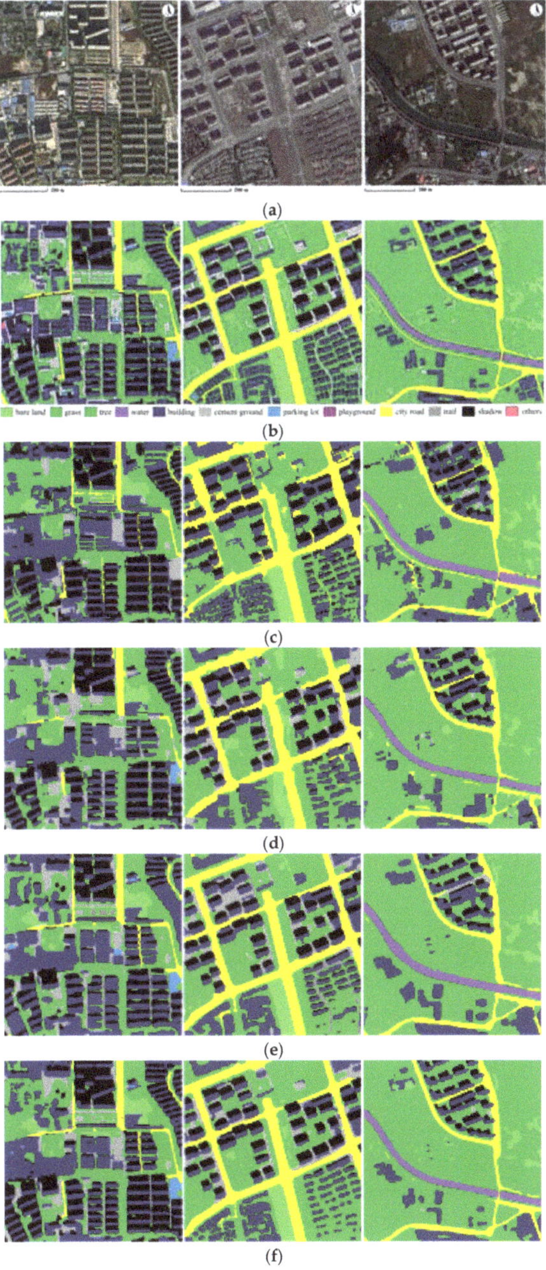

Figure 12. Classification result on IKONOS images (Experiment B). (**a**) Original images; (**b**) GT labels corresponding to the images in (**a**); (**c–e**) Results of the MR-SVM object-oriented classification, patch-based CNN classification, and FCN-8s classification corresponding to the images in (**a**), respectively; (**f**) Our classification results corresponding to the images in (**a**).

Table 3 lists the partial confusion matrix (only involves the above three classes) of our classification results. From the table, we can see that our approach achieves higher classification performance. In the above example, our recall for "cement ground" is 0.79. The proportions that are wrongly classified as "building" and "city road" are 0.05 and 0.06, respectively.

Table 3. Partial confusion matrix of our approach for "building", "cement ground", and "city road".

Experiment	GT/Predicted Class	Building	Cement Ground	City Road
Exp.A-(1)	Building	**0.91**	0.05	0.02
	Cement ground	0.13	**0.76**	0.02
	City road	0.02	0.01	**0.95**
Exp.A-(2)	Building	**0.92**	0.03	0.03
	Cement ground	0.05	**0.79**	0.06
	City Road	0.01	0.04	**0.89**
Exp.A-(3)	Building	**0.91**	0.02	0.05
	Cement ground	0.10	**0.82**	0.03
	City road	0.05	0.04	**0.82**
Exp.A-(4)	Building	**0.95**	0.03	0.00
	Cement ground	0.07	**0.81**	0.05
	City road	0.01	0.01	**0.93**
Exp.B-(1)	Building	**0.90**	0.02	0.01
	Cement ground	0.26	**0.65**	0.01
	City road	0.11	0.03	**0.84**
Exp.B-(2)	Building	**0.83**	0.01	0.00
	Cement ground	0.08	**0.75**	0.15
	City road	0.01	0.01	**0.96**
Exp.B-(3)	Building	**0.87**	0.06	0.01
	Cement ground	0.03	**0.70**	0.04
	City road	0.10	0.01	**0.87**

4. Discussion

This paper presents a classification approach for high resolution images using the improved FCN model. Compared with the object-oriented method and two typical deep learning-based approaches, the classification accuracy is obviously improved. In the following sections, we will discuss the reasons.

4.1. MR-SVM vs. Our Approach

Most of the traditional object-oriented classification approaches employ their classification in a "segmentation-classification" manner. In an ideal segmentation, each segment represents a single ground object. In other words, an ideal image object is neither over-covered nor over-segmented. However, most of the segmentation was conducted in an unsupervised way, which relies only on image information, but no prior class information. When the spectral and geometric features are similar, it is difficult to obtain high-quality image objects. Once the image objects are incorrect, subsequent object-oriented classification cannot lead to an accurate result. For an image, it is difficult to find universal segmentation parameters so that all image objects can be correctly generated. Figure 13 shows one image object (with a yellow boundary) generated by MR segmentation that incorrectly covers both building and cement ground.

In the classification stage, it is very difficult to choose expressive features for an image object as the input of the classifier. The feature selection usually needs many attempts and largely depends on experience. Therefore, the uncertainty introduced by the two stages, together affects the final classification accuracy.

In our FCN-based approach, the class information, which is the ultimate objective for classification, is taken as the supervisory signal that controls the whole process including both feature extraction and classification. Our approach combines the segmentation and classification stages, and achieves high quality classification in an end-to-end way. This is also the most obvious advantage of the deep learning theory.

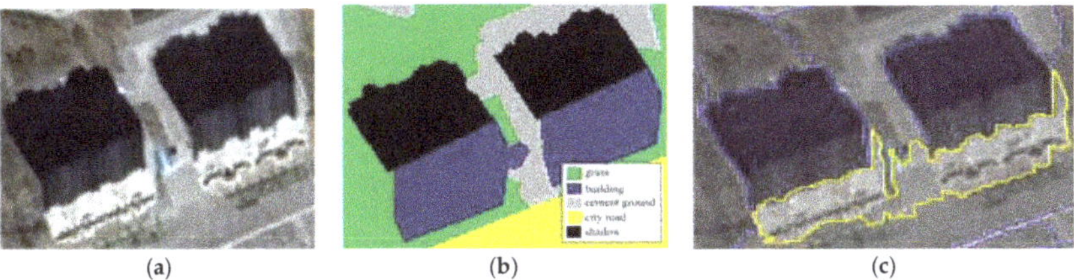

Figure 13. Incorrect image object generated by MR segmentation. (**a**) Original images; (**b**) GT labels corresponding to the images in (**a**); (**c**) Incorrect image object covers both the building and cement ground (with yellow boundary).

4.2. Patch-Based CNN vs. Our Approach

In the patch-based CNN approach, each image patch is input to the model independently, which means that only the "intra-patch" context information is considered. However, correlations between patches are not taken into account, which might lead to obvious gaps between patches. Especially for objects with strong continuity, such as road and building edges, the problem is more serious. Figure 14 shows the differences between patch-based CNN and our approach for building heat map generation.

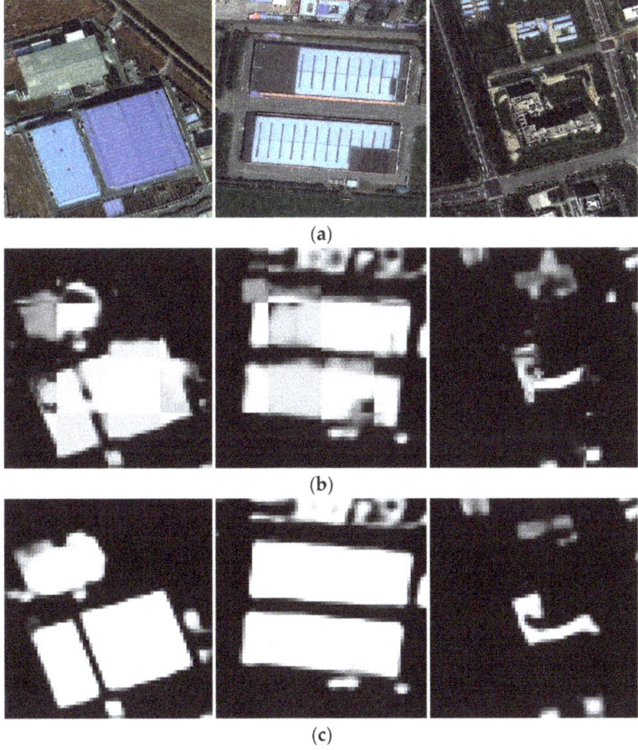

Figure 14. Heat map for the building generated by patch-based CNN and our approach. (**a**) Original images; (**b**) Heat map generated by patch-based CNN classification using 128 × 128 patches; (**c**) Heat map generated by the FCN model.

Compared with the patch-based approaches, our model takes the whole image as the input, and performs the classification in a single-loop manner, which considers the context information overall and seamlessly. Our model eliminates the discontinuities at the patch boundaries. This is also the most remarkable advantage of FCN.

4.3. FCN-8s vs. Our Approach

FCN model is a *convolutionalized* version of standard CNN through a simple modification. The most significant feature of the FCN model is: on the one hand, FCN inherits the high accuracy feature for image-label classification from standard CNN. On the other hand, it maintains the 2-D spatial information of the input image, thus achieving dense class prediction. However, pooling operations cause serious reduction of the resolution. The output is not fine enough, which will result in the loss of valuable detail information. As can be seen from Figure 15, our approach outperforms FCN-8s in terms of detail preserving. Therefore, the classification accuracy is greatly improved.

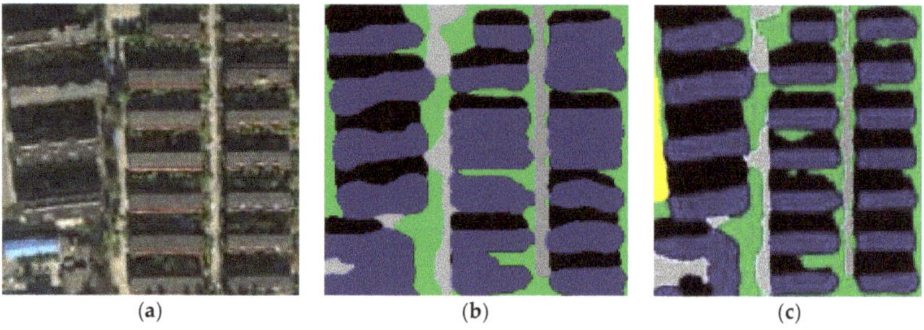

(a)   (b)   (c)

Figure 15. Detail comparison between FCN-8s and our approach. (**a**) Original images; (**b**) Classification result from FCN-8s; (**c**) Classification result from our approach.

As the most accurate model in the FCN family, FCN-8s combines the feature maps with different resolutions from different pooling stages, to obtain a more intensive class prediction. In FCN models, the lost resolution is compensated by the deconvolution operation. However, deconvolution is difficult for efficiently restoring the resolution by way of learning. Benefiting from the "atrous" convolution, the resolution of the feature map is maintained naturally in our approach. Besides, FCN models do not consider the relationship between pixels, ignoring the spatial regularization that is commonly employed in remote sensing image analysis. In our approach, the relationship between pixels is taken into account by CRF-based post-processing. The class map predicted by FCN is further refined, and the accuracy is therefore improved.

5. Conclusions

This paper presents a classification approach for high resolution images using an improved FCN model. Compared with the object-oriented method and two typical deep learning-based approaches, the classification accuracy is obviously improved.

Our FCN-based classification combines the segmentation and classification stages, taking the class accuracy as the only constraint, and achieves high quality classification in an end-to-end way. The GT classes of ground objects are taken as the supervised information that guides both the feature extraction and the region generation. The classification results of using "atrous" convolution and CRF-based post-processing allows us to obtain a high resolution class prediction. In addition, due to the use of a multi-scale model, the model trained from the GF-2 images also has high classification

Remote Sens. **2017**, *9*, 498

accuracy on the IKONOS images. It is proven that our approach has a strong applicability for images with different resolutions.

The main limitation of our approach is that it needs a large number of high quality GT-labels for the model training, which relies on professional interpretation experiences and lots of manual work. Therefore, the main aspect of our future work is training the model in a weak supervision way, to further enhance its applicability.

Acknowledgments: This work was jointly supported by the National Natural Science Foundation of China (Grant No. 41571414. Title: Eco-environment assessment of Yanhe watershed based on temporal-spatial entropy), Beijing Municipal Science and Technology Project (Grant No. Z161100001116102. Title: Research on Remote Sensing Technology in Soil and Water Conservation and Demonstrative Application in Beijing), and the Fundamental Research Project in China Institute of Water Resources and Hydropower Research (Grant No. JZ0145B2017. Title: Research on Spatial-Temporal Variable Source Runoff Model and Mechanism).

Author Contributions: Gang Fu and Changjun Liu proposed and designed the technique roadmap, and performed the programming works; Gang Fu and Tao Sun designed and performed the experiments; Rong Zhou, Tao Sun, and Qijian Zhang collected the training and testing image data, and analyzed the experimental results.

Conflicts of Interest: The authors declare no conflict of interest.

References

1. MacQueen, J.B. Some Methods for classification and Analysis of Multivariate Observations. Proceedings of 5th Berkeley Symposium on Mathematical Statistics and Probability; University of California Press: Berkeley, CA, USA, 1967.; pp. 281–297.
2. Miller, D.M.; Kaminsky, E.J.; Rana, S. Neural network classification of remote-sensing data. *Comput. Geosci.* **1995**, *21*, 377–386.
3. Mas, J.; Flores, J. The application of artificial neural networks to the analysis of remotely sensed data. *Int. J. Remote Sens.* **2008**, *29*, 617–663.
4. Camps-Valls, G.; Bruzzone, L. Kernel-based methods for hyperspectral image classification. *IEEE Trans. Geosci. Remote Sens.* **2005**, *43*, 1351–1362.
5. Mountrakis, G.; Im, J.; Ogole, C. Support vector machines in remote sensing: A review. *ISPRS J. Photogramm. Remote Sens.* **2011**, *66*, 247–259.
6. Yuan, Y.; Lin, J.; Wang, Q. Hyperspectral Image Classification via Multitask Joint Sparse Representation and Stepwise MRF Optimization. *IEEE Trans. Cybern.* **2016**, *46*, 2966–2977.
7. Wang, Q.; Lin, J.; Yuan, Y. Salient Band Selection for Hyperspectral Image Classification via Manifold Ranking. *IEEE Trans. Neural Netw. Learn. Syst.* **2016**, *27*, 1279–1289.
8. Walter, V. Object-based classification of remote sensing data for change detection. *ISPRS J. Photogramm. Remote Sens.* **2004**, *58*, 225–238.
9. Definiens Image. *eCognition User's Guide 4*; Definiens Image: Bernhard, Germany, 2004.
10. Feature Extraction Module Version 4.6. In *ENVI Feature Extraction Module User's Guide*; ITT Corporation: Boulder, CO, USA, 2008.
11. Baatz, M.; Schäpe, A. Multiresolution Segmentation: An Optimization Approach for High Quality Multi-scale Image Segmentation. In *Angewandte Geographische Information Sverarbeitung XII*; Herbert Wichmann Verlag: Heidelberg, Germany, 2000; pp. 12–23.
12. Robinson, D.J.; Redding, N.J.; Crisp, D.J. *Implementation of a Fast Algorithm for Segmenting SAR Imagery*; DSTO Electronics and Surveillance Research Laboratory: Edinburgh, Australia, 2002.
13. Cheng, Y. Mean shift, mode seeking, and clustering. *IEEE Trans. Pat.* **1995**, *17*, 790–799.
14. Fu, G.; Zhao, H.; Li, C.; Shi, L. Segmentation for High-Resolution Optical Remote Sensing Imagery Using Improved Quadtree and Region Adjacency Graph Technique. *Remote Sens.* **2013**, *5*, 3259–3279.
15. Hinton, G.; Osindero, S.; Welling, M.; Teh, Y.-W. Unsupervised Discovery of Nonlinear Structure Using Contrastive Backpropagation. *Science* **2006**, *30*, 725–732.
16. Deep Learning. Available online: https://en.wikipedia.org/wiki/Deep_learning (accessed on 3 May 2017).
17. Hinton, G.E.; Osindero, S.; Teh, Y.W. A Fast Learning Algorithm for Deep Belief Nets. *Neural Comput.* **2006**, *18*, 1527–1554.

18. Convolutional Neural Networks (LeNet)—DeepLearning 0.1 Documentation. DeepLearning 0.1. LISA Lab. Retrieved 31 August 2013. Available online: http://deeplearning.net/tutorial/lenet.html (accessed on 5 May 2017).

19. Graves, A.; Liwicki, M.; Fernandez, S.; Bertolami, R.; Bunke, H.; Schmidhuber, J. A Novel Connectionist System for Improved Unconstrained Handwriting Recognition. *IEEE Trans. Pattern Anal. Mach. Intell.* **2009**, *31*, 855–868.

20. Krizhevsky, A.; Sutskever, I.; Hinton, G.E. Imagenet classification with deep convolutional neural networks. In Proceedings of the Neural Information Processing Systems (NIPS) Conference, La Jolla, CA, USA, 3–8 December 2012.

21. Ciresan, D.; Meier, U.; Schmidhuber, J. Multi-column deep neural networks for image classification. In Proceedings of the Conference on Computer Vision and Pattern Recognition (CVPR), Providence, RI, USA, 16–21 June 2012; pp. 3642–3649.

22. Nguyen, T.; Han, J.; Park, D.C. Satellite image classification using convolutional learning. In Proceedings of the AIP Conference, Albuquerque, NM, USA, 7–10 October 2013; pp. 2237–2240.

23. Wang, J.; Song, J.; Chen, M.; Yang, Z. Road network extraction: A neural-dynamic framework based on deep learning and a finite state machine. *Int. J. Remote Sens.* **2015**, *36*, 3144–3169.

24. Castelluccio, M.; Poggi, G.; Sansone, C.; Verdoliva, L. Land Use Classification in Remote Sensing Images by Convolutional Neural Networks. *arXiv*, **2015**, arXiv:1508.00092.

25. Hu, F.; Xia, G.S.; Hu, J.; Zhang, L. Transferring deep convolutional neural networks for the scene classification of high-resolution remote sensing imagery. *Remote Sens.* **2015**, *7*, 14680–14707.

26. Zhou, W.; Newsam, S.; Li, C.; Shao, Z. Learning Low Dimensional Convolutional Neural Networks for High-Resolution Remote Sensing Image Retrieval. *arXiv*, **2016**, arXiv:1610.03023.

27. Mnih, V. Machine Learning for Aerial Image Labeling. Ph.D. Thesis, University of Toronto, Toronto, ON, Canada, 2013.

28. Lagkvist, M.; Kiselev, A.; Alirezaie, M.; Loutfi, A. Classification and Segmentation of Satellite Orthoimagery Using Convolutional Neural Networks. *Remote Sens.* **2016**, *8*, 329.

29. Long, J.; Shelhamer, E.; Darrell, T. Fully Convolutional Networks for Semantic Segmentation. In Proceedings of the Conference on Computer Vision and Pattern Recognition (CVPR), Boston, MA, USA, 7–12 June 2015.

30. Chen, L.C.; Kokkinos, I.; Murphy, K.; Yuille, A.L. Semantic Image Segmentation with Deep Convolutional Nets and Fully Connected CRFs. In Proceedings of the International Conference on Learning Representations (ICLR), San Diego, CA, USA, 7–9 May 2015.

31. Paisitkriangkrai, S.; Sherrah, J.; Janney, P.; Van den Hengel, A. Effective Semantic Pixel labelling with Convolutional Networks and Conditional Random Fields. In Proceedings of the Conference on Computer Vision and Pattern Recognition (CVPR), Boston, MA, USA, 7–12 June 2015.

32. Zheng, S.; Jayasumana, S.; Romera-Paredes, B.; Vineety, V.; Su, Z. Conditional Random Fields as Recurrent Neural Networks. In Proceedings of the Conference on Computer Vision and Pattern Recognition (CVPR), Las Vegas, NV, USA, 26 June–1 July 2016.

33. Sherrah, J. Fully Convolutional Networks for Dense Semantic Labelling of High-Resolution Aerial Imagery. *arXiv*, **2016**, arXiv:1606.02585.

34. Marmanis, D.; Wegner, J.D.; Galliani, S.; Schindler, K.; Datcu, M.; Stilla, U. Semantic segmentation of aerial images with an ensemble of CNSS. In Proceedings of the ISPRS Annals of the Photogrammetry, Remote Sensing and Spatial Information Sciences, Prague, Czech Republic, 12–19 July 2016.

35. Maggiori, E.; Tarabalka, Y.; Charpiat, G.; Alliez, P. Fully Convolutional Neural Networks for Remote Sensing Image Classification. In Proceedings of the 2016 IEEE International Geoscience and Remote Sensing Symposium (IGARSS), Beijing, China, 10–15 July 2016; pp. 5071–5074.

36. Maggiori, E.; Tarabalka, Y.; Charpiat, G.; Alliez, P. Convolutional Neural Networks for Large-Scale Remote Sensing Image Classification. *IEEE Trans. Geosci. Remote Sens.* **2017**, *2*, 645–657.

37. Maggiori, E.; Tarabalka, Y.; Charpiat, G.; Alliez, P. High-Resolution Semantic Labeling with Convolutional Neural Networks. *arXiv*, **2016**, arXiv:1611.01962.

38. Simonyan, K.; Zisserman, A. Very deep convolutional networks for large-scale image recognition. *arXiv*, **2014**, arXiv:1409.1556.

39. He, K.; Zhang, X.; Ren, S.; Sun, J. Deep residual learning for image recognition. *arXiv*, **2015**, arXiv:1512.03385.

40. Szegedy, C.; Ioffe, S.; Vanhoucke, V.; Alemi, A. Inception-v4, Inception-ResNet and the Impact of Residual Connections on Learning. *arXiv*, **2016**, arXiv:1602.07261.
41. Bertasius, G.; Shi, J.; Torresani, L. Deepedge: A multiscale bifurcated deep network for top-down contour detection. In Proceedings of the Conference on Computer Vision and Pattern Recognition (CVPR), Boston, MA, USA, 7–12 June 2015.
42. Xie, S.; Tu, Z. Holistically-Nested Edge Detection. *arXiv*, **2015**, arXiv:1504.06375.
43. Krahenbuhl, P.; Koltun, V. Efficient Inference in Fully Connected CRFs with Gaussian Edge Potentials. In Proceedings of the 24th International Conference on Neural Information Processing Systems (NIPS), Granada, Spain, 12–15 December 2011.
44. Nussbaum, S.; Niemeyer, I.; Canty, M.J. SEATH—A new tool for automated feature extraction in the context of object-based image analysis. In Proceedings of the 1st International Conference on Object-Based Image Analysis, Salzburg, Austria, 4–5 July 2006. XXXVI-4/C42.
45. Chang, C.C.; Lin, C.J. LIBSVM: A library for support vector machines. *ACM Trans. Intell. Syst. Technol.* **2011**, 2.

Article

Hyperspectral Dimensionality Reduction by Tensor Sparse and Low-Rank Graph-Based Discriminant Analysis

Lei Pan [1], Heng-Chao Li [1,*], Yang-Jun Deng [1], Fan Zhang [2], Xiang-Dong Chen [1] and Qian Du [3]

[1] School of Information Science & Technology, Southwest Jiaotong University, Chengdu 610031, China; mapan.lei@163.com (L.P.); dyj2012@yeah.net (Y.-J.D.); xdchen@home.swjtu.edu.cn (X.-D.C.)

[2] College of Information Science & Technology, Beijing University of Chemical Technology, Beijing 100029, China; zhangf@mail.buct.edu.cn

[3] Department of Electrical & Computer Engineering, Mississippi State University, Starkville, MS 39762, USA; du@ece.msstate.edu

* Correspondence: lihengchao_78@163.com; Tel.: +86-139-8212-3202

Academic Editors: Qi Wang, Nicolas H. Younan, Carlos López-Martínez, Lenio Soares Galvao and Prasad S. Thenkabail

Received: 14 March 2017; Accepted: 3 May 2017; Published: 6 May 2017

Abstract: Recently, sparse and low-rank graph-based discriminant analysis (SLGDA) has yielded satisfactory results in hyperspectral image (HSI) dimensionality reduction (DR), for which sparsity and low-rankness are simultaneously imposed to capture both local and global structure of hyperspectral data. However, SLGDA fails to exploit the spatial information. To address this problem, a tensor sparse and low-rank graph-based discriminant analysis (TSLGDA) is proposed in this paper. By regarding the hyperspectral data cube as a third-order tensor, small local patches centered at the training samples are extracted for the TSLGDA framework to maintain the structural information, resulting in a more discriminative graph. Subsequently, dimensionality reduction is performed on the tensorial training and testing samples to reduce data redundancy. Experimental results of three real-world hyperspectral datasets demonstrate that the proposed TSLGDA algorithm greatly improves the classification performance in the low-dimensional space when compared to state-of-the-art DR methods.

Keywords: hyperspectral image; sparse and low-rank graph; tensor; dimensionality reduction

---

1. Introduction

A hyperspectral image contains a wealth of spectral information about different materials by collecting the reflectance of hundreds of contiguous narrow spectral bands from the visible to infrared electromagnetic spectrum [1–3]. However, the redundant information in a hyperspectral image not only increases computational complexity but also degrades classification performance when training samples are limited. Some research has demonstrated that the redundancy can be reduced without a significant loss of useful information [4–7]. As such, reducing the dimensionality of hyperspectral images is a reasonable and important preprocessing step for subsequent analysis and practical applications.

Dimensionality reduction (DR) aims to reduce the redundancy among features and simultaneously preserve the discriminative information. In general, existing DR methods may belong to one of three categories: unsupervised, supervised, and semisupervised. The unsupervised methods do not take the class label information of training samples into consideration. The most commonly used unsupervised DR algorithm is principal component analysis (PCA) [8], which is to find a linear transformation by maximizing the variance in the projected subspace. Linear discriminant analysis (LDA) [9], as a simple supervised DR method, is proposed to maximize the trace ratio of between-class and within-class scatter matrices. To address the application limitation in data distribution of LDA, local Fisher's discriminant analysis (LFDA) [10] is developed. In order to overcome the difficulty that the number of training samples is usually limited, some semisupervised DR methods in [11,12] are proposed.

The graph, as a mathematical data representation, has been successfully embedded in the framework of DR, resulting in the development of many effective DR methods. Recently, a general graph embedding (GE) framework [13] has been proposed to formulate most of the existing DR methods, in which an undirected graph is constructed to characterize the geometric information of the data. k-nearest neighbors and ε-radius ball [14] are two traditional methods to construct adjacency graphs. However, these two methods are sensitive to the noise and may lead to incorrect data representation. To construct an appropriate graph, a graph-based discriminant analysis with spectral similarity (GDA-SS) measurement was recently proposed by considering curves changing description among spectral bands in [15]. Sparse representation (SR) [16,17] has attracted much attention because of its benefits of data-adaptive neighborhoods and noise robustness. Based on this work, a sparse graph embedding (SGE) model [18] was developed by exploring the sparsity structure of the data. In [19], a sparse graph-based discriminant analysis (SGDA) model was developed for hyperspectral image dimensionality reduction and classification by exploiting the class label information, improving the performance of SGE. In [20], a weighted SGDA integrated both the locality and sparsity structure of the data. To reduce the computational cost, collaborative graph-based discriminant analysis (CGDA) [21] was introduced by imposing an l_2 regularization on sparse coefficient vector. In [22], Laplacian regularization was imposed on CGDA, resulting in the LapCGDA algorithm. SR is able to reveal the local structure but fails in capturing the global structure. To solve this problem, a sparse and low-rank graph-based discriminant analysis (SLGDA) [23] was proposed to simultaneously preserve the local and global structure of hyperspectral data.

However, the aforementioned graph-based DR methods only deal with spectral vector-based (first-order) representations, which do not take the spatial information of hyperspectral data into consideration. Aiming to overcome this shortcoming, simultaneous sparse graph embedding (SSGE) was proposed to improve the classification performance in [24]. Although SSGE has obtained enhanced performance, it still puts the spectral-spatial feature into first-order data for analysis and ignores the cubic nature of hyperspectral data that can be taken as a third-order tensor. Some researchers have verified the advantage of tensor representation when processing the hyperspectral data. For example, multilinear principal component analysis (MPCA) [25] was integrated with support vector machines (SVM) for tensor-based classification in [26]. A group based tensor model [27] by exploiting clustering technique was developed for DR and classification. In addition, a tensor discriminative locality alignment (TDLA) [28] algorithm was proposed for hyperspectral image spectral-spatial feature representation and DR, which has been extended in [29] by combining with well-known spectral-spatial feature extraction methods (such as extended morphological profiles (EMPs) [30], extended attribute profiles (EAPs) [31], and Gabors [32]) for classification. Though the previous tensor-based DR methods have achieved great improvement on performance, they do not consider the structure property from other perspectives, such as representation-based and graph-based points.

In this context, we propose a novel DR method, i.e., tensor sparse and low-rank graph-based discriminant analysis (TSLGDA), for hyperspectral data, in which the information from three perspectives (tensor representation, sparse and low-rank representation, and graph theory) is exploited to present the data structure for hyperspectral image. It is noteworthy that the proposed method aims to exploit the spatial information through tensor representation, which is different from the work in [23] only considering the spectral information. Furthermore, tensor locality preserving projection (TLPP) [33] is exploited to obtain three projection matrices for three dimensions (one spectral dimension and two spatial dimensions) in TSLGDA, while SLGDA [23] only considers one spectral projection matrix by locality preserving projection. The contributions of our work lie in the following aspects: (1) tensor representation is utilized in the framework of sparse and low-rank graph-based discriminant analysis for DR of hyperspectral image. To the best of our knowledge, this is the first time that tensor theory, sparsity, and low-rankness are combined in graph embedding framework; (2) Tensorial structure contains the spectral-spatial information, sparse and low-rank representation reveals both local and global structure and a graph preserves manifold structure. The integration of these three techniques remarkably promotes discriminative ability of reduced features in low-dimensional subspaces; (3) The proposed method can effectively deal with small training size problem, even for the class with only two labeled samples.

The rest of this paper is organized as follows. Section 2 briefly describes the tensor basics and some existing DR methods. The proposed TSLGDA algorithm for DR of hyperspectral imagery is provided in detail in Section 3. Parameters discussions and experimental results compared with some state-of-the-art methods are given in Section 4. Finally, Section 5 concludes this paper with some remarks.

2. Related Work

In this paper, if not specified otherwise, lowercase italic letters denote scalars, e.g., i, j, k, bold lowercase letters denote vectors, e.g., $\mathbf{x}$, $\mathbf{y}$, bold uppercase letters denote matrices, e.g., $\mathbf{U}$, $\mathbf{X}$, and bold uppercase letters with underline denote tensors, e.g., $\underline{\mathbf{A}}$, $\underline{\mathbf{X}}$.

2.1. Tensor Basics

A multidimensional array is defined as a tensor, which is represented as $\underline{\mathbf{A}} \in \mathbf{R}^{I_1 \times \cdots I_n \times \cdots I_N}$. We regard $\underline{\mathbf{A}} \in \mathbf{R}^{I_1 \times \cdots I_n \times \cdots I_N}$ as an N-order tensor, corresponding to an N-dimensional data array, with its element denoted as $\underline{\mathbf{A}}_{i_1 \ldots i_n \ldots i_N}$, where $1 \leq i_n \leq I_n$, and $1 \leq n \leq N$. Some basic definitions related to tensor operation are provided as follows [28,33,34].

Definition 1. *(Frobenius norm):* *The Frobenius norm of a tensor $\underline{\mathbf{A}}$ is defined as* $\|\underline{\mathbf{A}}\|_F = (\sum_{i_1 \ldots i_N} (\underline{\mathbf{A}}_{i_1 \ldots i_N})^2)^{1/2}$.

Definition 2. *(Mode-n matricizing):* *The n-mode vector of an N-order tensor $\underline{\mathbf{A}} \in \mathbf{R}^{I_1 \times \cdots I_n \times \cdots I_N}$ is defined as an n-dimensional vector by fixing all indices except i_n. The n-mode matrix is composed of all the n-mode vectors in column form, denoted as $\mathbf{A}^n \in \mathbf{R}^{I_n \times (I_1 \ldots I_{n-1} I_{n+1} \ldots I_N)}$. The obtained n-mode matrix is also known as n-mode unfolding of a tensor $\underline{\mathbf{A}}$.*

Definition 3. *(Mode-n product):* *The mode-n product of a tensor $\underline{\mathbf{A}}$ with a matrix $\mathbf{U} \in \mathbf{R}^{I'_n \times I_n}$ yields $\underline{\mathbf{C}} = \underline{\mathbf{A}} \times_n \mathbf{U}$, and $\underline{\mathbf{C}} \in \mathbf{R}^{I_1 \cdots I_{n-1} I'_n I_{n+1} \cdots I_N}$, whose entries are computed by*

$$\underline{\mathbf{C}}_{i_1 \ldots i_{n-1} i'_n i_{n+1} \ldots i_N} = \sum_{i_n=1}^{I_n} \underline{\mathbf{A}}_{i_1 \ldots i_{n-1} i_n i_{n+1} \ldots i_N} \mathbf{U}_{i'_n i_n} \tag{1}$$

where $i_k = 1, 2, \ldots, I_k, (k \neq n)$ and $i'_n = 1, 2, \ldots, I'_n$. Note that the n-mode product can also be expressed in terms of unfolding tensor

$$\underline{\mathbf{C}} = \underline{\mathbf{A}} \times_n \mathbf{U} \Leftrightarrow \mathbf{C}^n = \mathbf{U} \mathbf{A}^n \tag{2}$$

where $\times_n$ denotes mode-n product between a tensor and a matrix.

Definition 4. *(Tensor contraction):* *The contraction of tensors $\underline{\mathbf{A}} \in \mathbf{R}^{I_1 \times \cdots \times I_N \times I'_1 \times \cdots \times I'_{N'}}$ and $\underline{\mathbf{B}} \in \mathbf{R}^{I_1 \times \cdots \times I_N \times I''_1 \times \cdots \times I''_{N''}}$ is defined as*

$$[\underline{\mathbf{A}} \otimes \underline{\mathbf{B}}; (1 : N)(1 : N)]_{i_1, i_2, \ldots, i_N} = \sum_{i_1=1}^{I_1} \cdots \sum_{i_N=1}^{I_N} \underline{\mathbf{A}}_{i_1, \ldots, i_N, i'_1, \ldots, i'_{N'}} \underline{\mathbf{B}}_{i_1, \ldots, i_N, i''_1, \ldots, i''_{N''}} \tag{3}$$

The condition for tensor contraction is that both two tensors should have the same size at the specific mode. For example, when the contraction is conducted on all indices except for the index n on tensors $\underline{\mathbf{A}}, \underline{\mathbf{B}} \in \mathbf{R}^{I_1 \times \cdots I_n \times \cdots I_N}$, *this operation can be denoted as* $[\underline{\mathbf{A}} \otimes \underline{\mathbf{B}}; (\overline{n})(\overline{n})]$. *According to the property of tensor contraction, we have*

$$[\underline{\mathbf{A}} \otimes \underline{\mathbf{B}}; (\overline{n})(\overline{n})] = \mathbf{A}^n \mathbf{B}^{n\,T} \tag{4}$$

2.2. Sparse and Low-Rank Graph-Based Discriminant Analysis

In [19], sparse graph-based discriminant analysis (SGDA), as a supervised DR method, was proposed to extract important features for hyperspectral data. Although SGDA can successfully reveal the local structure of the data, it fails to capture the global information. To address this problem, sparse and low-rank graph-based discriminant analysis (SLGDA) [23] was developed to preserve local neighborhood structure and global geometrical structure simultaneously by combining the sparse and low-rank constraints. The objective function of SLGDA can be formulated as

$$\arg\min_{\mathbf{W}^{(l)}} \frac{1}{2} \|\mathbf{X}^{(l)} - \mathbf{X}^{(l)}\mathbf{W}^{(l)}\|_F^2 + \beta\|\mathbf{W}^{(l)}\|_* + \lambda\|\mathbf{W}^{(l)}\|_1,$$
$$s.t.\ diag(\mathbf{W}^{(l)}) = 0 \tag{5}$$

where β and λ are two regularization parameters to control the effect of low-rank term and sparse term, respectively, $\mathbf{X}^{(l)}$ represents samples from the *l*th class in a vector-based way, and $l = [1, 2, \ldots, c]$, in which c is the number of total classes. After obtaining the complete graph weight matrix $\mathbf{W} = diag(\mathbf{W}^{(1)}, \mathbf{W}^{(2)}, \ldots, \mathbf{W}^{(c)})$, the projection operator can be solved as

$$\begin{aligned}
\mathbf{P}^* &= \arg\min_{\mathbf{P}^\mathbf{T}\mathbf{X}\mathbf{L}_p\mathbf{X}^\mathbf{T}\mathbf{P}} \sum_{i \neq j} \|\mathbf{P}^T\mathbf{x}_i - \mathbf{P}^T\mathbf{x}_j\|_2^2 \mathbf{W}_{ij} \\
&= \arg\min_{\mathbf{P}^\mathbf{T}\mathbf{X}\mathbf{L}_p\mathbf{X}^\mathbf{T}\mathbf{P}} tr(\mathbf{P}^\mathbf{T}\mathbf{X}\mathbf{L}_s\mathbf{X}^\mathbf{T}\mathbf{P})
\end{aligned} \tag{6}$$

where $\mathbf{L}_s = \mathbf{D} - \mathbf{W}$ is defined as the Laplacian matrix, $\mathbf{D}$ is a diagonal matrix with the *i*th diagonal entry being $\mathbf{D}_{ii} = \sum_{j=1}^{N} \mathbf{W}_{ij}$, and $\mathbf{L}_p$ may be a simple scale normalization constraint [13].

The projection can be further formulated as

$$\mathbf{P}^* = \arg\min_{\mathbf{P}} \frac{|\mathbf{P}^T\mathbf{X}\mathbf{L}_s\mathbf{X}^T\mathbf{P}|}{|\mathbf{P}^T\mathbf{X}\mathbf{L}_p\mathbf{X}^T\mathbf{P}|} \tag{7}$$

which can be solved as a generalized eigendecomposition problem

$$\mathbf{X}\mathbf{L}_s\mathbf{X}^T\mathbf{p}_b = \lambda_b\mathbf{X}\mathbf{L}_p\mathbf{X}^T\mathbf{p}_b \tag{8}$$

The *b*th projection vector $\mathbf{p}_b$ is the eigenvector corresponding to the *b*th smallest nonzero eigenvalue. The projection matrix can be formed as $\mathbf{P} = [\mathbf{p}_1, \ldots, \mathbf{p}_B] \in \mathbf{R}^{d \times B}$, $B \ll d$. Finally, the reduced features are denoted as $\widehat{\mathbf{X}} = \mathbf{P}^T\mathbf{X} \in \mathbf{R}^{B \times M}$.

2.3. Multilinear Principal Component Analysis

In order to obtain a set of multilinear projections that will map the original high-order tensor data into a low-order tensor space, MPCA performs to directly maximize the total scatter matrix on the subspace $\mathbf{U}_i (i \neq n)$

$$\max_{\mathbf{U}_n\mathbf{U}_n^T = \mathbf{I}_n} tr(\mathbf{U}_n\mathbf{S}_T^n\mathbf{U}_n^T) = \max_{\mathbf{U}_n\mathbf{U}_n^T = \mathbf{I}_n} tr\left(\mathbf{U}_n(\sum_{k=1}^{M} \mathbf{X}_k^n\mathbf{X}_k^{n\,T})\mathbf{U}_n^T\right), \tag{9}$$

where $\mathbf{S}_T^n = \sum_{k=1}^{M} \mathbf{X}_k^n\mathbf{X}_k^{n\,T}$ and $\mathbf{X}_k^n$ is the *n*-mode unfolding matrix of tensor $\underline{\mathbf{X}}_k$.

The optimal projections of MPCA can be obtained from the eigendecomposition

$$\mathbf{S}_T^n \mathbf{U}_n^T = \mathbf{U}_n^T \mathbf{D}_n \tag{10}$$

where $\mathbf{U}_n = [\mathbf{u}_n^1, \ldots, \mathbf{u}_n^{d_n}]$ is the eigenvector matrix and $\mathbf{D}_n = diag(\lambda_n^1, \ldots, \lambda_n^{d_n})$ is the eigenvalue matrix of $\mathbf{S}_T^n$, in which the eigenvalues are ranked in descending order, and λ_n^j is the eigenvalue corresponding to the eigenvector $\mathbf{u}_n^j$. The optimal projection matrix for mode-n is composed of the eigenvectors corresponding to the first B_n largest eigenvalues, e.g., $\mathbf{U}_n = [\mathbf{u}_n^1, \ldots, \mathbf{u}_n^{B_n}]$. After obtained the projection matrix for each mode, the reduced features can be formulated as

$$\widehat{\mathbf{X}}_k = \mathbf{X}_k \times_1 \mathbf{U}_1 \ldots \times_N \mathbf{U}_N \tag{11}$$

where $\mathbf{U}_i \in \mathbf{R}^{B_n \times I_n} (B_n \leq I_n)$.

3. Tensor Sparse and Low-Rank Graph-Based Discriminant Analysis

Consider a hyperspectral image as a third-order tensor $\underline{\mathbf{A}} \in \mathbf{R}^{I_1 \times I_2 \times I_3}$, in which I_1 and I_2 refer to the width and height of the data cube, respectively, and I_3 represents the number of spectral bands, $I_3 = d$. Assume that the kth small patch is composed of the kth training sample and its $i_1 \times i_2$ neighbors, which is denoted as $\underline{\mathbf{X}}_k \in \mathbf{R}^{i_1 \times i_2 \times d}$. M patches construct the training set $\{\underline{\mathbf{X}}_k\}_{k=1}^M$. The training patches belonging to the lth class are expressed as $\{\underline{\mathbf{X}}_{k,l}\}_{k=1}^{M_l}$, where M_l represents the number of patches belonging to the lth class and $l \in \{1, 2, \ldots, c\}$. For the purpose of convenient expression, a fourth-order tensor $\underline{\mathbf{X}}^{(l)} \in \mathbf{R}^{i_1 \times i_2 \times d \times M_l}$ is defined to represent these M_l patches, and $\underline{\mathbf{X}} \in \mathbf{R}^{i_1 \times i_2 \times d \times M}$ denotes all training patches for c classes, where $M = \sum_{l=1}^{c} M_l$. A visual illustration of 3-mode vectors, 3-mode unfolding, and 3-mode product is shown in Figure 1.

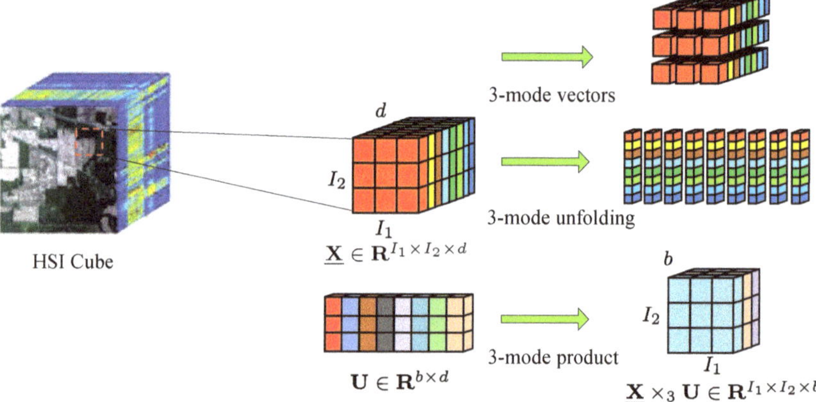

Figure 1. Visual illustration of n-mode vectors, n-mode unfolding, and n-mode product of a third-order tensor from a hyperspectral image.

3.1. Tensor Sparse and Low-Rank Graph

The previous SLGDA framework can capture the local and global structure of hyperspectral data simultaneously by imposing both sparse and low-rank constraints. However, it may lose some important structural information of hyperspectral data, which presents an intrinsic tensor-based data structure. To overcome this drawback, a tensor sparse and low-rank graph is constructed with the objective function

$$\arg\min_{\mathbf{W}^{(l)}} \frac{1}{2}\|\underline{\mathbf{X}}^{(l)} - \underline{\mathbf{X}}^{(l)} \times_4 \mathbf{W}^{(l)}\|_F^2 + \beta\|\mathbf{W}^{(l)}\|_* + \lambda\|\mathbf{W}^{(l)}\|_1,$$
$$s.t.\ diag(\mathbf{W}^{(l)}) = 0, \tag{12}$$

where $\mathbf{W}^{(l)} \in \mathbf{R}^{M_l \times M_l}$ denotes the graph weigh matrix using labeled patches from the lth class only. As such, with the help of class-specific labeled training patches, the global graph weigh matrix $\mathbf{W}$ can be designed as a block-diagonal structure

$$\mathbf{W} = \begin{bmatrix} \mathbf{W}^{(1)} & & \mathbf{0} \\ & \ddots & \\ \mathbf{0} & & \mathbf{W}^{(c)} \end{bmatrix} \tag{13}$$

To obtain the lth class graph weight matrix $\mathbf{W}^{(l)}$, the alternating direction method of multipliers (ADMM) [35] is adopted to solve problem (12). Two auxiliary variables $\mathbf{Z}^{(l)}$ and $\mathbf{J}^{(l)}$ are first introduced to make the objective function separable

$$\arg\min_{\mathbf{Z}^{(l)},\mathbf{J}^{(l)},\mathbf{W}^{(l)}} \frac{1}{2}\|\underline{\mathbf{X}}^{(l)} - \underline{\mathbf{X}}^{(l)} \times_4 \mathbf{W}^{(l)}\|_F^2 + \beta\|\mathbf{Z}^{(l)}\|_* + \lambda\|\mathbf{J}^{(l)}\|_1,$$
$$s.t.\ \mathbf{W}^{(l)} = \mathbf{Z}^{(l)},\ \mathbf{W}^{(l)} = \mathbf{J}^{(l)} - diag(\mathbf{J}^{(l)}) \tag{14}$$

The augmented Lagrangian function of problem (14) is given as

$$L(\mathbf{Z}^{(l)},\mathbf{J}^{(l)},\mathbf{W}^{(l)},\mathbf{D}_1,\mathbf{D}_2)$$
$$= \frac{1}{2}\|\underline{\mathbf{X}}^{(l)} - \underline{\mathbf{X}}^{(l)} \times_4 \mathbf{W}^{(l)}\|_F^2 + \beta\|\mathbf{Z}^{(l)}\|_* + \lambda\|\mathbf{J}^{(l)}\|_1 + \langle\mathbf{D}_1, \mathbf{W}^{(l)} - \mathbf{Z}^{(l)}\rangle + \langle\mathbf{D}_2, \mathbf{W}^{(l)} - \mathbf{J}^{(l)} + diag(\mathbf{J}^{(l)})\rangle \tag{15}$$
$$+ \frac{\mu}{2}(\|\mathbf{W}^{(l)} - \mathbf{Z}^{(l)}\|_F^2 + \|\mathbf{W}^{(l)} - \mathbf{J}^{(l)} + diag(\mathbf{J}^{(l)})\|_F^2)$$

where $\mathbf{D}_1$ and $\mathbf{D}_2$ are Lagrangian multipliers, and μ is a penalty parameter.

By minimizing the function $L(\mathbf{Z}^{(l)},\mathbf{J}^{(l)},\mathbf{W}^{(l)})$, each variable is alternately updated with other variables being fixed. The updating rules are expressed as

$$\mathbf{Z}_{t+1}^{(l)} = \arg\min_{\mathbf{Z}^{(l)}} \beta\|\mathbf{Z}^{(l)}\|_* + \langle\mathbf{D}_{1,t}, \mathbf{W}_t^{(l)} - \mathbf{Z}^{(l)}\rangle + \frac{\mu_t}{2}\|\mathbf{W}_t^{(l)} - \mathbf{Z}^{(l)}\|_F^2$$
$$= \arg\min_{\mathbf{Z}^{(l)}} \frac{\beta}{\mu_t}\|\mathbf{Z}^{(l)}\|_* + \frac{1}{2}\|\mathbf{Z}^{(l)} - (\mathbf{W}_t^{(l)} + \frac{\mathbf{D}_{1,t}}{\mu_t})\|_F^2 \tag{16}$$
$$= \Omega_{\frac{\beta}{\mu_t}}(\mathbf{W}_t^{(l)} + \frac{\mathbf{D}_{1,t}}{\mu_t})$$

$$\mathbf{J}_{t+1}^{(l)} = \arg\min_{\mathbf{J}^{(l)}} \lambda\|\mathbf{J}^{(l)}\|_1 + \langle\mathbf{D}_{2,t}, \mathbf{W}_t^{(l)} - \mathbf{J}\rangle + \frac{\mu_t}{2}\|\mathbf{W}_t^{(l)} - \mathbf{J}^{(l)}\|_F^2$$
$$= \arg\min_{\mathbf{J}^{(l)}} \frac{\lambda}{\mu_t}\|\mathbf{J}^{(l)}\|_1 + \frac{1}{2}\|\mathbf{J}^{(l)} - (\mathbf{W}_t^{(l)} + \frac{\mathbf{D}_{2,t}}{\mu_t})\|_F^2 \tag{17}$$
$$= \mathcal{S}_{\frac{\lambda}{\mu_t}}(\mathbf{W}_t^{(l)} + \frac{\mathbf{D}_{2,t}}{\mu_t}),$$
$$\mathbf{J}_{t+1}^{(l)} = \mathbf{J}_{t+1}^{(l)} - diag(\mathbf{J}_{t+1}^{(l)}),$$

where μ_t denotes the learning rate, $\Omega_\tau(\Delta) = \mathbf{Q}\mathcal{S}_\tau(\Sigma)\mathbf{V}^T$ is the singular value thresholding operator (SVT), in which $\mathcal{S}_\tau(x) = sgn(x)\max(|x| - \tau, 0)$ is the soft thresholding operator [36]. By fixing $\mathbf{Z}_{t+1}^{(l)}$ and $\mathbf{J}_{t+1}^{(l)}$, the formulation of $\mathbf{W}_{t+1}^{(l)}$ can be written as

$$
\begin{aligned}
\mathbf{W}_{t+1}^{(l)} =\ & \arg\min_{\mathbf{W}^{(l)}} \frac{1}{2}\|\underline{\mathbf{X}}^{(l)} - \underline{\mathbf{X}}^{(l)} \times_4 \mathbf{W}^{(l)}\|_F^2 + \langle \mathbf{D}_{1,t}, \mathbf{W}^{(l)} - \mathbf{Z}_{t+1}^{(l)}\rangle + \langle \mathbf{D}_{2,t}, \mathbf{W}^{(l)} - \mathbf{J}_{t+1}^{(l)}\rangle \\
& + \frac{\mu_t}{2}(\|\mathbf{W}^{(l)} - \mathbf{Z}_{t+1}^{(l)}\|_F^2 + \|\mathbf{W}^{(l)} - \mathbf{J}_{t+1}^{(l)}\|_F^2) \\
=\ & (\mathbf{H}^{(l)} + 2\mu_t\mathbf{I})^{-1}(\mathbf{H}^{(l)} + \mu_t\mathbf{Z}_{t+1}^{(l)} + \mu_t\mathbf{J}_{t+1}^{(l)} - (\mathbf{D}_{1,t} + \mathbf{D}_{2,t})),
\end{aligned}
\tag{18}
$$

where $\mathbf{H}^{(l)} = [\underline{\mathbf{X}}^{(l)} \otimes \underline{\mathbf{X}}^{(l)}; (\overline{4})(\overline{4})] \in \mathbf{R}^{M_l \times M_l}$, $\mathbf{W}^{(l)} \in \mathbf{R}^{M_l \times M_l}$, and $\mathbf{I} \in \mathbf{R}^{M_l \times M_l}$ is an identity matrix.

The global similarity matrix $\mathbf{W}$ will be obtained depending on Equation (13) when each sub-similarity matrix corresponding to each class is calculated from problem (12). Until now, a tensor sparse and low-rank graph $G = \{\underline{\mathbf{X}}, \mathbf{W}\}$ is completely constructed with vertex set $\underline{\mathbf{X}}$ and similarity matrix $\mathbf{W}$. How to obtain a set of projection matrices $\{\mathbf{U}_n \in \mathbf{R}^{B_n \times I_n}, B_n \leq I_n, n = 1, 2, \ldots, N\}$ is the following task.

3.2. Tensor Locality Preserving Projection

The aim of tensor LPP is to find transformation matrices $\{\mathbf{U}_1, \mathbf{U}_2, \ldots, \mathbf{U}_N\}$ to project high-dimensional data $\underline{\mathbf{X}}_i$ into low-dimensional representation $\widehat{\underline{\mathbf{X}}}_i$, where $\widehat{\underline{\mathbf{X}}}_i = \underline{\mathbf{X}}_i \times_1 \mathbf{U}_1 \times_2 \mathbf{U}_2 \cdots \times_N \mathbf{U}_N$.

The optimization problem for tensor LPP can be expressed as

$$
\begin{aligned}
\arg\min J(\mathbf{U}_1, \mathbf{U}_2, \ldots, \mathbf{U}_N) &= \sum_{i,j} \|\widehat{\underline{\mathbf{X}}}_i - \widehat{\underline{\mathbf{X}}}_j\|^2 \mathbf{W}_{ij} \\
&= \sum_{i,j} \|\underline{\mathbf{X}}_i \times_1 \mathbf{U}_1 \cdots \times_N \mathbf{U}_N - \underline{\mathbf{X}}_j \times_1 \mathbf{U}_1 \cdots \times_N \mathbf{U}_N\|^2 \mathbf{W}_{ij} \\
s.t.\ \sum_{i} \|\underline{\mathbf{X}}_i \times_1 \mathbf{U}_1 \cdots \times_N \mathbf{U}_N\|^2 \mathbf{C}_{ii} &= 1
\end{aligned}
\tag{19}
$$

where $\mathbf{C}_{ii} = \sum_j \mathbf{W}_{ij}$. It can be seen that the corresponding tensors $\widehat{\underline{\mathbf{X}}}_i$ and $\widehat{\underline{\mathbf{X}}}_j$ in the embedded tensor space are expected to be close to each other if original tensors $\underline{\mathbf{X}}_i$ and $\underline{\mathbf{X}}_j$ are greatly similar.

To solve the optimization problem (19), an iterative scheme is employed [33]. First, we assume that $\{\mathbf{U}_1, \ldots, \mathbf{U}_{n-1}, \mathbf{U}_{n+1}, \ldots, \mathbf{U}_N\}$ are known, then, let $\widehat{\underline{\mathbf{X}}}_{i,(n)} = \underline{\mathbf{X}}_i \times_1 \mathbf{U}_1 \ldots \times_{n-1} \mathbf{U}_{n-1} \times_{n+1} \mathbf{U}_{n+1} \ldots \times_N \mathbf{U}_N$. With properties of tensor and trace, the objective function (19) is rewritten as

$$
\begin{aligned}
\arg\min J_n(\mathbf{U}_n) &= \sum_{i,j} \|\widehat{\underline{\mathbf{X}}}_{i,(n)} \times_n \mathbf{U}_n - \widehat{\underline{\mathbf{X}}}_{j,(n)} \times_n \mathbf{U}_n\|^2 \mathbf{W}_{ij} \\
&= \sum_{i,j} \|\mathbf{U}_n\widehat{\mathbf{X}}_i^n - \mathbf{U}_n\widehat{\mathbf{X}}_j^n\|^2 \mathbf{W}_{ij} \\
&= \sum_{i,j} tr\left(\mathbf{U}_n((\widehat{\mathbf{X}}_i^n - \widehat{\mathbf{X}}_j^n)(\widehat{\mathbf{X}}_i^n - \widehat{\mathbf{X}}_j^n)^T\mathbf{W}_{ij})\mathbf{U}_n^T\right) \\
&= tr\left(\mathbf{U}_n(\sum_{i,j}(\widehat{\mathbf{X}}_i^n - \widehat{\mathbf{X}}_j^n)(\widehat{\mathbf{X}}_i^n - \widehat{\mathbf{X}}_j^n)^T\mathbf{W}_{ij})\mathbf{U}_n^T\right), \\
s.t.\ tr\left(\mathbf{U}_n(\sum_{i}\widehat{\mathbf{X}}_i^n\widehat{\mathbf{X}}_i^{nT}\mathbf{C}_{ii})\mathbf{U}_n^T\right) &= 1,
\end{aligned}
\tag{20}
$$

where $\widehat{\mathbf{X}}_i^n$ denotes the n-mode unfolding of tensor $\underline{\widehat{\mathbf{X}}}_{i,(n)}$. Finally, the optimal solution of problem (20) is the eigenvectors corresponding to the first B_n smallest nonzero eigenvalues of the following generalized eigenvalue problem

$$\Big(\sum_{i,j}(\widehat{\mathbf{X}}_i^n - \widehat{\mathbf{X}}_j^n)(\widehat{\mathbf{X}}_i^n - \widehat{\mathbf{X}}_j^n)^T \mathbf{W}_{ij}\Big)\mathbf{u} = \lambda\Big(\sum_i \widehat{\mathbf{X}}_i^n \widehat{\mathbf{X}}_i^{nT} \mathbf{C}_{ii}\Big)\mathbf{u} \tag{21}$$

Assume $\boldsymbol{\Phi} = \sum_{i,j}(\widehat{\mathbf{X}}_i^n - \widehat{\mathbf{X}}_j^n)(\widehat{\mathbf{X}}_i^n - \widehat{\mathbf{X}}_j^n)^T \mathbf{W}_{ij}$, $\boldsymbol{\Psi} = \sum_i \widehat{\mathbf{X}}_i^n \widehat{\mathbf{X}}_i^{nT} \mathbf{C}_{ii}$, then, problem (21) can be transformed into

$$\boldsymbol{\Phi}\mathbf{u} = \lambda\boldsymbol{\Psi}\mathbf{u} \tag{22}$$

To solve this problem, the function $eig(\cdot)$ embedded in the MATLAB software (R2013a, The MathWorks, Natick, Massachusetts, USA) is adopted, i.e., $[\mathbf{u}, \boldsymbol{\Lambda}] = eig(\boldsymbol{\Phi}, \boldsymbol{\Psi})$, and the eigenvectors in $\mathbf{u}$ corresponding to the first B_n smallest nonzero eigenvalues in $\boldsymbol{\Lambda}$ are chosen to form the projection matrix. The other projection matrices can be obtained in a similar manner. The complete TSLGDA algorithm is outlined in Algorithm 1.

Algorithm 1: Tensor Sparse and Low-Rank Graph-Based Discriminant Analysis for Classification.

Input: Training patches $\underline{\mathbf{X}} = [\underline{\mathbf{X}}^{(1)}, \underline{\mathbf{X}}^{(2)}, \ldots, \underline{\mathbf{X}}^{(c)}]$, testing patches $\underline{\mathbf{Y}}$, regularization parameters β and λ, reduced dimensionality $\{B_1, B_2, B_3\}$.

Initialize: $\mathbf{Z}_0^{(l)} = \mathbf{J}_0^{(l)} = \mathbf{W}_0^{(l)} = 0$, $\mathbf{Y}_{1,0} = \mathbf{Y}_{2,0} = 0$, $\mu_0 = 0.1$, $\mu_{max} = 10^3$, $\rho_0 = 1.1$, $\varepsilon_1 = 10^{-4}$, $\varepsilon_2 = 10^{-3}$, maxIter = 100, $t = 0$.

1. **for** $l = 1, 2, \ldots, c$ **do**
2.   **repeat**
3.   Compute $\mathbf{Z}_{t+1}^{(l)}, \mathbf{J}_{t+1}^{(l)}$, and $\mathbf{W}_{t+1}^{(l)}$ according to (16)–(18).
4.   Update the Lagrangian multipliers:

        $\mathbf{Y}_{1,t+1} = \mathbf{Y}_{1,t} + \mu_t(\mathbf{W}_{t+1}^{(l)} - \mathbf{Z}_{t+1}^{(l)})$, $\mathbf{Y}_{2,t+1} = \mathbf{Y}_{2,t} + \mu_t(\mathbf{W}_{t+1}^{(l)} - \mathbf{J}_{t+1}^{(l)})$.
5.   Update μ: $\mu_{t+1} = \min(\rho\mu_t, \mu_{max})$, where

$$\rho = \begin{cases} \rho_0, & if\ \mu_t \max(\|\mathbf{W}_{t+1}^{(l)} - \mathbf{W}_t^{(l)}\|_F, \|\mathbf{Z}_{t+1}^{(l)} - \mathbf{Z}_t^{(l)}\|_F, \|\mathbf{J}_{t+1}^{(l)} - \mathbf{J}_t^{(l)}\|_F)/\|\underline{\widehat{\mathbf{X}}}^{(l)}\|_F < \varepsilon_2, \\ 1, & otherwise. \end{cases}$$
6.   Check convergence conditions: $\|\mathbf{W}_{t+1}^{(l)} - \mathbf{Z}_{t+1}^{(l)}\|_\infty < \varepsilon_1$, $\|\mathbf{W}_{t+1}^{(l)} - \mathbf{J}_{t+1}^{(l)}\|_\infty < \varepsilon_1$.
7. $t \leftarrow t + 1$.
8.   **until** convergence conditions are satisfied or $t >$ maxIter.
9. **end for**
10. Construct the block-diagonal weight matrix $\mathbf{W}$ according to (13).
11. Compute the projection matrices $\{\mathbf{U}_1, \mathbf{U}_2, \mathbf{U}_3\}$ according to (21).
12. Compute the reduced features:

    $\underline{\widehat{\mathbf{X}}} = \underline{\mathbf{X}} \times_1 \mathbf{U}_1 \times_2 \mathbf{U}_2 \times_3 \mathbf{U}_3$, $\underline{\widehat{\mathbf{Y}}} = \underline{\mathbf{Y}} \times_1 \mathbf{U}_1 \times_2 \mathbf{U}_2 \times_3 \mathbf{U}_3$.
13. Determine the class label of $\underline{\widehat{\mathbf{Y}}}$ by NN classifier.
14. **Output:** The class labels of test patches.

---

4. Experiments and Discussions

In this section, three hyperspectral datasets are used to verify the performance of the proposed method. The proposed TSLGDA algorithm is compared with some state-of-the-art approaches, including unsupervised methods (e.g., PCA [8], MPCA [25]) and supervised methods (e.g., LDA [9], LFDA [10], SGDA [19], GDA-SS [15], SLGDA [23], G-LTDA (local tensor discriminant analysis with Gabor filters) [29]). SGDA is implemented using the SPAMS (SPArse Modeling Software) toolbox [38]. The nearest neighbor classifier (NN classifier) is exploited to classify the projected features obtained by these DR methods. The class-specific accuracy , overall accuracy (OA), average accuracy (AA), and kappa coefficient (κ) are reported for quantitative assessment after ten runs. All experiments are implemented on an Inter Core i5-4590 CPU personal computer (Santa Clara, CA, USA).

4.1. Experimental Datasets

The first dataset [39] was acquired by Airborne Visible/Infrared Imaging Spectrometer (AVIRIS) sensor over northwest Indiana's Indian Pine test site in June 1992. The AVIRIS sensor generates the wavelength range of 0.4–2.45-μm covered 220 spectral bands. After removing 20 water-absorption bands (bands 104–108, 150–163, and 220), a total of 200 bands is used in experiments. The image with 145 × 145 pixels represents a rural scenario having 16 different land-cover classes. The numbers of training and testing samples in each class are listed in Table 1.

Table 1. Number of training and testing samples for the Indian Pines and University of Pavia datasets.

	Indian Pines			University of Pavia		
Class	Name	Training	Testing	Name	Training	Testing
1	Alfalfa	5	41	Asphalt	40	6591
2	Corn-notill	143	1285	Meadows	40	18,609
3	Corn-mintill	83	747	Gravel	40	2059
4	Corn	24	213	Tree	40	3024
5	Grass-pasture	48	435	Painted metal sheets	40	1305
6	Grass-trees	73	657	Bare Soil	40	4989
7	Grass-pasture-mowed	3	25	Bitumen	40	1290
8	Hay-windrowed	48	430	Self-blocking bricks	40	3642
9	Oats	2	18	Shadows	40	907
10	Soybean-notill	97	875			
11	Soybean-mintill	246	2209			
12	Soybean-clean	59	534			
13	Wheat	21	184			
14	Woods	127	1138			
15	Buildings-Grass-Trees-Drive	39	347			
16	Stone-Steel-Towers	9	84			
Total		1027	9222		360	42,416

The second dataset [39] is the University of Pavia collected by the Reflective Optics System Imaging Spectrometer (ROSIS) sensor in Italy. The image has 103 bands after removing 12 noisy bands with a spectral coverage from 0.43 to 0.86 μm, covering a region of 610 × 340 pixels. There are nine ground-truth classes, from which we randomly select training and testing samples as shown in Table 1.

The third dataset [39] was also collected by the AVIRIS sensor over the Valley of Salinas, Central Coast of California, in 1998. The image comprises 512 × 217 pixels with a spatial resolution of 3.7 m, and only preserves 204 bands after 20 water-absorption bands removed. Table 2 lists 16 land-cover classes and the number of training and testing samples.

Table 2. Number of training and testing samples for the Salinas dataset.

	Salinas		
Class	Name	Training	Testing
1	Brocoli-green-weeds-1	40	1969
2	Brocoli-green-weeds-2	75	3651
3	Fallow	40	1936
4	Fallow-rough-plow	28	1366
5	Fallow-smooth	54	2624
6	Stubble	79	3880
7	Celery	72	3507
8	Grapes-untrained	225	11,046
9	Soil-vinyard-develop	124	6079
10	Corn-senesced-green-weeds	66	3212
11	Lettuce-romaine-4wk	21	1047
12	Lettuce-romaine-5wk	39	1888
13	Lettuce-romaine-6wk	18	898
14	Lettuce-romaine-7wk	21	1049
15	Vinyard-untrained	145	7123
16	Vinyard-vertical-trellis	36	1771
Total		1083	53,046

4.2. Parameters Tuning

For the proposed method, four important parameters (i.e., regularization parameters β and λ, window size, and the number of spectral dimension) that can be divided into three groups need to be determined before proceeding to the following experiments. β and λ control the effect of sparse term and low-rank term in the objective function, respectively, which can be tuned together, while window size and the number of spectral dimension are another two groups that can be determined separately. When analyzing one group specific parameter, the other group parameters are fixed on their corresponding chosen values. According to many existing DR methods [22–24] and tensor-based research [26,28], window size is the first set as 9 for the Indian Pines and Salinas datasets, and 7 for the University of Pavia dataset; the initial value for the number of spectral dimension is given as 30 for all three datasets, and the performance basically reaches steady state with this dimension.

4.2.1. Regularization Parameters for TSLGDA

With the initial values of window size and the number of spectral dimension fixed, β and λ are first tuned to achieve better classification performance. Figure 2 shows the overall classification accuracy with respect to different β and λ by fivefold cross validation for three experimental datasets. It can be clearly seen that the OA values can reach the maximum values for some β and λ. Accordingly, for the Indian Pines dataset, the optimal values of β and λ can be set as $(0.01, 0.1)$, which is also an appropriate choice for the University of Pavia dataset, while $(0.001, 0.1)$ is chosen for the Salinas data.

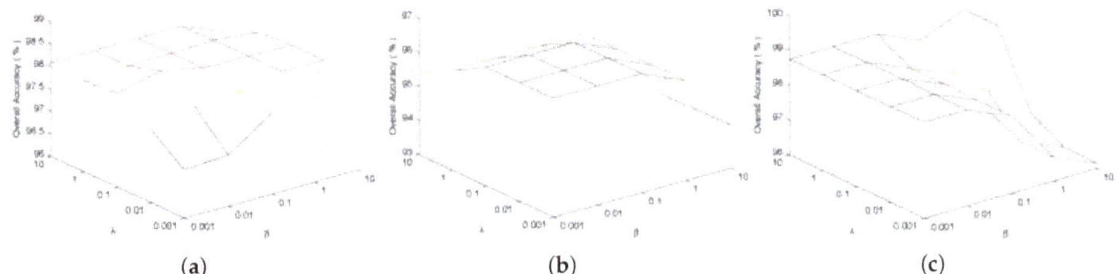

(a)   (b)   (c)

Figure 2. Parameter tuning of β and λ for the proposed TSLGDA algorithm using three datasets: (**a**) Indian Pines; (**b**) University of Pavia; (**c**) Salinas.

4.2.2. Window Size for Tensor Representation

For tensor-based DR methods, i.e., MPCA and TSLGDA, window size (or patch size) is another important parameter. Note that small windows may fail to cover enough spatial information, whereas large windows may contain multiple classes, resulting in complicated analysis and heavy computational burden. Therefore, the window size is searched in the range of $\{3 \times 3, 5 \times 5, 7 \times 7, 9 \times 9\}$. β and λ are fixed on the tuned values, while the numbers of spectral dimension are still set as initial values for three datasets, respectively. Figure 3 presents the variation of classification performances of MPCA and TSLGDA with different window sizes for experimental datasets. It can be seen that the window sizes for MPCA and TSLGDA can be both chosen as 9×9 for the Indian Pines and Salinas datasets, while the optimal values are 5×5 and 7×7, respectively, for the University of Pavia dataset. This may be because the formers represent a rural scenario containing large spatial homogeneity while the Pavia University data is obtained from an urban area with small homogeneous regions. To evaluate the classification performance using the low-dimensional data, 1NN classifier is adopted in this paper.

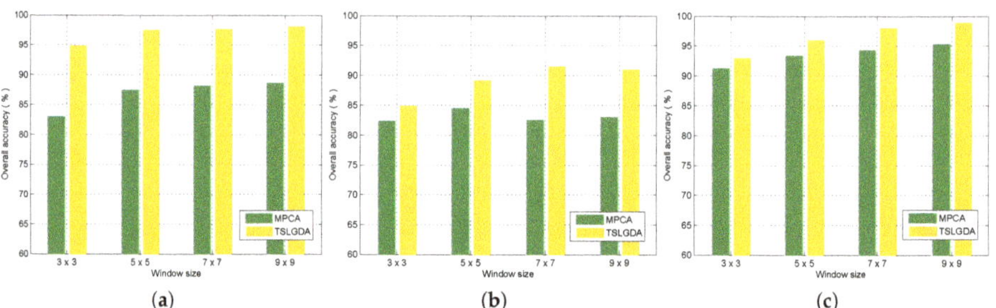

Figure 3. Parameter tuning of window size for MPCA and TSLGDA using three datasets: (**a**) Indian Pines; (**b**) University of Pavia; (**c**) Salinas.

4.2.3. The Number of Spectral Dimension for TSLGDA

According to [28], $\{1,1\}$ is set as the reduced dimensionality of the first two dimensions (i.e., two spatial dimensions). The third dimension (i.e., spectral dimension) is considered carefully by keeping the tuned values of β, λ, and window size is fixed. Figure 4 shows the overall classification accuracy with respect to spectral dimension for three hyperspectral datasets. Obviously, due to the spatial information contained in tensor structure, tensor-based DR methods (i.e., MPCA, TSLGDA) outperform vector-based DR methods (i.e., PCA, SGDA, GDA-SS, SLGDA). According to [29,37], G-LTDA can automatically obtain the optimal reduced dimensions during the optimization procedure; therefore, the number of spectral dimension for G-LTDA is not discussed here. For the Indian Pines dataset, the performances of all considered methods increase when the spectral dimension increases, and then keep stable at the maximum values. The similar results can also be observed from the University of Pavia and Salinas datasets. In any case, TSLGDA outperforms other DR methods even when the spectral dimension is as low as 5. In the following assessment, $\{1,1,30\}$ and $\{1,1,20\}$ dimensions are used to conduct classification for two AVIRIS datasets and one ROSIS dataset, respectively.

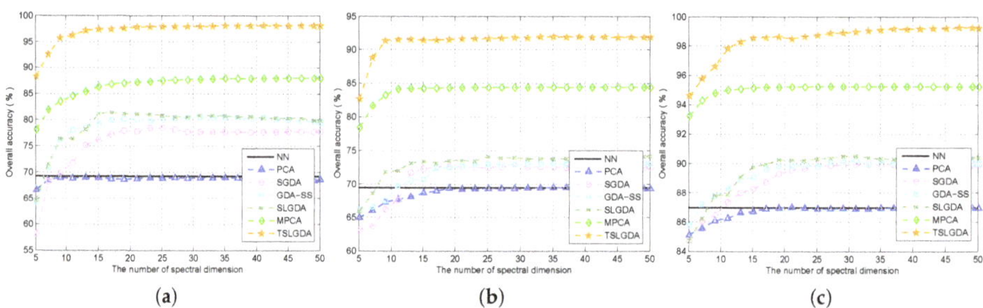

Figure 4. Overall accuracy versus the reduced spectral dimension for different methods using three datasets: (**a**) Indian Pines; (**b**) University of Pavia; (**c**) Salinas.

4.3. Classification Results

4.3.1. Classification Accuracy

Tables 3–5 present the classification accuracy of individual class, OA, AA, and kappa coefficient for three experimental datasets, respectively. Obviously, the proposed method provides the best results than other compared methods on almost all of classes; meanwhile, OA, AA, and kappa coefficient are also better than those of other methods. Specifically, by comparing to all considered methods, TSLGDA yields about 2% to 30%, 5% to 20%, and 2% to 12% gain in OA with limited training sets for three datasets, respectively. Even for classes with few labeled training samples, such as class 1, class 7, and class 9 in the Indian Pines data, the proposed TSLGDA algorithm offers great improvement in performance as well. Besides TSLGDA, MPCA and G-LTDA also obtain much higher accuracies than other vector-based methods, which effectively demonstrates the advantage of tensor-based techniques. In addition, SLGDA yields better results than SGDA (about 3%, 1%, and 0.6% gain) by simultaneously exploiting the properties of sparsity and low-rankness, while GDA-SS is superior to SGDA by considering the spectral similarity measurement based on spectral characteristics when constructing the graph.

Table 3. Classification accuracy (%) and standard deviation of different methods for the Indian Pines data when the reduced dimension is 30.

No.	Origin	PCA	LDA	LFDA	SGDA	GDA-SS	SLGDA	MPCA	G-LTDA	TSLGDA
1	39.02	54.15	33.66	44.88	65.04	49.59	48.78	71.34	**92.20**	91.71
	±8.27	±11.1	±17.8	±15.5	±7.45	±12.2	±6.90	±9.63	±4.69	±8.02
2	55.92	52.96	57.28	67.78	69.31	74.24	73.04	81.09	96.47	**97.32**
	±2.68	±1.53	±2.13	±3.56	±2.37	±3.95	±1.93	±2.74	±1.01	±0.68
3	49.83	50.15	58.34	66.75	62.65	69.57	67.00	82.26	93.98	**97.51**
	±2.68	±2.34	±2.57	±2.82	±1.76	±5.56	±0.28	±2.74	±2.34	±0.91
4	42.07	40.19	38.12	54.93	49.14	58.06	62.68	87.91	96.53	**97.37**
	±7.75	±4.56	±4.00	±7.69	±5.40	±8.24	±12.3	±4.65	±3.93	±1.90
5	82.95	84.47	81.20	88.25	89.55	92.03	93.32	91.13	93.15	**97.00**
	±2.93	±4.58	±3.87	±2.41	±1.74	±1.34	±0.98	±2.00	±1.44	±2.50
6	90.75	93.06	93.36	94.64	95.38	96.91	96.27	97.53	94.76	**99.27**
	±1.00	±2.95	±1.47	±1.59	±0.61	±0.89	±0.11	±1.14	±2.94	±0.46
7	81.60	72.00	76.00	79.20	88.00	88.00	88.00	94.00	95.20	**96.80**
	±8.29	±13.6	±12.3	±22.5	±4.00	±8.00	±5.66	±7.66	±7.15	±3.35
8	96.28	93.02	95.26	99.12	99.53	97.91	99.19	98.37	97.81	**99.86**
	±1.78	±1.52	±2.71	±1.47	±0.40	±2.02	±0.49	±1.66	±0.67	±0.31
9	26.67	34.44	25.56	43.33	50.00	37.04	25.00	54.17	78.89	**93.33**
	±4.65	±12.0	±16.5	±9.94	±33.8	±16.9	±11.8	±19.4	±15.4	±7.24
10	66.06	63.91	65.40	69.04	69.64	73.64	74.03	84.12	95.93	**96.52**
	±2.04	±3.49	±3.61	±3.05	±5.81	±3.02	±0.32	±1.32	±1.35	±1.56
11	71.75	71.41	73.65	72.43	78.18	79.45	79.52	90.30	96.32	**98.53**
	±3.00	±2.00	±1.81	±1.83	±1.42	±1.23	±2.08	±0.78	±1.41	±0.59
12	43.41	41.46	48.63	67.20	67.29	74.78	76.83	73.73	93.60	**96.17**
	±6.34	±2.55	±3.25	±1.56	±2.19	±4.59	±1.99	±2.38	±1.70	±1.75
13	91.41	94.02	93.59	98.70	96.01	97.83	98.64	98.23	91.85	**99.46**
	±2.44	±2.40	±1.11	±0.62	±0.63	±1.63	±1.15	±1.12	±4.21	±0.67
14	90.04	89.65	89.44	93.83	94.58	94.00	96.05	95.78	97.72	**99.67**
	±1.96	±2.10	±2.16	±1.56	±0.89	±1.18	±0.87	±0.40	±0.66	±0.43
15	37.98	36.54	41.15	61.04	48.90	56.20	56.48	88.26	95.91	**98.67**
	±2.18	±2.30	±3.73	±2.89	±1.92	±3.20	±2.85	±4.69	±1.62	±1.16
16	88.43	88.67	91.08	89.64	92.37	91.27	93.98	93.07	84.29	**97.35**
	±6.30	±3.02	±3.47	±5.56	±3.03	±2.99	±1.70	±4.33	±8.68	±1.32
OA	69.25	68.52	70.86	76.60	77.65	80.51	80.76	88.34	95.67	**98.08**
	±1.16	±0.88	±0.76	±0.82	±1.44	±0.31	±0.08	±0.51	±0.49	±0.30
AA	65.89	66.26	66.36	74.42	75.97	76.91	76.80	86.33	93.41	**97.28**
	±1.19	±1.62	±2.30	±1.79	±2.37	±2.38	±1.98	±1.17	±0.56	±0.85
κ	64.90	64.04	66.73	73.32	74.40	77.70	78.01	86.70	95.07	**97.81**
	±1.30	±0.98	±0.92	±0.93	±1.68	±0.38	±0.14	±0.59	±0.56	±0.34

Table 4. Classification accuracy (%) and standard deviation of different methods for the University of Pavia data when the reduced dimension is 20.

No.	Origin	PCA	LDA	LFDA	SGDA	GDA-SS	SLGDA	MPCA	G-LTDA	TSLGDA
1	56.13	55.98	64.77	60.56	47.44	52.88	52.84	84.20	72.41	**91.15**
	±1.99	±2.90	±2.11	±5.24	±2.00	±6.58	±1.98	±1.49	±2.03	±1.46
2	69.68	70.30	68.75	77.05	82.15	78.88	80.92	84.60	89.24	**92.59**
	±5.59	±3.27	±3.44	±4.42	±2.71	±2.80	±3.74	±3.31	±0.93	±2.68
3	68.02	67.34	69.90	66.47	63.83	64.27	61.17	80.24	**89.48**	86.83
	±3.95	±1.49	±3.10	±3.94	±10.5	±3.28	±3.26	±3.01	±5.68	±2.44
4	90.21	86.98	88.92	91.33	90.73	91.26	92.54	92.20	71.28	**96.04**
	±4.43	±3.70	±2.23	±2.01	±2.25	±2.10	±0.07	±1.85	±4.90	±2.23
5	99.39	99.49	99.51	99.88	99.73	99.79	99.66	99.72	98.41	**100**
	±0.38	±0.23	±0.25	±0.10	±0.18	±0.08	±0.27	±0.26	±1.10	±0.00

Table 4. *Cont.*

No.	Origin	PCA	LDA	LFDA	SGDA	GDA-SS	SLGDA	MPCA	G-LTDA	TSLGDA
6	59.11	61.68	66.35	65.36	59.47	65.07	63.97	77.99	**95.04**	93.06
	±2.25	±6.60	±6.62	±7.09	±5.18	±2.72	±0.50	±4.68	±2.35	±3.12
7	83.36	83.22	86.34	75.78	82.25	79.04	81.71	89.22	**98.26**	97.50
	±4.59	±3.57	±2.25	±1.97	±5.40	±3.64	±1.75	±2.09	±1.37	±0.90
8	68.06	66.89	68.24	60.81	61.16	64.67	65.46	76.30	**93.31**	86.07
	±2.72	±4.34	±3.24	±4.18	±8.92	±4.21	±2.87	±3.07	±1.32	±3.27
9	95.94	95.90	97.00	83.95	84.04	87.81	85.17	**99.49**	88.00	98.39
	±1.52	±1.36	±1.82	±4.64	±6.01	±2.20	±1.01	±0.32	±2.23	±1.03
OA	69.47	69.65	71.38	73.04	72.59	73.01	73.80	84.30	86.92	**92.33**
	±2.16	±0.88	±1.10	±0.70	±0.68	±1.47	±1.91	±1.05	±0.42	±0.93
AA	76.66	76.42	78.86	75.69	74.53	75.96	75.94	87.11	88.38	**93.52**
	±0.52	±0.70	±0.92	±1.55	±1.82	±0.74	±0.25	±0.71	±0.43	±0.53
κ	61.22	61.43	63.79	65.31	64.39	65.22	66.10	79.57	82.88	**89.93**
	±2.30	±0.88	±1.19	±0.83	±0.89	±1.74	±2.14	±1.24	±0.50	±1.17

Table 5. Classification accuracy (%) and standard deviation of different methods for the Salinas data when the reduced dimension is 30.

No.	Origin	PCA	LDA	LFDA	SGDA	GDA-SS	SLGDA	MPCA	G-LTDA	TSLGDA
1	98.07	98.73	98.98	99.44	99.49	99.39	99.61	98.00	96.94	**99.92**
	±0.44	±0.80	±0.81	±0.10	±0.13	±0.14	±0.23	±0.98	±1.63	±0.15
2	98.68	98.90	98.88	99.23	99.54	99.25	99.50	99.47	98.73	99.98
	±0.38	±0.25	±0.29	±0.17	±0.28	±0.21	±0.37	±0.55	±0.81	±0.03
3	96.20	96.85	95.13	99.16	99.28	99.59	99.57	98.17	93.65	**99.97**
	±0.25	±0.61	±1.05	±0.25	±0.05	±0.15	±0.17	±0.19	±1.88	±0.06
4	99.24	99.39	99.51	99.12	99.41	99.12	99.15	**99.71**	93.92	98.41
	±0.08	±0.35	±0.18	±0.46	±0.13	±0.41	±0.30	±0.87	±3.27	±0.68
5	94.55	93.45	95.63	98.79	98.64	98.42	**99.03**	97.95	96.50	98.87
	±0.66	±1.85	±0.81	±0.09	±0.87	±0.62	±0.12	±1.28	±1.76	±1.33
6	99.67	99.63	99.56	99.79	99.77	99.70	99.87	99.24	98.74	**100**
	±0.16	±0.25	±0.11	±0.21	±0.05	±0.13	±0.13	±1.27	±0.52	±0.00
7	98.87	99.40	99.34	99.43	99.44	99.64	99.64	98.18	96.21	**99.99**
	±0.53	±0.11	±0.24	±0.24	±0.09	±0.30	±0.08	±0.35	±2.39	±0.02
8	72.41	73.59	74.13	73.01	76.25	78.11	78.86	90.80	**97.93**	97.73
	±2.03	±2.33	±0.49	±3.40	±4.74	±0.42	±1.50	±0.19	±0.60	±0.22
9	97.82	97.91	98.79	98.92	99.10	98.78	99.65	99.54	98.71	**100**
	±0.01	±0.88	±0.50	±0.18	±0.19	±1.46	±0.12	±0.07	±1.07	±0.00
10	87.70	89.62	91.68	95.24	96.07	94.88	95.42	94.77	94.96	**99.77**
	±4.21	±0.33	±1.05	±0.44	±1.28	±1.65	±1.12	±0.67	±2.25	±0.37
11	93.82	96.85	93.47	95.03	96.49	95.61	97.29	94.58	90.58	**100**
	±1.38	±1.92	±4.81	±2.28	±3.75	±2.83	±3.54	±1.72	±4.90	±0.00
12	99.75	99.93	99.45	99.95	99.91	99.95	99.82	99.44	97.17	**100**
	±0.16	±0.12	±0.46	±0.09	±0.06	±0.07	±0.17	±0.98	±1.53	±0.00
13	97.29	96.14	97.14	98.36	97.84	97.94	98.59	99.74	95.01	**100**
	±0.17	±1.56	±0.17	±0.73	±0.89	±0.08	±0.84	±0.28	±2.11	±0.00
14	92.49	93.89	95.00	94.91	96.91	95.23	97.23	94.97	93.16	**99.87**
	±1.53	±0.87	±0.98	±1.63	±1.39	±2.02	±0.25	±2.23	±5.57	±0.15
15	62.04	58.38	64.37	69.36	67.05	67.51	66.31	88.63	96.22	**96.77**
	±1.48	±2.25	±1.98	±4.08	±5.23	±1.65	±1.88	±0.62	±1.10	±1.47
16	94.75	94.44	98.00	98.78	98.57	98.76	99.30	96.95	91.91	**100**
	±1.41	±0.85	±0.58	±0.40	±0.31	±0.16	±0.46	±1.68	±7.30	±0.00
OA	86.97	86.96	88.23	89.34	89.86	90.13	90.43	95.27	96.73	**98.98**
	±0.63	±0.49	±0.27	±0.79	±0.45	±0.42	±0.07	±0.04	±0.89	±0.15
AA	92.71	92.94	93.69	94.91	95.24	95.12	95.55	96.70	95.65	**99.46**
	±0.58	±0.23	±0.40	±0.43	±0.38	±0.24	±0.18	±0.06	±1.41	±0.08
κ	85.50	85.48	86.90	88.15	89.02	88.33	89.34	94.74	96.35	**98.86**
	±0.70	±0.53	±0.30	±0.88	±0.49	±0.46	±0.08	±0.05	±0.99	±0.16

4.3.2. Classification Maps

In order to show the classification results more directly, classification maps of all considered methods are provided in Figures 5–7 for three experimental datasets, respectively. From Figure 5, it can be clearly seen that the proposed method can obtain much smoother classification regions than other methods, especially for class 1 (Alfalfa), class 2 (Corn-notill), class 3 (Corn-mintill), and class 12

(Soybean-clean) whose spectral characteristics are highly correlated with other classes. The similar results can also be observed from Figures 6 and 7, where class 1 (Asphalt), class 6 (Bare Soil), and class 8 (Self-blocking bricks) in the second dataset, and class 8 (Grapes untrained), class 15 (Vineyard untrained) in the third dataset are labeled more precisely. These observations are consistent with the quantitative results listed in Tables 3–5.

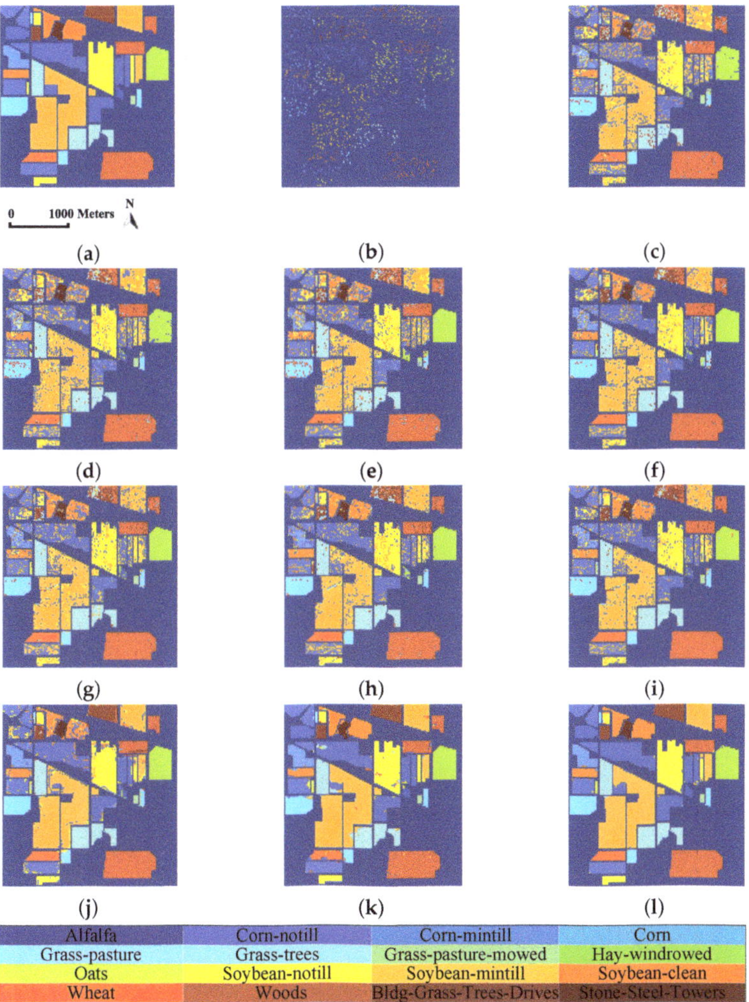

Figure 5. Classification maps of different methods for the Indian Pines dataset: (**a**) ground truth; (**b**) training set; (**c**) origin; (**d**) PCA; (**e**) LDA; (**f**) LFDA; (**g**) SGDA; (**h**) GDA-SS; (**i**) SLGDA; (**j**) MPCA; (**k**) G-LTDA; and (**l**) TSLGDA.

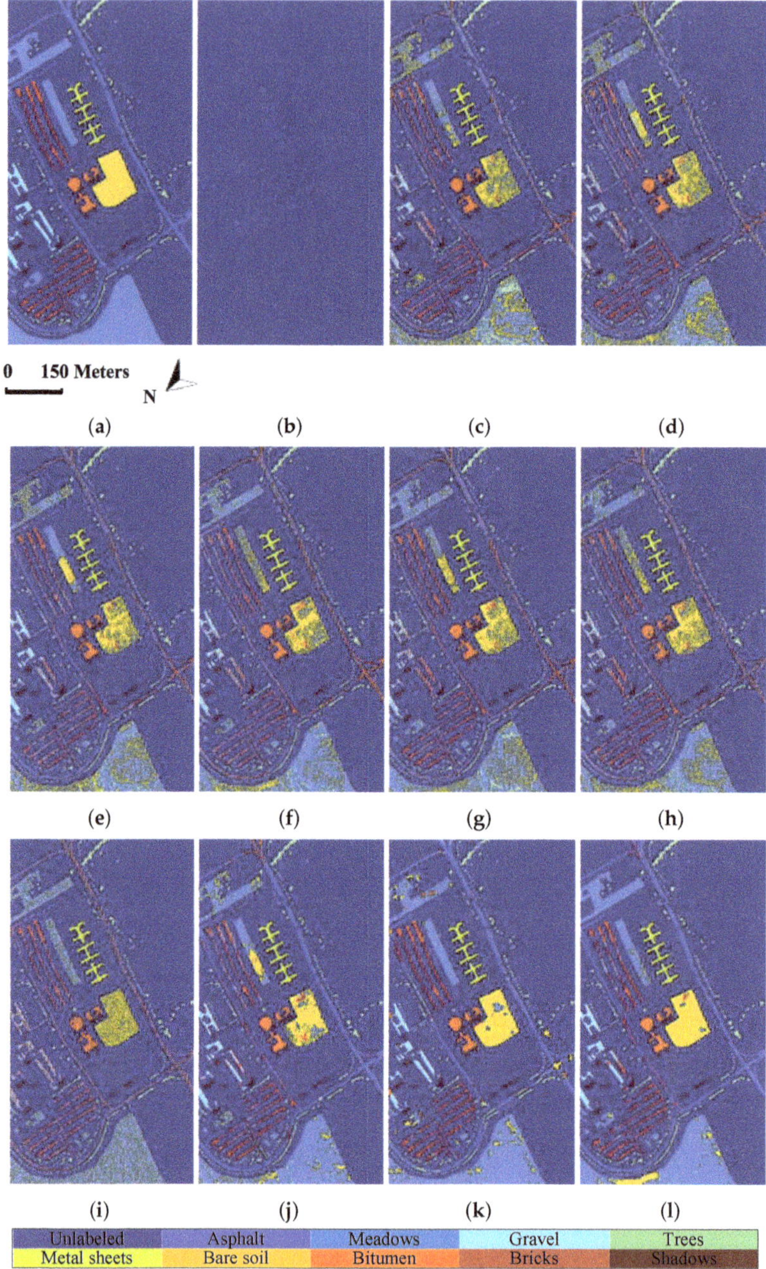

Figure 6. Classification maps of different methods for the University of Pavia dataset: (**a**) ground truth; (**b**) training set; (**c**) origin; (**d**) PCA; (**e**) LDA; (**f**) LFDA; (**g**) SGDA; (**h**) GDA-SS; (**i**) SLGDA; (**j**) MPCA; (**k**) G-LTDA; and (**l**) TSLGDA.

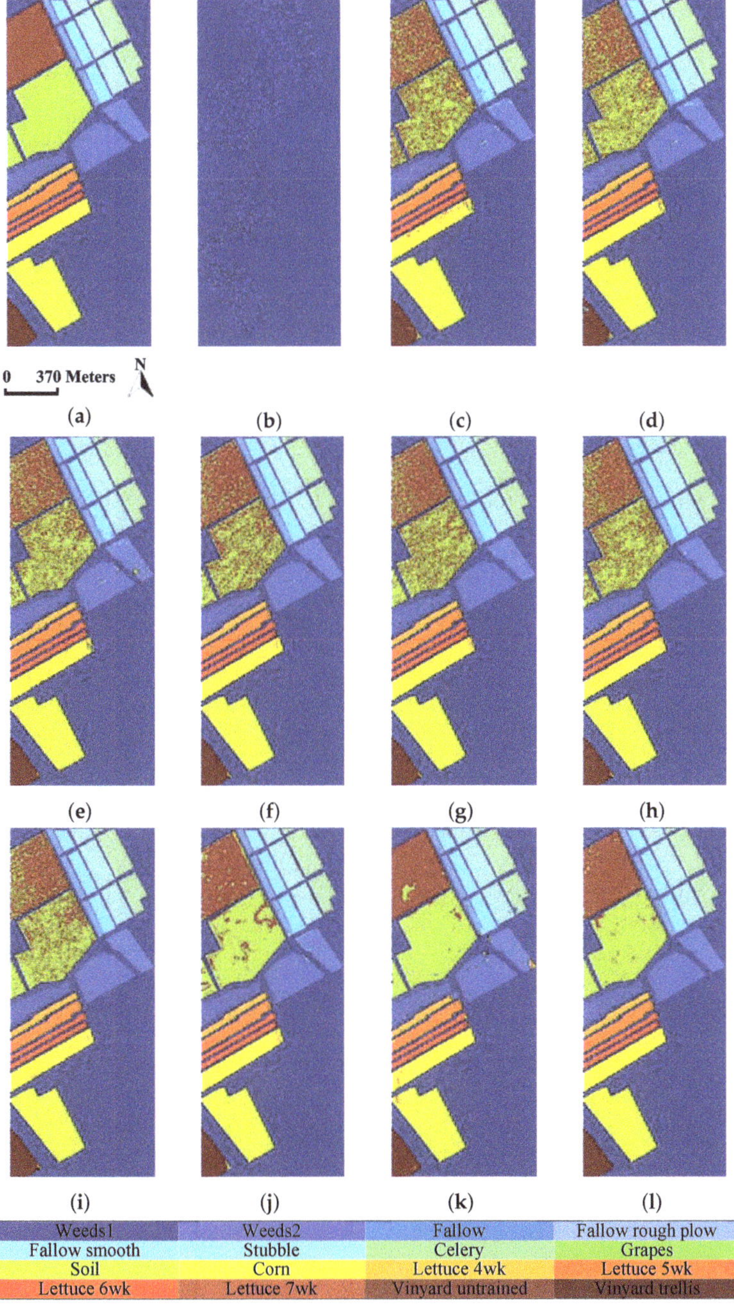

Figure 7. Classification maps of different methods for the Salinas dataset: (**a**) ground truth; (**b**) training set; (**c**) origin; (**d**) PCA; (**e**) LDA; (**f**) LFDA; (**g**) SGDA; (**h**) GDA-SS; (**i**) SLGDA; (**j**) MPCA; (**k**) G-LTDA; and (**l**) TSLGDA.

4.3.3. The Influence of Training Size

To show the influence of training size, some considered DR methods are tested. The results are given in Figure 8, from which we can see that the OA values of all methods are improved when the number of training samples increases for three datasets. Due to the spatial structure information contained in the tensor, the proposed method always performs better than other methods in all cases. In addition, with the label information, the supervised DR methods (i.e., SGDA, GDA-SS, SLGDA, G-LTDA, TSLGDA) achieve better results than the corresponding unsupervised DR methods (i.e., PCA, MPCA).

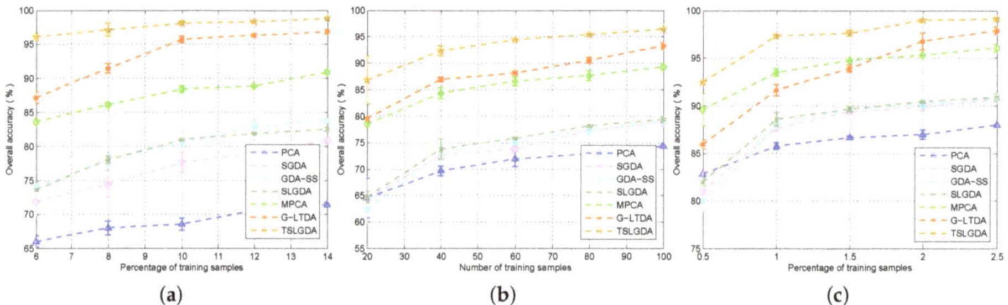

Figure 8. Overall classification accuracy and standard deviation versus different numbers of training samples per class for all methods using three datasets: (**a**) Indian Pines; (**b**) University of Pavia; (**c**) Salinas.

4.3.4. The Analysis of Computational Complexity

For the comparison of computational complexity, we take the Indian Pines data as an example. Table 6 shows the time requirements of all considered methods, from which it can be clearly seen that traditional methods (e.g., PCA, LDA, LFDA) run faster than other recently proposed methods. In addition, due to complicated tensor computation, tensor-based DR methods (e.g., MPCA, G-LTDA, TSLGDA) cost more time than vector-based methods (e.g., SGDA, GDA-SS, SLGDA). Although TSLGDA has the highest computational complexity, it yields the best classification performance. In practice, the general-purpose graphics processing units (GPUs) can be adopted to greatly accelerate the TSLGDA algorithm.

Table 6. Execution time (in seconds) of different methods for the Indian Pines data with different training size.

Methods	6%	8%	10%	12%	14%
PCA	1.23	1.49	1.86	2.35	2.54
LDA	1.23	1.51	1.88	2.34	2.54
LFDA	1.24	1.57	1.93	2.40	2.62
SGDA	10.60	14.11	18.53	23.90	29.30
GDA-SS	1.13	1.36	1.67	2.15	2.45
SLGDA	3.24	4.81	7.20	10.19	13.09
MPCA	115.94	150.00	161.06	182.37	203.94
G-LTDA	30.96	40.24	49.86	62.41	74.83
TSLGDA	183.91	225.06	281.19	349.44	456.84

5. Conclusions

In this paper, we have proposed a tensor sparse and low-rank graph-based discriminant analysis method (i.e., TSLGDA) for dimensionality reduction of hyperspectral imagery. The hyperspectral data cube is taken as a third-order tensor, from which sub-tensors (local patches) centered at the training samples are extracted to construct the sparse and low-rank graph. On the one hand, by imposing both the sparse and low-rank constraints on the objective function, the proposed method is capable of capturing the local and global structure simultaneously. On the other hand, due to the spatial structure information introduced by tensor data, the proposed method can improve the graph structure and enhance the discriminative ability of reduced features. Experiments conducted on three hyperspectral datasets have consistently confirmed the effectiveness of our proposed TSLGDA algorithm, even for small training size. Compared to some state-of-the-art methods, the overall classification accuracy of TSLGDA in the low-dimensional space improves about 2% to 30%, 5% to 20%, and 2% to 12% for three experimental datasets, respectively, with increased computational complexity.

Acknowledgments: This work was supported by the National Natural Science Foundation of China under Grant 61371165 and Grant 61501018, and by the Frontier Intersection Basic Research Project for the Central Universities under Grant A0920502051714-5. The authors would like to thank Prof. David A. Landgreve from Purdue University for providing the AVIRIS image of Indian Pines and Prof. Paolo Gamba from University of Pavia for providing the ROSIS dataset. The authors would like to thank Dr. Zisha Zhong for sharing the code of Gabor filters and giving some useful suggestions. Last but not least, we would like to thank the editors and the anonymous reviewers for their detailed comments and suggestions, which greatly helped us to improve the clarity and presentation of our manuscript.

Author Contributions: All of the authors made significant contributions to the work. Lei Pan and Heng-Chao Li designed the research model, analyzed the results and wrote the paper. Yang-Jun Deng provided codes about tensor processing. Fan Zhang and Xiang-Dong Chen reviewed the manuscript. Qian Du contributed to the editing and review of the manuscript.

Conflicts of Interest: The authors declare no conflict of interest.

References

1. He, Z.; Li, J.; Liu, L. Tensor block-sparsity based representation for spectral-spatial hyperspectral image classification. *Remote Sens.* **2016**, *8*, 636.
2. Peng, B.; Li, W.; Xie, X.M.; Du, Q.; Liu, K. Weighted-fusion-based representation classifiers for hyperspectral imagery. *Remote Sens.* **2015**, *7*, 14806–14826.
3. Yu, S.Q.; Jia, S.; Xu, C.Y. Convolutional neural networks for hyperspectral image classification. *Neurocomputing* **2017**, *219*, 88–98.
4. Jimenez, L.O.; Landgrebe, D.A. Supervised classification in high-dimensional space: Geometrical, statistical, and asymptoticla properitier of multivariate data. *IEEE Trans. Syst. Man Cybern. Part C Appl. Rev.* **1998**, *28*, 39–54.
5. Chang, C.-I.; Safavi, H. Progressive dimensionality reduction by transform for hyperspectral imagery. *Pattern Recognit.* **2011**, *44*, 2760–2773.
6. Yuan, Y.; Lin, J.Z.; Wang, Q. Dual-clustering-based hyperspectral band selection by contextual analysis. *IEEE Trans. Geosci. Remote Sens.* **2016**, *54*, 1431–1445.
7. Wang, Q.; Lin, J.Z.; Yuan, Y. Salient band selection for hyperspectral image classification via manifold ranking. *IEEE Trans. Neural Netw. Learn. Syst.* **2016**, *27*, 1279–1289.
8. Jolliffe, I.T. *Principal Component Analysis*; Springer-Verlag: New York, NY, USA, 2002.
9. Bandos, T.V.; Bruzzone, L.; Camps-Valls, G. Classification of hyperspectral images with regularized linear discriminant analysis. *IEEE Trans. Geosci. Remote Sens.* **2009**, *47*, 862–873.
10. Li, W.; Prasad, S.; Fowler, J.E.; Bruce, L.M. Locality-preserving dimensionality reduction and classification for hyperspectral image analysis. *IEEE Trans. Geosci. Remote Sens.* **2012**, *50*, 1185–1198.
11. Tan, K.; Zhou, S.Y.; Du, Q. Semisupervised discriminant analysis for hyperspectral imagery with block-sparse graph. *IEEE Geosci. Remote Sens. Lett.* **2015**, *12*, 1765–1769.

12. Chatpatanasiri, R.; Kijsirikul, B. A unifier semi-supervised dimensionality reduction framework for manifold learning. *Neurocomputing* **2010**, *73*, 1631–1640.

13. Yan, S.C.; Xu, D.; Zhang, B.Y.; Zhang, H.-J.; Yang, Q.; Lin, S. Graph embedding and extensions: A general framework for dimensionality reduction. *IEEE Trans. Pattern Anal. Mach. Intell.* **2007**, *29*, 40–51.

14. He, X.F.; Cai D.; Yan, S.C.; Zhang, H.-J. Neighborhood preserving embedding. In Proceedings of the 2005 IEEE Conference on Computer Vision (ICCV), Beijing, China, 17–20 October 2005; pp. 1208–1213.

15. Feng, F.B.; Li, W.; Du, Q.; Zhang, B. Dimensionality reduction of hyperspectral image with graph-based discriminant analysis considering spectral similarity. *Remote Sens.* **2017**, *9*, 323.

16. Wright, J.; Yang, A.Y.; Ganesh, A.; Sastry, S.S.; Ma, Y. Robust face recognition via sparse representation. *IEEE Trans. Pattern Anal. Mach. Intell.* **2009**, *31*, 210–227.

17. Wright, J.; Ma, Y.; Mairal, J.; Sapiro, G.; Huang, T.S.; Yan, S.C. Sparse representation for computer vision and pattern recognition. *Proc. IEEE* **2010**, *98*, 1031–1044.

18. Cheng, B.; Yang, J.C.; Yan, S.C.; Fu, Y.; Huang, T.S. Learning with l_1-graph for image analysis. *IEEE Trans. Image Process.* **2015**, *23*, 2241–2253.

19. Ly, N.H.; Du, Q.; Fowler, J.E. Sparse graph-based discriminant analysis for hyperspectral imagery. *IEEE Trans. Geosci. Remote Sens.* **2014**, *52*, 3872–3884.

20. He, W.; Zhang, H.Y.; Zhang, L.P.; Philips, W.; Liao, W.Z. Weighted sparse graph based dimensionality reduction for hyperspectral images. *IEEE Geosci. Remote Sens. Lett.* **2016**, *13*, 686–690.

21. Ly, N.H.; Du, Q.; Fowler, J.E. Collaborative graph-based discriminant analysis for hyperspectral imagery. *IEEE J. Sel. Top. Appl. Earth Observ. Remote Sens.* **2014**, *7*, 2688–2696.

22. Li, W.; Du, Q. Laplacian regularized collaborative graph for discriminant analysis of hyperspectral imagery. *IEEE Trans. Geosci. Remote Sens.* **2016**, *54*, 7066–7076.

23. Li, W.; Liu, J.B.; Du, Q. Sparse and low-rank graph for discriminant analysis of hyperspectral imagery. *IEEE Trans. Geosci. Remote Sens.* **2016**, *54*, 4094–4105.

24. Xue, Z.H.; Du, P.J.; Li, J.; Su, H.J. Simultaneous sparse graph embedding for hyperspectral image classification. *IEEE Trans. Geosci. Remote Sens.* **2015**, *53*, 6114–6132.

25. Lu, H.P.; Plataniotis, K.N.; Venetsanopoulos, A.N. MPCA: Multilinear principal component analysis of tensor objects. *IEEE Trans. Neural Netw.* **2008**, *19*, 18–39.

26. Guo, X.; Huang, X.; Zhang, L.F.; Zhang, L.P.; Plaza, A.; Benediktssom, J.A. Support tensor machines for classification of hyperspectral remote sensing imagery. *IEEE Trans. Geosci. Remote Sens.* **2016**, *54*, 3248–3264.

27. An, J.L.; Zhang, X.R.; Jiao, L.C. Dimensionality reduction based on group-based tensor model for hyperspectral image classification. *IEEE Geosci. Remote Sens. Lett.* **2016**, *13*, 1497–1501.

28. Zhang, L.P.; Zhang, L.F.; Tao, D.C.; Huang, X. Tensor discriminative locality alignment for hyperspectral image spectral-spatial feature extraction. *IEEE Trans. Geosci. Remote Sens.* **2013**, *51*, 242–256.

29. Zhong, Z.S.; Fan, B.; Duan, J.Y.; Wang, L.F.; Ding, K.; Xiang, S.M.; Pan, C.H. Discriminant tensor spectral-spatial feature extraction for hyperspectral image classification. *IEEE Geosci. Remote Sens. Lett.* **2015**, *12*, 1028–1032.

30. Benediktsson, J.A.; Palmason, J.A.; Sveinsson, J.R. Classification of hyperspectral data from urban areas based on extended morphological profiles. *IEEE Trans. Geosci. Remote Sens.* **2005**, *43*, 480–491.

31. Dallal Mura, M.; Benediktsson, J.A.; Waske, B.; Bruzzone, L. Morphological attribute profiles for the analysis of very high resolution images. *IEEE Trans. Geosci. Remote Sens.* **2010**, *48*, 3747–3762.

32. Rajadell, O.; Garcia-Sevilla, P.; Pla, F. Spectral-spatial pixel characterization using Gabor filters for hyperspectral image classification. *IEEE Geosci. Remote Sens. Lett.* **2013**, *10*, 860–864.

33. Zhao, H.T.; Sun, S.Y. Sparse tensor embedding based multispectral face recognition. *Neurocomputing* **2014**, *133*, 427–436.

34. Lai, Z.H.; Xu, Y.; Chen, Q.C.; Yang, J.; Zhang, D. Multilinear sparse principal component analysis. *IEEE Trans. Neural Netw. Learn. Syst.* **2014**, *25*, 1942–1950.

35. Boyd, S.; Parikh, N.; Chu, E.; Peleato, B.; Eckstein, J. Distributed optimization and statistical learning via the alternating direction method of multipliers. *Found. Trends Mach. Learn.* **2011**, *3*, 1–122.
36. Cai, J.-F.; Candés, E.J.; Shen, Z. A singular value thresholding algorithm for matrix completion. *SIAM J. Optim.* **2010**, *24*, 1956–1982.
37. Nie, F.P.; Xiang, S.M.; Song, Y.Q.; Zhang, C.S. Extracting the optimal dimensionality for local tensor discriminant analysis. *Pattern Recognit.* **2009**, *42*, 105–114.
38. SPArse Modeling Software. Available online: http://spams-devel.gforge.inria.fr/index.html (accessed on 20 January 2017).
39. Hyperspectral Remote Sensing Scenes. Available online: http://www.ehu.eus/ccwintco/index.php?title=Hyperspectral_Remote_Sensing_Scenes (accessed on 20 January 2017).

Article

Sea Ice Concentration Estimation during Freeze-Up from SAR Imagery Using a Convolutional Neural Network

Lei Wang, K. Andrea Scott * and David A. Clausi

Department of Systems Design Engineering, University of Waterloo, Waterloo, ON N2L 3G1, Canada; alphaleiw@gmail.com (L.W.); dclausi@uwaterloo.ca (D.A.C.)
* Correspondence: ka3scott@uwaterloo.ca; Tel.: +1-519-888-4567 (ext. 32811)

Academic Editors: Qi Wang, Nicolas H. Younan, Carlos López-Martínez, Xiaofeng Li and Prasad S. Thenkabail
Received: 27 January 2017; Accepted: 21 April 2017; Published: 26 April 2017

Abstract: In this study, a convolutional neural network (CNN) is used to estimate sea ice concentration using synthetic aperture radar (SAR) scenes acquired during freeze-up in the Gulf of St. Lawrence on the east coast of Canada. The ice concentration estimates from the CNN are compared to those from a neural network (multi-layer perceptron or MLP) that uses hand-crafted features as input and a single layer of hidden nodes. The CNN is found to be less sensitive to pixel level details than the MLP and produces ice concentration that is less noisy and in closer agreement with that from image analysis charts. This is due to the multi-layer (deep) structure of the CNN, which enables abstract image features to be learned. The CNN ice concentration is also compared with ice concentration estimated from passive microwave brightness temperature data using the ARTIST sea ice (ASI) algorithm. The bias and RMS of the difference between the ice concentration from the CNN and that from image analysis charts is reduced as compared to that from either the MLP or ASI algorithm. Additional results demonstrate the impact of varying the input patch size, varying the number of CNN layers, and including the incidence angle as an additional input.

Keywords: ice concentration; SAR imagery; convolutional neural network

---

1. Introduction

In the operational sea ice community, visual analyses of SAR imagery by expert ice analysts are a key contribution to ice charts, which are used to assist navigation and operations in ice-covered waters [1]. However, the generation of these analyses is time consuming. Upcoming and new satellite missions, such as the Canadian RADARSAT Constellation Mission (RCM), and the European Sentinel mission, will lead to significantly increased volumes of SAR imagery [2], increasing the need for automated methods to analyze the imagery.

There are several previous studies extracting information from SAR imagery using automated methods. Many of these studies use 'engineered' or hand-crafted features, which are features designed and selected to carry out a specific task. Examples include, the HH autocorrelation, normalized polarization difference and cross-polarization ratio all of which have been used in ice concentration estimation [3,4], grey level co-occurrence matrix features, Gabor filters and Markov random fields, which have been used to classify imagery into ice type and ice/water [5–8], and curvelet features used to locate the ice edge [9]. One of the challenges with using a set of engineered features to automatically extract information from SAR imagery is the difficulty of developing a set of robust features that can be applied to different geographic regions and seasons and for different imaging geometries. To capture various ice conditions, features may need to be designed for different locations or times of the year. For example, a large database of HH and HV backscatter values that represent typical signatures of

100% ice cover has been generated to retrieve ice observations for use in data assimilation. In the database, the backscatter values are estimated for each month as a function of incidence angle and windspeed on a region dependent-basis [10]. Such an extensive database may be necessary to assess the robustness of engineered features for large-scale applications, such as estimating ice concentration for assimilation in an operational prediction system [11]. Data assimilation requires high quality observations due to the nature of the assimilation cycle, in which erroneous observations will lead to an erroneous analysis, the influence of which will persist when the analysis is used to initialize the next assimilation cycle. For example, the open water regions that are estimated by Karvonen [4] as having an ice concentration of 10% or 15% would generate an incorrect analysis in a sea ice data assimilation system. A similar situation would arise upon assimilating a consolidated ice cover estimated with passive microwave data, in the event that the real ice cover has cracks and leads. Such openings in the ice are crucial for heat transfer from the ocean to the atmosphere. When the ice cover is used as a boundary condition for numerical weather prediction, an accurate estimate of the sea ice concentration is critical [12].

When an analyst estimates ice concentration from a SAR image, they combine their knowledge of ice conditions in the region with visual cues in the image. This may involve looking at the SAR image features over a range of scales. For example, at large scale, tonal changes across a region can be used to identify the region as either ice or open water, while at small scale visible ridges in the ice cover may indicate a region of high ice concentration, or small-scale ice floes may indicate a marginal ice zone. Thus, if it is desired to emulate the analyst's task, the goal can be viewed as emulating the human visual system's ability to assimilate information at various scales with prior knowledge. Convolutional neural networks (CNNs) are a known method to learn features from images, taking into account information at various scales. The training takes place by minimizing a difference between output of the CNN and training data, which represents prior knowledge. Remarkable similarities between CNNs and the human visual system have been demonstrated in numerous studies [13].

The present study uses a CNN trained with image analysis charts to estimate ice concentration from SAR imagery acquired over the Gulf of St. Lawrence during freeze-up in the winter of 2014. A previous study [14] has evaluated a similar architecture for the problem of ice concentration estimation in the Beaufort Sea for the 2010-2011 melt period. The present study builds on that work, addressing the following questions: (i) Can a CNN estimate sea ice concentration accurately during freeze-up, when the ice is very thin and may be difficult to distinguish from open water [15,16]? (ii) How is the performance of the CNN affected when some of the parameters (e.g., number of layers and input patch size) are modified? (iii) Can a CNN manage to interpret ice concentration for environments, such as the Gulf of St. Lawrence, where the ice characteristics are dynamic?

2. Background

Learning image features from SAR imagery to estimate ice concentration, as compared to first calculating engineered features from the image, builds on previous work in feature learning, which is a promising method to analyze complex and large volumes of data [17–21]. Deep learning is a type of feature learning method that can automatically extract complex data representations at high levels of abstraction [18,22,23]. For image recognition tasks, deep convolutional neural networks (CNN) are widely used due to their ability to model local image structures at multiple scales efficiently [24–27].

There has been limited research in using CNNs to learn features from satellite images. Related studies include using CNNs for road classification from aerial images [28] and the detection of vehicles [29] and buildings [30] from high resolution satellite images. Training of CNN models requires a large quantity of high quality training samples. For many remote sensing problems, gathering high quality ground truth is expensive and sometimes not feasible, due to the vast study area and diversity of surface conditions. This is in particular the case for ice concentration mapping. Due to harsh environmental conditions and in the interest of safety, obtaining adequate in situ samples coincident or near-coincident in time with a SAR scene is not usually feasible. Normally such in-situ studies are limited to small geographic regions and a limited time period.

Using other sources of satellite data or output from ice-ocean models may not be very suitable choices for training data. For example, many algorithms that compute ice concentration from passive microwave data are known to be biased over thin ice and in regions with low ice concentration levels [16,31,32]. Training a CNN with this data will lead to a CNN model that generates similar biases. Ice concentration estimated by image analysts is considered the best available ice concentration information [33]. Hence, the extensive image analysis database at the Canadian Ice Service (CIS) represents a promising archive that can be used to provide data to investigate the use of a CNN to estimate ice concentration from SAR imagery.

3. Data and Study Area

The study area is located in the Gulf of Saint Lawrence, which is situated on the east coast of Canada (Figure 1). The period of study extends from 17 January 2014 to 10 February 2014. This time of year corresponds to freeze-up in the Gulf of Saint Lawrence, with both ice concentration and thickness increasing from January into February. For the duration of the study, the ice cover is composed of new ice (less than 10 cm in thickness) and grey and grey-white ice (10–30 cm in thickness), with thicker first-year ice near Prince Edward Island. Definitions for the various ice types are provided by the World Meteorological Organization (WMO) [34].

A total of 25 RADARSAT-2 dual-pol (HH and HV) ScanSAR Wide [35] images are used for the present study. The full list of the SAR images used is provided in Table 1. The nominal pixel spacing of the acquired SAR images is 50 m by 50 m, and the incidence angle ranges from 20° to 49°. The image size is roughly 10 k × 10 k covering a spatial extent of about 500 km × 500 km. The outlines of all the SAR images in the dataset are shown in Figure 1.

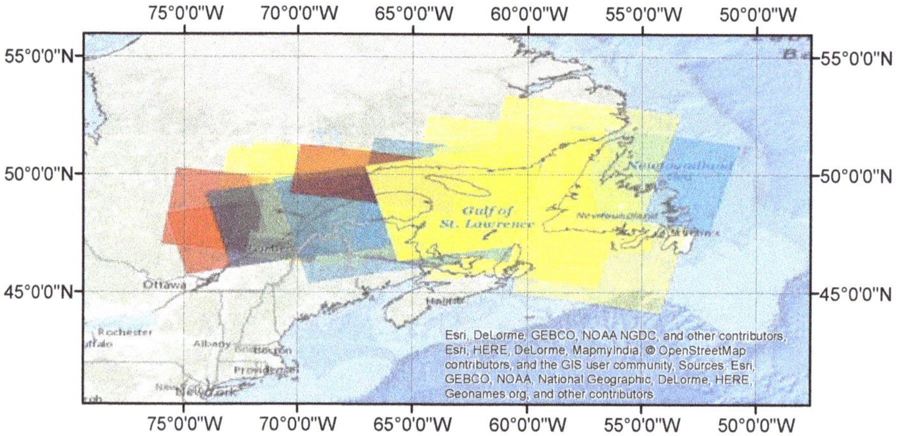

Figure 1. Study area and the dataset for the Gulf of Saint Lawrence. There are 25 scenes of dual-pol SAR images acquired between 16 January 2014 and 10 February 2014 in this area. The coverage for each scene is marked in a translucent polygon with different colors. Yellow scenes are used for training, red are used for validation and blue for testing.

Each SAR image has an accompanying image analysis chart, which is used to provide the training data to the ice concentration estimation methods. Compared to other types of ice charts (daily ice chart and regional ice chart), image analysis charts provide a more detailed interpretation of SAR images and are valid at the SAR image acquisition time [34]. Image analyses are prepared manually by a trained analyst who identifies regions (polygons) in which the ice conditions appear to be uniform, in terms of the total ice concentration and the relative mix of ice types. The ice types are defined according to their stage of development following World Meteorological Organization standards [34]. The ice concentration label given to a polygon is assigned in increments of 10%, hence the the precision of the image analyses cannot be higher than 10%. In addition, since each polygon of the image analysis is labeled with a single ice concentration value for the entire polygon, the actual ice concentration at the grid-point locations may be different from that indicated by the polygon label, depending on the spatial distribution of ice within the polygon.

As is the case with other sources of ice concentration data, it is difficult to quantify the accuracy of the image analysis charts. In comparing image analyses with other sources of data there are several factors that should be taken into account. First of all, the preparation of image analyses is subjective, and interpretation of image data by different analysts can lead to biases [36]. There are also errors due to converting continuous image data to discrete ice thickness categories, for example small scale details such as cracks in the ice or streaks of new ice are typically lost. Finally, the ice charts may have a slight tendency to over predict the ice concentration in the interest of marine safety.

The image analysis training data obtained from CIS in this study are grid-point data from the image analysis charts. The sampling interval is about 8 km in the north-south direction and 5 km in the east-west direction. The number of image analysis grid points for each SAR image varies from a few hundred to several thousand (Table 1) which depends on the area of sea surface in that scene. Note that while most of the validation data were acquired in February, these validation images overlay a large part of the study area. Visual inspection of the images reveals that they contain a variety of ice types, representative of those seen in the training and test data.

Table 1. Details of the Gulf of Saint Lawrence dataset. Each image analysis point covers an area of approximately 5 km × 8 km.

Set	Scene ID	Date Acquired	Number of Image Analysis Points
Training	20140131_103053	31 January 2014	8231
	20140127_221027	27 January 2014	1319
	20140203_104323	3 February 2014	3019
	20140116_223042	16 January 2014	530
	20140208_095758	8 February 2014	13,872
	20140210_220111	10 February 2014	8358
	20140207_214938	7 February 2014	612
	20140125_100500	25 January 2014	5200
	20140131_215240	31 January 2014	11,111
	20140124_103501	24 January 2014	6900
	20140120_105149	20 January 2014	829
	20140118_101002	18 January 2014	7492
	20140128_101751	28 January 2014	12,791
	20140130_222234	30 January 2014	1407
	20140123_222627	23 January 2014	950
	20140127_104734	27 January 2014	3427
	20140124_215646	24 January 2014	10,964
	20140121_214420	21 January 2014	15,897
Validation	20140122_095247	22 January 2014	5014
	20140206_221744	6 February 2014	3395
	20140209_223030	9 February 2014	545
	20140207_102631	7 February 2014	9228
Testing	20140210_103911	10 February 2014	2918
	20140130_110029	30 January 2014	425
	20140126_223850	26 January 2014	165
	20140117_103914	17 January 2014	2922

Corresponding daily AMSR2 ice concentration maps for each SAR scene are downloaded from the website of PHAROS group at the University of Bremen. These AMSR2 ice concentration maps are reprojected to their corresponding SAR image pixel grids with cubic interpolation, and are referred to as ASI ice concentration in the remainder of this paper, where ASI refers to the ARTIST sea ice concentration algorithm [31]. The ice cover during the study period is generally thin, with significant regions of thickness less than 30 cm. Based on previous studies [16] it is expected that the ice concentration calculated from passive microwave data will be underestimated in these regions of thin ice. However, the ASI ice concentration is based on the 89GHz channels of the AMSR2 sensor, and is known to have less of an underestimation than other products [16]. No modifications were made to the ASI algorithm, such as a recalibration of the algorithm tie-points, in order to compare our ice concentration against that from an available product. Note that the ASI algorithm contains a weather filter that on average removes all ice up to 15% concentration, and that the ASI data are daily averages whereas the CNN results and image analyses are snapshots valid at the image acquisition time.

4. Methodology

4.1. Preprocessing of SAR Images

All the SAR images are sub-sampled by 8×8 block averaging to reduce data volume while also reducing image speckle noise. Learning at this reduced scale requires a smaller spatial context window and therefore smaller neural networks. This is desired because of the limited number of training samples available (0.152 million image analysis sample points) for our study compared to model size ($\approx$3.9 million parameters). The sub-sampled images have 400 m pixel spacing with pixel values between 0 and 255. Input normalization is a common practice to improve the performance of CNNs [26,37]. In this study, the pixel values of the dual-polarized SAR images are normalized by first calculating the mean and standard deviation of pixel values over the entire dataset for each channel, then subtracting from each pixel value this mean, and dividing by the standard deviation.

If training sample patches are selected near land, when the patches are processed by the CNN, the land pixels may lead to signatures in the adjacent water regions that could be interpreted as ice. This may lead to overestimation (contamination) of ice concentration estimates near land. The size of land contaminated regions depends on the size of training sample patches. In our case, an image patch size 45 by 45 pixels is used, which corresponds to 18 km $\times$ 18 km ground distance. Therefore, land contamination can potentially affect regions within 18 km distance to the coast. Direct masking out land pixels to 0 is not used because the masked pixels may be confused with dark new ice or calm open water. Instead, a land mask is applied to the SAR images and land pixels are replaced by their corresponding mirrored ice or water pixels to reduce land contamination. By doing this, the estimated ice concentration only depends on local ice or water pixels. The actual ice concentration may be changed by the land mirroring process, depending on the shape of the coastline. However, in our testing, the mirroring was found to significantly reduce the effect of land on the estimated ice concentration. Therefore, no further investigation of alternative methods to mask land pixels is performed at this time.

The incidence angle for each SAR image pixel is calculated from the image meta data using linear interpolation and stored as incidence angle images. These incidence angle images are also normalized to have similar value ranges as the normalized SAR images. For the experiments that use incidence angle, each image patch is a three dimensional matrix of size $3 \times 45 \times 45$, while for the experiments that do not use incidence angle, each image patch is a two dimensional matrix of size $2 \times 45 \times 45$.

Each extracted patch and the ice concentration located at the patch center from the image analysis is one sample used to train the CNN. Polygon boundaries were not considered in selecting samples from the image analyses due to the limited number of samples available. Patches chosen that contain a polygon boundary are assigned the label corresponding to the polygon of the central pixel of the patch, but could be better described with a label the specifies the ice concentration as the mixture of the two polygons. These issues should be considered in a future study.

4.2. Overview and Structure of the CNN

CNN is a trainable architecture composed of multiple stages [38–40]. Each stage is composed of three consecutive operations (layers): convolutional filtering, non-linear transformation and sub-sampling (pooling). A CNN normally contains multiple stages that learn the image features, followed by a stack of fully connected (FC) layers [40]. The structure of the CNN used in this study is illustrated in Table 2. The CNN contains three convolutional layers followed by two fully connected layers. An excellent overview of CNNs can be found in [13].

Table 2. Structure and configuration of the CNN model used in the present study. Each row for a given layer corresponds to: the layer dimension (top row), the layer configuration (middle row) and the dimension the output (bottom row). For example for the layer *Conv1* there are 64 filters of dimension $3 \times 5 \times 5$ that are applied to an input patch of size $3 \times 45 \times 45$ with a stride of 1 and using a pad 2, to produce an output of dimension $64 \times 45 \times 45$.

Layer	
Data	$3 \times 45 \times 45$
Conv1	$64 \times 3 \times 5 \times 5$ stride 1, pad 2, ReLU $64 \times 45 \times 45$
Pool1	2×2 stride 2, pad 1, Max $64 \times 23 \times 23$
Conv2	$128 \times 64 \times 5 \times 5$ stride1, pad 2, ReLU $128 \times 23 \times 23$
Pool2	$128 \times 23 \times 23$ stride 2, pad 1, Max $128 \times 12 \times 12$
Conv3	$128 \times 128 \times 5 \times 5$ stride 1 , pad 2 , ReLU $128 \times 12 \times 12$
FC4	$1024 \times 128 \times 5 \times 5$ ReLU 1024×1
Dropout	$1024 \times 1 \times 1$ Drop rate: 0.5 1024×1
FC5	1×1024 Linear 1

In the convolutional layers, the layer input matrix x (width S_x pixels, height S_y pixels and number of channels S_z), which is a patch extracted from the SAR image, is convolved with K convolution filters of size (C_x, C_y, S_z), denoted by $C^k, k = 1, \ldots, K$. Each filter is applied to the image patch with a step size (stride) P (convolution is carried out for locations that are P pixels apart). A total of K feature maps, denoted as h^k of dimension M_x and M_y will be generated as the output of this convolutional layer as described in Equation (1),

$$h^k = (C^k * x) + b, \text{in which}, k = 1, \ldots, K \tag{1a}$$

$$M_x = \frac{S_x - C_x}{P} + 1 \tag{1b}$$

$$M_y = \frac{S_y - C_y}{P} + 1, \tag{1c}$$

where the operation of convolution is denoted by $*$ and the size of the feature maps ($M_x \times M_y$) is given for the case with zero padding. For a discussion of padding see [41]. Each convolutional layer is mainly characterized by the size and number of filters. The values of the filter weights and the bias term, b, are learned from the training data [42].

A convolutional layer is followed by a nonlinear transformation layer, which applies a nonlinear function to each element in the feature maps. This nonlinear function is also referred as the activation function, and is a well known feature used in neural networks to ensure the output is not simply a linear transformation of the input [43]. The rectified linear unit, ReLU is used as the activation function in the present study. ReLU activation has been demonstrated to lead to faster learning and better features than traditionally used sigmoid activation function, because ReLU activation does not saturate, as compared to sigmoid activation [26,44].

The nonlinear transformation layer is followed by the sub-sampling layer, also known as the pooling layer. Max pooling is used in the present study due to its simplicity and effectiveness [25,26,40,45]. It outputs the maximum value over each pooling window. For example, when pooling window size and step size are both set to 2, a max-pooling layer outputs the maximum value of every two by two non-overlapping window of its input.

The convolutional layers are followed by fully connected layers that serve as classification modules using the features extracted by the previous multiple stages. These layers have structure that is similar to that of a basic neural network [43]. Every neuron in a fully connected layer is connected to all the neurons of its input layer. The first fully connected layer takes a stack of feature maps, h^k as input. The feature maps are flattened to a vector and transformed to the output space by a weight matrix W and bias b. This is followed by the application of an activation function, f, to generate the output,

$$h = f((W * x) + b). \tag{2}$$

4.3. Training and Testing

Our network is trained to output the ice concentration from SAR image patches. Instead of using softmax loss [26], which is commonly used in classification CNNs, the L_2 loss is used (3) for this regression problem to penalize the discrepancy between the CNN output and the ice concentration provided by the image analysis charts. The loss function is,

$$\mathbb{L}(F(x; \theta), z) = \frac{1}{M} \sum_{m=1}^{M} (F(x; \theta)_m - z_m)^2, \tag{3}$$

where $F(x; \theta)$ is the network output given input x and parameterization θ, z_m is the ice concentration for the mth sample from image analyses, and M is the number of samples used in each training sample batch. For batch sizes larger than 1, the overall loss of this mini-batch is the average loss of all samples in that mini-batch.

Backpropagation and mini-batch stochastic gradient descent (SGD) [46] are used as the training algorithm. This method uses the derivatives of loss function (3) with respect to the network parameters

$$\frac{\partial \mathbb{L}}{\partial \theta} = \frac{2}{M} \sum (F(x; \theta)_m - z_m) \frac{\partial F(x; \theta)_m}{\partial \theta}, m = 1, ..., M. \tag{4}$$

The derivatives are backpropagated through each pixel in the predictions. The network parameters are updated according to the derivative of the loss to the parameters over each mini-batch, which is described by (5).

$$V_{t+1} = \alpha \cdot V_t - r \cdot \epsilon \cdot \theta_t - \epsilon \frac{\partial \mathbb{L}}{\partial \theta}|_{\theta_t} \tag{5a}$$

$$\theta_{t+1} = \theta_t + V_{t+1}. \tag{5b}$$

The weights θ are updated by V_{i+t} at iteration $t+1$ with learning rate $\epsilon = 10^{-3}$ and weight decay of $r = 2 \times 10^{-5}$ with momentum, α, of 0.9. The setting of the training parameters for SGD is similar to the published setting by Krizhevsky et al. [26]. Adjustments are made by tuning the training parameters sequentially. ϵ is first tuned due to its significant effect on the training results. Then r and α are tuned. Similar to Krizhevsky et al. [26], the parameters of the CNN are initialized by uniform random sampling between -0.05 and 0.05. Stochastic gradient descent is used to iteratively update the model weights using the gradient of loss with respect to the model parameters calculated using a subset of the training samples (mini-batch). The gradients of the loss with respect to the network parameters ($\partial \mathbb{L}/\partial \theta$) are calculated and averaged over the mini-batch. An epoch training scheme [46] is adopted. For each epoch, all the training samples are iterated once by the training algorithm. The learning rate is reduced by a factor of 10 for every 20 thousand mini-batches (about 17 epochs). To accelerate the training process, the training is set to stop when the score of the loss function is changing less than 0.001 for 20 consecutive epochs, in case the training converges early (which is typical [47]).

Overfitting is a common problem with CNNs. It is common practice to use a validation dataset to validate the CNN model during training time [26]. The derived CNN model is evaluated after each training epoch by calculating the loss function on the validation dataset using the current model. The CNN model with the smallest validation error will be selected as the trained CNN. Note that validation is used for model selection and it is therefore part of the training scheme. In this case, the 25 scenes are randomly divided to 17 training images, 4 testing images and 4 validation images, as described in Table 1.

To further reduce overfitting, training sample augmentation and dropout are used. Training sample augmentation artificially enlarges the training dataset by label-preserving transformations, such as rotation and flipping [26,48]. In our experiment, training samples are augmented on-the-fly by random rotating and flipping. These transformed SAR image patches are used for forward-propagation, which corresponds to increasing the training set by a factor of several hundred times. Dropout is a different and complementary technique used to reduce overfitting. A dropout layer randomly sets the outputs of neurons (also referred as units) in a layer to zero with predefined probability [49]. Those dropped neurons are not contributing to the forward pass and therefore are not updated in the backpropagation. The use of dropout can reduce the co-adaptations between neurons because a neuron cannot rely on the presence of other neurons [26,49]. The network is therefore forced to learn more representative features. A dropout layer with drop rate 0.5, i.e., half of the neurons are randomly chosen and their outputs are set to zero, is used in the present study.

Once the CNN model is trained, ice concentration for each pixel location is estimated by applying the trained model on the target SAR images. Since the CNN can only predict a single location in one forward-propagation, the CNN model is used on input images with stride 1, i.e., the input window moves one pixel every time.

4.4. Implementation

Caffe [50], a popular C++ open-source deep learning package, is used in this study. It provides a ready-to-use implementation of the CNN. SAR image preprocessing and patching are implemented in Python. A data layer is implemented using C++ under Caffe to read the image patches and their corresponding image analyses ice concentration values. In-situ training sample augmentation is also implemented in the data layer.

5. An MLP for Ice Concentration Estimation

For the purpose of evaluation, a fully connected neural network, known as MLP (multilayer perceptron) has also been developed to estimate sea ice concentration from the set of SAR images. The structure of this MLP is similar to that of a fully connected layer, and is described in [43]. The MLP used here is a variation of that used in the ice concentration estimation algorithm developed by Karvonen [4]. Karvonen's method [4] uses a preliminary ice concentration estimated from the autocorrelation of HH pol SAR images by a segmentation based approach [3] and four other SAR image features (HV, HV/HH, (HH-HV)/HH, and incidence angle) as input to an MLP with one hidden layer of 10 units. The MLP developed in [4] was trained using data from Finnish Ice Service (FIS) ice charts.

In our implementation, the ice concentration is estimated on a pixel-by-pixel basis using an MLP with one hidden layer of size 40. Ten GLCM features are used in addition to the four features used by Karvonen (HV, HV/HH, (HH-HV)/HH, and incidence angle). These ten GLCM features are identified as the most important ten SAR image features from a pool of 172 SAR image features used to distinguish ice and water [7] and should also benefit the ice concentration estimation task. The features input to the MLP are listed in Table 3. In Leigh et al. [7], image features are extracted from 4 by 4 block averaged SAR images. For consistency with the 8 by 8 block averaged SAR images used here, the image features are first calculated from 4 by 4 block averaged SAR images as done in [7], and are then averaged for every 2 by 2 block.

Table 3. Image features used for method MLP40.

#	Pol	Feature
1	HV	GLCM mean 25 by 25 step 5
2	HH	GLCM correlation 51 by 51 step 5
3	HH	GLCM mean 25 by 25 step 1
4	HH	GLCM dissimilarity 51 by 51 step 20
5	HH	GLCM second moment 101 by 101 step 5
6	HH	Intensity
7	HV	Average 25 by 25 window
8	HH	Average 5 by 5 window
9	HH	GLCM dissimilarity 51 by 51 step 5
10	HH	GLCM mean 101 by 101 step 20
11	HV	Intensity
12	HH, HV	HV/HH
13	HH, HV	(HH-HV)/HH
14	HH	Intensity autocorrelation
15		Incidence angle

Due to the larger number of input image features in our MLP as compared to [4], the number of hidden neurons needs to be increased. The resulting MLP has higher ratio of hidden neurons to input features (40/15) as compared to Karvonen's implementation (10/6). Note that Karvonen [4] made a correction to the images to account for the variation of backscatter with incidence angle, while in our implementation such a correction was not applied due to the fact that such a correction depends on whether the underlying surface is ice or water [10], and also varies with ice type, none of which can be assumed known in advance. The same training scheme used by Karvonen is used to train the MLP [4].

6. Results

6.1. Evaluation

The ice concentration estimated from the SAR images using the CNN described in Section 4, as well as ice concentration from ASI and MLP40 are evaluated against image analyses in the SAR image space. In other words, each image analysis sample point is compared to the ice concentration of its nearest pixel in the associated SAR scene, which means the image analysis samples are used at a finer spatial resolution than what the analyst intended. The mean error (E_{sgn}), mean absolute error (E_{L1}), error standard deviation (E_{std}) and root mean squared error (E_{rmse}) are calculated for evaluation purposes using (6)

$$E_{sgn} = mean(IC - ImA) \tag{6a}$$

$$E_{L1} = mean(|IC - ImA|) \tag{6b}$$

$$E_{std} = std(IC - ImA) \tag{6c}$$

$$E_{rmse} = \sqrt{(mean[(IC - ImA)^2])}. \tag{6d}$$

The term IC denotes the ice concentration estimated using the CNN and ImA denotes the ice concentration from the image analysis charts.

While the ice concentration derived from the image analysis is a discrete number (0–10) scaled between 0 and 1 (0, 0.1, ..., 1.0), the ice concentration from the CNN is determined as a real number between 0 and 1. This difference may introduce errors into the evaluation statistics. To investigate this, the ice concentration estimates are also quantized by rounding to 11 levels between 0 and 1 and re-evaluated against the image analyses. The evaluation results are similar with slight improvement after quantization, and are therefore not shown.

The evaluation results for training, testing and validation datasets are given in Table 4. The E_{rmse} is lower for the ice concentration estimated by the CNN than that from either MLP or ASI. The statistical significance of the E_{rmse} for each of the test datasets is assessed using a z-test, with the E_{rmse} assumed to follow a chi-squared distribution [51]. For Table 4, the null hypothesis is that the E_{rmse} of the CNN and MLP have the same distribution. The calculated p-value is $<<0.001$, indicating that the difference between the two is statistically significant for significance level of 0.01. Similar tests were done for the other experiments (discussed in Sections 6.3.2 and 6.3.3) and in all cases the p-value is $<<0.001$, with the exception of the experiment comparing two convolutional layers with three convolutional layers, in which case the p-value is 0.0019. For each experiment it was the E_{rmse} of the test dataset that was evaluated.

Table 4. Average error statistics across different methods for Gulf of Saint Lawrence dataset.

Method	Set	E_{sgn}	E_{L1}	E_{std}	E_{rmse}
	Training	−0.2423	0.2605	0.3207	0.4020
ASI	Validation	−0.3416	0.3768	0.3693	0.5031
	Testing	−0.2717	0.2877	0.3097	0.4121
	Training	0.0002	0.1460	0.2050	0.2049
MLP40	Validation	−0.0410	0.2381	0.2986	0.3015
	Testing	−0.0819	0.1727	0.2325	0.2466
	Training	−0.0039	0.0845	0.1506	**0.1507**
CNN	Validation	−0.0123	0.1253	0.2056	0.2059
	Testing	−0.0274	0.1295	0.2197	0.2214

In Table 4 it can be seen that ASI underestimates ice concentration by around 24% when compared with image analyses (Table 4). Since the CNN is trained using image analysis charts, while ASI ice concentration is not, it is expected to have lower error than ASI when the error is calculated with respect to image analysis charts. Previous studies reported that the ASI ice concentration normally has errors less than 10% for intermediate and high ice concentrations [31]. The large underestimation of ice concentration observed in this study is mainly caused by the large regions of thin ice, and the magnitude of the error is consistent with that reported in other studies [16]. The underestimation of ice concentration is improved by the CNN compared to MLP40. Note that the error standard deviation (E_{std}) for testing is at the same level as training and validation for the CNN, which indicates a low level of over-fitting for the trained CNN model. The validation errors are larger than testing errors for MLP40. This might be caused by the insufficient testing samples used, which could lead to different distributions of image surface types for validation and testing images.

Figure 2 shows the mean value of the estimated ice concentration ± one standard deviation of the ice concentration estimate errors for different ice concentration bins from the image analysis charts. Results are shown separately for training, validation and testing datasets. There is a clear trend between image analyses and ice concentration estimates generated from SAR images for all three sets in general. ASI shows underestimation for almost all ice concentration levels, with larger underestimation for higher ice concentration values. MLP40 overestimates ice concentration for water regions by about 15% for all three datasets, and underestimates ice concentration by 20% to 40% for training, testing and validation in the highest ice concentration bin. The CNN has relatively less overestimation for water regions and less underestimation for ice regions compared to MLP40. For water, CNN overestimates ice concentration on average by approximately 5% for training and 10% for testing and validation. For ice (where ice concentration is equal to 1), CNN underestimates ice concentration by less than 10% on average for all three sets. The estimation of pure water or ice generally has smaller error standard deviation than the estimate for intermediate ice concentration levels. This might be caused by the abundant water samples and ice samples in the training dataset (Figure 3), or the better quality (less errors) of ice/water samples than samples of intermediate ice concentration levels. It is reasonable to assume that the ice concentration estimates could be improved by using more training samples of intermediate ice concentration levels.

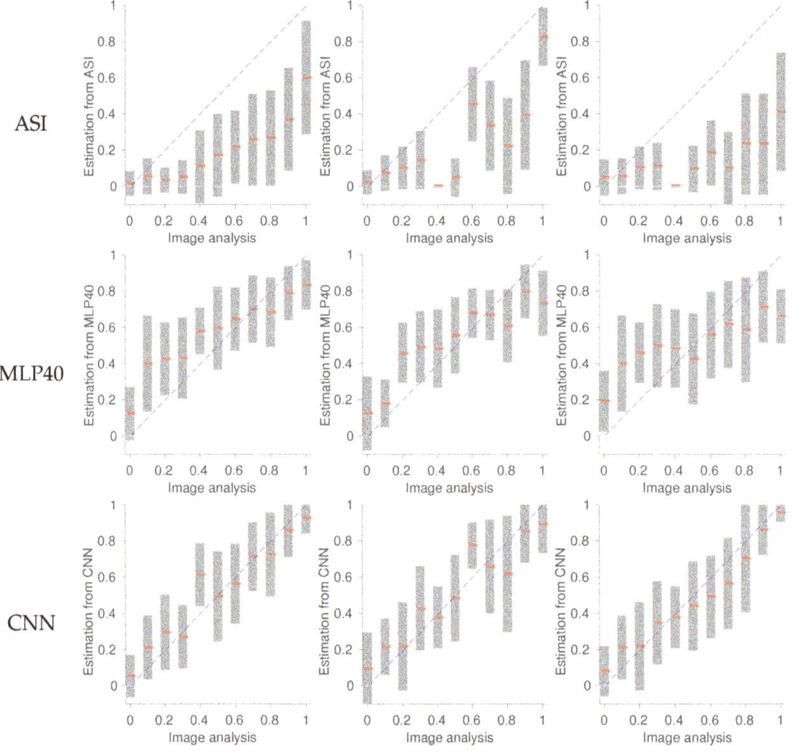

Figure 2. Errors at different ice concentration levels for ASI (1st row), MLP40 (2nd row), and CNN (3rd row) for training (1st column), validation (2nd column) and testing (3rd column) sets. The red lines represent the mean ice concentration, and half length of a bar represents the error standard deviation.

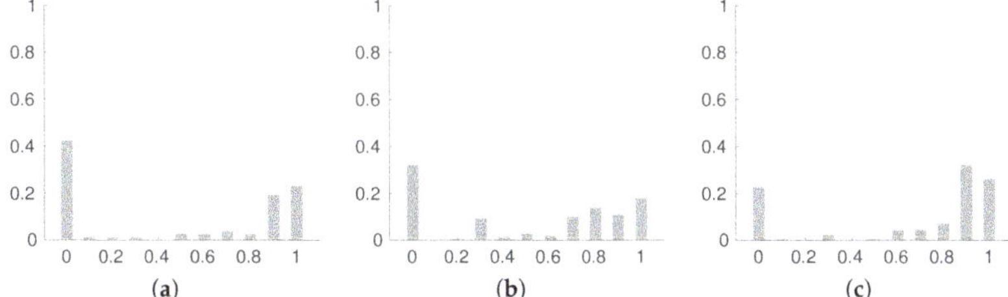

Figure 3. Histogram of the percentage of samples from each 10% interval of the image analyses for training, validation and testing dataset of the Gulf of Saint Lawrence. The training samples are strongly biased since the majority of the training samples are either water or ice. (**a**) Training; (**b**) Validation; (**c**) Testing.

6.2. Comparison between MLP and CNN

All SAR based algorithms produce ice concentration estimates with more details and sharper ice-water boundaries than the ASI data (see Figures 4 and 5), which may be due to the higher resolution of SAR images, and the fact that regions of thin ice are reasonably well captured in the training data used for the SAR based methods. Figure 4e,f shows that MLP40 is more sensitive to backscatter changes in SAR images than the CNN. Therefore, MLP40 produces more details in the ice concentration estimates, as well as an ice cover that appears noisy (e.g., spurious ice can be seen over open water regions). This can sometimes introduce errors, noted in the lower left portion of Figure 6d. The ice concentration estimates by the CNN contain fewer visible errors in assignment of ice concentration than the result of MLP40, but more details than the image analysis charts, especially in low ice concentration regions and marginal ice zones (Figure 6). These differences may be caused by the difficulty to manually identify accurate boundaries of low ice concentration regions by ice analysts or the limited number of polygons they can use for each image analysis, or simply the fact that the ice charts contain an estimate of ice concentration in 10% intervals over a region (polygon) identified as homogeneous.

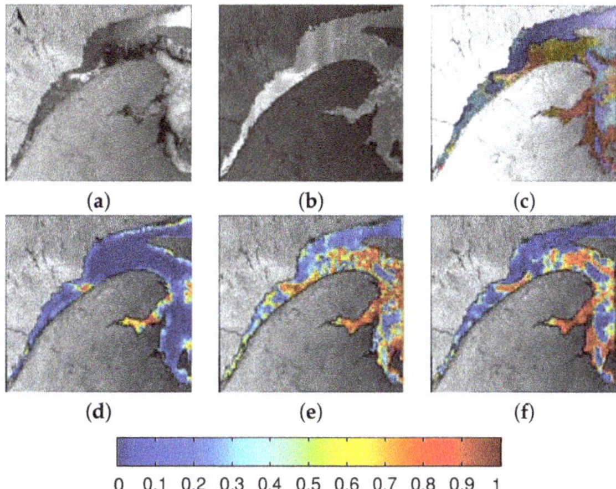

Figure 4. Ice concentration estimated by CNN compared to that from other methods. The HH and HV images are shown in panels (**a**) and (**b**) repectively. Panel (**c**) is the image analysis, (**d–f**) are the ice concentration from ASI, MLP40 and CNN, repectively. Scene shown is 20140117_103914, which is used for testing. Scene centered at 47.99°N, 66.85°W with extent of 500 km by 500 km.

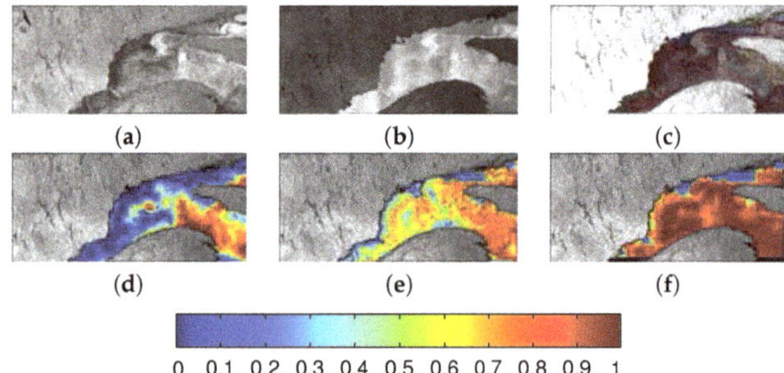

Figure 5. Ice concentration estimated by CNN compared to that from other methods. The HH and HV images are shown in panels (**a**) and (**b**) respectively. Panel (**c**) is the image analysis. Panels (**d–f**) are ice concentration from ASI, MLP40 and CNN respectively. Scene shown is 20140210_103911, which is used for testing. Scene centered at 49.90°N, 66.42°W with extent of 500 km by 230 km.

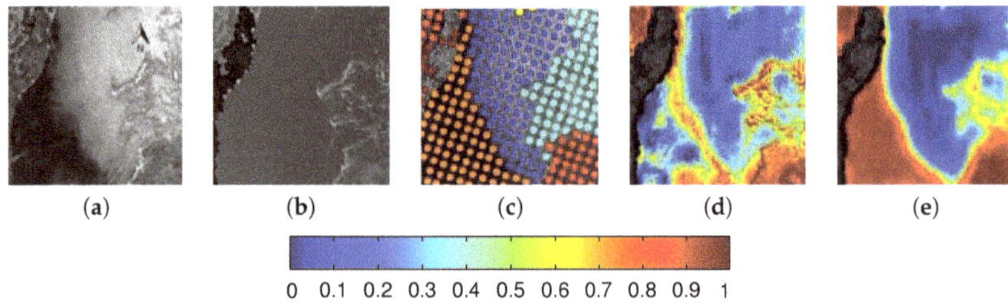

Figure 6. An example shows the details for a region with new ice and water. The ASI result is mainly water for this region. It can be seen MLP40 (**d**) produces noisy ice concentration estimates with new ice in the bottom left identified as water with some ice of low ice concentration. The CNN (**e**) is able to correctly identify new ice and water with higher accuracy. Subscene of dimension 60 km × 60 km from 20140117_103914 centered at 47.60°N, 64.13°W. The HH image, HV image and image analysis are shown in panels (**a–c**) respectively.

Strong banding in the HV channel of the RADARSAT-2 imagery may cause overestimation of ice concentration for water regions. Such an example is given in Figure 7, where MLP and CNN overestimate ice concentration for water regions with strong banding in the HV pol. The level of overestimation is reduced slightly when a larger patch size (55 vs. 45) is used for the CNN.

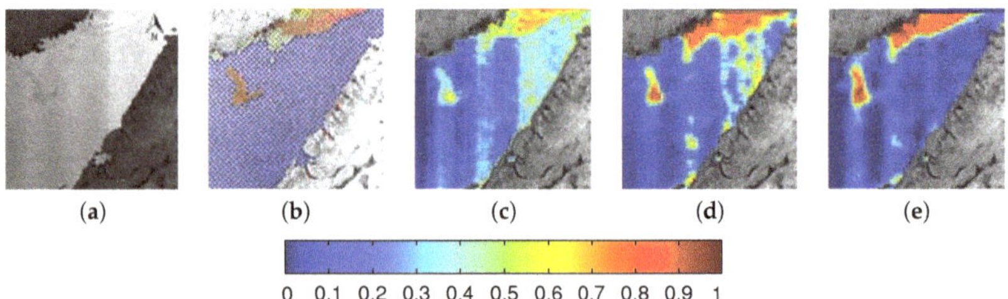

Figure 7. Example of water misidentified as ice for both MLP40 and CNN due to the banding effect in HV pol. Water in the right part of HV pol (**a**) is obviously brighter than water in the left. Water regions are estimated incorrectly for MLP40 (**c**), and CNN with patch size 45 (**d**). Results from the CNN are improved when a patch size of 55 is used, as shown in panel (**e**), although the features are also less sharp. Subscene centered at 49.72°N, 59.11°W of dimension 200 km × 200 km from 20140121_214420. Image analysis is shown in panel (**b**).

6.3. Evaluation of CNN Architecture and Parameters

6.3.1. Patch Size

The size of the input patches, and the support of the convolutional filters, are related to the intrinsic scale and complexity of the problem. The impact of patch size was evaluated by examining the output of the CNN for patch sizes of 25, 35, 45 and 55, corresponding to 10 km (25 × 400 m), 14 km (35 × 400 m), 18 km (45 × 400 m) and 22 km (55 × 400 m). With larger patch size, the model is a better fit to the training data and the E_{rmse} of the training data decreases. The E_{rmse} for test and validation data decreases when the patch size increases from 25 to 45. However, when the patch size increased from 45 to 55, the E_{rmse} for the test and validation data increased slightly, which could be an indication of slight overfitting for the dataset used. Therefore, a patch size of 45 was used in this study. Note that for a different dataset, the patch size selected may be different.

The impact of patch size on the estimated ice concentration can be seen in the regions contaminated with either banding or wind roughened open water. Examples are shown in Figure 8. The smaller patch sizes (Figure 8e,f) lead to spurious ice in water regions due to wind and banding. These results suggest that the separation of water and ice requires spatial context information over a larger region. This is also seen in studies using GLCM statistics to separate ice from water, in which case the separation of the two generally improves when larger patches are considered [7]. In contrast, ice is generally well identified for all tested patch sizes. Using small patch sizes tends to slightly underestimate ice concentration, leading to ice cover that is less homogeneous, as compared to larger patch sizes. For the patch size of 25, in some cases openings (i.e., open water) can be seen in the ice cover (not shown) for polygons corresponding to 100% ice concentration in the image analysis chart.

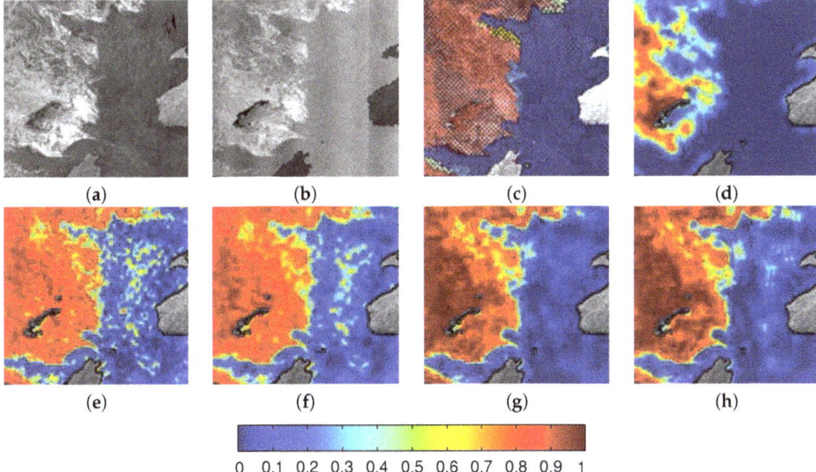

Figure 8. Visual comparison of different patch sizes, (**e**) 25 × 25 pixels, (**f**) 35 × 35 pixels, (**g**) 45 × 45 pixels, (**h**) 55 × 55 pixels. Estimate of ice concentration is improved when patch size increases. Patch size 45, corresponding to ground distance of 18 km, has cleaner water estimates than the others. Subscene of dimension 270 km × 270 km from 20140124_215646 centered at 47.86°N, 60.94°W. Panels (**a–d**) are the HH image, HV image, image analysis chart and ASI ice concentration respectively.

6.3.2. Use of Incidence Angle Data

The results shown in previous sections used input image patches consisting of HH pol, HV pol and incidence angle. To investigate the impact of including incidence angle on the estimated ice concentration, CNNs are trained, validated and tested, with HH pol and HV pol only. The network structure used is the same as that for the CNN without incidence angle (Table 2). The ice concentration from the CNN is evaluated against image analysis charts, results are given in Table 5. The errors are higher in all cases when incidence angle is included. This is in part likely due to the fact that including the incidence angle information leads to greater dependency of the CNN on the HH channel. This may also be due to the fact that with a third channel of input, the model is larger (there are more weights that need to be trained), and is therefore has more potential to overfit the training data.

Table 5. The average error statistics for networks trained with or without incidence angle data using CNN on the Gulf of Saint Lawrence data.

	Set	E_{sgn}	E_{L1}	E_{std}	E_{rmse}
with incidence angle	Training	−0.0039	0.0845	0.1506	0.1507
	Validation	−0.0123	0.1253	0.2056	0.2059
	Testing	−0.0274	0.1295	0.2197	0.2214
without incidence angle	Training	0.0052	0.0817	0.1434	**0.1435**
	Validation	0.0035	0.1183	0.1837	**0.1836**
	Testing	−0.0119	0.1220	0.2031	**0.2035**

Due to the reduced dependency of the CNN on the HV pol, and more significant extraction of information from the HH pol with the use of incidence angle, the banding effect from HV is reduced, but the ice concentration estimates appear to be more sensitive to wind roughening. New ice is more likely to be correctly identified when incidence angle is used (Figure 9), in particular for cases when there are features visible in the HH image that appear to indicate a region of new ice.

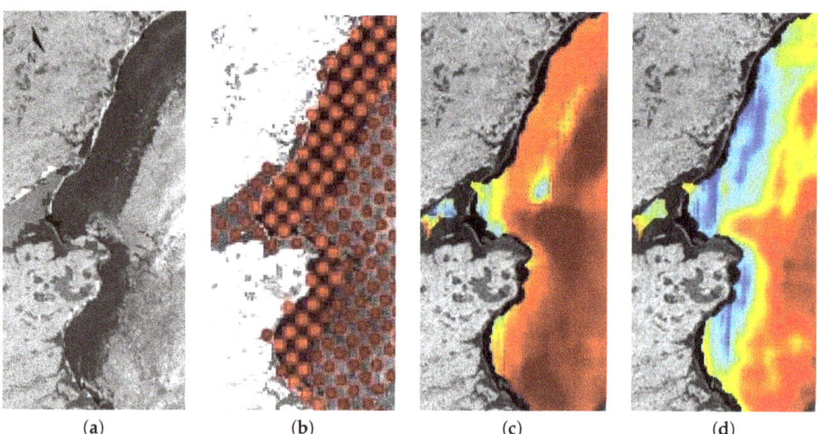

(a)   (b)   (c)   (d)

Figure 9. New ice can be seen in the HH image as the dark regions along the coast (**a**). This ice is correctly identified when incidence angle data are used (**c**), as compared to when the incidence angle data is not used (**d**). Subscene of dimension 120 km × 52 km from 20140206_221744 centered at 47.12°N, 64.72°W. Image analysis is shown in panel (**b**).

6.3.3. Network Depth

Network depth is the number of convolutional layers in the CNN, where each layer contains a filtering, non-linear activation and pooling operation. The network depth is an important parameter that determines the level of abstraction used for classification or regression. Here, CNN models with two and three convolutional layers are trained and evaluated. In both cases, there are two fully connected layers after the convolutional layers. The error statistics against image analyses are illustrated in Table 6. Although the use of two or three convolutional layers in the networks generates similar error statistics, visually, the network with three convolutional layers produces smoother and more reasonable ice concentration estimates, as shown in Figure 10. This makes sense as deeper networks extract more abstract features so that the results are less sensitive to raw pixel values. The ice-covered regions in Figure 10a that are incorrectly identified by the network with two convolutional layers (Figure 10c) are correctly identified by the network with three convolutional layers (Figure 10d). Regions that can be visually identified as open water in Figure 11a look cleaner when three layers are used, as shown in Figure 11d. While similar results (meaning sharper features with increasing layers) are obtained when more convolutional layers are used, as adding more layers leads to increased computational complexity, the three-convolutional-layer structure is deemed adequate.

Table 6. Average error statistics for networks with two convolutional layers and three convolutional layers on the Gulf of Saint Lawrence dataset.

	Two Convolutional Layers				Three Convolutional Layers			
Set	E_{sgn}	E_{L1}	E_{std}	E_{rmse}	E_{sgn}	E_{L1}	E_{std}	E_{rmse}
Training	−0.0055	0.0874	0.1266	**0.1269**	−0.0039	0.0845	0.1506	0.1507
Validation	−0.0028	0.1229	0.1933	**0.1934**	−0.0123	0.1253	0.2056	0.2059
Testing	0.0054	0.1556	0.2300	0.2302	−0.0274	0.1295	0.2197	**0.2214**

Figure 10. The network with three convolutional layers (**d**), improves the estimation for new ice compared to network with two convolutional layers (**c**). Panel (**a**) is the HH image, and (**b**) is the image analysis chart. Subscene of dimension 8 km × 8 km centered at 47.06°N and 64.46°W from 20140117_103914.

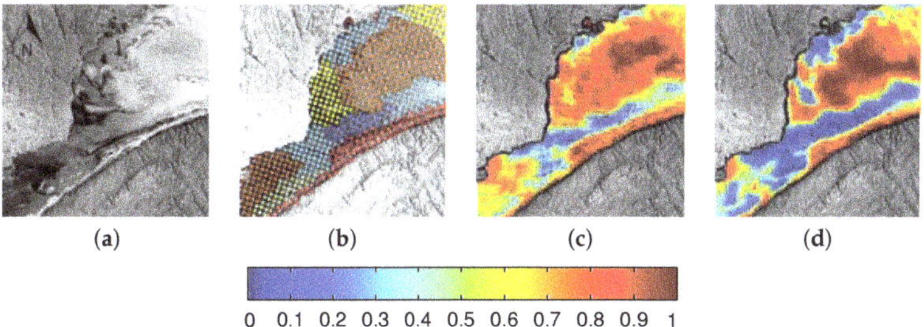

Figure 11. Comparison of results produced by networks with two-convolutional-layer (**c**) and three-convolutional-layer structures (**d**) for a sample location centered at 49.57°N, 66.59°W with size 200 km × 200 km in scene 20140127_104734 in Gulf of Saint Lawrence. Estimate by the two-convolutional-layer network is noisier. The three-convolutional-layer network produces smoother and more reasonable results. Panel (**a**) is the HH image and (**b**) is the image analysis chart for the subregion.

7. Discussion

In this study, a CNN has been applied to estimate sea ice concentration from dual-polarized SAR images in the Gulf of St. Lawrence. State-of-the-art ice concentration estimates with finer details than the image analysis chart are generated. Experiments using HV pol or HH pol only have also been carried out (results not shown here). Using dual-pol SAR imagery leads to improved ice concentration estimates as compared to using HH pol or HV pol only. When using HH pol only, the results are strongly affected by the incidence angle, which causes overestimation of ice concentration for water regions at low incidence angles. Using only HV pol shows banding in the estimated ice concentration. Similar results have been demonstrated in previous studies [4,52].

Sea ice concentration from image analysis charts was selected as the training data for this study. These charts contain regions (polygons) labelled by a trained analyst as having homogeneous ice conditions. When the image analysis charts were sampled, a single pixel from the image analysis (representing an area of 8 km $\times$ 5 km) was associated with a patch from the SAR image (representing an area of 18 km $\times$ 18 km). This means the SAR image patches could overlap polygon boundaries. While it may have been more appropriate to sample the image analysis charts to avoid this overlap, the accuracy of the polygon boundaries is not known. The image analyses are also subjective manual analyses, and are known to contain errors [36], as is the case with any ice concentration analysis. Even if it can be assumed the polygon boundaries are accurate, the use of spatially discrete polygons to represent the ice concentration over an image of continuous grey levels, introduces sampling errors in the ice concentration estimates. Preliminary work on the impact of errors in the training data, and alternative methods to train a CNN to estimate sea ice concentration, can be found in [53]. Learning a sparse representation of the data could improve the ice concentration estimates when training sample quality and quantity are not sufficient [54].

Testing demonstrates that the CNN is robust to the changes in image tone with incidence angle, even without explicitly including incidence angle data as an input. When the incidence angle data was included, an increased dependence on the HH pol image was observed in the ice concentration. Windspeed information could also be included as an additional input, which could help reduce the spurious ice that appears in some cases over open water when it appears to be wind-roughened. This would require accurate windspeed information at a sufficiently high spatial resolution, which is not presently available.

A linear activation function has been chosen for the last fully connected layer, which means that ice concentration values can be estimated that are greater than 1 or less than zero. For comparison between the different methods these ice concentration values were truncated to remain in the range of [0,1]. A sigmoid activation would be a more intuitive choice, as it naturally bounds the output of the CNN to 0 and 1. However, in our experiment, sigmoid activation was found to produce saturated ice concentration predictions close to 0 or 1, and large errors for intermediate ice concentration levels.

8. Conclusions

The CNN has been found to generate ice concentration estimates with improved details and accuracy as compared to ASI passive microwave ice concentration products when IA charts are used as the verification data. Our CNN ice concentration is also improved as compared to that from a method that uses an MLP to regress ice concentration from a set of engineered SAR image features. Because of the shallow network structure, MLP40 is more sensitive to the SAR image backscatter values than the CNN, which causes noisy ice concentration estimates. The small model used by MLP40 does not have the large learning capacity as the CNN. Some complex cases, such as dark new ice, are not recognized correctly. This causes systematic errors in the results, which cannot be corrected by segmentation based post-processing. Therefore, the deeper and larger CNNs used here can generate more accurate ice concentration estimates than MLP40. Note that while a multilayer version of MLP40 could be developed, maintaining full connectivity between the weights in these layers would require many weights to be learned, making such networks prone to overfitting [13]. Compared to standard fully connected neural networks with similar number of units, CNNs are able to model local spatial information more efficiently with fewer trainable parameters, which also makes them easier to train [26,55]. The success of CNNs as multi-layer networks is due to weight sharing and the local connectivity between adjacent layers [38], and methods developed to reduce overfitting [26], such as training sample augmentation and dropout, which have been implemented in the present study.

We note that there are alternative approaches to using a CNN for this problem that may be more efficient than that presented here. For example, methods that predict dense labelling as compared to a label [30,56] at a single pixel location (as has been done in the present study). Preliminary work using such an architecture for the GSL data has been presented in [53], and will be investigated further in a future study.

Acknowledgments: This study was funded through the Chinese Scholarship Council, the National Science and Engineering Research Council of Canada, ArcticNet Networks of Centres of Excellence, and the Grants and Contributions program through Environment Canada. The authors would like to thank Lynn Pogson and Alain Caya for providing the SAR imagery and image analysis charts. RADARSAT-2 Data and Products ©MacDonald, Dettwiler and Associates Ltd. 2010. All Rights Reserved. RADARSAT is an official mark of the Canadian Space Agency.

Author Contributions: Lei Wang carried out the data processing and analysis, and contributed to the research design and manuscript writing. Andrea Scott led manuscript writing, contributed to the research design and co-supervised this study. David Clausi contributed to manuscript writing and research design, and co-supervised this study.

Conflicts of Interest: The authors declare no conflict of interest.

References

1. Carrieres, T.; Greenan, B.; Prinsenberg, S.; Peterson, I. Comparison of Canadian daily ice charts with surface observations off Newfoundland, winter 1992. *Atmos. Ocean* **1996**, *34*, 207–226.

2. Arkett, M.; Braithwaite, L.; Pestieau, P.; Carrieres, T.; Pogson, L.; Fabi, C.; Geldsetzer, T. Preparation by the Canadian Ice Service for the operational use of the RADARSAT Constellation Mission in their ice and oil spill monitoring programs. *Can. J. Remote Sens.* **2015**, *41*, 380–389.

3. Karvonen, J. Baltic sea ice concentration estimation based on C-band HH-polarized SAR data. *Sel. Top. Appl. Earth Obs. Remote Sens.* **2012**, *5*, 1874–1884.

4. Karvonen, J. Baltic sea ice concentration estimation based on C-band dual-polarized SAR data. *IEEE Trans. Geosci. Remote Sens.* **2014**, *52*, 5558–5566.

5. Clausi, D.A. Comparison and fusion of co-occurrence, Gabor, and MRF texture features for classification of SAR sea ice imagery. *Atmos. Ocean* **2001**, *39*, 183–194.

6. Deng, H.; Clausi, D.A. Unsupervised segmentation of synthetic aperture radar sea ice imagery using a novel Markov random field model. *IEEE Trans. Geosci. Remote Sens.* **2005**, *43*, 528–538.

7. Leigh, S.; Wang, Z.; Clausi, D.A. Automated ice-water classification using dual polarization SAR satellite imagery. *IEEE Trans. Geosci. Remote Sens.* **2014**, *52*, 5529–5539.

8. Zakhvatkina, N.Y.; Alexandrov, V.Y.; Johannessen, O.M.; Sandven, S.; Frolov, I.Y. Classification of Sea Ice Types in ENVISAT Synthetic Aperture Radar Images. *IEEE Trans. Geosci. Remote Sens.* **2013**, *51*, 2587–2600.

9. Liu, J.; Scott, K.; Gawish, A.; Fieguth, P. Automatic detection of the ice edge in SAR imagery using curvelet transform and active contour. *Remote Sens.* **2016**, *8*, doi:10.3390/rs8060480.

10. Pogson, L.; Geldsetzer, T.; Buehner, M.; Carrieres, T.; Ross, M.; Scott, K. A collection of empirically-derived characteristic values from SAR across a year of sea ice environments for use in data assimilation. *Mon. Weather Rev.* **2016**, in press.

11. Buehner, M.; Caya, A.; Pogson, L.; Carrieres, T.; Pestieau, P. A new Environment Canada regional ice analysis system. *Atmos. Ocean* **2013**, *51*, 18–34.

12. Drusch, M. Sea ice concentration analyses for the Baltic Sea and their impact on numerical weather prediction. *J. Appl. Meteorol. Climatol.* **2006**, *45*, 982–994.

13. LeCun, Y.; Bengio, J.; Hinton, G. Deep Learning. *Nature* **2015**, *521*, 436–444.

14. Wang, L.; Scott, K.A.; Xu, L.; Clausi, D.A. Sea Ice Concentration Estimation During Melt From Dual-Pol SAR Scenes Using Deep Convolutional Neural Networks: A Case Study. *IEEE Trans. Geosci. Remote Sens.* **2016**, *54*, 4524–4533.

15. Geldsetzer, T.; Yackel, J. Sea ice type and open water discrimination using dual co-polarized C-band SAR. *Can. J. Remote Sens.* **2009**, *35*, 73–84.

16. Ivanova, N.; Tonboe, R.; Pedersen, L.T. *SICCI Product Validation and Algorithm Selection Report (PVASR)—Sea Ice Concentration*; Technical Report; European Space Agency: Paris, France, 2013.

17. Dumbill, E. *Strata 2012: Making Data Work*; O'Reilly: Santa Clara, CA, USA, 2012.

18. Najafabadi, M.M.; Villanustre, F.; Khoshgoftaar, T.M.; Seliya, N.; Wald, R.; Muharemagic, E. Deep learning applications and challenges in big data analytics. *J. Big Data* **2015**, *2*, doi:10.1186/s40537-014-0007-7.

19. National Research Council. *Frontiers in Massive Data Analysis*; The National Academies Press: Washington, DC, USA, 2013.

20. Domingos, P. A Few Useful Things to Know About Machine Learning. *Commun. ACM* **2012**, *55*, 78–87.

21. Bengio, Y.; Courville, A.; Vincent, P. Representation learning: A review and new perspectives. *IEEE Trans. Pattern Anal. Mach. Intell.* **2013**, *35*, 1798–1828.

22. Hinton, G.E. Learning multiple layers of representation. *Trends Cogn. Sci.* **2007**, *11*, 428–434.

23. Bengio, Y. Learning deep architectures for AI. *Found. Trends Mach. Learn.* **2009**, *2*, 1–127.

24. Lee, H.; Grosse, R.; Ranganath, R.; Ng, A.Y. Convolutional deep belief networks for scalable unsupervised learning of hierarchical representations. In Proceedings of the 26th Annual International Conference on Machine Learning, Montreal, QC, Canada, 14–18 June 2009; pp. 609–616.

25. Ciresan, D.C.; Meier, U. Flexible, high performance convolutional neural networks for image classification. In Proceedings of the Twenty-Second International Joint Conference On Artificial Intelligence, Barcelona, Spain, 16–22 July 2011; pp. 1237–1242.

26. Krizhevsky, A.; Sutskever, I.; Hinton, G.E. ImageNet classification with deep convolutional neural networks. In Proceedings of the 25th International Conference on Neural Information Processing Systems, Lake Tahoe, NV, USA, 3–6 December 2012; pp. 1097–1105.

27. Karpathy, A.; Toderici, G.; Shetty, S.; Leung, T.; Sukthankar, R.; Fei-Fei, L. Large-scale video classification with convolutional neural networks. In Proceedings of the 2014 IEEE Conference on Computer Vision and Pattern Recognition, Columbus, OH, USA, 23–28 June 2014; pp. 1725–1732.

28. Mnih, V.; Hinton, G.E. Learning to detect roads in high-resolution aerial images. In *Computer Vision-ECCV 2010*; Springer: Berlin/Heidelberg, Germany, 2010; pp. 210–223.

29. Chen, X.; Xiang, S.; Liu, C.L.; Pan, C.H. Vehicle Detection in Satellite Images by Hybrid Deep Convolutional Neural Networks. *IEEE Geosci. Remote Sens. Lett.* **2014**, *11*, 1797–1801.

30. Maggiori, E.; Tarabalka, Y.; Charpiat, G.; Alliez, P. Fully convolutional neural networks for remote sensing image classification. In Proceedings of the 2016 IEEE Geoscience and Remote Sensing Symposium, Beijing, China, 10–15 July 2016.

31. Spreen, G.; Kaleschke, L.; Heygster, G. Sea ice remote sensing using AMSR-E 89-GHz channels. *J. Geophys. Res.* **2008**, *113*, doi:10.1029/2005JC003384.

32. Agnew, T.; Howell, S. The use of operational ice charts for evaluating passive microwave ice concentration data. *Atmos. Ocean* **2003**, *41*, 317–331.

33. Karvonen, J.; Vainio, J.; Marnela, M.; Eriksson, P.; Niskanen, T. A comparison between high-resolution EO-based and ice analyst-assigned sea ice concentrations. *J. Sel. Top. Appl. Earth Obs. Remote Sens.* **2015**, *8*, 1799–1807.

34. Fequest, D. *MANICE: Manual of Standard Procedures for Observing and Reporting Ice Conditions*; Environment Canada: Ottawa, ON, Canada, 2002.

35. Slade, B. *RADARSAT-2 Product Description*; MacDonald, Dettwiler and Associates Ltd.: Richmond, BC, Canada, 2009.

36. Moen, A.; Doulgeris, P.; Anfinsen, S.; Renner, A.; Hughes, N.; Gerland, S.; Eltoft, T. Comparison of feature based segmentation of full polarimetric SAR satellite sea ice images with manually drawn ice charts. *Cryosphere* **2013**, *7*, 1693–1705.

37. De Andrade, A. *Best Practices for Convolutional Neural Networks Applied to Object Recognition in Images*; Technical Report; Department of Computer Science, University of Toronto: Toronto, ON, USA, 2014.

38. LeCun, Y.; Bottou, L.; Bengio, Y.; Haffner, P. Gradient-based learning applied to document recognition. *Proc. IEEE* **1998**, *86*, 2278–2324.

39. LeCun, Y.; Huang, F.J.; Bottou, L. Learning methods for generic object recognition with invariance to pose and lighting. In Proceedings of the 2004 IEEE Computer Society Conference on Computer Vision and Pattern Recognition, Washington, DC, USA, 27 June–2 July 2004.

40. LeCun, Y.; Kavukcuoglu, K.; Farabet, C. Convolutional networks and applications in vision. In Proceedings of 2010 IEEE International Symposium on Circuits and Systems (ISCAS), Paris, France, 30 May–2 June 2010; pp. 253–256.

41. Chen, L.C.; Papandreou, G.; Kokkinos, I.; Murphy, K.; Yuille, A.L. Semantic image segmentation with deep convolutional nets and fully connected CRFs. *arXiv* **2016**, arXiv:1412.7062.

42. Hastie, T.; Tibshirani, R.; Friedman, J. *The Elements of Statistical Learning*; Springer: Berlin/Heidelberg, Germany, 2009; Volume 2.

43. Bishop, C.M. *Pattern Recognition and Machine Learning*; Springer: Berlin/Heidelberg, Germany, 2006.

44. Nair, V.; Hinton, G.E. Rectified linear units improve restricted Boltzmann machines. In Proceedings of the 27th International Conference on Machine Learning (ICML-10), Haifa, Israel, 21–24 June 2010; pp. 807–814.

45. Scherer, D.; Müller, A.; Behnke, S. Evaluation of pooling operations in convolutional architectures for object recognition. In *Artificial Neural Networks–ICANN 2010*; Springer: Berlin/Heidelberg, Germany, 2010; pp. 92–101.

46. LeCun, Y.; Bottou, L.; Orr, G.; Müller, K. Efficient backprop. In *Neural Networks: Tricks of the Trade*; Springer: Berlin/Heidelberg, Germany, 2012.

47. Prechelt, L. Early stopping-but when? In *Neural Networks: Tricks of the Trade*; Springer: Berlin/Heidelberg, Germany, 2012; pp. 53–67.

48. Chatfield, K.; Simonyan, K.; Vedaldi, A.; Zisserman, A. Return of the Devil in the Details: Delving Deep into Convolutional Nets. *arXiv* **2014**, arXiv:1405.3531.

49. Hinton, G.E.; Srivastava, N.; Krizhevsky, A.; Sutskever, I.; Salakhutdinov, R.R. Improving neural networks by preventing co-adaptation of feature detectors. *arXiv* **2012**, arXiv:1207.0580.

50. Jia, Y.; Shelhamer, E.; Donahue, J.; Karayev, S.; Long, J.; Girshick, R.; Guadarrama, S.; Darrell, T. Caffe: Convolutional architecture for fast feature embedding. In Proceedings of the ACM International Conference on Multimedia, Orlando, FL, USA, 3–7 November 2014; pp. 675–678.

51. Watkins, J.C. Probability Theory. In *Course Note for Probability Theory*; University of Arizona: Tucson, AZ, USA, 2006.

52. Wang, L.; Scott, K.; Clausi, D. Automatic feature learning of SAR images for sea ice concentration estimation using feed-forward neural networks. In Proceedings of the 2014 IEEE Geoscience and Remote Sensing Symposium, Quebec City, QC, Canada, 13–18 July 2014; pp. 3969–3971.

53. Wang, L. Learning to Estimate Sea Ice Concentration from SAR Imagery. Ph.D. Thesis, University of Waterloo, Waterloo, ON, Canada, 2016.

54. Wang, Q.; Lin, J.; Yuan, Y. Salient band selection for hyperspectral image classification via manifold ranking. *IEEE J. Neural Netw. Learn. Syst.* **2016**, *27*, 1279–1289.

55. LeCun, Y. Generalization and network design strategies. In *Connections in Perspective*; Elsevier: Amsterdam, The Netherlands, 1989; pp. 143–155.

56. Maggiori, E.; Tarabalka, Y.; Chariot, G.; Alliez, P. High-resolution semantic labeling with convolutional neural networks. *arXiv* **2016**, arXiv:1611.01962v1.

Article

A New Spatial Attraction Model for Improving Subpixel Land Cover Classification

Lizhen Lu [1,*], Yanlin Huang [1], Liping Di [2,*] and Danwei Hang [1]

[1]   School of Earth Sciences, Zhejiang University, Hangzhou 310027, Zhejiang, China;
      hylgis@zju.edu.cn (Y.H.); hangdanwei@zjzhd.com (D.H.)
[2]   Center for Spatial Information Science and Systems, George Mason University, Fairfax, VA 22030, USA
*   Correspondence: llz_gis@zju.edu.cn (L.L.); ldi@gmu.edu (L.D.);
      Tel.: +86-571-8795-1336 (L.L.); +1-703-993-6114 (L.D.)

Academic Editors: Qi Wang, Nicolas H. Younan, Carlos López-Martínez, Parth Sarathi Roy and Prasad S. Thenkabail
Received: 14 January 2017; Accepted: 7 April 2017; Published: 11 April 2017

Abstract: Subpixel mapping (SPM) is a technique that produces hard classification maps at a spatial resolution finer than that of the input images produced when handling mixed pixels. Existing spatial attraction model (SAM) techniques have been proven to be an effective SPM method. The techniques mostly differ in the way in which they compute the spatial attraction, for example, from the surrounding pixels in the subpixel/pixel spatial attraction model (SPSAM), from the subpixels within the surrounding pixels in the modified SPSAM (MSPSAM), or from the subpixels within the surrounding pixels and the touching subpixels within the central pixel in the mixed spatial attraction model (MSAM). However, they have a number of common defects, such as a lack of consideration of the attraction from subpixels within the central pixel and the unequal treatment of attraction from surrounding subpixels of the same distance. In order to overcome these defects, this study proposed an improved SAM (ISAM) for SPM. ISAM estimates the attraction value of the current subpixel at the center of a moving window from all subpixels within the window, and moves the window one subpixel per step. Experimental results from both Landsat and MODIS imagery have proven that ISAM, when compared with other SAMs, can improve SPM accuracies and is a more efficient SPM technique than MSPSAM and MSAM.

Keywords: spatial attraction model (SAM); subpixel mapping (SPM); land cover; mixed pixel; spatial distribution; hard classification

---

1. Introduction

Land use and land cover (LULC) information is very important in many scientific studies and applications. Remote sensing is the only feasible way of obtaining LULC information for large geographic areas. Many algorithms have been developed to classify various remote sensing data to obtain LULC maps [1–4]. However, remote sensing images often contain mixed pixels, since the sensor's instantaneous field of view (IFOV) includes more than one land cover class [5,6]. The existence of mixed pixels leads to three main problems which need be solved: (1) What classes of land cover does a mixed pixel contain? (2) What are the proportions of land cover classes in a pixel? (3) What is the subpixel spatial distribution of land cover classes [7]? For the first problem, end-member extraction algorithms [8], such as the pixel purity index (PPI), N-FINDER, iterative error analysis (IEA), etc., have been developed. For the second problem, soft or fuzzy classification algorithms, which allocate all classes, in varying proportions, to each pixel [9], have been proposed. These algorithms can be broadly categorized as linear spectral mixed models (LSMMs) and nonlinear mixture models [10–12]. Due to the intrinsic complexity of the mixture modeling and the difficulty in obtaining scene parameters, nonlinear mixture models (NLMMs) have not been applied as widely as LSMMs [10,11]. For the third problem, subpixel mapping (SPM) or super resolution mapping (SRM) methods, which produce hard classified maps at a spatial resolution finer than that of the input images [13], have been developed in recent decades. This paper focuses on SPM, which has been proved as an alternative method for obtaining land use/land cover with an acceptable accuracy [14–19].

In 1993, Schneider first introduced a knowledge-based analysis technique for the automatic localization of field boundaries in agricultural areas [20]. Atkinson formally proposed the concept of SPM and mentioned that SPM can be considered as the post-processing of soft classification based on spatial dependence theory [21]. With the assumption of spatial dependence, Verhoeye et al. [6] proposed a spatial dependence mathematical model and employed linear optimization techniques to find the maximum of the dependence. Considering each pixel as a neuron, Tatem et al. [22–24] and Wang et al. [25] applied a Hopfield neural network (HNN) to map subpixel land cover. The HNN increases the spatial correlation between neighboring subpixels and minimizes iterations to obtain SPM results. Atkinson [13] utilized a two-point histogram method to optimize the match between the target and the current realization of the two-point histograms for subpixel classes within pixels. Atkinson [9,26] developed a pixel swapping algorithm (PSA) to maximize the spatial correlation between neighboring subpixels, by changing the spatial arrangement of subpixels. PSA was initially designed to work for binary-class images, and was later expanded to work on multiple-class images [27–29]. Mertens et al. [30] proposed a subpixel/ pixel spatial attraction model (SPSAM) to calculate the spatial attractions between subpixels and their neighboring pixels. In addition, the Markov random field [31,32], genetic algorithms [33,34], and indicator cokriging-based geostatistical methods [35,36], have also been successfully applied in SPM.

Among all of the aforementioned SPM methods, SPSAM has several advantages in terms of both its simplicity and its explicit physical meanings [30]. For example, spatial attraction, which calculates the spatial correlation between subpixels and their surrounding pixels, is used in SPSAM as a simple tool to directly convey spatial dependence. Without requiring prior knowledge on the spatial structure, which is essential in some learning-based SPM methods, such as a two-point histogram, indicator cokriging-based methods, and genetic algorithms, etc., SPSAM can obtain satisfactory SPM results. However, SPSAM ignores the uncertainty of the spatial distribution of subpixels within surrounding pixels and fails to adequately consider the spatial correlation between subpixels within the central pixel. Consequently, the SPM results obtained by SPSAM are noisy and its accuracy is limited [37]. Therefore, based on SPSAM, Wang et al. proposed a modified SPSAM (MSPSAM) [37] which estimates the spatial attractions according to the distribution of subpixels within neighboring pixels. They also proposed a mixed spatial attraction model (MSAM) for improving the SPM result. MSAM integrates the spatial attraction from both the immediate surrounding subpixels of the current subpixel within the central pixel, and all of the subpixels within the immediate neighboring pixels of the central pixel.

Among the abovementioned spatial attraction models (SAMs), MSAM is the only SAM which considers the spatial attractions generated by not only the subpixels of neighboring pixels, but also the subpixels of the central pixel. However, MSAM assumes that the spatial attraction of a subpixel being considered (called the current subpixel hereafter) is only influenced by the neighboring subpixels, instead of all the subpixels within the central pixel. Yet, according to the spatial dependence theory, the subpixels within the central pixel can exert stronger spatial attractions than those within neighboring pixels because they are spatially closer to the current subpixel. In MSAM, after spatial attraction of all subpixels within the central pixel is calculated, the calculation moves to the next pixels. As a result of this, the same set of subpixels within the neighboring pixels is used in calculating the spatial attraction of all the subpixels within the central pixel. When the current pixel, of which the spatial attraction is being calculated, is not located at the center of the central pixels, the subpixels within the pixel next to the neighboring pixels, which are closer to the current pixel than many of the subpixels within the neighboring pixels, are not considered. This results in the unequal treatment of attraction from surrounding subpixels of the same distance.

This study proposes an improved spatial attraction model (ISAM) to overcome the shortcomings of MSAM. ISAM estimates the attraction value of the current subpixel at the center of a moving window from all the subpixels within the window, and moves the window one subpixel per step, to improve the SPM result.

2. Methodology

2.1. Subpixel Mapping (SPM): Theory

SPM aims to determine the most likely locations of the class fractions within a pixel. The general methods of SPM include three steps: (1) Utilizing spectral mixture analysis models to obtain soft class fraction (proportion) images at an original (coarse resolution) pixel resolution; (2) Dividing the original pixels into a series of subpixels, assuming that one subpixel only contains a specific class, to determine the number of subpixels for each class; (3) Applying spatial distribution features of classes and other prior knowledge, to map the subpixel spatial distribution of classes. From the abovementioned steps, it is obvious that the spatial distribution features of classes are the critical factor of SPM. A random subpixel distribution of classes can be assumed if prior knowledge is lacking. However, according to the spatial dependence theory, the land covers of two adjacent subpixels are more similar than those of two distant subpixels. Therefore, Atkinson considered the spatial dependence theory as the basis for SPM [21].

Figure 1 illustrates the spatial dependence theory of SPM. It shows a raster grid of 3×3 original (coarse resolution or mixed) pixels, with associated fractions of a specific class (Figure 1a). Each pixel is divided into S^2 subpixels (S is scale factor), each corresponding to $1/S^2$ area of the original pixel. Although both Figure 1b,c can present the possible results of the subpixel allocation of the gray class corresponding to the indicated proportion in Figure 1a, according to spatial dependence theory, this is more likely to represent the ground truth.

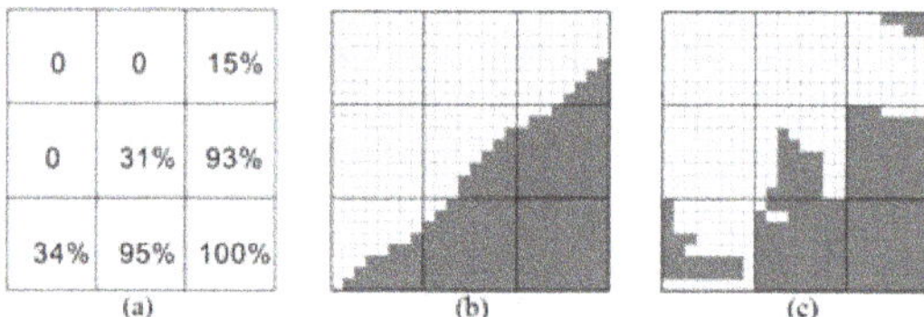

Figure 1. Illustration of spatial dependence theory for subpixel mapping in an 8×8 subpixel scene. (a) 3×3 coarse resolution pixels with the indicated proportion of a specific (gray) class; (b) and (c) The possible results of the subpixel allocation of the gray specific class.

Based on Atkinson's study [21], Verhoeye et al. [6] presented a mathematical model for SPM, which transformed the SPM problem into one of assigning classes to the subpixels using linear optimization techniques. Suppose that the coarse resolution pixels are to be divided into S^2 subpixels. The number of subpixels that have to be assigned to class c is NSP_c and has been derived from soft class fraction images. A measure for spatial dependence $SDV_{c,j}$ will be computed for class c at each subpixel j. Each subpixel has to be assigned a value of one or zero for each class, one indicating an assignment to a particular class. Following this, the problem of assigning each subpixel to a specific class emerges, which has the maximum value of the spatial dependence.

The mathematical model can be expressed as Equation (1):

$$Maximize\ Z = \sum_c \sum_j x_{cj} \cdot SDV_{cj} \tag{1}$$

where $c \in \{1, 2, \ldots, C\}$, C is the total number of classes in the study case; SDV_{cj}, the model key parameter, respresents the spatial dependence values (SDV) of subpixel p_j when it is assigned to class c; x_{cj}, the choice variable of subpixel p_j when it is assigned to class c, is defined in Equation (2):

$$x_{cj} = \begin{cases} 1, \ if \text{ subpix } p_j \text{ is assigned to class } c \\ 0, \text{ otherwise} \end{cases} \tag{2}$$

The model meets two constraints:

$$\sum_c x_{cj} = 1 \tag{3}$$

$$\sum_j x_{cj} = NSP_c \tag{4}$$

Equation (3) means that only one subpixel can be assigned to a specific class and Equation (4) means that the number of subpixels belonging to class c within an original pixel has to be NSP_c.

2.2. SPSAM, MSPSAM, and MSAM

2.2.1. SPSAM

SPSAM was proposed based on the theory of spatial dependence. The assumptions of SPSAM are: (1) the fraction values of neighboring pixels exert the attraction toward subpixels within a central pixel; (2) a subpixel within the central pixel can only be attracted by pixels surrounding the central one; and (3) other pixels are assumed to be too distant to exert any attraction. Assuming that closer pixels attract the subpixel more than the distant ones, SPSAM calculates the attraction value of a neighboring pixel to a subpixel, based on their Euclidean distance.

Figure 2 illustrates the labeled pixels and subpixels, the coordinate system, and the distance between pixels and subpixels in SPSAM. A scale factor of $S = 4$ means that the original central pixel P_{11} contains 16 subpixels with labels: $p_{44}, p_{45}, p_{46}, p_{47}, \ldots, p_{74}, p_{75}, p_{76}, p_{77}$. The distance between subpixel p_{ij} within the central pixel and the neighboring pixel P_{MN} can be defined as:

$$d(P_{MN}, p_{ij}) = \sqrt{[i + 0.5 - S(M + 0.5)]^2 + [j + 0.5 - S(N + 0.5)]^2} \tag{5}$$
$$(i, j = 0, 1, \ldots, 8; \ M, N = 0, 1, 2)$$

$SDV_{c,ij}$, the attraction values of subpixel p_{ij}, which is assigned class c, by the neighboring pixels, can be defined using Equation (6).

$$SDV_{c,ij} = \sum_M \sum_N \frac{1}{d(P_{MN}, p_{ij})} F_c(P_{MN}) \tag{6}$$

where $F_c(P_{MN})$ is the fraction value of class c of the neighboring pixel P_{MN}.

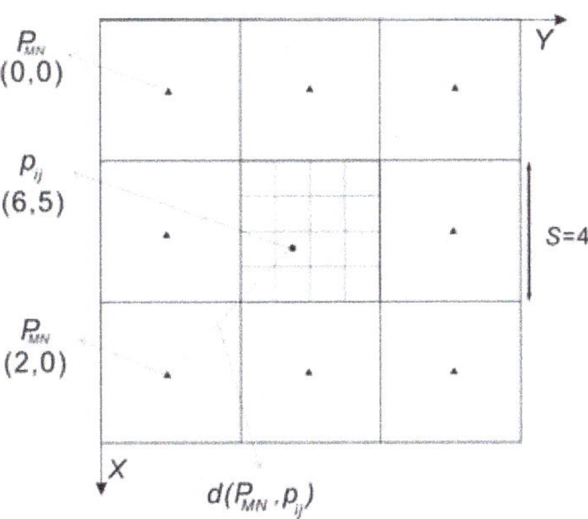

Figure 2. Illustration of the subpixel/pixel spatial attraction model (SPSAM) (adapted from [30]).

2.2.2. MSPSAM and MSAM

SPSAM estimates the spatial attractions of subpixel p_{ij} by the neighboring pixel, ignoring that the other subpixels within the central pixel can exhibit spatial attraction toward the subpixel p_{ij}, and the different spatial distribution of classes of the neighboring pixels can also have different spatial attraction values. Therefore, Wang et al., 2012b, proposed MSPSAM and MSAM to improve the SPM results. As illustrated in Figure 3a, MSPSAM calculates the spatial attractions of subpixel p_{ij} within the central pixel for a given class by using all of the subpixels within the neighboring pixels that have been assigned to the same class as the given class of subpixel p_{ij}. MSAM, illustrated in Figure 3b, computes the spatial attraction of subpixel p_{ij} by using not only the subpixels within the neighboring pixels, but also the neighboring subpixels of subpixel p_{ij} within the central pixel.

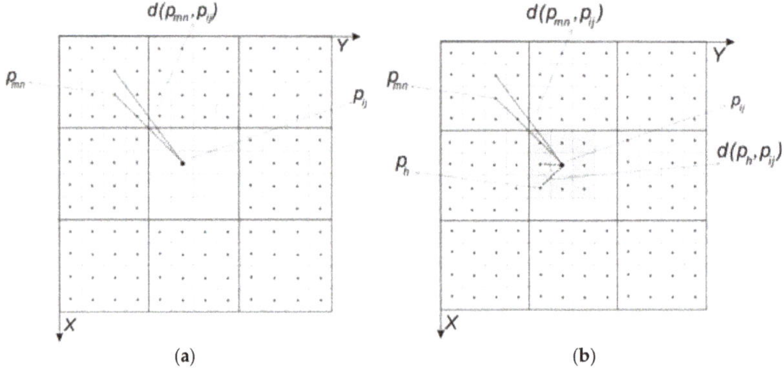

Figure 3. Illustration of the modified subpixel/pixel spatial attraction model (MSPSAM) and the mixed spatial attraction model (MSAM) (adapted from [37]). (**a**) MSPSAM; (**b**) MSAM.

2.3. Improved Spatial Attraction Model (ISAM)

Referring to PSA in Atkinson [9,26] and the modified pixel swapping algorithm (MPSA) in [29], ISAM computes the spatial attractions of the current subpixel at the center of a moving window by the surrounding subpixels within the window, which can be $2S + 1$ times the size of the subpixel and moves the window one subpixel per step. As an illustration of ISAM, Figure 4 shows that subpixel p_{ij} within the central pixel P_{cen} is attracted by the surrounding subpixels within a moving window that is double the size of the original pixel. In Figure 4, S is the scale factor, which divides an original pixel into S^2 subpixels, each corresponding to $1/S^2$ area of the original one.

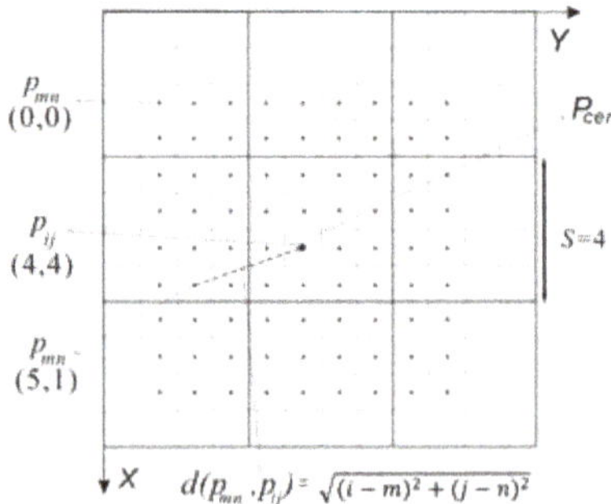

Figure 4. Illustration of the Improved Spatial Attraction Model (ISAM) (the size of the moving window is equal to $2S + 1$).

Therefore, defined in Equation (7), $J_{c,ij}$, the spatial attraction of subpixel p_{ij} which is assigned to class c (c can be any class in the study case), can be estimated as an inverse-distance weighted function of its surrounding subpixels within the moving window.

$$J_{c,ij} = \sum_m \sum_n \frac{x_{c,ij}}{d(p_{mn}, p_{ij})} \tag{7}$$

where $d(p_{mn}, p_{ij})$ is the distance between subpixel p_{ij} and the surrounding subpixel p_{mn} defined in Equation (8), and $x_{c,ij}$ is a choice variable defined in Equation (9).

$$d(p_{mn}, p_{ij}) = \sqrt{(i-m)^2 + (j-n)^2} \tag{8}$$

$$x_{c,ij} = \begin{cases} 1, & if \text{ subpixel } p_{ij} \text{ and } p_{mn} \text{ are assigned to the same class } c \\ 0, & \text{otherwise} \end{cases} \tag{9}$$

The mathematical model thus becomes Equation (10):

$$\text{Maximize } J = \sum_c \sum_i \sum_j \sum_m \sum_n \frac{x_{c,ij}}{d(p_{mn}, p_{ij})} \tag{10}$$

The model constraints of ISAM are shown as Equations (11) and (12):

$$\sum_c x_{c,ij} = 1 \tag{11}$$

$$\sum_i \sum_j x_{c,ij} = n_c \tag{12}$$

Equation (11) means that only one subpixel can be assigned a specific class, and Equation (12) means that the number of subpixels that have to be assigned class c is n_c, which has been determined from the fraction images.

Based on spatial dependence theory, maximum J will be retrieved when the top n_c subpixels within the central pixel are assigned to class c.

The ISAM proposed in this study is similar to the MPSA proposed by Shen et al., 2009 [29], but there are three differences between them, including: (1) the initialization of subpixel class allocation. The former uses the random allocation and the latter allocates the subpixel class based on spatial attractiveness; (2) the size of the moving window. The former's is $2S + 1$ times the size of the sub-pixel, and the latter's is unfixed; and (3) the calculation of the distance weighting parameter. The former takes the Euclidean distance as the weighting parameter of two subpixels and the latter uses an exponential model containing the Euclidean distance and a non-linear parameter. These differences make ISAM computationally more efficient.

As seen for other SPM methods, theoretically, ISAM also has a few limitations, including: (1) the classification accuracy of ISAM depends on the accuracy of the soft class fraction image, which is the result of spectral mixture analysis; and (2) ISAM prefers a subpixel mapping H-resolution-case image, of which the pixels are smaller than the objects of interest or landcover, to the L-resolution-case one, of which the pixels are much larger than the objects of interest or landcover [38,39].

2.4. The Algorithm of ISAM

The algorithm flowchart of ISAM is shown in Figure 5, and the detailed steps of the algorithm are given below:

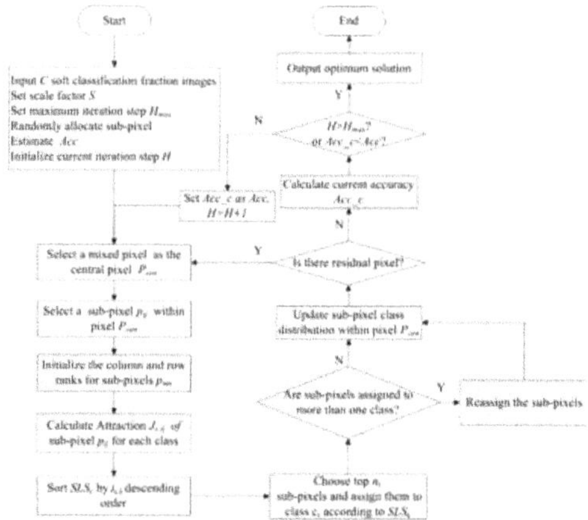

Figure 5. The algorithm flowchart of the improved spatial attraction model (ISAM): H_{max}—maximum steps of iteration; H—current step of iteration; Acc—the accuracies of SPM of previous iteration step; Acc_c—the accuracies of SPM of current iteration step; P_{cen}—the central pixel; p_{ij}—the subpixel which spatial attractions are currently calculated; C—the number of classes in the study case; $J_{c,ij}$—the spatial attractions of subpixel p_{ij} when it is assigned to class c, SLS_c—the spatial location sequence of class c of pixel P_{cen}.

Input a soft classification fraction image of C number of classes

---

Set scale factor S
Set maximum iteration step H_{max}
Randomly allocate subpixel to classes based on the pixel-level class fraction
Estimate Acc, the accuracies of SPM of previous iteration step
Initialize current iteration step H
FOR each iteration//H
  FOR *each pixel//Select a pixel as the central pixel P_{cen}*
    FOR *each subpixel p_{ij} within the central pixel*
      Initialize *the* column and row ranks for subpixels within a moving window around *subpixel p_{ij}*
      FOR each class
        FOR *each subpixel p_{mn} within the moving window*
          Calculate the *spatial attraction of subpixel p_{ij} exercised by p_{mn}*
        END FOR *each subpixel p_{mn} within the moving window*
          Summarize $J_{c,ij}$, the *spatial attractions of subpixel p_{ij} exercised by subpixels within the*
            moving window
      END FOR
    END FOR
    Sort SLS_c (spatial location sequence for class c) by $J_{c,ij}$ descending order
    Choose top n_c subpixels and assign them to class c, according to SLS_c
    Reassign the subpixels, which have been assigned to more than one class, to a specific class of
    which the spatial attractions reach the maximum. Make sure every subpixel is uniquely assigned to
    a specific class.
  END FOR
  Estimate Acc_c, the accuracies of SPM of current iteration step
  IF $Acc \geq Acc\_c$ or $H = H_{max}$
    break
  ELSE
    $Acc = Acc\_c$
  ENDIF
END FOR

---

3. Experiments and Results

To test and validate the advantages of the proposed ISAM algorithm, this study compared the SPM accuracies of ISAM with those of other SAMs by using Landsat OLI and MODIS imagery. ISAM, SPSAM, MSPSAM, and MSAM were implemented with ENVI IDL 8.3, and the following experiments were all accomplished in ENVI 5.1. A workstation computer with an Intel Quad 2.67 GHz processor and 4 GB RAM was used for this study. In all experiments, the moving window for ISAM is set to two original pixels plus one subpixel in size, so that the current subpixel is always at the center of the window.

3.1. Experiment with Landsat OLI Imagery

3.1.1. Data Sets

A scene of the Landsat-8 Operational Land Imager (OLI) image with its identifier LC81460322015267LGN00 was downloaded from the U.S. Geological Survey (USGS) official website [40] and the region of interest (ROI) of 552×424 pixels in size was subset from the scene. By applying a support vector machine (SVM, of which the training samples were selected through visually interpreting both the high spatial resolution Google earth and the Landsat-8 images) to the Landsat image of ROI, a hard land cover classification map, which is used as a reference map, was created for the ROI at 30-m resolution. Then, by using a bi-cubic resampling algorithm, the land cover map at the original 30-m resolution was aggregated to 60-, 120- and 240-m resolution to form soft land cover fraction maps which were 276×212, 138×106, and 69×53 pixels in size, respectively.

3.1.2. Experiment Results

The accuracy is measured by comparing the SPM results from ISAM, SPSAM, MSPSAM, and MSAM with the reference map. The Overall Accuracy (OA) and Kappa Coefficient (κ), the most commonly used indices for classification accuracy assessment, are applied in this study. The experimental results are displayed in Figures 6–8 and the accuracy measures are shown in Tables 1–3. From Figures 6–8, a visual assessment of the image quality reveals that: (1) the SPM of the four SAM algorithms can reveal more details than hard classification results at scale factors of $S = 2, 4$, and 8; (2) the SPM from ISAM can obtain more details than those from other SAMs (see the details within red rectangles in Figure 8c). From Tables 1–3, a quantitative comparison analysis proves that: (1) the OA values of ISAM and the other SAMs at different scale factors are all above 95%, while all κ values are greater than 0.92, which means that all SAMs are effective SPM techniques; (2) both the OA and κ values of ISAM are the highest among all SAMs; (3) both the OA and κ values of all SAMs decrease with an increase of the scale factor, since the bigger the scale factor is, the coarser the aggregated image can be, and the less the detail of an initial image can convey; (4) the OA and κ of SPSAM are lower than those of MSPSAM and MSAM when the scale factor, S, is 2 or 4, while OA and κ of SPSAM are higher than those of MSPSAM and MSAM when the scale factor, S, is 8. From both visual and quantitative assessments, it is concluded that ISAM is a more accurate SPM technique than the other SAMs. From Tables 1–3, it can be also found that OA and κ of the four SAMs decreases by about 1.816%~4.035% and 0.029~0.065, respectively, when the scale factor S increases from 2 to 8. The sensitivity of the scale factor to the accuracy of the four SAMs is not obvious in this experiment and S can be determined according to the goal of experiment.

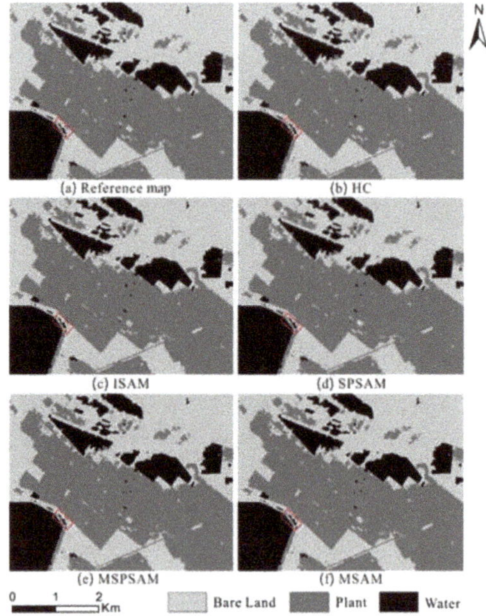

Figure 6. The comparison of SPM results among ISAM, SPSAM, MSPSAM, and MSAM (scale factor $S = 2$): (**a**) The classification result from Landsat data; (**b**) The hard classification result at scale factor S; (**c**–**f**) the results from ISAM, SPSAM, MSPSAM, and MSAM, respectively.

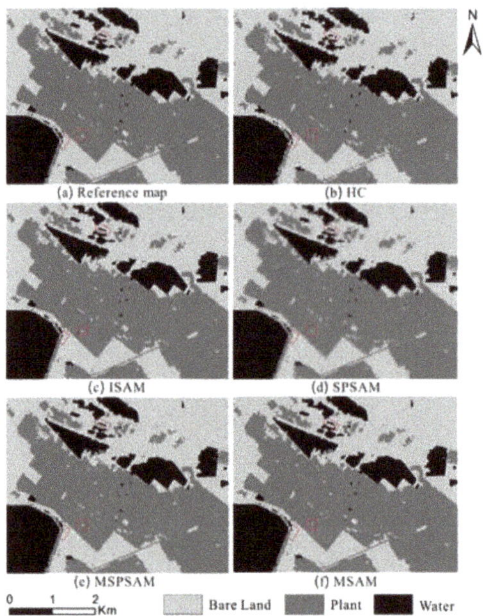

Figure 7. The comparison of SPM results among ISAM, SPSAM, MSPSAM, and MSAM (scale factor $S = 4$): (**a**) The classification result from Landsat data; (**b**) The hard classification result at scale factor S; (**c**–**f**) the results from ISAM, SPSAM, MSPSAM, and MSAM, respectively.

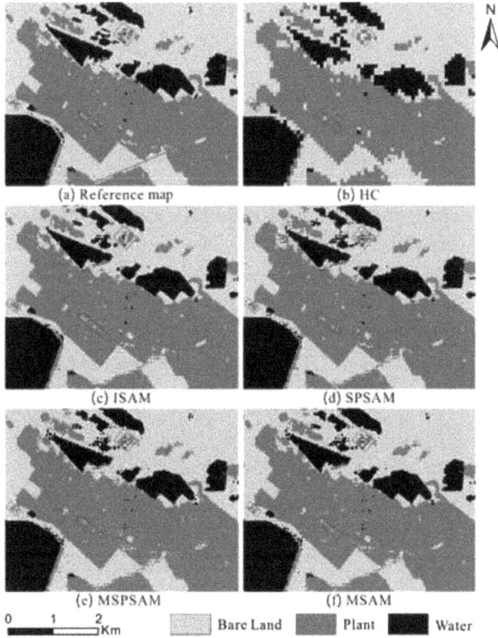

Figure 8. The comparison of SPM results among ISAM, SPSAM, MSPSAM, and MSAM (scale factor $S = 8$): (**a**) The classification result from Landsat data; (**b**) The hard classification result at scale factor S, (**c–f**) the results from ISAM, SPSAM, MSPSAM, and MSAM respectively.

Table 1. The comparison of SPM accuracies among ISAM, SPSAM, MSPSAM, and MSAM.

SAM Type	Accuracies (Scale Factor $S = 2$)	
	Overall Accuracy (OA, %)	Kappa Coefficient (κ)
ISAM	99.806	0.996
SPSAM	97.970	0.967
MSPSAM	99.629	0.994
MSAM	99.781	0.996

Table 2. The comparison of SPM accuracies among ISAM, SPSAM, MSPSAM, and MSAM.

SAM Type	Accuracies (Scale Factor $S = 4$)	
	Overall Accuracy (OA, %)	Kappa Coefficient (κ)
ISAM	98.776	0.980
SPSAM	95.852	0.933
MSPSAM	98.116	0.969
MSAM	98.734	0.979

Table 3. The comparison of SPM accuracies among ISAM, SPSAM, MSPSAM, and MSAM.

SAM Type	Accuracies (Scale Factor $S = 8$)	
	Overall Accuracy (OA, %)	Kappa Coefficient (κ)
ISAM	96.671	0.947
SPSAM	96.154	0.938
MSPSAM	95.594	0.929
MSAM	96.001	0.936

The comparison results of computational efficiency among ISAM, SPSAM, MSPSAM, and MSAM are shown in Table 4 when the scale factor S is set to 8 and the image size is 424 × 552 subpixels. Among the four SAMs, SPSAM needs the fewest number of iterations and the least time to achieve the optimal results, while ISAM needs three more iterations than SPAM, but one and five iterations fewer than MSPSAM and MSPSAM, respectively. Furthermore, ISAM reduces to almost 900 s per iteration or 2.2 h and 7.8 h less per entire computation than MSPSAM and MSPSAM. In other words, ISAM is more efficient than MSPSAM and MSPSAM, but less efficient than SPSAM. The reason for this is that SPSAM only considers the attraction from eight neighboring pixels at the original resolution to the subpixels of the central pixels, resulting in a significant reduction in the computational requirement, while the others all consider the attraction from the subpixels of the neighboring pixels. Although the computing power is not a significant limit factor nowadays for processing remote sensing images, timesaving is significant if applying the ISAM algorithm to large-scale subpixel hard classification, which may need to classify hundreds of remote sensing images, instead of MSPSAM and MSAM. Nevertheless, if the computational efficiency is the main concern, SPSAM is the better choice since it is 67 times faster than ISAM.

Table 4. The comparison of computational efficiency among ISAM, SPSAM, MSPSAM, and MSAM (scale factor S = 8).

Iterations	ISAM	SPSAM	MSPSAM	MSAM
Steps	4	1	5	9
Optimization time per step (*s*)	≈4000	240	≈4890	≈4890

3.2. Experiment with MODIS Imagery

3.2.1. Data Sets

The experiment in this section, taking the land cover classification results from the Landsat OLI image with the support vector machine (SVM) as the reference map, focuses on extracting the subpixel land cover from MODIS imagery.

The MODIS image, which covered the area of the Landsat OLI image and was acquired on 16 May 2014, was downloaded from the U.S. NASA official website [41]. The MODIS image was re-projected from Sinusoidal to Universal Transverse Mercator (UTM) projection with the MODIS Re-projection Tool (MRT), so that it could be co-registered with the Landsat image. Smoothing filter-based intensity modulation (SFIM) [42] was utilized to sharpen the MOD09GA bands 3–7 data to a 250-m pixel resolution of the MOD09GQ bands 1–2. After using the pixel purity index (PPI) method to select the end member of the land cover classes, the linear spectral mixing model (LSMM) was applied to extract the soft classification fraction from MODIS bands 1-2 and sharpened bands 3–7 data.

The Landsat OLI image (data identifier: LC81460322014136LGN00), which was acquired on the same day as the MODIS image, was downloaded from the U.S. Geological Survey (USGS) official website [40]. The Landsat image then was strip-repaired, atmospherically corrected, ROI clipped, and resampled into a pixel resolution of 31.25 m, to meet the requirement of SPM from the 250-m resolution MODIS image with an integral number of scale factors. The preprocessed image was used to extract the land cover classification map, which was used as the ground truth in this MODIS experiment, by utilizing the support vector machine (SVM).

3.2.2. Experiment Results

Setting scale factor S to 8, the subpixel resolution of the MODIS image will be 31.25 m, the same as the reference map. The soft classification fraction image is used as the input to the SPM algorithms of ISAM, SPSAM, MSPSAM, and MSAM. Similar to the experiment with the Landsat OLI image, the accuracy is measured by comparing the SPM results of ISAM and the other SAMs with the reference map. The SPMs from different SAM algorithms are displayed in Figure 9 and the accuracy measures are shown in Table 5.

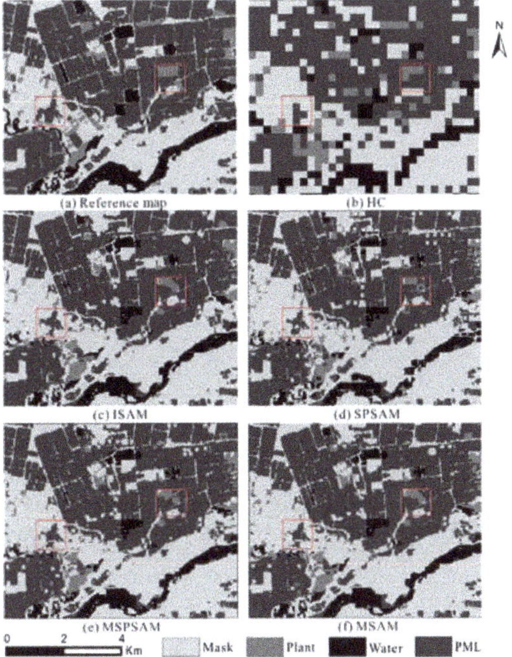

Figure 9. The comparison of subpixel mapping results among ISAM, SPSAM, MSPSAM, and MSAM (Scale factor $S = 8$; Mask represents the class of nonagricultural land; PML represents the class of plastic mulched landcover which is a type of farmland covered by plastic mulch film): (**a**) The classification results from Landsat data; (**b**) The hard classification results at scale factor S; (**c–f**) the results from ISAM, SPSAM, MSPSAM, and MSAM, respectively.

Table 5. The comparison of SPM accuracies among ISAM, SPSAM, MSPSAM, and MSAM (Scale factor $S = 8$).

Accuracies	ISAM	SPSAM	MSPSAM	MSAM
Overall accuracy (*OA*, %)	82.44	70.22	82.13	82.25
Kappa coefficient (κ)	0.66	0.46	0.66	0.66

By making a visual assessment of SPM maps in Figure 9, it can be found that the SPM map from ISAM contains more details than those from other SAMs. For instance, the details within the red rectangular areas in the SPM Map from ISAM match the same areas in the reference map much better than those from other SAMs. Table 5 shows that the *OA* of the SPM results from ISAM is 82.44%, which is higher than those of other SAMs; and κ *is* 0.66, which is higher than that of SPSAM and is equal to those of MSPSAM and MSAM. From both a visual assessment and quantitative analysis, it can be concluded that ISAM is more effective than other SAMs in SPM.

The comparison results of computational efficiency among ISAM, SPSAM, MSPSAM, and MSAM are shown in Table 6. Among the four SAMs, SPSAM is the most efficient SPM technique, while ISAM is the second most efficient one.

Comparing ISAM with SPAM, OA and κ increase by 12.22% and 0.2, respectively, in the experiment with MOIDS (though the accuracies of ISAM increase slightly, compared with SPSAM, and

MSPSAM and MSAM in the experiment with Landsat). Therefore, ISAM can improve SPM accuracies more than SPSAM and is a more efficient SPM technique than MSPSAM and MSAM.

Table 6. The comparison of computational efficiency among ISAM, SPSAM, MSPSAM, and MSAM.

SAM Type	Scale Factor $S = 2$		Scale Factor $S = 4$		Scale Factor $S = 8$	
	Optimization Time per Step (s)	Steps	Optimization Time per Step (s)	Steps	Optimization Time per Step (s)	Steps
ISAM	1.18	3	5.20	4	35.30	5
SPSAM	0.90	1	1.10	1	2.6	1
MSPSAM	1.20	3	5.60	4	40.25	6
MSAM	1.25	3	6.80	7	47.10	11

4. Conclusions

In order to overcome the defects in the existing SAM techniques, this study has proposed an improved SAM (ISAM) for SPM, through extending the existing SAM techniques. Instead of computing the spatial attraction by the surrounding pixels in SPSAM, or by the subpixels within the surrounding pixels and the touching subpixels within the central pixel in MSAM, ISAM estimates the attraction of the current subpixel at the center of a moving window by using all of the subpixels within the window and moves the window one subpixel at a time. The design of the algorithm is more straightforward and logically consistent than existing SAM algorithms, resulting in the simplification of the algorithm implementation and efficiency in the algorithm execution. Experimental results from both Landsat and MODIS imagery show that ISAM improves the SMP accuracy over the existing SAMs and is computationally more efficient than SPSAM and MSAM. Overall, ISAM is an effective and efficient technique for SPM.

Acknowledgments: This research is supported in part by a grant from China's National Science and Technology Support Program (grant # 41471277). The author would like to thank the four anonymous reviewers for the comments and suggestions that significantly helped to improve the quality of the paper.

Author Contributions: All the authors made significant contributions to the study. Yanlin Huang and Deiwei Hang conceived and designed the experiments, as well as performed the experiments; Lizhen Lu analyzed the experimental results and wrote the paper; Liping Di provided advice for the paper preparation and revised the paper.

Conflicts of Interest: The authors declare no conflict of interest.

References

1. Lu, L.Z.; Di, L.P.; Ye, Y.M. A Decision-tree classifier for extracting transparent plastic-mulched landcover from Landsat-5 TM images. *IEEE J. Sel. Top. Appl. Earth Obs. Remote Sens.* **2014**, *7*, 4548–4558. [CrossRef]
2. Lu, L.Z.; Hang, D.W.; Di, L.P. Threshold model for detecting transparent plastic mulched landcover using MODIS time series data: A case study in southern Xinjiang, China. *J. Appl. Remote Sens.* **2015**, *9*. [CrossRef]
3. Wang, Q.; Lin, J.; Yuan, Y. Salient band selection for hyperspectral image classification via manifold ranking. *IEEE Trans. Neural Netw. Learn. Syst.* **2016**, *27*, 1–11. [CrossRef] [PubMed]
4. Yuan, Y.; Lin, J.; Wang, Q. Dual-clustering-based hyperspectral band selection by contextual analysis. *IEEE Trans. Geosci. Remote Sens.* **2016**, *54*, 1431–1445. [CrossRef]
5. Smith, M.O.; Ustin, S.L.; Adams, J.B.; Gillespie, A.R. Vegetation in deserts: I. A regional measure of abundance from multi-spectral images. *Remote Sens. Environ.* **1990**, *31*, 1–26. [CrossRef]
6. Verhoeye, J.; Wulf, R.D. Land cover mapping at sub-pixel scales using linear optimization techniques. *Remote Sens. Environ.* **2002**, *79*, 96–104. [CrossRef]
7. Ling, F.; Wu, S.J.; Xiao, F.; Wu, K. Sub-pixel mapping of remotely sensed imagery: A review. *J. Image Graph.* **2011**, *16*, 1335–1345.
8. Plaza, A.; Martinerz, P.; Perez, R.; Plaza, J. A quantitative and comparative analysis of endmember extraction algortihms from hyperspectral data. *IEEE Trans. Geosci. Remote Sens.* **2004**, *42*, 650–663. [CrossRef]

9.   Atkinson, P.M. Sub-pixel target mapping from soft-classified remotely sensed imagery. *Photogramm. Eng. Remote Sens.* **2005**, *71*, 839–846. [CrossRef]

10.   Shi, C.; Wang, L. Incorporating spatial information in spectral unmixing: A review. *Remote Sens. Environ.* **2014**, *149*, 70–87. [CrossRef]

11.   Bioucas-Dias, J.M.; Plaza, A.; Dobigeon, N.; Pario, P.; Du, Q.; Gader, P. Hyperspectral unmixing overview: Geometrical, statistical, and sparse regression-based approaches. *IEEE J. Sel. Top. Appl. Earth Obs. Remote Sens.* **2012**, *5*, 354–379. [CrossRef]

12.   Keshava, N.; Mustard, J.F. Spectral unmixing. *IEEE Signal Process. Mag.* **2002**, *19*, 44–57. [CrossRef]

13.   Atkinson, P.M. Super-resolution land cover classification using the two-point histogram. In *GeoENV VI—Geostatistics for Environmental Applications*; Springer: Berlin/Heidelberg, Germany, 2004; pp. 15–28.

14.   Feng, R.Y.; Zhong, Y.F.; Wu, Y.Y.; He, D.; Xu, X.; Zhang, L.P. Nonlocal total variation subpixel mapping for hyperspectral remote sensing imagery. *Remote Sens.* **2016**, *8*, 250. [CrossRef]

15.   Ge, Y.; Jiang, Y.; Chen, Y.H.; Stein, A.; Jiang, D.; Jia, Y.X. Designing an experiment to investigate subpixel mapping as an alternative method to obtain land use/land cover maps. *Remote Sens.* **2016**, *8*, 360. [CrossRef]

16.   He, D.; Zhong, Y.F.; Feng, R.Y.; Zhang, L.P. Spatial-temporal sub-pixel mapping based on swarm intelligence theory. *Remote Sens.* **2016**, *8*, 894. [CrossRef]

17.   Johnson, B.; Tateishi, R.; Kobayashi, T. Remote sensing of fractional green vegetation cover using spatially-interpolated endmembers. *Remote Sens.* **2012**, *4*, 2619–2634. [CrossRef]

18.   Ling, F.; Foody, G.M.; Li, X.D.; Zhang, Y.H.; Du, Y. Assessing a temporal change strategy for sub-pixel land cover change mapping from multi-scale remote sensing imagery. *Remote Sens.* **2016**, *8*, 642. [CrossRef]

19.   Okujeni, A.; van der Linden, S.; Jakimow, B.; Rabe, A.; Verrelst, J.; Hostert, P. A comparison of advanced regression algorithms for quantifying urban land cover. *Remote Sens.* **2014**, *6*, 6324–6346. [CrossRef]

20.   Schneider, W. Land use mapping with subpixel accuracy from Landsat TM image data. In Proceedings of the 25th International Symposium on Remote Sensing and Global Environmental Changes, Graz, Austria, 4–8 April 1993; pp. 155–161.

21.   Atkinson, P.M. Mapping subpixel boundaries from remotely sensed images. In *Innovations in GIS 4*; Taylor and Francis: London, UK, 1997; pp. 166–180.

22.   Tatem, A.J.; Lewis, H.G.; Atkinson, P.M.; Nixon, M.S. Super-resolution target identification from remotely sensed images using a Hopfield neural network. *IEEE Trans. Geosci. Remote Sens.* **2001**, *39*, 781–796. [CrossRef]

23.   Tatem, A.J.; Lewis, H.G.; Atkinson, P.M.; Nixon, M.S. Super-resolution land cover pattern prediction using a Hopfield neural network. *Remote Sens. Environ.* **2002**, *79*, 1–14. [CrossRef]

24.   Tatem, A.J.; Lewis, H.G.; Atkinson, P.M.; Nixon, M.S. Increasing the spatial resolution of agricultural land cover maps using a Hopfield neural network. *Int. J. Remote Sens.* **2003**, *24*, 4241–4247. [CrossRef]

25.   Wang, Q.M.; Atkinson, P.M.; Shi, W.Z. Fast subpixel mapping algorithms for subpixel resolution change detection. *IEEE Trans. Geosci. Remote Sens.* **2015**, *53*, 1692–1706. [CrossRef]

26.   Atkinson, P.M. Super-resolution target mapping from soft-classified remotely sensed imagery. In Proceedings of the 5th International Conference on GeoComputation, London, UK, 23–25 August 2000.

27.   Thornton, M.W.; Atkinson, P.M.; Holland, D.A. Sub-pixel mapping of rural land cover objects from fine spatial resolution satellite sensor imagery using super resolution pixel swapping. *Int. J. Remote Sens.* **2006**, *27*, 473–491. [CrossRef]

28.   Makido, Y.; Shortridge, A.; Messina, J.P. Assessing alternatives for modeling the spatial distribution of multiple land-cover classes at sub-pixel scales. *Photogramm. Eng. Remote Sens.* **2007**, *73*, 935–943. [CrossRef]

29.   Shen, Z.Q.; Qi, J.G.; Wang, K. Modification of pixel-swapping algorithm with initialization from a sub-pixel/pixel spatial model. *Photogramm. Eng. Remote Sens.* **2009**, *75*, 557–567. [CrossRef]

30.   Mertens, K.C.; Baets, B.D.; Verbeke, L.P.C.; Wulf, R.R.D. A sub-pixel mapping algorithm based on sub-pixel/pixel spatial attraction model. *Int. J. Remote Sens.* **2006**, *27*, 3293–3310. [CrossRef]

31.   Kasetkasem, T.; Arora, M.K.; Varshney, P.K. Super-resolution land-cover mapping using a Markov random field based approach. *Remote Sens. Environ.* **2005**, *96*, 302–314. [CrossRef]

32.   Wang, L.G.; Wang, Q.M. Subpixel mapping using Markov random field with multiple spectral constraints from subpixel shifted remote sensing images. *IEEE Trans. Geosci. Remote Sens.* **2013**, *10*, 598–602. [CrossRef]

33.   Mertens, K.C.; Verbeke, L.P.C.; Ducheyne, E.I.; Wulf, R.R.D. Using genetic algorithms in sub-pixel mapping. *Int. J. Remote Sens.* **2003**, *24*, 4241–4247. [CrossRef]

34. Wang, Q.M.; Wang, L.G.; Liu, D.F. Particle swarm optimization-based sub-pixel mapping for remote-sensing imagery. *Int. J. Remote Sens.* **2012**, *33*, 6480–6496. [CrossRef]

35. Boucher, A.; Kyriakidis, P.C.; Cronkite-Ratcliff, C. Geostatistical solutions for super-resolution land cover mapping. *IEEE Trans. Geosci. Remote Sens.* **2008**, *46*, 272–283. [CrossRef]

36. Wang, Q.M.; Shi, W.Z.; Wang, L.G. Indicator cokriging-based subpixel land cover mapping with shifted images. *IEEE Trans. Geosci. Remote Sens.* **2014**, *7*, 327–339.

37. Wang, Q.M.; Wang, L.G.; Liu, D.F. Integration of spatial attractions between and within pixels for sub-pixel mapping. *J. Syst. Eng. Electron.* **2012**, *23*, 293–303. [CrossRef]

38. Woodcock, C.E.; Strahler, A.H. The factor of scale in remote sensing. *Remote Sens. Environ.* **1987**, *21*, 311–332. [CrossRef]

39. Atkinson, P.M. Issues of uncertainty in super-resolution mapping and their implications for the design of an inter-comparison study. *Int. J. Remote Sens.* **2009**, *30*, 5293–5308. [CrossRef]

40. USGS Official Website. Available online: http://earthexplorer.usgs.gov/ (accessed on 8 August 2015).

41. NASA Official Website. Available online: http://reverb.echo.nasa.gov/reverb/ (accessed on 10 August 2015).

42. Liu, J.G. Smoothing filter-based intensity modulation: A spectral preserve image fusion technique for improving spatial details. *Int. J. Remote Sens.* **2000**, *21*, 3461–3472. [CrossRef]

Article

Supervised and Semi-Supervised Multi-View Canonical Correlation Analysis Ensemble for Heterogeneous Domain Adaptation in Remote Sensing Image Classification

Alim Samat [1,2], Claudio Persello [3], Paolo Gamba [4], Sicong Liu [5], Jilili Abuduwaili [1,2,*] and Erzhu Li [6]

1   State Key Laboratory of Desert and Oasis Ecology, Xinjiang Institute of Ecology and Geography, Chinese Academy of Sciences, Urumqi 830011, China; alim.smt@gmail.com
2   CAS Research Center for Ecology and Environment of Central Asia, Chinese Academy of Sciences, Urumqi 830011, China
3   Department of Earth Observation Science, Faculty of Geo-Information Science and Earth Observation (ITC), University of Twente, 7500 AE Enschede, The Netherlands; c.persello@utwente.nl
4   Department of Electrical, Computer and Biomedical Engineering, University of Pavia, 27100 Pavia, Italy; paolo.gamba@unipv.it
5   College of Surveying and Geoinformatics, Tongji University, Shanghai 200092, China; sicongliu.rs@gmail.com
6   Department of Geographical Information Science, Nanjing University, Nanjing 210000, China; lierzhu2008@126.com
*   Correspondence: jilil@ms.xjb.ac.cn

Academic Editors: Qi Wang, Nicolas H. Younan, Carlos López-Martínez, Xiaofeng Li and Prasad S. Thenkabail
Received: 7 January 2017; Accepted: 29 March 2017; Published: 1 April 2017

Abstract: In this paper, we present the supervised multi-view canonical correlation analysis ensemble (SMVCCAE) and its semi-supervised version (SSMVCCAE), which are novel techniques designed to address heterogeneous domain adaptation problems, i.e., situations in which the data to be processed and recognized are collected from different heterogeneous domains. Specifically, the multi-view canonical correlation analysis scheme is utilized to extract multiple correlation subspaces that are useful for joint representations for data association across domains. This scheme makes homogeneous domain adaption algorithms suitable for heterogeneous domain adaptation problems. Additionally, inspired by fusion methods such as Ensemble Learning (EL), this work proposes a weighted voting scheme based on canonical correlation coefficients to combine classification results in multiple correlation subspaces. Finally, the semi-supervised MVCCAE extends the original procedure by incorporating multiple speed-up spectral regression kernel discriminant analysis (SRKDA). To validate the performances of the proposed supervised procedure, a single-view canonical analysis (SVCCA) with the same base classifier (Random Forests) is used. Similarly, to evaluate the performance of the semi-supervised approach, a comparison is made with other techniques such as Logistic label propagation (LLP) and the Laplacian support vector machine (LapSVM). All of the approaches are tested on two real hyperspectral images, which are considered the target domain, with a classifier trained from synthetic low-dimensional multispectral images, which are considered the original source domain. The experimental results confirm that multi-view canonical correlation can overcome the limitations of SVCCA. Both of the proposed procedures outperform the ones used in the comparison with respect to not only the classification accuracy but also the computational efficiency. Moreover, this research shows that canonical correlation weighted voting (CCWV) is a valid option with respect to other ensemble schemes and that because of their ability to balance diversity and accuracy, canonical views extracted using partially joint random view generation are more effective than those obtained by exploiting disjoint random view generation.

Keywords: heterogeneous domain adaptation; transfer learning; multi-view canonical correlation analysis ensemble; semi-supervised learning; canonical correlation weighted voting; ensemble learning; image classification

---

1. Introduction

Supervised learning algorithms predominate over all other land cover mapping/monitoring techniques that use remote sensing (RS) data. However, the performance of supervised learning algorithms varies as a function of labeled training data properties, such as the sample size and the statistically unbiased and discriminative capabilities of the features extracted from the data [1]. As monitoring requires multi-temporal images, radiometric differences, atmospheric and illumination conditions, seasonal variations, and variable acquisition geometries can affect supervised techniques, potentially causing a distribution shift in the training data [2,3]. Regardless of the cause, any distribution change or domain shift that occurs after learning a classifier can degrade performance.

In the pattern recognition (PR) and RS image classification communities, this challenge is commonly referred to as covariate shift [4] or sample selection bias [5]. Many solutions have been proposed to resolve this problem, including image-to-image normalization [6], absolute and relative image normalization [7,8], histogram matching [9], and a multivariate extension of the univariate matching [10]. Recently, domain adaptation (DA) techniques, which attempt to mitigate performance the degradation caused by a distribution shift, has attracted increasing attention and is widely considered to provide an efficient solution [11–16].

According to the technical literature in PR and machine learning (ML), DA is a special case of transductive transfer learning (TTL). Its goal is to learn a function that predicts the label of a novel test sample in the target domain [12,15]. Depending on the availability of the source and the target domain data, the DA problem can result into supervised domain adaptation (SDA), semi-supervised domain adaptation (SSDA), unsupervised domain adaptation (UDA), multisource domain adaptation (MSDA) and heterogeneous domain adaption (HDA) [14–19].

Moreover, according to the "knowledge" transferred across domains or tasks, classical approaches to DA can be grouped into parameter adapting, instance transferring, feature representation, and relational knowledge transfer techniques.

Parameter adapting approaches aim to transfer and adapt a classification model and/or its parameters to the target domain; the model and/or parameters are learned from the source domain (SD) [20]. The seminal work presented by Khosla et al. [5] and Woodcock et al. [7], which features parameter adjustment for a maximum-likelihood classifier in a multiple cascade classifier system by retraining, can be categorized into this group.

In instance transferring, the samples from the SD are reweighted [21] or resampled [22] for their use in the TD. In the RS community, active learning (AL) has also been applied to address DA problems. For example, AL for DA in the supervised classification RS images is proposed by Persello and Bruzzone [23] via iteratively labeling and adding to the training set the minimum number of the most informative samples from the target domain, while removing the source-domain samples that do not fit with the distributions of the classes in the TD.

For the third group, feature representation-based adaptation searches for a set of shared and invariant features using feature extraction (FE), feature selection (FS) or manifold alignment to reduce the marginal, conditional and joint distributions between the domains [16,24–26]. Matasci et al. [14] investigated the semi-supervised transfer component analysis (SSTCA) [27] for both hyperspectral and multispectral high resolution image classification, whereas Samat et al. [16] analyzed a geodesic Gaussian flow kernel based support vector machine (GFKSVM) in the context of hyperspectral image classification, which adopts several unsupervised linear and nonlinear subspace feature transfer techniques.

Finally, relational knowledge transfer techniques address the problem of how to leverage the knowledge acquired in SD to improve accuracy and learning speed in a related TD [28].

Among these four groups, it is easy to recognize the importance of RS image classification of adaptation strategies based on feature representation. However, most previous studies have assumed that data from different domains are represented by the same types of features with the same dimensions. Thus, these techniques cannot handle the problem of data from source and target domains represented by heterogeneous features with different dimensions [18,29]. One example of this scenario is land cover updating using current RS data; each time, there are different features with finer spatial resolution and more spectral bands (e.g., Landsat 8 OLI with nine spectral bands at 15–30 m spatial resolution, and Airborne Visible/Infrared Imaging Spectrometer (AVIRIS) with 224 spectral bands at 20 m spatial resolution), when the training data are only available at coarser spatial and spectral resolutions (e.g., MSS with four spectral bands and 60 m spatial resolution).

One of the simplest feature-based DA approaches is the feature augmentation proposed in [17], whose extended versions, called heterogeneous feature augmentation (HFA) and semi-supervised HFA (SHFA), were recently proposed in [18]. Versions that consider the intermediate domains as being manifold-based were proposed in [30,31]. However, none of these approaches have been considered in RS image classification.

Finding a joint feature representation between the source and target domains requires FS [12,19] or FE [16] to select the most effective feature set. To accomplish this aim, canonical correlation analysis (CCA), which aims to maximize the correlation between two variable sets (in this case, the different domains) could be a very effective technique. Indeed, CCA and kernel CCA (KCCA) have already been applied with promising results in object recognition and text categorization [29], action recognition and image-to-text classification [32]. However, existing joint optimization frameworks such as [32] are limited to scenarios in which the labeled data from both domains are available. This is not the case in many practical situations. To solve this problem, CTSVM was proposed in [29], incorporating the DA ability into the classifier design for a cross-domain recognition scenario of labeled data that is available only in the SD. However, the CTSVM might fail to balance the possible mismatches between the heterogeneous domains.

One solution might be to multi-view learning (MVL), a procedure that implies the splitting of high-dimensional data into multiple "views" [33,34]. If multiple views are available, then multiple classification results must be reconciled, and this step is efficiently performed using Ensemble Learning (EL) [35,36]. Accordingly, this work introduces an EL technique based on supervised multi-view CCA, which is called supervised multi-view canonical correlation analysis ensemble (SMVCCAE), and we prove its effectiveness for DA (and specifically heterogeneous DA) problems.

Additionally, in real applications, it is typical to experience situations in which there are very limited or even no labeled samples available. In this case, a semi-supervised learning (SSL) technique (e.g., [37]), which uses of unlabeled data to improve performance using a small amount of labeled data from the same domain, might be an appropriate solution. As a matter of fact, many SSDAs have been proposed. However, most existing studies, such as asymmetric kernel transforms (AKT) [38], domain-dependent regularization (DDR) [32], TCA, SSTCA [14,27], and co-regularization based SSDA [39], were designed for homogeneous DA. Very recently, Li et al. [18] proposed a semi-supervised heterogeneous DA by convex optimization of standard multiple kernel learning (MKL) with augmented features. Unfortunately, this optimization is quite challenging in real-world applications. This work instead proposes a semi-supervised version of the above-mentioned multi-view canonical correlation analysis ensemble (called SSMVCCAE), incorporating multiple speed-up spectral regression kernel discriminant analysis (SRKDA) [40] into the original supervised algorithm.

2. Related Work

2.1. Notation for HDA

According to the technical literature, feature-based approaches to HDA can be grouped into the following three clusters, depending on the features used to connect the target and the SD:

(1) If data from the source and target domains share the same features [41–43], then latent semantic analysis (LSA) [44], probabilistic latent semantic analysis (pLSA) [45], and risk minimization techniques [46] may be used.

(2) If additional features are needed, "feature augmentation" approaches have been proposed, including the method in [37], HFA and SHFA [18], manifold alignment [31], sampling geodesic flow (SGF) [47], and geodesic flow kernel (GFK) [16,30]. All of these approaches introduce a common subspace for the source and target data so that heterogeneous features from both domains.

(3) If features are adapted across domains through learning transformations, feature transformation-based approaches are considered. This group of approaches includes the HSMap [48], the sparse heterogeneous feature representation (SHFR) [49], and the correlation transfer SVM (CTSVM) [29]. The algorithms that we propose fit into this group.

Although all of the approaches reviewed above have achieved promising results, they also have some limitations of all the approaches reviewed above. For example, the co-occurrence features assumption used in [41–43] may not hold in applications such as object recognition, which uses only visual features [32]. For the feature augmentation based approaches discussed in [18,30,31], the domain-specific copy process always requires large storage space, and the kernel version requires even more space and computational complexity because of the parameter tuning. Finally, for the feature transformation based approaches proposed in [29,32,48], they do not optimize the objective function of a discriminative classifier directly, and the computational complexity is highly dependent on the total number of samples or features used for adaptation [12,19].

In this work, we assume that there is only one SD (S_D) and one TD (T_D). We also define $\mathbf{X}_S = \left[x_1^S, ..., x_{n_S}^S\right]^\dagger \in \Re^{d_S \times n_S}$ and $\mathbf{X}_T = \left[x_1^T, ..., x_{n_T}^T\right]^\dagger \in \Re^{d_T \times n_T}$ as the feature spaces in the two domains, with the corresponding marginal distributions $p(\mathbf{X}_S)$ and $p(\mathbf{X}_T)$ for S_D and T_D, respectively. The parameters d_S and d_T represent the size of $x_i^S, i = 1, ..., n_S$ and $x_j^T, j = 1, ..., n_T$, n_S and n_T are the sample sizes for $\mathbf{X}_S$ and $\mathbf{X}_T$, and we have $S_D = \{\mathbf{X}_S, P(\mathbf{X}_S)\}$, $T_D = \{\mathbf{X}_T, P(\mathbf{X}_T)\}$. The labeled training samples from the SD are denoted by $\left\{\left(x_j^S, y_j^S\right)\Big|_{j=1}^{n_S}\right\}$, $y_j^S \in \Omega = \{\omega_l\}_{l=1}^{c}$, and they refer to c classes. Furthermore, let us consider as "task" Υ the task to assign to each element of a set a label selected in a label space by means of a predictive function f, so that $v = \{y, f\}$.

In general, if the feature sets belong to different domains, then either $\mathbf{X}_S \neq \mathbf{X}_T$ or $p(\mathbf{X}_S) \neq p(\mathbf{X}_T)$, or both. Similarly, the condition $v_S \neq v_T$ implies that either $\Upsilon_S \neq \Upsilon_T$ ($\Upsilon_S = [y_1^S, ..., y_{n_S}^S]$, $\Upsilon_T = [y_1^T, ..., y_{n_T}^T]$) or $p(\Upsilon_S|\mathbf{X}_S) \neq p(\Upsilon_T|\mathbf{X}_T)$, or both. In this scenario, a "domain adaptation algorithm" is an algorithm that aims to improve the learning of the predictive function f_T in the TD T_D using the knowledge available in the SD S_D and in the learning task v_S, when either $S_D \neq T_D$ or $v_S \neq v_T$. Moreover, in heterogeneous problems, the additional condition $d_S \neq d_T$ holds.

2.2. Canonical Correlation Analysis

Let us now assume that $n_S = n_T$ for the feature sets (called "views" here) in the source and target domains. The CCA is the procedure for obtaining the transformation matrices ω_S and ω_T which maximize the correlation coefficient between the two sets [50]:

$$\max_{\omega_S, \omega_T} \rho = \frac{\omega_S^\dagger \Sigma_{ST} \omega_T}{\sqrt{\omega_S^\dagger \Sigma_{SS} \omega_S}\sqrt{\omega_T^\dagger \Sigma_{TT} \omega_T}} \tag{1}$$

where $\Sigma_{ST} = \mathbf{X}_S \mathbf{X}_T^{\dagger}$, $\Sigma_{SS} = \mathbf{X}_S \mathbf{X}_S^{\dagger}$, $\Sigma_{TT} = \mathbf{X}_T \mathbf{X}_T^{\dagger}$, $\rho \in [0,1]$, and "$\dagger$" means the matrix transpose. In practice, $\boldsymbol{\omega}_S$ can be obtained by a generalized eigenvalue decomposition problem:

$$\Sigma_{ST}(\Sigma_{TT})^{-1}\Sigma_{ST}^{\dagger}\boldsymbol{\omega}_S = \eta(\Sigma_{SS})\boldsymbol{\omega}_S \tag{2}$$

where η is a constraint factor. Once $\boldsymbol{\omega}_S$ is obtained, $\boldsymbol{\omega}_T$ can be obtained by $\Sigma_{TT}^{-1}\Sigma_{ST}\boldsymbol{\omega}_S/\eta$. By adding the regularization terms $\lambda_S \mathbf{I}$ and into Σ_{SS} and Σ_{TT} to avoid overfitting and singularity problems, Equation (2) becomes:

$$\Sigma_{ST}(\Sigma_{TT} + \lambda_T \mathbf{I})^{-1}\Sigma_{ST}^{\dagger}\boldsymbol{\omega}_S = \eta(\Sigma_{SS} + \lambda_S \mathbf{I})\boldsymbol{\omega}_S \tag{3}$$

As a result, the source and target view data can be transformed into correlation subspaces by:

$$\mathbf{X}_S^C = \mathbf{X}_S \cdot \boldsymbol{\omega}_S, \boldsymbol{\omega}_S \in \Re^{d_S \times d} \tag{4}$$

$$\mathbf{X}_T^C = \mathbf{X}_T \cdot \boldsymbol{\omega}_T, \boldsymbol{\omega}_T \in \Re^{d_T \times d} \tag{5}$$

Note that one can derive more than one pair of transformation matrices $\{\omega_i^S\}_{i=1}^d$ and $\{\omega_i^T\}_{i=1}^d$, where $d = \min\{d_S, d_T\}$ is the dimension of the resulting CCA subspace. Once the correlation subspaces $\mathbf{X}_S^C$ and $\mathbf{X}_T^C$ spanned by $\boldsymbol{\omega}_S$ and $\boldsymbol{\omega}_T$ are derived, test data in the target view can be directly labeled by any model M_S^C that is trained using the source features $\mathbf{X}_S^C$.

2.3. Fusion Methods

If multiple "views" are available, then for each view, a label can be associated with each pixel used, for instance, CCA. If multiple labels are present, then they must be fused to obtain a single value using a so-called decision-based fusion procedure. Decision-based fusion aims to provide the final classification label for a pixel by combining the labels obtained, in this case, by multiple view analysis. This usually is obtained using two classes of procedures: weighted voting methods and meta-learning methods [51].

For weighted voting, the labels are combined using the weights assigned to each result. Many variants have been proposed in past decades. For the sake of comparison and because we must consider these options to evaluate the performance of the canonical correlation weighted voting (CCWV) scheme proposed in this paper, here, we consider only the following state-of-the-art techniques:

- Accuracy weighted voting (AWV), in which the weight of each member is set proportionally to its accuracy performance on a validation set [51]:

$$w_i = \frac{a_i}{\sum_{j=1}^{T} a_j} \tag{6}$$

where a_i is a performance evaluation of the i-th classifier on a validation set.
- Best–worst weighted voting (BWWV), in which the best and the worst classifiers are given a weight of 1 or 0, respectively [51], and for the ones the weights are compute according to:

$$\alpha_i = 1 - \frac{e_i - \min_i(e_i)}{\max_i(e_i) - \min_i(e_i)} \tag{7}$$

where e_i is the error of the i-th classifier on a validation set.
- Quadratic best–worst weighted voting (QBWWV), that computes the intermediate weights between 0 and 1 via squaring the above-mentioned BWWV:

$$\alpha_i = \left(\frac{\max_i(e_i) - e_i}{\max_i(e_i) - \min_i(e_i)} \right)^2 \tag{8}$$

3. The (Semi) Supervised Canonical Correlation Analysis Ensemble

3.1. Supervised Procedure

The idea of this procedure is to adopt MVL to decompose the target domain data into multiple disjoint or partial joint feature subsets (views), where each view is assumed to bring complementary information [52]. Next, these multiple views are used for DA, providing multiple matches between the source and the target domains. Eventually, the labeling task in the SD is transferred into the target domain through CCA, and the results of this "multi-view" CCA are combined to achieve a more efficient heterogeneous DA.

Specifically, without loss of generality, let us assume a heterogeneous DA from a low-dimensional $\mathbf{X}_S$ to a high-dimensional $\mathbf{X}_T$, with $d_S < d_T$, which requires that $\mathbf{X}_T$ is decomposed into N views, i.e., $\mathbf{X}_T = \{\mathbf{X}_T^i\}_{i=1}^N, \mathbf{X}_T^i \in \Re^{d_i \times n_T}, d_T = \sum_{i=i}^N d_i$. In this case, the implementation of MVCCA corresponds to searching for the following:

$$\underset{(\omega_S^i, \omega_T^i), \dots, (\omega_S^N, \dots, \omega_T^N)}{\text{argmax}} (\rho_1, \dots, \rho_N) = \sum_{i=1}^N \frac{\left(\omega_S^i\right)^\dagger \Sigma_{ST}^i \omega_T^i}{\sqrt{\left(\omega_S^i\right)^\dagger \Sigma_{SS}^i \omega_S^i} \sqrt{\left(\omega_T^i\right)^\dagger \Sigma_{TT}^i \omega_T^i}} \tag{9}$$

where $\Sigma_{ST}^i = \mathbf{X}_S\left(\mathbf{X}_T^i\right)^\dagger, \Sigma_{SS}^i = \mathbf{X}_S\mathbf{X}_S^\dagger$ and $\Sigma_{TT}^i = \mathbf{X}_T^i\left(\mathbf{X}_T^i\right)^\dagger$. Generalizing the standard CCA, Equation (9) can be rewritten as:

$$\underset{(\omega_S^i, \omega_T^i), \dots, (\omega_S^N, \dots, \omega_T^N)}{\text{argmax}} (\rho_1, \dots, \rho_N) = \sum_{i=1}^N \left(\omega_S^i\right)^\dagger \Sigma_{ST}^i \omega_T^i$$
$$s.t. \left(\omega_S^1\right)^\dagger \Sigma_{ST}^1 \omega_T^i = 1, \dots, \left(\omega_S^N\right)^\dagger \Sigma_{ST}^N \omega_T^N = 1 \tag{10}$$

As a result, by using the solutions $\omega_S^i\big|_{i=1}^N$ and $\omega_T^i\big|_{i=1}^N$, we will have multiple transformed correlation subspaces, each one considering the SD and one of the target "views":

$$\mathbf{X}_S^{Ci} = \mathbf{X}_S \cdot \omega_S^i, \omega_S^i \in \Re^{d_S \times \hat{d}_i} \tag{11}$$

$$\mathbf{X}_T^{Ci} = \mathbf{X}_T^i \cdot \omega_T^i, \omega_T^i \in \Re^{d_T \times \hat{d}_i} \tag{12}$$

For any new instance of the target domain, i.e., $\mathbf{x} = \{x_i\}\big|_{i=1}^N, x_i \in \mathbf{X}_T^{Ci}$, the decision function of this SMVCCAE, trained with labeled training samples $\left\{\left(x_j^{SC}, y_j^S\right)\big|_{j=1}^{n_S}\right\}, x_j^{SC} \in \mathbf{X}_S^{Ci}, i = \forall N$, can be implemented via majority voting (MV):

$$\begin{aligned}
H(\mathbf{x}) &= sign\left(\sum_{i=1}^N h_i(x_i)\right) \\
&= \begin{cases} \omega_l, & \text{if } \sum_{i=1}^N h_i^l(x_i) \succ \frac{1}{2} \sum_{k=1}^c \sum_{i=1}^N h_i^k(x_i) \\ reject, & \text{otherwise} \end{cases}
\end{aligned} \tag{13}$$

However, to further optimize the ensemble results, one can also recall that the canonical correlations $\rho = \left\{ \{\rho_1, \dots, \rho_j\}\big|_{j=1}^{\hat{d}_1}, \dots, \{\rho_1, \dots, \rho_j\}\big|_{j=1}^{\hat{d}_N} \right\}$ obtained together with the transformation matrices ω_S^i and ω_T^i provide information about correlation between the SD and each target view. Since larger values of $\forall \{\rho_j\}\big|_{j=1}^{\hat{d}_i} \in \{\rho_i\}\big|_{i=1}^N$ show a greater correlation, this can also be considered a hint to obtain a better domain transfer ability for the corresponding view. We expect that poor correlation values (i.e., low values of $\sum_{j=1}^{\hat{d}_i} \rho_j$) will result in poor domain transfer abilities. Therefore, $\sum_{j=1}^{\hat{d}_i} \rho_j$ may be used to quantitatively evaluate the domain transfer ability of the transformation matrices ω_S^i and

ω_T^i. Accordingly, we propose to include the following canonical correlation coefficient in the voting strategy of Equation (13):

$$H(\mathbf{x}) = sign\left(\sum_{i=1}^{N}\sum_{j=1}^{\hat{d}_i}\rho_j h_i(\mathbf{x}_i)\right) \tag{14}$$

The algorithmic steps of the new algorithm (called Supervised MVCCA Ensemble, or SMVCCAE for short) are summarized in Algorithm 1.

Algorithm 1. Algorithmic details of SMVCCAE.

---

1.   **Inputs:** SD $\mathbf{X}_S = [x_1^S,...,x_{n_S}^S] \in \Re^{d_S \times n_S}$; TD $\mathbf{X}_T = [x_1^T,...,x_{n_T}^T] \in \Re^{d_T \times n_T}$; id for labeled training samples

2. $\left\{\left(x_j^S, y_j^S\right)\Big|_{j=1}^{n_S}\right\}, y_j^S \in \Omega = \{\omega_l\}_{l=1}^c$ from $\mathbf{X}_S$, where the superscript C represents the number of class types;

3.   Supervised classifier ζ; N the number of views of the TD; and $min(d_S, d_T) \leq \left\lfloor \frac{max(d_S, d_T)}{N} \right\rfloor$.

4.   **Train:** *for i = 1 to N*

5.   generate the target domain view $\mathbf{X}_T^i \in \Re^{d_i \times n_T}, d_T = \sum_{i=i}^N d_i$;

6.   return the transformation matrices ω_S^i and ω_T^i according to Equation (10);

7.   obtain the correlation subspaces $\mathbf{X}_S^{Ci}$ and $\mathbf{X}_T^{Ci}$ according to Equations (11) and (12);

8.   compute the transformed training samples $\left\{\left(x_j^{SC}, y_j^S\right)\Big|_{j=1}^{n_S}\right\}$ from $\mathbf{X}_S^{Ci}$ according to id;

9.   train the classifier $h_i = \zeta(x^{SC}, y^S)$;

10.   *end*

11.   **Output:** return the classifier pool $\{h_1,...,h_N\}$;

12.   **Classification:** For a given new instance $\mathbf{x} = \{x_i\}|_{i=1}^N, x_i \in \mathbf{X}_T^{Ci}$, predict the label according to Equation (14).

3.2. Semi-Supervised Version

To implement a semi-supervised version of the proposed algorithm, the multiple speed-up SRKDA approach has been incorporated into the supervised procedure. SRDKA essentially improves the original idea of the spectral regression proposed in [53] for linear discriminant analysis (LDA), by transforming the eigenvector decomposition based discriminant analysis into a regression framework via spectral graph embedding [40]. For the sake of clarity, we briefly recall here the SRKDA notation before formalizing its implementation in the new procedure.

Given the labeled samples $\left\{\left(x_j^S, y_j^S\right)\Big|_{j=1}^{n_S}\right\}, y_j^S \in \Omega = \{\omega_l\}_{l=1}^c$, the LDA objective function is:

$$\begin{aligned}
a_{LDA} &= \operatorname{argmax}\frac{a^\dagger \psi_b a}{a^\dagger \psi_w a} \\
\psi_b &= \sum_{k=1}^{c} n_k\left(u^{(k)} - u\right)\left(u^{(k)} - u\right)^\dagger \\
\psi_w &= \sum_{k=1}^{c}\left(\sum_{q=1}^{n_k}(\mathbf{x}_q^{(k)} - u^{(k)})(\mathbf{x}_q^{(k)} - u^{(k)})^\dagger\right)
\end{aligned} \tag{15}$$

where u is the global centroid, n_k is the number of samples in the k-th class, $u^{(k)}$ is the centroid of the k-th class, $\mathbf{x}_q^{(k)}$ is the q-th sample in the k-th class, and ψ_w and ψ_b represent the within-class scatter matrix and the between-class scatter matrix respectively, so that the total scatter matrix is computed as $\psi_t = \psi_b + \psi_w$. The best solutions for Equation (15) are the eigenvectors that correspond to the nonzero eigenvalues of:

$$\psi_b a_{LDA} = \lambda \psi_t a_{LDA} \tag{16}$$

To address the nonlinearities, the kernel extension of this procedure maps the input data to a kernel Hilbert space through nonlinear positive semi-definite kernel functions, such as the Gaussian kernel $K(\mathbf{x}, y) = \exp\left(-\|\mathbf{x} - y\|^2 / 2\sigma^2\right)$, the polynomial kernel $K(\mathbf{x}, y) = \left(1 + \mathbf{x}^\dagger y\right)^d$ and the sigmoid kernel $K(\mathbf{x}, y) = \tanh\left(\mathbf{x}^\dagger y + a\right)$. Generalizing Equation (15), the projective function of KDA is therefore:

$$
\begin{aligned}
\upsilon_{KDA} &= \operatorname{argmax} \frac{\upsilon^\dagger \psi_b^\phi \upsilon}{\upsilon^\dagger \psi_t^\phi \upsilon} \\
\psi_b^\phi &= \sum_{k=1}^{c} n_k \left(u_\phi^{(k)} - u_\phi\right)\left(u_\phi^{(k)} - u_\phi\right)^\dagger \\
\psi_w^\phi &= \sum_{k=1}^{c} \left(\sum_{q=1}^{n_k} (\phi(\mathbf{x}_q^{(k)}) - u_\phi^{(k)})(\phi(\mathbf{x}_q^{(k)}) - u_\phi^{(k)})^\dagger \right) \\
\psi_t^\phi &= \psi_b^\phi + \psi_w^\phi
\end{aligned}
\tag{17}
$$

where ψ_b^ϕ, ψ_w^ϕ, and ψ_t^ϕ denote the between-class, within-class and total scatter matrices in the kernel space, respectively.

Because the eigenvectors of $\psi_b^\phi \upsilon_{KDA} = \lambda \psi_t^\phi \upsilon_{KDA}$ are linear combinations of $\phi(\mathbf{x}_q)$ [54], there is always a coefficient ε_q such as $\upsilon_{KDA} = \sum_{q=1}^{n_k} \varepsilon_q \phi(\mathbf{x}_q)$. This constrain makes Equation (17) equivalent to:

$$
\varepsilon_{KDA} = \operatorname{argmax} \frac{\varepsilon^\dagger \mathbf{KWK}\varepsilon}{\varepsilon^\dagger \mathbf{KK}\varepsilon}
\tag{18}
$$

where $\varepsilon_{KDA} = \left[\varepsilon_1, ..., \varepsilon_{n_k}\right]^\dagger$. Then, the corresponding eigenproblem becomes:

$$
\mathbf{KWK}\varepsilon_{KDA} = \lambda \mathbf{KK}\varepsilon_{KDA}
\tag{19}
$$

where $\mathbf{K}$ is the kernel matrix, and the affinity matrix $\mathbf{W}$ is defined using either HeatKernel [55] or the binary weight mode:

$$
W_{i,j} = \begin{cases} 1/n_k, & \text{if } \mathbf{x}_i \text{ and } \mathbf{x}_j \text{ both belong to the } k^{th} \text{ class;} \\ 0, & \text{otherwise.} \end{cases}
\tag{20}
$$

To efficiently solve the KDA eigenproblem in Equation (19), let us consider ϑ to be the solution of $\mathbf{W}\vartheta = \lambda\vartheta$. Replacing $\mathbf{K}\varepsilon_{KDA}$ on the left side of Equation (19) by ϑ, we have:

$$
\mathbf{KWK}\varepsilon_{KDA} = \mathbf{KW}\vartheta = \mathbf{K}\lambda\vartheta = \lambda \mathbf{K}\vartheta = \lambda \mathbf{KK}\varepsilon_{KDA}
\tag{21}
$$

To avoid singularities, a constant matrix δI is added to $\mathbf{K}$ to keep it positive definite:

$$
\varepsilon_{KDA} = (\mathbf{K} + \delta I)^{-1}\vartheta
\tag{22}
$$

where I is the identity matrix, and $\delta \geq 0$ represents the regularization parameter. It can be easily verified that the optimal solution given by Equation (22) is the optimal solution of the following regularized regression problem [56]:

$$
\min_{f \in F} \sum_{j=1}^{n_S} \left(f(\mathbf{x}_j) - y_j\right)^2 + \delta \|f\|_K^2
\tag{23}
$$

where F is the kernel space associated with the kernel K, and $\|f\|_K$ is the corresponding norm.

According to Equations (19) and (21), the solution can be reached in two steps: (1) solve the eigenproblem $\mathbf{W}\boldsymbol{\vartheta} = \lambda\boldsymbol{\vartheta}$ to obtain $\boldsymbol{\vartheta}$; and (2) find a vector ε_{KDA} that satisfies $\mathbf{K}\varepsilon_{KDA} = \boldsymbol{\vartheta}$. For Step 1, it is easy to check that the involved affinity matrix $\mathbf{W}$ has a block-diagonal structure:

$$\mathbf{W} = \begin{bmatrix} \mathbf{W}^{(1)} & 0 & \cdots & 0 \\ 0 & \mathbf{W}^{(2)} & \cdots & 0 \\ \vdots & \vdots & \ddots & \vdots \\ 0 & 0 & \cdots & \mathbf{W}^{(c)} \end{bmatrix} \tag{24}$$

where $\left\{\mathbf{W}^{(k)}\right\}_{k=1}^{c}$ is an $n_k \times n_k$ matrix with all of the elements defined in Equation (19), and it is straightforward to show that $\mathbf{W}^{(k)}$ has the eigenvector $\mathbf{e}^{(k)}$ associated with $e^{(k)} = [1, 1, ..., 1]^{\dagger}$. In addition, there is only one nonzero eigenvalue of $\mathbf{W}^{(k)}$ because the rank of $\mathbf{W}^{(k)}$ is always 1. Thus, there are exactly c eigenvectors of $\mathbf{W}$ with the same eigenvalue 1:

$$\boldsymbol{\vartheta}_k = [\underbrace{0, ..., 0}_{\sum_{i=1}^{k-1} n_i}, \underbrace{1, ..., 1}_{n_k}, \underbrace{0, ..., 0}_{\sum_{i=k+1}^{c} n_i}]^{\dagger} \tag{25}$$

According to the theorem proven by Cai and He in [57], the kernel matrix is positive definite, and the c-1 projective function of KDA gives exactly the same solutions as the c-1 linear equations systems $\mathbf{K}\varepsilon_{KDA}^k = \overline{\boldsymbol{\vartheta}}^k$. Then let $\boldsymbol{\Theta} = [\varepsilon_1, ..., \varepsilon_{c-1}]$ be the KDA transformation matrix which embeds the data into the KDA subspace:

$$\boldsymbol{\Theta}^{\dagger}\left[K(:, x_1), ..., K(:, x_{n_k})\right] = \overline{Y}^{\dagger} \tag{26}$$

where the columns of $\overline{Y}^{\dagger}$ are the embedding results. Accordingly, the data with the same label correspond to the same point in the KDA subspace when the kernel matrix is positive definite.

To perform SRKDA in a semi-supervised way, one straightforward solution is to use the label information to guide the construction of the affinity matrix $\mathbf{W}$, as in [57–59]. Let $G = (V, E)$ be a graph with set of vertices V, which is connected by a set of edges E. The vertices of the graph are the labeled and unlabeled instances $\left(x_j^S, y_j^S\right)\big|_{j=1}^{n_S} \cup \left\{\left(x_j^T\right)\big|_{j=1}^{n_T}\right\}$. An edge between two vertices (or labeled and unlabeled samples) i, j represents the similarity of two instances with an associated weight $\{W_{i,j}\}$. Then, the affinity matrix W is built using both labeled and unlabeled samples. To achieve this goal, p-nearest neighbors, ε-neighbors, or fully connected graph techniques can be adopted, where 0–1 weighting, Gaussian kernel weighting, Polynomial kernel weighting and Dot-product weighting can be considered to establish the graph weights [57,58]. Usually, graph-based SSL methods compute the normalized graph Laplacian:

$$L = I - D^{-1/2}WD^{-1/2} \tag{27}$$

where D denotes a diagonal matrix defined by $D_{ii} = \sum_j W_{i,j}$ (see [59,60] (Chapter 5) for more details on different families of graph based SSL methods).

According to this procedure, and inserting the notation for DA using multiple view CCA, the new semi-supervised procedure follows the steps reported in Algorithm 2.

Algorithm 2. Algorithmic details of SSMVCCAE.

---

1. ***Inputs:*** SD $\mathbf{X}_S = \left[x_1^S, ..., x_{n_S}^S\right] \in \Re^{d_S \times n_S}$; TD $\mathbf{X}_T = \left[x_1^T, ..., x_{n_T}^T\right] \in \Re^{d_T \times n_T}$; id_S^L for labeled training

2.   samples $\left\{ \left(x_j^S, y_j^S\right)\Big|_{j=1}^{n_S} \right\}, y_j^S \in \Omega = \{\omega_l\}_{l=1}^c$ from $\mathbf{X}_S$, where superscript C represents the number of class

3.   types; id_T^U for unlabeled candidates $\left\{ \left(x_j^T\right)\Big|_{j=1}^{n_T} \right\}$ from $\mathbf{X}_T$ Semi-supervised classifier ζ_{SRKDA}; $N =$

4.   Number of views of the target domain; and $\min(d_S, d_T) \leq \left\lfloor \frac{\max(d_S, d_T)}{N} \right\rfloor$.

5. ***Train:*** *for i = 1 to N*

6.   generate the target domain view $\mathbf{X}_T^i \in \Re^{d_i \times n_T}, d_T = \sum_{i=i}^N d_i$;

7.   return the transformation matrices $\boldsymbol{\omega}_S^i$ and $\boldsymbol{\omega}_T^i$ according to Equation (10);

8.   obtain the correlation subspaces $\mathbf{X}_S^{Ci}$ and $\mathbf{X}_T^{Ci}$ according to Equations (11) and (12);

9.   compute the transformed training samples $\left\{ \left(x_j^{SC}, y_j^S\right)\Big|_{j=1}^{n_S} \right\}$ from $\mathbf{X}_S^{Ci}$ according to id_S^L and the

10.   transformed unlabeled samples $\left\{ \left(x_j^{TC}\right)\Big|_{j=1}^{n_T} \right\}$ from $\mathbf{X}_T$ according to id_T^U;

11.   build the graph Laplacian L_i according to Equation (27) using $\left(x_j^{SC}, y_j^{SC}\right)\Big|_{j=1}^{n_S} \cup \left\{ \left(x_j^{TC}\right)\Big|_{j=1}^{n_T} \right\}$;

12.   obtain the KDA transformation matrix $\boldsymbol{\Theta}_i$ according to the solutions of Equation (26) and Equation (22);

13.   return the embedded results $\overline{Y}_i^\dagger$;

14.   *end*

15. ***Output:*** return the KDA transformation matrices $\{\boldsymbol{\Theta}_i\}_{i=1}^N$ and the full KDA subspace embedded results $\left\{\overline{Y}_i^\dagger\right\}_{i=1}^N$;

16. ***Classification:*** For a given new instance $x = \{x_i\}|_{i=1}^N, x_i \in \mathbf{X}_T^{Ci}$

17. *for i = 1 to N*

18.   first map $\mathbf{x}_i$ into RKHS with the specified kernel function $\phi(\mathbf{x}_i)$;

19.   obtain the embedded results $\overline{Y}_{iT}$ in KDA space according to Equation (26);

20.   return the decision function $h_i(x) = \mathrm{argmin} \sum_{j=1}^c \left(\|\overline{\mathbf{y}}_{iT} - u_j\|^2\right), \overline{\mathbf{y}}_{iT} \in \overline{Y}_{iT}$, and $u_j = \sum_{\mathbf{x} \in c_i} \mathbf{x}/\left|c_j\right|$, which represents the class center of c_i in the KDA embedded space.

21. *end*

22. obtain the final predicted label by a majority voting ensemble strategy using Equation (14).

Summing up algorithmic details of the SMVCCAE and SSMVCCAE as described in Sections 3.1 and 3.2, Figure 1 illustrate the general flowchart for the proposed heterogeneous DA algorithms for RS image classification.

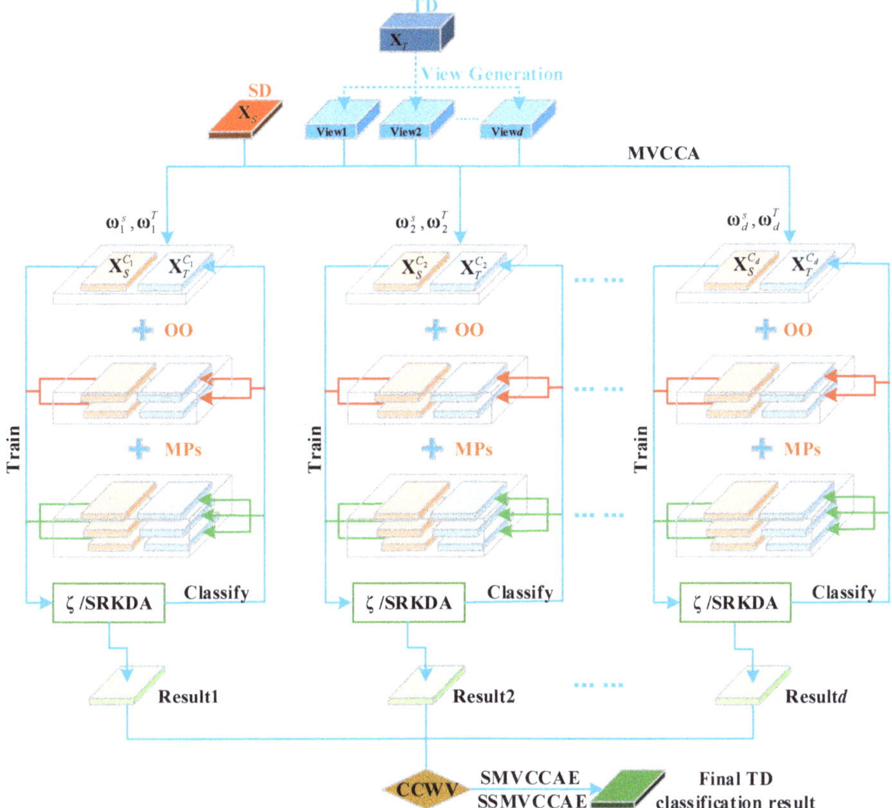

Figure 1. General flowchart for the proposed heterogeneous DA algorithms SMVCCAE and SSMVCCAE for RS image classification.

4. Data Sets and Setups

4.1. Datasets

For our analyses and evaluations, we consider two datasets, with different spatial and spectral resolutions. The first dataset is a 1.3 m spatial resolution image collected by the Reflective Optics Spectrographic Image System (ROSIS) sensor over the University of Pavia, with a size of 610×340 pixels (Figure 2). A total of 103 spectral reflectance bands that cover a region of the spectrum between 430 and 860 nm were retained for the analyses. The captured scene primarily represents a built-up setting with these thematic classes: asphalt, meadows, gravel, trees, metal sheets, bitumen, bare soil, bricks and shadows, as listed in Table 1. As described earlier, the main purpose of this article is to investigate the proposed methods in a heterogeneous DA problem. In this sense, the low-dimensional image is simulated by clustering the spectral space of the original ROSIS image. Specifically, the original bands of the original ROSIS image are clustered into seven groups using the K-Means algorithm, and the mean value of each cluster is considered as a new spectral band, providing a total of seven new bands. In the experiments, the new synthetic image is considered as the SD, whereas the original ROSIS image is considered as the TD.

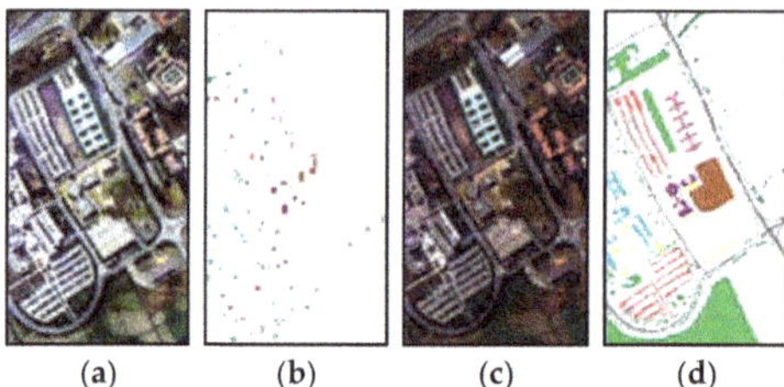

(a)   (b)   (c)   (d)

Figure 2. (**a–d**) False color composite of the: synthetic low spectral resolution (**a**); and the original hyperspectral (**c**) images of the University campus in Pavia, together with: training (**b**); and validation (**d**) data sets (legend and sample details are reported in Table 1). False color composites are obtained and are displayed as R, G, and B bands 7, 5, and 4 for the synthetic, and bands 60, 30, and 2 for the original image, respectively.

Table 1. Class legend and sample details for the ROSIS University data set.

No.	Class	Code	Source Train	Target Test
1	Asphalt		548	6631
2	Meadows		540	18649
3	Gravel		392	2099
4	Trees		524	3064
5	Metal sheets		265	1345
6	Bare soil		532	5029
7	Bitumen		375	1330
8	Bricks		514	3682
9	Shadows		231	947

The second dataset was gathered by the AVIRIS sensor over the Indian Pines test site in North-western Indiana in 1992, with 224 spectral reflectance bands in the wavelength range of 0.4 to 2.5 µm. It consists of 145 × 145 pixels with moderate spatial resolution of 20 m per pixel, and a 16-bit radiometric resolution. After an initial screening, the number of bands was reduced to 200 by removing bands 104–108, 150–163, and 220, due to noise and water absorption phenomena. This scene contains two-thirds agriculture, and one-third forest or other natural perennial vegetation. For the other Pavia data set, K-Means is used to simulate a low dimensional image with 10 bands. For illustrative purposes, Figure 3a,b shows false color composition of the simulated low dimensional and the original AVIRIS Indian Pines scene, whereas Figure 3b shows the ground truth map that is available for the scene, which is displayed in the form of a class assignment for each labeled pixel. In the experimenting stage, this ground truth map is subdivided into two parts for training and validation purposes, as detailed in Table 2.

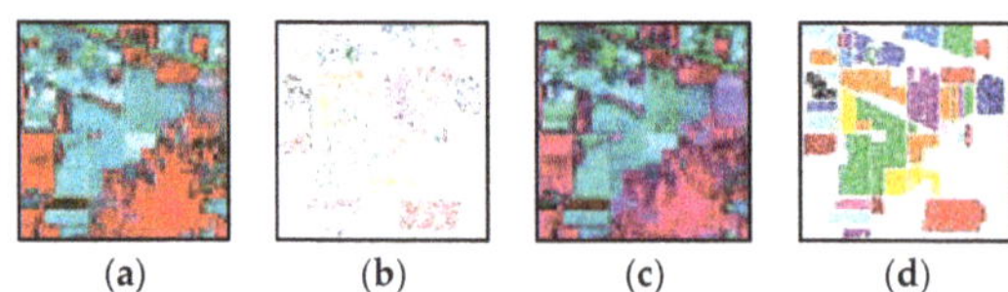

(a)   (b)   (c)   (d)

Figure 3. (**a–d**) False color composites of the: simulated low spectral resolution (**a**); and original hyperspectral (**c**) images of Indian Pines data, together with: training (**b**); and validation (**d**) data sets (color legend and sample details are reported in Table 2). False color composites are obtained displaying as R, G, and B bands, 6, 4, and 5 for the synthetic, and bands 99, 51, and 21 for the original image, respectively.

Table 2. Class legend and sample details for the AVIRIS Indian Pines data set.

No.	Class	Code	Source Train	Target Test
1	Alfalfa		23	23
2	Corn-notill		228	1200
3	Corn-mintill		130	700
4	Corn-notill		57	180
5	Grass-pasture		83	400
6	Grass-trees		130	600
7	Grass-pasture-mowed		14	14
8	Hay-windrowed		78	400
9	Oats		10	10
10	Soybean-notill		172	800
11	Soybean-mintill		255	2200
12	Soybean-clean		93	500
13	Wheat		55	150
14	Woods		265	1000
15	Buildings-grass-trees-drives		86	300
16	Stone-steel-towers		43	50

4.2. Experiment Setups

All of the experiments were performed using Matlab^{TM} on a Windows 10 64-bit system with Intel® Core^{TM} i7-4970 CPU, @3.60 GHz, 32GB RAM. For the sake of evaluation and comparison, a Random Forest classifier (RaF) is considered as benchmark classifier for both the SMVCCAE and SVCCA approaches, because of its proven velocity, and its generalized and easy-to-implement properties [61,62]. The number of decision trees in RaF is set by default to 100, whereas the number of features is set by default to the floor of the square root of the original feature dimensionality.

For both the ROSIS and Indian Pines data sets, all of the initial and derived features have been standardized to a zero mean and unit variance. For incorporated object oriented (OO), five statistics are utilized, including the pixels' mean and standard deviation, area, orientation and major axis length of the segmented objects via K-Means clustering algorithm, whereas the spatial feature morphology profiles (MPs) are applied to the three transferred features that have the highest canonical correlation coefficients. Specifically, MPs are constructed by applying closing by reconstruction (CBR) with a circular element with a radius of 3–11 pixels, and opening by reconstruction (OBR) with an element with a radius of 3–6 pixels, refer to works carried out in [63,64]. Therefore, the feature dimensionality set in the experiments is 7 (10) vs. 103 (200) when using spectral features only for ROSIS (Indian Pines), 7 + 5 (10 + 5) vs. 103 + 5 (200 + 5) when using spectral features stacked with OO ones, 7 + 39 (10 + 39) vs. 103 + 39 (200 + 39) when using spectral features stacked with MPs features, and finally 7 + 5 + 39 (10 + 5 + 39) vs. 103 + 5 + 39 (200 + 5 + 39) when using all spectral, OO, and MPs features.

To assess the classification performances of the proposed semi-supervised approach, two state-of-the-art semi-supervised classifiers, Logistic label propagation (LLP) [65] and Laplacian support vector machine (LapSVM) [66] were considered. For the critical parameters of the semi-supervised technique (SRKDA), such as the regularization parameter δ and the number of neighbors NN used to construct the graph Laplacian L with HeatKernel [40], their values are obtained by a heuristic search in the (0.01–1) and (1–15) ranges, respectively. The parameter settings for LLP and LapSVM are instead reported in Table 3. Because LapSVM was originally proposed for binary classification problems, a one-against-all (OAA) scheme was adopted to handle the multiclass classification in our experiments.

Table 3. Parameter details for LLP and LapSVM.

Classifier	Parameters	Meanings	Values
LLP	g	graph complete type	KNN
	τ	neighborhood type	Supervised
	N	neighbor size for constructing graph	5
	ω	weights for edge in graph	Heat Kernel
	σ	parameter for Heat Kernel	1
	C	regularization scale	0.001
	M	maxim iteration number	1000
	η	weight function for labeled samples	mean
LapSVM	γa	regularization parameter (ambient norm)	10^{-5}
	γi	regularization parameter (intrinsic norm)	1
	α	the initial weights	0
	κ	kernel type	RBF
	σ	RBF kernel parameter	0.01
	M	maximum iteration number	200
	c	LapSVM training type	primal
	η	Laplacian normalization	TRUE
	N	neighbor size for constructing graph	6

5. Experimental Results and Discussion

5.1. Domain Transfer Ability of MVCCA

As discussed in Section 3.1, each dimension in the derived CCA subspace is associated with a different canonical correlation coefficient which is a measure of its transfer ability. Moreover, in the MVCCA scenario, the transfer ability of each view and dimension is controlled not only by the number of views but also by the view generation technique. In this sense, Figure 4 presents the results of the average canonical correlation coefficient obtained using different view generation techniques, i.e., disjoint random sampling, uniform slice, clustering and partially joint random generation. Partially joint random view generation can apparently increase the chance of finding views with better domain transfer ability on the one hand, and to overcome the limitation ensemble techniques when the number of classifiers (equal to number of views in our case) is small on the other hand. Please note that for a more objective evaluation and comparison, each experiment was executed 10 times independently.

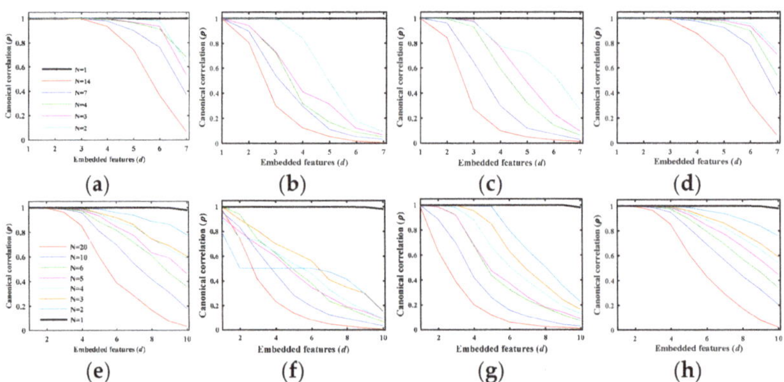

Figure 4. Average canonical correlation coefficient versus embedded features for: ROSIS (**a–d**); and Indian Pines (**e–h**) data sets using different view generation techniques: disjoint random sampling (**a,e**); uniform slice (**b,f**); clustering (**c,g**); and partially joint random generation (**d,h**).

In Figure 4, we see that the embedded features with the highest canonical correlation coefficient are obtained by directly applying CCA without multi view generation (i.e., $n = 1$). However, single view CCA may still fail to balance potential mismatches across heterogeneous domains by overfitting, as demonstrated in the results reported in the following sections. Additionally, the decreasing trend of the canonical correlation coefficient with an increasing number of views is obvious because of the increasing mismatch between the source and target views. However, the decreasing rates of the canonical correlation coefficient for disjoint random and partially joint random generation techniques are lower than those from disjoint uniform slice and disjoint clustering view generations. Therefore, partially joint random and disjoint random view generation techniques have been selected for the following experiments.

5.2. Parameter Analysis for SMVCCAE

In Figure 5, we report the results of a sensitivity analysis of SMVCCAE that involves its critical parameters: the dimension of the target view $d_T^i = \frac{d_T}{N}$, the view generating strategies including disjoint random (DJR) and partially joint random (PJR) generation, as well as the ensemble approaches MJV and CCWV. Please note that the number of views for PJR based SMCCAE was set to 35, which is a number that will be discussed later in this paper.

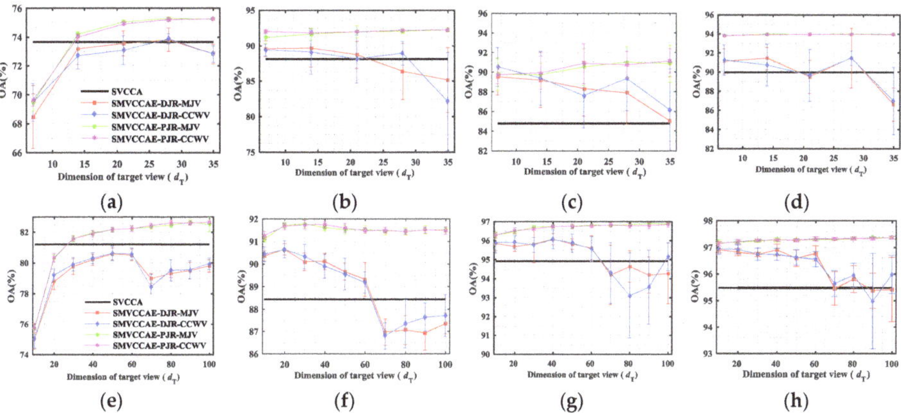

Figure 5. (**a–h**)Average OA values versus target view dimensionality for SMVCCAE with different fusion strategies using: spectral (**a,e**); spectral-OO (**b,f**); spectral-MPs (**c,g**); and spectral-OO-MPs (**d,h**) features on: ROSIS University (**a–d**); and Indian Pine datasets (**e–h**).

As illustrated in Figure 5 for the test data sets, the choice of PJR view generation with MJV and CCWV strategies allows the best overall accuracy values (OA curves in color green and pink). Concerning the dimensionality of the target views, they are different using different features. Specifically, for spectral features, the larger the dimensionality of the target views, the larger the OA values for PJR-based SMVCCAE because of the better domain transfer capacity with more ensemble classifiers. However, a dimensionality that is too large leads to too few view splits, i.e., a small number of ensemble elements, eventually resulting in a degraded performance. For example, when target view dimensionality is larger than four times the source view (7) dimensionality for ROSIS and larger than six times this value for Indian Pines, the OA value exhibits a decreasing trend (Figure 5a,e). Among the different types of features, (e.g., spectral and object-oriented features (labeled "spectral-OO"), spectral and morphological profile features (labeled "spectral-MPs"), and all of them together (labeled "spectral-OO-MPs"), the outcome is as expected, which is that the best results are obtained using spectral-OO-MPs. Interestingly, whereas the classification performances of the PJR-based approach are quite stable with respect to the dimensionality of the target views, the DJR-based results show a negative trend with an increasing number of target views. This finding is especially true when spatial (i.e., OO and morphological profiles) features are incorporated. This result can be explained by the trade-off between the diversity, OA and number of classifiers in an ensemble system. Specifically, the statistical diversity among spectral and spatial features tends to enhance the classification accuracy diversities more than using any view splitting strategy. As a result, the final classification performance could be limited or even degraded, especially when the number of classifiers is small.

Finally, in Figure 6, we focus on the computational complexity of the proposed approach by presenting OA, kappa statistics and CPU time values with respect to the number of views and the various fusion strategies.

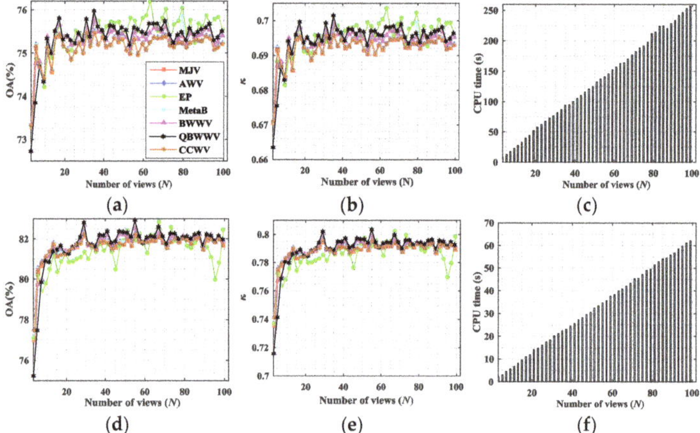

Figure 6. Average OA, Kappa (κ) and CPU time in seconds vs. the number of views for SMVCCA with PJR view generation and various fusion strategies applied to spectral features of ROSIS: University (**a–c**); and Indian Pines datasets (**d–f**).

According to Figure 6, the proposed CCWV fusion technique is effective as the other fusion techniques. Apparently, with regard to the improvements in the OA values (see Figure 6a,b,d,e), and the computational burden from the number of views (see Figure 6c,f), views between 30 and 40 produce the best tradeoff between computational burden and classification accuracy.

In summary, in a scenario in which low-dimensional and high-dimensional data sets require DA, a well-designed SMVCCAE requires us to set the dimensionality of each target view to three or four times the dimensionality of the source view, and to use a PJR view generation technique.

5.3. Validation of SMVCCAE

Figure 7 provides the SMVCCAE heterogeneous cross-domain classification maps with OA values for the ROSIS University dataset using spectral, spectral-OO, spectral-MPs and spectral-OO-MPs features. Compared with the maps produced by a single-view canonical correlation analysis (SVCCA) approach, the thematic maps obtained by SMVCCAE using the associated features are better, specifically with adequate delineations of the bitumen, gravel and bare soil areas (see the numbers in Table 4). These results experimentally verify our earlier assumptions that single view CCA could fail to balance potential mismatches across heterogeneous domains by overfitting. Additionally, the most accurate result is obtained with spectral-OO-MPs by SMVCCAE using the PJR view generation strategy, as shown by the results in Figure 7 and the numbers in bold in Table 4.

For the Indian Pines dataset, Figure 8 shows the thematic maps with OA values, whereas Table 5 reports the classification accuracies (Average accuracy (AA) and OA), and kappa statistics (k) with respect to various features. Once again, the thematic maps with larger OA values produced by SMVCCAE are better than the results produced by SVCCA, especially when the OO and MPs are incorporated. The numbers in bold in Table 5 show that the largest accuracies for various class types are obtained by the SMVCCAE with the PJR technique using spectral-OO-MPs features.

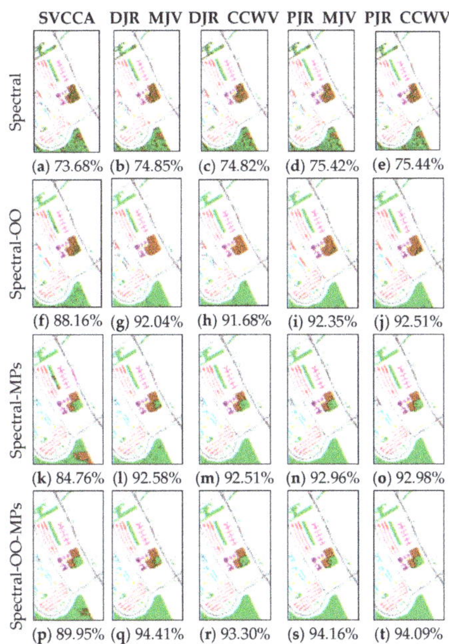

Figure 7. (**a–t**) Summary of the best classification maps with OA values for SMVCCAE with different fusion strategies using spectral, OO and MPs features of ROSIS University.

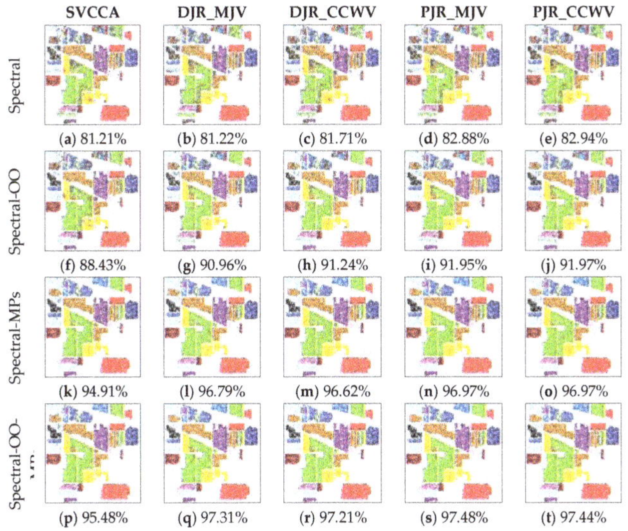

Figure 8. (**a–t**) Summary of the best classification maps with OA values for SMVCCAE with different fusion strategies using spectral, OO and MPs features of Indian Pines.

5.4. Parameter Analysis for the Semi-Supervised Version of the Algorithm

In Figures 9 and 10, we report the results of the sensitivity analysis for SSMVCCAE while considering the two critical parameters from the adopted SRKDA technique: (1) the regularization parameter δ; and (2) the number of neighbors NN used to construct the graph Laplacian L. The other parameters, such as the target view dimensionality, d_T^i and the number of total views N (i.e., the ensemble size), are set by default to $d_T^i = 4 \times d_s$ and $N = 35$, according to our previous experimental analysis for the supervised version of the same technique.

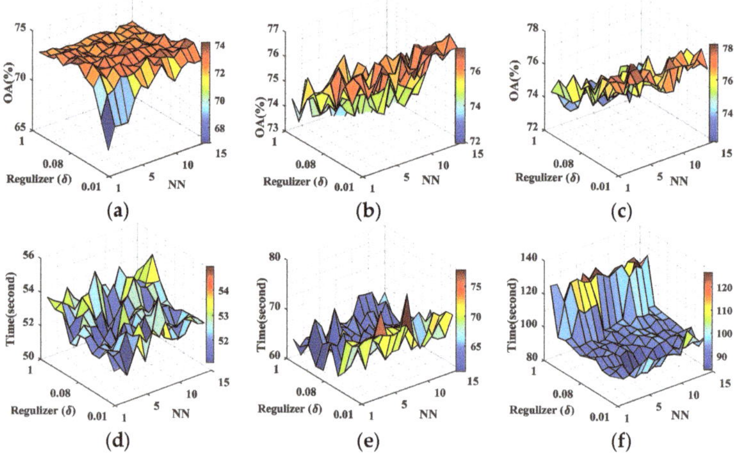

Figure 9. (a–f) OA values and CPU time (in seconds) versus the regularization parameter (δ) and nearest neighborhood size (NN) set of SSMVCCAE with DJR view generation strategy for ROSIS University using different sizes of labeled samples: 10 pixels/class (**a,d**); 50 pixels/class (**b,e**); and 100 pixels/class (**c,f**).

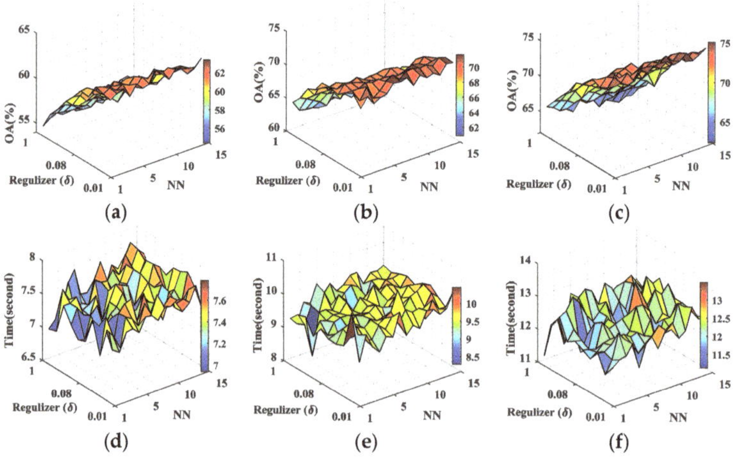

Figure 10. (a–f) OA values and CPU time (in seconds) versus the regularization parameter (δ) and nearest neighborhood size (NN) set of SSMVCCAE with the DJR view generation strategy for Indian Pine using different size of labeled samples: 10 pixels/class (**a,d**); 30 pixels/class (**b,e**); and 55 pixels/class (**c,f**).

Table 4. Classification accuracy values for the SVCCA and SMVCCAE ($d_T = 4 \times d_S$) methods for ROSIS University. Considered metrics: Overall accuracy (OA), Average accuracy (AA), Kappa statistic (Kappa).

Methods	Strategy	Features	Asphalt	Meadows	Gravel	Trees	Metal Sheets	Bare Soil	Bitumen	Bricks	Shadows	AA (%)	OA (%)	Kappa
SVCCA	~	F1	94.96	91.61	66.17	52.56	98.68	45.70	70.63	69.50	99.26	76.56	73.68	0.67
		F2	98.02	95.88	93.04	71.59	98.68	71.13	90.88	76.59	**100.00**	88.42	88.76	0.85
		F3	99.47	88.06	94.39	80.89	99.55	53.10	72.31	90.67	98.90	86.37	84.76	0.80
		F4	99.86	89.32	91.35	82.43	98.67	71.98	96.44	95.76	99.15	91.66	89.96	0.87
SMVCCAE	DJR_MJV	F1	94.72	93.38	73.72	51.80	99.40	45.96	73.73	68.49	99.62	77.87	73.80	0.68
		F2	95.35	97.59	77.93	61.68	99.61	82.74	81.94	68.45	99.90	85.02	86.37	0.82
		F3	99.36	90.58	95.88	74.91	99.37	72.69	94.79	85.28	99.21	90.23	88.16	0.85
		F4	99.49	92.05	96.76	79.38	99.77	88.84	96.45	86.15	99.26	93.13	91.44	0.89
	DJR_CCWV	F1	94.81	93.25	73.44	51.82	99.65	45.99	74.43	68.29	99.61	77.92	73.84	0.68
		F2	96.56	**98.56**	78.45	62.47	99.47	92.16	88.74	68.79	99.81	87.22	88.89	0.86
		F3	99.31	90.60	96.05	74.26	99.52	75.25	96.40	85.82	99.32	90.72	88.33	0.85
		F4	99.24	90.64	96.72	77.65	99.28	93.32	97.36	86.71	99.19	93.34	91.42	0.89
	PJR_MJV	F1	95.30	94.31	76.84	52.48	99.83	48.15	76.36	69.20	99.87	79.15	75.28	0.69
		F2	98.64	98.00	95.62	77.19	99.52	89.26	97.57	72.69	99.79	92.03	92.14	0.90
		F3	99.72	91.09	98.96	82.15	99.93	80.10	**99.62**	87.11	99.36	93.11	90.97	0.88
		F4	**99.89**	91.46	94.97	**84.63**	99.93	98.81	99.34	95.66	99.40	96.01	**93.97**	**0.92**
	PJR_CCWV	F1	95.26	94.33	77.45	52.44	99.83	47.96	76.56	69.06	99.86	79.19	75.20	0.69
		F2	98.55	98.02	95.55	77.33	99.54	89.40	97.57	72.62	99.79	92.04	92.16	0.90
		F3	99.71	90.90	**99.08**	82.14	**99.95**	77.94	99.56	86.99	99.36	92.85	90.69	0.88
		F4	**99.89**	91.36	95.16	84.40	**99.95**	**98.88**	99.35	**95.78**	99.38	**96.02**	93.92	**0.92**

F1: Spectral; F2: Spectral-OO; F3: Spectral-MPs; F4: Spectral-OO-MPs.

Table 5. Classification accuracy values (average) for the SVCCA and SMVCCAE methods for Indian Pines. Considered metrics: Overall accuracy (OA), Average accuracy (AA), Kappa statistic (Kappa).

Methods	SVCCA				SMVCCAE															
Strategy	~				DJR_MJV				DJR_CCWV				PJR_MJV				PJR_CCWV			
Features	F1	F2	F3	F4	F1	F2	F3	F4	F1	F2	F3	F4	F1	F2	F3	F4	F1	F2	F3	F4
Alfalfa	69.57	91.30	86.96	86.96	45.22	91.30	95.22	**95.65**	48.26	91.30	**95.65**	**95.65**	46.09	91.30	**95.65**	**95.65**	46.09	91.30	95.65	**95.65**
Corn-notill	81.42	87.42	90.67	93.92	78.04	87.86	90.45	91.92	77.91	87.05	90.41	91.70	80.83	89.12	91.06	92.78	80.82	89.38	91.14	**92.90**
Corn-mintill	70.71	88.71	96.86	96.57	64.70	84.54	97.00	98.16	65.34	83.29	97.31	97.91	65.87	86.54	98.03	99.20	65.43	86.93	97.97	**99.24**
Corn-notill	75.56	94.44	95.56	96.67	62.83	83.89	94.11	95.33	62.94	83.44	93.11	95.61	65.56	86.17	95.56	95.89	65.61	86.28	95.56	**95.95**
Grass-pasture	79.00	81.50	88.75	88.75	72.98	86.48	93.13	93.60	72.95	86.38	92.55	93.70	75.90	88.65	93.63	93.90	75.95	88.43	93.73	**94.00**
Grass-trees	91.00	92.17	99.00	99.00	96.03	96.80	99.70	99.69	95.68	96.73	99.67	99.64	96.58	97.33	**99.67**	**99.67**	96.50	97.49	**99.67**	**99.67**
Grass-pasture-mowed	85.71	85.71	85.71	85.71	91.43	**92.86**	**92.86**	**92.86**	**92.86**	**92.86**	**92.86**	**92.86**	**92.86**	**92.86**	**92.86**	**92.86**	**92.86**	**92.86**	**92.86**	**92.86**
Hay-windrowed	97.75	97.50	99.75	99.75	98.45	96.30	99.68	99.70	98.68	96.93	99.68	99.63	99.45	97.70	99.73	99.75	99.23	97.83	99.65	**99.75**
Oats	90.00	90.00	100.00	100.00	80.00	89.00	91.00	99.00	85.00	92.00	97.00	98.00	91.00	99.00	**100.**	**100.**	89.00	**98.00**	**100.**	**100.**
Soybean-notill	77.75	87.38	87.25	89.00	79.37	89.83	91.34	92.59	79.54	89.02	90.93	92.22	81.89	91.85	92.27	93.14	81.70	91.89	92.15	**92.92**
Soybean-mintill	78.55	87.45	95.77	95.64	76.94	91.20	97.35	98.44	77.20	91.22	97.54	98.16	78.52	92.82	98.16	98.54	78.74	92.88	98.25	**98.52**
Soybean-clean	71.60	82.80	93.80	93.80	73.42	81.86	95.20	96.36	73.90	82.72	95.18	95.94	77.90	86.10	97.14	97.16	77.50	86.16	96.90	**97.18**
Wheat	**99.33**	**99.33**	98.67	98.67	98.20	99.00	98.60	98.73	98.13	98.53	98.27	98.80	98.54	**99.33**	98.67	99.00	98.47	**99.33**	98.67	98.80
Woods	96.60	96.90	99.60	99.50	98.23	98.94	99.87	99.82	98.17	98.90	99.83	99.85	98.37	99.08	**99.91**	**99.91**	98.41	99.06	99.90	99.90
Buildings-grass-trees-drives	51.33	61.33	99.00	99.00	56.00	69.60	99.77	99.97	55.27	70.27	99.90	99.97	57.17	69.87	**100.**	**100.**	56.60	70.33	**100.**	**100.**
Stone-steel-towers	**100.**	**100.**	**100.**	**100.**	99.80	**100.**	**100.**	**100.**	99.60	**100.**	**100.**	**100.**	**100.**	**100.**	**100.**	**100.**	**100.**	**100.**	**100.**	**100.**
AA (%)	82.24	89.00	94.83	95.18	79.48	89.97	95.95	96.99	80.09	90.04	96.24	96.85	81.66	91.73	97.02	**97.34**	81.43	91.76	97.01	97.33
OA (%)	81.21	88.43	94.91	95.48	80.19	90.10	96.07	96.89	80.30	89.89	96.05	96.72	81.95	91.60	96.73	**97.27**	81.89	91.71	96.73	**97.27**
Kappa	0.78	0.87	0.94	0.95	0.77	0.89	0.95	0.96	0.77	0.88	0.95	0.96	0.79	0.90	0.96	**0.97**	0.79	0.90	0.96	**0.97**

F1: Spectral; F2: Spectral-OO; F3: Spectral-MPs; F4: Spectral-OO-MPs.

According to the results, the smaller the regularization parameter δ *is* and the larger the number of neighbors *NN*, the larger the OA values. Thus, $\delta = 0.01$ and *NN* = 12 were considered in all of the experiments. Computational complexity is primarily controlled by the labeled sample size (note the vertical axis in Figures 9d–f and 10d–f.

5.5. Validation of the Semi-Supervised MVCCAE

To validate the performances of the semi-supervised version of the proposed algorithm, comparisons with existing methods, specifically LLP and LapSVM, are presented for the ROSIS University data set, starting from a label set of increasing size.

Figure 11 shows the learning curves for SSMVCCAE, LLP, and LapSVM using different view generation and classifier ensemble strategies as a function of this size. Each point on the *x*-axis represents the size of the labeled samples (pixels) for each class type, while the *y*-axis represents the average overall classification accuracy. In Table 6, we report the average overall classification accuracies and kappa statistics (κ) over 10 independent runs, when a total of 100 labeled samples are considered for each class.

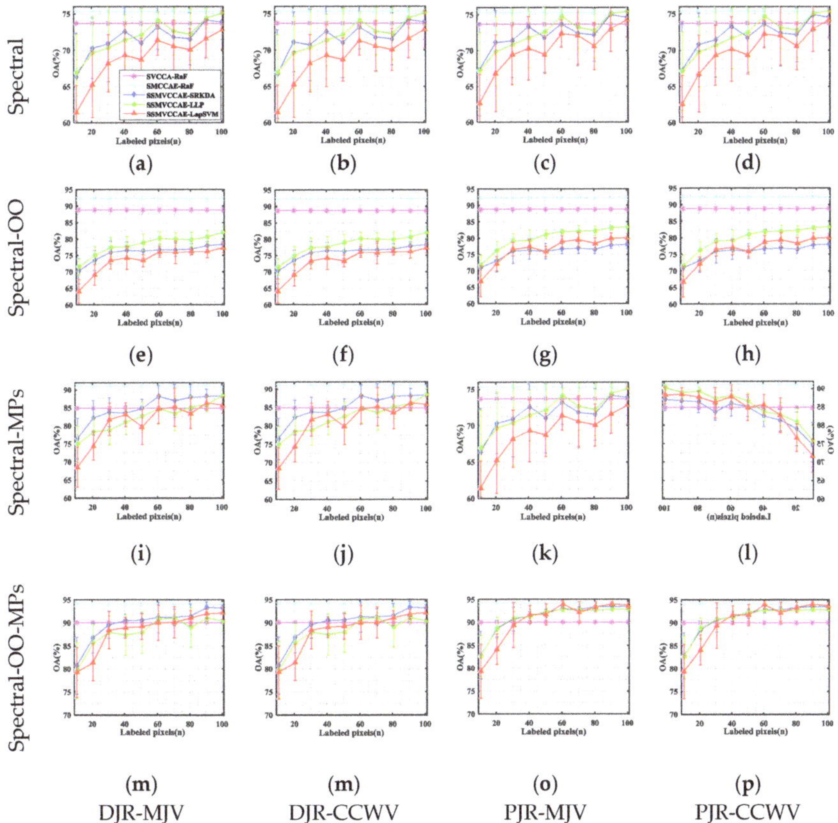

Figure 11. (**a–p**) Average OA values versus labeled pixels for SSMVCCAE with different view generation and fusion strategies for ROSIS University dataset.

According to the results in Figure 11 and Table 6, the proposed semi-supervised heterogeneous DA approach achieves comparable and sometimes better results in any case (see the learning curves in blue for SSMVCCAE-SRKDA vs. green for SSMVCCAE-LPP and red for SSMVCCAE-LapSVM in Figure 11). Moreover, larger OA values with faster convergence rates are shown by SSMVCCAE with PJR as opposed to DJR view generation, either by MJV fusion or by the CCWV fusion, especially using the spectral-OO-MPs features.

In Figure 12 and Table 7, the results of the same experiments are reported for the Indian Pines test set. Please note that because only a few samples are available for some classes in the Indian Pines case, class types that contain less than 70 pixels for training are not considered here. Even in this case, to obtain a more objective comparison and evaluation, each test is executed independently for 10 rounds.

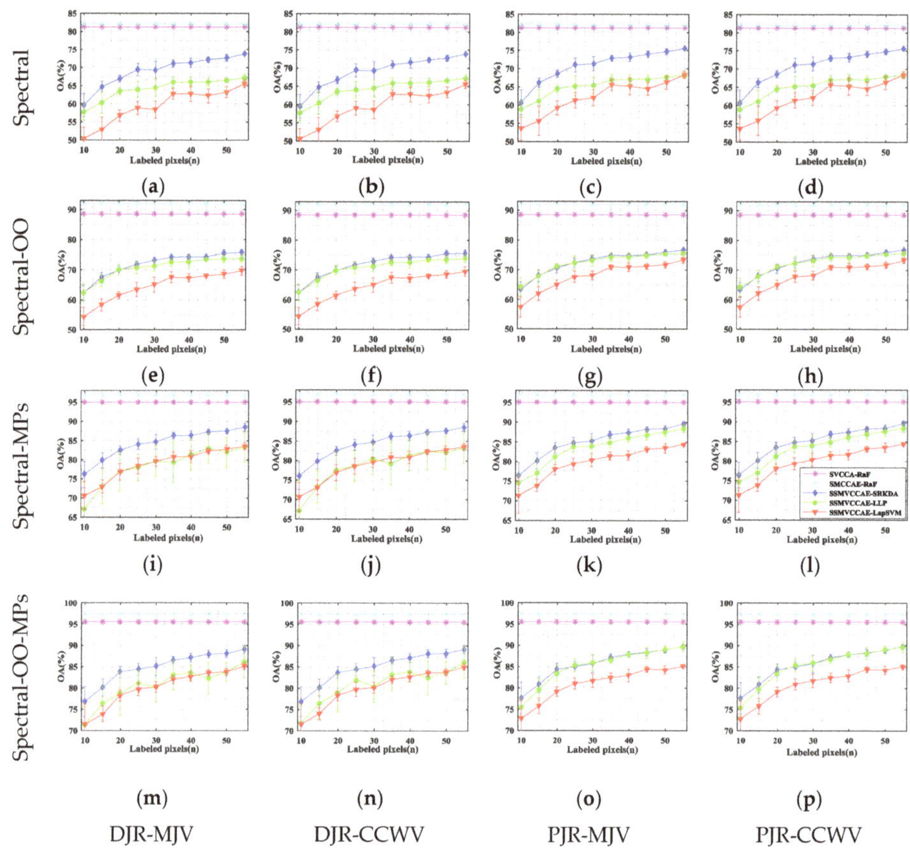

Figure 12. (a–p) Average OA values versus labeled pixels for SSMVCCAE with different view generation and fusion strategies on Indian Pines data.

Figure 12 shows that better classification results are obtained by the SSMVCCAE with SRKDA, not only using the original spectral features but also using spectral features that incorporate OO and MPs features (see the learning curves in blue vs. those in green and red). Moreover, the best classification results are obtained by SSMVCCAE-SRKDA with the PJR view generation technique, and when considering the spectral-OO-MPs stacked features (see the numbers in bold in Table 7).

Table 6. Average overall classification accuracies and kappa statistics (κ) for SSMVCCAE with different semi-supervised classifiers for the ROSIS University data. Total 100 labeled samples are available for each class over 10 independent runs.

Classifier	SSMVCCAE (SRKDA)								SSMVCCAE (LPP)								SSMVCCAE (LapSVM)							
View Generation	DJR				PJR				DJR				PJR				DJR				PJR			
Voting	MJV		CCWV		MJV		CCWV		MJV		CCWV		MJV		CCWV		MJV		CCWV		MJV		CCWV	
Statistics	OA	κ	OA	κ	OA	κ	OA	κ	OA	κ	OA	κ	OA	κ	OA	κ	OA	κ	OA	κ	OA	κ	OA	κ
Spectral	73.82	0.66	73.83	0.66	74.58	0.67	74.47	0.67	75.12	0.68	75.11	0.68	**75.45**	**0.68**	75.37	0.68	72.82	0.66	72.85	0.66	74.26	0.67	74.16	0.67
Spectral-OO	78.31	0.72	78.29	0.72	78.02	0.72	78.00	0.72	82.08	0.76	82.04	0.76	**83.44**	**0.78**	83.32	0.78	77.37	0.71	77.38	0.71	80.08	0.74	80.04	0.74
Spectral-MPs	88.23	0.85	88.24	0.85	86.73	0.82	86.89	0.83	88.44	0.85	88.45	0.85	90.16	0.87	**90.17**	**0.87**	85.65	0.82	85.72	0.82	88.14	0.85	88.12	0.85
Spectral-OO-MPs	93.17	0.91	93.14	0.91	93.47	0.91	93.46	0.91	90.36	0.87	90.31	0.87	92.78	0.90	92.77	0.90	92.08	0.90	92.10	0.90	**93.68**	**0.92**	93.67	0.92

Table 7. Average overall classification accuracies and kappa statistics (κ) for SSMVCCAE with different semi-supervised classifiers for the Indian Pines data. A total of 55 labeled samples are available for each class over 10 independent runs.

Classifier	SSMVCCAE (SRKDA)								SSMVCCAE (LPP)								SSMVCCAE (LapSVM)							
View Generation	DJR				PJR				DJR				PJR				DJR				PJR			
Voting	MJV		CCWV		MJV		CCWV		MJV		CCWV		MJV		CCWV		MJV		CCWV		MJV		CCWV	
Statistics	OA	κ	OA	κ	OA	κ	OA	κ	OA	κ	OA	κ	OA	κ	OA	κ	OA	κ	OA	κ	OA	κ	OA	κ
Spectral	73.67	0.70	73.81	0.70	75.49	0.72	**75.51**	**0.72**	67.05	0.62	67.13	0.62	68.18	0.64	68.17	0.64	65.43	0.61	65.48	0.61	68.34	0.64	68.38	0.64
Spectral-OO	75.64	0.72	75.53	0.72	76.61	0.73	**76.66**	**0.73**	73.69	0.70	73.75	0.70	75.42	0.72	75.47	0.72	69.59	0.65	69.54	0.65	73.20	0.69	73.18	0.69
Spectral-MPs	88.42	0.87	88.49	0.87	89.57	0.88	**89.54**	**0.88**	83.19	0.81	83.22	0.81	88.29	0.86	88.31	0.86	83.49	0.81	83.51	0.81	84.33	0.82	84.33	0.82
Spectral-OO-MPs	89.02	0.87	89.05	0.87	**89.66**	**0.88**	**89.66**	**0.88**	86.01	0.84	86.02	0.84	89.60	0.88	89.59	0.88	85.01	0.83	84.99	0.83	85.03	0.83	85.01	0.83

Finally, in Figures 13 and 14, the CPU time consumptions in seconds for the different implementations of the semi-supervised procedure are reported as a function of the labeled sample size for both Pavia and Indian Pines. According to the results, SSMVCCAE with SRKDA is only slightly more efficient than LapSVM for the ROSIS University data, but is much more efficient for the Indian Pines data. Moreover, the computational complexities of LapSVM and LLP increase linearly with the number of labeled samples, because they are more visible for the Indian Pines data, whereas the CPU time for SRKDA stays almost constant.

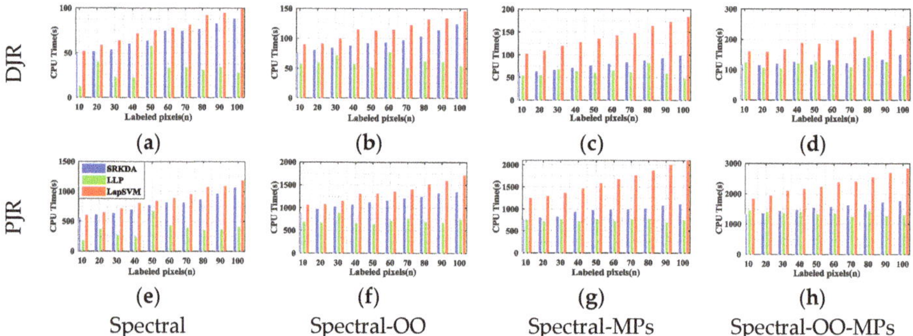

Figure 13. (a–h) CPU time consumption in seconds versus the size of the labeled samples for SSMVCCAE-SRKDA/-LLP/-LapSVM for the ROSIS University data.

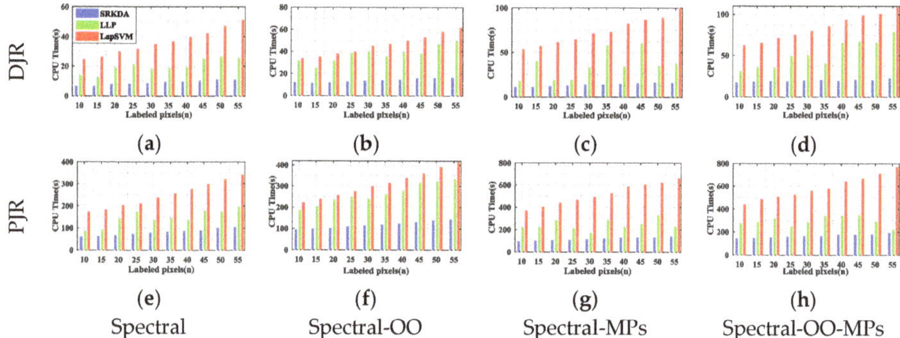

Figure 14. (a–h) CPU time versus the size of the labeled samples for SSMVCCAE-SRKDA/-LLP/-LapSVM for the Indian Pines data.

Summing the results presented in this section, it can be concluded that the novel proposed semi-supervised heterogeneous DA approach works properly and achieves satisfactory results better than the current state-of-the-art techniques when using a PJR view generation technique either with majority voting or with canonical correlation coefficient voting. A comparison of the results by SSMVCCAE with those by LLP and LapSVM shows that the performance of SRKDA is superior for both classification accuracy and computational efficiency. Finally, the computational burden caused by the sizes of the labeled samples and feature dimensionality is much smaller for SSMVCCAE with SRKDA, whereas it increases linearly with the sample size when using the other techniques.

6. Conclusions

In this paper, we have presented the implementation details, analyzed the parameter sensitivity, and proposed a comprehensive validation of two versions of an ensemble classifier that is suitable for heterogeneous DA and based on multiple view CCA. The main idea is to overcome the limitations of SVCCA by incorporating multi view CCA into EL. Superior results have been proven using two high dimensional (hyperspectral) images, the ROSIS Pavia University and the AVIRIS Indian Pine datasets, as high dimensional target domains, with synthetic low dimensional (multispectral) images as associated SDs. The best classification results were always obtained by jointly considering the original spectral features stacked with object-oriented features assigned to segmentation results, and the morphological profiles, which were subdivided into multiple views using the PJR view generation technique.

To further mitigate the marginal and/or conditional distribution gap between the source and the target domains, when few or even no labeled samples are available from the target domain, we propose a semi-supervised version of the same approach via training multiple speed-up SRKDA.

For new research directions, we are considering more complex problems, such as single SD vs. multiple TDs, as well as multiple SDs vs. multiple TDs supervised and semi-supervised adaptation techniques.

Acknowledgments: This work was partially supported by the Project funded by China Postdoctoral Science Foundation (2016M592872), the Xinjiang Uyghur Autonomous Region High Level Talents Introduction Project (Y648031) and the National Natural Science Foundation of China (No. 41601440, No. 41601354, and No. 41471098).

Author Contributions: Alim Samat developed the algorithms, executed all of the experiments, finished the original manuscript and the subsequent revisions, and provided part of the funding. Claudio Persello and Paolo Gamba offered valuable suggestions and comments, and carefully revised the original manuscript and its revisions. Jilili Abuduwaili provided part of the funding. Sicong Liu and Erzhu Li, contributed to revising of the manuscript.

Conflicts of Interest: The authors declare no conflict of interest.

References

1. Olofsson, P.; Foody, G.M.; Herold, M.; Stehman, S.V.; Woodcock, C.E.; Wulder, M.A. Good practices for estimating area and assessing accuracy of land change. *Remote Sens. Environ.* **2014**, *148*, 42–57. [CrossRef]
2. Curlander, J.C. Location of spaceborne SAR imagery. *IEEE Trans. Geosci. Remote Sens.* **1982**, *3*, 359–364. [CrossRef]
3. Bruzzone, L.; Cossu, R. A multiple-cascade-classifier system for a robust and partially unsupervised updating of land-cover maps. *IEEE Trans. Geosci. Remote Sens.* **2002**, *40*, 1984–1996. [CrossRef]
4. Torralba, A.; Efros, A.A. Unbiased Look at Dataset Bias. In Proceedings of the IEEE Conference on Computer Vision and Pattern Recognition, Colorado Springs, CO, USA, 20–25 June 2011; pp. 1521–1528.
5. Khosla, A.; Zhou, T.; Malisiewicz, T.; Efros, A.A.; Torralba, A. Undoing the Damage of Dataset Bias. In Proceedings of the IEEE Conference on Computer Vision and Pattern Recognition, Providence, RI, USA, 20–25 June 2012; Springer: Berlin/Heidelberg, Germany, 2012; pp. 158–171.
6. Schott, J.R.; Salvaggio, C.; Volchok, W.J. Radiometric scene normalization using pseudoinvariant features. *Remote Sens. Environ.* **1988**, *26*, 1–16. [CrossRef]
7. Woodcock, C.E.; Macomber, S.A.; Pax-Lenney, M.; Cohen, W.B. Monitoring large areas for forest change using Landsat: Generalization across space, time and Landsat sensors. *Remote Sens. Environ.* **2001**, *78*, 194–203. [CrossRef]
8. Olthof, I.; Butson, C.; Fraser, R. Signature extension through space for northern landcover classification: A comparison of radiometric correction methods. *Remote Sens. Environ.* **2005**, *95*, 290–302. [CrossRef]
9. Rakwatin, P.; Takeuchi, W.; Yasuoka, Y. Stripe noise reduction in MODIS data by combining histogram matching with facet filter. *IEEE Trans. Geosci. Remote Sens.* **2007**, *45*, 1844–1856. [CrossRef]
10. Inamdar, S.; Bovolo, F.; Bruzzone, L.; Chaudhuri, S. Multidimensional probability density function matching for preprocessing of multitemporal remote sensing images. *IEEE Trans. Geosci. Remote Sens.* **2008**, *46*, 1243–1252. [CrossRef]
11. Bruzzone, L.; Marconcini, M. Domain adaptation problems: A DASVM classification technique and a circular validation strategy. *IEEE Trans. Pattern Anal. Mach. Intell.* **2010**, *32*, 770–787. [CrossRef] [PubMed]
12. Pan, S.J.; Yang, Q. A survey on transfer learning. *IEEE Trans. Knowl. Data Eng.* **2010**, *22*, 1345–1359. [CrossRef]

13. Banerjee, B.; Bovolo, F.; Bhattacharya, A.; Bruzzone, L.; Chaudhuri, S.; Buddhiraju, K.M. A Novel Graph-Matching-Based Approach for Domain Adaptation in Classification of Remote Sensing Image Pair. *IEEE Trans. Geosci. Remote Sens.* **2015**, *53*, 4045–4062. [CrossRef]

14. Matasci, G.; Volpi, M.; Kanevski, M.; Bruzzone, L.; Tuia, D. Semisupervised Transfer Component Analysis for Domain Adaptation in Remote Sensing Image Classification. *IEEE Trans. Geosci. Remote Sens.* **2015**, *53*, 3550–3564. [CrossRef]

15. Tuia, D.; Persello, C.; Bruzzone, L. Domain Adaptation for the Classification of Remote Sensing Data: An Overview of Recent Advances. *IEEE Geosci. Remote Sens. Mag.* **2016**, *4*, 41–57. [CrossRef]

16. Samat, A.; Gamba, P.; Abuduwaili, J.; Liu, S.; Miao, Z. Geodesic Flow Kernel Support Vector Machine for Hyperspectral Image Classification by Unsupervised Subspace Feature Transfer. *Remote Sens.* **2016**, *8*, 234. [CrossRef]

17. Daumé, H., III; Kumar, A.; Saha, A. Frustratingly Easy Semi-Supervised Domain Adaptation. In Proceedings of the 2010 Workshop on Domain Adaptation Natural Language Processing, Uppsala, Sweden, 15 July 2010; pp. 53–59.

18. Li, W.; Duan, L.; Xu, D.; Tsang, I.W. Learning with augmented features for supervised and semi-supervised heterogeneous domain adaptation. *IEEE Trans. Pattern Anal. Mach. Intell.* **2014**, *36*, 1134–1148. [CrossRef] [PubMed]

19. Patel, V.M.; Gopalan, R.; Li, R.; Chellappa, R. Visual domain adaptation: A survey of recent advances. *IEEE Sign. Process. Mag.* **2015**, *32*, 53–69. [CrossRef]

20. Gao, J.; Fan, W.; Jiang, J.; Han, J. Knowledge Transfer via Multiple Model Local Structure Mapping. In Proceedings of the 14th ACM SIGKDD International Conference on Knowledge Discovery and Data Mining, Las Vegas, NV, USA, 24–27 August 2008; pp. 283–291.

21. Jiang, J.; Zhai, C. Instance Weighting for Domain Adaptation in NLP. In Proceedings of the ACL, Prague, Czech Republic, 23–30 June 2007; Volume 7, pp. 264–271.

22. Sugiyama, M.; Nakajima, S.; Kashima, H.; Buenau, P.V.; Kawanabe, M. Direct Importance Estimation with Model Selection and Its Application to Covariate Shift Adaptation. In *Advances in Neural Information Processing Systems*; Springer: Vancouver, BC, Canada, 2008; pp. 1433–1440.

23. Persello, C.; Bruzzone, L. Active learning for domain adaptation in the supervised classification of remote sensing images. *IEEE Trans. Geosci. Remote Sens.* **2012**, *50*, 4468–4483. [CrossRef]

24. Bruzzone, L.; Persello, C. A novel approach to the selection of spatially invariant features for the classification of hyperspectral images with improved generalization capability. *IEEE Trans. Geosci. Remote Sens.* **2009**, *47*, 3180–3191. [CrossRef]

25. Pan, S.J.; Kwok, J.T.; Yang, Q. Transfer Learning via Dimensionality Reduction. In Proceedings of the AAAI, 8, Stanford, CA, USA, 26–28 March 2008; pp. 677–682.

26. Long, M.; Wang, J.; Ding, G.; Pan, S.J.; Yu, P.S. Adaptation regularization: A general framework for transfer learning. *IEEE Trans. Knowl. Data Eng.* **2014**, *26*, 1076–1089. [CrossRef]

27. Pan, S.J.; Tsang, I.W.; Kwok, J.T.; Yang, Q. Domain adaptation via transfer component analysis. *IEEE Trans. Neural Netw.* **2011**, *22*, 199–210. [CrossRef] [PubMed]

28. Mihalkova, L.; Huynh, T.; Mooney, R.J. Mapping and Revising Markov Logic Networks for Transfer Learning. In Proceedings of the AAAI, 7, Vancouver, BC, Canada, 22–26 July 2007; pp. 608–614.

29. Yeh, Y.R.; Huang, C.H.; Wang, Y.C.F. Heterogeneous domain adaptation and classification by exploiting the correlation subspace. *IEEE Trans. Image Proc.* **2014**, *23*, 2009–2018.

30. Gopalan, R.; Li, R.; Chellappa, R. Domain Adaptation for Object Recognition: An Unsupervised Approach. In Proceedings of the IEEE International Conference on Computer Vision, Barcelona, Spain, 6–13 November 2011; pp. 999–1006.

31. Gopalan, R.; Li, R.; Chellappa, R. Unsupervised adaptation across domain shifts by generating intermediate data representations. *IEEE Trans. Pattern Anal. Mach. Intell.* **2014**, *6*, 2288–2302. [CrossRef] [PubMed]

32. Duan, L.; Xu, D.; Tsang, I.W. Domain adaptation from multiple sources: A domain-dependent regularization approach. *IEEE Trans. Neural Netw. Learn. Syst.* **2012**, *23*, 504–518. [CrossRef] [PubMed]

33. Wang, W.; Zhou, Z.H. A New Analysis of Co-Training. In Proceedings of the 27th International Conference on Machine Learning, (ICML-10) 2010, Haifa, Israel, 21–24 June 2010; pp. 1135–1142.

34. Di, W.; Crawford, M.M. View generation for multiview maximum disagreement based active learning for hyperspectral image classification. *IEEE Trans. Geosci. Remote Sens.* **2012**, *50*, 1942–1954. [CrossRef]

35. Sun, S. A survey of multi-view machine learning. *Neural Comput. Appl.* **2013**, *23*, 2031–2038. [CrossRef]
36. Kuncheva, L.I.; Rodríguez, J.J.; Plumpton, C.O.; Linden, D.E.; Johnston, S.J. Random subspace ensembles for fMRI classification. *IEEE Trans. Med. Imaging* **2010**, *29*, 531–542. [CrossRef] [PubMed]
37. Samat, A.; Du, P.; Liu, S.; Li, J. E2LMs: Ensemble extreme learning machines for hyperspectral image classification. *IEEE J. Sel. Top. Appl. Earth Obs. Remote Sens.* **2014**, *7*, 1060–1069. [CrossRef]
38. Hady, M.F.A.; Schwenker, F. Semi-Supervised Learning. In *Handbook on Neural Information Processing*; Springer: Berlin/Heidelberg, Germany, 2013; pp. 215–239.
39. Kulis, B.; Saenko, K.; Darrell, T. What you Saw Is not What you Get: Domain Adaptation Using Asymmetric Kernel Transforms. In Proceedings of the IEEE International Conference on Computer Vision and Pattern Recognition (CVPR), Colorado Springs, CO, USA, 20–25 June 2011; pp. 1785–1792.
40. Kumar, A.; Saha, A.; Daume, H. Co-regularization based semi-supervised domain adaptation. In *Advances in Neural Information Processing Systems 23 (NIPS 2010)*; Springer: Vancouver, BC, Canada, 2010; pp. 478–486.
41. Cai, D.; He, X.; Han, J. Speed up kernel discriminant analysis. *VLDB J. Int. J. Very Large Data Bases* **2011**, *20*, 21–33. [CrossRef]
42. Dai, W.; Chen, Y.; Xue, G.R.; Yang, Q.; Yu, Y. Translated learning: Transfer learning across different feature spaces. In *Advances in Neural Information Processing Systems*; Springer: Vancouver, BC, Canada, 2008; pp. 353–360.
43. Yang, Q.; Chen, Y.; Xue, G.R.; Dai, W.; Yu, Y. Heterogeneous Transfer Learning for Image Clustering via the Social Web. In Proceedings of the Joint Conference 47th Annual Meeting of the ACL and the 4th International Joint Conference Natural Language Process, AFNLP, Singapore, 2–7 August 2009; Volume 1, pp. 1–9.
44. Zhu, Y.; Chen, Y.; Lu, Z.; Pan, S.J.; Xue, G.R.; Yu, Y.; Yang, Q. Heterogeneous Transfer Learning for Image Classification. In Proceedings of the AAAI, San Francisco, CA, USA, 7–11 August 2011.
45. Evangelopoulos, N.; Zhang, X.; Prybutok, V.R. Latent semantic analysis: Five methodological recommendations. *Eur. J. Inf. Syst.* **2012**, *21*, 70–86. [CrossRef]
46. Hong, L. A Tutorial on Probabilistic Latent Semantic Analysis. Available online: https://arxiv.org/pdf/1212.3900.pdf (accessed on 21 December 2012).
47. Koltchinskii, V. Rademacher penalties and structural risk minimization. *IEEE Trans. Inf. Theory* **2001**, *47*, 1902–1914. [CrossRef]
48. Gong, B.; Shi, Y.; Sha, F.; Grauman, K. Geodesic Flow Kernel for Unsupervised Domain Adaptation. In Proceedings of the 2012 IEEE Conference Computer Vision and Pattern Recognition (CVPR), Providence, RI, USA, 16–21 June 2012; pp. 2066–2073.
49. Shi, X.; Liu, Q.; Fan, W.; Yu, P.S.; Zhu, R. Transfer Learning on Heterogenous Feature Spaces via Spectral Transformation. In Proceedings of the IEEE 10th International Conference on Data Mining, Sydney, Australia, 13–17 December 2010; pp. 1049–1054.
50. Zhou, J.T.; Tsang, I.W.; Pan, S.J.; Tan, M. Heterogeneous Domain Adaptation for Multiple Classes. In Proceedings of the AISTATS, Reykjavik, Iceland, 22–25 April 2014; pp. 1095–1103.
51. Hardoon, D.R.; Szedmak, S.; Shawe-Taylor, J. Canonical correlation analysis: An overview with application to learning methods. *Neural Comput.* **2004**, *16*, 2639–2664. [CrossRef] [PubMed]
52. Rokach, L. *Pattern Classification Using Ensemble Methods*; World Scientific Publishing Company: Singapore, 2010; Volume 75.
53. Xu, C.; Tao, D.; Xu, C. Multi-View Learning with Incomplete Views. *IEEE Trans. Image Proc.* **2015**, *24*, 5812–5825. [CrossRef] [PubMed]
54. Cai, D.; He, X.; Han, J. Spectral Regression: A Unified Subspace Learning Framework for Content-Based Image Retrieval. In Proceedings of the 15th International Conference on Multimedia, Augsburg, Germany, 24–29 September 2007; pp. 403–412.
55. Baudat, G.; Anouar, F. Generalized discriminant analysis using a kernel approach. *Neural Comput.* **2000**, *12*, 2385–2404. [CrossRef] [PubMed]
56. Vassilevich, D.V. Heat kernel expansion: User's manual. *Phys. Rep.* **2003**, *388*, 279–360. [CrossRef]
57. Vapnik, V.N. An overview of statistical learning theory. *IEEE Trans. Neural Netw.* **1999**, *10*, 988–999. [CrossRef] [PubMed]
58. Cai, D.; He, X.; Han, J. Document clustering using locality preserving indexing. *IEEE Trans. Knowl. Data Eng.* **2005**, *17*, 1624–1637. [CrossRef]

59. Subramanya, A.; Talukdar, P.P. Graph-based semi-supervised learning. *Synth. Lect. Arti. Intell. Mach. Learn.* **2014**, *8*, 1–125. [CrossRef]
60. Camps-Valls, G.; Marsheva, T.V.B.; Zhou, D. Semi-supervised graph-based hyperspectral image classification. *IEEE Trans. Geosci. Remote Sens.* **2007**, *45*, 3044–3054. [CrossRef]
61. Breiman, L. Random forests. *Mach. Learn.* **2001**, *45*, 5–32. [CrossRef]
62. Du, P.; Samat, A.; Waske, B.; Liu, S.; Li, Z. Random Forest and Rotation Forest for fully polarized SAR image classification using polarimetric and spatial features. *ISPRS J. Photogramm. Remote Sens.* **2015**, *105*, 38–53. [CrossRef]
63. Benediktsson, J.A.; Palmason, J.A.; Sveinsson, J.R. Classification of hyperspectral data from urban areas based on extended morphological profiles. *IEEE Trans. Geosci. Remote Sens.* **2005**, *43*, 480–491. [CrossRef]
64. Fauvel, M.; Benediktsson, J.A.; Chanussot, J.; Sveinsson, J.R. Spectral and spatial classification of hyperspectral data using SVMs and morphological profiles. *IEEE Trans. Geosci. Remote Sens.* **2008**, *46*, 3804–3814. [CrossRef]
65. Kobayashi, T.; Watanabe, K.; Otsu, N. Logistic label propagation. *Pattern Recognit. Lett.* **2012**, *33*, 580–588. [CrossRef]
66. Melacci, S.; Belkin, M. Laplacian support vector machines trained in the primal. *J. Mach. Learn. Res.* **2011**, *12*, 1149–1184.

Article

Refinement of Hyperspectral Image Classification with Segment-Tree Filtering

Lu Li [1,2], Chengyi Wang [1,*], Jingbo Chen [1] and Jianglin Ma [1]

[1] Institute of Remote Sensing and Digital Earth, Chinese Academy of Sciences, Datun Road North 20A, Beijing 100101, China; lilu@radi.ac.cn (L.L.); chenjb@radi.ac.cn (J.C.); majianglin2003@gmail.com (J.M.)

[2] The University of Chinese Academy of Sciences, Beijing 100049, China

[*] Correspondence: wangcycastle@163.com; Tel.: +86-170-9008-6991

Academic Editors: Qi Wang, Nicolas H. Younan, Carlos López-Martínez, Lenio Soares Galvao and Prasad S. Thenkabail

Received: 11 November 2016; Accepted: 9 January 2017; Published: 16 January 2017

Abstract: This paper proposes a novel method of segment-tree filtering to improve the classification accuracy of hyperspectral image (HSI). Segment-tree filtering is a versatile method that incorporates spatial information and has been widely applied in image preprocessing. However, to use this powerful framework in hyperspectral image classification, we must reduce the original feature dimensionality to avoid the Hughes problem; otherwise, the computational costs are high and the classification accuracy by original bands in the HSI is unsatisfactory. Therefore, feature extraction is adopted to produce new salient features. In this paper, the Semi-supervised Local Fisher (SELF) method of discriminant analysis is used to reduce HSI dimensionality. Then, a tree-structure filter that adaptively incorporates contextual information is constructed. Additionally, an initial classification map is generated using multi-class support vector machines (SVMs), and segment-tree filtering is conducted using this map. Finally, a simple Winner-Take-All (WTA) rule is applied to determine the class of each pixel in an HSI based on the maximum probability. The experimental results demonstrate that the proposed method can improve HSI classification accuracy significantly. Furthermore, a comparison between the proposed method and the current state-of-the-art methods, such as Extended Morphological Profiles (EMPs), Guided Filtering (GF), and Markov Random Fields (MRFs), suggests that our method is both competitive and robust.

Keywords: hyperspectral image classification; SELF; SVMs; Segment-Tree Filtering

1. Introduction

Hyperspectral image (HSI) classification is important for urban land use monitoring, crop growth monitoring, environmental assessment, etc. Various machine learning algorithms that process high-dimension data can be employed in pixel-wise classification, such as Support Vector Machines (SVMs) [1], Logistic Regression [2,3], Artificial Neural Networks (ANNs) [4], etc. However, these conventional approaches do not consider spatial HSI information between neighboring pixels, which can lead to noisy classification output. Including the spatial relationships between pixels can enhance the classification accuracy. For example, there is a high probability that a pixel shares the same class as its neighboring pixels if the similarity measure between them is high. Otherwise, if the similarity measure is low, this probability decreases. Therefore, HSI classification could be improved further by combining spatial and spectral features.

Many spatial-spectral methods have been proposed to incorporate spatial or contextual information. For example, spatial information was represented using Markov Random Fields (MRFs) in [5,6], and classification has been performed using α–Expansion [7] and Belief Propagation [8], which are commonly used max-flow/min-cut algorithms in MRF optimization. Another method is presented in [9], namely Extended Morphological Profiles (EMPs). After the first two principal components of the HSI are computed using the Principal Component Analysis (PCA) method, spatial features are extracted by morphological operations. Together with spectral information, they are concatenated for HSI classification. As morphological operations such as opening and closing involve neighboring pixel calculations, contextual information is naturally utilized in this manner. Another example of employing contextual information is via texture analysis. In [10], a Gray Level Co-occurrence Matrix (GLCM) is used to extract this type of contextual information, which is then employed to concatenate spectral features used for classification. In [11], segmentation is employed to represent spatial information based on a minimum spanning tree method, and majority voting is used to assign a class label to each region. Similar to [11], methods based on segmentation [12–15] have attracted increased attention because they produce satisfactory results. However, there are some drawbacks to algorithms based on hard segmentation. For example, they assume that all pixels in the same region are homogenous. After segmentation is completed, the relationship between pixels in different regions is fully disconnected; thus, if the segmentation is incorrect, the accuracy decreases dramatically. Although an over-segmentation approach is applied in [11,15] to improve the similarity in a region, the computational complexity increases considerably. Therefore, these algorithms are not efficient because of the complex voting processes in thousands of regions. In [16], super-pixel segmentation is applied to feature extraction and then classification is conducted in a novel framework via multiple kernels, which avoid voting but the super-pixel method still needs over-segmentation. To make classification more efficient, Edge-Aware Filtering and Edge-Preserving Filtering (EAF and EPF) methods [17,18] can be applied. These methods have been adopted successfully in many computer vision applications, such as stereo matching [19], optical flow [20], image fusion [21], etc. Unlike image segmentation, the most prominent merit of the EAF method is that in homogeneous image areas, EAFs can generate smooth output, while in inhomogeneous image areas, they can adaptively preserve boundaries, even in challenging situations. In this paper, we implement a tree-structure EAF for HSIs that is based on the segment-tree algorithm [22,23] and combines the advantages of segmentation and EAF. Unlike other EAF methods, the window size does not need to be set in this scheme. It is difficult to establish a proper window size for bilateral and guided filters [17], largely because objects of interest display the most prominent features at different scales. Another merit of this scheme is that the segment-tree filter is more efficient than other EAFs because of its tree structure [24]. By traversing the tree in two sequential passes, from the leaves to the root and from the root to the leaves, every pixel in HSI can be filtered and labeled.

However, the Segment-Tree Filter cannot be used for original HSI directly because the computational cost of this method is extremely high and the Hughes phenomenon always makes the classification accuracy unsatisfactory. The hyperspectral bands that are contaminated by noise may destroy the true connection between neighboring pixels. To avoid this problem, there are several literature that introduce how to choose the bands of original HSI [25,26] or produce new salient features. In this paper, the Semi-supervised Local Fisher (SELF) discriminant analysis method [27] is employed to reduce dimensionality. The SELF method of feature reduction is used because it retains prior knowledge from training sets and statistical distribution of clusters, unlike methods such as PCA, Linear Discriminant Analysis (LDA)/Fisher Discriminant Analysis (FDA) [28], and Local FDA (LFDA) [29]. In practice, the segmentation will be less sensitive to the number of training samples based on the SELF method. Additionally, we can construct the Segment-Tree Filter using a limited number of bands, which can reduce the computational cost of segmentation. Because the extracted SELF bands can reduce the effect of noise, a limited number of bands can well represent the inherent spatial structure of the image, which can lead to better output.

The remainder of this paper is organized as follows. In Section 1, we discuss some related methods and processes, including initial classification, SELF, Graph-based Segment-Tree Filter construction, and filtering. In Section 2, the proposed HSI classification scheme is described in detail. The experimental results are presented in Section 3. Finally, we draw our conclusions and present our outlooks for future research in Section 4.

2. HSI Classification Refinement Using Segment-Tree Filtering

A schematic diagram of the proposed method is shown in Figure 1.

1. Step 1: Construct the Segment-Tree Filter, which involves feature extraction using the SELF method followed by building a tree-structure filter for an HSI based on dimensionality reduction.
2. Step 2: Use a Multi-class SVM method to obtain the initial classification map.
3. Step 3: Perform Segment-Tree Filtering based on the Multi-class SVM, pixel-based initial classification map. By combining this initial classification map and the Segment-Tree Filter, we can incorporate spatial information and spectral features, adaptively. Finally, the HSI classification map can be derived from the result of Segment-Tree Filtering.

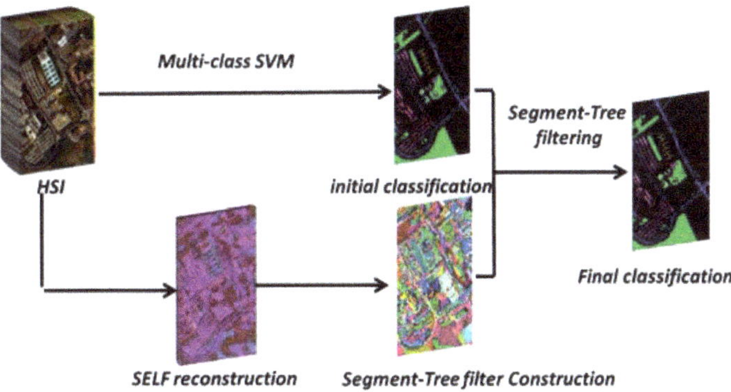

Figure 1. Workflow of Segment-Tree Filtering for HSI classification.

2.1. Initial Classification

In this paper, a Multi-class SVM classifier is adopted in the initial classification step. SVMs are widely used classifiers in remote sensing image classification. These supervised learning models are used for classification and regression in binary classification problems. In this paper, we utilize a Multi-class SVM from LIBSVM library with a radial basis function (RBF) kernel. In this method, a "one against one" strategy [30] is employed to extend the binary SVM to multi-class cases. The punishment parameter C and the spread of the kernel gamma are optimally determined by cross-validation.

In most cases, the output of the initial classification is a probability map, which can be represented as a tensor [18] as follows:

$$\{\mathbf{M}_p^k \mid p(i,j); i = 1, 2, \ldots, H; j = 1, 2, \ldots, W; k = 1, 2, \ldots, S\} \tag{1}$$

where (i, j) is the position of sample p in the image; H and W are the height and width of the image, respectively; k is the label of the sample; S is the total number of classes in the classification; and $\mathbf{M}_p^k$ is the probability that the sample p belongs to the kth class. Based on the Multi-class SVM classifier, $\mathbf{M}_p^k$ is either 0 or 1 depending on whether the sample belongs to the kth class.

$$\mathbf{M}_p^k = \begin{cases} 1 \; if & class(p) = k \\ 0 & otherwise \end{cases} \tag{2}$$

2.2. Semi-Supervised Local Fisher Discriminant Analysis

In this section, we review SELF briefly. The SELF method seeks an embedding transformation such that the local, between-class scatter is maximized and the local, within-class scatter is minimized in both the training and test sets. We assume that HSI $\mathbf{X}$ has m hyperspectral bands and n samples, and the training set $\mathbf{X}'$ has n' samples. Then, the test set has $n - n'$ samples. There are three pre-defined input parameters: the trade-off parameter β, the dimensionality of the reconstruction space r, and the KNN parameter K. The five steps in this process are as follows:

1. Local scaling coefficient σ_i is pre-computed for each sample in the training set, which is equal to the Euclidean distance between the sample x_i and its Kth nearest neighbor x_i^K among all samples in both the training and test sets.

$$\sigma_i = \|x_i - x_i^K\| \tag{3}$$

2. Local between-class weight matrix $\mathbf{W}^{lb}$ and local within-class weight matrix $\mathbf{W}^{lw}$ are computed as Equations (4) and (5), respectively. In this step, if two samples have the same label in the training set, σ_i is used to scale the local geometric structure with heat kernel weighting.

$$\mathbf{W}_{i,j}^{lb} = \begin{cases} (\frac{1}{n'} - \frac{1}{n'_{y_i}}) \exp(\frac{-\|x_i - x_j\|^2}{\sigma_i \sigma_j}) & if \quad y_i = y_j \\ \frac{1}{n'} & otherwise \end{cases} \tag{4}$$

$$\mathbf{W}_{i,j}^{lw} = \begin{cases} \frac{1}{n'_{y_i}} \exp(\frac{-\|x_i - x_j\|^2}{\sigma_i \sigma_j}) & if \quad y_i = y_j \\ 0 & otherwise \end{cases} \tag{5}$$

3. The local between-class scatter matrix $\mathbf{S}^{lb}$ and local, within-class scatter matrix $\mathbf{S}^{lw}$ are calculated by Equations (6) and (7):

$$\mathbf{S}^{lb} = \mathbf{X}'\{diag(\mathbf{W}^{lb}\mathbf{1}_{n'})\}\mathbf{X}'^T; \tag{6}$$

$$\mathbf{S}^{lw} = \mathbf{X}'\{diag(\mathbf{W}^{lw}\mathbf{1}_{n'})\}\mathbf{X}'^T; \tag{7}$$

Note that $\mathbf{1}_{n'}$ is a unit column vector of size $n' \times 1$. Steps 1–3 are the same as those used in the LFDA procedure. In our procedure, only samples in the training set have been used at this point, and the statistical distribution of clusters has not been assessed or applied.

4. The covariance matrix $\mathbf{S}^t$ is computed based on all samples in both the training and test sets as below:

$$\mathbf{S}^t = \frac{\sum_{i=1}^{n} (x_i - \bar{x})(x_i - \bar{x})^T}{n}; \tag{8}$$

where $\bar{x}$ is the mean of all samples. Then, the regularized, local, between-class scatter matrix $\mathbf{S}^{rlb}$ and the regularized, local, within-class scatter matrix $\mathbf{S}^{rlw}$ are derived by Equations (9) and (10), respectively.

$$\mathbf{S}^{rlb} = (1 - \beta)\mathbf{S}^{lb} + \beta\,\mathbf{S}^t; \tag{9}$$

$$\mathbf{S}^{rlw} = (1 - \beta)\mathbf{S}^{lw} + \beta\,\mathbf{I}_m; \tag{10}$$

β is the trade-off parameter based on prior knowledge from the training set and the statistical distribution of clusters. Therefore, SELF maintains the advantages of LFDA and PCA. Note that $\mathbf{I}_m$ is an $m \times m$ identity matrix.

5. Transformation matrix $\mathbf{T}$ can be computed based on generalized eigenvalue decomposition. $\mathbf{T}$ consists of weighted eigenvectors corresponding to the r largest eigenvalues. After $\mathbf{T}$ is determined, all the pixels in the HSI can be reprojected to a new low-dimensional space.

The parameter β plays an important role in the algorithm. When it is relatively small (e.g., $\beta = 0.01$), SELF is nearly identical to LFDA, and SELF becomes increasingly similar to PCA when β approaches 1. β balances prior knowledge regarding the labels in the training set and the statistical distribution of clusters in the test set. In our experiment, we set β to 0.6, as we found that this value fully utilizes the advantages of the algorithm.

As a Semi-Supervised Learning (SSL) method, SELF can adapt based on the number of training samples. When the number of samples in a training set is small and prior knowledge about labels is limited and/or noisy, SELF can use the statistical distribution of clusters in the test set to offset these issues. We demonstrate this advantage in Figures 2 and 3. Figure 2 illustrates the reconstructed image of the Indian Pines dataset using PCA, LDA, LFDA, and SELF when the training samples accounted for only 1% of all samples. Figure 3 shows the same reconstructed image when the training percentage increases to 20%. In both figures, the color images (R, G, and B) are composed of the first three bands extracted using the corresponding feature-transformation methods. In Figure 2a, because the reconstruction based on LDA only relies on a small number of training set samples, the image exhibits considerable noise and error. When the number of training samples increases, LDA reconstruction is improved (e.g., there are fewer fractions and more homogenous areas in Figure 3a than in Figure 2a). Additionally, LFDA is more robust than LDA, even if the number of training samples is limited. However, as the number of samples increases, numerous false edges and fractions can be observed in the reconstructed image based on LFDA, as shown in Figures 2b and 3b. The boundary of the purple trapezoid in the bottom-left portion of Figure 2b was correctly extracted; however, it was incorrectly extracted in Figure 3b. As shown in Figures 2d and 3d (see the red rectangular region), SELF is robust regardless of the number of samples in the training set. Conversely, PCA does not depend on the training set; therefore, Figures 2c and 3c display the same reconstruction result. However, the comparison between PCA and SELF in the rectangular region in Figure 3d shows that PCA creates more segments and fractions because it aligns the boundaries of objects rather than classes, which causes more errors in subsequent processing steps compared to using SELF. In our experiment, the best reconstructed images based on SELF had 10 bands. Thus, the spectral dimension of the original HSI was dramatically reduced, but the most discriminatory information within the spectral bands was retained.

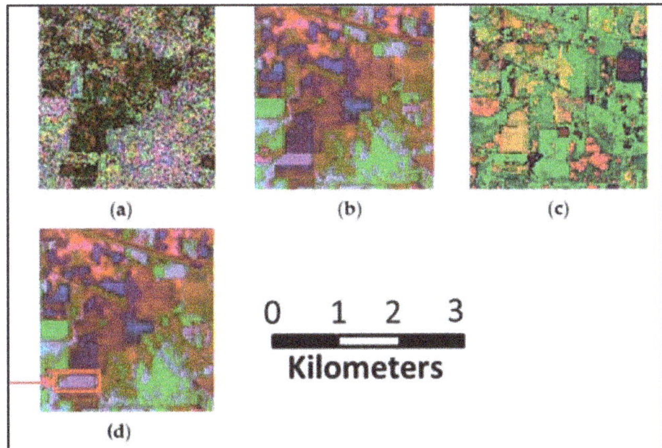

Figure 2. Indian Pines reconstructed using different methods of dimensional reduction: (**a**) LDA; (**b**) LFDA; (**c**) PCA; (**d**) SELF. The number of samples in the training set accounts for only 1% of all samples.

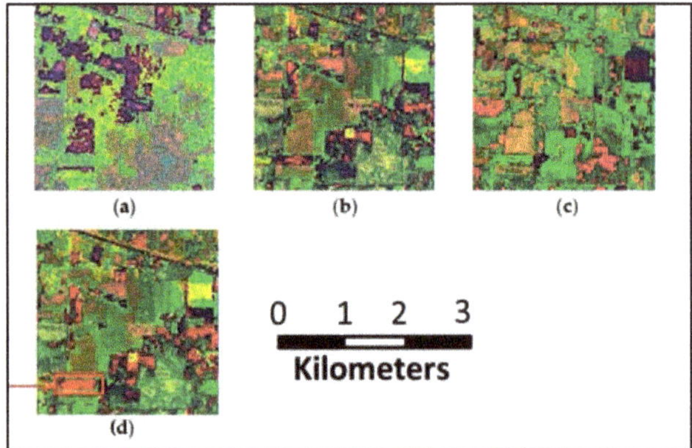

Figure 3. Indian Pines reconstructed using different methods of dimensional reduction: (**a**) LDA; (**b**) LFDA; (**c**) PCA; (**d**) SELF. The number of samples in the training set accounts for 20% of all samples.

2.3. Segment-Tree Filter Construction

The image transformed using SELF is used as input for the graph-based Segment-Tree Filter. The implementation of Segment-Tree Filtering is based on the methodology presented in [22,23], which use the Kruskal algorithm to construct a Minimum Spanning Tree (MST). The general workflow is summarized as follows. First, a graph $G = \{V, E\}$ is constructed for an image ($m \times n$ pixels), where V represents the vertices and each pixel is a vertex. E represents an edge that links four neighbors, and there are $m(n-1) + n(m-1)$ edges in total. A weight w_e is assigned for each edge E to represent the dissimilarity between the linked vertices. Several dissimilarity measures, such as the L1-norm, L2-norm, L∞-norm, and Spectral Angle Mapper (SAM), have been proposed in the literature [11]. In our experiment, SAM is used as the dissimilarity measure.

1. All the edges are sorted in ascending order according to their weights. This step can be performed efficiently using a quicksort algorithm [31], even if the number of edges is very large.
2. For each vertex, we initialize a tree $T_i(V_i, E_i)$.
3. A subtree is then built for each segment. Then, subtrees are merged based on the order of sorted edges. Segment-Tree Filtering is a variant of the conventional MST approach that considers an extra criterion to merge trees [22,32], as shown in Equation (11):

$$w_e \leq \min(\max(w_{Tp}) + \frac{k}{|Tp|}, \max(w_{Tq}) + \frac{k}{|Tq|}) \tag{11}$$

where w_e is the weight of the edge between subtrees T_p and T_q, $|T_p|$ is the number of vertices in the subtree T_p, and k is a constant. In our experiments, k is set to five times the standard deviation of all weights in the graph. If criterion (3) is satisfied, subtrees T_p and T_q are merged. Criterion (3) establishes a trade-off between the edge weights and the numbers of pixels in the subtrees. Initially, merging subtrees is easy because the number of pixels in each subtree is small. As the number of pixels increases, the criterion becomes increasingly rigorous; therefore, it is adaptive.

4. All the remaining edges that are not part of any subtree are sorted again. If the number of vertices in a subtree is smaller than a threshold T_0, then the subtrees should be merged. In our experiment, $T_0 = 6$. This processing step is based on the improvement presented in [23] to omit small fractions caused by noise. The obtained subtrees are illustrated in Figure 4, in which each color represents an obtained subtree. As shown, constructed subtrees can be used to segment HSIs adaptively.

5. Finally, subtrees are merged until all vertices are included in the trees. For each tree, all the connected vertices exhibit the highest similarity and are within the shortest possible distance. As shown in Figure 5b, the edges of the final tree minimally cross the boundaries between two regions.

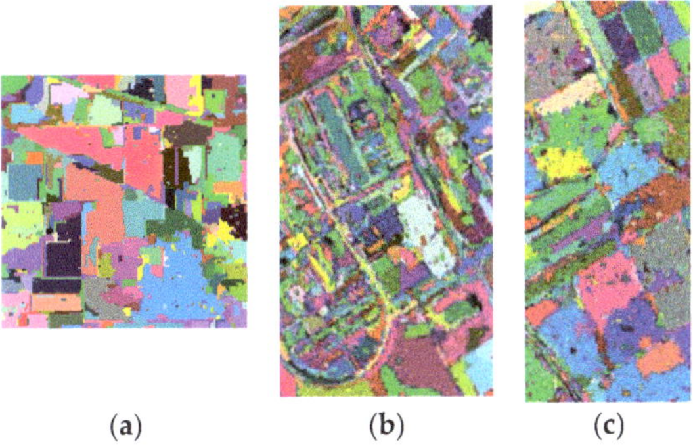

(a)   **(b)**   **(c)**

Figure 4. Subtrees constructed for different standard benchmarks: (**a**) Indian Pines; (**b**) University of Pavia; (**c**) Salinas. Each color segment represents a subtree.

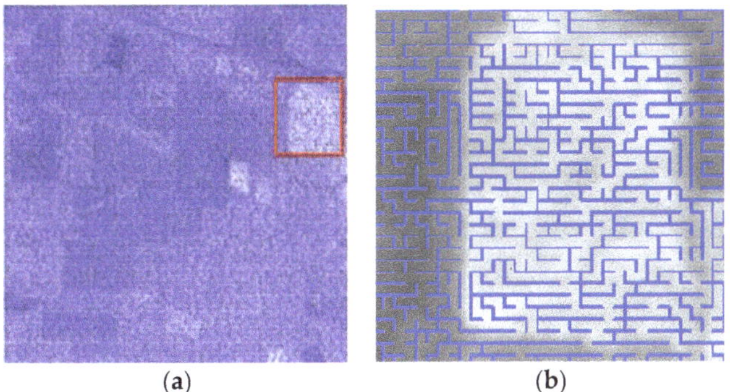

(a)   **(b)**

Figure 5. Tree structure of the Segment-Tree Filter for the Indian Pines dataset: (**a**) Image of the segment tree; (**b**) Close-up of the red rectangular region in (**a**).

2.4. Segment-Tree Filtering

The final step is to filter the initial probability maps using the tree-structure filter. The objective of the filtering process is to compute the aggregated probabilities. In the proposed approach, all vertices contribute to the aggregated probabilities, unlike using local neighbor methods. The non-local, aggregated probabilities $\overline{\mathbf{M}}_p^d$ can be defined as follows:

$$\overline{\mathbf{M}}_p^d = \sum_{q \in I} S(p,q)\mathbf{M}_q^d \tag{12}$$

where $\mathbf{M}_q^d$ is defined in Equation (1). $S(p,q)$ is a weighting function that denotes the weight contribution of pixel q to p:

$$S(p,q) = \exp(-\sum_{i \in path(p,q)} w_{ei}/\gamma) \tag{13}$$

where w_{ei} is the weight of an edge in the tree structure connecting p and q and γ is a constant parameter.

Due to the tree structure, all the aggregated probabilities of class d in the image can be computed efficiently through traversing the tree in two sequential passes. In the first pass, forward filtering occurs from the leaf pixels to the root:

$$\mathbf{M}_p^{d\uparrow} = \mathbf{M}_p^d + \sum_{q \in c(p)} S(p,q)\mathbf{M}_q^{d\uparrow} \tag{14}$$

where $c(p)$ represents all the children of vertex $c(p)$. In the second pass, backward filtering occurs from the root to the leaf pixels:

$$\overline{\mathbf{M}}_p^d = S(pa(p),p)\overline{\mathbf{M}}_{pa(p)}^d + (1 - S^2(pa(p),p))\mathbf{M}_q^{d\uparrow} \tag{15}$$

where $pa(p)$ represents the parent of vertex p.

As Figure 6 shows, vertex V_4 aggregates the probabilities of V_5, V_6, V_7, and itself during the forward filtering step using Equation (16). During the backward filtering step, the probabilities of V_1, V_2, and V_3 contribute to V_4 based on Equation (17). After only two filtering steps, the aggregated probabilities of all vertices are computed, which reflects an extremely low computational complexity. Finally, the classification map is obtained using a simple Winner-Take-All (WTA) rule.

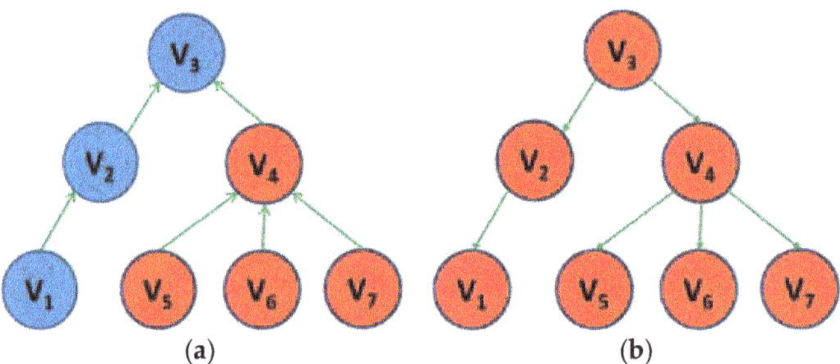

Figure 6. Segment-Tree Filtering in two sequential passes: (**a**) Forward filtering from the leaves to root; (**b**) Backward filtering from the root to leaves.

3. Experiments and Results

The proposed method has been implemented in C++ with the OpenCV library and Lapack library. The implemented code is available by contracting author. Evaluations were performed using three hyperspectral benchmark datasets as below:

1. The first HSI is a 2×2 mile portion of agricultural area over the Indian Pines region in Northwest Indiana, which was acquired by NASA's Airborne Visible/Infrared Imaging Spectrometer (AVIRIS) sensor. This scene with a size of 145×145 pixels, comprises 202 spectral bands in the wavelength range from 0.4 to $2.5\mu m$, with spatial resolution of 20 m. The ground truth of scene (see Figure 7a) contains 16 classes of interest and total 10,366 samples. Due to the imbalanced number of available labeled pixels and a large number of mixed pixels per class, this dataset creates a challenge in HSI classification.

2. The second HSI is a 103-band image acquired by Reflective Optics Spectrographic Image System (ROSIS-03) sensor over the urban area of the University of Pavia, Italy. The spatial resolution is 1.3 m and the scene contains 610×340 pixels and nine classes. The number of samples is 42,776 in total. The ground truth of the scene is shown in Figure 8a.

3. The third HSI is also derived by AVIRIS sensor over Salinas Valley, California. This scene with a size of 512×217 pixels, and 204 spectral bands is used for classification. There are 16 classes in the ground truth image, which is shown in Figure 9a.

The overall accuracy (OA), average accuracy (AA), Kappa coefficient, and producer accuracy (PA) are used to assess the classification accuracy.

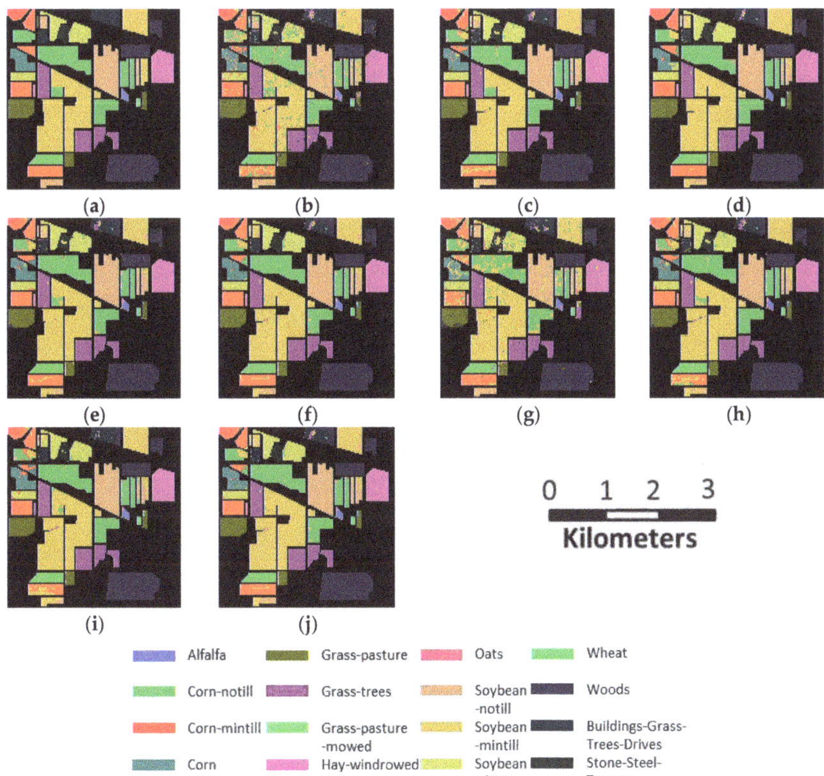

Figure 7. Classification results for Indian Pines: (**a**) Actual values; (**b**) Multi-class SVM; (**c**) ST; (**d**) PCA + ST; (**e**) LDA + ST; (**f**) LFDA + ST; (**g**) EMPs; (**h**) SVM + MRF; (**i**) PCA + GF ([18]); (**j**) The proposed method; (**d–f**) combine different dimensionality reduction methods (before "+") with Segment-Tree Filtering (after "+"); (**g–i**) are other methods of spatial-spectral classification for HSIs.

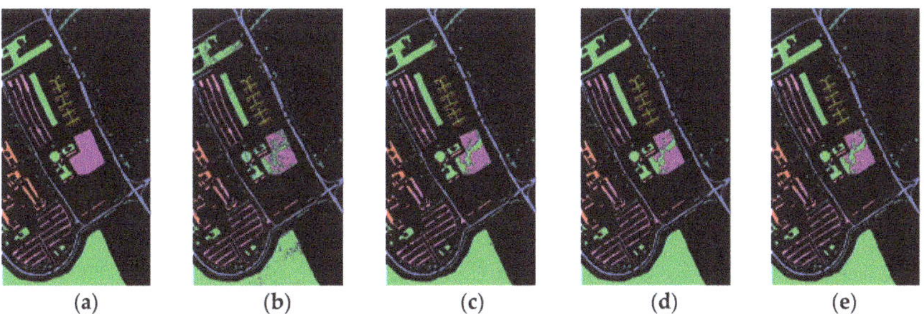

Figure 8. *Cont.*

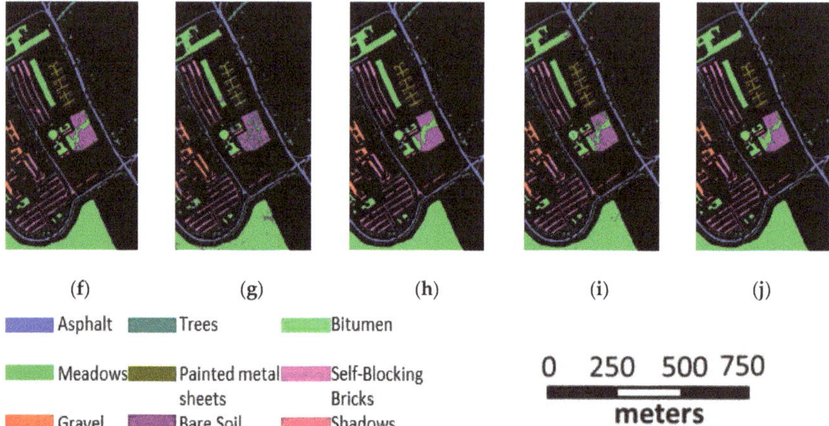

Figure 8. Classification results for Pavia University: (**a**) Actual values; (**b**) Multi-class SVM; (**c**) ST; (**d**) PCA + ST; (**e**) LDA + ST; (**f**) LFDA +ST; (**g**) EMPs; (**h**) SVM + MRF; (**i**) PCA + GF ([18]); (**j**) The proposed method. (**d–f**) combine different dimensionality reduction methods (before "+") with Segment-Tree Filtering (after "+"); (**g–i**) are other methods of spatial-spectral classification for HSIs.

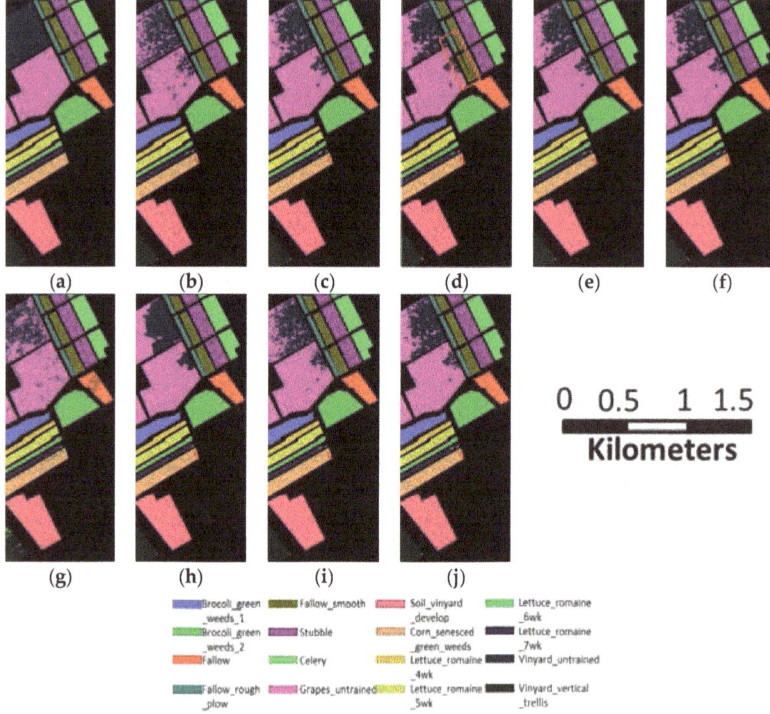

Figure 9. Classification results for Salinas; (**a**) Actual values; (**b**) Multi-class SVM; (**c**) ST; (**d**) PCA + ST; (**e**) LDA + ST; (**f**) LFDA + ST; (**g**) EMPs; (**h**) SVM + MRF; (**i**) PCA + GF ([18]); (**j**) The proposed method; (**d–f**) combine different dimensionality reduction methods (before "+") with Segment-Tree Filtering (after "+"); (**g–i**) are other methods of spatial-spectral classification for HSIs.

3.1. Influence of Different Parameters

Some parameters in our proposed method may affect the classification accuracy, such as β, K, and r. Therefore, the Indian Pines dataset is used to test the importance of these parameters to the classification. In this case, the training samples account for 15% of all samples, regardless of their class. When one of the parameters is measured, the other parameters are fixed. Five-fold cross validation is used to tune all parameters. The influences of β, K, and r on the classification accuracy are shown in Figures 10–12, respectively. The influences of β and r are less than 1%, while the influence of K is greater than 1%. Figures 10–12 illustrate that the classification accuracy is the most sensitive to the influence of parameter K. Different dissimilarity measures are adopted during graph-based Segment-Tree Filter construction in our experiments, including the Minkowski distance (from 1 to 6 and infinity) and SAM, as shown in Figure 13. All the parameters affect the classification accuracy by approximately 1% to 2%, and the SAM dissimilarity measure was the largest in our Segment-Tree Filtering approach.

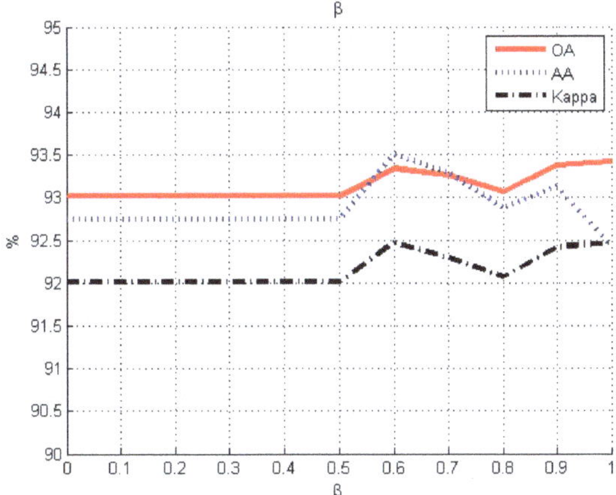

Figure 10. Influence of parameter β on the classification accuracy.

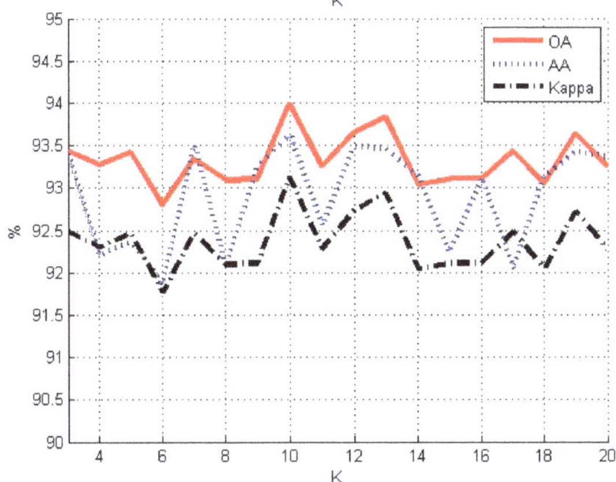

Figure 11. Influence of parameter K on the classification accuracy.

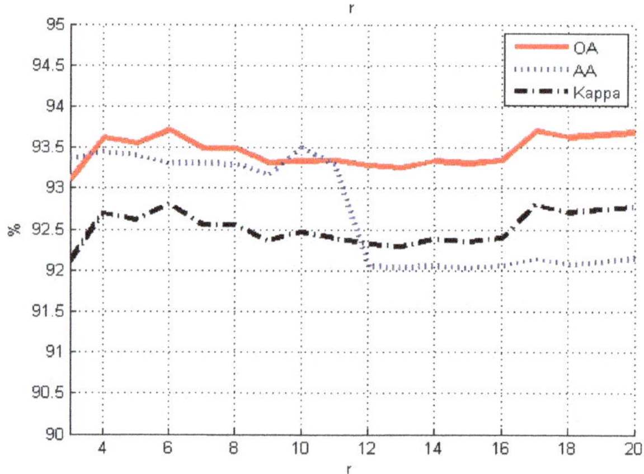

Figure 12. Influence of parameter *r* on the classification accuracy.

Figure 13. Influences of different dissimilarity measures on the classification accuracy.

3.2. Classification Accuracy Analysis

In this experiment, the training samples account for 15% of all the available samples, regardless of their class. The parameter settings are summarized as follows. In the initial classification step, the parameters were based on observed values, as discussed in Section 2.1. In the SELF transformation step, $\beta = 0.6$, $K = 7$, and $r = 10$. In the graph-based Segment-Tree construction step, SAM is used as the dissimilarity measure, and in the Segment-Tree Filtering step, γ is set as three times the standard deviation of w_e.

All experiments would be repeated five times according to different sampling training-set. The average of the five classification accuracies is recorded. The results of our proposed method based on analyses of the Indian Pines, University of Pavia, and Salinas datasets are shown in Tables 1–3, respectively. The visual results of the initial classification of each HSI are shown in Figure 7b, Figure 8b, and Figure 9b, respectively. Although SVMs are powerful classifiers, the results of the initial classification based solely on spectral features contain substantial noise. However, our proposed method greatly improves the classification accuracy after Segment-Tree Filtering, as shown in Figure 7j, Figure 8j, and Figure 9j. The OA increases by 8.56% for the Indian Pines dataset, 4.64% for the Pavia University dataset, and 1.22% for the Salinas dataset. The largest PA increase is 32.60% for the Indian Pines dataset, followed by 22.71% for the Pavia University dataset and 3.41% for the Salinas dataset.

Table 1. Number of training and test samples from the Indian Pines dataset and the classification accuracies (in percentages) of different methods (the bolded item in each line means the best accuracy).

Class	Training/Test	SVM	ST	PCA + ST	LDA + ST	LFDA + ST	EMP	SVM + MRF	PCA + GF	Proposal
Alfalfa	7/46	58.70	71.74	**91.30**	76.09	82.61	82.61	83.30	80.43	**91.30**
Corn-N	214/1428	81.65	**92.86**	89.22	90.68	89.64	71.57	88.51	89.29	92.37
Corn-M	125/830	75.90	83.25	96.51	91.81	92.65	76.99	80.84	81.20	**92.16**
Corn	36/237	64.56	85.23	76.79	91.56	**93.67**	62.87	87.34	89.87	88.61
Grass-Pa	73/483	89.23	90.89	92.75	91.10	92.13	78.05	91.72	93.17	**93.37**
GrassT	109/730	96.99	**99.73**	99.45	99.59	99.45	98.36	99.18	100	**99.73**
GrassP	5/28	89.29	96.43	92.85	**100**	96.42	89.29	96.43	96.43	96.43
Hay-W	72/478	98.74	99.79	**100**	**100**	**100**	98.95	**100**	**100**	**100**
Oats	5/20	75.00	**100**	**100**	90.00	**100**	90.00	0.00	0.00	**100**
Soy-N	146/972	82.10	**89.20**	86.31	88.17	88.16	84.77	87.14	84.26	88.17
Soy-M	368/2455	85.62	**94.70**	95.62	95.11	94.50	93.40	94.87	95.52	94.58
Soy-C	89/593	74.20	94.77	**99.66**	96.46	97.64	71.16	93.76	95.45	97.98
Wheat	31/205	96.59	99.51	99.51	99.51	99.51	97.56	99.51	**100**	99.51
Woods	190/1265	95.42	97.23	98.50	97.94	98.26	98.26	96.60	**98.66**	98.10
Building	58/386	61.14	59.07	60.62	58.55	60.33	**85.23**	62.79	76.42	64.88
Stone-ST	14/93	87.10	87.10	**98.92**	87.10	**98.92**	60.22	88.17	94.62	**98.92**
OA		84.78	92.11	93.32	92.83	93.01	70.48	91.22	92.20	**93.34**
AA		82.01	90.09	92.44	90.85	92.74	67.26	89.07	85.96	**93.50**
Kappa		82.60	90.97	**92.47**	91.80	92.00	67.28	90.11	91.08	**92.47**

Table 2. Number of training and test samples from the Pavia University dataset and the classification accuracies (in percentages) of different methods (the bolded item in each line means the best accuracy).

Class	Training/Test	SVM	ST	PCA + ST	LDA + ST	LFDA + ST	EMP	SVM + MRF	PCA + GF	Proposal
Asphalt	995/6631	93.03	96.95	95.97	96.03	95.99	93.53	**97.10**	96.44	96.67
Meadows	2797/18,649	95.06	99.33	99.88	99.81	99.88	95.69	**100**	99.18	99.79
Gravel	315/2099	66.32	72.46	71.46	72.74	71.46	76.13	69.03	**73.80**	71.08
Trees	460/3064	93.05	94.65	94.39	94.09	94.45	98.63	90.31	**97.03**	93.79
P-M-S	202/1345	99.70	99.55	99.78	99.63	99.78	84.31	**100**	**100**	99.70
Bare Soil	754/5029	66.65	70.33	71.01	70.01	71.12	76.89	70.87	68.50	**71.30**
Bitumen	200/1330	77.21	96.99	97.07	95.78	97.74	84.81	83.38	97.22	**99.92**
Self-B B	552/3682	91.55	98.37	97.99	98.09	97.83	89.19	98.29	99.76	**98.80**
Shadows	142/947	100	98.94	96.09	91.12	96.09	77.82	98.10	**100**	98.32
OA		89.25	93.74	93.76	93.51	93.78	90.75	93.21	93.78	**93.89**
AA		86.95	91.95	91.52	90.81	91.59	86.34	89.68	**92.43**	92.15
Kappa		85.60	91.58	91.59	91.26	91.62	87.72	90.82	91.62	**91.77**

Table 3. Number of training and test samples from the Salinas dataset and the classification accuracies (in percentages) of different methods (the bolded item in each line means the best accuracy).

Class	Training/Test	SVM	ST	PCA + ST	LDA + ST	LFDA + ST	EMP	SVM + MRF	PCA + GF	Proposal
g_w_1	301/2009	98.80	**100**	**100**	**100**	**100**	98.95	**100**	99.80	**100**
g_w_2	491/3276	99.97	**100**	99.97	**100**	99.97	99.68	**100**	99.97	99.97
Fallow	296/1976	98.68	**100**	**100**	99.75	**100**	90.13	**100**	99.89	**100**
Fallow_r_p	209/1394	99.35	98.21	60.04	99.50	98.92	99.14	99.43	**100**	98.92
Fallow_s	401/2678	98.28	98.81	**99.22**	98.62	98.62	96.83	99.10	98.92	98.62
Stubble	593/3959	99.97	99.92	99.90	99.97	99.87	99.75	**100**	99.97	99.87
Celery	536/3579	99.35	99.61	**99.66**	99.52	99.64	98.46	99.89	99.78	99.64
Grapes_u	1690/11,271	92.11	95.03	95.20	95.16	95.51	95.40	94.58	95.11	**95.52**
Soil_v_d	930/6203	99.43	99.50	**99.87**	99.48	99.69	96.45	99.79	99.47	99.68
C_s_g_w	491/3278	93.62	96.06	94.63	95.18	95.79	94.97	**96.86**	95.73	95.64
L_r_4	160/1068	96.44	99.25	96.72	97.94	**99.63**	94.66	98.69	99.25	**99.63**
L_r_5	289/1927	99.53	**100**	95.69	**100**	**100**	99.79	**100**	100	**100**
Le_r_6	137/916	98.03	97.82	98.25	97.49	98.14	95.09	98.25	**98.80**	98.14
L_r_7	160/1070	92.05	93.74	93.74	93.93	93.48	96.07	**96.26**	93.64	93.49
V_u	1090/7268	56.89	57.33	56.70	56.84	57.75	50.30	57.04	57.66	**57.85**
V_v	271/1807	98.83	99.06	**99.11**	99.00	99.06	89.60	99.39	99.45	99.06
OA		91.56	92.59	91.35	92.49	92.77	90.32	92.76	92.72	**92.78**
AA		95.08	95.89	93.05	95.77	96.00	93.45	**96.17**	96.09	96.00
Kappa		90.57	91.73	90.33	91.60	91.91	89.17	**91.92**	91.85	**91.92**

3.3. Influences of Different Techniques for Dimensionality Reduction

In the above section, we illustrated that incorporating spatial information can improve the classification accuracy. In the following section, we will evaluate how different techniques for dimensionality reduction can affect the classification accuracy. First, we assess the classification accuracy with/without dimensionality reduction. If no dimensionality reduction method is used, the Segment-Tree Filter is constructed using the original HSI. Figure 7c, Figure 8c, and Figure 9c show the results of classification using this scheme. Because redundant bands negatively affect segmentation, the classification accuracy using the original bands in the three HSI datasets is less than that produced using the proposed method. The fourth column in Tables 1–3 illustrates that reducing the dimensionality is necessary to increase the classification accuracy, and the average OA increased by approximately 0.53%. In addition, dimensionality can considerably improve the computational speed.

Next, we examine how different methods of dimensionality reduction can affect the classification accuracy. Figures 7–9 show the classification results for various methods, including the PCA, LDA, and LFDA methods; however, the classification accuracy produced by SELF is better than the accuracies of those methods.

Figure 7d–f, Figure 8d–f, and Figure 9d–f show the classification results for PCA, LDA, and LFDA, respectively. As expected, the OA and Kappa coefficient of SELF is the highest among these methods and the AA is the highest for the Indian Pines dataset and the second highest for the Pavia University and Salinas datasets. Although PCA sometimes performed better than SELF in some PAs, PCA with Segment-Tree Filtering is not a robust algorithm and can easily over-smooth spatial information, as illustrated in Figure 9d. The results illustrated in the red rectangle exhibit considerable classification error-based PCA, and the PA of Fallow_r_p decreases from 99.35% to 60.04% in the fourth row of Table 3.

3.4. Comparison to Other Methods of Spectral-Spatial Classification

As discussed in Section 1, spectral-spatial classification is a powerful method of combining contextual information. Therefore, we compared the proposed method to other common methods of spectral-spatial classification. We implemented the following spectral-spatial classification algorithms in our analysis.

1. The first algorithm is based on EMPs [9]. In [9], a neural network classifier was applied; however, an SVM is used instead of a back-propagation neural network to create a fair comparison. The EMPs are shown in Figure 7g, Figure 8g, and Figure 9g.
2. The second approach uses MRFs [6] with Multi-class SVM, which is, to the best of our knowledge, the state of the art method for spatial-spectral image classification based on remote sensing. Multi-class SVM is used as the initial classifier, and the spatial optimization is performed using the max-flow/min-cut algorithms. In our experiment, α-expansion is adopted, and the regularization coefficient is fixed to 0.5. The results of the SVM with MRFs are shown in Figure 7h, Figure 8h, and Figure 9h.
3. The third approach is based on a Guided Filter with PCA [18]. The size and blur degree in Guided Filtering are tuned adaptively by cross-validation. The results of this classification are shown in Figure 7i, Figure 8i, and Figure 9i.

The proposed method produced results that were more accurate than those of the EMP-based method for the Indian Pines dataset; however, the results were similar for the other datasets. This result suggests that the proposed method is more suitable for different datasets compared to the EMP-based approach.

The classification accuracies of the proposed method and the SVM method with MRFs were nearly equal. This result indicates that the proposed method achieved an accuracy comparable to that of a state of the art method for spatial-spectral HSI classification. Furthermore, when the number of training samples within a class is very small, e.g., the PAs of the "Oats" class in Table 1, the classification accuracy of the proposed approach is perfect, while the SVM with MRFs method fails. This occurs because MRFs over smooth spatial features; thus, the regularization parameter requires complex tuning steps. Therefore, our proposed approach is more robust than the SVM with MRFs method.

The classification accuracy of the proposed method is slightly higher than that of the Guided Filter based on the OAs of the three datasets.

However, we computed the computational times associated with the three HSIs based on GF with PCA [18] and our method. We assume that N pixels, M bands, D classes, and local window size R are used for the reconstruction of the HSIs. The complexity of Segment-Tree Filtering is O (ND), and that of Guided Filtering is O (NDM). For the Indian Pines dataset, GF needed 2.6138 s to process 10 bands in the compressed dataset, while the proposed method required only 0.0536 s (all programs were executed using an Intel(R) Xeon(R) CPU E5-2620 with 24 GB of RAM.). Guided Filtering is slower because it computes the inverse covariance matrix for each sample. In extreme cases, Guided Filtering using an original HSI as the guide image can be time consuming and ineffective.

3.5. Effect of the Training Set on Classification

In this section, we assess how the number of training samples affects the classification accuracy of the proposed method. Thus, we varied the training sample size from 1% of all samples to 20% of all samples. We found that when the training sample size increases, the classification accuracy also increases. Therefore, we only illustrate how the number of training samples affects the classification accuracy of the Indian Pines dataset, as shown in Figure 14. The classification accuracy improves considerably until the number of pixels in the training set reaches 5% of the total pixel number. Then, the accuracy continues to improve but at a lower rate.

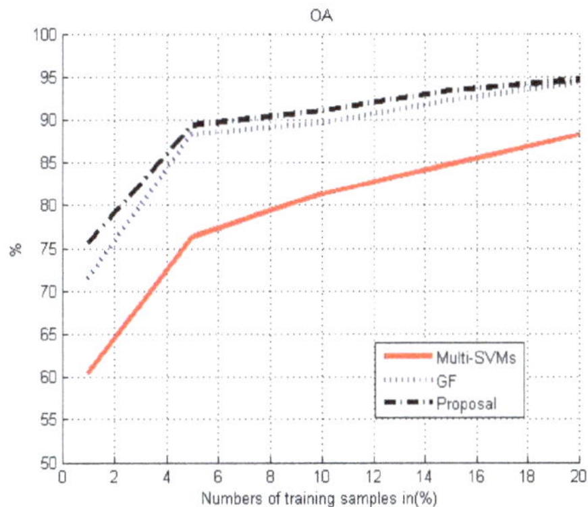

Figure 14. Classification accuracy based on the number of training samples for the Indian Pines dataset.

We also evaluate the effects of the training sample size on the classification accuracies of the Guided Filter [18] and Multi-class SVM methods. As shown in Figure 14, the proposed method and Guided Filter approach improve the classification accuracy regardless of the size of the training set, and the proposed method yields better results. Furthermore, the advantage is larger when the size of the training set is small.

4. Conclusions

A novel and efficient approach based on a Segment-Tree Filter has been proposed for hyperspectral image classification. Our proposed approach is based on spatial-spectral filtering, which is a special EAF. This filter construction utilizes both spectral features using a SELF transformation and spatial information using a Segment-Tree algorithm. After an initial classification map is generated by Multi-class SVM, we can filter the map using the Segment-Tree Filter. One advantage of our proposed approach is that the classification accuracy has been improved dramatically. Experimental results show that the proposed method produced a high classification accuracy for hyperspectral image benchmark sets, including 93.34% for the Indian Pines dataset, 93.89% for the Pavia University dataset, and 92.78% for the Salinas dataset. Compared to other spatial-spectral methods, another advantage of the proposed method is that it provides a more robust classification approach for different datasets and training sets of different sizes.

In the future, two major aspects of our approach could be improved. First, dimensionality reduction using could be performed in SELF to reconstruct HSIs with nonlinear projections. Second, other classifiers, including fuzzy classifiers, could be applied to improve the classification accuracy.

Acknowledgments: The authors would like to thank. D. Landgrebe and P. Gamba for providing the Indian Pines and Pavia University respectively hyperspectral data set available to the community, and Website http://www.ehu.eus/ccwintco/index.php?title=Hyperspectral_Remote_Sensing_Scenes for downloading all the three hyperspectral data sets. This research was supported in part by the Natural Science Foundation of China with Project IDs 41301499 and 41401474, and the National Science and Technology Major Project with Project ID 30-Y20A03-9003-15/16.

Author Contributions: Lu Li and Chengyi Wang conceived and designed the experiments; Lu Li performed the experiments; Lu Li and Jingbo Chen analyzed the data; Lu Li and Jianglin Ma wrote the paper.

Conflicts of Interest: The authors declare no conflict of interest.

References

1. Melgani, F.; Bruzzone, L. Classification of hyperspectral remote sensing images with support vector machines. *IEEE Trans. Geosci. Remote Sens.* **2004**, *42*, 1778–1790. [CrossRef]
2. Böhning, D. Multinomial logistic regression algorithm. *Ann. Inst. Stat. Math.* **1992**, *44*, 197–200. [CrossRef]
3. Li, J.; Bioucas-Dias, J.; Plaza, A. Semi-supervised hyperspectral image segmentation using multinomial logistic regression with active learning. *IEEE Trans. Geosci. Remote Sens.* **2010**, *48*, 4085–4098.
4. Ratle, F.; Camps-Valls, G.; Weston, J. Semi-supervised neural networks for efficient hyperspectral image classification. *IEEE Trans. Geosci. Remote Sens.* **2010**, *48*, 2271–2282. [CrossRef]
5. Li, W.; Prasad, S.; Fowler, E. Hyperspectral image classification using Gaussian mixture models and Markov random fields. *IEEE Lett. Geosci. Remote Sens.* **2014**, *11*, 153–157. [CrossRef]
6. Li, J.; Bioucas, M.; Antonio, P. Spectral-spatial hyperspectral image segmentation using subspace multinomial logistic regression and Markov random fields. *IEEE Trans. Geosci. Remote Sens.* **2012**, *50*, 809–823. [CrossRef]
7. Boykov, O.; Veksler, O.; Zabih, R. Fast approximate energy minimization via graph cuts. *IEEE Trans. Pattern Anal. Mach. Intell.* **2001**, *23*, 1222–1239. [CrossRef]
8. Li, J.; Bioucas, M.; Antonio, P. Spectral-spatial classification of hyperspectral data using loopy belief propagation and active learning. *IEEE Trans. Geosci. Remote Sens.* **2013**, *51*, 844–856. [CrossRef]
9. Benediktsson, A.; Palmason, A.; Sveinsson, R. Classification of hyperspectral data from urban areas based on extended morphological profiles. *IEEE Trans. Geosci. Remote Sens.* **2005**, *43*, 480–491. [CrossRef]
10. Zortea, M.; de Martino, M.; Serpico, S. A SVM Ensemble approach for spectral-contextual classification of optical high spatial resolution imagery. In Proceeding of the IEEE International Conference on Geoscience and Remote Sensing Symposium, Boston, MA, USA, 23–28 July 2007.
11. Yuliya, T.; Jocelyn, C.; Jón Atli, B. Segmentation and classification of hyperspectral images using minimum spanning forest grown from automatically selected markers. *IEEE Trans. Syst. Man Cybern. B Cybern.* **2010**, *40*, 1267–1279. [CrossRef]
12. Fu, W.; Li, S.; Fang, L. Spectral-spatial Hyperspectral image classification via superpixel merging and sparse representation. In Proceeding of the IEEE Proceedings on Geoscience and Remote Sensing Symposium, Milan, Italy, 26–31 July 2015.
13. Duan, W.; Li, S.; Fang, L. Spectral-spatial hyperspectral image classification using superpixel and extreme learning machines. In *Pattern Recognition, Proceedings the 6th Chinese Conference, Changsha, China, 17–19 November 2014*; Springer: Berlin/Heidelberg, Germany, 2014; Volume 483, pp. 159–167. [CrossRef]

14. Weihua, S.; David, M. Trilateral filter on multispectral imagery for classification and segmentation. *Proc. SPIE* **2011**. [CrossRef]

15. Tarabalka, Y.; Benediktsson, A.; Chanussot, J. Spectral-spatial classification of hyperspectral imagery based on partitional clustering techniques. *IEEE Trans. Geosci. Remote Sens.* **2009**, *47*, 2973–2987. [CrossRef]

16. Fang, L.; Li, S.; Duan, W. Classification of hyperspectral images by exploiting spectral-spatial information of superpixel via multiple kernels. *IEEE Trans. Geosci. Remote Sens.* **2015**, *53*, 6663–6673. [CrossRef]

17. He, K.; Sun, J.; Tang, X. Guided image filtering. *IEEE Trans. Pattern Anal. Mach. Intell.* **2013**, *35*, 1397–1409. [CrossRef] [PubMed]

18. Kang, X.; Li, S.; Jón Alti, B. Spectral-spatial hyperspectral image classification with edge-preserving filtering. *IEEE Trans. Geosci. Remote Sens.* **2014**, *52*, 2666–2677. [CrossRef]

19. Hosni, A.; Rhemann, C.; Bleyer, M.; Rother, C.; Gelautz, M. Fast cost-volume filtering for visual correspondence and beyond. *IEEE Trans. Pattern Anal. Mach. Intell.* **2013**, *35*, 504–511. [CrossRef] [PubMed]

20. Hosni, A.; Rhemann, C.; Bleyer, M.; Gelautz, M. Temporally consistent disparity and optical flow via efficient spatio-temporal filtering. In Proceedings of the 5th Pacific Rim Symposium, Gwangju, Korea, 20–23 November 2011; Springer: Berlin, Germany, 2011; pp. 165–177.

21. Shutao, L.; Xudong, K.; Jianwen, H. Image fusion with guided filtering. *IEEE Trans. Image Process.* **2013**, *22*, 2864–2875. [CrossRef] [PubMed]

22. Felzenszwalb, F.; Huttenlocher, P. Efficient graph-based image segmentation. *Int. J. Comput. Vis.* **2004**, *59*, 167–181. [CrossRef]

23. Mei, X.; Sun, X.; Dong, W.; Wang, H.; Zhang, X. Segment-tree based cost aggregation for stereo matching. In Proceeding of the 2013 IEEE Conference on Computer Vision and Pattern Recognition, Portland, OR, USA, 23–28 June 2013.

24. Yang, X. A Non-local cost aggregation method for stereo matching. In Proceeding of the 2012 IEEE Conference on Computer Vision and Pattern Recognition, Providence, RI, USA, 16–21 June 2012.

25. Wang, Q.; Lin, J.; Yuan, Y. Salient band selection for hyperspectral image classification via manifold ranking. *IEEE Trans. Neural Netw. Learn. Syst.* **2016**, *27*, 1279–1289. [CrossRef] [PubMed]

26. Yuan, Y.; Lin, J.; Wang, Q. Dual clustering based hyperspectral band selection by contextual analysis. *IEEE Trans. Geosci. Remote Sens.* **2016**, *54*, 1431–1445. [CrossRef]

27. Sugiyama, M.; Idé, T.; Nakajima, S.; Sese, J. Semi-supervised local Fisher discriminant analysis for dimensionality reduction. *Mach. Learn.* **2010**, *78*, 35–61. [CrossRef]

28. Fisher, R.A. The use of multiple measurements in taxonomic problems. *Ann. Eugen.* **1936**, *7*, 179–188. [CrossRef]

29. Sugiyama, M. Dimensionality reduction of multimodal labeled data by local fisher discriminant analysis. *J. Mach. Learn. Res.* **2007**, *8*, 1027–1061.

30. Huang, T.K.; Weng, R.C.; Lin, C.J. Generalized bradley-terry models and multi-class probability estimates. *J. Mach. Learn. Res.* **2006**, *7*, 85–115.

31. Cormen, T.; Leiserson, C.; Rivest, R.; Stein, C. *Introduction to Algorithms*, 3rd ed.; MIT Press: London, UK, 2005; pp. 170–174.

32. Shi, J.; Malik, J. Normalized cuts and image segmentation. *IEEE Trans. Pattern Anal. Mach. Intell.* **2000**, *22*, 888–905. [CrossRef]

Article

Automatic Counting of Large Mammals from Very High Resolution Panchromatic Satellite Imagery

Yifei Xue [1,*], Tiejun Wang [1,*] and Andrew K. Skidmore [1,2]

[1] Faculty of Geo-Information Science and Earth Observation (ITC), University of Twente, P.O. Box 217, 7500 AE Enschede, The Netherlands; a.k.skidmore@utwente.nl

[2] Department of Environmental Science, Macquarie University, Sydney, NSW 2109, Australia

* Correspondence: y.xue@utwente.nl (Y.X.); t.wang@utwente.nl (T.W.); Tel.: +31-53-487-4274 (T.W.)

Academic Editors: Qi Wang, Nicolas H. Younan and Carlos López-Martínez
Received: 22 June 2017; Accepted: 21 August 2017; Published: 23 August 2017

Abstract: Estimating animal populations by direct counting is an essential component of wildlife conservation and management. However, conventional approaches (i.e., ground survey and aerial survey) have intrinsic constraints. Advances in image data capture and processing provide new opportunities for using applied remote sensing to count animals. Previous studies have demonstrated the feasibility of using very high resolution multispectral satellite images for animal detection, but to date, the practicality of detecting animals from space using panchromatic imagery has not been proven. This study demonstrates that it is possible to detect and count large mammals (e.g., wildebeests and zebras) from a single, very high resolution GeoEye-1 panchromatic image in open savanna. A novel semi-supervised object-based method that combines a wavelet algorithm and a fuzzy neural network was developed. To discern large mammals from their surroundings and discriminate between animals and non-targets, we used the wavelet technique to highlight potential objects. To make full use of geometric attributes, we carefully trained the classifier, using the adaptive-network-based fuzzy inference system. Our proposed method (with an accuracy index of 0.79) significantly outperformed the traditional threshold-based method (with an accuracy index of 0.58) detecting large mammals in open savanna.

Keywords: GeoEye-1; wavelet transform; fuzzy neural network; remote sensing; conservation

---

1. Introduction

Global biodiversity loss is a pressing environmental issue [1]. Populations of a number of wild animals have been reduced by half over the past four decades [2,3]. Counting wild animals to determine population size is an essential element of wildlife conservation and environmental management [4]. However, accurate population estimation using ground-based methods remains challenging, requiring considerable investment in resources and time [5]. Aerial surveys have been used as an alternative approach to detect large mammal populations and generate statistical estimates of their abundance in open areas [6]. In developed countries, wildlife such as caribou, elk, deer and moose have been monitored using aerial surveys [7–9]. For developing nations, where scores of endangered and threatened fauna are found, such an alternative is not always feasible due to limitations in access, technology, aircraft availability and skilled human resources [10,11]. It is therefore desirable to develop alternative approaches for conducting wildlife population counts in such regions.

Advances in satellite technology have provided new avenues in remote sensing for environmental applications, including the remote counting and mapping of animal populations. Lower spatial resolution satellite images have proven inadequate to detect and count individual animals [12], but the availability of commercial satellite images with a spatial resolution of one meter or less (e.g., IKONOS,

QuickBird, GeoEye and WorldView) has made such an undertaking more feasible [13]. As a result, studies have been undertaken utilizing satellite remote sensing data to detect animals. For example, Fretwell et al. [14] successfully estimated the abundance of penguins from fecal staining of ice by using a combination of medium resolution (15–30 m) Landsat-7 ETM+ and very high resolution (0.6–2.5 m) QuickBird satellite images, but they did not attempt to count individual birds. Stapleton et al. [15] used different very high resolution (VHR) satellite images (i.e., QuickBird, WorldView-1 and WorldView-2) to track the distribution and abundance of polar bears. Although their findings demonstrated the potential of remote sensing applications for wildlife detection and monitoring, they also revealed the need for more automated detection processes to expedite analysis. Yang et al. [16] explored mammal detection in open savanna country from VHR (0.5–2 m) GeoEye-1 satellite images, using a hybrid image classification approach. Through a two-step process of pixel-based and object-based image classification, they were able to demonstrate the feasibility of automated detection and counting of large wild animals in vast open spaces. However, the method they proposed requires the input by an expert of a number of parameters, and therefore this method remains subjective and labor-intensive. Fretwell et al. [17] compared a number of classification techniques endeavoring to automatically detect whale-like objects. They found that a simple thresholding technique of the panchromatic and coastal band delivered the best results. Neither Stapleton et al. [15] nor Fretwell et al. [17] made full use of the multispectral band, while the panchromatic band played an important role in their research. To our knowledge, there has been no substantial exploration of the feasibility of using a single panchromatic (black and white) band for wildlife detection. The typical panchromatic band data obtained from airborne platforms have a much wider spectral range than is utilized by multispectral bands (red, green, blue) [18], and also have a higher radiometric resolution (number of bits per pixel). Moreover, panchromatic satellite images have a higher spatial resolution than multispectral images [19].

Object counting can also be achieved with computer vision techniques, such as local feature-based subspace clustering algorithms [20,21] and global feature-based saliency detection approaches [22–25]. The conventional clustering method, such as the K-means clustering algorithm, has been used to extract local features, but its performance relies on finding "similar" records in the training data and could therefore be highly influenced by noise [21]. Data in a specific category can also be well-represented by low-dimensional subspace where noise can be reduced [26]. To achieve a good result by eliminating the influence of errors (e.g., noise, outliers), Peng et al. [20] proposed a graph-oriented learning method, which applied the L2-Graph for subspace learning and subspace clustering, for facial recognition and moving-vehicle detection [26]. However, studies on subspace clustering mainly concentrate on high-dimensional data clustering, such as facial recognition and motion image segmentation. Saliency detection is a well-researched problem in computer vision. It aims at indicating the saliency likelihood of each pixel by generating bounding boxes, binary foreground and background segmentation, or saliency maps [27]. The aforementioned methods have proven to be useful for multi-level features with multi-band images, but are difficult to apply to a single-band image where the object consists of few pixels.

Aerial photographs have been used for bird censuses since the 1980s, counting image points falling below an established threshold [28,29]. Bajzak and Piatt [29] studied the greater snow goose, contrasting its white plumage against the surrounding mud flats by size and tonal class. Similarly, a panchromatic image can use thresholding as a simple image segmentation method that divides an image into objects and background [30–32]. It works well when targets contrast sharply with their background. However, thresholding methods have their limitations: (1) targets cannot be separated from ground elements with similar brightness values; (2) gray value thresholding does not make full use of geometric information; and (3) threshold values are defined manually and depend heavily on the user's expertise.

Animal detection using remote sensing then predominantly switched to a two-step process [33]: (1) highlighting suspected targets; and then (2) classifying them, using geometric information. Groom et al. [33] proposed a scheme using geometric feature (object-size) filters to count birds against a monochromatic background. As targets were visually small and dim, they were not easily discerned against their background [34]. Using filters and image processing techniques, targets embedded in the scene could be visualized and detected [35–38]. However, the performance of such filters remains dependent on the brightness contrast between the target and background [34]. Several studies have employed wavelet-based techniques to address this concern [39–41]. The discernibility of targets from the background may vary at different scales, which can be problematic for object detection [19,42]. Wavelet analysis can transform signals into multiple resolutions, using an adaptive window [43], and thereby latently detect targets in cluttered backgrounds.

After highlighting the targets, the major challenge becomes how to make full use of geometric features to help separate a target from its surroundings. Spectral characteristics, cluster size, shape and other spatial features have been used in rule sets for image segmentation [44]. McNeill et al. [45] analyzed potential regions using shapes, by rejecting those with a compactness greater than a specified threshold value. Descamps et al. [46] counted large birds by fitting suspected objects (birds) into bright ellipses surrounded by a darker background. Expert knowledge can also play a critical role in image classification [16,47,48]. For example, Yang et al. [16] developed a specific rule set using expert knowledge to remove misclassified objects generated by object-based analysis. In another study, Wang et al. [47] proposed a hybrid neural network and expert system to quantify understory bamboo from satellite imagery, and they concluded that integration of a neural network and expert system appeared to be more efficient than when using either a neural network or an expert system alone. However, these methods rely on experts' subjective experience and knowledge, which can be challenging for practical applications.

An alternative approach to using an expert system is machine learning: a data analysis technique that automates model building through algorithms that iteratively learn from a given dataset. Though different classifiers based on machine learning generate varying levels of accuracy for different datasets [49], the most recent machine-learning techniques have a proven ability to solve complex problems [50]. For example, convolutional neural networks (CNNs) [51] have emerged as state-of-the-art models for image classification and object detection [52–57]. Local connections, shared weight, pooling and multiple layers are four architectural factors that make CNNs excel in processing natural signals [58]. However, the human involvement level is high when tailoring the CNN algorithm to a specific task [59], and large data sets are required for training purposes to ensure a high quality output [60]. Another major limitation of CNNs is their intrinsic black-box nature: their internal workings are hidden and not easily understood [61], so the models they generate are unexplainable [62]. The fuzzy neural network (FNN) is an alternative model that incorporates both the explicit knowledge representation of an fuzzy inference system (FIS) and the learning ability of an artificial neural network [63,64].The McCulloch–Pitts model [65] was one of the earliest applications to use fuzzy sets with a neural network concept. Since the 1990s, Takagi and others have developed a solid foundation for the fuzzy neural network [66]. In 1993, Jang proposed the adaptive-network-based fuzzy inference system (ANFIS) [67]. This algorithm has been widely employed in applied mathematics [68–71], and, unlike traditional expert systems, does not require a high level of expert knowledge when developing decision rules.

This study aims to detect and count large mammals in open spaces from a single, VHR GeoEye-1 panchromatic image, using a novel semi-supervised object-based scheme that combines a wavelet algorithm and a fuzzy neural network.

2. Materials and Methods

2.1. Study Area and Animal Species

The study area is located in the Maasai Mara National Reserve (also known as Maasai Mara or the Mara), a large game reserve in the Great Rift Valley in the southern part of Kenya (Figure 1).

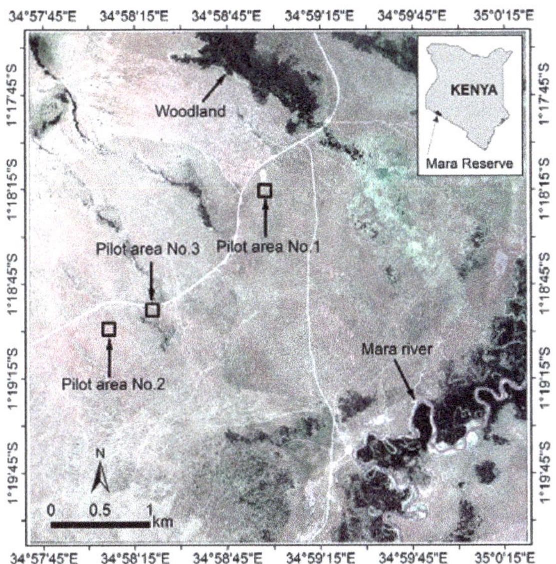

Figure 1. Location of the Maasai Mara National Reserve in Kenya and the three pilot study areas on a natural color composite of a GeoEye-1 image, acquired on 11 August 2009.

The reserve's topography is mainly open savanna (grassland) with clusters of acacia trees along the southeastern area of the park [72]. The reserve not only protects the habitat of resident species, but also preserves a critical part of the route used by wildebeests and zebras during the great migration that traverses the Maasai Mara via the Serengeti National Park. The wildebeest is the dominant species of the Maasai Mara, and herd sizes can range from a few individuals to many thousands [73]. Serengeti wildebeests migrate seasonally, and are seen intermittently in the Mara between August and November [74]. The sheer numbers of animals that congregate during migration make the wildebeest an ideal candidate species to map through the use of satellite technology.

2.2. Satellite Images

We acquired two GeoEye-1 satellite images of part of the Maasai Mara National Reserve through the DigitalGlobe Foundation (www.digitalglobefoundation.org/), each covering an area of 25 km^2. Both images are cloud free, and include one panchromatic (0.5 m) and four multispectral (2 m) bands. The image captured on 11 August 2009 depicts large numbers of animals. The other image, without any large animals present, was captured on 10 August 2013. To address our research objective, we carefully selected three small pilot study areas from the first image, each covering an area of 120 × 120 m (Figure 2). These pilot study areas were chosen to represent different levels of complexity regarding three criteria: (a) complexity of the landscape; (b) abundance of animals; and (c) feasibility and reliability of the visual interpretation of target animals. Pilot area No. 1 represents low complexity, with a few dozen animals viewed against a uniform background; Pilot area No. 2 represents moderate complexity, with more than one hundred animals viewed against a slightly less uniform background; and Pilot area No. 3 represents high complexity, with several hundred animals viewed against a non-uniform background.

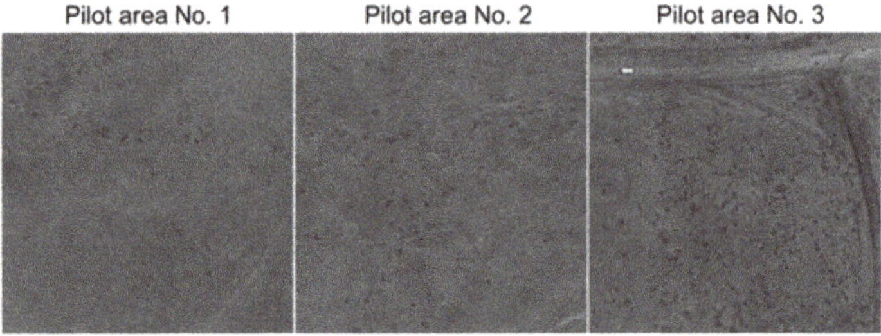

Figure 2. The panchromatic band of the GeoEye-1 image taken on 11 August 2009, showing large mammals in the Maasai Mara National Reserve. Pilot area No. 1 represents low complexity regarding animal numbers and uniformity of background; Pilot area No. 2 represents moderate complexity; and Pilot area No. 3 represents high complexity. The rectangle visible in the top-left corner of Pilot area No. 3 is a white vehicle.

2.3. Visual Interpretation to Establish Ground Truth for Large Animals Discerned on GeoEye-1 Imagery

Ground truth is required to calibrate the model, as well as validate the classification result. Using the panchromatic band of the GeoEye-1 image, large mammals (e.g., wildebeests and zebras) are visualized as 3–4 pixels long and 1–2 pixels wide [16]. Due to their similarity in size, large animals can be confused with small ground features such as bushes and termite mounds [75]. To facilitate the visual interpretation of target animals and avoid the problem of subjectivity, we used one pan-sharpened GeoEye-1 image with, and one without, the presence of large animals (Figure 3). We invited two experienced wildlife researchers from Africa as independent visual interpreters. Together we visually compared the two separate temporal images of the three pilot study locations at multiple scales under the ArcGIS 10.3.1 environment (ESRI Inc., Redlands, CA, USA). After the observers had discussed their interpretation results, especially regarding uncertain objects, and had agreed which identified objects were indeed large mammals, their knowledge was recorded as confirmed animal ground truth points. In total, we identified 50, 128 and 426 large mammals in the pilot study areas 1, 2 and 3, respectively.

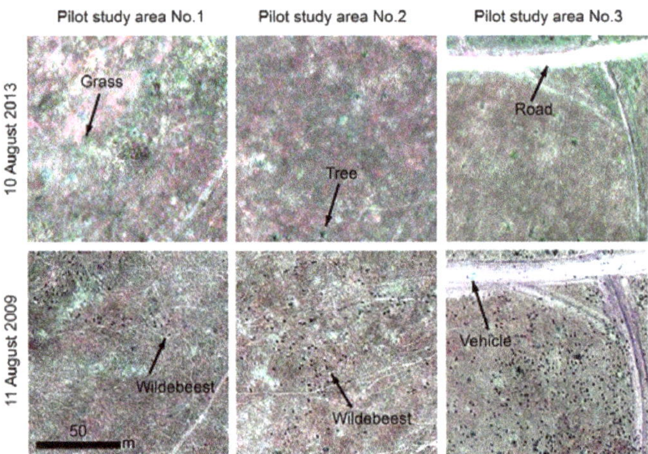

Figure 3. Visual interpretation of target animals by comparing two pan-sharpened GeoEye-1 images (0.5 m): one acquired 10 August 2013, without large animals present (top), and one acquired 11 August 2009, with large animals (bottom). The three pilot study areas represent the complexity of the landscape and the abundance of animals appearing in these images, from left to right: low, moderate and high.

2.4. Semi-Automatic Animal Detection Algorithm

Large mammals were identified by a series of multistage, semiautomatic techniques in VHR panchromatic satellite images. Our proposed scheme includes four principal steps (Figure 4): image preprocessing, preclassification, reclassification and accuracy assessment. Visual interpretation was incorporated for the purpose of reclassification and accuracy assessment.

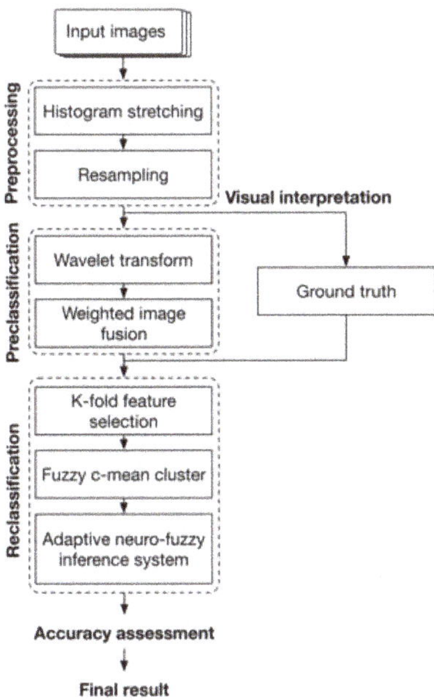

Figure 4. Workflow of the proposed method for counting large mammals from a single, very high resolution panchromatic GeoEye-1 satellite image.

2.4.1. Image Preprocessing

To highlight large mammals in the panchromatic imagery, we applied a histogram stretch in ENVI 5.2 (Exelis Visual Information Solutions, Inc., Boulder, CO, USA). Due to the limited resolution of the panchromatic band of VHR satellite images, an individual animal is represented as a cluster of pixels consisting of no more than eight pixels. To fully use their geometric information, we resampled the original image. Bicubic interpolation, which uses weighted arithmetic means, was chosen, as it maintains the quality of detailed information through antialiasing [76]. The image was carefully resized to eight times the original size, taking the wavelet decomposition performance into account, as well as memory and computation time, using

$$I = \left[a_{i,j} \right]_{m \times n} \tag{1}$$

where the original image $\left[a_{i,j} \right]_{m \times n}$ is a matrix with m rows and n columns. We describe the resampled image as

$$I\prime = f\left(\lambda \left[a_{i,j} \right]_{m \times n} \right) \tag{2}$$

where $I\prime$ is the new image, λ represents the diagonal matrix of the resized scale and f is the bicubic interpolation function.

2.4.2. Wavelet-Based Preclassification

Based on the generally accepted methodology of image decomposition and reconstruction, we used the wavelet-based method when highlighting suspected large mammals, to enhance their contrast against the immediate surroundings and to suppress irrelevant background [77,78]. Wavelet transform (WT) is based on the theory of Short-Time Fourier Transform (STFT) [79]. The WT differs from STFT in that it replaces infinite triangle function bases with finite decay wavelet bases. The finite decay wavelet bases, which are stretched (or squeezed) and translated from the mother wavelet, have an average value of 0 [80]. The WT of a continuous signal is defined as

$$T(a,b) = w(a) \int_{-\infty}^{\infty} x(t)\psi^*(\frac{t-b}{a})dt \tag{3}$$

where a is scale, b is the position parameter, $w(a)$ is a weighting function and $\psi^*(\frac{t-b}{a})$ is the wavelet base [81]. If the wavelet base sufficiently corresponds to an input signal, the WT coefficient at this position is high [82]. The optimal mother wavelet and parameters were selected by comparing the performance of mainstream wavelet families regarding maintaining geometry features of suspected targets in our experimental imagery. A Haar wavelet (or db1 wavelet) was selected as it is not continuous and is therefore able to detect signals containing a sudden transition [83].

The image was transformed into a series of sub-images: A1 (low-frequency image), H1 (high-frequency image in the horizontal direction) and V1 (high-frequency image in the vertical direction); and then the same procedure was applied to the low frequency image (A1). Such a method permits multiresolution processing in both directions. After three transformation iterations, nine sub-images were generated, containing details as well as background. To highlight suspected targets and suppress background information, a weighted fusion algorithm was used. We then calculated the mean-square error (MSE) [84] between sub-images (resized to the original) and the original image. Sub-images containing more high-frequency information yielded higher MSE values. The weight of each sub-image should be

$$\omega_i = \frac{\sigma_i^2}{\sum_{j=1}^{n} \sigma_j^2}(i,j = 1,2,\ldots,n) \tag{4}$$

where i,j are the serial numbers of the current image, $\sigma_{i(j)}$ is the MSE of the current sub-image, and n is the total number of calculated sub-images. The weighted fusion algorithm creates a high signal-to-noise ratio (SNR) image. We then used Ostu's method [85] in MATLAB (The Mathworks Inc., Natick, MA, USA), to discriminate between each suspected animal blob and the background.

2.4.3. Selecting Geometric Features

The next concern was how to identify which suspected large mammals were true large mammals. This entailed deciding which geometric features to use, typically length and area. We also considered gray value (hue) pixels. We used cross-validation (a model assessment technique) to verify the performance of classifiers [86]. This basically involves grouping raw data: one group is used as training set and the other for validation. K-fold cross-validation (K-CV) is a commonly used validation technique in object detection [86,87]. We divided the data into ten groups, and used each group once as the training dataset while the other nine groups acted as the validation dataset. We determined the most suitable combination for this experiment by calculating the average value of the training errors and checking errors using the dataset mentioned above at situations of different feature combinations. After employing the K-fold cross-validation multiple times, we decided a combination of feature area, major axis length, minor axis length and bounding box area was most suitable for this experiment.

2.4.4. ANFIS-Based Reclassification

A total of 100 blobs (or unknown objects) were randomly selected from the database to train the final model. The distribution of training data was comparable to the distribution of the whole dataset.

Before we trained these data using ANFIS, a number of rules was decided upon. The Fuzzy C-Mean (FCM, or Fuzzy ISODATA), which was originally designed by Dunn [88], is a well-accepted clustering algorithm ideally suited to solving a natural problem [89,90]. As shown in Figure 5, this algorithm generated 10 cluster centers (corresponding to 10 membership functions for each variable). To limit the number of feature fields, we used expert knowledge to eliminate redundant classes. Finally, we input the 100 randomly selected blobs to train ANFIS in MATLAB. With the function /genfis2/, we built an initial fuzzy inference system (FIS) structure. We then loaded the initial FIS structure into the function /anfis/ to train the ANFIS and develop the model. A hybrid method, including least-squares and backpropagation gradient descent, was applied to optimise the model. ANFIS model evaluation was conducted according to the 'evalfis' function. Required parameters for the 'anfis' function, including training error goal, initial training step size, step size decrease rate and step size increase rate, were set to default values (0, 0.01, 0.9, 1.1), which were proven to be adequate for most situations [91]. In order to avoid overfitting, we set the epoch number to 75 by considering both training error and checking error (see Appendix A). The adaptive tuning stops when the least-squares error is less than the training error goal, or has reached the epoch number. By loading all the datasets containing feature values into the model, all suspected blobs were classified by the inference system into targets and non-targets.

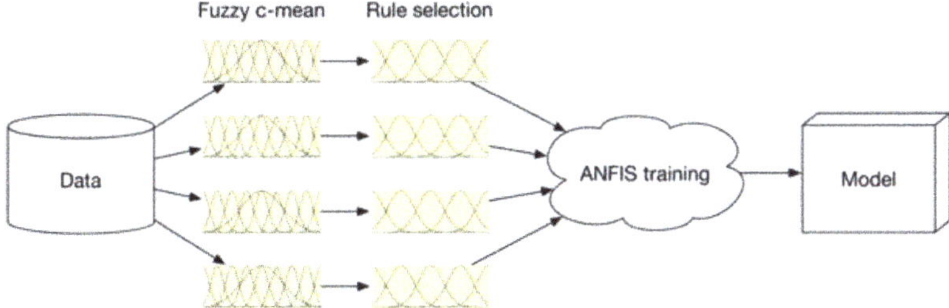

Figure 5. Flow diagram of the adaptive-network-based fuzzy inference system (ANFIS) based reclassification system.

2.5. Accuracy Assessment

We assessed the accuracy of the classification results by comparing the number of large mammals detected by the computer model with the ground truthing, and then calculated the omission error and commission error [92]. Detection accuracy (DA), which is the most commonly used metric, is highly inversely correlated ($DA + omission\ error = 1$) [93]. The values for both the omission error and the commission error are always between 0 and 1. The closer their values are to 0, the better the result.

The accuracy index (AI), which was devised by Pouliot et al. [94], was computed as:

$$AI = \frac{N - TP - FN}{N} \tag{5}$$

where TP (true positive) denotes the number of targets occurring in both the ground truth and our processing result; FN (false negative) denotes the number of targets that do appear in the ground truth, but not in our processing result; FP (false positive) denotes the number of targets occurring in our processing result, but not in the ground truth data; and N is the number of ground truth targets in the study area. The higher the value of the accuracy index, the better the result.

3. Results

In Figure 6, the visual results of our semi-automated ANFIS-wavelet approach to detecting large mammals are compared with the results gained with the thresholding method.

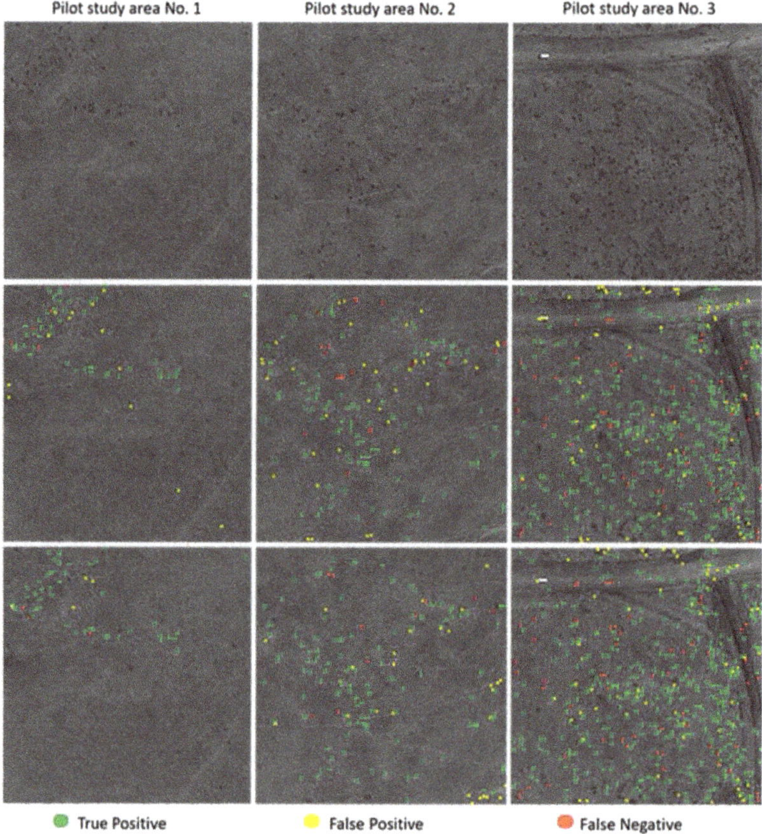

Figure 6. Results regarding large mammal detection in the three different pilot study areas. The columns show images of the three pilot areas: No. 1 is of low complexity, No. 2 of moderate complexity and No. 3 of high complexity. The first row contains the original panchromatic satellite images; the second row illustrates results based on the thresholding method; and the third row illustrates the results obtained using the method proposed in this study (i.e., ANFIS-wavelet). The green, red and yellow dots indicate true positive, false negative and false positive results, respectively.

The accuracy index regarding the proposed method for the low complexity study area (No. 1) was as high as 0.86 (Table 1). For the higher-complexity sites, the results also yielded acceptable accuracy indices: 0.79 and 0.72, respectively, for the moderately (No. 2) and highly (No. 3) complex sites. As shown in Table 2, the thresholding method produced accuracy indices of 0.64, 0.56 and 0.54, respectively, for the low, moderate and high complexity areas, with an average accuracy index of 0.58. The average accuracy index of our proposed method, depicted in Table 1, is 0.79, which is 0.21 higher than that of the thresholding method. Also, the calculated omission and commission errors of our approach (0.09 and 0.12, respectively) are lower than those of the thresholding method (0.15 and 0.24, respectively). It should also be noted that, if the study area is more complex, this does not necessarily mean that the detection is less accurate. As shown in Figure 6, specific ground features can introduce inaccuracies, such as the errors appearing in this study close to roads and edges of forests. In absolute terms of detected targets, the thresholding technique and our semi-automated ANFIS-wavelet approach showed different accuracies for each pilot study area. The statistical results regarding this study area illustrate that a higher detection accuracy is obtained with the ANFIS-wavelet method than with the threshold-based method.

Table 1. Accuracy assessment of the ANFIS-wavelet method for the three pilot study areas: No. 1, No. 2 and No. 3, with low, moderate and high complexity, respectively.

	Pilot Area No. 1	Pilot Area No. 2	Pilot Area No. 3	Average
Ground truth	50	128	416	198
True positive	47	118	370	178
False positive	4	17	64	28
False negative	3	10	56	23
Omission error	0.06	0.08	0.13	0.09
Commission error	0.08	0.13	0.15	0.12
Accuracy index	0.86	0.79	0.72	0.79

Table 2. Accuracy assessment of the threshold-based method for the three pilot study areas with low, moderate and high complexity, respectively.

	Pilot Area No. 1	Pilot Area No. 2	Pilot Area No. 3	Average
Ground truth	50	128	416	198
True positive	45	105	354	168
False positive	13	33	126	57
False negative	5	23	72	33
Omission error	0.10	0.18	0.17	0.15
Commission error	0.22	0.24	0.26	0.24
Accuracy index	0.64	0.56	0.54	0.58

4. Discussion

The results from this study demonstrate that it is feasible to use VHR panchromatic satellite imagery to detect and count large mammals in extensive open areas. In comparison with the traditional thresholding technique, our ANFIS-wavelet method produced a higher accuracy index and less commission/omission errors.

Although the thresholding method performs adequately when the targets share similar gray values and are dissimilar to their background, it is less accurate in more complex areas. There are two main reasons for the higher commission error found when using the thresholding method. Firstly, when the gray values of suspected objects (animals) are similar to those of the surroundings, they may be ignored by the threshold-based segmentation. In the ANFIS-wavelet method, the representation of the target is considered at different spatial scales. Suspected animals that do contrast with their immediate background, once different spatial scales are considered, will contribute to a higher weighted value in the preclassification results. Secondly, when animal objects and terrain have similar gray values, they cannot be altered simply by using thresholds: more information is required before further processing can be undertaken [32]. We statistically selected four geometric features to distinguish non-target objects from large mammals in the feature space. This approach proved more accurate than merely using a simple threshold value.

The commission error derived from our method was found to be three percentage points greater than the omission error, resulting in more non-target objects being incorrectly classified as large mammals than large mammals being incorrectly omitted. Further analysis revealed that commission errors always appeared near roads and vegetation. Bushes were confused with large mammals because of similarities in geometric features. Rough road surfaces or vehicles may result in discontinuous blobs and may thus also be recognized as large mammals by our method. Two reasons for omission include targets that are not clearly distinguishable from the background and targets that are too close to each other.

The geometric features chosen to distinguish an animal from its background were area, major axis length, minor axis length and bounding area. These features differ between target animals and non-targets such as shrubs or boulders. Even though some features were highly correlated, they can also help us in detecting animals. For example, defining both major and minor axis length can help to eliminate objects that do not have a correct length–width ratio.

The ANFIS-wavelet method has proved to be a feasible method for detecting animals in open savanna landscapes. This method is based on wavelet preclassification followed by ANFIS reclassification. The wavelet-based classification is able to highlight objects and maintain their geometric features. This is critical because the targets are dim and small, and as much useful information as possible needs to be retained. By using multiscale analysis, targets can be precisely located in poorer quality (i.e., low SNR) imagery without information loss. The ANFIS, which combines the advantages of machine learning and a fuzzy system, makes it possible to learn from data and concomitantly use existing expert knowledge, resulting in a method that is both efficient and stable.

5. Conclusions

We developed a novel semi-supervised object-based method that combines a wavelet algorithm and a fuzzy neural network for detecting and counting large mammals (e.g., wildebeests and zebras) from a single, very high resolution GeoEye-1 panchromatic image in open savanna. To discern large mammals from their surroundings and discriminate between animals and non-targets, we used the wavelet technique to highlight potential objects. To make full use of geometric attributes, we carefully trained the classifier, using the adaptive-network-based fuzzy inference system. We then compared our method with the traditional threshold-based method. The results showed that our proposed method (with an accuracy index of 0.79) significantly outperformed the traditional threshold-based method (with an accuracy index of 0.58) in detecting large mammals in open savanna. The greater availability of VHR images, and the advances in image segmentation techniques, mean that animal detection by means of remote sensing technology is a pragmatic alternative to direct animal counting. Further developments in image processing should eventually make it feasible to detect and monitor medium-sized and small animals remotely from space as well.

Acknowledgments: Yifei Xue was supported by the China Scholarship Council (CSC) and co-funded by the ITC Research Fund from the Faculty of Geo-Information Science and Earth Observation (ITC), University of Twente, the Netherlands. We acknowledge the satellite imagery support received from the DigitalGlobe Foundation. We also thank Festus Ihwagi and Tawanda Gara for their assistance with the visual interpretation of the GeoEye-1 satellite images.

Author Contributions: Yifei Xue, Tiejun Wang and Andrew K. Skidmore conceived and designed the experiment. Yifei Xue analyzed the data and wrote the paper. All authors contributed to the editing of manuscript.

Conflicts of Interest: The authors declare no conflict of interest.

Appendix A

ANFIS is a hybrid method which combines both least-square and backpropagation algorithms. The training datasets were used to construct the initial model, and the validation datasets were used for tuning. The training algorithm stops when either the training error goal value is satisfied, or the number of training epochs is reached. The training error goal was always being used as default value 0 when solving an unknown problem [91]. After a certain epoch number, the model will overfit the training data. To avoid overfitting, an optimal epoch number is required, but it is also difficult to determine. We evaluated the training error and the checking error (also known as validation error) with increasing the epoch number (Figure A1). Root-mean-square error (RMSE) is one of the most used indexes for performance indication [95]. The RMSE of the training data decreases along with the epoch number, but the tendency is slowed down after around 120 epochs and does not seem to have an obvious descent after 200 epochs. The RMSE of the checking data decreases along with the epoch number until around 75 epochs, and increases rapidly before around 120 epochs. According to this quantitative analysis, we found that it is proper to set the epoch number to around 75.

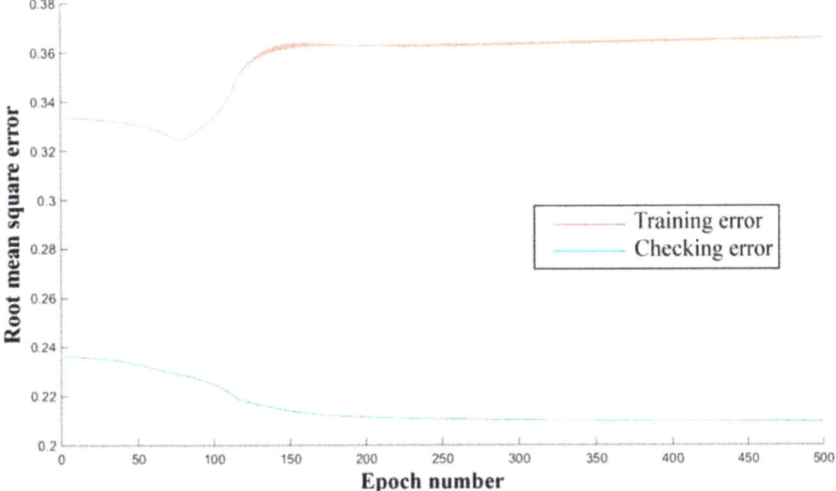

Figure A1. Indentification of optimum epoch number based on the root-mean-square error of both training error and checking error.

References

1. Skidmore, A.K.; Pettorelli, N.; Coops, N.C.; Geller, G.N.; Hansen, M.; Lucas, R.; Mücher, C.A.; O'Connor, B.; Paganini, M.; Pereira, H.M.; et al. Environmental science: Agree on biodiversity metrics to track from space. *Nature* **2015**, *523*, 403–405. [CrossRef] [PubMed]
2. Cuttelod, A.; Garcia, N.; Malak, D.A.; Temple, H.; Katariya, V. The Mediterranean: a biodiversity hotspot under threat. In *Wildlife in a Changing World: An Analysis of the 2008 IUCN Red List of Threatened Species*; Vié, J.-C., Hilton-Taylor, C., Stuart, S.N., Eds.; IUCN: Gland, Switzerland, 2009.
3. Carrington, D. Earth has lost half of its wildlife in the past 40 years, says WWF. Available online: https://www.theguardian.com/environment/2014/sep/29/earth-lost-50-wildlife-in-40-years-wwf (accessed on 30 August 2016).
4. Ramono, W.; Rubianto, A.; Herdiana, Y. Spatial distributions of Sumatran rhino calf at Way Kambas National Park based on its footprint and forest fire in one decade (2006 to 2015). In Proceedings of the Scientific Program of the 15th International Elephant & Rhino Conservation and Research Symposium, Singapore, 14–18 November 2016; p. 63.
5. Witmer, G.W. Wildlife population monitoring: Some practical considerations. *Wildl. Res.* **2005**, *32*, 259–263. [CrossRef]
6. Jones, G.P. *The Feasibility of Using Small Unmanned Aerial Vehicles for Wildlife Research*; University of Florida: Gainesville, FL, USA, 2003.
7. Gasaway, W.C.; DuBios, S.D.; Reed, D.J.; Harbo, S.J. *Estimating Moose Population Parameters from Aerial Surveys*; University of Alaska: Fairbanks, AK, USA, 1986.
8. Couturier, S.; Courtois, R.; Crépeau, H.; Rivest, L.-P.; Luttich, S.N. Calving photocensus of the Rivière George Caribou Herd and comparison with an independent census. *Rangifer* **1996**, *16*, 283–296. [CrossRef]
9. Pettorelli, N.; Côté, S.D.S.; Gingras, A.; Potvin, F.; Huot, J. Aerial surveys vs hunting statistics to monitor deer density: The example of Anticosti Island, Quebec, Canada. *Wildl. Biol.* **2007**, *3*, 321–327. [CrossRef]
10. Barnes, R.F.W. The problem of precision and trend detection posed by small elephant populations in West Africa. *Afr. J. Ecol.* **2002**, *40*, 179–185. [CrossRef]

11. Ransom, J.I.; Kaczensky, P.; Lubow, B.C.; Ganbaatar, O.; Altansukh, N. A collaborative approach for estimating terrestrial wildlife abundance. *Biol. Conserv.* **2012**, *153*, 219–226. [CrossRef]

12. Löffler, E.; Margules, C. Wombats detected from space. *Remote Sens. Environ.* **1980**, *9*, 47–56. [CrossRef]

13. Maglione, P. Very high resolution optical satellites: An overview of the most commonly used. *Am. J. Appl. Sci.* **2016**, *13*, 91–99. [CrossRef]

14. Fretwell, P.T.; LaRue, M.A.; Morin, P.; Kooyman, G.L.; Wienecke, B.; Ratcliffe, N.; Fox, A.J.; Fleming, A.H.; Porter, C.; Trathan, P.N. An emperor penguin population estimate: The first global, synoptic survey of a species from space. *PLoS ONE* **2012**, *7*. [CrossRef]

15. Stapleton, S.; LaRue, M.; Lecomte, N.; Atkinson, S.; Garshelis, D.; Porter, C.; Atwood, T. Polar bears from space: Assessing satellite imagery as a tool to track arctic wildlife. *PLoS ONE* **2014**, *9*. [CrossRef] [PubMed]

16. Yang, Z.; Wang, T.; Skidmore, A.K.; de Leeuw, J.; Said, M.Y.; Freer, J. Spotting East African Mammals in Open Savannah from Space. *PLoS ONE* **2014**, *9*, 1–16. [CrossRef] [PubMed]

17. Fretwell, P.T.; Staniland, I.J.; Forcada, J. Whales from space: Counting southern right whales by satellite. *PLoS ONE* **2014**, *9*, 1–9. [CrossRef] [PubMed]

18. Liu, J.G.; Mason, P.J. *Essential Image Processing and GIS for Remote Sensing*; John Wiley & Sons Ltd.: London, UK, 2009; ISBN 9780470510322.

19. Zhang, K.; Wang, M.; Yang, S.; Member, S.; Xing, Y.; Qu, R. Fusion of panchromatic and multispectral images via coupled sparse non-negative matrix factorization. *IEEE J. Sel. Top. Appl. Earth Obs. Remote Sens.* **2016**, *9*, 5740–5747. [CrossRef]

20. Peng, X.; Member, S.; Zhang, L.; Yi, Z.; Member, S. Constructing the L2-Graph for Subspace Learning and Subspace Clustering. *IEEE Trans. Cybern.* **2016**, *47*, 1053–1066. [CrossRef] [PubMed]

21. Otto, C.; Wang, D.; Jain, A. Clustering Millions of Faces by Identity. *IEEE Trans. Pattern Anal. Mach. Intell.* **2016**. [CrossRef] [PubMed]

22. Li, Z.; Itti, L. Saliency and gist features for target detection in satellite images. *IEEE Trans. Image Process.* **2011**, *20*, 2017–2029. [PubMed]

23. Wang, Q.; Yuan, Y.; Yan, P.; Li, X. Saliency detection by multiple-instance learning. *IEEE Trans. Cybern.* **2013**, *43*, 660–672. [CrossRef] [PubMed]

24. Wang, Z.; Du, L.; Wang, F.; Su, H.; Zhou, Y. Multi-Scale Target Detection in SAR Image Based on Visual Attention Model. In Proceedings of the 2015 IEEE 5th Asia-Pacific Conference on Synthetic Aperture Radar (APSAR), Singapore, 1–4 September 2015; pp. 704–709.

25. Wang, Q.; Lin, J.; Yuan, Y. Salient Band Selection for Hyperspectral Image Classification via Manifold Ranking. *IEEE Trans. Neural Netw. Learn. Syst.* **2016**, *27*, 1279–1289. [CrossRef] [PubMed]

26. Elhamifar, E.; Rene, V. Sparse Subspace Clustering: Algorithm, Theory, and Applications Ehsan. *IEEE Trans. Pattern Anal. Mach. Intell.* **2013**, *35*, 1–19. [CrossRef] [PubMed]

27. Yang, C.; Zhang, L.; Lu, H.; Ruan, X.; Yang, M.H. Saliency detection via graph-based manifold ranking. *Proc. IEEE Comput. Soc. Conf. Comput. Vis. Pattern Recognit.* **2013**, 3166–3173.

28. Gilmer, D.S.; Brass, J.A.; Strong, L.L.; Card, D.H. Goose counts from aerial photographs using an optical digitizer. *Wildl. Soc. Bull.* **1988**, *16*, 204–206.

29. Bajzak, D.; Piatt, J.F. Computer-aided procedure for counting waterfowl on aerial photographs. *Wildl. Soc. Bull.* **1990**, *18*, 125–129.

30. Glasbey, C.A.; Horgan, G.W.; Darbyshire, J.F. Image analysis and three-dimensional modelling of pores in soil aggregates. *J. Soil Sci.* **1991**, *42*, 479–486. [CrossRef]

31. Cunningham, D.J.; Anderson, W.H.; Anthony, R.M. An image-processing program for automated counting. *Wildl. Soc. Bull.* **1996**, *24*, 345–346.

32. Laliberte, A.S.; Ripple, W.J. Automated wildlife counts from remotely sensed imagery. *Wildl. Soc. Bull.* **2003**, *31*, 362–371.

33. Groom, G.; Krag Petersen, I.; Anderson, M.D.; Fox, A.D. Using object-based analysis of image data to count birds: Mapping of Lesser Flamingos at Kamfers Dam, Northern Cape, South Africa. *Int. J. Remote Sens.* **2011**, *32*, 4611–4639. [CrossRef]

34. Bai, X.; Zhang, S.; Du, B.; Liu, Z.; Jin, T.; Xue, B.; Zhou, F. Survey on dim small target detection in clutter background: Wavelet, inter-frame and filter based algorithms. *Procedia Eng.* **2011**, *15*, 479–483. [CrossRef]

35. Soni, T.; Zeidler, J.R.; Ku, W.H. Performance evaluation of 2-D adaptive prediction filters for detection of small objects in image data. *IEEE Trans. Image Process.* **1993**, *2*, 327–340. [CrossRef] [PubMed]

36. Shirvaikar, M.V. A neural network filter to detect small targets in high clutter backgrounds. *IEEE Trans. Neural Netw.* **1995**, *6*, 252–257. [CrossRef] [PubMed]

37. Casasent, D.; Ye, A. Detection filters and algorithm fusion for ATR. *IEEE Trans. Image Process.* **1997**, *6*, 114–125. [CrossRef] [PubMed]

38. Trathan, P.N.; Ratcliffe, N.; Masden, E.A. Ecological drivers of change at South Georgia: The krill surplus, or climate variability. *Ecography* **2012**, *35*, 983–993. [CrossRef]

39. Boccignone, G.; Chianese, A.; Picariello, A. Small target detection using wavelets. *Proc. Fourteenth Int. Conf. Pattern Recognit.* **1998**, *2*, 1776–1778.

40. Davidson, G.; Griffiths, H.D. Wavelet detection scheme for small targets in sea clutter. *Electron. Lett.* **2002**, *38*, 1128–1130. [CrossRef]

41. Kim, S. High-speed incoming infrared target detection by fusion of spatial and temporal detectors. *Sensors* **2015**, *15*, 7267–7293. [CrossRef] [PubMed]

42. Zhao, J.; Liu, F.; Mo, B. An algorithm of dim and small target detection based on wavelet transform and image fusion. In Proceedings of the 2012 Fifth International Symposium on Computational Intelligence and Design, Hangzhou, China, 28–29 October 2012; pp. 43–45.

43. Duk, V.; Ng, B.; Rosenberg, L. The potential of 2D wavelet transforms for target detection in sea-clutter. In Proceedings of the 2015 IEEE Radar Conference (RadarCon), Arlington, VA, USA, 10–15 May 2015; pp. 901–906.

44. Groom, G.; Stjernholm, M.; Nielsen, R.D.; Fleetwood, A.; Petersen, I.K. Remote sensing image data and automated analysis to describe marine bird distributions and abundances. *Ecol. Inform.* **2013**, *14*, 2–8. [CrossRef]

45. McNeill, S.; Barton, K.; Lyver, P.; Pairman, D. Semi-automated penguin counting from digital aerial photographs. In Proceedings of the 2011 IEEE International Geoscience and Remote Sensing Symposium (IGARSS), Vancouver, BC, Canada, 24–29 July 2011; pp. 4312–4315.

46. Descamps, S.; Béchet, A.; Descombes, X.; Arnaud, A.; Zerubia, J. An automatic counter for aerial images of aggregations of large birds. *Bird Study* **2011**, *58*, 302–308. [CrossRef]

47. Wang, T.J.; Skidmore, A.K.; Toxopeus, A.G. Improved understorey bamboo cover mapping using a novel hybrid neural network and expert system. *Int. J. Remote Sens.* **2009**, *30*, 965–981. [CrossRef]

48. Dagnino, A.; Allen, J.I.; Moore, M.N.; Broeg, K.; Canesi, L.; Viarengo, A. Development of an expert system for the integration of biomarker responses in mussels into an animal health index. *Biomarkers* **2007**, *12*, 155–172. [CrossRef] [PubMed]

49. Fernández-Delgado, M.; Cernadas, E.; Barro, S.; Amorim, D. Do we need hundreds of classifiers to solve real world classification problems? *J. Mach. Learn. Res.* **2014**, *15*, 3133–3181.

50. Schmidhuber, J. Deep Learning in neural networks: An overview. *Neural Netw.* **2015**, *61*, 85–117. [CrossRef] [PubMed]

51. LeCun, Y.; Bottou, L.; Bengio, Y.; Haffner, P. Gradient-based learning applied to document recognition. *Proc. IEEE* **1998**, *86*, 2278–2323. [CrossRef]

52. Johnson, J.; Karpathy, A.; Fei-Fei, L. DenseCap: Fully Convolutional Localization Networks for Dense Captioning. In Proceedings of the IEEE Conference Computer Vision and Pattern Recognition, Washington, WA, USA, 27–30 June 2016; pp. 4565–4574.

53. Krizhevsky, A.; Sutskever, I.; Hinton, G.E. ImageNet Classification with Deep Convolutional Neural Networks. *Adv. Neural Inf. Process. Syst.* **2012**, *25*, 1–9. [CrossRef]

54. Papandreou, G.; Kokkinos, I.; Savalle, P.A. Modeling local and global deformations in Deep Learning: Epitomic convolution, Multiple Instance Learning, and sliding window detection. *Proc. IEEE Comput. Soc. Conf. Comput. Vis. Pattern Recognit.* **2015**, 390–399. [CrossRef]

55. Wei, Y.; Xia, W.; Lin, M.; Huang, J.; Ni, B.; Dong, J.; Zhao, Y.; Yan, S. HCP: A Flexible CNN Framework for Multi-Label Image Classification. *IEEE Trans. Pattern Anal. Mach. Intell.* **2016**, *38*, 1901–1907. [CrossRef] [PubMed]

56. Wu, H.; Zhang, H.; Zhang, J.; Xu, F. Typical target detection in satellite images based on convolutional neural networks. In Proceedings of the IEEE International Conference on System, Man and Cybernetics, Hong Kong, China, 9–12 October 2015; pp. 2956–2961.

57. Ren, S.; He, K.; Girshick, R.; Sun, J. Faster R-CNN: Towards Real-Time Object Detection with Region Proposal Networks. *IEEE Trans. Pattern Anal. Mach. Intell.* **2017**, *39*, 1137–1149. [CrossRef] [PubMed]

58. LeCun, Y.; Yoshua, B.; Geoffrey, H. Deep learning. *Nature* **2015**, *521*, 436–444. [CrossRef] [PubMed]
59. Bengio, Y.; LeCun, Y. Scaling Learning Algorithms towards AI. In *Large-Scale Kernel Machines*; MIT Press: Cambridge, MA, USA, 2007; pp. 1–41, ISBN 1002620262.
60. Kala, R.; Shulkla, A.; Tiwari, R. Fuzzy Neuro Systems for Machine Learning for Large Data Sets. In Proceedings of the 2009 IEEE International Advance Computing Conference, Patiala, India, 6–7 March 2009; pp. 6–7.
61. Yager, R.R.; Zadeh, L.A. (Eds.) *An Introduction to Fuzzy Logic Applications in Intelligent Systems*; Springer Science & Business Media: Berlin, Germany, 2012.
62. Ma, H.; Ma, X.; Liu, W.; Huang, Z.; Gao, D.; Jia, C. Control flow obfuscation using neural network to fight concolic testing. *Lect. Notes Inst. Comput. Sci. Soc. Telecommun. Eng. LNICST* **2015**, *152*, 287–304.
63. Buckley, J.J.; Hayashi, Y. Fuzzy neural networks: A survey. *Fuzzy Sets Syst.* **1994**, *66*, 1–13. [CrossRef]
64. Hosseini, M.S.; Zekri, M. Review of Medical Image Classification using the Adaptive Neuro-Fuzzy Inference System. *J. Med. Signals Sens.* **2012**, *2*, 49–60. [PubMed]
65. McCulloch, W.S.; Pitts, W.H. A logical calculus of the idea immanent in nervous activity. *Bull. Math. Biophys.* **1943**, *5*, 115–133. [CrossRef]
66. Takagi, H.; Suzuki, N.; Koda, T.; Kojima, Y. Neural networks designed on approximate reasoning architecture and their applications. *IEEE Trans. Neural Netw.* **1992**, *3*, 752–760. [CrossRef] [PubMed]
67. Jang, J.-S.R. ANFIS: Adaptive-Network-Based Fuzzy Inference System. *IEEE Trans. Syst. Man Cybern.* **1993**, *23*, 665–685. [CrossRef]
68. Kurian, C.P.; George, V.I.; Bhat, J.; Aithal, R.S. Anfis model for the time series prediction of interior daylight illuminance. *ICGST Int. J. Artif. Intell. Mach. Learn.* **2006**, *6*, 35–40.
69. Yun, Z.; Quan, Z.; Caixin, S.; Shaolan, L.; Yuming, L.; Yang, S. RBF neural network and ANFIS-based short-term load forecasting approach in real-time price environment. *IEEE Trans. Power Syst.* **2008**, *23*, 853–858.
70. Boyacioglu, M.A.; Avci, D. An adaptive network-based fuzzy inference system (ANFIS) for the prediction of stock market return: The case of the Istanbul stock exchange. *Expert Syst. Appl.* **2010**, *37*, 7908–7912. [CrossRef]
71. Hiremath, S. Transmission rate prediction for cognitive radio using adaptive neural fuzzy inference system. Proceedings of 2010 5th International Conference on Industrial and Information Systems, ICIIS 2010, Mangalore, India, 29 July–1 August 2010; pp. 92–97.
72. Ford, A.T.; Fryxell, J.M.; Sinclair, A.R.E. Conservation challenges facing African savanna ecosystems. In *Antelope Conservation: From Diagnosis to Action*; Bro-Jørgensen, J., Mallon, D.P., Eds.; John Wiley & Sons Ltd.: London, UK, 2016; pp. 11–31. ISBN 9781118409572.
73. Hopcraft, J.G.C.; Sinclair, A.R.E.; Holdo, R.M.; Mwangomo, E.; Mduma, S.; Thirgood, S.; Borner, M.; Fryxell, J.M.; Olff, H. Why are wildebeest the most abundant herbivore in the Serengeti ecosystem? In *Serengeti IV: Sustaining Biodiversity in a Coupled Human-Natural System*; University of Chicago Press: Chicago, IL, USA, 2015; pp. 35–72.
74. Boone, R.B.; Thirgood, S.J.; Hopcraft, J.G.C. Serengeti Wildebeest Migratory Patterns Modeled from Rainfall and New Vegetation Growth. *Ecology* **2006**, *87*, 1987–1994. [CrossRef]
75. Pringle, R.M.; Doak, D.F.; Brody, A.K.; Jocque, R.; Palmer, T.M. Spatial pattern enhances ecosystem functioning in an african savanna. *PLoS Biol.* **2010**, *8*. [CrossRef] [PubMed]
76. Han, D. Comparison of commonly used image interpolation methods. In Proceedings of the 2nd International Conference on Computer Science and Electronics Engineering (ICCSEE 2013), Hangzhou, China, 22–23 March 2013; pp. 1556–1559.
77. Li, H.; Manjunath, B.S.; Mitra, S.K. Multisensor image fusion using the wavelet transform. *Graph. Model. Image Process.* **1995**, *57*, 235–245. [CrossRef]
78. Zhang, Y.; Dong, Z.; Wang, S.; Ji, G.; Yang, J. Preclinical diagnosis of magnetic resonance (MR) brain images via discrete wavelet packet transform with tsallis entropy and generalized eigenvalue proximate support vector machine (GEPSVM). *Entropy* **2015**, *17*, 1795–1813. [CrossRef]
79. Daubechies, I. The wavelet transform, time-frequency localization and signal analysis. *Inf. Theory IEEE Trans.* **1990**, *36*, 961–1005. [CrossRef]
80. Young, R.K. *Wavelet Theory and Its Applications*; Springer Science & Business Media: Berlin, Germany, 2012.

81. Addison, P.S. *The Illustrated Wavelet Transform Handbook: Introductory Theory and Applications in Science, Engineering, Medicine and Finance*; IOP Publishing: Bristol, UK, 2002.
82. Ye, X.; Wang, T.; Skidmore, A.K.; Fortin, D.; Bastille-Rousseau, G.; Parrott, L. A wavelet-based approach to evaluate the roles of structural and functional landscape heterogeneity in animal space use at multiple scales. *Ecography* **2015**, *38*, 740–750. [CrossRef]
83. Lee, B.Y.; Tarng, Y.S. Application of the discrete wavelet transform to the monitoring of tool failure in end milling using the spindle motor current. *Int. J. Adv. Manuf. Technol.* **1999**, *15*, 238–243. [CrossRef]
84. Ephraim, Y.; Malah, D. Speech enhancement using a minimum mean-square error short-time spectral amplitude estimator. *IEEE Trans. Acoust. Speech Signal Process.* **1984**, *32*, 1109–1122. [CrossRef]
85. Otsu, N. A threshold selection method from gray-level histograms. *IEEE Trans. Syst. Man Cybern.* **1979**, *9*, 62–66. [CrossRef]
86. Kohavi, R. A study of cross-validation and bootstrap for accuracy estimation and model selection. In Proceedings of the International Joint Conference on Artificial Intelligence, New York, NY, USA, 9–15 July 1995; pp. 1137–1143.
87. Bengio, Y.; Grandvalet, Y. No unbiased estimator of the variance of k-fold cross-validation. *J. Mach. Learn. Res.* **2004**, *5*, 1089–1105.
88. Dunn, J.C. A fuzzy relative of the ISODATA process and its use in detecting compact well-separated clusters. *Cybern. Syst.* **1973**, *3*, 32–57. [CrossRef]
89. Güler, C.; Thyne, G.D. Delineation of hydrochemical facies distribution in a regional groundwater system by means of fuzzy c-means clustering. *Water Resour. Res.* **2004**, *40*, 1–11. [CrossRef]
90. Shahi, A. An effective fuzzy C-Mean and Type-2 fuzzy logic for weather forecasting. *J. Theor. Appl. Inf. Technol.* **2009**, *5*, 556–567.
91. Ozkan, C. Surface interpolation by adaptive neuro-fuzzy inference system based local ordinary kriging. *Lect. Notes Comput. Sci.* **2006**, *3851*, 196–205.
92. Congalton, R.G. A review of assessing the accuracy of classification of remotely sensed data. *Remote Sens. Environ.* **1991**, *37*, 35–46. [CrossRef]
93. Yin, D.; Wang, L. How to assess the accuracy of the individual tree-based forest inventory derived from remotely sensed data: A review. *Int. J. Remote Sens.* **2016**, *37*, 4521–4553. [CrossRef]
94. Pouliot, D.A.; King, D.J.; Bell, F.W.; Pitt, D.G. Automated tree crown detection and delineation in high-resolution digital camera imagery of coniferous forest regeneration. *Remote Sens. Environ.* **2002**, *82*, 322–334. [CrossRef]
95. Dragomir, O.E.; Dragomir, F.; Stefan, V.; Minca, E. Adaptive Neuro-Fuzzy Inference Systems as a Strategy for Predicting and Controlling the Energy Produced from Renewable Sources. *Energies* **2015**, *8*, 13047–13061. [CrossRef]

 *remote sensing*

Article

Saliency Analysis via Hyperparameter Sparse Representation and Energy Distribution Optimization for Remote Sensing Images

Libao Zhang [1,2,*], Xinran Lv [1] and Xu Liang [1]

[1] The College of Information Science and Technology, Beijing Normal University, Beijing 100875, China; 201211211009@mail.bnu.edu.cn (X.L.); 201321210018@mail.bnu.edu.cn (X.L.)
[2] The State Key Laboratory of Remote Sensing Science, Beijing Normal University, Beijing 100875, China
* Correspondence: libaozhang@163.com; Tel.: +86-10-6225-8850

Academic Editors: Qi Wang, Nicolas H. Younan, Carlos López-Martínez and Prasad S. Thenkabail
Received: 10 May 2017; Accepted: 16 June 2017; Published: 21 June 2017

Abstract: In an effort to detect the region-of-interest (ROI) of remote sensing images with complex data distributions, sparse representation based on dictionary learning has been utilized, and has proved able to process high dimensional data adaptively and efficiently. In this paper, a visual attention model uniting hyperparameter sparse representation with energy distribution optimization is proposed for analyzing saliency and detecting ROIs in remote sensing images. A dictionary learning algorithm based on biological plausibility is adopted to generate the sparse feature space. This method only focuses on finite features, instead of various considerations of feature complexity and massive parameter tuning in other dictionary learning algorithms. In another portion of the model, aimed at obtaining the saliency map, the contribution of each feature is evaluated in a sparse feature space and the coding length of each feature is accumulated. Finally, we calculate the segmentation threshold using the saliency map and obtain the binary mask to separate the ROI from the original images. Experimental results show that the proposed model achieves better performance in saliency analysis and ROI detection for remote sensing images.

Keywords: saliency analysis; remote sensing; ROI detection; hyperparameter sparse representation; dictionary learning; energy distribution optimizing

---

1. Introduction

With the rapid progress of remote sensing technology, it is becoming easier to acquire high spatial resolution remote sensing images from various satellites and sensors. However, the analysis and processing of high spatial resolution images in more effective and efficient ways still remains a great challenge, particularly in images with complicated spatial information, clear details, and well-defined geographical objects [1–4].

The detection of the region of interest (ROI) has become a popular research topic, with valuable applications in many fields, such as object segmentation [5,6], image compression [7,8], video summarization [9], and photo collage [10,11]. Introducing ROI detection into remote sensing image processing has raised great concern among some scholars.

The human visual system serves as a filter for selecting a certain subset of visual information, based on visual saliency, while ignoring irrelevant information for further processing [12,13]. The region that draws human attention in an image is called ROI. There has been a lot of work done on saliency analysis and ROI extraction based on visual saliency, which is generally constructed based on low-level visual features, pure computation or a combination of these.

Itti et al. [14] developed a biologically-based model ITTI, which was named after the presenter, using "Difference of Gaussians" across multiple scales to implement "center-surround" contrast in color, intensity, and orientation features. Li et al. [15] presented a model based on Itti's method and additionally extracted GIST features trained by a support vector machine (SVM). Klein et al. [16] extracted ROIs with the knowledge of information theory. Although the models calculated visual saliency based on biological plausibility, the computing of center-surround involved the tuning of many parameters that determined the final performance.

In addition, pure computation based algorithms for ROI extraction have also been developed. Saliency analysis based on frequency domain has been shown in [17–19]. Imamoglu et al. [20] utilized the lower-level features produced by wavelet transform (WT). The above methods based on pure computing improve the efficiency of saliency processing. However, problems related to the complexity of modeling catering to different feature distributions and the lack of sufficient plausibility of biological visual saliency mechanisms are still unsolved.

With regard to mixed models, the Graph-based visual saliency (GBVS) model proposed by Harel et al. [21] applied the principles of Markov Chain theory to normalize activation maps on each extracted feature under the ITTI model. In 2012, Borji and Itti [22] utilized the sparse representation of the image and used local and global contrast in combination to detect saliency. Goferman et al. [23] combined local underlying clues and visual organization rules with methods of local contrast to highlight significant objects, and proposed a different model based on context-aware (CA) salient information. The CA model can detect the salient object in certain scenes, but the inevitably high false detection rate affects the accuracy. Another drawback of the model is that the time complexity is much higher than for other spatial-based saliency models. Wang et al. [24] proposed a visual saliency model based on selective contrast. Additionally, methods utilizing learning have also attracted attention in recent years, such as the model for saliency detection by multiple-instance learning [25].

In terms of the application of saliency analysis in remote sensing images, some have employed support vector machines (SVM) to extract bridges and airport runways from remote sensing images [26,27]. Some have constructed parameterized models to extract roads and airports from remote sensing images with prior information of targets [28–30]. Zhang et al. [31] proposed a frequency domain analysis (FDA) model based on the principle of Quaternion Fourier Transform to attain better experimental results compared with those that only used the information of amplitude spectrum or phase spectrum in the frequency domain. Zhang et al. also adopted multi-scale feature fusion (MFF) based on integer wavelet transform (IWT) to extract residential areas along the feature channels of intensity and orientation [32]. For some remote sensing images corrupted by noise, the saliency analysis of co-occurrence histogram (SACH) model uses a co-occurrence histogram to improve robustness against Gaussian and Salt and Pepper noises [33]. In addition, global clustering methods for image pre-classification or ROI detection are also introduced in remote sensing images [34–36]. For example, Lu et al. [36] first produced an initial clustering map, and then utilized a multiscale cluster histogram to analyze the spatial information around each pixel.

It is noticeable that the data sets of remote sensing images have a high volume of dimensional information, which is usually too large to handle effectively. Aiming at this problem, sparse codes have been introduced into image processing. Sparse codes learned from image patches are similar to the receptive fields of simple-cells in the primary visual cortex (V1) [37], which shows that the mechanism of human visual saliency is consistent with sparse representation. Sparse representation has also been shown to be a quite effective technique for wiping out non-essential or irrelevant information in order to reduce the dimensions. Furthermore, it has greater flexibility for data structure capture, and better stability against perturbations of the signal, which suggests that we can obtain the sparse coefficients produced by those basic functions with good robustness against noise or corruption.

Researchers have proposed a number of methods for dictionary learning. Independent Component Analysis (ICA) is a good method for learning a dictionary in order to obtain compact basic functions. Thus, ICA is mainly utilized for the learning of basic functions based on a large number of randomly selected image patches. In addition, there are also some other methods, such as DCT [38], DWT [39], K-SVD [40], and FOCUSS [41], which also perform well at forming sparse representation of datasets.

However, these methods are difficult to use when faced with different data modalities requiring specific extensive hyper-parameter tuning on each modality when learning a dictionary in remote sensing images. For DCT and DWT, there are three parameters that need to be considered: the number of extracted features; the sparsity penalty, which is used to balance sparsity and distortion during the learning process; and the size of mini-batch, which helps improve processing efficiency. For K-SVD, sparsity and dictionary size of the target should also be considered. For FOCUSS, the calculation of the final results needs a posteriori information. Therefore, the efficiency of these dictionary learning algorithms may run into a bottleneck when applied to remote sensing images.

Considering the problems mentioned above, we propose a model based on the integration of hyperparameter sparse representation and energy distribution optimization for saliency analysis. In this study, we focus on the ROI in optical remote sensing images. As a whole, the combination has full biological plausibility in terms of the human visual mechanism. In terms of sparse representation of remote sensing images, we adopt a novel feature learning algorithm—hyperparameter sparse representation—to train a dictionary. This algorithm is simple, clear and can be quickly implemented with high effectiveness, as well as being almost parameter-free, as the feature number is the only item to be decided. As for the measure of saliency, we use an energy distribution optimization algorithm to define saliency as entropy gain. Similarly, computation of this algorithm does not involve any parameter tuning, and is computationally efficient.

In the experimental process, we first transform the image from the RGB color space to the HSI color space as a preprocessing step. Subsequently, the input remote sensing images are divided into overlapping patches, and the patches are further decomposed over the learned dictionary. Then, an algorithm is utilized to maximize the entropy of visual saliency features for energy redistribution, so as to generate a final saliency map. Finally, Otsu's threshold segmentation method is implemented in the acquisition of binary masks from saliency maps, and the masks are then used for ROI extraction from the original remote sensing images. Experimental results show that the proposed model achieves better performance than other traditional models for saliency analysis of and ROI detection in remote sensing images.

There are three major contributions in our paper: (1) we introduce hyperparameter sparse representation into dictionary learning for remote sensing images. The algorithm converges faster and has fewer parameters; (2) while training the dictionary, we define every single pixel as a feature. Thus, the sparse representation of an image is equal to the optimal features used for further saliency analysis; and (3) hyperparameter sparse representation and energy distribution optimization of features are integrated to compute the saliency map. This method is biologically rational, and consistent with cortical visual information processing.

The work in this paper is organized as followed: the proposed model is thoroughly illustrated in Section 2, Section 3 focuses on the experimental results and discussion, Sections 4 and 5 provide the applications and conclusion, respectively.

2. Methodology

In the proposed model, the whole process of ROIs detection for remote sensing images can be divided into three parts: (1) obtain sparse representation of the image feature; (2) compute saliency contribution of all sparse features; (3) extract the ROIs from saliency maps. Figure 1 illustrates the framework of the proposed model. As we can see, in the first part, an unsupervised feature learning algorithm—Hyperparameter Sparse Representation—is utilized to create a dictionary for sparse representation of remote sensing images. We define every single pixel as a feature. Thus, the sparse representation of an image is equal to the optimal features that are used for further saliency analysis. The second part measures the entropy gain of each feature. On the basis of the general principle of predictive coding [42], the rarity of features can be seen as their average energy, which is redistributed to features in terms of their code length: frequently activated features receive less energy. The final saliency map is generated by summing up the activity of all features. Finally, we segment ROI from the original remote sensing image with the mask of saliency map based on the threshold segmentation algorithm [43].

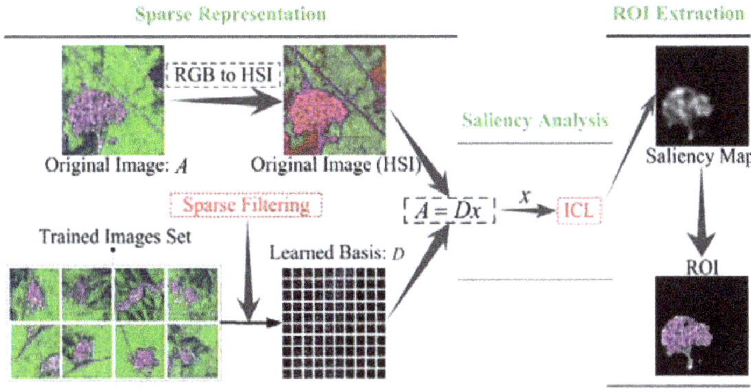

Figure 1. The framework of the proposed model.

Due to the characters of the simple computation, time efficiency and consistency in terms of the human color perception system of an HSI-based model [44], we preprocess images from RGB to HSI color space. Then the represented image is divided into overlapping patches and each patch is vectored as a column where all the pixel features were columned to form a feature matrix. Section 2.2, Section 2.3, Section 2.4 separately introduce the details of the three parts of our proposed model.

2.1. The Inadequacy of Traditional Algorithms

As we mentioned in Section 1, traditional visual saliency analysis methods have played an increasingly important role in the field of remote sensing image processing. Remote sensing images generally have high resolution and complex structure, which means that it is difficult to process directly. Visual attention models are first proposed for natural scene images. This kind of image is mostly obtained by different types of cameras, which means that we can highlight the significant targets by adjusting the aperture and the shutter. Targets will contain more information than background by selecting artificially. However, in remote sensing images, all objects have the same clarity. In other words, there is no difference in terms of clarity between the residential areas and the mountains, the roads and the ponds. Because of the clear and complex background, the problem of background interference is serious, which makes the saliency analysis hard.

The traditional methods need to combine the difference of the data distribution characteristics to select the effective calculation method for analysis, which will undoubtedly increase the diversity and complexity of the analysis. Moreover, the primary visual cortex shows that the receptive field of the single cell is similar to the sparse coding of the natural image block [45]. The human visual system also exhibits the characteristics of multilayer sparse representation of the image data. It shows that the sparse representation is consistent with the principle of human visual saliency mechanism, and can well explain the visual significance, which is biologically rational.

As shown in Figure 2, the ITTI model always mistakenly detects the background and sometimes misses the target region. The results of the frequency domain based model, Frequency-tuned (FT) model, contain a lot of debris and holes. The algorithms, which are designed specifically for ROI detection of remote sensing images, FDA and our model, obtain acceptable results. However, our results are clearly more accurate. In general, the ITTI and FT model are likely to get more inaccurate results, the FDA model makes some relative progress, and our model works best.

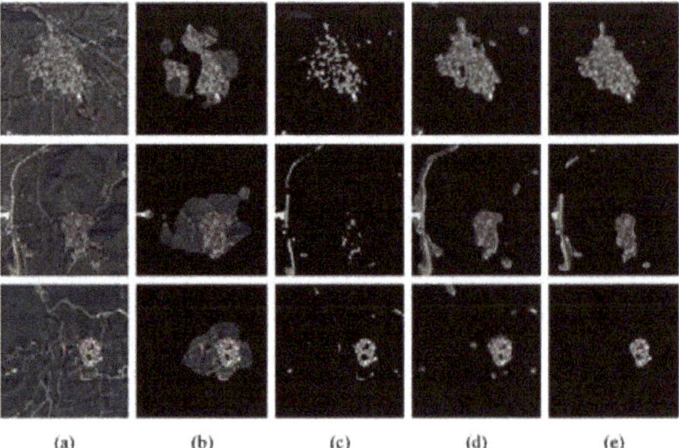

Figure 2. Region-of-interest (ROI) detection results produced by our model and the other 3 models. (**a**) origin images; (**b**) ITTI; (**c**) FT; (**d**) frequency domain analysis (FDA) and (**e**) our model.

2.2. Hyperparameter Sparse Representation

The method of dictionary learning can be considered as the generation of a particular feature distribution. For example, sparse representations are designed to use several nonzero coefficients to represent each sample, which highlight the main features of the sample. To achieve this goal, the ideal characteristics of the feature distribution should be optimized.

The desirable properties of feature distribution should meet with and include the three criteria [46]: population sparsity, lifetime sparsity and high dispersal. Population sparsity means that for each column in the feature matrix, there should be finite active (non-zero) elements. Moreover, it provides an effective coding method which is a theoretical basis for early visual cortex studies. Lifetime sparsity refers to that each row of feature matrix having only a small number of non-zero elements. This is because the features which are needed for further calculation ought to be characteristic of discrimination. High dispersal indicates that all features should have similar contributions, and the activity value of each row is supposed to be the same for every feature. Under certain circumstances, high dispersal is not completely necessary for good feature representation, on account of the same features which may be active and can prevent feature degeneration [46].

According to the characteristics that the sparse features should have, we apply a simple algorithm—hyperparameter sparse representation—which can optimize the three properties of features. Specifically, we illustrate these properties with a feature matrix of each sample. Figure 3 shows the structure of this algorithm.

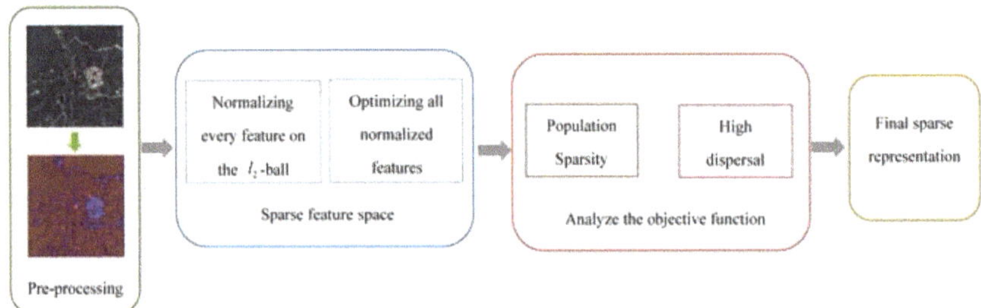

Figure 3. The structure of Hyperparameter Sparse Representation algorithm.

Each pixel column is viewed as a feature in our model. A feature matrix will be obtained after remote sensing image preprocessing. Each row of the matrix represents a feature and each column is a patch divided from the image. $f_j^{(i)}$ represents the jth feature value (rows) for the ith patch (columns). This sparse representation method aims to optimize and normalize the feature matrix by rows (feature values), then by columns (vectored image patch) and finally sums up the absolute value of all entries.

Firstly, by dividing each feature by its l_2-norm across all patches, each feature is normalized to be equally active:

$$\tilde{f}_j = f_j / \|f_j\|_2 \tag{1}$$

Then, analogously, by computing $\hat{f}^{(i)} = \tilde{f}^{(i)} / \|\tilde{f}^{(i)}\|_2$, all these features are normalized by each patch to put them on the l_2-norm ball. All normalized features are further optimized for sparsity by l_1 penalty. If there are M patches, then the sparse filtering objective function can be written as follows:

$$\min \sum_{i=1}^{M} \|\hat{f}^{(i)}\|_1 = \sum_{i=1}^{M} \left\| \frac{\tilde{f}^{(i)}}{\|\tilde{f}^{(i)}\|_2} \right\|_1 \tag{2}$$

Now it is essential to analyze whether the objective function meets with the three properties of desire features. First, population sparsity of features on the ith patch is measured by the equation as follows:

$$\|\hat{f}^{(i)}\|_1 = \left\| \frac{\tilde{f}^{(i)}}{\|\tilde{f}^{(i)}\|_2} \right\|_1 \tag{3}$$

when the features are sparse, an objective function can reach a minimum for the constraint of $\hat{f}^{(i)}$ in the l_2-norm ball. Contrarily, a patch that has similar values for each feature would incur a high penalty. Normalization of all features would cause competition between features: if only one element of $f^{(i)}$ increases, all the other elements in $f^{(i)}$ will decrease in the normalization, and vice versa. Minimal optimization of the objective function aims to make the normalization features sparse and mostly close to zero. With the principle of the competition between features, some features in $f^{(i)}$ have to be of large values while most of the rest of them are very small. To sum up, the objective function has been optimized for population sparsity.

Meanwhile, to satisfy the quality of high dispersion, each feature should equally active. As mentioned above, each feature is divided by its l_2-norm across all patches and normalized to be equally active by Equation (1). This is equal to constraining each feature to have the same expected squared value, thus contributing high dispersion. In the work of Ngiam et al. [47], they found that we can obtain over-complete sparse representation when realizing population sparsity and high dispersion in feature optimization, which also means that it is sufficient to learn good features as long as the condition of population sparsity and high dispersion are satisfied.

Therefore, obviously, the sparse filtering satisfies the three properties of desirable feature distribution and at the same time is also proved to be a fast and easy algorithm to implement. The entire optimization can be seen as the process of dictionary learning. When the objective function is optimized to reach a minimum under constraints, a dictionary D for sparse representation of the original image would appear to be the natural next-step before going on to process the image.

Notably, the entire optimization process of the feature matrix is automatically operated with the only tunable parameter: the number of the features. We can change the number of features by resizing the row number of the feature matrix to satisfy different requirements in image and signal processing. We can also learn that the dictionary learning process of the proposed model is approximately similar to the multi-layer sparsity by which the human vision system reacts to an image with the salient region from its surroundings.

2.3. Energy Distribution Optimizing

In this part, we describe the saliency of images with the optimized energy distribution (Algorithm 1), where different feature responses should have different energy intensity based on the principle of predictive coding. Therefore, incremental coding length is introduced to measure the distribution of energy on different features [48], which implies that different features have different rarity. The energy of the jth feature is defined as the ensemble's entropy gain during the activity of the jth feature. So the rarity of a dictionary feature is computed as its average energy. That is to say, rarely activated features will receive higher energy than activated ones. Then the final visually saliency is obtained by energy measurement, which shows that saliency computation by energy distribution conforms to the mechanism of human visual saliency in some degree.

Algorithm 1. Energy Distribution Optimizing

Input: A remote sensing image $A = [a_1, a_2, \cdots a_k, \cdots]$ and the liner filter $W = [w_1, w_2, \cdots w_k, \cdots]$.
    Vectorize the image patch a_k
for each feature **do**
   compute the activity ratio of the jth feature p_j.
   maximize the entropy $H(\mathbf{p})$.
   when a new excitation add a variation ε to p_i
     if $i = j$ $\hat{p}_i = (p_i + \varepsilon)/(1 + \varepsilon)$
     else $\hat{p}_i = p_i/(1 + \varepsilon)$
   end
   calculate the change of entropy of the jth feature $COE(p_j)$.
   get the salient features group $G = \{i | COE(p_i) > 0\}$
   compute the energy of the jth feature d_j
end
   obtain the saliency map m_k of image patch a_k

With the dictionary D for sparse representation mentioned above, the spare feature matrix X of image A on D can be acquired by $X = WA$, where $W = D^{-1}$. Then we can compute the activity ration p_j as follows:

$$p_j = \frac{\sum_k |w_j a_k|}{\sum_j \sum_k |w_j a_k|} \tag{4}$$

To fully consider the reaction degree of each feature in the sparse code and achieve optimality, maximizing the entropy $H(\mathbf{p})$ of the probability function $\mathbf{p}$ is a key principle to efficient coding. The probability function $\mathbf{p}$ varies at different points of time, depending upon whether there is a new perturbation on a feature, which means a variation ε will be added to p_i and further change the whole probability distribution.

This variation will change the entropy of the feature activities. We define the change of entropy of the jth feature $COE(p_j)$ as the following equation:

$$COE(p_j) = \frac{\partial H(\mathbf{p})}{\partial p_j} = -H(\mathbf{p}) - p_j - \log p_j - p_j \log p_j \tag{5}$$

The features with COE value above zero are viewed as salient and a salient feature set is obtained as G. Then the energy among features are redistributed according to their COE values. Denote the amount of energy that every sparse feature obtains d_j is computed as follows:

$$d_j = \begin{cases} \dfrac{COE(p_j)}{\sum\limits_{j \in G} COE(p_j)} & j \in G \\ 0 & j \notin G \end{cases} \tag{6}$$

Finally, the saliency map $M = [m_1, m_2, \cdots m_k, \cdots]$ of image A can be obtained as the equation below:

$$m_k = \sum_{j \in G} d_j w_j a_k \tag{7}$$

The final saliency map can be obtained by restoring all the vectorization image patches to the whole original remote sensing image.

2.4. Threshold Segmentation

To further evaluate the performance of the proposed model, we segment the saliency maps from the original images and obtain masks of the ROIs with the threshold algorithm proposed by Otsu [43].

Assume that the total number of pixels in an image is N, gray values of the image range from 1 to L, and the number of pixels with gray value i in the entire image is n_i. The occurrence ratio of pixels is computed as follows:

$$p_i = n_i / N \; (i = 1, 2, \ldots L)$$

$$\sum_{i=1}^{L} p_i = 1 \tag{8}$$

Suppose that the gray threshold value is k, pixels of the whole image is thus divided into two classes: A and B. Values in class A range from 1 to k, and values in class B from $k + 1$ to L. Their respective ratio is:

$$\omega_A = \sum_{i=1}^{k} p_i = \omega(k)$$
$$\omega_B = \sum_{i=k+1}^{k} p_i = 1 - \omega(k) \tag{9}$$

Then, the average gray value of each cluster is:

$$\lambda_A = \sum_{i=1}^{k} i p_i / \omega_A = \frac{\lambda(k)}{\omega(k)}$$
$$\lambda_B = \sum_{i=1+k}^{L} i p_i / \omega_B = \frac{\lambda_T - \lambda(k)}{1 - \omega(k)} \tag{10}$$

where $\lambda(k) = \sum_{i=1}^{k} i p_i$ and $\lambda_T = \sum_{i=1}^{L} i p_i$. λ_T is the average gray value of the whole image. The variance between A and B are calculated as follows:

$$\sigma^2(k) = \frac{[\lambda_T \omega(k) - \lambda(k)]^2}{\omega(k)[1 - \omega(k)]} \tag{11}$$

Then, the optimal segmentation threshold can be obtained by:

$$k^* = \underset{1 \leq k \leq L}{\mathrm{argmax}}\, \sigma^2(k) \tag{12}$$

The segmentation threshold value varies for different saliency maps. With the image binary segmentation, the masks of the ROIs are produced, and the masks are overlaid onto the original images to extract the final ROI in the next step.

3. Experimental Results and Discussion

To evaluate the performance of the proposed model, we used 300 remote sensing images of two different kinds as the experimental data. One is the remote sensing images from the SPOT 5 satellite with a spatial resolution of 2.5 m; the other is the remote sensing images from Google Earth with a higher spatial resolution of 1.0 m. The size of the experimental data are all 512×512 pixels. Among experiment images, we define the rural residential regions as ROIs, which should be detected primarily. As we have presented before, these regions typically include rich texture, irregular boundary, the area of brightness and color highlighting.

For the proposed model, the size of all these images used for learning a dictionary is down-sampled to 128×128 pixels, considering that we chose each pixel as a feature for saliency detection and ROI extraction. Therefore, the time consumed will be unbelievably excessive if we directly process images of original size. For remote sensing images of each kind, we randomly selected 60 images of to train the dictionary for sparse representation and all the 150 images were demonstrated for saliency analysis and ROIs extraction. The performance of the proposed model was compared qualitatively and quantitatively with other nine models including the Itti's model (ITTI) [14], the frequency-tuned (FT) model [17], the spectral residual (SR) model [18], the Graph-based visual saliency (GBVS) model [21], the Wavelet-transform-based (WT) model [20], the context aware (CA) model [23], the multiscale feature fusion (MFF) model [32], the frequency domain analysis (FDA) model [31] and the saliency analysis of co-occurrence histogram (SACH) model [33]. These nine models are selected for the following reasons:

- high citation rate: The classic model ITTI and SR have been widely cited;
- variety: ITTI is biologically motivated; FT, SR, and WT model all are the purely computational based models and estimate saliency in the frequency domain; GBVS and CA both belong to biological models and partly to the computational model;
- affinity: MFF, FDA and SACH model all are specially designed for saliency analysis in remote sensing images.

Notably, we use resized original images of 128×128 pixels to test their respective performance on different models. Finally, we resized the saliency maps of all models uniformly to the size of 128×128 pixels for fair comparison. Here, in each kind of image, we choose eight out of all the 150 images to make up the display figures for our experimental results.

After the transformation from RGB to HSI color space, we divide all the input remote sensing images used for dictionary training into overlapped patches of the size of 8×8 pixels with 192-dimension and further form an up to 130,000 large set of vectorization image patches.

Here, what we should pay attention to is the selecting feature number which is the only tunable parameter in the process of dictionary learning. Generally, a greater numbers of features correlates to a better performance. For consistency with the input dimension of the vectorization image set to form a square matrix, we choose 192 features for dictionary learning and saliency analysis. In our experiments, we adopted the off-the-shelf L-BFGS [49] package to optimize the sparse filtering objective until convergence with a maximum iteration number of 100. The learned dictionary we have obtained is shown in Figure 4.

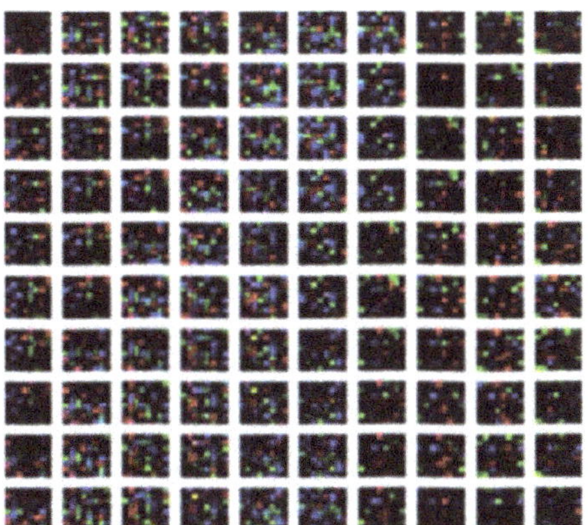

Figure 4. The learned dictionary.

3.1. Qualitative Experiment

As shown in Figures 5 and 6, the comparison among saliency maps generated by the proposed model and the other nine competing models on remote sensing images from SPOT 5 satellite and Google Earth, respectively. We can see that the saliency maps obtained by the proposed method focus on the residential areas and hardly have any background information. In contrast to the original images, the results of our model detected almost all salient objects. However, the other nine models detected some redundant information from the original images and cannot accurately locate the salient region. Although the CA model detects a clear boundary, it also includes the non-residential areas, thus enlarging the fall-out ratio and meanwhile is quite time-consuming.

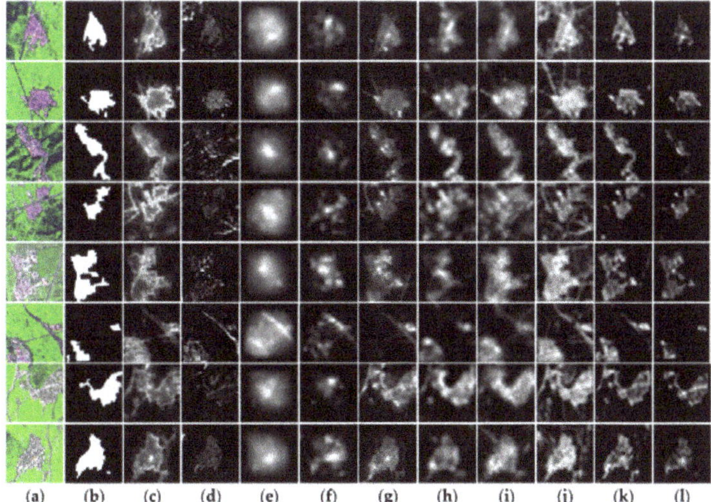

Figure 5. Saliency maps by our proposed model and nine competing models on SPOT 5 images. (**a**) Origin images; (**b**) Ground truth; (**c**) CA; (**d**) FT; (**e**) GBVS; (**f**) ITTI; (**g**) WT; (**h**) SR; (**i**) MFF; (**j**) SACH; (**k**) FDA and (**l**) Ours.

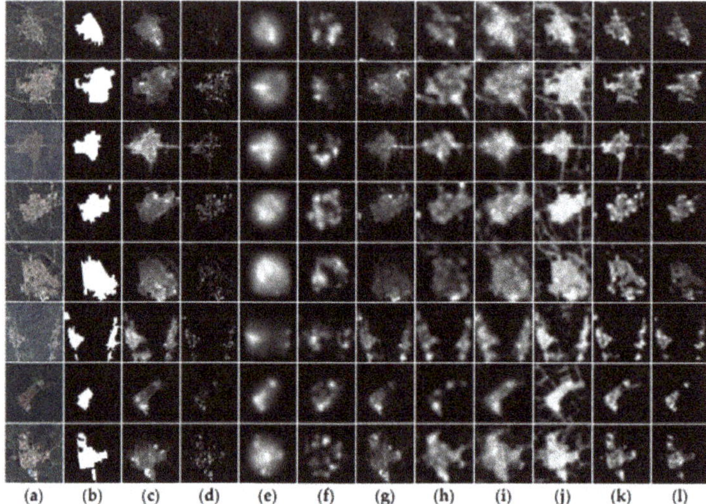

Figure 6. Saliency maps by our proposed model and nine competing models on Google Earth images. (**a**) Origin images; (**b**) Ground truth; (**c**) CA; (**d**) FT; (**e**) GBVS; (**f**) ITTI; (**g**) WT; (**h**) SR; (**i**) MFF; (**j**) SACH; (**k**) FDA and (**l**) Ours.

For SPOT 5 images, the experimental results of FDA model seem close to ours but we can see that there are still some little non-salient regions such as roads contained in the last four saliency maps in Figure 5. The MFF and SACH model can also obtain saliency maps which are not bad, but they are not accurate enough. Other models such as the ITTI, GBVS, and SR generate the final saliency maps of low resolution with blurred boundaries, which do not contribute to further ROI extraction. The CA and WT model always get acceptable results, but the inevitable needless background information can always be highlighted, too. Conversely, FT model fails to highlight the entire salient area, which results in the so-called hole effect that is the incomplete description of the salient area's interior. Meanwhile, for Google Earth images, although the performance of all the other models on saliency details such as border information is a little worse than that on SPOT images because of the higher spatial resolution, the proposed model still performs better intuitively.

Similarly, we can see the ROIs extraction results for two kinds of images from Figures 7 and 8 after Otsu's threshold segmentation. For the other nine models, some extracted ROIs are not able to completely contain the residential areas while some ROIs include excessively large redundant background information such as roads, especially in the ROI extraction results of the ITTI model and the GBVS model. In contrast, the proposed model exactly extracts the ROIs with clear boundaries and also has a good performance for remote sensing images with complex background, especially for the images with non-salient regions inside the outline of the residential areas and those with more than one salient region, as is shown in the ROI extraction result on the fifth and sixth images in Figure 7.

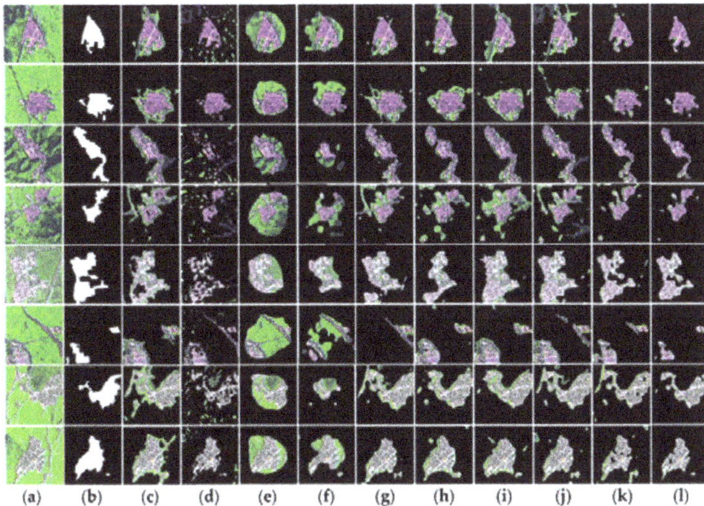

Figure 7. ROIs extracted by our proposed model and nine competing models on SPOT 5 images. (**a**) Origin images; (**b**) Ground truth; (**c**) CA; (**d**) FT; (**e**) GBVS; (**f**) ITTI; (**g**) WT; (**h**) SR; (**i**) MFF; (**j**) SACH; (**k**) FDA and (**l**) ours.

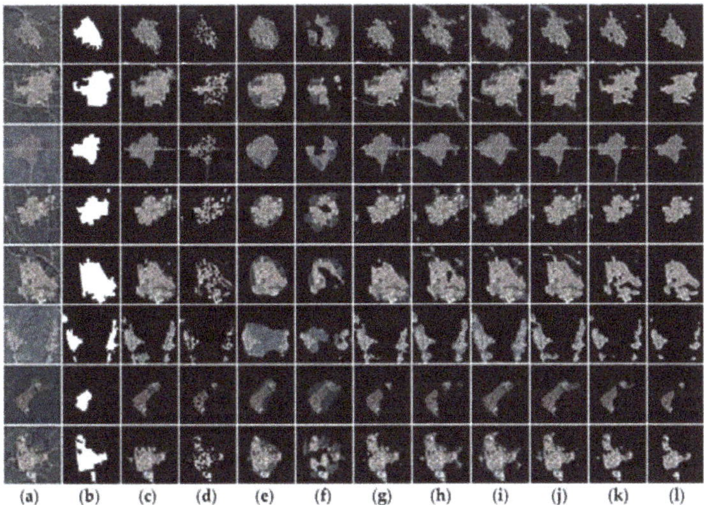

Figure 8. ROIs extracted by our proposed model and nine competing models on Google Earth images. (**a**) Origin images; (**b**) Ground truth; (**c**) CA; (**d**) FT; (**e**) GBVS; (**f**) ITTI; (**g**) WT; (**h**) SR; (**i**) MFF; (**j**) SACH; (**k**) FDA and (**l**) ours.

On a qualitative level, the experimental results show that the proposed model can not only generate saliency maps with a clear boundary with no excessive redundant background information, but also extracts exactly the ROIs with irregular shape and multi-saliency.

3.2. Quantitative Experiment

In the quantitative analysis of the experiment results, the ROC (Receiver Operator Characteristic) curve is adopted to measure the performance of different models. The ROC curve is derived by thresholding a saliency map at the threshold within the range [0, 255] and further classifying the saliency map into the ROIs and the background. The True Positive Rate (TPR) and the False Positive Rate (FPR) are two dimensions for spanning the ROC curve and respectively denote the percentage of the ROIs from the ground truth intersecting with the ROI from the saliency map and the percentage of the remaining background except for the ROIs. They are both computed as follows:

$$TPR = \frac{\sum\limits_{i=1}^{M}\sum\limits_{j=1}^{N} g(i,j)s(i,j)}{\sum\limits_{i=1}^{M}\sum\limits_{j=1}^{N} g(i,j)} \tag{13}$$

$$FPR = \frac{\sum\limits_{i=1}^{M}\sum\limits_{j=1}^{N} [1 - g(i,j)]s(i,j)}{\sum\limits_{i=1}^{M}\sum\limits_{j=1}^{N} [1 - g(i,j)]} \tag{14}$$

where, for an $M \times N$ image, g denotes the ground truth, s denotes the saliency map after the binary image, and (i,j) denotes the coordinate of the images. A higher TPR value indicates a better performance when the FPR value is the same and, conversely, better performance depends on a smaller FPR value at the same TPR value. The area beneath the curve is called the Area Under the Curve (AUC). Thus, a larger AUC indicates better performance. The AUCs of all the models are shown in Tables 1 and 2. From the Tables we can see that our model obtains the largest value of AUC compared to the other nine competing models, thus achieving better performance.

Table 1. The Area Under the Curve (AUC)s of our proposed model and nine competing models on SPOT 5 images.

Model	CA	FT	GBVS	ITTI	WT	SR	MFF	SACH	FDA	OURS
AUC	0.8832	0.9008	0.8216	0.7973	0.8934	0.9107	0.9278	0.9350	0.9408	0.9629

Table 2. The AUCs of our proposed model and nine competing models on Google Earth images.

Model	CA	FT	GBVS	ITTI	WT	SR	MFF	SACH	FDA	OURS
AUC	0.9274	0.9227	0.9267	0.8634	0.9531	0.9354	0.9639	0.9889	0.9789	0.9887

Similarly, we used two kinds of resized remote sensing images of 128×128 pixel size to test our model's performance. For each image, a manually segmented binary map using graphic software was generated as the ground truth. The average TPR and FPR values of every model are computed, and their ROCs on two kinds of images are shown in Figure 9a,b, respectively. From Figure 9a, we can conclude that the ROC curve that our model generated seems to show better performance than the others. However, we can see from Figure 9b that the performance of the SACH model is slightly better than our model whose ROC trace almost coincides with the other one. Therefore, we can know that the same model may have different performance for different kinds of remote sensing images, such as the FDA model and SACH model. The AUC comparison in Figure 10a,b further verifies our conclusion exactly, meanwhile, the Tables 1 and 2 also show the clear value of AUC.

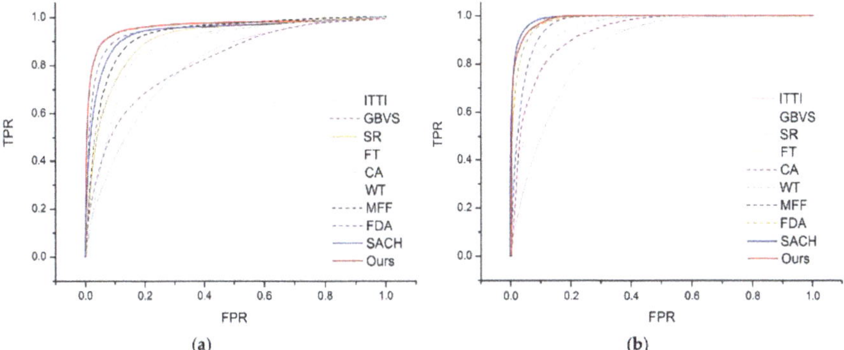

Figure 9. ROC curves of our proposed model and nine competing models on (**a**) SPOT 5 and (**b**) Google Earth images.

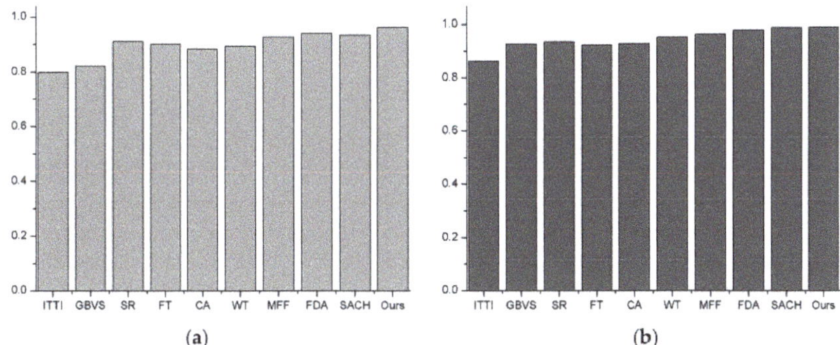

Figure 10. AUC of ROC curves of our proposed model and nine competing models on (**a**) SPOT 5 and (**b**) Google Earth images.

Another method based on Precision, Recall and the F-Measure which are denoted as P, R and F is also adopted to further evaluate the model's performance. They are computed as follows and the comparison of different models is shown in Figure 11a,b.

$$P = \frac{\sum\limits_{x=1}^{M}\sum\limits_{y=1}^{N} t(x,y)s(x,y)}{\sum\limits_{x=1}^{M}\sum\limits_{y=1}^{N} s(x,y)} \tag{15}$$

$$R = \frac{\sum\limits_{x=1}^{M}\sum\limits_{y=1}^{N} t(x,y)s(x,y)}{\sum\limits_{x=1}^{M}\sum\limits_{y=1}^{N} t(x,y)} \tag{16}$$

$$F_\beta = (1 + \beta^2)\frac{P \cdot R}{\beta^2 \cdot P + R} \tag{17}$$

where, for an image with size of $M \times N$, $t(x,y)$ denotes the ground truth, and $s(x,y)$ denotes the saliency map. The β serves as an indicator for the relative importance between precision and recall.

The larger the value of β, the more emphasis we put on recall than precision and vice versa. We choose $\beta = 1$ to equally balance the weight in our experiment.

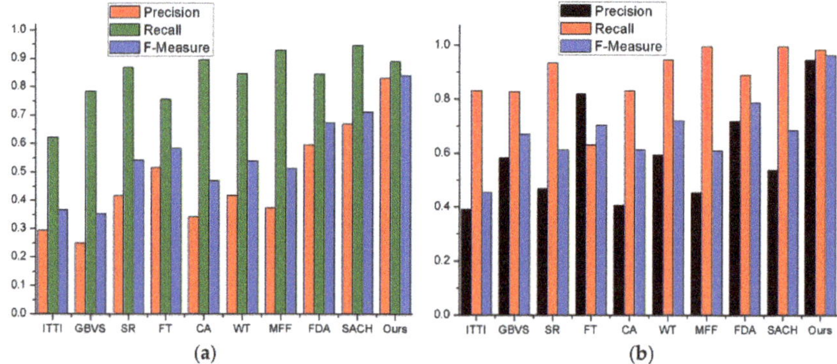

Figure 11. Precision, Recall and F-Measure of ROIs by our proposed model and nine competing models on (**a**) SPOT 5 and (**b**) Google Earth images.

From Figure 11a,b the precision of our model is obviously much higher than the other nine competing models, which means our model returns substantially more salient regions than background regions. Based on the previous qualitative analysis, the CA, WT, SR, MFF, SACH and FDA models achieve higher recall than the proposed model, probably because these models capture not only salient areas but some little non-salient regions with blurred boundaries. Meanwhile, this can be obtained clearly and reasonably according to Equation (17). Although the Recall is not the highest among these models, and in Google Earth dataset our ROC curve is slightly worse than SACH, our model still achieves the highest F-measure, thus showing better performance than others on different kinds of remote sensing images.

Additionally, we have compared the computational time for each method using matlab on a PC with 8 G RAM, Intel Core i3-4170 CPU @ 3.70 GHz. For the proposed model, the size of all these images used for learning a dictionary is down-sampled to 128 × 128 pixels. Here, we resized all images to the size of 128 × 128 pixels for fair comparison. From the Table 3 we can see that the run time of our proposed model is in the middle of the ten methods.

The FDA, FT, SR, ITTI and SACH model have a shorter run time than our model. The ITTI, FT and SR model are not proposed for remote sensing images. They do not take into account the complex background of remote sensing images, and use only a few simple features for analysis. The models FDA and SACH are specially designed for remote sensing images. For the former, there remain some holes in ROIs and the latter is not as high as our F-measure evaluation.

The MFF, GBVS, WT and CA model have a longer run time than our model. GBVS generates the final saliency maps of low resolution with blurred boundaries. WT and CA can always get acceptable results some non-salient regions were still extracted. Although MFF does not perform badly, it is not accurate enough.

Table 3. Running time comparisons for 10 models.

Model	FDA	FT	SR	ITTI	SACH	MFF	GBVS	WT	CA	OURS
AUC	0.85	1.72	2.04	3.68	4.83	6.81	18.43	106.51	1664	5.72

4. Applications

Because of the development of remote sensing technology, remote sensing image registration and fusion have been paid more and more attention in this field. Some researchers have applied region based image fusion algorithms to remote sensing images [50]. In the previous section, our experiments show that our model can extract ROI accurately from high resolution remote sensing images. Therefore, according to the region information provided by our model and the Gauss Pyramid decomposition, we can obtain more details from different scales of the original images, and then carry out image fusion to construct a clearer and accurate map.

The JPEG 2000 standard demonstrates many attractive features, including the ROI definition. In this case, ROI needs to encode with higher quality than the background [51]. However, knowing how to accurately select investment returns is still a prominent problem. Therefore, the results of our model can also be applied to image compression. The saliency map of the image can be detected and the visual importance [52] of the image pixels is measured, so that ROI can be considered as a step in the process of image compression priority encoding. According to Figure 12, the ROI still has a high subjective quality even at low bit rates (e.g., 0.5 bpp).

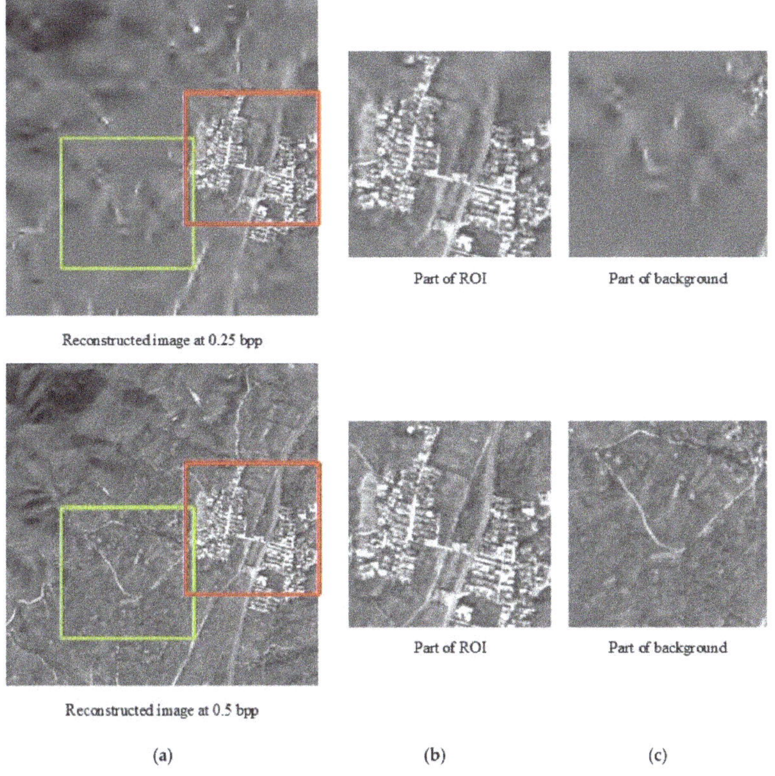

Figure 12. ROI compression example of remote sensing image. (**a**) reconstructed image; (**b**) part of ROI; and (**c**) part of background region. From top to bottom: reconstructed images are 0.5 bpp and 2.0 bpp, respectively.

5. Conclusions

This paper proposes a novel model based on hyperparameter sparse representation and energy distribution optimizing for saliency analysis and ROI detection in remote sensing images. The proposed model is simple to use and makes up the deficiency of biological plausibility as well as achieving better performance on saliency analysis and ROI detection. In this model, we firstly down-sample the original images and then transform them to HSI color space to increase the efficiency for further processing. After the overlapped patches segmentation and vectorization, a feature learning algorithm is adopted to train the dictionary for sparse representation. Then, energy distribution optimizing based on the principle of predictive coding is used to maximize the entropy of the feature of visual saliency, thereby generating the final saliency map. Finally, ROIs are extracted from original images with Otsu's segmentation method implemented in the obtained saliency map. Experimental results in two different kinds of remote sensing images demonstrate that the proposed model outperforms the other nine models in ROI extraction, qualitatively and quantitatively. In our experiments, each pixel is simply used as feature and only the number of features need to be chosen. Thus, there is no need to consider the specific structural information of different remote sensing images, which may provide a new unified method for feature extraction for image processing areas such as object compression, segmentation and recognition in the future.

Acknowledgments: This work was supported by the National Natural Science Foundation of China under grant numbers 61571050; the Beijing Natural Science Foundation under grant number 4162033; and the Open Fund of State Key Laboratory of Remote Sensing Science under grant number OFSLRSS201621.

Author Contributions: Libao Zhang, Xinran Lv and Xu Liang had the original idea for the study; Libao Zhang supervised the research and contributed to the article's organization; Libao Zhang and Xinran Lv conceived and designed the experiments; Xinran Lv performed the experiments; Xinran Lv and Xu Liang analyzed the data; Libao Zhang and Xinran Lv wrote the paper. All of the authors read and approved the submitted manuscript.

Conflicts of Interest: The authors declare no conflict of interest.

References

1. Zhang, L.; Li, A.; Zhang, Z.; Yang, K. Global and local saliency analysis for the extraction of residential areas in high-spatial-resolution remote sensing image. *IEEE Trans. Geosci. Remote Sens.* **2016**, *54*, 3750–3763. [CrossRef]
2. Sedaghat, A.; Mokhtarzade, M.; Ebadi, H. Uniform robust scale-invariant feature matching for optical remote sensing images. *IEEE Trans. Geosci. Remote Sens.* **2011**, *49*, 4516–4527. [CrossRef]
3. Liu, Z.; Dezert, J.; Mercier, G.; Pan, Q. Dynamic evidential reasoning for change detection in remote sensing images. *IEEE Trans. Geosci. Remote Sens.* **2012**, *50*, 1955–1967. [CrossRef]
4. Yi, L.; Zhang, G.; Wu, Z. A scale-synthesis method for high spatial resolution remote sensing image segmentation. *IEEE Trans. Geosci. Remote Sens.* **2012**, *50*, 4062–4070. [CrossRef]
5. Zhang, L.; Li, A.; Li, X.; Xu, S.; Yang, X. Remote Sensing Image Segmentation Based on an Improved 2-D Gradient Histogram and MMAD Model. *IEEE Geosci. Remote Sens. Lett.* **2015**, *12*, 58–62. [CrossRef]
6. Faur, D.; Gavat, I.; Datcu, M. Salient remote sensing image segmentation based on rate-distortion measure. *IEEE Geosci. Remote Sens. Lett.* **2009**, *6*, 855–859. [CrossRef]
7. Giusto, D.; Murroni, M.; Petrou, M. Region-based remote sensing image compression in wavelet domain using free angle segmentation model. *Electron. Lett.* **2002**, *38*, 1335–1337. [CrossRef]
8. Ancis, M.; Murroni, M.; Giusto, D.; Petrou, M. Region-based remote-sensing image compression in the wavelet domain. In Proceedings of the IEEE Conference on Geoscience and Remote Sensing Symposium, Hamburg, Germany, 28 June–2 July 1999; pp. 2054–2056.
9. Ma, Y.; Hua, X.; Lu, L.; Zhang, H. A generic framework of user attention model and its application in video summarization. *IEEE Trans. Multimedia* **2005**, *7*, 907–919.
10. Wang, J.; Sun, J.; Quan, L.; Tang, X.; Shum, H.Y. Picture collage. In Proceedings of the IEEE Conference on Computer Vision and Pattern Recognition, New York, NY, USA, 17–22 June 2006; pp. 347–354.
11. Goferman, S.; Tal, A.; Zelnik-Manor, L. Puzzle-like collage. *Comput. Gr. Forum* **2010**, *29*, 459–468. [CrossRef]

12. Maunsell, J.; Treue, S. Feature-based attention in visual cortex. *Trends Neurosci.* **2006**, *29*, 317–322. [CrossRef] [PubMed]

13. Najemnik, J.; Geisler, W. Optimal eye movement strategies in visual search. *Nature* **2005**, *434*, 387–391. [CrossRef] [PubMed]

14. Itti, L.; Koch, C.; Niebur, E. A Model of Saliency-Based Visual Attention for Rapid Scene Analysis. *IEEE Trans. Pattern Anal. Mach. Intell.* **1998**, *20*, 1254–1259. [CrossRef]

15. Li, Z.; Itti, L. Saliency and gist features for target detection in satellite images. *IEEE Trans. Image Process.* **2011**, *20*, 2017–2029. [PubMed]

16. Klein, D.; Frintrop, S. Center-surround Divergence of Feature Statistics for Salient Object Detection. In Proceedings of the IEEE Conference on Computer Vision and Pattern Recognition, Colorado Springs, CO, USA, 20–25 June 2011; pp. 2204–2219.

17. Achanta, R.; Hemami, S.; Estrada, F.; Susstrunk, S. Frequency-tuned salient region detection. In Proceedings of the IEEE Conference on Computer Vision and Pattern Recognition, Miami, FL, USA, 20–25 June 2009; pp. 1597–1604.

18. Hou, X.; Zhang, L. Saliency detection: A spectral residual approach. In Proceedings of the IEEE Conference on Computer Vision and Pattern Recognition, Los Angeles, CA, USA, 17–22 June 2007; pp. 1–8.

19. Guo, C.; Ma, Q.; Zhang, L. Spatio-temporal saliency detection using phase spectrum of quaternion fourier transform. In Proceedings of the IEEE Conference on Computer Vision and Pattern Recognition, Anchorage, AK, USA, 23–28 June 2008; pp. 1–8.

20. Imamoglu, N.; Lin, W.; Fang, Y. A saliency detection model using low-level features based on wavelet transform. *IEEE Trans. Multimedia* **2013**, *15*, 96–105. [CrossRef]

21. Harel, J.; Koch, C.; Perona, P. Graph-based visual saliency. *Neural Inf. Process. Syst.* **2006**, *19*, 545–552.

22. Borji, A.; Itti, L. Exploiting local and global patch rarities for saliency detection. In Proceedings of the IEEE Conference on Computer Vision and Pattern Recognition, Providence, RI, USA, 16–21 June 2012.

23. Goferman, S.; Zelnik-Manor, L.; Tal, A. Context-aware saliency detection. *IEEE Trans. Pattern Anal. Mach. Intell.* **2012**, *34*, 1915–1926. [CrossRef] [PubMed]

24. Wang, Q.; Yuan, Y.; Yan, P. Visual saliency by selective contrast. *IEEE Trans. Circuits Syst. Video Technol.* **2013**, *23*, 1150–1155. [CrossRef]

25. Wang, Q.; Yuan, Y.; Yan, P.; Li, X. Saliency detection by multiple-instance learning. *IEEE Trans. Cybern.* **2013**, *43*, 660–672. [CrossRef] [PubMed]

26. Tong, X.; Xie, H.; Weng, Q. Urban Land Cover Classification with Airborne Hyperspectral Data: What Features to Use? *IEEE J. Sel. Top. Appl. Earth Obs. Remote Sens.* **2014**, *7*, 3998–4009. [CrossRef]

27. Li, L.; Wang, C.; Chen, J.; Ma, J. Refinement of Hyperspectral Image Classification with Segment-Tree Filtering. *Remote Sens.* **2017**, *9*, 69. [CrossRef]

28. Valero, S.; Chanussot, J.; Benediktsson, J.A.; Talbot, H.; Waske, B. Directional mathematical morphology for the detection of the road network in very high resolution remote sensing images. *Pattern Recogn. Lett.* **2010**, *31*, 1120–1127. [CrossRef]

29. Chao, T.; Tan, Y.; Cai, H.; Tian, J. Airport detection from large IKONOS images using clustered SIFT keypoints and region information. *IEEE Geosci. Remote Sens. Lett.* **2011**, *8*, 128–132.

30. Lyu, C.; Jiang, J. Remote Sensing Image Registration with Line Segments and Their Intersections. *Remote Sens.* **2017**, *9*, 439. [CrossRef]

31. Zhang, L.; Yang, K. Region-of-interest extraction based on frequency domain analysis and salient region detection for remote sensing image. *IEEE Geosci. Remote Sens. Lett.* **2014**, *11*, 916–920. [CrossRef]

32. Zhang, L.; Yang, K.; Li, H. Regions of interest detection in panchromatic remote sensing images based on multiscale feature fusion. *IEEE J. Sel. Top. Appl. Earth Obs. Remote Sens.* **2014**, *7*, 4704–4716. [CrossRef]

33. Zhang, L.; Li, A. Region-of-Interest Extraction Based on Saliency Analysis of Co-occurrence Histogram in High Spatial Resolution Remote Sensing Images. *IEEE J. Sel. Top. Appl. Earth Obs. Remote Sens.* **2015**, *8*, 2111–2124. [CrossRef]

34. Martinez-Uso, A.; Pla, F.; Sotoca, J.M.; Garcia-Sevilla, P. Clustering-based hyperspectral band selection using information measures. *IEEE Trans. Geosci. Remote Sens.* **2007**, *45*, 4158–4171. [CrossRef]

35. Chen, J.; Zhang, L. Joint Multi-Image Saliency Analysis for Region of Interest Detection in Optical Multispectral Remote Sensing Images. *Remote Sens.* **2016**, *8*, 461. [CrossRef]

36. Lu, Q.; Huang, X.; Zhang, L. A Novel Clustering-Based Feature Representation for the Classification of Hyperspectral Imagery. *Remote Sens.* **2014**, *6*, 5732–5753. [CrossRef]

37. Huang, K.; Aviyente, S. Sparse representation for signal classification. *Adv. Neural Inf. Process. Syst.* **2006**, *19*, 609–616.

38. Lam, E.Y.; Goodman, J.W. A Mathematical Analysis of the DCT Coefficient Distributions for Images. *IEEE Trans. Image Process.* **2000**, *9*, 1661–1666. [CrossRef] [PubMed]

39. Bruce, L.M.; Koger, C.H.; Jiang, L. Dimensionality reduction of hyperspectral data using discrete wavelet transform feature extraction. *IEEE Trans. Geosci. Remote Sens.* **2002**, *40*, 2331–2338. [CrossRef]

40. Elad, M.; Aharon, M. Image denoising via sparse and redundant representations over learned dictionary. *IEEE Trans. Image Process.* **2006**, *15*, 3736–3745. [CrossRef] [PubMed]

41. Gorodnitsky, I.; Rao, B. Sparse signal reconstruction from limited data using FOCUSS: A re-weighted minimum norm algorithm. *IEEE Trans. Signal Process.* **1997**, *45*, 600–616. [CrossRef]

42. Rao, R.; Ballard, D. Predictive coding in the visual cortex: A functional interpretation of some extra-classical receptive-field effects. *Nat. Neurosci.* **1999**, *2*, 79–87. [CrossRef] [PubMed]

43. Otsu, N. A threshold selection algorithm from gray-level histograms. *IEEE Trans. Syst. Man Cybern.* **1979**, *9*, 62–66. [CrossRef]

44. Rahmani, S.; Strait, M.; Merkurjev, D.; Moeller, M.; Wittman, T. An adaptive IHS pan-sharpening method. *IEEE Geosci. Remote Sens. Lett.* **2010**, *7*, 746–750. [CrossRef]

45. Han, J.; He, S.; Qian, X.; Wang, D.; Guo, L.; Liu, T. An object-oriented visual saliency detection framework based on sparse coding representations. *IEEE Trans. Circuits Syst. Video Technol.* **2013**, *23*, 2009–2021. [CrossRef]

46. Willmore, B.; Tolhurst, D.J. Characterizing the sparseness of neural codes. *Network* **2001**, *12*, 255–270. [CrossRef] [PubMed]

47. Ngiam, J.; Koh, P.W.; Chen, Z.; Bhaskar, S.; Ng, A.Y. Sparse filtering. *Proc. Neural Inf. Process. Syst.* **2011**, *11*, 1125–1133.

48. Hou, X.; Zhang, L. Dynamic Visual Attention: Searching for coding length increments. *Adv. Neural Inf. Process. Syst.* **2008**, *21*, 681–688.

49. Schmidt, M. minFunc: Unconstrained Differentiable Multivariate Optimization in Matlab. Available online: http://www.cs.ubc.ca/~schmidtm/Software/minFunc.html (accessed on 1 January 2005).

50. Younggi, B.; Jaewan, C.; Youkyung, H. An Area-Based Image Fusion Scheme for the Integration of SAR and Optical Satellite Imagery. *IEEE J. Sel. Top. Appl. Earth Obs. Remote Sens.* **2013**, *6*, 2212–2220. [CrossRef]

51. Skodras, A.; Christopoulos, C.; Ebrahimi, T. The JPEG 2000 still image compression standard. *IEEE Signal Process. Mag.* **2001**, *18*, 36–58. [CrossRef]

52. Zhang, L.; Chen, J.; Qiu, B. Region-of-interest coding based on saliency detection and directional wavelet for remote sensing images. *IEEE Geosci. Remote Sens. Lett.* **2017**, *14*, 23–27. [CrossRef]

Article

Road Detection by Using a Generalized Hough Transform

Weifeng Liu [1]**, Zhenqing Zhang** [1]**, Shuying Li** [2,*] **and Dapeng Tao** [3]

[1] College of Information and Control Engineering, China University of Petroleum (East China),
    Qingdao 266580, China; liuwf@upc.edu.cn (W.L.); zhenqingz@163.com (Z.Z.)
[2] The 16th Institute, China Aerospace Science and Technology Corporation, Xi'an 710100, China
[3] School of Information Science and Engineering, Yunnan University, Kunming 650091, China;
    dapeng.tao@gmail.com
* Correspondence: angle_lisy@163.com; Tel.: +029-85619024

Academic Editors: Qi Wang, Nicolas H. Younan, Carlos López-Martínez and Prasad S. Thenkabail
Received: 28 April 2017; Accepted: 8 June 2017; Published: 10 June 2017

Abstract: Road detection plays key roles for remote sensing image analytics. Hough transform (HT) is one very typical method for road detection, especially for straight line road detection. Although many variants of Hough transform have been reported, it is still a great challenge to develop a low computational complexity and time-saving Hough transform algorithm. In this paper, we propose a generalized Hough transform (i.e., Radon transform) implementation for road detection in remote sensing images. Specifically, we present a dictionary learning method to approximate the Radon transform. The proposed approximation method treats a Radon transform as a linear transform, which then facilitates parallel implementation of the Radon transform for multiple images. To evaluate the proposed algorithm, we conduct extensive experiments on the popular RSSCN7 database for straight road detection. The experimental results demonstrate that our method is superior to the traditional algorithms in terms of accuracy and computing complexity.

Keywords: Hough transform; dictionary learning; road detection; Radon transform

---

1. Introduction

The determination of the location and orientation of a straight line road is a fundamental task for many computer vision applications such as road network extraction [1–23], image registration [4],visual tracking [5], robot autonomous navigation [6], hyperspectral image classification [7,8], Global Navigation Satellite System(GNSS) [9,10], unmanned aerial vehicle images [11], and sports video broadcasting [12,13]. A Hough transform (HT) [14–16] is one of the very typical methods and has been widely applied to computer processing, image processing, and digital image processing. It transforms the problem of a global detection in a binary image into peaks detection in a Hough parameter space. Dozens of HT extensions have been developed for solving straight line road detection problem. And particularly, these methods can be divided into the following four groups: generalized HT (GHT) [17–21], randomized HT (RHT) [22–25], probabilistic HT (PHT) [26–29], and fuzzy HT (FHT) [30–32].

Generalized HT (GHT) [17–21] detects arbitrary object curves (i.e., shapes having no or complex analytical form) by transforming the curves in image space into a four dimensional parameter space. For example, Lo et al. [18] developed a perspective-transformation-invariant GHT (PTIGHT) by using a new perspective reference table (PR-table) to detect perspective planar shapes. Ji et al. [19] proposed fuzzy GHT by using fuzzy set theory to focus the vote peaks to one point. Yang et al. [20] proposed polygon-invariant GHT (PI-GHT) by exploiting the scale-and rotation invariant polygon triangles characteristic to accomplish High-Speed Vision-Based Positioning. Xu et al. [21] developed robust invariant GHT (RIGHT) based on a robust shape model by utilizing an iterative training method.

Randomized Hough transform (RHT) [22–25] reduces the calculation and storage by using random sampling in image space, converging mapping and dynamic storage. Lu et al. [23] proposed an iterative randomized HT (IRHT) by the iteration to gradually reduce the target area from the entire image to the region of interest. Jiang [24] determined sample points and candidate circles by probability sampling and optimized methods to avoid false detection. Lu et al. [25] developed a direct inverse RHT (DIRHT) by incorporating inverse HT with RHT, this method is able to enhance the target ellipse in strong noisy images.

Probabilistic Hough transform (PHT) [26–29] defines a Hough transform in a mathematically "correct" form with a likelihood function in the output parameters. Matas et al. [27] proposed Progressive PHT (PPHT) utilized the difference in the fraction of votes to greatly reduce the amount of calculation of line detections. Galambos et al. [28] controlled the vote process by gradient information to improve the performance of PPHT. Qiu and Wang [29] proposed an improved PPHT by exploiting segment-weighted voting and density-based segment filtering to improve accuracy rate.

Fuzzy Hough transform (FHT) [30–32] finds the target shapes in noisy images by fitting data points approximately. Basak and Pal [31] utilized gray level images in FHT (gray FHT) to process the shape distortion. Pugin and Zhiznyakov [32] proposed a new method of filter or fusion of straight lines after performing FHT and thus avoiding detecting unnecessary linear features.

Although Hough transform and its many variants have achieved better results, it is still a great challenge to develop a low computational complexity and time-saving HT algorithm. In this paper, we propose a new method based on a generalized HT (i.e., Radon transform) and apply it for straight road detection in remote sensing images. We adopt a dictionary learning method [33] to approximate the Radon transform. The proposed approximation method has two significant contributions: (1) our method treats Radon transform as a linear transform, which greatly reducing the computational complexity; and (2) linear transformation makes it possible to realize parallel implementation of the Radon transform for multiple images, which can save time. To evaluate the proposed algorithm, we conduct extensive experiments on the popular RSSCN7 database for straight road detection. The experimental results demonstrate that our method is superior to the traditional HT algorithm in terms of accuracy and computing complexity.

The rest of this paper is arranged as follows. Section 2 briefly reviews the related works including the Hough transform and Radon transform. Section 3 presents the dictionary learning method to approximate the Radon transform. Section 4 describes the extensive experiments and discusses the experimental results. Finally, Section 5 gives some conclusions.

2. Related Work

In this section, we review some related works including Hough transform and Radon transform.

A Hough transform [14–16] detects shape in binary images by using an array named parameter space. Each point in binary images votes for the parameters space. The highest values of votes in the parameter space represent a parameter shape with the same linear features in the original image. Generally, linear features of a straight line on two dimensional plane (s_1, s_2) are parameterized by the slope (k) and intercept (b). Each point of a straight line will focus on one point in the (k, b) parameter space (Figure 1).

However, when the values of parameters are infinite (i.e., $k = \infty$), the parametrization of a straight line exists a singularity. Duda and Hart [34] proposes that straight lines can be parameterized by ρ, θ (Figure 2). And the mapping relations between image point (s_1, s_2) and (ρ, θ) parameter space satisfy the following:

$$\rho = s_1 cos(\theta) + s_2 sin(\theta) \tag{1}$$

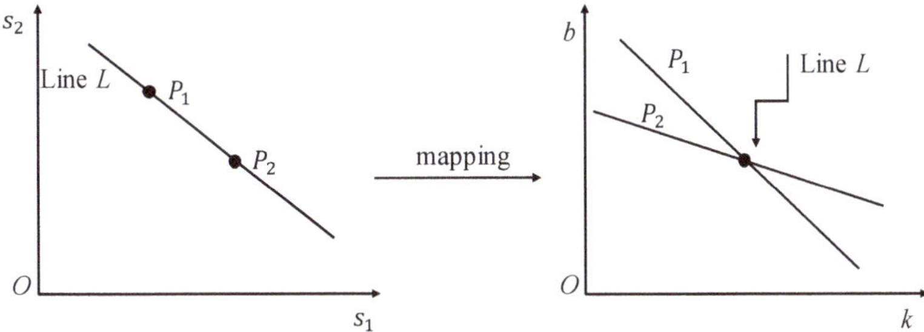

Figure 1. Mapping of P_1 and P_2 from Cartesian space to the slope-intercept parameter space.

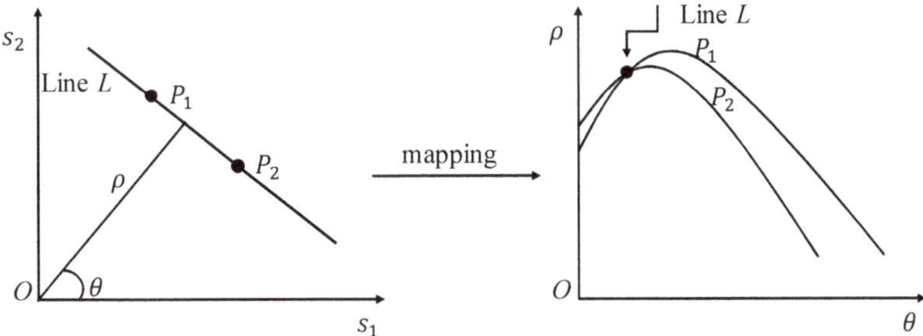

Figure 2. Mapping of P_1 and P_2 from Cartesian space to the (ρ, θ) parameter space.

Considering that a Hough transform can only be used for binary images, a Radon transform extends this concept to the problem of straight line detection in grayscale images [35]. If we denote $y(s_1, s_2)$ as an image on a two-dimensional Euclidean plane space, the Radon transform $x(\rho, \theta)$ of image y can be expressed as follows [36]:

$$x = \mathcal{R}$$
$$= \int_{\mathbb{R}^2} y(s_1, s_2)\delta(\rho - s_1 cos(\theta) - s_2 sin(\theta))ds_1 ds_2) \tag{2}$$

where $\delta(.)$ is the Dirac delta function, $\mathcal{R}$ is the Radon operator, $y(s_1, s_2)$ is the grayscale value of the point of (s_1, s_2), ρ is the distance between the origin and the vertical of straight line, and θ is the angle between the normal of straight line and the s_1 axis. Each point $y(s_1, s_2)$ can be mapped into a sinusoidal curve in the parameterized space, and a single point (ρ, θ) in the parameter space can be used to represent a line in image space.

The inverse Radon transform is defined as

$$y(s_1, s_2) = \mathcal{C}x(\rho, \theta) = \int_0^\pi z[s_1 cos(\theta) + s_2 sin(\theta), \theta]d\theta \tag{3}$$

$$z(\rho, \theta) \triangleq \int_{-\infty}^{+\infty} |\omega| X(\omega, \theta)e^{j2\pi\omega t}d\omega \tag{4}$$

where $\mathcal{R} = \mathcal{C}^{-1}$ is the Radon operator, $X(\omega, \theta)$ is the Fourier transform of $x(\rho, \theta)$ at angle θ. In addition, the Formulas (3) and (4) are the filtered back projection algorithm which is introduced to compute the inverse Radon transform.

3. Dictionary Learning Based Radon Transform

In this section, we introduced a dictionary learning method to approximate the Radon transform. Specifically, we use linear transform to approximate the discretized form of Formula (3) in practice. The relationship between the discretized parameter space image x and the discretized image data y can be defined as [37]:

$$y = Cx \tag{5}$$

where C is the discrete inverse Radon operator, $y \in R^{mn}$ denotes the vectorized $y \in R^{mn}$, and $x \in R^{pq}$ denotes the vectorized $x \in R^{pq}$.

In this paper, we employ a dictionary learning method to obtain the matrix C. Suppose the N training samples is $Y = (y_1, y_2, \cdots, y_N) \in R^{mn \times N}$, where $y_i \in R^{mn}$ denotes the vectorized $y_i \in R^{mn}$. $X = (x_1, x_2, \cdots, x_N) \in R^{pq \times N}$, and $x_i \in R^{pq}$ denotes the vectorized $x_i \in R^{pq}$. Our purpose is to learn a dictionary $C \in R^{mn \times pq}$ based on Equation (5):

$$(y_1, y_2, \cdots, y_N) = C(x_1, x_2, \cdots, x_N) \tag{6}$$

Since X is not a square matrix, matrix C can be calculate by the least squares method through minimizing the following objection function:

$$J = \| Y - CX \|^2 \tag{7}$$

where $\| * \|$ denotes the 2-norm of $*$. By minimizing the objective function (7), we have

$$C = Y\left(X^T X\right)^{-1} X^T, \text{ when } pq > N; \tag{8}$$

or

$$C = YX^T\left(XX^T\right)^{-1}, \text{ when } pq < N; \tag{9}$$

since matrix XX^T or $X^T X$ may be a singular matrix or approach a singular matrix, we add a damping factor α (with range from 0.1 to 1) to ensure the stability of numerical value:

$$C = Y\left(X^T X + \alpha I\right)^{-1} X^T, \text{ when } pq > N; \tag{10}$$

or

$$C = YX^T\left(XX^T + \alpha I\right)^{-1}, \text{ when } pq < N; \tag{11}$$

where matrix X^T is the transpose of the matrix X and I is a unit matrix.

Hence, the Radon transform of an image can be treated as a two matrix multiplication (i.e., linear transform):

$$X = C^{-1} Y \tag{12}$$

Since C is not a square matrix, we can obtain the value of X by minimizing the following target function:

$$J = \| Y - CX \|^2 \tag{13}$$

we have

$$X = \left(C^T C\right)^{-1} C^T Y, \text{ when } mm > pq; \tag{14}$$

or

$$X = C^T\left(CC^T\right)^{-1} Y, \text{ when } mm < pq. \tag{15}$$

Similarly, to ensure the stability of a numerical value, we add a damping factor α.

$$X = \left(C^T C + \alpha I\right)^{-1} C^T Y, \text{ when } mm > pq; \tag{16}$$

or

$$X = C^T \left(C C^T + \alpha I\right)^{-1} Y, \text{ when } mm < pq; \tag{17}$$

where matrix C^T is the transpose of the matrix C.

Our method treats a Radon transform as a linear transform, which can be realized by parallel computation of the Radon transform for multiple images:

$$(x_1, x_2, \cdots, x_N) = \left(C^T C + \alpha I\right)^{-1} C^T (y_1, y_2, \cdots, y_N), \text{ when } mm > pq; \tag{18}$$

or

$$(x_1, x_2, \cdots, x_N) = C^T \left(C C^T + \alpha I\right)^{-1} (y_1, y_2, \cdots, y_N), \text{ when } mm > pq; \tag{19}$$

The advantages of our solution is two-fold. Firstly, the transform (5) of the Radon operator makes it convenient and reasonable to leverage the performance by adding some special regularizations. For example, we can incorporate our objective function (5) into the regularization framework:

$$\hat{x} = \underset{x}{\arg\min} \|y - Cx\|^2 + \alpha^2 \varphi(x) \tag{20}$$

where $\varphi(x)$ is a regularization term which includes norm regularizer terms, log regularizer term, etc. Norm regularization terms take the form of $\varphi_{l_1}(x) = \|x\|_1 = \sum_i |x_i|$ for l_1- regularization, $\varphi_{l_2}(x) = \|x\|_2 = \sum_i x_i^2$ for l_2- regularization, $\varphi_{l_p}(x) = 1/p(\sum_i |x_i|^p), (p < 1)$ for l_p- regularization, etc. The log regularization term is in the form of $\varphi_{\log}(x) = \sum_i \log|x_i|$. We will verify the effect of adding regularization items in the future work.

Secondly, the linear transformation makes it possible to detect a straight line road of multiple images at one time, which will significantly reduce the time consuming aspect of this process.

4. Experiments and Discussion

In order to evaluate the performance of our method, we implement extensive experiments on RSSCN7 [38]. The RSSCN7 database is a remote sensing database which was issued in 2015, and the size of each remote sensing image is 400×400 pixels. There are 2800 remote sensing scene images in the RSSCN7 database, and they are from seven typical scene categories, which are a grassland, forest, farmland, parking lot, residential region, industrial region, river and lake. In this paper, we selected 170 remote sensing images with a straight line road to verify the proposed algorithm, and those 170 color images are converted to grayscale images in the preprocessing stage. Particularly, 150 images are used as a training set and the others as a test set. Some selected remote sensing images are shown in Figure 3.

In order to obtain sufficient training images, we rotate those 150 images from 0 to 180 degrees with a fixed step length, i.e., 10 degrees. Thus, we totally have 2700 grayscale images with the same size by intercepting those rotating images. Finally, the 2700 grayscale images are resized to 128×128. Further, all the test images are also adjusted to the size 128×128.

In this section, we demonstrate some experimental results of test samples and illustrate how our method is superior to the traditional algorithms in terms of accuracy and computing complexity.

Figures 4–7 illustrate the experimental results of four test samples. Now we discuss the experimental results of our methods with the experimental results of a traditional Radon transform.

Figure 3. Some remote sensing images with straight road examples from the RSSCN7 dataset.

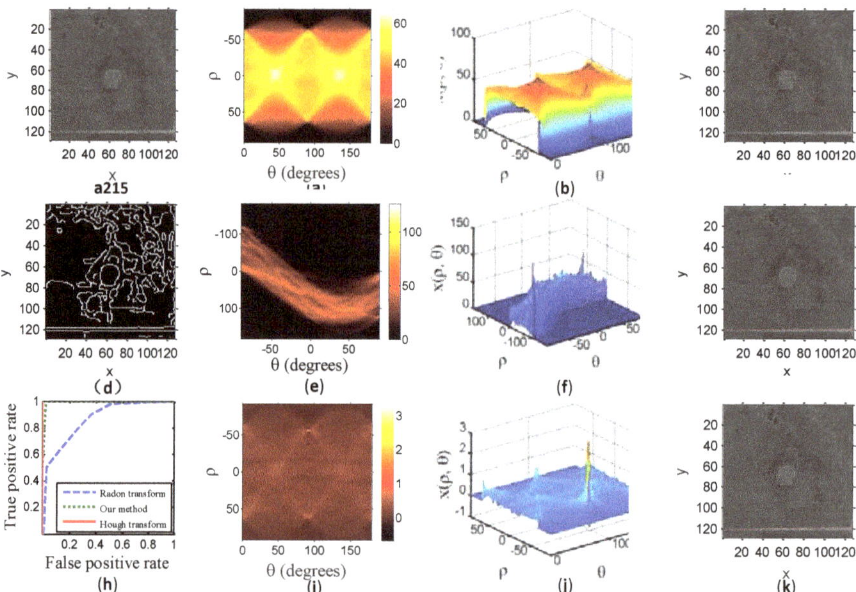

Figure 4. a215 is a test image. (**a**) Radon transform of test image in two-dimensional parameter space. (**b**) Three-dimensional form of (**a**). (**c**) Detected line from (**b**) overlaid on test image. (**d**) Binary image of the test image. (**e**) Hough transform of (**d**). (**f**) Three-dimensional form of (**e**). (**g**) Detected line from (**f**). (**h**) Receiver Operator Curves of the evaluated detection methods. (**i**) Transform image obtained by our method. (**j**) Three-dimensional form of (**i**). (**k**) Detected line from (**j**).

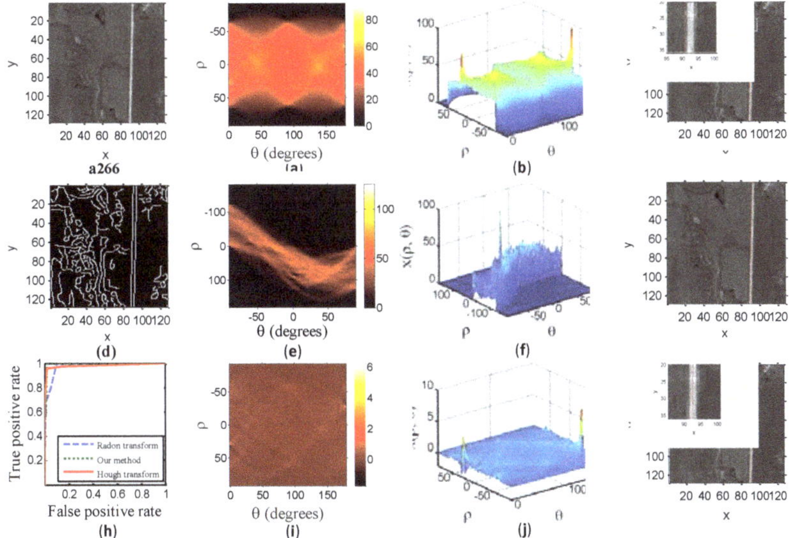

Figure 5. a266 is a test image. (**a**) Radon transform of test image in two-dimensional parameter space. (**b**) Three-dimensional form of (**a**). (**c**) Detected line from (**b**) overlaid on test image. (**d**) Binary image of the test image. (**e**) Hough transform of (**d**). (**f**) Three-dimensional form of (**e**). (**g**) Detected line from (**f**). (**h**) Receiver Operator Curves of the evaluated detection methods. (**i**) Transform image obtained by our method. (**j**) Three-dimensional form of (**i**). (**k**) Detected line from (**j**).

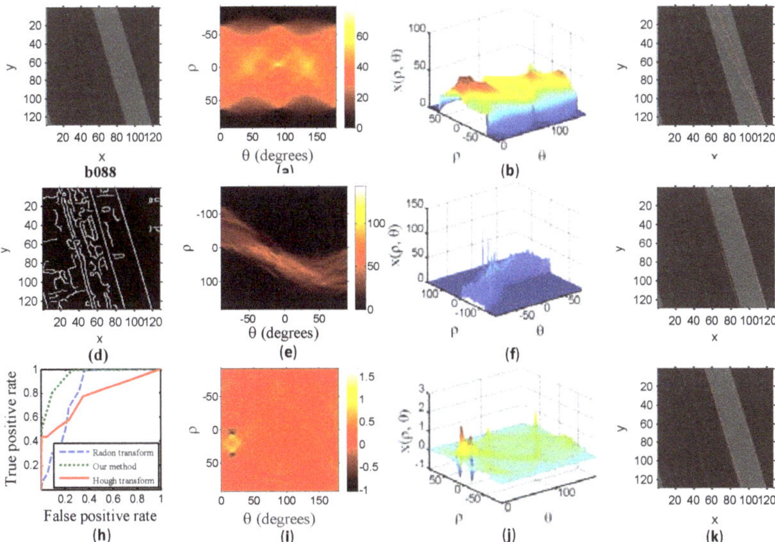

Figure 6. b088 is a test image. (**a**) Radon transform of test image in two-dimensional parameter space. (**b**) Three-dimensional form of (**a**). (**c**) Detected line from (**b**) overlaid on test image. (**d**) Binary image of the test image. (**e**) Hough transform of (**d**). (**f**) Three-dimensional form of (**e**). (**g**) Detected line from (**f**). (**h**) Receiver Operator Curves of the evaluated detection methods. (**i**) Transform image obtained by our method. (**j**) Three-dimensional form of (**i**). (**k**) Detected line from (**j**).

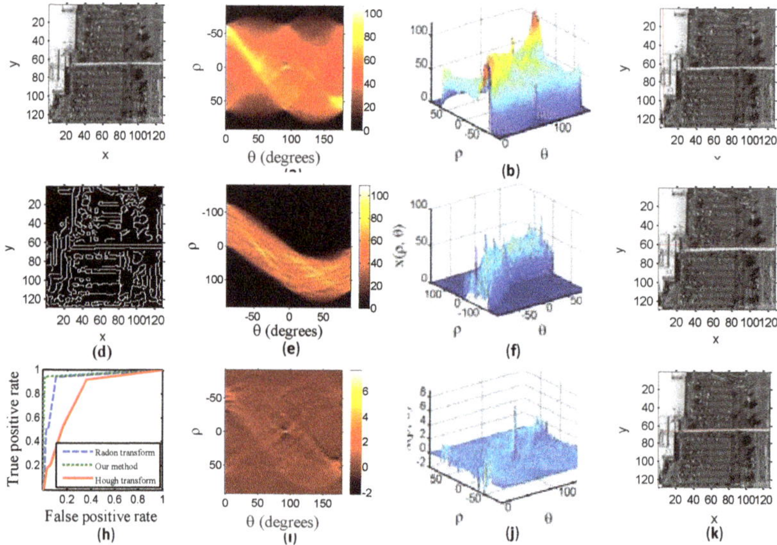

Figure 7. g146 is a test image. (**a**) Radon transform of test image in two-dimensional parameter space. (**b**) Three-dimensional form of (**a**). (**c**) Detected line from (**b**) overlaid on test image. (**d**) Binary image of the test image. (**e**) Hough transform of (**d**). (**f**) Three-dimensional form of (**e**). (**g**) Detected line from (**f**). (**h**) Receiver Operator Curves of the evaluated detection methods. (**i**) Transform image obtained by our method. (**j**) Three-dimensional form of (**i**). (**k**) Detected line from (**j**).

Figures 4a–7a show the Radon transform of a test sample in a two-dimensional parameter space and Figures 4i–7i show the transform image from our method in a two-dimensional parameter space. The one distinctly bright spot in Figures 4a–7a and Figures 4i–7i corresponds to the detected line (i.e., a red line) overlaid on the test image. It cannot be easy to isolate this one distinctly bright spot which matches with the straight road in test images from transform domain due to a lot of interference highlights in Figures 4a–7a. However, Figures 4i–7i show a bright spot corresponding to the detected line overlaid on the test image. The bright spot area in Figures 4a–7a is cluttered in visual effect. However, our algorithm reduces the effect of cluttered interference bright spots. By comparing Figures 4a–7a with Figures 4i–7i, we can see that the proposed method is superior to the conventional Radon transform in terms of the visual effect.

Figures 4b–7b show the three-dimensional form of Radon transform and Figures 4j–7j show the three-dimensional form of our method. The peak (i.e., bright spot in Figures 4a–7a) in Figures 4b–7b and Figures 4j–7j corresponds to the detected line overlaid on the test image. As seen in Figures 4b–7b, it cannot be easy to isolate the actual peak corresponding to the road in the test image from test samples owing to the mess in the transform domain. Particularly, the clutter of the peak in the transform domain will lead to false road detection or missed detection. From Figures 4j–7j, we can see that our method greatly accentuates the peak amplitudes relative to the background and it is possible to visually distinguish the peak point corresponding to the actual location of the straight road. Figures 4j–7j show that our method reduces the clutter interference to a large extent, and we are very easily able to isolate the true peak corresponding to the road in the test image.

Figures 4c–7c show the detected line from our method overlaid on the test samples and Figures 4k–7k show the detected line from Radon transform overlaid on the test samples. The location of the true and estimated straight line road are shown in Table 1. The ground truth parameters (ρ, θ) of the straight road are obtained by manual marking in sample images.

Table 1. The orientation of true and detected straight line.

Test Sample	a215	a266	b088	g146
True (ρ,θ)	$(-56.1,\ 90.7°)$	$(-27.6,\ 178.4°)$	$(8.3,\ 16.95°),(33.2,\ 17.6°)$	$(-0.8,\ 91.4°)$
Our Method (ρ,θ)	$(-56,\ 91°)$	$(-28,\ 179°)$	$(9,\ 18°),(33,\ 18°)$	$(-1,\ 92°)$
Radon Transform (ρ,θ)	$(0,\ 46°)$	$(-27,\ 180°)$	$(20,\ 28°),(26,\ 23°)$	$(1,\ -60°)$

It can be seen from the Figure 4b,c that the peak point does not match with the straight road in test sample a215. Figure 4j,k of test sample a215 show a conspicuous peak point which corresponds to the straight road in test sample a215. The experimental results of the test sample a215 illustrate that our method has a better detected result than traditional Radon transform if the detection target is not obvious.

The enlarged part in the Figure 5c shows the detected line from Radon transform. The enlarged part in the Figure 5k shows the detected line from our method. We can see that our detected results are closer to the true straight road.

By observing the Figure 6b, we can see that the peaks in a three-dimensional parameter space do not focus on one point. Scattered peaks result in a wrong detection, while Figure 6j illustrates that the peak point obtained by our method is more concentrated and easier to distinguish. From Figure 6k, we can see that the detected lines from our method correspond to the actual location of roads.

Test sample g146 has some noises which are similar to the straight road. From Figure 7c, we see that the detected line from the traditional Radon transform does not match with the straight road in the noisy image very well, whereas our method has good robustness for noisy images, as is shown in Figure 7k.

The above experimental results indicate that our method can accurately detect the position of the straight road when the noise is high or the road characteristics are not obvious, which illustrates that our method has stronger robustness, and our detected results are closer to the actual road location.

We also compared our method with a traditional Hough transform. A Hough transform can only be used for binary images. Although the binary images weaken the background noise, they also cause the loss of some road information.

Figures 4d–7d are the binary images of the test samples. By comparing the images of two-dimensional parameter space in Figures 4–7, we see that Figures 4e–7e also have many interference bright spots although the binary image weakens the background noise. However, Figures 4i–7i only include true bright spots. From the transform images of three-dimensional form in Figures 4–7, we see that our method greatly accentuates an area of high intensity in the transform domain relative to the background.

A binary image causes the loss of some road information. It can be seen from the Figure 7g,k that the detected line from Hough transform does not correspond to the true position of the straight road.

To clearly compare our method with the Radon transform and Hough transform, we also report the Receiver Operator Curves (ROC) result in Figures 4h–7h. The ROC was produced by changing the threshold parameter. Specifically, we first determine a threshold parameter, if peak points surpass the threshold, it was classified as road pixels, or otherwise as noise pixels. The ground truth data was obtained by manual marking in remote sensing image. The x-axis is the false positive rate (FPR) which can be calculated by:

$$FPR = \frac{Positives\ correctly\ classified}{Total\ positive}$$

the y-axis is the true positive rate (TPR) which can be calculated by:

$$TPR = \frac{negatives\ incorrectly\ classified}{Total\ negatives}$$

The accuracy of detected methods is measured through the area under the ROC curve. As shown in Figures 4h–7h, we can see that the accuracy of our method outperforms the traditional Radon transform and Hough transform.

To further demonstrate the performance of our method, we show the experimental results of another two test samples in Figures 8 and 9. The description of the experimental results in Figures 8 and 9 is the same as above.

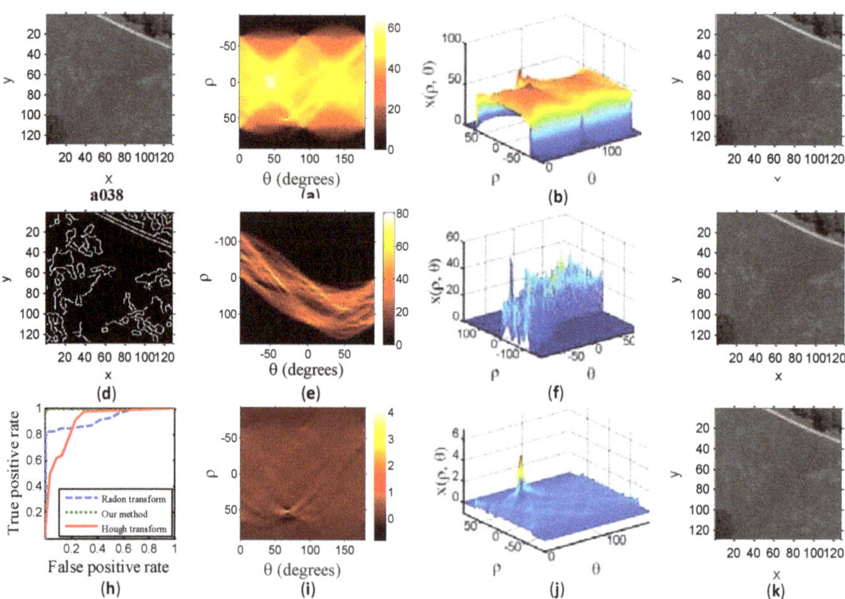

Figure 8. a038 is a test image. (**a**) Radon transform of test image in two-dimensional parameter space. (**b**) Three-dimensional form of (**a**). (**c**) Detected line from (**b**) overlaid on test image. (**d**) Binary image of the test image. (**e**) Hough transform of (**d**). (**f**) Three-dimensional form of (**e**). (**g**) Detected line from (**f**). (**h**) Receiver Operator Curves of the evaluated detection methods. (**i**) Transform image obtained by our method. (**j**) Three-dimensional form of (**i**). (**k**) Detected line from (**j**).

Specifically, test sample a038 shows a grayscale image with a shorter straight road. Figure 8b shows an undistinguishable peak point due to the mess in transform domain, and the detected line overlaid on a038 does not match with the straight road. From Figure 8j, we see that our method greatly accentuates an area of high intensity in the transform domain relative to the background. The experimental results in Figure 8 illustrate that our method can well detect a shorter straight road. The same conclusion can be drawn in the experimental result of test sample b230. This indicates that our algorithm is more sensitive to a shorter line road.

Particularly, our method is able to complete the line road detection of multiple images at one time. In dealing with a large number of images, our method facilitates parallel implementation of the Radon transform for multiple images (i.e., replace vector y_i with a matrix). Table 2 shows the time-consuming comparison between our method and the traditional Radon transform. We record the average running time of 20 test samples. Radon transform takes 0.106 s for per test image, but our method only takes 0.027 s. Experimental results of Table 2 show that the computation of our method is nearly 4 times faster than Radon transform.

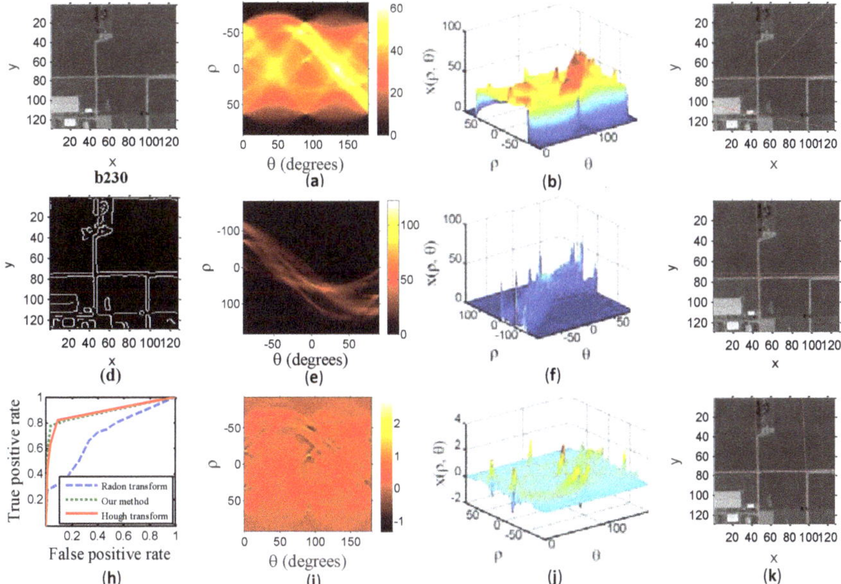

Figure 9. b230 is a test image. (**a**) Radon transform of test image in two-dimensional parameter space. (**b**) Three-dimensional form of (**a**). (**c**) Detected line from (**b**) overlaid on test image. (**d**) Binary image of the test image. (**e**) Hough transform of (**d**). (**f**) Three-dimensional form of (**e**). (**g**) Detected line from (**f**). (**h**) Receiver Operator Curves of the evaluated detection methods. (**i**) Transform image obtained by our method. (**j**) Three-dimensional form of (**i**). (**k**) Detected line from (**j**).

Table 2. Time-consuming comparison of two methods.

Methods	Our Method	Radon Transform
Test Samples	20	20
Average Running Time	0.027 s	0.106 s

Above all, our method is superior to the traditional Radon transform in terms of accuracy and computing complexity.

Table 3 illustrates the mean-error and variance of error. We can see that the mean-error of our method is much lower than traditional Radon transform. Hence, the detected parameters (ρ, θ) using our method is closer to the ground truth parameters. From the values of variance, we see that our method is more stable in detecting straight line.

Table 3. The mean-error and variance of two methods.

Methods	Our Method		Radon Transform	
Test Samples	20		20	
Line Parameters	ρ	θ	ρ	θ
Mean-Error	0.32	0.911°	11.46	15.65°
Variance of Error	0.089	0.286°	528.788	1105.48°

5. Conclusions

Road detection plays a key role for remote sensing image analytics and has attracted intensive attention. A Hough transform (HT) is a very typical method for road detection, especially for straight line road detection, and many variants have been proposed based on Hough transforms. However, developing a low computational complexity and time-saving Hough transform algorithm is still a great challenge. To solve the above problems, we present an approximation method by treating a Radon transform as a linear transform, which facilitates parallel implementation of the Radon transform for multiple images. Extensive experiments which are conducted on the RSSCN7 database show that our method is superior to the traditional Radon transform in terms of both accuracy and computing complexity. In the future, we will further study the regularization function being based on our algorithm to optimize our method.

Acknowledgments: This paper was supported by the National Natural Science Foundation of China under Grants 61671480, 61572486; the Fundamental Research Funds for the Central Universities, China University of Petroleum (East China), under Grants 14CX02203A.

Author Contributions: Weifeng Liu, Zhenqing Zhang and Shuying Li conceived and designed the experiments; Zhenqing Zhang performed the experiments; Shuying Li and Dapeng Tao analyzed the data, Weifeng Liu and Zhenqing Zhang contributed to the writing of the manuscript.

References

1. Zhu, L.; Lehtomäki, M.; Hyyppä, J.; Puttonen, E.; Krooks, A.; Hyyppä, H. Automated 3D scene reconstruction from open geospatial data sources: Airborne laser scanning and a 2D topographic database. *Remote Sens.* **2015**, *7*, 6710–6740. [CrossRef]

2. Cheng, L.; Wu, Y.; Tong, L.; Chen, Y.; Li, M. Hierarchical Registration Method for Airborne and Vehicle LiDAR Point Cloud. *Remote Sens.* **2015**, *7*, 13921–13944. [CrossRef]

3. Maboudi, M.; Amini, J.; Hahn, M.; Saati, M. Road Network Extraction from VHR Satellite Images Using Context Aware Object Feature Integration and Tensor Voting. *Remote Sens.* **2016**, *8*, 637. [CrossRef]

4. Han, J.; Pauwels, E.J.; De Zeeuw, P. Visible and infrared image registration in man-made environments employing hybrid visual features. *Pattern Recognit. Lett.* **2013**, *34*, 42–51. [CrossRef]

5. Wang, Q.; Fang, J.; Yuan, Y. Multi-cue based tracking. *Neurocomputing* **2014**, *131*, 227–236. [CrossRef]

6. Wang, Q.; Fang, J.; Yuan, Y. Adaptive road detection via context-aware label transfer. *Neurocomputing* **2015**, *158*, 174–183. [CrossRef]

7. Ghamisi, P.; Plaza, J.; Chen, Y.; Li, J.; Plaza, A.J. Advanced Spectral Classifiers for Hyperspectral Images: A review. *IEEE Geosci. Remote Sens. Mag.* **2017**, *5*, 8–32. [CrossRef]

8. Wang, Q.; Lin, J.; Yuan, Y. Salient band selection for hyperspectral image classification via manifold ranking. *IEEE Trans. Neural Netw. Learn. Syst.* **2016**, *27*, 1279–1289. [CrossRef] [PubMed]

9. Gao, Z.; Shen, W.; Zhang, H.; Ge, M.; Niu, X. Application of Helmert Variance Component Based Adaptive Kalman Filter in Multi-GNSS PPP/INS Tightly Coupled Integration. *Remote Sens.* **2016**, *8*, 553. [CrossRef]

10. Qian, C.; Liu, H.; Tang, J.; Chen, Y.; Kaartinen, H.; Kukko, A.; Zhu, L.; Liang, X.; Chen, L.; Hyyppä, J. An Integrated GNSS/INS/LiDAR-SLAM Positioning Method for Highly Accurate Forest Stem Mapping. *Remote Sens.* **2016**, *9*, 3. [CrossRef]

11. Duan, F.; Wan, Y.; Deng, L. A Novel Approach for Coarse-to-Fine Windthrown Tree Extraction Based on Unmanned Aerial Vehicle Images. *Remote Sens.* **2017**, *9*, 306. [CrossRef]

12. Han, J.; Farin, D.; de With, P.H. Broadcast court-net sports video analysis using fast 3-D camera modeling. *IEEE Trans. Circuits Syst. Video Technol.* **2008**, *18*, 1628–1638.

13. Han, J.; Farin, D.; de With, P. A mixed-reality system for broadcasting sports video to mobile devices. *IEEE MultiMed.* **2011**, *18*, 72–84. [CrossRef]

14. Ye, H.; Shang, G.; Wang, L.; Zheng, M. A new method based on hough transform for quick line and circle detection. In Proceedings of the International Conference on Biomedical Engineering and Informatics, Shenyang, China, 14–16 October 2015; pp. 52–56.

15. Hough Paul, V.C. Method and Means for Recognizing Complex Patterns. U.S. Patent 3,069,654, 18 December 1962.

16. Mukhopadhyay, P.; Chaudhuri, B.B. A survey of Hough Transform. *Pattern Recognit.* **2015**, *48*, 993–1010. [CrossRef]

17. Ballard, D.H. Generalizing the Hough transform to detect arbitrary shapes. *Pattern Recognit.* **1981**, *13*, 111–122. [CrossRef]

18. Lo, R.C.; Tsai, W.H. Perspective-transformation-invariant generalized Hough transform for perspective planar shape detection and matching. *Pattern Recognit.* **1997**, *30*, 383–396. [CrossRef]

19. Ji, Y.; Mao, L.; Huang, Q.; Gao, Y. Research on object shape detection from image with high-level noise based on fuzzy generalized Hough Transform. In Proceedings of the Multimedia and Signal Processing (CMSP), Guilin, Guangxi, China, 14–15 May 2011; pp. 209–212.

20. Xu, J.; Sun, X.; Zhang, D.; Fu, K. Automatic detection of inshore ships in high-resolution remote sensing images using robust invariant generalized Hough transform. *IEEE Geosci. Remote Sens. Lett.* **2014**, *11*, 2070–2074.

21. Yang, H.; Zheng, S.; Lu, J.; Yin, Z. Polygon-Invariant Generalized Hough Transform for High-Speed Vision-Based Positioning. *IEEE Trans. Autom. Sci. Eng.* **2016**, *13*, 1367–1384. [CrossRef]

22. Xu, L.; Oja, E.; Kultanen, P. A new curve detection method: Randomized Hough transform (RHT). *Pattern Recognit. Lett.* **1990**, *11*, 331–338. [CrossRef]

23. Lu, W.; Tan, J. Detection of incomplete ellipse in images with strong noise by iterative randomized Hough transform (IRHT). *Pattern Recognit.* **2008**, *41*, 1268–1279. [CrossRef]

24. Jiang, L. Efficient randomized Hough transform for circle detection using novel probability sampling and feature points. *Opt. Int. J. Light Electron. Opt.* **2012**, *123*, 1834–1840. [CrossRef]

25. Lu, W.; Yu, J.; Tan, J. Direct inverse randomized Hough transform for incomplete ellipse detection in noisy images. *J. Pattern Recognit. Res.* **2014**, *1*, 13–24. [CrossRef]

26. Stephens, R.S. Probabilistic approach to the Hough transform. *Image Vis. Comput.* **1991**, *9*, 66–71. [CrossRef]

27. Matas, J.; Galambos, C.; Kittler, J. Robust detection of lines using the progressive probabilistic hough transform. *Comput. Vis. Image Underst.* **2000**, *78*, 119–137. [CrossRef]

28. Galambos, C.; Kittler, J.; Matas, J. Gradient based progressive probabilistic Hough transform. *IEE Proc. Vis. Image Signal. Process.* **2001**, *148*, 158–165. [CrossRef]

29. Qiu, S.; Wang, X. The improved progressive probabilistic hough transform for paper wrinkle detection. In Proceedings of the International Conference on Signal Processing (ICSP), Beijing, China, 21–25 October 2012; pp. 783–786.

30. Han, J.H.; Kóczy, L.; Poston, T. Fuzzy hough transform. *Pattern Recognit. Lett.* **1994**, *15*, 649–658. [CrossRef]

31. Basak, J.; Pal, S.K. Theoretical quantification of shape distortion in fuzzy Hough transform. *Fuzzy Sets Syst.* **2005**, *154*, 227–250. [CrossRef]

32. Pugin, E.V.; Zhiznyakov, A.L. In Proceedings of the Filtering of meaningful features of fuzzy hough transform. In Proceedings of the Dynamics of Systems, Mechanisms and Machines (Dynamics), Omsk, Russia, 15–17 November 2016; pp. 1–5.

33. Liu, T.; Tao, D. On the performance of manhattan nonnegative matrix factorization. *IEEE Trans. Neural Netw. Learn. Syst.* **2016**, *27*, 1851–1863. [CrossRef] [PubMed]

34. Duda, R.O.; Hart, P.E. Use of the Hough transformation to detect lines and curves in pictures. *Commun. ACM* **1972**, *15*, 11–15. [CrossRef]

35. Deans, S.R. Hough transform from the Radon transform. *IEEE Trans. Pattern Anal. Mach. Intell.* **1981**, *2*, 185–188. [CrossRef]

36. Deans, S.R. *The Radon Transform and Some of Its Application*; John Wiley & Sons Inc.: New York, NY, USA, 1983; Volume 223, pp. 3–4.

37. Aggarwal, N.; Karl, W.C. Line detection in images through regularized Hough transform. *IEEE Trans. Image Process.* **2006**, *15*, 582–591. [CrossRef] [PubMed]

38. Zou, Q.; Ni, L.; Zhang, T.; Wang, Q. Deep learning based feature selection for remote sensing scene classification. *IEEE Geosci. Remote Sens. Lett.* **2015**, *12*, 2321–2325. [CrossRef]

 *remote sensing*

Article

Cost-Effective Class-Imbalance Aware CNN for Vehicle Localization and Categorization in High Resolution Aerial Images

Feimo Li [1,2,*], **Shuxiao Li** [1,2,*], **Chengfei Zhu** [1,2], **Xiaosong Lan** [1,2] and **Hongxing Chang** [1,2]

[1]   Institute of Automation Chinese Academy of Sciences, Beijing 100190, China;
       chengfei.zhu@ia.ac.cn (C.Z.); lanxiaosong2012@ia.ac.cn (X.L.); hongxing.chang@ia.ac.cn (H.C.)
[2]   University of Chinese Academy of Science, Beijing 100049, China
*   Correspondence: lifeimo2012@ia.ac.cn (F.L.); shuxiao.li@ia.ac.cn (S.L.);
     Tel.: +86-188-0012-4228 (F.L.); +86-138-1077-1030 (S.L.)

Academic Editors: Qi Wang, Nicolas H. Younan, Carlos López-Martínez, Gonzalo Pajares Martinsanz, Xiaofeng Li and Prasad S. Thenkabail
Received: 26 February 2017; Accepted: 15 May 2017; Published: 18 May 2017

Abstract: Joint vehicle localization and categorization in high resolution aerial images can provide useful information for applications such as traffic flow structure analysis. To maintain sufficient features to recognize small-scaled vehicles, a regions with convolutional neural network features (R-CNN) -like detection structure is employed. In this setting, cascaded localization error can be averted by equally treating the negatives and differently typed positives as a multi-class classification task, but the problem of class-imbalance remains. To address this issue, a cost-effective network extension scheme is proposed. In it, the correlated convolution and connection costs during extension are reduced by feature map selection and bi-partite main-side network construction, which are realized with the assistance of a novel feature map class-importance measurement and a new class-imbalance sensitive main-side loss function. By using an image classification dataset established from a set of traditional real-colored aerial images with 0.13 m ground sampling distance which are taken from the height of 1000 m by an imaging system composed of non-metric cameras, the effectiveness of the proposed network extension is verified by comparing with its similarly shaped strong counter-parts. Experiments show an equivalent or better performance, while requiring the least parameter and memory overheads are required.

Keywords: vehicle localization; vehicle classification; high resolution; aerial image; convolutional neural network (CNN); class imbalance

---

1. Introduction

For most of the sliding window-based vehicle detection methods involving localization and categorization, predictions are often performed in a separated manner, where the categories are estimated after the positional information is obtained. In the localization process—also called vehicle detection in its narrow sense—the positional existence of vehicles is estimated by analyzing the features extracted from the sliding window that moves across the region of interest with a pre-defined route and stepping pattern. The features used for vehicle detection can either be hand-crafted shallow descriptors or the deep features generated by convolutional neural network (CNN). Shallow features such as Haar [1], histogram of oriented gradients (HOG) [2,3], and local binary pattern (LBP) [3], etc.—although they are less robust and accurate as the deep ones—can make a good compromise between speed and efficiency when the computational resources or the quantity of training samples are very limited. However, once these limitations no longer exist, the detection methods based on deep features are often superior with strong resistance to disturbances in scale, lighting condition, and shadow, and their supreme performances have been repeatedly verified in many studies [4–8]. For these CNN-based methods, their underlying structures generally follow the regions with convolutional neural network features (R-CNN) [9] or its accelerated variants [10–13] with region of interest (ROI)-pooling [14]. More specifically, the R-CNN detector—whose features are calculated from the full-scale input image without sub-sampling—despite being primitive, turns out to be informative for recognizing small objects. Because of this, in large aerial images with small-scaled vehicles, R-CNN-like structure [5–8] is often preferred over those with ROI-pooling [4,15], which is also used in this article. Moreover, it can be accelerated by lossless preprocessing means such as saliency detection [16,17] and objectness filtering [8].

Once the vehicle locations are obtained, they are fed to the subsequent categorization process as positional indications to extract features. Similar to the localization process, features for classification can be produced by either shallow or deep models. At present, limited by the number of publicly available high-resolution aerial image datasets, only a small number of vehicle detection methods involve a classification procedure [18–20]. Among these limited publications, authors in both [19] and [20] tried to categorize vehicles by the "SVM + feature" strategy, while in [20] the strong influence of the class-imbalance issue on classification accuracies has been observed.

The separated estimation scheme discussed above is quite natural, and has been adopted for the positional classification of many general objects [10,12,13,21]. However, it could be troublesome for classifying targets as small as vehicles. Considering a private car only six pixels in width, any location error greater than four pixels will miss the main body of the vehicle and make the following categorization meaningless. Detecting objects in dense scenes can be untangled via density estimation [22] or object counting [23], which has already been validated for congested traffic scene classification [24]. While in this article, without loss of generality, taking the R-CNN detector as a common CNN-based classifier as in [7,8], the previously mentioned cascaded localization error can be avoided by treating the samples with deviation as a negative class and classifying them alongside the accurately centered but differently typed positives.

This arrangement primarily solves the problems caused by the small target scale, and strictly constrains type classification to those accurately located situations. Except for that, however, the introduction of a large quantity of negatives further skews the unbalanced categorical distributions between vehicle types. To address this problem, a bi-partite network extension driven by a class-imbalance-aware cost function is proposed. This cost function is designed based on the idea of providing the two network components with different training losses, intentionally correlating the extended component to the minority classes which are badly classified. Moreover, to reduce the extension costs, the extended components are built with feature maps from lower convolutional layers selected by a novel importance measurement. Notably, compared with other similarly-shaped structures, this proposed modification scheme is capable of achieving equal or better performance with much less extension overhead.

The rest of the paper is arranged as follows: Related and similar works are discussed in Section 2. The CNN basics and the semantic interpretation of convolutional kernels are given in Section 3. The proposed extension and its details are introduced in Section 4. Dataset preparation, experiment setup, and analysis of experimental results are presented in Section 5. Conclusive discussions on the experiments are given in Section 6. Section 7 concludes the paper.

2. Related Work

Class imbalance is a ubiquitous issue existing in nearly every real-life classification problem. As it has been intensively studied for more than two decades, many comprehensive and insightful reviews have been published to generalize the methods on this topic [25–28]. According to [28], these proposed treatments generally fall within three categories: data-level, algorithm-level, and hybrid treatments. The data-level methods focus on balancing the training samples, modifying their distributions via over-sampling or under-sampling. Typical techniques would include synthetic minority over-sampling technique (SMOTE) [29] and many of its variants, such as adaptive synthetic sampling (ADASYN) [30] and cluster-based oversampling (CBO) [31]. The algorithm-level methods—which are mostly based on the cost-sensitive principle [32,33]—alleviate the bias with majority classes by assigning greater penalties for the minority ones in training. The hybrid methods (e.g., the ensemble style classifiers [34]) take the advantages of the previous two for further performance enhancement, which is common, as mentioned in [25,28].

All of the previously mentioned means are for "shallow" models, but their class-imbalance-addressing principles still apply to the deep learning-based classifiers [35]. For instance, the re-sampling tricks work fine [36,37], although some more advanced dealing methods (e.g., the generative adversarial network (GAN) [38]) should be used to avoid noise and over-fitting in the re-sampling. Similarly, algorithm-level cost function reformation is also widely applicable [39–41], where the softmax loss [42,43], cross-entropy loss [39], and logistic regression [44] are mostly taken as the basis format. More recently, a new branch of cost-sensitive methods based on improving the underlying micro feature space structure have appeared, and they have achieved a significant improvement by constraining the relative sample distances [35,45–47]. Representative methods in this category include the triplet loss [43,45], quintuplet loss [35], and the center loss [47], which are now hotly debated in the academy.

Although the proposed method in this article generally follows the algorithm-level principle, it is more concerned about achieving a robust performance improvement with less or no influence on the original structure. This goal is achieved by re-balancing the classification bias with the assistance of an extra network component, where the structural expansion cost is kept at a minimum by the incorporative usage of feature map selection.

Plain extension of the convolutional kernel was theoretically analyzed in [48] without involving the class-imbalance issue. Structural extension is a common method for network performance enhancement whose underlying intentions focus either on feature space enhancement [41,48–50] or strong prior generation [51,52], and it has been applied to numerous topics, including classification [49,51], tracking [52], edge detection [41], etc. Specifically, only one paper [53] has been found to directly address the class-imbalance issue by combining the feature vectors outputted from a dual arrangement of auto-encoders, where the issue of cost-efficiency has not been emphasized.

Feature map selection can be viewed as a special case of feature selection based on the CNN structure. Consistent with the feature selection methods, it also has two categories with three types [54]: the first category includes the filters [55–57], where ranks of the features are obtained without the help of classifiers; the second category employs the predictor, and for the included types, wrappers [58] explicitly score the feature, while the embedded methods [59–61] do it implicitly in the training process. Mostly, feature map selection is used for the enhancement of network performance. However, for the purpose of structural simplification, the wrappers principle would be more appropriate in our case.

Due to such specialized requirement, per the brief review above, few studies have tried to make a combinatorial usage of these two methods to seek effective network performance improvement with optimized expansion costs. So, the method proposed in this article acts as a novel approach to the class-imbalance problem with convenient usage, where no tricky hard negative mining or parameter selection is involved.

3. Background

3.1. Basic Knowledge of Convolutional Neural Networks

Convolutional neural networks (CNNs) currently dominate computer vision studies, with constant state-of-the-art performance in almost every topic to which they are applied. CNNs are a special kind of deep belief network (DBN) with components called convolutional layers, composed of units called kernels or filters. Due to space limitations, a very brief introduction based on [62] is given for the principles of DBN and CNN and to help with the clarity of symbols. Firstly, a normal

DBN can be viewed as a stack of fully-connected layers, where each layer has a set of learnt parameters θ composed of connection weights $\mathbf{W}$ and bias $\mathbf{b}$. During the forward propagation, every input vector $\mathbf{x}$ will be processed by an affine transformation to get the output $\mathbf{z}$, as in Equation (1).

$$\mathbf{z} = \mathbf{W}^T \mathbf{x} + \mathbf{b} \tag{1}$$

In practice, the output $\mathbf{z}$ will be further corrected by a nonlinear function such as $\mathbf{h} = g(\mathbf{z})$ to overcome the XOR problem, where the rectified linear unit (or ReLU) [63,64] will always be chosen as the $g(\cdot)$. At the final stage of forward propagation, an output vector from the topmost fully-connected layer would be transformed by a probability distribution function (e.g., the softmax function) before being outputted. The softmax function defined in Equation (2) is one of the most commonly used Bernoulli distribution outputs calculated through normalized exponential transformation.

$$\begin{aligned} P(y = i|x) &= \text{softmax}(z_i) \\ &= \frac{\exp(z_i)}{\sum_j \exp(z_j)} \end{aligned} \tag{2}$$

To obtain the highest probability on the correct class label y on the input $\mathbf{x}$, this output for softmax function is minimized by its negative log-likelihood format, which is defined in Equation (3).

$$\begin{aligned} J(\theta; \mathbf{x}, y) &= L(\hat{y}, y) + \lambda \cdot \Omega(\theta) \\ L(\hat{y}, y) &= -\log(\text{softmax}(\mathbf{z})_i) \\ &= \log \sum_j \exp(z_j) - z_i \end{aligned} \tag{3}$$

Here, $J(\cdot)$ is the loss to be minimized during training, and $L(\hat{y}, y)$ is the softmax-based loss term in which y and $\hat{y}$ are the true and estimated labels for input $\mathbf{x}$. $\Omega(\cdot)$ is some regularization term with restrictions defined on the network parameters θ (e.g., the weights $\mathbf{W}$ or biases $\mathbf{b}$). More often than not, gradient descent-based optimization is employed to reduce the value of $J(\cdot)$, where the updating gradient from the softmax loss is $\mathbf{g} = \nabla_{\hat{y}} J$, based on the estimated label. Similarly, the updating gradients for $\mathbf{W}$ and $\mathbf{b}$ are defined in Equation (4), calculated by the chain rule.

$$\nabla_{\mathbf{W}^{(k)}} J = \mathbf{h}^{(k-1)T} \mathbf{g}, \ \nabla_{\mathbf{b}^{(k)}} J = \mathbf{g} \tag{4}$$

$$\mathbf{W}^{(k)} \leftarrow \mathbf{W}^{(k)} + \alpha \cdot \nabla_{\mathbf{W}^{(k)}} J, \ \mathbf{b}^{(k)} \leftarrow \mathbf{b}^{(k)} + \alpha \cdot \nabla_{\mathbf{b}^{(k)}} J \tag{5}$$

$\mathbf{W}^{(k)}$ and $\mathbf{b}^{(k)}$ are the weights and bias for the fully connected layer at level k, whose rectified output is denoted as $\mathbf{h}^{(k-1)}$. During the back propagation, at each layer, the weights and bias are updated by adding the deviations $\nabla_{\mathbf{W}^{(k)}} J$ and $\nabla_{\mathbf{b}^{(k)}} J$, with the latter ones multiplied by a learning rate α to control the convergence rate, as in Equation (5).

Those are the cases for the DBN, while all things are almost identical in the case of CNN, except for the part involving the convolutional layers. Convolutional layers can be treated as a special kind of fully-connected layer with shared connection weights held by kernels. Take the network in Figure 1 for illustration; considering a 4-D kernel tensor $\mathbf{K}^{(k)}$ from the kth convolutional layer, during the back propagation, the input signal data $\mathbf{V}^{(k-1)}$ is convoluted with $\mathbf{K}^{(k)}$ with step s to get the output $\mathbf{Z}^{(k)}$. The produced activation map $\mathbf{Z}^{(k)}$ is also called the *feature map*, which will always be under-sampled in practice by an operation called *pooling* to get the input data for the next layer, denoted as $\mathbf{Z}^{(k)} \rightarrow \mathbf{V}^{(k+1)}$. After the input image $\mathbf{V}^{(0)}$ has gone through all five convolutional layers in Figure 1, the final feature map $\mathbf{V}^{(5)}$ will be flattened into a 1-D vector $\mathbf{h}^{(5)}$ to be fed to the fully-connected trailing layer FC6 and the following FC7, FC8 to get the final predicted probabilities. Likewise, in the back-propagation, the 1-D difference $\mathbf{g}^{(5)}$ from the FC6 layer is reshaped into 3-D as $\mathbf{G}^{(5)}$ to update the feature maps. Assuming the objective function value is $J(\mathbf{V}, \mathbf{K})$ on the feature maps **V** and kernels **K**, its back-propagated differences from the upper layer should be calculated as $\mathbf{G}^{(k)} = \nabla_{\mathbf{V}^{(k)}} J\left(\mathbf{V}^{(k)}, \mathbf{K}^{(k)}\right)$ and $\nabla_{\mathbf{K}^{(k)}} J\left(\mathbf{V}^{(k)}, \mathbf{K}^{(k)}\right)$. Then, the feature maps and kernels are updated in a manner identical to Equation (5), where the convolutional kernels and feature maps are updated by adding with the derivations multiplied by a learning rate coefficient α, as in Equation (6).

$$\mathbf{V}^{(k)} \leftarrow \mathbf{V}^{(k)} + \alpha \cdot \nabla_{\mathbf{V}^{(k)}} J\left(\mathbf{V}^{(k)}, \mathbf{K}^{(k)}\right)$$
$$\mathbf{K}^{(k)} \leftarrow \mathbf{K}^{(k)} + \alpha \cdot \nabla_{\mathbf{K}^{(k)}} J\left(\mathbf{V}^{(k)}, \mathbf{K}^{(k)}\right)$$

(6)

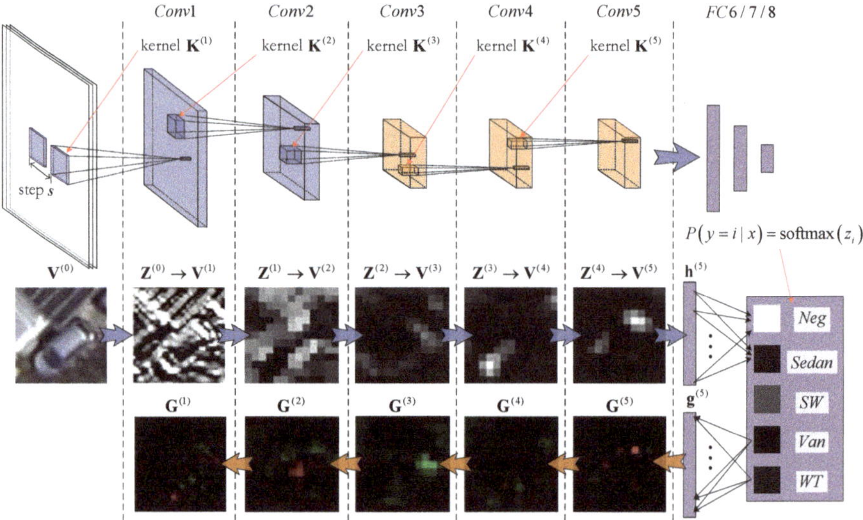

Figure 1. A typical convolutional neural network (CNN) structure, with feature and difference maps produced by the forward and backward propagations. SW: station wagon; WT: working truck.

3.2. The Semantic Texture Encoding Pattern for Convolutional Kernels

Despite of all the symbols and equations listed above, studies like [65] sought to produce more interpretable results, helping to better understand and improve the network. One of the important functional components of the DeepVis toolbox proposed in [65] is to find and show the image crops causing the top-most activations by each kernel. This kind of data-centric visualization measure [66–68] differs from other means such as deconvolution [69] or image synthesis [70], showing the correlations between kernel and image samples more directly.

The manifestation effectiveness of the previously mentioned data-centric max-activation illustration method is shown in Figure 2. Therein, six kernels from the CONV5 layer are arranged into two separated groups, denoted as $\{S_i\,|\,i=1,2,3\}$ and $\{W_i\,|\,i=1,2,3\}$ by their correlation strengths with the input image **x** shown in the column *Raw Image*. Under the column *Top Activation Image Crops*, the max-activation image crops are listed for each kernel, from which a stable image content can be observed, and that represents the textural pattern being encoded. Finally, for each kernel, the correlation between its texture and the input image can be measured by the corresponding feature maps being listed under the *Feature Map* column. Clearly, the feature maps from the kernels $\{S_i\}$ have greater activation values, while those belonging to $\{W_i\}$ are almost black. Considering that these pixel-wise activations will be fed to the trailing fully-connected layers to produce the class-wise likelihoods, strongly activated feature maps from $\{S_i\}$ indicate that they have stronger correlations with the input image.

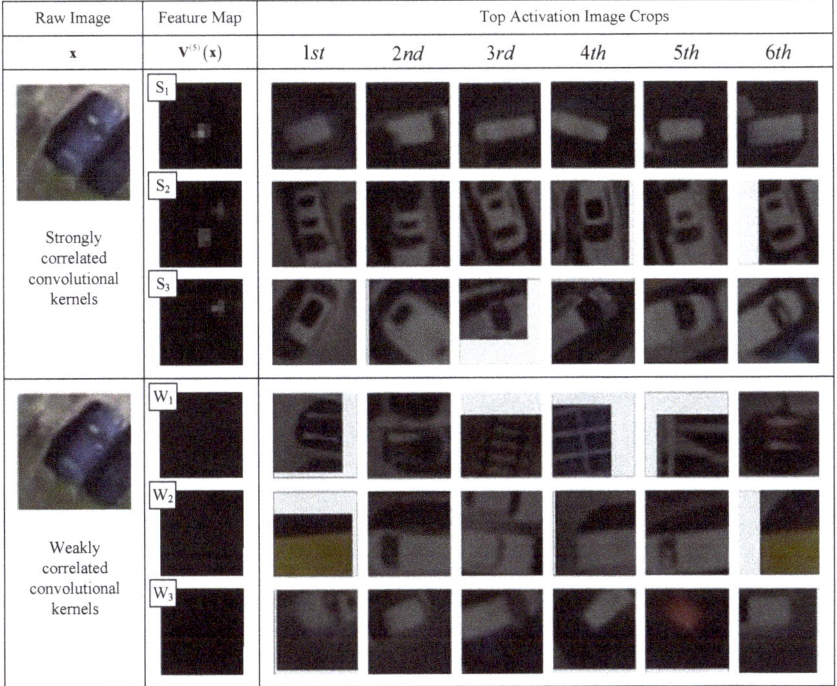

Figure 2. Illustration of the semantic meaning of the convolutional kernels. The raw input image is displayed in the *Raw Image* column; the six feature maps produced by six different kernels at the CONV5 layer are shown in the *Feature Map* column; and six arrays of local image crops on which the top six feature map activations are produced are shown in the *Top Activation Image Crops* column.

In fact, the way in which the high activations in feature maps from the last convolutional layer help with efficient classification can be exemplified by using Equation (5). Considering two activations $h_{l_1}^{(k-1)}$ and $h_{l_2}^{(k-1)}$ at the same position i, m, n from two feature maps $Z_{q_1}^{(k-1)}$ and $Z_{q_2}^{(k-1)}$ at layer level $k - 1$, with that $h_{l_1}^{(k-1)} = Z_{q_1,i,m,n}^{(k-1)}$ and $h_{l_2}^{(k-1)} = Z_{q_2,i,m,n}^{(k-1)}$. The connection weights bounded with these two activations are $W_{l_1}^{(k)}$ and $W_{l_2}^{(k)}$ in a single trailing fully-connected layer with its final categorical probabilities generated by transformation $z_j^{(k)} = \sum_l W_l^{(k)} h_l + b_j^{(k)}$. Then, by Equation (4), the updating differences for $W_{l_1,j}^{(k)}$ and $W_{l_2,j}^{(k)}$ can be calculated by Equation (7), where $g_j^{(k)} = \frac{\partial}{\partial z_j^{(k)}} J$.

$$\nabla_{\mathbf{W}_{l_1,j}^{(k)}} = g_j^{(k)} \cdot h_{l_1}^{(k-1)}, \ \nabla_{\mathbf{W}_{l_2,j}^{(k)}} = g_j^{(k)} \cdot h_{l_2}^{(k-1)} \tag{7}$$

So, when there is $h_{l_1}^{(k-1)} > h_{l_2}^{(k-1)}$, greater updating differences will be generated for the $W_{l_1}^{(k)}$ as $\nabla_{\mathbf{W}_{l_1,j}^{(k)}} > \nabla_{\mathbf{W}_{l_2,j}^{(k)}}$. Assuming activations $h_{l_1}^{(k-1)}$ and $h_{l_2}^{(k-1)}$ are all beneficial for the final probabilistic estimation on class j, the weighted connection $W_{l_1}^{(k)}$ will grow faster and larger with respect to $W_{l_2}^{(k)}$. This means that the feature map $Z_{q_1}^{(k-1)}$ produced by convolutional kernel $\mathbf{K}_{q_1}^{(k-1)}$ is more effective for recognizing samples from class j.

4. Methods

4.1. Overview of the Proposed CNN Extension Scheme

So, being aware of the fact that the modeling power of a CNN is strongly correlated with the diversity of feature maps at the last convolutional layer, this article sets out to tackle the problem of class-imbalance by adopting a cost-effective imbalance-aware feature map extension. Commonly, two kinds of overheads will be introduced when new feature maps are added: the *convolution overhead* and the *connection overhead*. Specifically, the *convolution overhead* refers to the extra convolution operation and extra feature map storage. The *connection overhead* happens in the fully-connected layer right above the extended convolutional layer, where every connection between pixels in the new feature map and the hidden-neurons in the fully-connected layers should be added. In order to reduce these two overheads, two general measures are adopted, which are illustrated in Figure 3: (1) the selective feature map extension by a newly derived class-importance measurement; (2) a class-imbalance-sensitive softmax loss function for optimizing the extended component. As a result, after these two modifications, the original network is turned into a bi-partite structure with enhanced sensitivities to the samples in the minority classes.

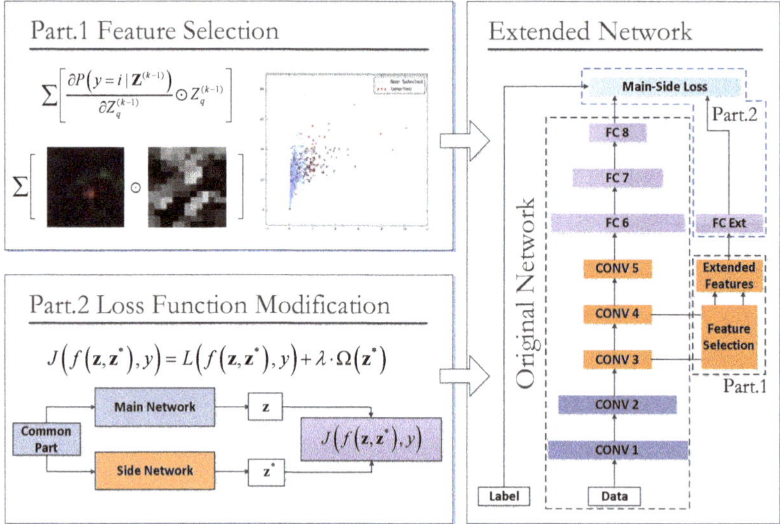

Figure 3. The general structure of the proposed network enhancement method.

(1)   Part 1: The selective feature map extension by class-importance measurement. This measure aims to reduce the *convolution overhead* by reusing feature maps selected from the preceding layers. The criteria adopted in the feature selection process—named feature map class-importance—are similar to that in [58], but are further extended for a multi-class problem with slight modification. Additionally, according to [58], these selected feature maps are further filtered by an extra convolutional layer to reduce noise before being used as the *Extended Features* component in Figure 3.

(2)   Part 2: the class-imbalance-sensitive softmax loss function. This measure aims at reducing the *connection overhead* and increasing the class-imbalance awareness of the improved structure. Firstly, the extended network components holding the *Extended Features* are isolated from the main part of the Original Network by a single-layered fully-connected (FC) layer *FC Ext*. This FC layer has hidden neurons only as few as the number of output classes; thus, the additional connection

quantity for the new maps is largely reduced. Secondly, as shown in the right-most text-box of Figure 3, a new loss function named main-side loss is adopted in place of the original softmax loss to raise the sensitivities of the *Extended Features* to the minority classes.

For the rest of Section 4, the proposed extension is described in detail based on a network prototype miniature visual geometry group (VGG-M) shown in Figure 3, which is very similar to AlexNet [71], but has slight improvements on the local convolutional parameters. This illustrative network has five convolutional layers (denoted as CONV1 to CONV5) and three fully-connected layers (denoted as FC6 to FC8), and feature maps for extension are selected from layers CONV3 and CONV4. All of these terms will be used in the following explanations.

4.2. The Network Extension by Selected Feature Maps

The idea of using quadratic expansion of the loss function to reduce less-effective network connections is not new—similar studies can be seen in [72], dating back to 1989. However, loss function-based feature map significance cannot be used to make class related pruning. Instead, the class-wise importance measurement for the feature maps is not hard to obtain—it can be produced by using a similar expansion technique on the output class likelihoods from the output neurons. Considering a general case where $\mathbf{Z}^{(k-1)}$ is the collection feature maps at the $k-1$th layer generated from input image $\mathbf{x}$, and the predicted probability for class i is $P\left(y = i | Z_q^{(k-1)}\right)$. Then, the contribution of feature map $Z_q^{(k-1)}$ to the estimated likelihood on class i can be approximated by Equation (8).

$$P\left(y = i | Z_q^{(k-1)}\right) \approx P\left(y = i | \mathbf{Z}^{(k-1)}\right) - P\left(y = i | \mathbf{Z}^{(k-1)}{}_{/q}\right)$$

$$= \sum \left[\frac{\partial P\left(y = i | \mathbf{Z}^{(k-1)}\right)}{\partial Z_q^{(k-1)}} \odot Z_q^{(k-1)} \right] + R_2\left(Z_q^{(k-1)}\right) \tag{8}$$

In Equation (8), $\mathbf{Z}^{(k-1)}{}_{/q}$ is the collection of feature maps $\mathbf{Z}^{(k-1)}$ without $Z_q^{(k-1)}$, and $R_2\left(Z_q^{(k-1)}\right)$ denotes the other higher-order expansions based on $Z_q^{(k-1)}$. In the first expansion term, $\frac{\partial P\left(y=i|\mathbf{Z}^{(k-1)}\right)}{\partial Z_q^{(k-1)}}$ is the feature map differences back-propagated from the probability value at the ith output neuron, and $\odot$ is the element-wise multiplication between matrices. In practice, this difference can be efficiently obtained by back-propagation. By summing the pixel-wise production of the feature map and its differences, the class-importance for the feature map on class i can be obtained. This is vividly shown in Figure 4.

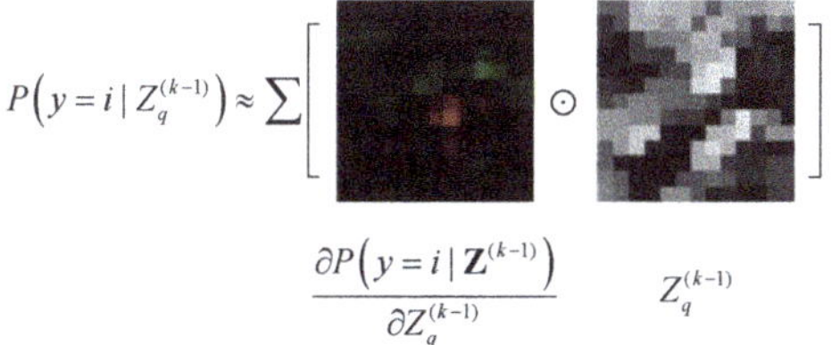

Figure 4. The first-order term of the Taylor expansion in Equation (8). $\frac{\partial P\left(y=i|\mathbf{Z}^{(k-1)}\right)}{\partial Z_q^{(k-1)}}$ denotes the feature map difference, positive, negative, and zero values marked as green, red, and black.

The class-important measure is validated in Figure 5, where the correlations for the maximal feature map activation and maximal feature significance to the probability values on negative samples are presented. Specifically, the x-axis max activations in Figure 5a means the topmost activation value measured from all the feature maps from CONV5. This is also the case for the x-axis class importance in Figure 5b. As can be seen, the data points in Figure 5b are much tighter and dense, roughly distributed on a curve with shape $y = K \cdot \frac{x}{a+x}$, where $a > 0$. Such strong correlation also indicates that the final categorical estimation is mostly based on a single feature map, which again emphasizes the importance of effective feature map selection.

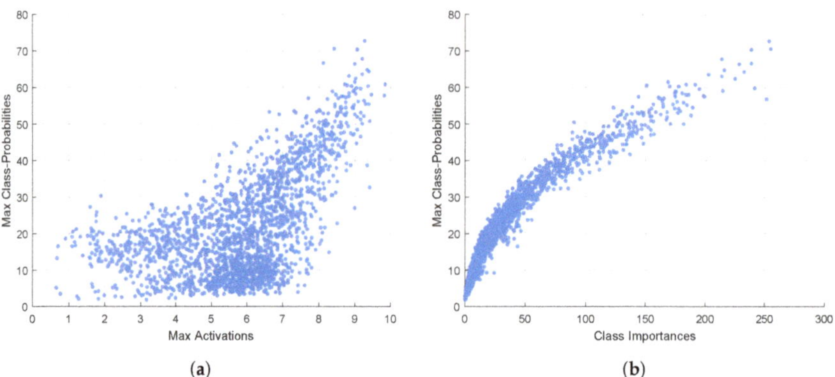

Figure 5. Correlations of the max-activations and class-importance with the class probability of the negative class. (**a**) Max-activation vs. class probability. (**b**) Max class-importance vs. class probability.

Figure 6a shows the distribution pattern of feature maps from the CONV3 and CONV4 layers in the max class-importance vs. max-activation space. From Figure 6a, it can be determined that feature maps from the CONV4 are slightly more significant than those from CONV3, with elements in the high class-importance section distributed closer to the x-axis. The categorical inclination of a specific feature map Z_q can be calculated by getting the index i of its largest class importance as $i = \arg\max_{j} P\left(y = j | Z_q\right)$, and their categorical distributions are shown in Figure 6b for five vehicle classes. As can be observed, feature maps belonging to all five classes have similar distributions in the importance section either high and low. Accordingly, in picking the most relevant feature maps for extension, it would be reasonable to select the ones with highest importance scores from each class and control that class-wise quantity according to their classification deficiencies, as in Algorithm 1.

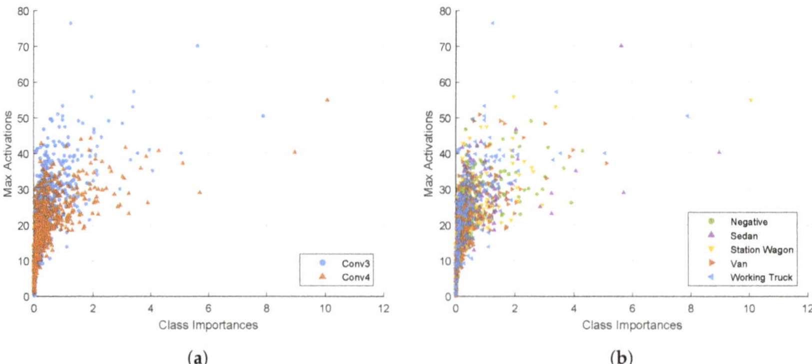

Figure 6. Scatter plots showing the distribution of the feature maps $\left\{Z_q\right\}$ from CONV3 and CONV4 in the class-importance vs. max-activation space. (**a**) The distributions of CONV3 and CONV4 feature maps. (**b**) Feature maps correlated to the five classes by the class-importance measurement.

Algorithm 1 Class Imbalance-Aware Extension Feature Map Selection

---

Input: Classification accuracies $\{ACC\,(j)\}$, class-importance $\{P\,(y = i|Z_q)\}$ for feature maps $\{Z_q\}$

from the CONV3 and CONV4 layers, and the total number of maps to be selected N_{sel}.

Output: Selected feature map indexes $\{i\}_{CONV3,CONV4}$ on CONV3 and CONV4

1: Calculate the number of extension maps needed for each class. For instance, for class j, denote the

required extension quantity as $N_{sel}^{(j)}$, then there is $N_{sel}^{(j)} = \left[\frac{1-ACC(j)}{\sum_i (1-ACC(i))}\right] \cdot N_{sel}$.

2: For each class j, sort the CONV3 and CONV4 feature maps $\{Z_q\}$ by their class importance

values $\{P\,(y = i|Z_q)\}$ in descending order, with the indexes denoted as $\{m_i\}_{CONV3,CONV4}^{DESC(j)} =$

$\left\{m_i \,\middle|\, P\,(y = j|Z_{m_1}) \geq \ldots \geq P\left(y = j|Z_{m_{N_{all}}}^{(k-1)}\right)\right\}$, where $N_{all} = |\{Z_q\}|$.

3: For each class j, get the top $N_{sel}^{(j)}$ map indexes from the descending order set as $\{m_i\}_{CONV3,CONV4}^{TOP\left(N_{sel}^{(j)}\right)} =$

$\left\{n_i \,\middle|\, i = 1, \ldots, N_{sel}^{(j)}, n_i \in \{m_i\}_{CONV3,CONV4}^{DESC(j)}\right\}$.

4: Merge the class-wise top indexes $\{m_i\}_{CONV3,CONV4}^{TOP(j)}$ from the previous step, and get the output

feature map index set as $\{i\}_{CONV3,CONV4} = \bigcup_j \{m_i\}_{CONV3,CONV4}^{TOP\left(N_{sel}^{(j)}\right)}$.

More specifically, as in Algorithm 1, the selection ratio for each class is measured by their pro rata accuracy deficiencies $\frac{1-ACC(j)}{\sum_i (1-ACC(i))}$, so the class-wise selection quantity is $N_{sel}^{(j)} = \left[\frac{1-ACC(j)}{\sum_i (1-ACC(i))}\right] \cdot N_{sel}$. Two exemplified CONV3 and CONV4 feature map selections are illustrated in Figure 7, where the total selection quantities are $N_{sel} = 64$ and $N_{sel} = 160$. Therein, the extended feature map candidates mainly reside in the high class-importance region.

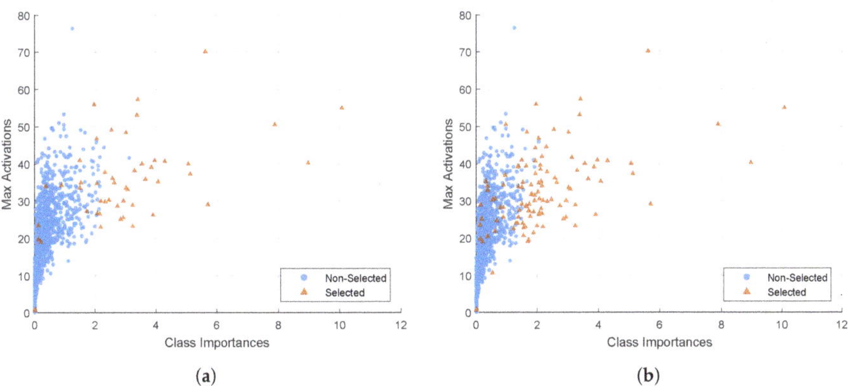

Figure 7. (**a**) The 50 selected maps for $N_{sel} = 64$. (**b**) The 109 selected maps for $N_{sel} = 160$.

4.3. Class Imbalance-Sensitive Softmax Loss Function

Up to the present, explanations for the cost-effective network extension have been focused on the feature map selection process which reduces the *convolution overhead*. However, the *connection overhead* is also significant if the newly extended feature maps are encoded directly by the trailing fully-connected layer FC6. Typically, for a network with structure similar to that in Figure 3, there can be as many as 4096 hidden neurons in FC6. Supposing the feature maps from CONV5 are of shape

13×13, then as many as $4096 \times 13 \times 13$ real-valued connection weights will be introduced for every newly added feature map. This kind of overhead can be greatly reduced if these extended feature maps are encoded by a single-layered fully-connected layer independent of the original network, which has hidden neurons with quantity equal to the number of output classes. As shown in Figure 8, the resulting bi-partite network is generalized as composed by three structural components: the common part, the main network, and the side network. For the eight-layered network in Figure 3, the common part refers to the shared layers CONV1 and CONV2, the Main Network refers to layers CONV3 through FC8 in the Original Network, and the Side Network refers to the *Extended Features* along with the isolated *FC Ext* layer.

In this structure, the output values from *FC Ext* can be viewed as an extra categorical estimation based purely on the newly added feature maps, whereas the final categorical prediction from the extended network can be calculated as the summation of these two. Taking the predicted likelihoods from the Main and Side Network components as $\mathbf{z}$ and $\mathbf{z}^*$, this kind of summarization-based likelihood mixture can be viewed as applying a hard connection on these two likelihoods as $f(\mathbf{z}, \mathbf{z}^*) = 1 \cdot \mathbf{z} + 1 \cdot \mathbf{z}^*$, in which both predictions are equally weighted. However, according to the analysis in Section 3.2, this straightforward means does not promise that the extended part will be more correlated with minority class samples. Take the $h_l^{(k-1)}$ as some activation from a feature map in the Side Network component at layer $k-1$, and its connection weights to a majority class i and a minority class j are denoted as $W_{l,i}^{(k)}$ and $W_{l,j}^{(k)}$. Then, according to Equation (9), in the case of using softmax loss, the updating differences $g_i^{(k)}$ and $g_j^{(k)}$ from upper layer will be almost equal.

$$\nabla_{\mathbf{W}_{l,i}^{(k)}} = g_i^{(k)} \cdot h_l^{(k-1)}, \ \nabla_{\mathbf{W}_{l,j}^{(k)}} = g_j^{(k)} \cdot h_l^{(k-1)} \tag{9}$$

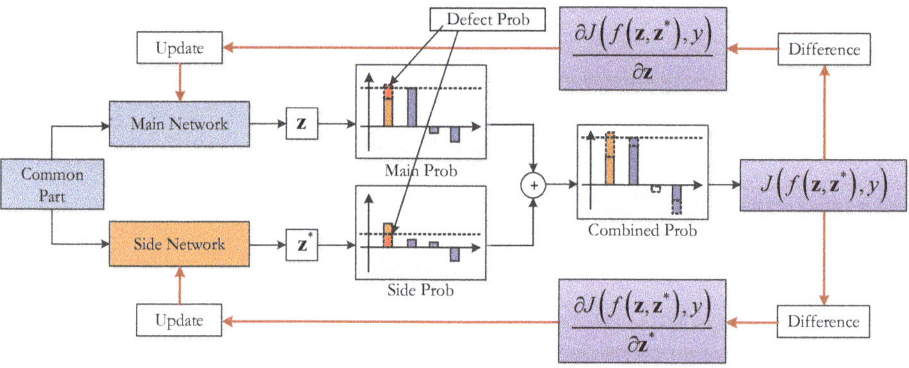

Figure 8. Principle structure of the class-imbalance aware Main-Side Network.

So, in order to achieve class-imbalance sensitivity, the loss function should differ the back-propagated values for the Side Network between majority and minority classes. This setting is manageable. By Figure 8, considering the likelihood summation format as employing the $\mathbf{z}^*$ from Side Network to rectify the estimates $\mathbf{z}$ from the Main Network, then the $\mathbf{z}^*$ acts as a filling for the probability deficiencies of $\mathbf{z}$ marked by the red bar in Figure 8. Then, if this kind of likelihood amendment is intentionally diminished for the majority classes and encouraged for the minority classes, the predictions from the Side Network are more likely to be correlated with samples from the minority classes.

More specifically, as in Equation (10), the newly introduced Main-Side loss is denoted as $J\left(f\left(\mathbf{z},\mathbf{z}^*\right),y\right)$ at the right-side of the picture, which takes the softmax loss $L\left(f\left(\mathbf{z},\mathbf{z}^*\right),y\right)$ as its main component. Then, in order to make these two updating values vary from each other, an extra regularization only relevant with $\mathbf{z}^*$ is added to the loss function, which is denoted as $\Omega\left(\mathbf{z}^*\right)$ with a global penalization coefficient λ. Since $\Omega\left(\mathbf{z}^*\right)$ is only dependent on the Side Network output $\mathbf{z}^*$, the back-propagated differences for the Main and Side Network components $\frac{\partial J\left(f\left(\mathbf{z},\mathbf{z}^*\right),y\right)}{\partial \mathbf{z}}$ and $\frac{\partial J\left(f\left(\mathbf{z},\mathbf{z}^*\right),y\right)}{\partial \mathbf{z}^*}$ will be different, as in Equation (11).

$$
\begin{aligned}
J\left(f\left(\mathbf{z},\mathbf{z}^*\right),y\right) &= L\left(f\left(\mathbf{z},\mathbf{z}^*\right),y\right) + \lambda \cdot \Omega\left(\mathbf{z}^*\right) \\
L\left(f\left(\mathbf{z},\mathbf{z}^*\right),y\right) &= -\log\left[\text{softmax}(\mathbf{z}+\mathbf{z}^*)_{y=i}\right]
\end{aligned}
\tag{10}
$$

$$
\begin{aligned}
\frac{\partial J\left(f\left(\mathbf{z},\mathbf{z}^*\right),y\right)}{\partial \mathbf{z}} &= \text{softmax}(\mathbf{z}+\mathbf{z}^*)_{y=i} - \mathbf{1}\left(y=i\right) \\
\frac{\partial J\left(f\left(\mathbf{z},\mathbf{z}^*\right),y\right)}{\partial \mathbf{z}^*} &= \text{softmax}(\mathbf{z}+\mathbf{z}^*)_{y=i} - \mathbf{1}\left(y=i\right) + \lambda \cdot \frac{\partial \Omega\left(\mathbf{z}^*\right)}{\partial \mathbf{z}^*}
\end{aligned}
\tag{11}
$$

Recalling that the softmax loss term $L\left(f\left(\mathbf{z},\mathbf{z}^*\right),y\right)$ should be diminished during training, this Side Network correlated regularization $\Omega\left(\mathbf{z}^*\right)$ should produce small penalty values for the minority classes, but large values for the majority classes. The simplest way to achieve this is to assign varied penalty coefficients for class-wise likelihood values in $\mathbf{z}^*$, and the classification accuracies for these classes measured on the cross-validation dataset serves such needs. So, as in Equation (12), the additional loss function regularization term $\Omega\left(\mathbf{z}^*\right)$ is defined as the Norm-2 of the element-wise multiplication of $\mathbf{z}^*$ and the class-wise accuracies measured on the Main-Network.

$$
\begin{aligned}
\Omega\left(\mathbf{z}^*\right) &= \|\mathbf{B}\odot\mathbf{z}^*\|_2 = \sqrt{\sum_j\left(\beta_j\cdot z_j^*\right)^2} \\
\beta_j &\propto ACC(\mathbf{X})_j, \quad ACC(\mathbf{X})_j = \frac{TP(\mathbf{X})_j}{TP(\mathbf{X})_j + FP(\mathbf{X})_j}
\end{aligned}
\tag{12}
$$

The $ACC(\mathbf{X})_j$ in Equation (12) is the averaged accuracy for the given image set $\mathbf{X}$ on class j measured by $\mathbf{z}$ from the Main Network, B is the categorical penalization coefficient applied on $\mathbf{z}^*$, and $\odot$ means element-wise multiplication between two vectors. Following this definition, for a majority class i already having very high accuracy $ACC(\mathbf{X})_i$, its penalization will be higher than a minority class j with lower $ACC(\mathbf{X})_i$, and vice versa. Besides, due to the flexibilities in choosing the set of input images $\mathbf{X}$, three penalization modes can thus be derived, here denoted as Global, Local, and Batch-wise, as shown in Figure 9.

Conceptually, these three penalization modes have specific pros and cons of their own. According to Figure 9, the global penalization β based on the overall sample set O stays unchanged for all training subsets, and thus is insensitive to abnormalities in local space. The local penalization $\beta_{i,k}$ partially improves the flexibility by using accuracy local cluster S_i for each training sample that k belongs to, but such accuracy must still be measured beforehand and could be obsolete during the training. Instead, for the batch-wise mode, a real-time tracking of accuracy can be acquired from the training mini-batch B_i, while the additional price is the increased non-linearity in convergence.

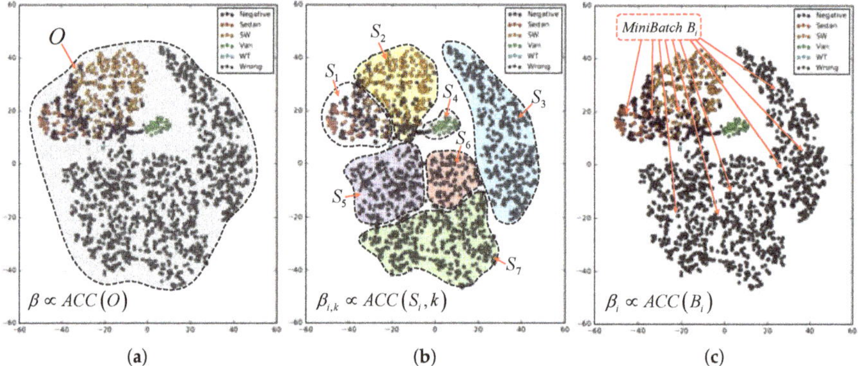

Figure 9. The t-Distribution stochastic neighbor embedding (t-SNE) -based visualization [73] of the negatives and vehicle types in the FC8 output space, and the three penalization modes used for B: (**a**) global, (**b**) local, and (**c**) batch-wise.

5. Experiments and Analysis

5.1. Data Set Description and Experiment Setup

5.1.1. DLR 3K Aerial Image Dataset

The DLR 3K aerial image dataset is an aerial image dataset made publicly available online by the Germany Aerospace Center, which has been studied in [19]. It contains 20 aerial images with resolution of 5616×3744 captured over the city of Munich by a low-cost airborne imaging system called DLR 3K+ Cam, which is composed of three non-metric Canon Eos 1Ds Mark III cameras with Zeiss lenses. This system is intended to be fixed on an airplane or a glider with a ZEISS shock mount, where images are taken at the height of 1000 m with real-time ortho-rectification made either on-board or at ground station. All pictures are in RGB real-colored spectral bands (each being digitalized by 8 bits) with ground sampling distance (GSD) at 13 cm.

Although there is no modern skyscraper, these pictures contain quantities of medium-height residential buildings, workshops, trees, lawns, railway track, and streets filled with kinds of vehicles either wide or narrow. All of these put together form a rich set of scenarios which would include most of the typical conditions that cause false detections. Figure 10 shows some of the image samples. The four sub-figures marked as $b_1 \sim b_4$ are cropped from spots marked by yellow squares in the main image *a* on the left, which represent classical detection disturbances: tight parking (b_1), shadows from trees and houses (b_1, b_2, and b_3), and partial occlusion (b_4). In addition, buildings and man-made facilities in this area have complex textures similar to vehicles, which further increases the localization and categorization difficulties.

Instead of using the original vehicle classes in the dataset, we defined a new set of classes, with the main focus being put on small and medium-sized vehicles; that is, Sedan, Station Wagon (i.e., private SUV), Van, and Working Truck. Quantitative distributions and averaged scales of these vehicle types are listed in Table 1, by which a highly skewed inter-class distribution of samples can be clearly observed. In it, the Station Wagon class has the top-most quantity with the Sedan and Van lagging far behind. The quantity of Working Truck is trivial, with occupation ratios at merely 0.8% in the training set and 0.6% in the testing set.

Figure 10. (**a**) A typical frame from the training sample. (**b**₁ ∼ **b**₄) Typical difficult detection cases. (**c**) The close-to-vehicle region (shaded blue) and categorical sampling positions.

Table 1. The vehicle types defined in this paper and the basic statistics.

Type	Samples	Training Set			Testing Set		
		L (px)	W (px)	N	L (px)	W (px)	N
Sedan		21.45	10.47	776	20.83	10.16	1075
Station Wagon		19.99	9.76	2302	19.14	9.32	4178
Van		24.65	12.06	312	24.14	11.83	512
Working Truck		27.17	13.31	29	26.58	13.02	34

Note: **L (px)** and **W (px)** denote the length and width of vehicles in pixels, and **N** denotes the quantity.

5.1.2. Training and Testing Preparation as a Classification Problem

Since the R-CNN detection structure is employed, it can be regarded as a common CNN-classifier making categorization on full-scaled input images. To facilitate the analysis and verification, 48×48 sized patches are uniformly extracted from the original image for a simplified experimental environment. Furthermore, to reduce the quantity of unnecessary negative samples with redundant textural patterns, these image patches are produced from three different regions by their distance to vehicle centers $Dist_V$, which are shown in Figure 11:

- The *Centered* category: position marked by yellow square in sub-figure c in Figure 10 with $Dist_V$ no more than 3 pixels;
- The *Close Range* category: positions marked by red squares within the blue shaded region in sub-figure c in Figure 10, whose $Dist_V$ are in range from 4 to 20 pixels;
- The *Far Range* category: in sub-figure c from Figure 10, positions marked by green squares outside the blue shaded region with $Dist_V$ more than 20 pixels.

Centered			Close Range			Far Range		
$Dist_V$	$N_{aug.}$	$\Delta\theta$	$Dist_V$	$N_{aug.}$	$\Delta\theta$	$Dist_V$	$N_{aug.}$	$\Delta\theta$
≤ 3	$16\times$	$22.5°$	$4 \sim 20$	$8\times$	$45°$	> 20	$1\times$	-

Figure 11. The sample categories used on the three regions: Centered, Close Range, and Far Range.

Only samples in the *Centered* category are treated as positives, which will be further categorized into different vehicle types. Samples from the *Close Range* and *Far Range* categories are taken as negatives with different classification difficulties. By Figure 11, data enhancements are performed on these samples by rotation with different times $N_{aug.}$, where rotated angle spacing $\Delta\theta$ is calculated by $\Delta\theta = 360° / N_{aug.}$. Since samples in the *Centered* and *Close Range* categories are less populated, their rotate angle spacings are $22.5°$ and $45°$ with augmentation times at $16\times$ and $8\times$. Finally, sample quantities in these categories are kept equal (approximately 33.3% for each), which results in 210,944 training samples and 534,624 testing samples.

5.1.3. The Baseline Network Structure and Extension Styles for Analysis

To manifest the effectiveness of feature selection and Main-Side loss-based fine-tuning, the VGG-M [74] network is employed as the baseline for the optimized extension. The VGG-M and its full version the 16-layered VGG [75] are powerful holistically structured networks, and have achieved a top-5 error at only 13.7% and 7.4% on the ILSVRC-2012-val dataset, which are the best scores until 2014. Different from its ancestor AlexNet [71], VGG-M uses small kernels of size 3×3 with 1 pixel-sized padding, making them ideal for encoding the local structural differences. After that, the development on CNN have either sought greater depth by shortcut connection [76–78] or more miscellaneous structural complexities [21,50,79].

Three typical kinds of extension structures based on VGG-M are illustrated in Figure 12, which will be studied in the following subsections. Figure 12a shows the case when the network is extended with blank randomly initialized kernels, and Figure 12b shows the case when selected feature maps from the preceding layers are used for extension. Figure 12c shows the case when both the feature selection and Main-Side loss techniques are employed for extension.

During the experimental analysis in the rest of the section, six kinds of network extension in total are involved for general or specific analysis, and their principle structures are shown in tables in Figure 13. Therein, the miniature VGG-M and full-sized VGG-16 are abbreviated as *Orig.M* and *Orig.16* in Figures 13a,b. Plain network extension by blank kernels and selected feature maps with the original softmax loss are abbreviated as *New Ext.* and *Select Ext.*, shown by Figures 13c,d. Blank kernel-based and selected feature map-based extension with the class-imbalance-sensitive Main-Side loss are denoted as *New S-Ext.* and *Select S-Ext.*, shown by Figures 13e,f.

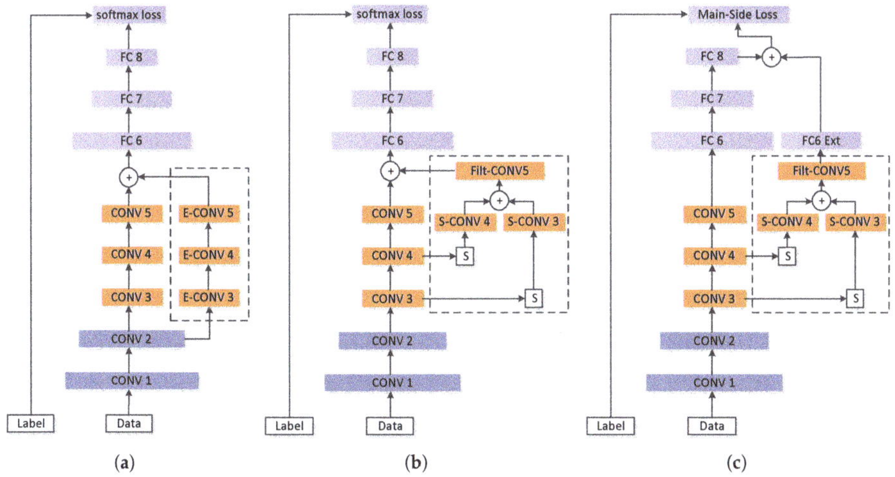

Figure 12. Three typical extension schemes. (**a**) Plain extension with blank kernel generated feature maps; (**b**) Plain extension with selected feature maps; (**c**) Main-Side bi-parted extension with selected feature maps.

Orig.M
Loss Softmax
FC6 ~ FC8
Conv5
Conv4
Conv3
Conv1 ~ Conv2
Input, Label

(**a**)

Orig.16
Loss Softmax
FC6 ~ FC8
Conv5_1, 5_2, 5_3
Conv4_1, 4_2, 4_3
Conv3_1, 3_2, 3_3
Conv1_1, 1_2 ~ Conv2_1, 2_2
Input, Label

(**b**)

New Ext.	
Loss Softmax	
FC6 ~ FC8	
Conv5	Conv5 Ext.N
Conv4	Conv4 Ext.N
Conv3	Conv3 Ext.N
Conv1 ~ Conv2	
Input, Label	

(**c**)

Select Ext.		
Loss Softmax		
FC6 ~ FC8		
Conv5	Conv5 Filt	
Conv4	Conv3 Sel.N_1	Conv4 Sel.N_2
Conv3		
Conv1 ~ Conv2		
Input, Label		

(**d**)

New S-Ext.	
Main-Side Loss	
FC6 ~ FC8	FC6 Ext.
Conv5	Conv5 Ext.N
Conv4	Conv4 Ext.N
Conv3	Conv3 Ext.N
Conv1 ~ Conv2	
Input, Label	

(**e**)

Select S-Ext.		
Main-Side Loss		
FC6 ~ FC8	FC6 Ext.	
Conv5	Conv5 Filt	
Conv4	Conv3 Sel.N_1	Conv4 Sel.N_2
Conv3		
Conv1 ~ Conv2		
Input, Label		

(**f**)

Figure 13. The five network structures studied in the experimental section. (**a**) The baseline network miniature miniature visual geometry group (VGG-M) (*Orig.M*) and (**b**) 16-layered VGG (*Orig.16*), the comparative extensions with either (**c**,**d**) the Loss of Softmax (*New Ext.*, *Select Ext.*) or (**e**,**f**) the proposed Main-Side Loss (*New S-Ext.*, *Select S-Ext.*).

More specifically, the network structures *Orig.M*, *Orig.16*, *New Ext.*, *Select Ext.*, and *Select S-Ext.* with the three penalization modes are compared and studied in Section 5.2 for a holistic comparison. After that, the structures *New Ext.* and *Select Ext.* are compared in Section 5.3 to showcase the effect of using selected features in the plain softmax loss-based network extension instead of the blank kernels. Finally, the main factors including the coefficient λ, coefficients **B**, and the three penalization modes are compared based on the *New S-Ext.* structure to analyze the behavior of the Main-Side loss function in Section 5.4.

5.2. Experimental Results

The proposed network extension scheme is verified in this section. The networks chosen for comparison are the baseline VGG-M (*Orig.M*), the 16-layered full-sized VGG (*Orig.16*), extensions based on the softmax loss (*New Ext.* and *Sel. Ext.*), and extensions based on the selected features and Main-Side loss (*Sel. S-Ext.*).

The parameter model file sizes, memory consumption sizes, and their overheads are shown in Table 2, in which the memory consumption is measured with batch size 96. All data are measured based on the Caffe CNN platform. Generally, Main-Side loss-based network extensions have the least overhead compared to those using softmax loss. The parameter file size increments are trivial since the *FC6 Ext.* layer has only five hidden neurons. For the memory consumptions, extra memory space saving is done by reusing existing feature maps from preceding layers. Moreover, there are also implicit computation savings by eliminating the convolutions in layers *Conv3 Ext.* and *Conv4 Ext.*.

Table 2. Trained model file sizes and GPU-memory consumption for batch size of 96.

Net Struct.	Orig.M	Orig.16	New Ext. 128	New Ext. 256	Sel. Ext. 128	Sel. Ext. 256	Sel. S-Ext. 128	Sel. S-Ext. 256
Model (Mb)	361.7	537.1	439.6	519.8	426.1	460.9	362.2	362.8
Δ Model (Mb)	-	175.4	77.9	158.1	64.4	99.2	**0.5**	**1.1**
Mem (Mb)	1820.3	10547.1	1988.4	2093.0	2018.5	2053.7	1977.4	2004.3
Δ Mem (Mb)	-	8726.8	168.0	272.7	192.7	223.1	**157.1**	**183.9**

Class-wise classification performances measured by accuracies and F1 scores are presented in Tables 3 and 4, based on extensions with $N_{sel} = 128$ and $N_{sel} = 256$ by Algorithm 1. In them, the global, local and batch-wise based penalization modes for *Select S-Ext.* are abbreviated as *Glb.*, *Lcl.*, and *Bat.*. Due to the limitation of page space, the *Select Ext.* is further abbreviated as *Sel. Ext.*. The trailing keyword ReLU indicates the usage of ReLU layer to constrain the Side-Network probabilities. In each column, the first-, second-, and third-highest scores are marked by bold, underline, and double-underline.

From these two tables, several important phenomena need to be taken care of. Firstly, compared to the small version *Orig.M*, the full-sized *Orig.16* is superior in achieving high F1 scores and high accuracy for recognizing negatives, but it is bad for making accurate predictions on the positive classes. This means that the depth-based network extension is more likely to be affected by the class-imbalance. Secondly, the softmax loss-based *Sel Ext.* has more high scores when $N_{sel} = 128$, meaning that selected features are better utilized for minority classes under smaller extension quantity. Thirdly, the Main-Side loss-based selective feature map extensions are stabler at maintaining high performance for the minority classes (Sedan, Van) except for ones too trivial in size (Working Truck). Fourthly, the usage of ReLU slightly decreases the improvement in accuracies while helping with the enhancement of F1 score. Considering the small overhead cost for the *Select S-Ext.* variants, their network extension efficiencies are better than the others.

Table 3. Best averaged F1 score cases of classification performance for 128 feature map extension.

	Negative		Sedan		Station Wagon		Van		Working Truck	
	ACC	F1	ACC	F1	ACC	F1	ACC	F1	ACC	F1
Orig.M	96.83%	0.9791	58.40%	0.6247	81.81%	0.8010	90.11%	0.8422	69.72%	0.5435
Orig.16	**99.68%**	0.9624	57.13%	0.6433	82.04%	**0.8329**	91.64%	**0.8650**	70.05%	**0.5914**
New Ext.	97.20%	0.9822	63.38%	0.6474	82.13%	0.8245	91.92%	0.8459	**74.52%**	0.5666
Sel. Ext.	96.90%	0.9808	63.56%	**0.6487**	**82.25%**	0.8247	**93.00%**	0.8501	68.16%	0.5609
Glb.	97.01%	0.9810	65.73%	0.6438	81.51%	0.8303	92.38%	0.8471	71.29%	0.5377
*Glb.*ReLU	97.22%	0.9820	**65.95%**	0.6410	81.27%	0.8315	92.69%	0.8477	71.25%	0.5406
Lcl.	97.00%	0.9813	65.45%	0.6408	81.65%	0.8310	92.66%	0.8497	69.63%	0.5418
*Lcl.*ReLU	97.27%	**0.9823**	64.61%	0.6404	81.53%	0.8285	92.56%	0.8498	70.70%	0.5375
Bat.	97.12%	0.9814	64.40%	0.6417	81.54%	0.8276	92.89%	0.8471	70.38%	0.5351
*Bat.*ReLU	97.30%	0.9820	63.87%	0.6407	81.67%	0.8273	92.66%	0.8505	72.78%	0.5556

Note: The first, second and third topmost values in each column are marked by **bold**, underline and double-underline. Meanings of abbreviations are: the baseline VGG-M (*Orig.M*), the 16-layered full-sized VGG (*Orig.16*), the softmax loss based extensions (*New Ext.* and *Sel. Ext.*), and Main-Side loss based extensions (*Sel. S-Ext.*).

Table 4. Best averaged F1 score cases of classification performance for 256 feature map extension.

	Negative		Sedan		Station Wagon		Van		Working Truck	
	ACC	F1	ACC	F1	ACC	F1	ACC	F1	ACC	F1
Orig.M	96.83%	0.9791	58.40%	0.6247	81.81%	0.8010	90.11%	0.8422	69.72%	0.5435
Orig.16	**99.68%**	0.9624	57.13%	0.6433	82.04%	**0.8329**	91.64%	**0.8650**	70.05%	**0.5914**
New Ext.	97.23%	**0.9823**	61.97%	0.6431	82.26%	0.8207	92.26%	0.8484	71.97%	0.5804
Sel. Ext.	96.96%	0.9808	61.98%	**0.6453**	**82.39%**	0.8192	91.69%	0.8451	70.85%	0.5439
Glb.	97.12%	0.9816	64.26%	0.6419	81.47%	0.8263	92.83%	0.8453	70.31%	0.5409
*Glb.*ReLU	97.16%	0.9818	64.47%	0.6441	81.80%	0.8290	**92.94%**	0.8505	**73.60%**	0.5472
Lcl.	96.94%	0.9809	**65.91%**	0.6384	81.45%	0.8306	92.46%	0.8507	68.53%	0.5469
*Lcl.*ReLU	97.11%	0.9816	65.11%	0.6439	81.69%	0.8296	92.46%	0.8481	72.05%	0.5564
Bat.	97.01%	0.9809	63.75%	0.6413	81.52%	0.8242	92.92%	0.8457	69.94%	0.5442
*Bat.*ReLU	97.31%	**0.9823**	65.12%	0.6420	81.45%	0.8303	92.70%	0.8482	71.70%	0.5419

Note: The first, second and third topmost values in each column are marked by **bold**, underline and double-underline. Meanings of abbreviations are: the baseline VGG-M (*Orig.M*), the 16-layered full-sized VGG (*Orig.16*), the softmax loss based extensions (*New Ext.* and *Sel. Ext.*), and Main-Side loss based extensions (*Sel. S-Ext.*).

Finally, a brief illustration of the effectiveness of the proposed network extension is given in Figure 14, where *Orig.M* and *Select S-Ext.* with $N_{sel} = 256$ and $\lambda = \exp(-2)$ are chosen for comparison. In Figure 14a, newly recognized images by *Select S-Ext.* are listed in Figure 14a by their types in each row. According to the common characteristics in appearance, three categories can be established in the columns: those with rare structures or confusing appearances (*Rare Instances*), those being blurred by shadows (*Shadowing*), and those being partially covered by trees and buildings (*Covering*). These are the challenging conditions to which the extended network structure is devoted. At last, prediction accuracies of *Orig.M* and *Select S-Net.* on the three sample categories discussed in Section 5.1.2 are illustrated in Figure 14b, abbreviated as *Orig.* and *Imprv..* Therein, accuracy values of *Imprv.* are marked above its curve markers, and the improvement values *Diff.* are shown as bars. As expected, samples with greater vehicle center distances (*Far Distance*) are better predicted by their recognition easiness. Additionally, consistent with the design pattern of Main-Side Loss, greater improvement happens on positives in the *Centered* category.

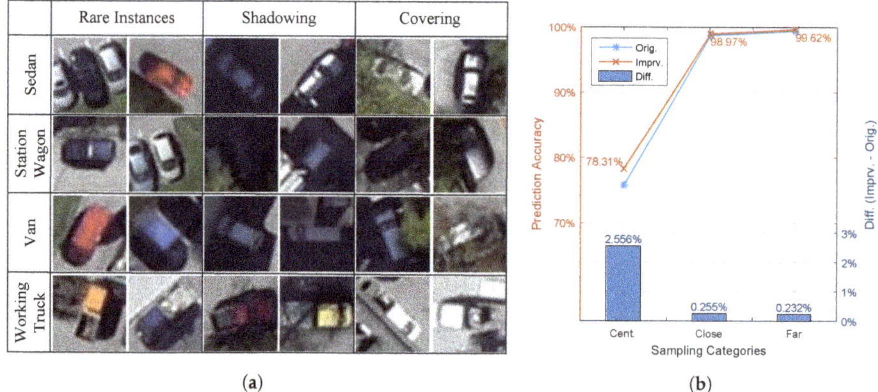

Figure 14. Network classification performance improvement illustrated by the established classification dataset. (**a**) Newly recognized positives after extension. (**b**) Prediction accuracies and the increments on sample categories: Centered (Cent.), Close Range (Close), and Far Range (Far).

5.3. Network Extension Efficiency by Selected Feature Maps

This sub-section discusses the network extension efficiency in using the selected convolutional feature maps. To justify the comparisons, only the extensions *New Ext.* and *Select Ext.* based on the softmax loss are adopted, so all kernels will be penalized equally over different classes.

Table 5 shows the classification accuracies between the original VGG-M network and its two extended counterparts, *New Ext.* and *Select Ext.*. Seven extension quantities are involved in the comparison, ranging from 64 to 256. Since the feature maps selection scheme described in Algorithm 1 will introduce duplications, the number of feature maps used in the selective extension is always smaller. As can be observed from Table 5, outperforming instances frequently occur on large and medium-sized classes (e.g., Sedan and Station Wagon) which have occupation ratios at 23.06% and 66.96%. For class Van, which has an occupation ratio of 9.10%, only one outperforming is detected. Accuracy differences on class Working Truck fluctuate radically, a class which has the smallest data occupation ratio at 0.88%.

Table 5. Classification accuracies for softmax loss-based extensions *New Ext.* and *Select Ext.*.

Original	Sedan		Station Wagon		Van		Working Truck	
	ACC 58.40%		ACC 81.81%		ACC 90.11%		ACC 69.72%	
New Ext. & Sel. Ext.	New	Select	New	Select	New	Select	New	Select
N64/S50	63.02%	**63.19%**	81.85%	**82.27%**	92.58%	91.81%	74.06%	**76.30%**
N96/S71	63.00%	62.78%	82.11%	**82.35%**	92.76%	91.90%	75.84%	67.97%
N128/S89	63.38%	**63.56%**	82.13%	**82.25%**	91.92%	**93.00%**	74.52%	68.16%
N160/S109	63.23%	**63.59%**	82.07%	81.96%	92.62%	92.48%	75.30%	**75.73%**
N192/S130	62.55%	62.30%	81.99%	**82.40%**	92.53%	92.07%	72.54%	**73.62%**
N224/S150	63.38%	63.10%	81.84%	**82.05%**	92.46%	91.95%	69.97%	68.73%
N256/S168	61.97%	**61.98%**	82.26%	**82.39%**	92.26%	91.69%	71.97%	70.85%

Note: For each pair of accuracies given by *New Ext.* and *Select Ext.*, instances where the *Select Ext.* outperforms the *New Ext.* are emphasized by **bold** font.

The phenomenon mentioned above can be regarded as the equal penalization nature of the softmax loss. As most of the feature maps selected by Algorithm 1 have high class-significance for all classes, they are more likely to be assigned to majority classes. For the kernels only efficient on minority classes, fluctuations occur as softmax loss attempts to bias them to the majority ones. As a result, poor overall performance refinement is obtained by *Select Ext.*. As in Figure 15, averaged F1 scores and accuracies are shown for the three networks, with differences between *Select Ext.* (*Select*) and *New Ext.* (*Simple*) displayed as bars *Diff.*. Instances where *Select Ext.* is comparable to *New Ext.* are marked by arrows, and values for *Select Ext.* are listed above the markers. For the aforementioned reasons, these instances are rare, and the superiorities of *Select Ext.* are less significant.

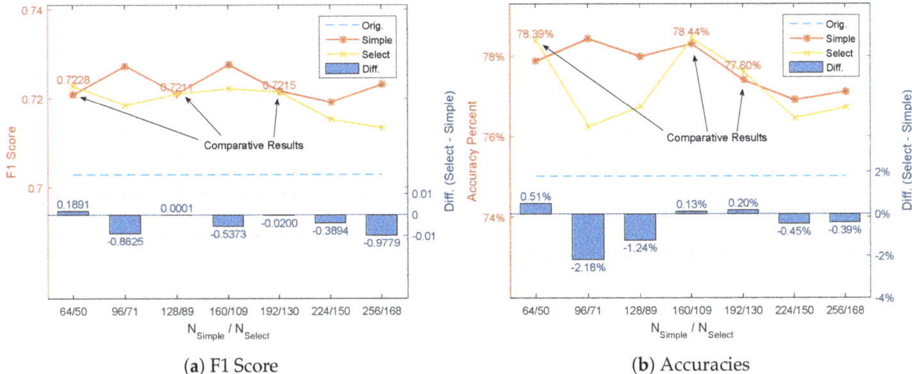

(a) F1 Score (b) Accuracies

Figure 15. Overall performance comparisons between the *Orig.M*, *New Ext.* and *Select Ext.* under different extension sizes. (**a**) the averaged F1 scores, (**b**) the averaged accuracies. Instances where *Select Ext.* is comparable to *New Ext.* are marked by arrows.

Finally, in Figure 16, a more fair comparison for showing the feature map extension efficiency is performed based on a per-kernel evaluation, where the increase in F1 score for each newly added feature map is calculated by $\left(F1_{ext} - F1_{orig} \right) / N_{ext}$, in which $F1_{orig}$ and $F1_{ext}$ for the baseline and extended network, and N_{ext} is the number of extended feature maps. As can be observed from Figure 16, the selective feature map-based extension is more efficient in medium-sized minority classes (Sedan and Van) for small extension quantity, while dropping more rapidly than the blank kernel-based one since the selected ones lack enough flexibility.

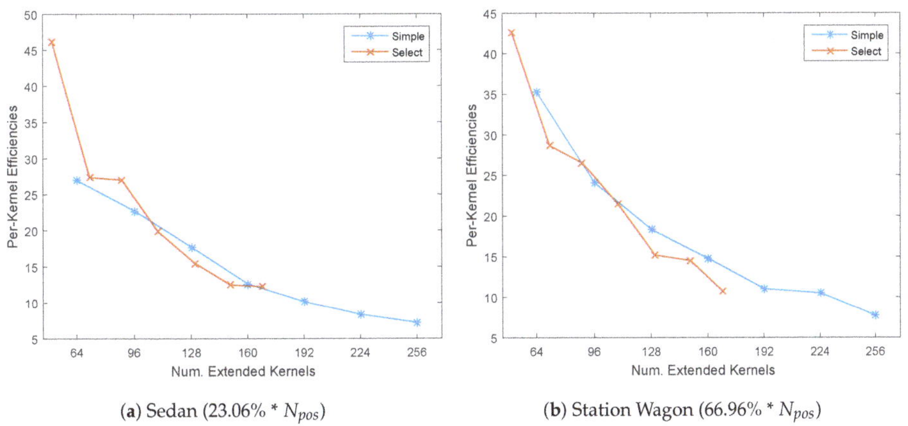

(a) Sedan ($23.06\% * N_{pos}$) (b) Station Wagon ($66.96\% * N_{pos}$)

Figure 16. *Cont.*

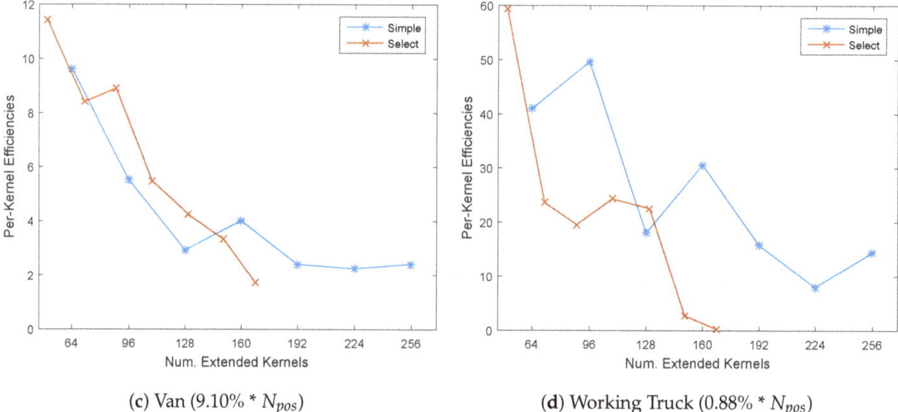

(c) Van (9.10% * N_{pos})   (d) Working Truck (0.88% * N_{pos})

Figure 16. Efficiency comparison of extended feature maps (kernels). N_{pos} is the quantity of all vehicles. Selected feature maps (kernels) are more effective for small extension and minority classes.

5.4. Main Factors in Main-Side Loss Function-based Fine-Tuning

Three major configurations have to be considered when using the Main-Side loss to fine-tune the bi-parted Main-Side network, which will be analyzed on the *New S-Ext.* extension: the first one is whether to fix the FC layers in the Main Network during the fine-tuning; the second one is the penalization coefficient λ and the positive constraint imposed on the single layered *FC6 Ext.* by an extra ReLU layer; and the third one is the three penalization modes. The reason for choosing the *New S-Ext.* extension for inspection is that it uses feature maps generated by blank kernels, which ensures that all extended kernels are equally flexible, and thus can be useful for an objective illustration of the impact caused by different configurations.

The first configuration—which involves partial fixation or joint optimization—determines whether the FC6 to FC8 layers should be updated during the fine-tuning. This configuration is only examined on the global penalization version of *New S-Ext.*, with the class-wise performances shown in Table 6. It is then obvious from the table that the joint optimization settings outperform the partially fixed ones in almost every class, including the accuracies and F1 scores, except the trivially populated class Working Truck. The superiority in performance for the joint optimization version is caused by the simultaneous adjustment of the estimation accuracies by the Main Network component, which means that kernels in the Main and Side Networks are optimally re-assigned. It is worth note that the existence of the positive constraint by ReLU layer is less significant for the joint optimization versions, in which the scores are almost identical.

Table 6. Categorization accuracies for fixed-Main and joint optimization, best average F1 cases.

	Sedan		Station Wagon		Van		Working Truck	
	ACC	F1	ACC	F1	ACC	F1	ACC	F1
Global No ReLU, Fix-M	62.12%	0.6275	81.10%	0.8212	91.46%	0.8479	<u>72.67%</u>	<u>0.5492</u>
Global ReLU, Fix-M	60.26%	0.6289	<u>81.48%</u>	0.8132	91.03%	0.8463	72.33%	**0.5542**
Global No ReLU, Joint	<u>65.42%</u>	<u>0.6435</u>	81.44%	<u>0.8320</u>	**93.29%**	**0.8497**	**73.77%**	0.5508
Global ReLU, Joint	**65.66%**	**0.6449**	**81.58%**	**0.8325**	<u>92.96%</u>	<u>0.8484</u>	72.06%	0.5490

Note: Fixed and non-fixed optimization settings are abbreviated as *Fix-M* and *Joint*, and the top-2 highest scores are marked as **bold** and <u>underline</u>.

For the second configuration involving the coefficient λ and the positive constraint ReLU, comparing results are shown in Figures 17 and 18. As can be observed from Figure 17a, the influences of λ are more correlated with the prediction accuracies, as they arise when the coefficient decreases. This is because smaller penalization encourages larger likelihood rectifications from the Side Network. This rectification effect is more clear in Figure 18, where medium-sized minority classes (e.g., class Sedan and Van) have greater accuracy improvements compared with majority ones (e.g., Station Wagon). However, the class that is too small (e.g., Working Truck) seems to benefit less from this effect because of the possibility of over-fitting.

In contrast, as seen previously in both figures, the existence of the ReLU layer has little or no influence on the resulting accuracies, while the removal of the ReLU layer seems to help stabilize the fluctuations in accuracies and F1 scores as the penalization λ changes. This is reasonable, since by permitting negative adjustments from the Side Network, they help with pruning the Main Network likelihoods too high to cause over-fitting.

For the third configuration—which involves the comparison between the three penalization modes (Global, Local, and Batch-wise)—experimental results are presented in Table 7. Judging from the scores, there is no apparent winner: Batch-wise penalization is more suitable for improving the small-sized classes (e.g., Working Truck), the Global penalization is more suitable for medium-sized classes (e.g., Sedan and Van), and the Local penalization performs better for the large and medium-sized ones (e.g., Station Wagon and Sedan).

Table 7. Best accuracies and F1s for three modes with or without the ReLU layer on FC6 Ext. layer.

	Sedan		Station Wagon		Van		Working Truck	
	ACC	**F1**	**ACC**	**F1**	**ACC**	**F1**	**ACC**	**F1**
Global No ReLU, Joint	65.42%	0.6435	81.44%	0.8320	93.29%	<u>0.8497</u>	<u>73.77%</u>	0.5508
Global ReLU, Joint	<u>65.66%</u>	**0.6449**	81.58%	<u>0.8325</u>	**92.96%**	0.8484	72.06%	0.5490
Local No ReLU, Joint	**65.79%**	0.6415	<u>81.63%</u>	**0.8335**	<u>92.91%</u>	0.8494	69.67%	0.5491
Local ReLU, Joint	65.53%	0.6441	81.55%	0.8320	92.88%	0.8468	72.17%	0.5432
Batch-wise No ReLU, Joint	64.79%	<u>0.6442</u>	**81.95%**	0.8308	92.40%	**0.8498**	71.04%	<u>0.5548</u>
Batch-wise ReLU, Joint	65.00%	0.6435	81.72%	0.8307	92.58%	0.8477	**74.92%**	**0.5662**

Note: In each column, the first and second topmost values are emphasized by **bold** and <u>underline</u>. Implementations with and without ReLU layer are marked by 'ReLU' and 'No ReLU'. 'Joint' means non-fixed optimization same as that in Table 6.

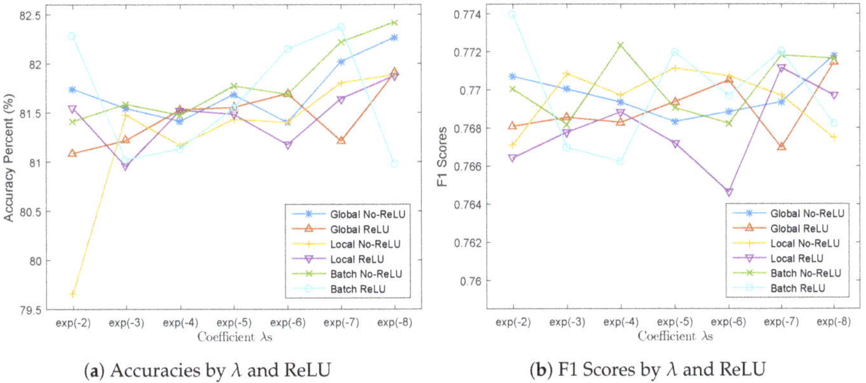

(a) Accuracies by λ and ReLU

(b) F1 Scores by λ and ReLU

Figure 17. Influences of the coefficient λ and ReLU constraint on the overall accuracy and $F1$ score in three modes. (a) the averaged accuracies; (b) the averaged $F1$ scores.

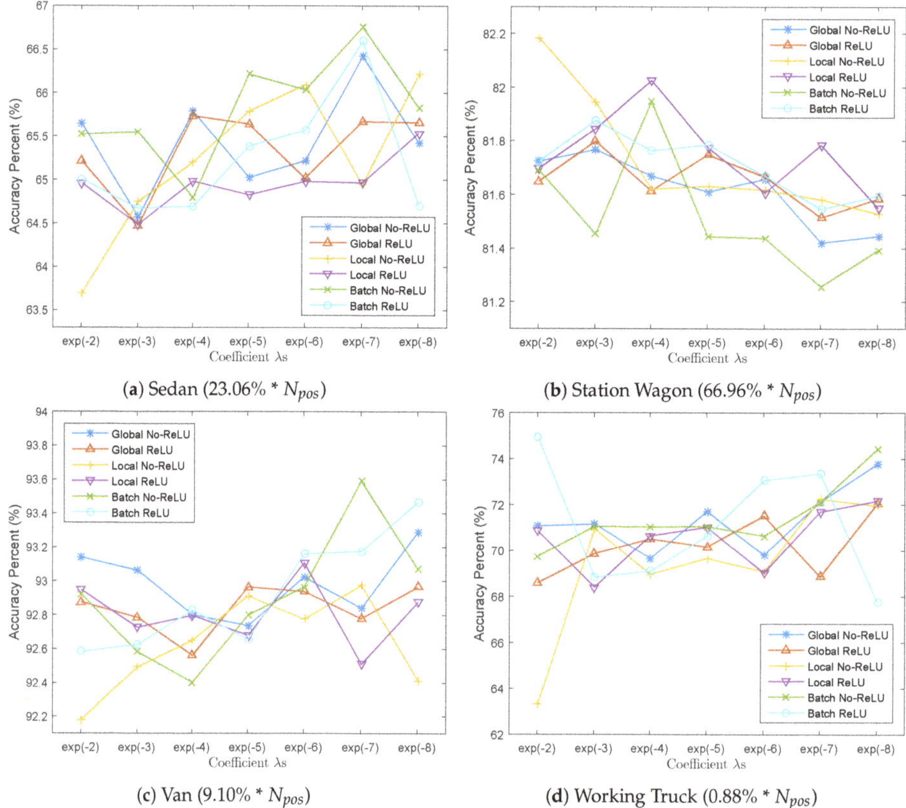

(a) Sedan (23.06% * N_{pos})

(b) Station Wagon (66.96% * N_{pos})

(c) Van (9.10% * N_{pos})

(d) Working Truck (0.88% * N_{pos})

Figure 18. Influences of the penalization mode and the coefficient λ on accuracy and $F1$ score for different vehicle types. N_{pos} is the quantity of positives, which is all the vehicles.

6. Discussion

As mentioned in Section 1, few articles have been found to address the class-imbalance issue in high-resolution aerial image-based vehicle localization and categorization using CNN structure extension; this article serves as an exploration of such methods. A principally similar work named hierarchical deep CNN (HD-CNN) [50] has studied the effectiveness of a tree-structured CNN ensemble on general object classification problems involving dozens of classes. However, with only a few classes, it is inconvenient to build multi-level class taxonomy, and appending a near-full-sized CNN structure might not be sufficiently cost-efficient considering the size of the problem.

The effectiveness of the proposed extension scheme is exemplified in a moderately-sized VGG-M network in a self-proven manner. According to the analysis in the previous experimental section, several general conclusions can be drawn on the network extension-based class-imbalance dealing methods, which can be useful for applying the methods on other similar applications:

(a)   According to Tables 3 and 4, using wider and deeper network structure with plain extension (blank kernels and softmax loss) will generally improve the classification performances on all classes, while using deeper structure will help more with the generalized performance measured by F1 score.

(b)   According to Table 5, the effectiveness of the softmax loss-based plain width extension with either blank kernels or selected feature maps will decrease rapidly as the extension quantity increases. Additionally, the selected feature maps are more effective under small extension quantity, while losing their advantage in large extension, as they lack flexibility.

(c)   As can be seen from Tables 3–5, selected feature maps are more helpful for improving the classification accuracies, while they can barely keep up with the blank kernel-based extension in overall F1 score by Figure 15a. To maintain a reasonably high F1 score performance, the penalization mode *Glb.ReLU* and *Bat.ReLU* are preferred, as in Tables 3 and 4.

(d)   As seen by Figure 17a, penalization modes without ReLU constraint in the Main-Side loss-related fine-tuning can produce a more significant increment in accuracies as the global penalization λ decreases. The existence of a ReLU layer helps to stabilize the fluctuation in F1 scores when λ changes, as in Figure 17b.

(e)   By Figure 18, the class-imbalance-sensitive penalization term $\Omega(\mathbf{z}^*)$ helps to improve the classification accuracies for the medium-sized minority classes (Sedan and Van), but is not so ideal for classes with an absolutely trivial sample quantity (Working Truck).

(f)   The sizes of most effective vehicle classes for the three penalization modes are different. Shown by Table 7, the Global penalization mode is effective on medium-sized classes (Sedan and Van), the Local mode is effective for large- and medium-sized classes (Station Wagon and Sedan), while the Batch-wise mode is effective for small-sized classes (Working Truck).

7. Conclusions

Methods for joint vehicle localization and categorization in aerial images helps with important applications such as traffic flow analysis and suspicious vehicle detection. By treating samples who exceed the permitted location deviation as negatives and classifying them along with the other vehicle classes, the problem of cascaded localization error in separated estimation is eliminated. Top-3 accuracy as high as 99% can be achieved when a typical CNN-based classifier is employed (e.g., the 16-layered VGG network), but it still suffers from the class-imbalance issue, which causes poor classification performances on minority classes.

Based on the R-CNN detection structure, a cost-effective network extension scheme is proposed in this paper to address this issue by introducing less computation and memory consumption overhead. Such efficiency is achieved by two means: the feature map selection and bi-partite Main-Side Network extension, which are performed with the help of a feature map class-importance measurement and a class-imbalance-aware loss function newly proposed in this article. The resulting extended network structure is verified along with its similarly-shaped strong counterparts on a 0.13 m GSD aerial image dataset captured over the urban region of Munich. Experimental results show that the selectively extended feature maps are more effective than those produced by randomly initialized new kernels. By applying the Main-Side loss on this bi-partite network, classification performances on medium-sized minority classes can be further improved. The three Main-Side loss penalizing schemes help with this performance improvement differently, showing varied refinement effect on different-sized classes. Generally, by jointly employing the feature map selection and Main-Side loss optimization schemes, comparable vehicle categorization results can be achieved compared to the counterparts with less parameter and memory overheads.

Key contributions of this study are as follows: First, a novel multi-class feature map importance measurement is proposed by extending the existing significance score for binary classification problems. Second, an easy-to-use cost-effective network extension scheme called Main-Side Network is proposed to greatly improve the classification performances on minority classes with small amount of overhead. Third, three penalization modes are proposed for regularizing the Main-Side loss adopted in this extension, which are simple to implement and beneficial for minority classes with different properties.

In future work, the existing classification deficiencies on tiny classes (e.g., the Working Truck class) is planned to be deeply investigated by using stronger models from the one-class classification. Difficult detection conditions involving shadowed and partially sheltered vehicles caused by skyscrapers and street trees will be further analyzed with harder experimental dataset. Behaviors of the three penalization modes for the Main-Side Loss should be further analyzed in detail to enhance the performance. The Main-Side Network extension structure is intended to be replaced by a network splitting method; thus, the convolution and memory consumption overhead can be completely eliminated.

Acknowledgments: This work is jointly supported by the National Science Foundation of China (NSFC) with granting No. 61302154 and No. 61573350, which mainly focus on aerial image and video analysis. The author would like to acknowledge the editor and reviewers by contributing their precious time to view this article. The authors would also like to thank authors Jason Yosinski et al. in [65] for their selflessness in sharing the great visualization tool.

Author Contributions: Feimo Li designed the experiment and prepared the manuscript; both Hongxing Chang, Shuxiao Li and Chengfei Zhu directed the research project and provided conceptual advices. Xiaosong Lan helped in the revision the manuscript.

Conflicts of Interest: The authors declare no conflict of interest.

Abbreviations

The following abbreviations are used in this manuscript:

ADASYN	Adaptive Synthetic Sampling
CBO	Cluster-based Oversampling
CNN	Convolutional Neural Network
DBN	Deep Belief Network
FCN	Fully Convolutional Neural Network
HOG	Histogram of Oriented Gradients
GAN	Generative Adversarial Network
GSD	Ground Sampling Distance
LBP	Local Binary Pattern
R-CNN	Regions with Convolutional Neural Network Features
ROI	Region of Interest
SIFT	Scale Invariant Feature Transform
SMOTE	Synthetic Minority Over-sampling Technique
SVM	Support Vector Machine
t-SNE	t-Distributed Stochastic Neighbor Embedding
VGG	Visual Geometry Group

References

1. Xu, Y.; Yu, G.; Wang, Y.; Wu, X.; Ma, Y. A Hybrid Vehicle Detection Method Based on Viola-Jones and HOG + SVM from UAV Images. *Sensors* **2016**, doi:10.3390/s16081325.
2. Tuermer, S.; Kurz, F.; Reinartz, P.; Stilla, U. Airborne vehicle detection in dense urban areas using HoG features and disparity maps. *IEEE J. Sel. Top. Appl. Earth Obs. Remote Sens.* **2013**, *6*, 2327–2337.
3. Hinz, S.; Schlosser, C.; Reitberger, J. Automatic car detection in high resolution urban scenes based on an adaptive 3D-model. In Proceedings of the 2nd GRSS/ISPRS Joint Workshop on Remote Sensing and Data Fusion over Urban Areas, Berlin, Germany, 22–23 May 2003; pp. 167–171.
4. Qu, T.; Zhang, Q.; Sun, S. Vehicle detection from high-resolution aerial images using spatial pyramid pooling-based deep convolutional neural networks. *Multimedia Tools Appl.* **2016**, doi:10.1007/s11042-016-4043-5.
5. Chen, X.; Xiang, S.; Liu, C.L.; Pan, C.H. Vehicle detection in satellite images by hybrid deep convolutional neural networks. *IEEE Geosci. Remote Sens. Lett.* **2014**, *11*, 1797–1801.
6. Cao, L.; Jiang, Q.; Cheng, M.; Wang, C. Robust vehicle detection by combining deep features with exemplar classification. *Neurocomputing* **2016**, *215*, 225–231.

7. Zhu, H.; Chen, X.; Dai, W.; Fu, K.; Ye, Q.; Jiao, J. Orientation robust object detection in aerial images using deep convolutional neural network. In Proceedings of the 2015 IEEE International Conference on Image Processing (ICIP), Quebec City, QC, Canada, 27–30 September 2015; pp. 3735–3739.

8. Qu, S.; Wang, Y.; Meng, G.; Pan, C. Vehicle Detection in Satellite Images by Incorporating Objectness and Convolutional Neural Network. *J. Ind. Intell. Inf.* **2016**, doi:10.18178/jiii.4.2.158-162.

9. Girshick, R.; Donahue, J.; Darrell, T.; Malik, J. Rich feature hierarchies for accurate object detection and semantic segmentation. In Proceedings of the IEEE Conference on Computer Vision and Pattern Recognition, Columbus, OH, USA, 23–28 June 2014; pp. 580–587.

10. Girshick, R. Fast r-cnn. In Proceedings of the IEEE International Conference on Computer Vision, Los Alamitos, CA, USA, 7–13 December 2015; pp. 1440–1448.

11. Ren, S.; He, K.; Girshick, R.; Sun, J. Faster r-cnn: Towards real-time object detection with region proposal networks. In Proceedings of the Advances in Neural Information Processing Systems, Montréal, QC, Canada, 7–12 December 2015.

12. Liu, W.; Anguelov, D.; Erhan, D.; Szegedy, C.; Reed, S.; Fu, C.Y.; Berg, A.C. SSD: Single shot multibox detector. In *European Conference on Computer Vision*; Springer: New York, NY, USA, 2016; pp. 21–37.

13. Redmon, J.; Divvala, S.; Girshick, R.; Farhadi, A. You only look once: Unified, real-time object detection. In Proceedings of the IEEE Conference on Computer Vision and Pattern Recognition, Stanford, CA, USA, 27–30 June 2016; pp. 779–788.

14. He, K.; Zhang, X.; Ren, S.; Sun, J. Spatial pyramid pooling in deep convolutional networks for visual recognition. In *European Conference on Computer Vision*; Springer: New York, NY, USA, 2014, pp. 346–361.

15. Tang, T.; Zhou, S.; Deng, Z.; Zou, H.; Lei, L. Vehicle Detection in Aerial Images Based on Region Convolutional Neural Networks and Hard Negative Example Mining. *Sensors* **2017**, doi:10.3390/s17020336.

16. Wang, Q.; Lin, J.; Yuan, Y. Salient band selection for hyperspectral image classification via manifold ranking. *IEEE Trans. Neural Netw. Learn. Syst.* **2016**, *27*, 1279–1289.

17. Zhang, F.; Du, B.; Zhang, L. Saliency-guided unsupervised feature learning for scene classification. *IEEE Trans. Geosci. Remote Sens.* **2015**, *53*, 2175–2184.

18. Holt, A.C.; Seto, E.Y.; Rivard, T.; Gong, P. Object-based detection and classification of vehicles from high-resolution aerial photography. *Photogramm. Eng. Remote Sens.* **2009**, *75*, 871–880.

19. Liu, K.; Mattyus, G. Fast multiclass vehicle detection on aerial images. *IEEE Geosci. Remote Sens. Lett.* **2015**, *12*, 1938–1942.

20. Razakarivony, S.; Jurie, F. Vehicle detection in aerial imagery: A small target detection benchmark. *J. Vis. Commun. Image Represent.* **2016**, *34*, 187–203.

21. Bell, S.; Lawrence Zitnick, C.; Bala, K.; Girshick, R. Inside-outside net: Detecting objects in context with skip pooling and recurrent neural networks. In Proceedings of the IEEE Conference on Computer Vision and Pattern Recognition, Stanford, CA, USA, 27–30 June 2016; pp. 2874–2883.

22. Ma, Z.; Yu, L.; Chan, A.B. Small instance detection by integer programming on object density maps. In Proceedings of the IEEE Conference on Computer Vision and Pattern Recognition, Boston, MA, USA, 7–12 June 2015; pp. 3689–3697.

23. Arteta, C.; Lempitsky, V.; Noble, J.A.; Zisserman, A. Interactive object counting. In *European Conference on Computer Vision*; Springer: New York, NY, USA, 2014, pp. 504–518.

24. Yuan, Y.; Wan, J.; Wang, Q. Congested scene classification via efficient unsupervised feature learning and density estimation. *Pattern Recognit.* **2016**, *56*, 159–169.

25. He, H.; Garcia, E.A. Learning from imbalanced data. *IEEE Trans. Knowl. Data Eng.* **2009**, *21*, 1263–1284.

26. Branco, P.; Torgo, L.; Ribeiro, R. A survey of predictive modelling under imbalanced distributions. *arXiv* **2015**, arXiv:1505.01658.

27. He, H.; Ma, Y. *Imbalanced Learning: Foundations, Algorithms, and Applications*; John Wiley & Sons: New York, NY, USA, 2013.

28. Krawczyk, B. Learning from imbalanced data: Open challenges and future directions. *Prog. Artif. Intell.* **2016**, *5*, 221–232.

29. Chawla, N.V.; Bowyer, K.W.; Hall, L.O.; Kegelmeyer, W.P. SMOTE: synthetic minority over-sampling technique. *J. Artif. Intell. Res.* **2002**, *16*, 321–357.

30. He, H.; Bai, Y.; Garcia, E.A.; Li, S. ADASYN: Adaptive synthetic sampling approach for imbalanced learning. In Proceedings of the IEEE International Joint Conference on Neural Networks, Hong Kong, China, 1–8 June 2008; pp. 1322–1328.

31. Jo, T.; Japkowicz, N. Class imbalances versus small disjuncts. *ACM Sigkdd Explor. Newsl.* **2004**, *6*, 40–49.

32. Zhou, Z.H.; Liu, X.Y. On Multi-Class Cost-Sensitive Learning. *Comput. Intell.* **2010**, *26*, 232–257.

33. Ting, K.M. A comparative study of cost-sensitive boosting algorithms. In Proceedings of the 17th International Conference on Machine Learning, Stanford, CA, USA, 29 June–2 July 2000.

34. Krawczyk, B.; Woźniak, M.; Schaefer, G. Cost-sensitive decision tree ensembles for effective imbalanced classification. *Appl. Soft Comput.* **2014**, *14*, 554–562.

35. Huang, C.; Li, Y.; Change Loy, C.; Tang, X. Learning deep representation for imbalanced classification. In Proceedings of the IEEE Conference on Computer Vision and Pattern Recognition, Stanford, CA, USA, 27–30 June 2016; pp. 5375–5384.

36. Jeatrakul, P.; Wong, K.W.; Fung, C.C. Classification of imbalanced data by combining the complementary neural network and SMOTE algorithm. In *International Conference on Neural Information Processing*; Springer: New York, NY, USA, 2010; pp. 152–159.

37. Simpson, A.J. Over-sampling in a deep neural network. *arXiv* **2015**, arXiv:1502.03648.

38. Goodfellow, I.; Pouget-Abadie, J.; Mirza, M.; Xu, B.; Warde-Farley, D.; Ozair, S.; Courville, A.; Bengio, Y. Generative adversarial nets. In Proceedings of the Advances in Neural Information Processing Systems, Montreal, QC, Canada, 8–13 December 2014; pp. 2672–2680.

39. Khan, S.H.; Bennamoun, M.; Sohel, F.; Togneri, R. Cost sensitive learning of deep feature representations from imbalanced data. *arXiv* **2015**, arXiv:1508.03422.

40. Cheng, G.; Zhou, P.; Han, J. Rifd-cnn: Rotation-invariant and fisher discriminative convolutional neural networks for object detection. In Proceedings of the IEEE Conference on Computer Vision and Pattern Recognition, Stanford, CA, USA, 27–30 June 2016; pp. 2884–2893.

41. Bertasius, G.; Shi, J.; Torresani, L. Deepedge: A multi-scale bifurcated deep network for top-down contour detection. In Proceedings of the IEEE Conference on Computer Vision and Pattern Recognition, Boston, MA, USA, 7–12 June 2015; pp. 4380–4389.

42. Shen, W.; Wang, X.; Wang, Y.; Bai, X.; Zhang, Z. Deepcontour: A deep convolutional feature learned by positive-sharing loss for contour detection. In Proceedings of the IEEE Conference on Computer Vision and Pattern Recognition, Boston, MA, USA, 7–12 June 2015; pp. 3982–3991.

43. Robinson, J.P.; Shao, M.; Wu, Y.; Fu, Y. Families in the Wild (FIW): Large-Scale Kinship Image Database and Benchmarks. In Proceedings of the 2016 ACM on Multimedia Conference, Amsterdam, The Netherlands, 15–19 October 2016; pp. 242–246.

44. Santos, C.N.d.; Xiang, B.; Zhou, B. Classifying relations by ranking with convolutional neural networks. *arXiv* **2015**, arXiv:1504.06580.

45. Schroff, F.; Kalenichenko, D.; Philbin, J. Facenet: A unified embedding for face recognition and clustering. In Proceedings of the IEEE Conference on Computer Vision and Pattern Recognition, Boston, MA, USA, 7–12 June 2015; pp. 815–823.

46. Oh Song, H.; Xiang, Y.; Jegelka, S.; Savarese, S. Deep metric learning via lifted structured feature embedding. In Proceedings of the IEEE Conference on Computer Vision and Pattern Recognition, Stanford, CA, USA, 27–30 June 2016; pp. 4004–4012.

47. Wen, Y.; Zhang, K.; Li, Z.; Qiao, Y., A Discriminative Feature Learning Approach for Deep Face Recognition. In *Computer Vision—ECCV 2016*; Springer International Publishing: Cham, The Netherlands, 2016; pp. 499–515.

48. Chu, J.L.; Krzyak, A. Analysis of feature maps selection in supervised learning using convolutional neural networks. In *Canadian Conference on Artificial Intelligence*; Springer: New York, NY, USA, 1994; pp. 59–70.

49. Marcu, A.; Leordeanu, M. Dual Local-Global Contextual Pathways for Recognition in Aerial Imagery. *arXiv* **2016**, arXiv:1605.05462.

50. Yan, Z.; Zhang, H.; Piramuthu, R.; Jagadeesh, V.; DeCoste, D.; Di, W.; Yu, Y. HD-CNN: hierarchical deep convolutional neural networks for large scale visual recognition. In Proceedings of the IEEE International Conference on Computer Vision, Los Alamitos, CA, USA, 7–13 December 2015; pp. 2740–2748.

51. Jaderberg, M.; Simonyan, K.; Zisserman, A.; Kavukcuoglu, K. Spatial transformer networks. In Proceedings of the Advances in Neural Information Processing Systems, Montréal, QC, Canada, 7–12 December 2015.

52. Wang, N.; Li, S.; Gupta, A.; Yeung, D.Y. Transferring rich feature hierarchies for robust visual tracking. *arXiv* **2015**, arXiv:1501.04587.

53. Ng, W.W.; Zeng, G.; Zhang, J.; Yeung, D.S.; Pedrycz, W. Dual autoencoders features for imbalance classification problem. *Pattern Recognit.* **2016**, *60*, 875–889.

54. Guyon, I.; Gunn, S.; Nikravesh, M.; Zadeh, L.A. *Feature Extraction: Foundations and Applications*; Springer: New York, NY, USA, 2008.

55. Bar, Y.; Diamant, I.; Wolf, L.; Lieberman, S.; Konen, E.; Greenspan, H. Chest pathology identification using deep feature selection with non-medical training. *Comput. Methods Biomech. Biomed. Eng. Imaging Vis.* **2016**, doi:10.1080/21681163.2016.1138324.

56. Matsugu, M.; Cardon, P. Unsupervised feature selection for multi-class object detection using convolutional neural networks. In *Advances in Neural Networks—ISNN 2004*; Springer: New York, NY, USA, 2004; pp. 864–869.

57. Zou, Q.; Ni, L.; Zhang, T.; Wang, Q. Deep Learning Based Feature Selection for Remote Sensing Scene Classification. *IEEE Geosci. Remote Sens. Lett.* **2015**, *12*, 2321–2325.

58. Wang, L.; Ouyang, W.; Wang, X.; Lu, H. Visual tracking with fully convolutional networks. In Proceedings of the IEEE International Conference on Computer Vision, Los Alamitos, CA, USA, 7–13 December 2015; pp. 3119–3127.

59. Liu, D.R.; Li, H.L.; Wang, D. Feature selection and feature learning for high-dimensional batch reinforcement learning: A survey. *Int. J. Autom. Comput.* **2015**, *12*, 229–242.

60. Yang, B.; Yan, J.; Lei, Z.; Li, S.Z. Convolutional channel features. In Proceedings of the IEEE International Conference on Computer Vision, Los Alamitos, CA, USA, 7–13 December 2015; pp. 82–90.

61. Zhong, B.; Zhang, J.; Wang, P.; Du, J.; Chen, D. Jointly Feature Learning and Selection for Robust Tracking via a Gating Mechanism. *PLoS ONE* **2016**, *11*, e0161808.

62. Goodfellow, I.; Bengio, Y.; Courville, A. *Deep Learning*; MIT Press: Cambridge, MA, USA, 2016; pp. 166–373.

63. Jarrett, K.; Kavukcuoglu, K.; LeCun, Y.; Ranzato, M. What is the best multi-stage architecture for object recognition? In Proceedings of the 2009 IEEE 12th International Conference on Computer Vision, Kyoto, Japan, 29 September–2 October 2009; pp. 2146–2153.

64. Nair, V.; Hinton, G.E. Rectified linear units improve restricted boltzmann machines. In Proceedings of the 27th International Conference on Machine Learning (ICML-10), Haifa, Israel, 21–25 June 2010; pp. 807–814.

65. Yosinski, J.; Clune, J.; Nguyen, A.; Fuchs, T.; Lipson, H. Understanding neural networks through deep visualization. *arXiv* **2015**, arXiv:1506.06579.

66. Simonyan, K.; Vedaldi, A.; Zisserman, A. Deep inside convolutional networks: Visualising image classification models and saliency maps. *arXiv* **2013**, arXiv:1312.6034.

67. Nguyen, A.; Yosinski, J.; Clune, J. Deep neural networks are easily fooled: High confidence predictions for unrecognizable images. In Proceedings of the IEEE Conference on Computer Vision and Pattern Recognition, Boston, MA, USA, 7–12 June 2015; pp. 427–436.

68. Szegedy, C.; Zaremba, W.; Sutskever, I.; Bruna, J.; Erhan, D.; Goodfellow, I.; Fergus, R. Intriguing properties of neural networks. *arXiv* **2013**, arXiv:1312.6199.

69. Zeiler, M.D.; Fergus, R. Visualizing and understanding convolutional networks. In *European Conference on Computer Vision*; Springer: New York, NY, USA, 2014; pp. 818–833.

70. Erhan, D.; Bengio, Y.; Courville, A.; Vincent, P. Visualizing Higher-Layer Features of a Deep Network. *Univ. Montr.* **2009**, *1341*, 3.

71. Krizhevsky, A.; Sutskever, I.; Hinton, G.E. Imagenet classification with deep convolutional neural networks. In Proceedings of the Advances in Neural Information Processing Systems, Lake Tahoe, ND, USA, 3–6 December 2012; pp. 1097–1105.

72. LeCun, Y.; Denker, J.S.; Solla, S.A.; Howard, R.E.; Jackel, L.D. *Optimal Brain Damage*; NIPs: Tokyo, Japan, 1989; Volume 2, pp. 598–605.

73. Maaten, L.v.d.; Hinton, G. Visualizing data using t-SNE. *J. Mach. Learn. Res.* **2008**, *9*, 2579–2605.

74. Chatfield, K.; Simonyan, K.; Vedaldi, A.; Zisserman, A. Return of the devil in the details: Delving deep into convolutional nets. *arXiv* **2014**, arXiv:1405.3531.

75. Simonyan, K.; Zisserman, A. Very deep convolutional networks for large-scale image recognition. *arXiv* **2014**, arXiv:1409.1556.

76. He, K.; Zhang, X.; Ren, S.; Sun, J. Deep residual learning for image recognition. In Proceedings of the IEEE Conference on Computer Vision and Pattern Recognition, Stanford, CA, USA, 27–30 June 2016; pp. 770–778.

77. Huang, G.; Liu, Z.; Weinberger, K.Q.; van der Maaten, L. Densely connected convolutional networks. *arXiv* **2016**, arXiv:1608.06993.

78. Targ, S.; Almeida, D.; Lyman, K. Resnet in Resnet: Generalizing residual architectures. *arXiv* **2016**, arXiv:1603.08029.

79. Szegedy, C.; Liu, W.; Jia, Y.; Sermanet, P.; Reed, S.; Anguelov, D.; Erhan, D.; Vanhoucke, V.; Rabinovich, A. Going deeper with convolutions. In Proceedings of the IEEE Conference on Computer Vision and Pattern Recognition, Boston, MA, USA, 7–12 June 2015; pp. 1–9.

Article

Hyperspectral Target Detection via Adaptive Joint Sparse Representation and Multi-Task Learning with Locality Information

Yuxiang Zhang [1], Ke Wu [1], Bo Du [2,*], Liangpei Zhang [3] and Xiangyun Hu [1]

[1] Hubei Subsurface Multi-Scale Imaging Key Laboratory, Institute of Geophysics and Geomatics, China University of Geosciences, Wuhan 430074, China; zyx_070504@163.com (Y.Z.); tingke2000@126.com (K.W.); xyhu@cug.edu.cn (X.H.)

[2] School of Computer, Wuhan University, Wuhan 430079, China

[3] State Key Laboratory of Information Engineering in Surveying, Mapping, and Remote Sensing, Wuhan University, Wuhan 430079, China; zlp62@whu.edu.cn

[*] Correspondence: gunspace@163.com; Tel.: +86-138-7146-1059

Academic Editors: Qi Wang, Nicolas H. Younan, Carlos López-Martínez, Xiaofeng Li and Prasad S. Thenkabail
Received: 16 April 2017; Accepted: 12 May 2017; Published: 14 May 2017

Abstract: Target detection from hyperspectral images is an important problem but encounters a critical challenge of simultaneously reducing spectral redundancy and preserving the discriminative information. Recently, the joint sparse representation and multi-task learning (JSR-MTL) approach was proposed to address the challenge. However, it does not fully explore the prior class label information of the training samples and the difference between the target dictionary and background dictionary when constructing the model. Besides, there may exist estimation bias for the unknown coefficient matrix with the use of ℓ_1/ℓ_2 minimization which is usually inconsistent in variable selection. To address these problems, this paper proposes an adaptive joint sparse representation and multi-task learning detector with locality information (JSRMTL-ALI). The proposed method has the following capabilities: (1) it takes full advantage of the prior class label information to construct an adaptive joint sparse representation and multi-task learning model; (2) it explores the great difference between the target dictionary and background dictionary with different regularization strategies in order to better encode the task relatedness; (3) it applies locality information by imposing an iterative weight on the coefficient matrix in order to reduce the estimation bias. Extensive experiments were carried out on three hyperspectral images, and it was found that JSRMTL-ALI generally shows a better detection performance than the other target detection methods.

Keywords: hyperspectral image; target detection; multi-task learning; sparse representation; locality information

---

1. Introduction

Target detection is essentially a binary classification problem, which aims to separate specific target pixels from various backgrounds with prior knowledge of the targets [1,2]. With the characteristic of high spectral resolution [3], hyperspectral images (HSIs) with hundreds or even thousands of spectral bands can distinguish subtle spectral differences, even between very similar materials, providing a unique advantage for target detection [4,5]. Target detection has therefore attracted much attention in many HSI applications, and it has been successfully used in real-world applications such as detecting rare minerals in geology, oil pollution in environmental research, landmines in the public safety and defense domain, and man-made objects in reconnaissance and surveillance applications [6–9].

The current target detection methods mainly utilize the detailed spectral information from the HSI data and use different techniques to distinguish the targets and the background, such as the statistical hypothesis testing theory [10–12], filtering or projection technique [13–15], and sparse representation technique [16–19]. These existing target detection methods, using a uniform vector of test pixel's spectrum as input, usually employ all the original bands to both construct the model and perform the detection. In other words, these methods fully and uniformly utilize the discriminative information within all single-band images, without considering the inherent similarity between the adjacent single-band images of HSI. In fact, the spectral resolution of HSIs is so high that the adjacent single-band images present a great spectral similarity or redundancy, and this spectral redundancy provides an obstacle for effective target detection. Many methods via dimension reduction for hyperspectral target detection have been proposed in order to relieve this problem [20–24]. However, none of them can guarantee that all the valuable discriminative spectral information underlying the HSI data is preserved, since the HSI data dimension is greatly reduced after the dimension reduction process. To summarize, there exists a dilemma to simultaneously reduce spectral redundancy and preserve discriminative information for Hyperspectral target detection.

In recent years, the multi-task learning (MTL) technique has attracted much interest [25–28] and has been employed to address the above dilemma for hyperspectral target detection in [29], labeled as the joint sparse representation and multi-task learning (JSR-MTL) approach. The approach explores the spectral similarity between the adjacent single-band images to construct multiple sub-HSIs with a band cross-grouping strategy, which leads to multiple related detection tasks. The approach further explores the similarity between the sub-HSIs to analyze the latent sparse representation of each task. Then multiple sparse representation models via the union target and background dictionary are integrated via a unified multitask learning technique. In this way, the redundancy in each detection task can be effectively avoided; and the spectral information behind the high dimension original HSI dataset fully used, so that the discriminative information is not lost [29].

However, there still exist several problems with the JSR-MTL approach. Firstly, it does not fully incorporate the class label (prior) information of the training samples, which only utilizes the class label information in post-processing when calculating the residuals for each class and ignores the class label information when constructing the sparse representation models. Secondly, it encourages shared sparsity among the columns of the coefficient matrix corresponding to the union dictionary, which lead to the same sparsity constraint among the tasks corresponding to both the target dictionary and background dictionary. However, as the size and the spectral variability of the target dictionary are much different from the background dictionary, it is therefore not appropriate to impose the same sparsity constraint for both the coefficient matrices corresponding to the target dictionary and background dictionary. Finally, it does not take the locality information between the test pixel and all the neighboring background training samples into consideration, which may make a contribution for better signal reconstruction, due to the fact that the samples similar to the test pixel are more likely to be selected for signal reconstruction.

To address the above problems, this paper proposes an adaptive joint sparse representation and multi-task learning detector with locality information (JSRMTL-ALI). The proposed method explores the prior class label information of the training samples to construct two joint sparse representation and multi-task learning models, where the test pixel is separately modeled via the target dictionary or background dictionary. Considering also the great difference between the target dictionary and background dictionary, different regularization strategies encoding the task relatedness are employed for the two joint sparse representation and multi-task learning models based on the target dictionary or background dictionary. Besides, a locality information descriptor is introduced to indicate the difference between the central test pixel and the neighboring background training samples. Additionally, inspired by the idea that the coefficient matrix may have estimation bias in [30,31], since the ℓ_1/ℓ_2 minimization used in the regularization strategy is usually inconsistent in variable selection, a locality information descriptor-based weight is employed to iteratively constrain the regularization term to reduce the estimation bias.

The rest of this paper is organized as follows. Section 2 briefly introduces the original JSR-MTL method. The proposed JSRMTL-ALI method is then presented in Section 3. The experimental results of the proposed method with several HSIs are presented in Section 4. Finally, the discussion and conclusions are drawn in Sections 5 and 6.

2. Brief Introduction to the JSR-MTL Method

For the hyperspectral imagery (HSI), as discussed in [29], the adjacent single band images are similar to each other and MTL technology is introduced to utilize the spectral similarity for hyperspectral target detection.

The MTL methodology was proposed by Caruana [28]. It is an inductive transfer method that uses the domain-specific information contained in the training signals of related tasks, which can guarantee that the related tasks can learn from each other and make the inductive transfer method work. There are two key techniques of MTL. One is the construction of multiple tasks with commonality. The other key technique is the relevance analysis of multiple tasks. The multiple tasks can be constructed in various ways, which may depend on the specific application [25,26]. Tasks can be related in various ways. There are two commonly used approaches: (1) tasks may be related by assuming that all the learned functions are close to each other in some norm, such as the linear regression function [25]; and (2) tasks may also be related in that they all share a common underlying representation [32], such as sparsity, a manifold constraint, or a graphical model structure.

In JSR-MTL [29], multiple related detection tasks are constructed through band cross-grouping strategy. In accordance with the band order of the original HSI, the multiple adjacent single-band images are cross-grouped into different groups. Each group then forms a sub-HSI, as shown in Figure 1. Based on the spectral similarity between the adjacent single-band images, multiple sub-HSIs from the original HSI are related with each other. Therefore, these multiple related sub-HSIs naturally correspond to multiple related detection tasks [29].

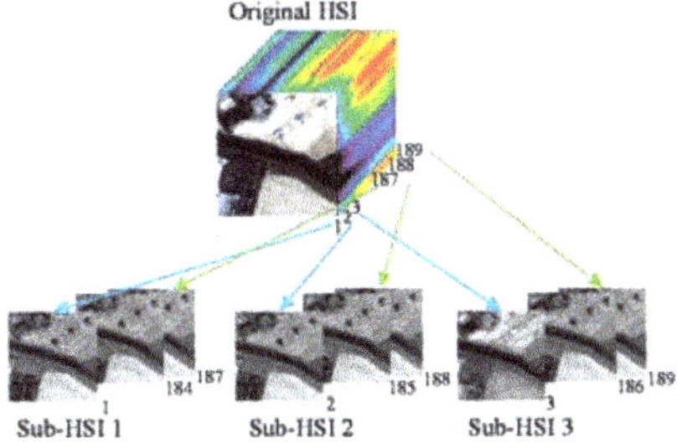

Figure 1. Illustration of the band cross-grouping strategy for the multiple detection tasks. HSI = hyperspectral image.

For the relevance analysis of the multiple tasks, the spectral similarity of the multiple sub-HSIs naturally guarantees the relevance of the multiple detection tasks. Therefore the multiple detection tasks are likely to share a common sparse representation [29], which has shown effectiveness in hyperspectral target detection [16–19].

Considering hyperspectral data $\mathbf{X} \in R^{h \times w \times B}$ with training samples $\mathbf{D} = \left[\mathbf{D}^t, \mathbf{D}^b\right]$, where $\mathbf{D}^t$ is the target dictionary generated via the target training samples $\{\mathbf{d}_i{}^t\}_{i=1}^{N_t} \in R^B$, and $\mathbf{D}^b$ is the background dictionary generated via the background training samples $\{\mathbf{d}_i{}^b\}_{i=1}^{N_b} \in R^B$. N_b and N_t are the number of background and target training samples, respectively. Let $\mathbf{x}$ be a test pixel in the original HSI, and $\left\{\mathbf{x}^k \in R^{B^k}\right\}_{k=1}^{K}$ represents the partial test pixel in each sub-HSI.

For the k-th sub-HSI, the partial test pixel $\left\{ \mathbf{x}^k \right\}_{k=1}^{K} \in R^{B^k}$ can be modeled to lie in the union of the background and target subspaces respectively spanned by the background training samples $\{\mathbf{d}_i^{kb} \in R^{B^k \times N_b}\}_{i=1}^{N_b}$ and the target training samples $\{\mathbf{d}_i^{kt} \in R^{B^k \times N_t}\}_{i=1}^{N_t}$. Therefore, $\mathbf{x}^k$ can be represented by a sparse linear combination of the training samples

$$
\begin{aligned}
\mathbf{x}^k &= \left(w_1^{kb}\mathbf{d}_1^{kb} + w_2^{kb}\mathbf{d}_2^{kb} + \cdots + w_{N_b}^{kb}\mathbf{d}_{N_b}^{kb} \right) + \left(w_1^{kt}\mathbf{d}_1^{kt} + w_2^{kt}\mathbf{d}_2^{kt} + \cdots + w_{N_t}^{kt}\mathbf{d}_{N_t}^{kt} \right) + \varsigma^k \\
&= \mathbf{D}^{kb}\mathbf{w}^{kb} + \mathbf{D}^{kt}\mathbf{w}^{kt} + \varsigma^k \\
&= \mathbf{D}^k\mathbf{w}^k + \varsigma^k
\end{aligned}
\tag{1}
$$

where ς^k is the random noise. $\mathbf{D}^{kb}$ and $\mathbf{D}^{kt}$ are the $B^k \times N_b$ background sub-dictionary and $B^k \times N_t$ target sub-dictionary, respectively. $\mathbf{w}^k \in R^{N_b+N_t}$ is a concatenation of $\mathbf{w}^{kb}$ and $\mathbf{w}^{kt}$, which are the coefficient sub-vectors over the k-th sub-dictionary $\mathbf{D}^{kb}$ and $\mathbf{D}^{kt}$.

Since the K groups of partial test pixels are highly related to each other, the sparse representation for a single-task case can be generalized to a multiple-task case. Thus, for the multiple detection tasks, the original pixel $\mathbf{x} \in R^B$ decomposed into K sub-vectors can be represented as

$$
\begin{aligned}
\mathbf{x}^1 &= \mathbf{D}^{1b}\mathbf{w}^{1b} + \mathbf{D}^{1t}\mathbf{w}^{1t} + \varsigma^1 = \mathbf{D}^1\mathbf{w}^1 + \varsigma^1 \\
&\vdots \qquad\qquad\qquad \vdots \\
\mathbf{x}^K &= \mathbf{D}^{Kb}\mathbf{w}^{Kb} + \mathbf{D}^{Kt}\mathbf{w}^{Kt} + \varsigma^K = \mathbf{D}^K\mathbf{w}^K + \varsigma^K
\end{aligned}
\tag{2}
$$

These can be incorporated into the joint sparse representation and multi-task learning model

$$
\widehat{\mathbf{W}} = \arg\min_{\mathbf{w}^k} \sum_{k=1}^{K} ||\mathbf{x}^k - \mathbf{D}^k\mathbf{w}^k||_2^2 + \rho||\mathbf{W}||_{2,1}
\tag{3}
$$

where $\mathbf{W} \in R^{(N_b+N_t) \times K}$ is the coefficient matrix formed by stacking the vectors $\mathbf{w}^k \in R^{N_b+N_t}$. ρ is the regularization parameter to trade off the data fidelity term and the regularization term, which penalizes the $\ell_{2,1}$-norm of the coefficient matrix $\mathbf{W}$. The $\ell_{2,1}$-norm of $\mathbf{W}$ is obtained by first computing the ℓ_2-norm of the rows $\{\mathbf{w}_i\}_{i=1}^{N_b+N_t}$ (across the tasks) of the matrix $\mathbf{W}$, and then computing the ℓ_1-norm of the vector $b(\mathbf{W}) = (||\mathbf{w}_1||_2, \cdots, ||\mathbf{w}_{N_b+N_t}||_2)^T$. This norm encourages the sparsity of each column of the matrix $\mathbf{W}$, and simultaneously encourages shared sparsity among the columns of the matrix $\mathbf{W}$.

3. Adaptive JSR-MTL with Locality Information Detector

3.1. Adaptive JSR-MTL Model

Some sparse representation classifiers employ the sparsity within a class for the classification, and show that a few background samples are adequate to reconstruct a test background sample in HSI [18]. Thus, If $\mathbf{x}$ is a background pixel, for the k-th sub-HSI, the partial test pixel $\left\{ \mathbf{x}^k \right\}_{k=1}^{K} \in R^{B^k}$ can be approximately represented as a linear combination of the background training samples $\{\mathbf{d}_i^{kb}\}_{i=1}^{N_b} \in R^{B^k}$ as follows:

$$
\begin{aligned}
\mathbf{x}^k &= \left(w_1^{kb}\mathbf{d}_1^{kb} + w_2^{kb}\mathbf{d}_2^{kb} + \cdots + w_{N_b}^{kb}\mathbf{d}_{N_b}^{kb} \right) + \varsigma^{kb} \\
&= \mathbf{D}^{kb}\mathbf{w}^{kb} + \varsigma^{kb}
\end{aligned}
\tag{6}
$$

where ς^{kb} is the random noise. $\mathbf{D}^{kb}$ is the $B^k \times N_b$ background sub-dictionary. $\mathbf{w}^{kb} \in R^{N_b}$ is the coefficient sub-vector over the sub-dictionary $\mathbf{D}^{kb}$.

For the multiple detection tasks, the original background pixel $\mathbf{x} \in R^B$ decomposed into K sub-vectors can be represented as

$$\mathbf{x}^1 = \mathbf{D}^{1b}\mathbf{w}^{1b} + \varsigma^{1b}$$
$$\vdots \qquad \qquad \vdots \tag{7}$$
$$\mathbf{x}^K = \mathbf{D}^{Kb}\mathbf{w}^{Kb} + \varsigma^{Kb}$$

These models can be incorporated into the following joint sparse representation and multi-task learning model

$$\widehat{\mathbf{W}}^b = \arg\min_{\mathbf{w}^{kb}} \sum_{k=1}^{K} ||\mathbf{x}^k - \mathbf{D}^{kb}\mathbf{w}^{kb}||_2^2 + \rho^b \Omega(\mathbf{W}^b) \tag{8}$$

where $\mathbf{W}^b \in R^{N_b \times K}$ is the matrix formed by stacking the vectors $\mathbf{w}^{kb} \in R^{N_b}$. $\Omega(\mathbf{W}^b)$ is the regularization term to further encode the task relatedness. ρ^b is the regularization parameter to trade off the data fidelity term and the regularization term.

Similarly, a target pixel $\mathbf{x} \in R^B$ decomposed into K sub-vectors can be represented as

$$\mathbf{x}^1 = \mathbf{D}^{1t}\mathbf{w}^{1t} + \varsigma^{1t}$$
$$\vdots \qquad \qquad \vdots \tag{9}$$
$$\mathbf{x}^K = \mathbf{D}^{Kt}\mathbf{w}^{Kt} + \varsigma^{Kt}$$

where ς^{kt} is the random noise. $\mathbf{D}^{kt}$ is the $B^k \times N_t$ target sub-dictionary. $\mathbf{w}^{kt} \in R^{N_t}$ is the coefficient sub-vector over the k-th sub-dictionary $\mathbf{D}^{kt}$.

These models can also be incorporated into the following joint sparse representation and multi-task learning model

$$\widehat{\mathbf{W}}^t = \arg\min_{\mathbf{w}^{kt}} \sum_{k=1}^{K} ||\mathbf{x}^k - \mathbf{D}^{kt}\mathbf{w}^{kt}||_2^2 + \rho^t \Omega(\mathbf{W}^t) \tag{10}$$

where $\mathbf{W}^t \in R^{N_t \times K}$ is the matrix formed by stacking the vectors $\mathbf{w}^{kt} \in R^{N_t}$.

In the detection problems, we are given a set of training samples with corresponding labels. The above two JSR-MTL models in Equations (8) and (10) make the assumption that a test sample should be represented by atoms from the same classes that the test sample belongs to, which means that the test sample is modeled separately for target and background pixel. Therefore, the above two JSR-MTL models in Equations (8) and (10) are more complete and realistic than the basic JSR-MTL model in [29]. In the above two JSR-MTL models in Equations (8) and (10), the test samples are modeled separately with more reasonable dictionaries, with only the background training samples for the null hypothesis, and the target training samples for the alternative hypothesis. In the case of the basic JSR-MTL model in [29], either the target test samples or the background test samples are represented by both the background and target training samples. In other words, the basic JSR-MTL model in [29] does not fully incorporate the class label (prior) information of the data set; it only utilizes the class label (background and target) information in post-processing when calculating the residuals for each class and ignores it when constructing models and calculating sub-vectors.

What is more, as noted, the regularization terms $\Omega(\mathbf{W})$ in Equations (8) and (10) are employed to further encode the task relatedness for the background pixel and target pixel, respectively. It can be seen that different assumptions on the task relatedness lead to different regularization terms. Whether the same regularization terms should be used for both the target and background pixel is an interesting problem, which needs further discussion. As we know, in the basic JSR-MTL model [29], multiple partial test pixels $\mathbf{x}^k$ in each sub-HSI are sparsely represented via the union target and background dictionary $\mathbf{D}^k = [\mathbf{D}^{kt}, \mathbf{D}^{kb}]$, and the $\ell_{2,1}$-norm of $\mathbf{W}$ encourages shared sparsity among the columns of the matrix $\mathbf{W}$ which is formed by stacking the vectors $\mathbf{w}^k \in R^{N_b + N_t}$. This will lead to the same sparsity constraint among the columns of the matrix $\mathbf{W}^b$ and $\mathbf{W}^t$ corresponding to the target dictionary and background dictionary. This is inappropriate when considering the construction of target and background dictionary. In target detection applications, the number of target pixels is usually small. The target dictionary is therefore constructed from some of the target pixels in the global image scene [17,18]. The background dictionary is generated locally for each test pixel through a dual concentric window which separates the local area around each pixel into two regions, a small inner window region (IWR) centered within a larger outer window region (OWR), which can better represent and capture the spectral signature of the test sample [17,18]. The background dictionary consists of many locally neighboring background training samples whose spectra are likely to be similar to each other. Thus, for the background pixel, multiple columns of the coefficient matrix $\mathbf{W}^b$ corresponding to multiple background sub-dictionaries are likely to share consistent sparsity among different tasks. However, the case for the target pixel is much different from the background pixel. The size of the target dictionary is smaller than the background dictionary, and the target training samples selected from the whole image are likely to show spectral variability [11]. Therefore it is inappropriate to assume consistent sparsity among multiple columns of the coefficient matrix $\mathbf{W}^t$ corresponding to multiple target sub-dictionaries. In brief, different regularization terms should be used for the target pixel and background pixel.

For the background pixel in (8), the $\ell_{2,1}$-norm can be enforced to the matrix $\mathbf{W}^b$ as is done in [29]. For the target pixel in Equation (10), the ℓ_1-norm is applied for the matrix $\mathbf{W}^t$, which is obtained by the sum of absolute values in the matrix. The difference between ℓ_1-norm and $\ell_{2,1}$-norm of the matrix $\mathbf{W}$ is that, ℓ_1-norm imposes element wise sparsity and does not require consistent feature selection among columns (tasks), while $\ell_{2,1}$-norm by grouping rows together can achieve consistent sparsity among different columns (tasks).

Therefore, Equations (8) and (10) can be rewritten as the following adaptive JSR-MTL model, which can be labeled as the JSRMTL-A model:

$$\widehat{\mathbf{W}}^b = \arg\min_{\mathbf{w}^{kb}} \sum_{k=1}^{K} ||\mathbf{x}^k - \mathbf{D}^{kb}\mathbf{w}^{kb}||_2^2 + \rho^b ||\mathbf{W}^b||_{2,1} \tag{11}$$

$$\widehat{\mathbf{W}}^t = \arg\min_{\mathbf{w}^{kt}} \sum_{k=1}^{K} ||\mathbf{x}^k - \mathbf{D}^{kt}\mathbf{w}^{kt}||_2^2 + \rho^t ||\mathbf{W}^t||_1 \tag{12}$$

3.2. Locality Information Descriptor-Based Weight

The background dictionary is further discussed in this section. It can be seen from Equation (11) that, all the training samples (atoms) in the background dictionary are treated equally for signal representation, which ignores locality information, such as differences between the neighboring pixels and the central test pixel. However, some surrounding pixels may be quite similar to the center pixel and are likely to be selected for signal representation; some are quite different from the center pixel, such as the pixel which has a different kind of material from the central pixel, which should be limited or even prohibited for signal representation. The differences between the test pixel and the target atoms are not discussed here due to the small size of the target atoms and the global target atoms selection method.

To preserve the locality difference between the central test pixel and the neighboring background atoms, a distance based locality information descriptor is introduced, which can be expressed as

$$\alpha_i^k = \exp\left(\frac{||\mathbf{x}^k - \mathbf{d}_i^{kb}||_2^2}{2}\right) \tag{13}$$

where α_i^k is the sample-specific descriptor for training sample $i(i = 1, 2, \cdots, N_b)$ in the k-th background sub-dictionary $\mathbf{D}^{kb}$. It is clear that a smaller α_i^k indicates $\mathbf{x}^k$ is more similar to the atom $\mathbf{d}_i^{kb}$, and vice versa.

Once the above descriptor is included, all the atoms in the background dictionary will be adaptively treated for signal representation via the $\ell_{2,1}$-norm. However, there may still exist estimation bias for the signal representation. As stated in [30,31] the estimation bias can be large due to the fact that the ℓ_1/ℓ_2 minimization is generally inconsistent in variable selection. Many efforts have been made to reduce the estimation bias, such as adaptive Lasso method [30] and the reweighted ℓ_1

minimization [31]. Inspired by the reweighted ℓ_1 minimization, a weight strategy on the $\ell_{2,1}$-based regularization term is introduced to reduce the estimation bias as follows.

$$\widehat{\mathbf{W}}^b = \arg\min_{\mathbf{w}^{kb}} \sum_{k=1}^{K} ||\mathbf{x}^k - \mathbf{D}^{kb}\mathbf{w}^{kb}||_2^2 + \rho^b||\mathbf{\Psi} \odot \mathbf{W}^b||_{2,1} \tag{14}$$

where $\mathbf{\Psi} = \left\{ \Psi_i^k \right\}$ is the weighting matrix, and Ψ_i^k is the weight for atom $i(i = 1, 2, \cdots, N_b)$ and column (task) $k(k = 1, 2, \cdots, K)$, $\odot$ denotes modifying the element in the coefficients matrix $\mathbf{W}^b$ by iteratively multiplying a weight during the coefficient optimization.

In order to impose a relatively higher penalty for smaller coefficients and a lower penalty for larger coefficients, the weight can be computed as inversely proportional to the sparse coefficient

$$\varphi_i^k = \frac{1}{|w_i^{kb}|} \tag{15}$$

Combining the above locality information descriptor and weight strategy, we obtain the locality information descriptor-based weight defined as

$$\Psi_i^k = \frac{\varphi_i^k \alpha_i^k}{\max\limits_{i,k} \varphi_i^k \alpha_i^k} \tag{16}$$

3.3. Model Optimization

For the model optimization, we use the popular accelerated proximal gradient (APG) algorithm [33,34] to efficiently solve the problem in Equations (12) and (14). The APG algorithm alternately updates a matrix sequence $\widehat{\mathbf{W}}^t = \left[w_i^{k,t} \right]$ and an aggregation matrix sequence $\widehat{\mathbf{V}}^t = \left[v_i^{k,t} \right]$.

Given the current matrix aggregation matrix $\widehat{\mathbf{V}}^t$, a generalized gradient mapping step is employed to update matrix $\widehat{\mathbf{W}}^{t+1}$ as follows

$$\begin{aligned} \widehat{\mathbf{w}}^{k,t+1} &= \widehat{\mathbf{v}}^{k,t} - \eta^t \nabla k,t, \quad t \geq 1, \\ \widehat{\mathbf{W}}^{t+1} &= f(\widehat{\mathbf{W}}^{t+1}), k = 1, 2, \cdots K \end{aligned} \tag{17}$$

where $\nabla^{k,t} = -(\mathbf{D}^k)^T \mathbf{x}^k + (\mathbf{D}^k)^T \mathbf{D}^k \widehat{\mathbf{v}}^{k,t}$, $\eta^t = 1/2^t$ is the step size. $f(\cdot)$ is a function of $\widehat{\mathbf{W}}^{t+1} = \left[\widehat{w}_i^{k,t+1} \right]$, which has a different format for (12) and (14).

For (12), the matrix $\widehat{\mathbf{W}}^{t+1}$ can be updated as follows

$$\widehat{\mathbf{W}}^{t+1} = \begin{cases} P_{\Omega_1}(\widehat{\mathbf{W}}^{t+1} - \frac{\rho}{2^t}), & \Omega_1 : (\widehat{\mathbf{W}}^{t+1})_{i,k\in\Omega_1} > \frac{\rho}{2^t} \\ P_{\Omega_2}(\widehat{\mathbf{W}}^{t+1} + \frac{\rho}{2^t}), & \Omega_2 : (\widehat{\mathbf{W}}^{t+1})_{i,k\in\Omega_2} < -\frac{\rho}{2^t} \\ P_{\Omega_3}(0 \in R^{N_t \times K}), & \Omega_3 : (\Omega_1 \cup \Omega_2)^\perp, \quad i = 1, 2, \cdots, N_b \end{cases} \tag{18}$$

where P_Ω is the projection of a matrix onto an entry set, and Ω is the index of the entry set.

For (14), the matrix $\widehat{\mathbf{W}}^{t+1}$ can be updated as follows

$$\begin{aligned} \widehat{\mathbf{w}}_i^{t+1} &= \left[1 - \frac{\rho}{2^t ||\widehat{\mathbf{w}}_i^{t+1}||_2} \right]_+ \widehat{\mathbf{w}}_i^{t+1}, \quad i = 1, 2, \cdots, N_b \\ \widehat{w}_i^{k,t+1} &= \widehat{w}_i^{k,t+1} \times \frac{\alpha_i^k / |\widehat{w}_i^{k,t+1}|}{\max\limits_{i=1,2,\cdots N_b, k=1,2,\cdots K} \alpha_i^k / |\widehat{w}_i^{k,t+1}|} \end{aligned} \tag{19}$$

where $[\cdot]_+ = \max(\cdot, 0)$.

An aggregation forward step is then employed to update $\widehat{\mathbf{V}}^{t+1}$ by linearly combining $\widehat{\mathbf{W}}^{t+1}$ and $\widehat{\mathbf{W}}^{t}$ as follows

$$\widehat{\mathbf{V}}^{t+1} = (1 + \tau^t)\widehat{\mathbf{W}}^{t+1} - \tau^t \widehat{\mathbf{W}}^{t} \tag{20}$$

where the sequence τ^t is conventionally set to $\tau^t = 2(t-1)/(1 + \sqrt{1 + 4t^2})$, as applied in our implementation.

The optimization methods for the problem in Equations (12) and (14) can be summarized as Algorithms 1 and 2, respectively.

Algorithm 1. The Coefficients over Target Dictionary Optimization Algorithm.

Input: Data $\left\{ \mathbf{D}^k, \mathbf{x}^k \right\}_{k=1}^{K}$, regularization parameter ρ

Output: Coefficient vectors $\left\{ \widehat{\mathbf{w}}^k \right\}_{k=1}^{K}$

Step (1): Initialization: $\widehat{\mathbf{w}}^{k,0} = (\mathbf{D}^k)^T \mathbf{x}^k$, $\widehat{\mathbf{v}}^{k,0} = \widehat{\mathbf{w}}^{k,0}$, $\tau^0 = -1, t := 0$

Step (2): Repeat {Main loop}

  a) $\widehat{\mathbf{w}}^{k,t+1} = \widehat{\mathbf{v}}^{k,t} - \frac{1}{2^t}\left[-(\mathbf{D}^k)^T \mathbf{x}^k + (\mathbf{D}^k)^T \mathbf{D}^k \widehat{\mathbf{v}}^{k,t} \right], \quad k = 1, \cdots K$

  b) $\widehat{w}_i^{k,t+1} = \begin{cases} \widehat{w}_i^{k,t+1} - \rho/2^t, & \Omega_1 \\ \widehat{w}_i^{k,t+1} + \rho/2^t, & \Omega_2 \\ 0, & \Omega_3 \end{cases}$

  c) $\tau^t = \frac{2(t-1)}{1+\sqrt{1+4t^2}}$, $\widehat{\mathbf{v}}^{k,t+1} = (1+\tau^t)\widehat{\mathbf{w}}^{k,t+1} - \tau^t \widehat{\mathbf{w}}^{k,t}$

  d) $t := t + 1$

Until: convergence is attained

Algorithm 2. The Coefficients over Background Dictionary Optimization Algorithm.

Input: Data $\left\{ \mathbf{D}^k, \mathbf{x}^k \right\}_{k=1}^{K}$, regularization parameter ρ, locality information descriptor $\left\{ \alpha_i^k \right\}$

Output: Coefficient vectors $\left\{ \widehat{\mathbf{w}}^k \right\}_{k=1}^{K}$

Step (1): Initialization: $\widehat{\mathbf{w}}^{k,0} = (\mathbf{D}^k)^T \mathbf{x}^k$, $\widehat{\mathbf{v}}^{k,0} = \widehat{\mathbf{w}}^{k,0}$, $\tau^0 = -1, t := 0$

Step (2): Repeat {Main loop}

  a) $\widehat{\mathbf{w}}^{k,t+1} = \widehat{\mathbf{v}}^{k,t} - \frac{1}{2^t}\left[-(\mathbf{D}^k)^T \mathbf{x}^k + (\mathbf{D}^k)^T \mathbf{D}^k \widehat{\mathbf{v}}^{k,t} \right], \quad k = 1, \cdots K$

  b) $\widehat{\mathbf{w}}_i^{t+1} = \left[1 - \frac{\rho}{2^t \|\widehat{\mathbf{w}}_i^{t+1}\|_2} \right]_+ \widehat{\mathbf{w}}_i^{t+1}, \quad i = 1, 2, \cdots, N_b$

  $\widehat{w}_i^{k,t+1} = \widehat{w}_i^{k,t+1} \times \dfrac{\alpha_i^k / |\widehat{w}_i^{k,t+1}|}{\max\limits_{i,k} \alpha_i^k / |\widehat{w}_i^{k,t+1}|}$

  c) $\tau^t = \frac{2(t-1)}{1+\sqrt{1+4t^2}}$, $\widehat{\mathbf{v}}^{k,t+1} = (1+\tau^t)\widehat{\mathbf{w}}^{k,t+1} - \tau^t \widehat{\mathbf{w}}^{k,t}$

  d) $t := t + 1$

Until: convergence is attained

3.4. Final Sketch of the JSRMTL-ALI Detector

Once given the recovery of the coefficient vectors $\widehat{\mathbf{w}}^{kb}$ and $\widehat{\mathbf{w}}^{kt}$ corresponding to the background dictionary $\mathbf{D}^{kb}$ and target dictionary $\mathbf{D}^{kt}$ for each task, we can then calculate the residual errors for the background and target between the multiple signals in the sub-HSIs $\left\{ \mathbf{x}^k \right\}_{k=1}^{K}$ and the approximations recovered via their corresponding sub-dictionaries $\left\{ \mathbf{D}^{kb} \right\}_{k=1}^{K}$ and $\left\{ \mathbf{D}^{kt} \right\}_{k=1}^{K}$ as follows.

$$r^b = \sum_{k=1}^{K} ||\mathbf{x}^k - \mathbf{D}^{kb}\widehat{\mathbf{w}}^{kb}||_2$$
$$r^t = \sum_{k=1}^{K} ||\mathbf{x}^k - \mathbf{D}^{kt}\widehat{\mathbf{w}}^{kt}||_2 \tag{21}$$

where $\widehat{\mathbf{w}}^{kb}$ and $\widehat{\mathbf{w}}^{kt}$ are the subsets of the coefficient vector $\widehat{\mathbf{w}}^{k}$ associated with the background and target. The output of the test pixel $\mathbf{x}$ is then calculated by

$$D(\mathbf{x}) = r^b - r^t \tag{22}$$

Finally, a visual illustration of the proposed LWAJSR-MTL algorithm for HSIs is shown in Figure 2. Given a hyperspectral image, multiple sub-HSIs are extracted via the band cross-grouping strategy. We construct the multiple-signals for each pixel $\left\{\mathbf{x}^k\right\}_{k=1}^{K}$, multiple background dictionary $\left\{\mathbf{D}^{kb}\right\}_{k=1}^{K}$ with the local dual window, and multiple target dictionary $\left\{\mathbf{D}^{kt}\right\}_{k=1}^{K}$ via the target training samples. Each pixel is represented by the multi-task sparse representation model via the target dictionary and background dictionary, respectively. The coefficient matrices corresponding to the target dictionary and dictionary are recovered via the Algorithms 1 and 2, respectively. Finally, the detection decision rules in favor of the target class or the background class with the lowest total reconstruction error difference accumulated over all the tasks.

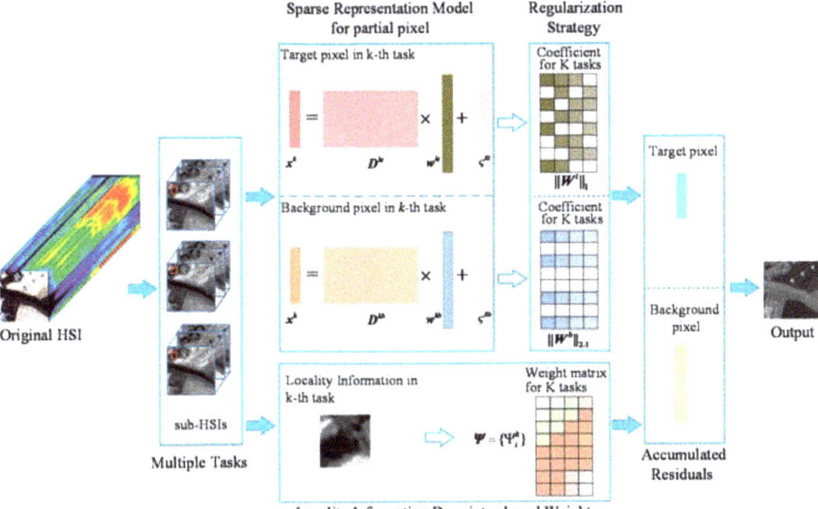

Figure 2. Schematic illustration of the adaptive joint sparse representation and multi-task learning detector with locality information (JSRMTL-ALI) algorithm.

4. Experiments and Analysis

4.1. Dataset Description

Three hyperspectral datasets were used in this study to evaluate the effectiveness of the proposed detector introduced in Section 3.

The first dataset was collected by the Airborne Visible/Infrared Imaging Spectrometer (AVIRIS) sensor from San Diego, CA, USA. The spatial resolution of this image is 3.5 m per pixel. The image has 224 spectral channels in wavelengths ranging from 370 to 2510 nm. After removing the bands that correspond to the water absorption regions, low-SNR, and bad bands (1–6, 33–35, 97, 107–113, 153–166, and 221–224), 189 bands were retained in the experiments. An area of 100×100 pixels was used for the experiments. The image scene is shown in Figure 3a. There are three planes in the image, which consist of 58 pixels, as shown in Figure 3b. We selected one pixel from each plane as the target atoms, $N_t = 3$.

The second dataset was gathered by the Airborne Visible/Infrared Imaging Spectrometer (AVIRIS) sensor over the Indian Pines test site in Northwest Indiana and consists of 145×145 pixels and 224 spectral reflectance bands in the wavelength range 0.4–2.5 µm. The false color image of the Indian Pines image is shown in Figure 4a. We also reduced the number of bands to 200 by removing bands covering the regions of water absorption: 104–108, 150–163, and 220, as referred to in [35]. This image contains 16 ground-truth classes via a ground truth labels, and the stone-steel-towers was selected as the target of interest to be detected, which has 93 pixels, as shown in Figure 4b. We selected three pixels from the target as the target atoms, $N_t = 3$.

The third data set was acquired by the Nuance Cri hyperspectral sensor. This sensor can acquire imagery with a spectral resolution of 10 nm. The image scene covers an area of 400×400 pixels, as shown in Figure 5a, with 46 spectral bands in wavelengths ranging from 650 to 1100 nm. There are ten rocks located in the grassy scene, which consist of 1254 pixels, as shown in Figure 5b. We selected one pixel from each rock as the target atoms, $N_t = 10$.

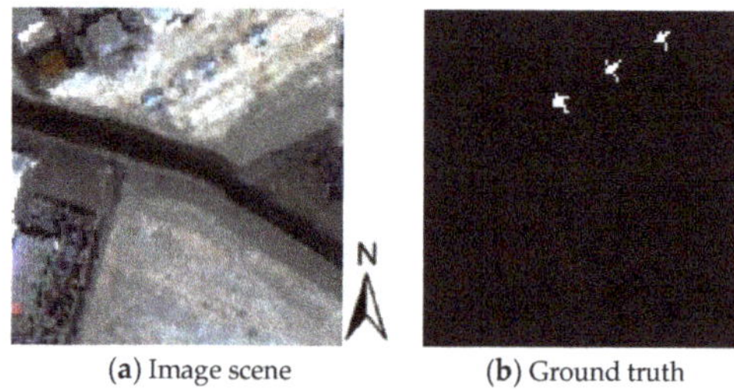

(a) Image scene   (b) Ground truth

Figure 3. The AVIRIS dataset.

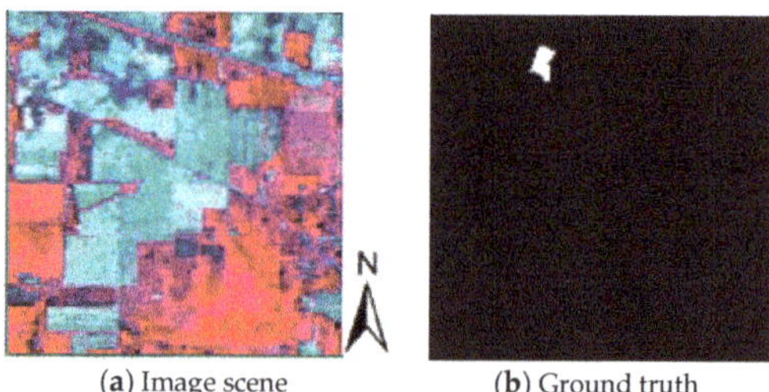

(a) Image scene   (b) Ground truth

Figure 4. The Indian dataset.

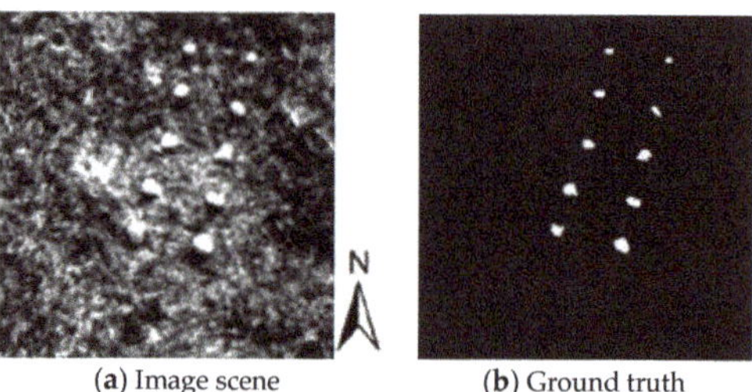

(a) Image scene   (b) Ground truth

Figure 5. The Cri dataset.

4.2. Evaluation of JSRMTL-ALI Model

Firstly, the effectiveness of the JSRMTL-ALI model was investigated and compared with the original JSR-MTL model in Equation (3) and the adaptive JSR-MTL (labeled as JSRMTL-A) model in Equations (11) and (12). We took three detection tasks ($K = 3$) as an example, and the JSR-MTL with $K = 1$ which indicates the detection performance without the multi-task learning technique. For simplicity, all regularization parameters used in the four models are set with the same value ($\rho = 0.1$). The sizes of the OWR for the three datasets were respectively set as 17×17, 23×23, and 23×23. The sizes of the IWR are related to the size of the target, and were set as 7×7, 15×15, and 15×15 for the AVIRIS, Indian, and Cri datasets, respectively. The numbers of the background training samples for the three datasets were therefore $N_b = 240$, $N_b = 304$, and $N_b = 304$, respectively. The detection performance for the four models with three datasets are provided by the area under the receiver operation characteristics (ROC) curves, as shown in Figure 6.

For the AVIRIS dataset, as shown Figure 6a, the ROC curve of JSRMTL-ALI is not above that of JSRMTL-A, however, it is above that of JSR-MTL with $K = 3$ and $K = 1$. For the Indian dataset, as shown in Figure 6b, the ROC curve of JSRMTL-ALI is always above those of the other models, and the ROC curve of JSRMTL-A is always above that of JSR-MTL with $K = 3$ and $K = 1$. For the Cri dataset, as shown Figure 6c, the ROC curve of JSRMTL-ALI is successively above that of JSRMTL-A, JSR-MTL with $K = 1$, and JSR-MTL with $K = 3$.

Overall, the results show that the performance of the JSR-MTL model is generally better than that without the multi-task learning technique, especially for the AVIRIS and Indian datasets. The JSRMTL-A model can also obtain a better detection performance compared to the JSR-MTL model for all three datasets, which shows the effectiveness of the adaptive JSR-MTL (JSRMTL-A) model. This result demonstrates that it is useful to explore the prior class label information of the training samples and the difference between the target dictionary and background dictionary for hyperspectral target detection. What is more, the JSRMTL-ALI model can further improve the detection performance of the JSRMTL-A model, especially for the Indian and Cri datasets. This result confirms that the locality information descriptor-based weight can improve the detection performance, which can remain as the locality information between the central test pixel and neighboring background training samples, and also reduce the estimation bias caused by the ℓ_1 / ℓ_2 minimization. In addition, we can further adjust the number of detection tasks, the regularization parameter, and the window size to obtain an even better performance.

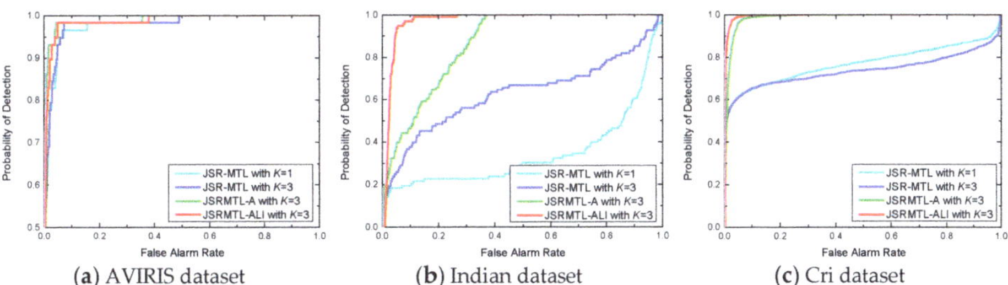

(a) AVIRIS dataset   (b) Indian dataset   (c) Cri dataset

Figure 6. Receiver operation characteristic (ROC) curves for the effectiveness investigation of JSRMTL-ALI model.

4.3. Parameter Analysis for the JSRMTL-ALI Algorithm

In this section, we examine the effect of the parameters on the detection performance of the JSRMTL-ALI algorithm with the three datasets. We fixed the other parameters and focused on one specific parameter at a time. There are three key parameters in the JSRMTL-ALI algorithm: the detection task number parameter K, the regularization parameter ρ, and the size of the dual window. As is done in [29], the range of K was set as [1, 2, 3, 4, 5, 6, 7, 8, 9] and the range of ρ was set as [1, 0.5, 10−1, 10−2, 10−3, 10−4, 10−5]. For the size of the dual window, the size of the IWR is related to the size of the target. When the size of the IWR is set too large, the background training samples in the OWR will not effectively represent the local background characteristic. Thus, the sizes of the IWR were fixed as above-mentioned 7×7, 15×15, and 15×15 for the AVIRIS, Indian, and Cri datasets, respectively. The range of the size of the OWR for AVIRIS dataset was set as [17, 19, 21, 23, 25], and it was set as [23, 25, 27, 29, 31] for the Indian and Cri datasets. The experimental results are provided through the AUC values, as shown in Figures 7–9. The X-axes and the Y-axes respectively represent the value range of the corresponding parameter and the AUC values.

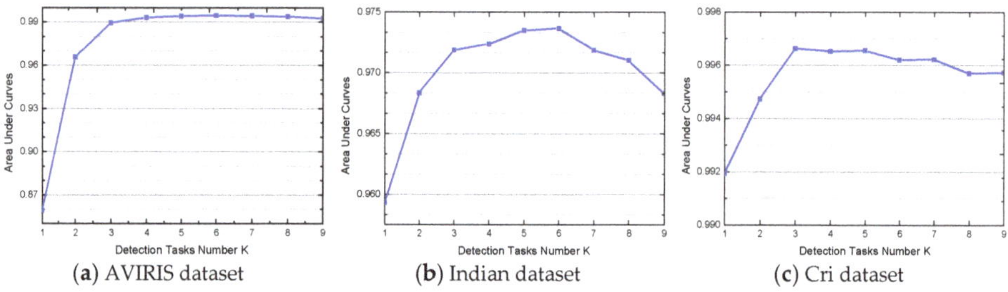

(**a**) AVIRIS dataset   (**b**) Indian dataset   (**c**) Cri dataset

Figure 7. Detection performance of JSRMTL-ALI versus the detection task number K.

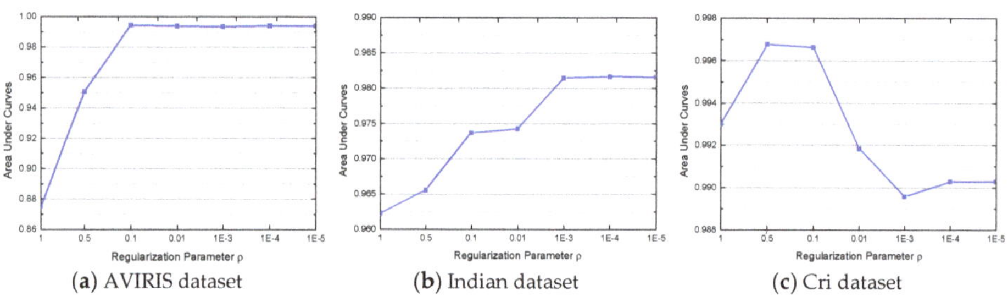

(**a**) AVIRIS dataset   (**b**) Indian dataset   (**c**) Cri dataset

Figure 8. Detection performance of JSRMTL-ALI versus the detection task number ρ.

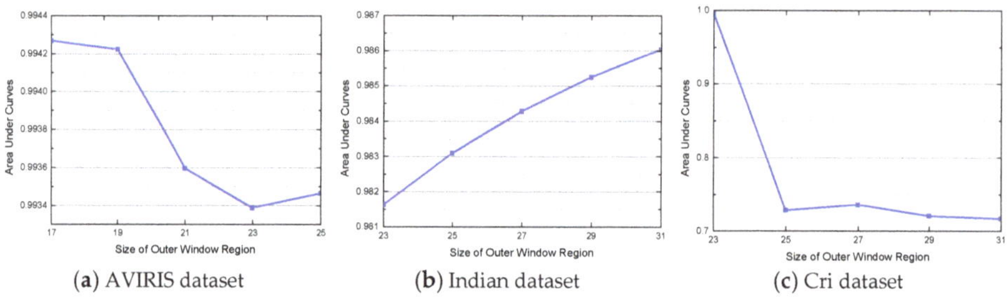

(**a**) AVIRIS dataset   (**b**) Indian dataset   (**c**) Cri dataset

Figure 9. Detection performance of JSRMTL-ALI versus the size of the outer window region (OWR).

For the AVIRIS dataset in Figure 7a, the AUC value of the JSRMTL-ALI algorithm improves as the detection task number parameter K increases to 6. After that, the detection performance slowly decreases as K increases to 9. For the Indian dataset in Figure 7b, the AUC value generally improves as K increases to 6 and then decreases as K increases to 9. For the Cri dataset in Figure 7c, the AUC value improves as K increases to 3, gently decreases as K increases to 9. Based on these results, it can be generally concluded that the performance of the JSRMTL-ALI algorithm improves as the detection task number parameter K increases and then begins to decrease after the maximum value. The reason for this may be as follows. As discussed in [29], a large detection task number K results in too many detection tasks which leads to too many unknown coefficients; however, the rows of the dictionary for the multiple representation models will be significantly decreased. This can lead to a weakened estimation for the unknown coefficient matrix, which will affect the detection performance. Besides, the advantage of the multi-task learning technique for hyperspectral image lies in the fact that it can explore the relatedness within the corresponding single-band images in the same position in each sub-HIS. However, a large detection task number is highly likely to reduce the relatedness within multiple sub-HSIs, and the effectiveness of MTL will decrease in return.

For the AVIRIS dataset in Figure 8a, the AUC value of the JSRMTL-ALI algorithm improves when the regularization parameter ρ decreases from 1 to 10^{-1}, and the AUC values gradually decrease as ρ decreases from 10^{-2} to 10^{-5}. For the Indian dataset in Figure 8b, the AUC value improves as ρ decreases from 1 to 10^{-4}, and decreases as ρ decreases to 10^{-5}. For the Cri dataset in Figure 8c, the AUC value improves as ρ decreases from 1 to 0.5, and generally decreases as ρ decreases to 10^{-5}. Based on these results, it can be generally concluded that a too small or too large regularization parameter ρ can decrease the detection performance of JSRMTL-ALI. The reasons may be listed as follows. A too small regularization parameter makes the dominant part of Equations (11) and (14) become the first term $||\mathbf{x}^k - \mathbf{D}^k\mathbf{w}^k||_2^2$, which will weaken the effect of the multiple detection task combination, and will affect the final detection performance of JSRMTL-ALI. A too large regularization parameter makes the dominant part of Equations (11) and (14) become the second term, which will weaken the effect of the data representation, and again affect the final detection performance of JSRMTL-ALI.

For the AVIRIS dataset in Figure 9a, the AUC value of the JSRMTL-ALI algorithm decreases as the size of the OWR increases to 23, and then slightly increases as the size of the OWR increases to 25. For the Indian dataset in Figure 9b, the AUC value improves as the size of the OWR increases to 31. For the Cri dataset in Figure 9c, the AUC value of the JSRMTL-ALI algorithm generally decreases as the size of the OWR increases to 31. Based on these results, it can be seen that the detection performance decreases as the size of Outer Window Region (OWR) increases for the AVIRIS dataset and Cri dataset, while the case is totally different for the Indian dataset. Although the regular patter of the size of the OWR for all datasets is not obvious; it can still generally be concluded that a too large or too small size of OWR can affect the detection performance of JSRMTL-ALI. The reason for this may be as follows. For a too large size of OWR, the background training samples in the OWR will not effectively represent the local background characteristic, which may include some other background materials. For a too small size of OWR, the background training samples in the OWR are not sufficient to represent the local background characteristic. Both cases will lead to a weakened detection performance. Therefore, it is not easy to select a proper value for the size of OWR in a practical application.

4.4. Detection Performance

In this section, the detection performance of the proposed JSRMTL-ALI algorithm was further analyzed and compared with traditional detectors of local adaptive coherence/cosine estimator (LACE), local constrained energy minimization (LCEM), reweighted adaptive coherence/cosine estimator (rACE) [10], hierarchical constrained energy minimization (hCEM) [14], STD [17], RBBHD [18], and JSR-MTL [29]. The parameters of the JSRMTL-ALI algorithm were set as the optimal parameter values for the three datasets. The detection task number parameter K was respectively set as 6, 6, and 3 for the three datasets. The regularization parameter ρ was respectively set as 10^{-1}, 10^{-4}, 0.5 for the three datasets. The size of the OWR was set as 17, 31, and 23 for the three datasets. For the comparison methods, the parameters were also tested, such as the sparsity level for the sparsity-based detectors (STD, SRBBHD), and so on. The optimal parameter values were experimentally set for the comparison methods. For all the detectors, we used the same given target spectra as a priori target spectra. In the case of hCEM and LCEM, the mean of the target atoms was used as the target signature. We adopted the pixels falling in the OWR to estimate the background covariance matrix for LACE, to estimate the background correlation matrix for LCEM, and to construct the background dictionary for STD, SRBBHD, JSR-MTL, and JSRMTL-ALI. The detection performance of the eight detectors are provided through the receiver operation characteristics (ROC) curves, as shown in Figure 10.

For the AVIRIS dataset, as shown in Figure 10a, the ROC curve of JSRMTL-ALI is above that of the other detectors, except for rACE. For the Indian dataset, as shown in Figure 10b, the ROC curve of JSRMTL-ALI is always above those of the other detectors. For the Cri dataset, as shown in Figure 10c, rACE and hCEM obtain the best result, and the ROC curve of JSRMTL-ALI is above those of the rest of the detectors.

Overall, the results generally show that the JSRMTL-ALI algorithm obtains a better detection performance than the other detectors, especially for the Indian dataset. For the AVIRIS and Cri dataset, JSRMTL-ALI does not perform as well as rACE or hCEM. However, the detection performances of rACE and hCEM are much different for the three datasets and a robust detection performance is not shown. For example, rACE obtains a good performance for AVIRIS and Cri datasets, while obtains a weak performance for the Indian dataset. hCEM obtains a good performance for Indian and Cri datasets, while obtaining a weak performance for the AVIRIS dataset.

The separability between target and background was evaluated via separability maps, as shown in Figure 11. After statistical calculation of the detection values of each pixel, boxes were drawn to enclose the main parts of the pixels, excluding the biggest 10% and the smallest 10%. There are target and background columns for each detector. The lines at the top and bottom of each column are the extreme values, which are normalized to [1]. The orange boxes illustrate the distribution of the target pixel values, and the line in the middle of the box is the mean of the pixels. In a similar way, the green boxes enclose the middle 80% of the pixels of the background pixels. The position of the boxes reflects the tendency and compactness of the distribution of the pixels. In other words, the position reflects the separability between target and background.

For the AVIRIS dataset, as shown in Figure 11a, STD and rACE can effectively suppress the background information; and LACE, LCEM, STD, SRBBHD, rACE and hCEM can effectively suppress the middle 80% of the background pixels. Compared to these detectors, the gaps between the target box and the background box for rACE, JSR-MTL, and JSRMTL-ALI are very obvious, and the gap for JSRMTL-ALI is larger than JSR-MTL. The target box and the background box for rACE, JSR-MTL, and JSRMTL-ALI are overlapping, but the overlapped region for JSR-MTL is slightly less. For the Indian dataset, as shown in Figure 11b, rACE can specially, effectively suppress the middle 80% of the background pixels. Compared to these detectors, the gap between the two boxes for JSRMTL-ALI is very obvious, and the two boxes for the other detectors are overlapping. For the Cri dataset, as shown in Figure 11c, JSRMTL-ALI, hCEM, and rACE can gradually and successively increase the gap between the target box and the background box. Based on these results, it can be seen that, the proposed JSRMTL-ALI algorithm can perform well at the distinguishing target from the background.

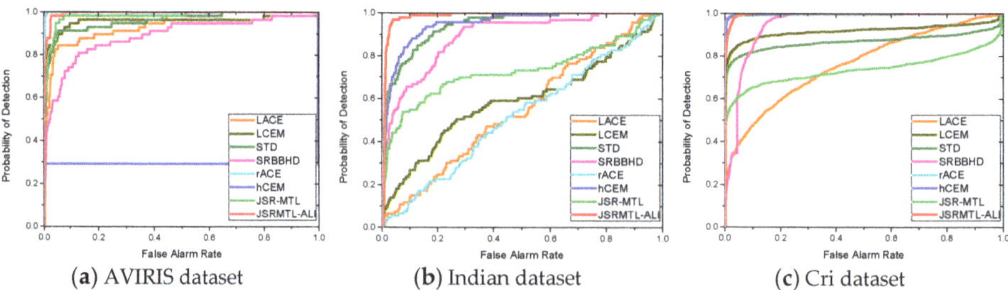

(**a**) AVIRIS dataset (**b**) Indian dataset (**c**) Cri dataset

Figure 10. Detection performance of eight detectors for three datasets.

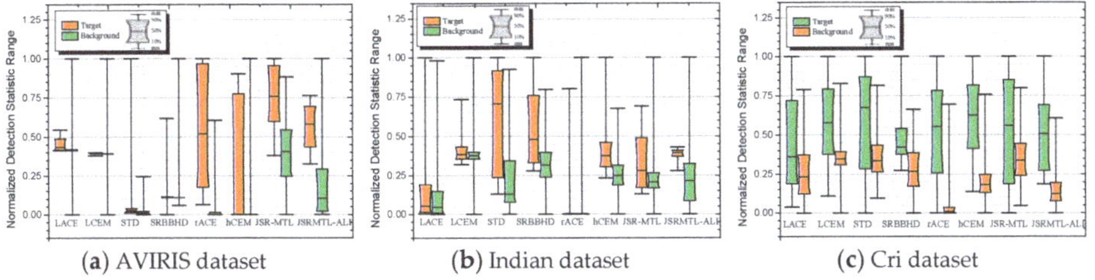

(a) AVIRIS dataset   (b) Indian dataset   (c) Cri dataset

Figure 11. The separability maps of eight detectors for three datasets.

Finally, 2-D plots of the detection map of all the comparison algorithms with the three data sets are shown in Figures 12–14. For the AVIRIS dataset, as shown in Figure 12, we can see that the proposed JSRMLT-ALI shows high statistical values for the target pixels as well as STD, rACE, and JSR-MTL. However, compared with JSRMLT-ALI, STD and JSR-MTL also show high values for some tree or grass pixels, particularly in the bottom/right left corner in the image. Also rACE shows a good performance for suppressing background. For the Indian dataset, as shown in Figure 13, none of these detectors show a clearly distinguishable statistic map, but JSRMLT-ALI generally shows relatively higher statistical values for the target pixels compared with all the other detectors. For the Cri dataset, as shown in Figure 14, the proposed JSRMLT-ALI shows low statistical values for the background pixels as well as rACE and hCEM. However, compared with rACE, JSRMTL-ALI does not show a clearly distinguishable statistic map between target and background.

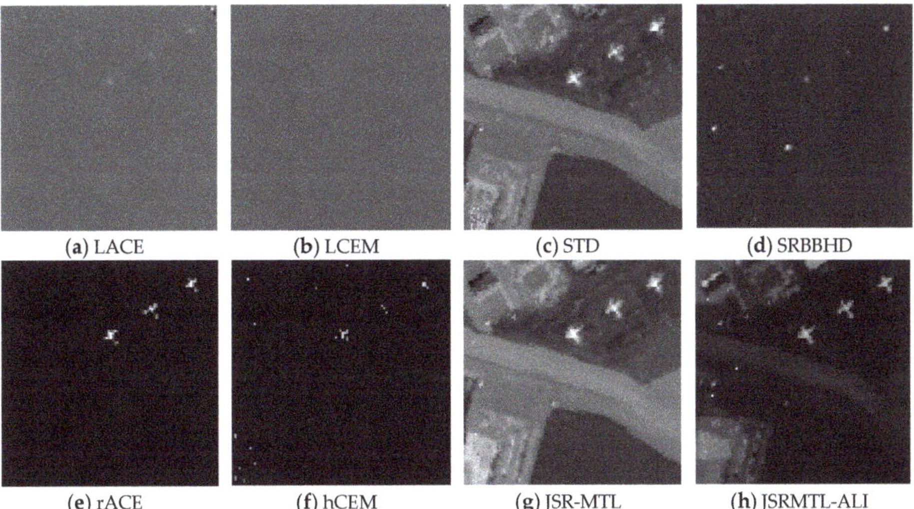

(a) LACE   (b) LCEM   (c) STD   (d) SRBBHD

(e) rACE   (f) hCEM   (g) JSR-MTL   (h) JSRMTL-ALI

Figure 12. Two-dimensional plots of the detection map for the AVIRIS dataset.

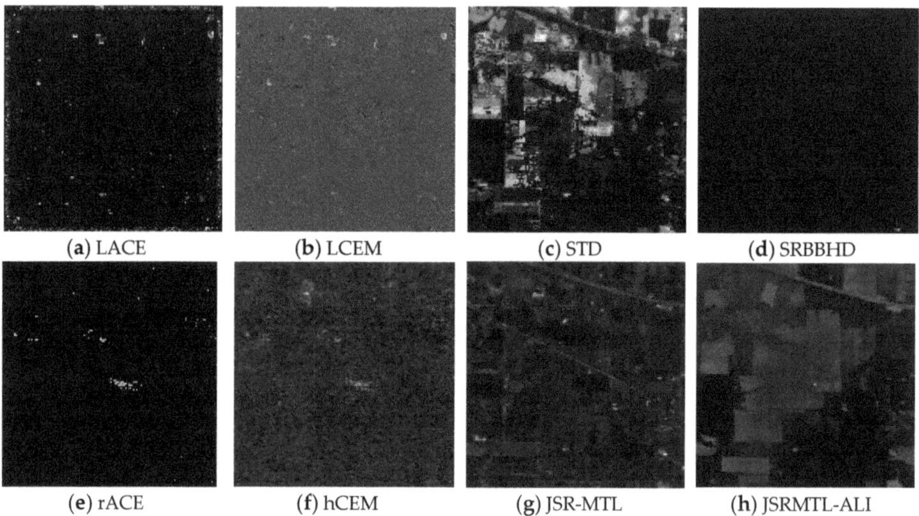

(**a**) LACE   (**b**) LCEM   (**c**) STD   (**d**) SRBBHD

(**e**) rACE   (**f**) hCEM   (**g**) JSR-MTL   (**h**) JSRMTL-ALI

Figure 13. Two-dimensional plots of the detection map for the Indian dataset.

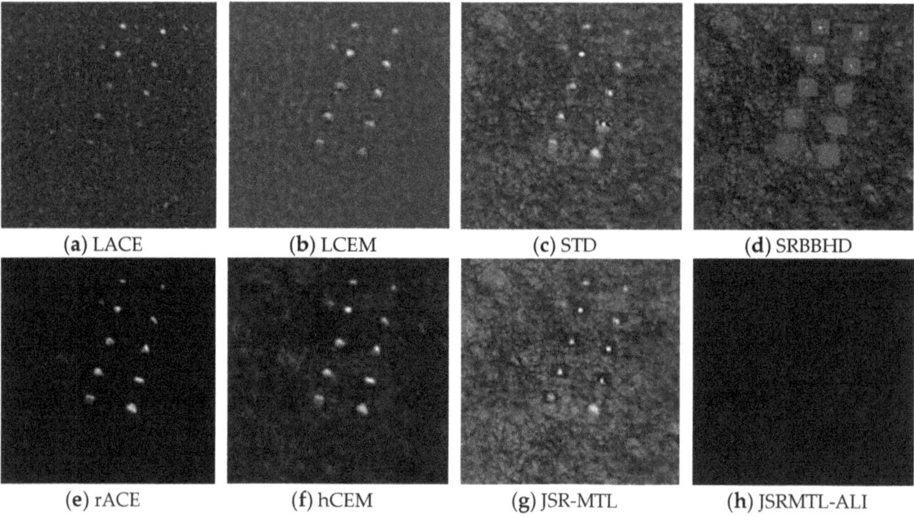

(**a**) LACE   (**b**) LCEM   (**c**) STD   (**d**) SRBBHD

(**e**) rACE   (**f**) hCEM   (**g**) JSR-MTL   (**h**) JSRMTL-ALI

Figure 14. Two-dimensional plots of the detection map for the Cri dataset.

5. Discussion

An adaptive joint sparse representation and multi-task learning detector with locality information (JSRMTL-ALI) is proposed in this paper. In order to fully explore the prior class label information of the training samples, JSRMTL-ALI constructs two joint sparse representation and multi-task learning models corresponding to the target and background classes. In order to consider the difference between the target dictionary and background dictionary, JSRMTL-ALI then employs different regularization strategies encoding the task relatedness for the two models, where the $\ell_{2,1}$-norm is enforced to the coefficient matrix $\mathbf{W}^b$ corresponding to the background dictionary, while the ℓ_1-norm is applied for the coefficient matrix $\mathbf{W}^t$ corresponding to the target dictionary. These two contributions lead to the so-called JSRMTL-A model. What is more, in order to keep the locality information between the central test pixel and neighboring background training samples, JSRMTL-ALI employs the locality information descriptor-based weight to the joint sparse representation and multi-task learning model corresponding to the background class, which can also reduce the estimation bias caused by the ℓ_1/ℓ_2 minimization.

From the above experimental results, it can be seen that Figure 6 shows the superiority of the JSRMTL-A model to the traditional JSR-MTL. The JSRMTL-ALI model can generally further improve the detection performance of the JSRMTL-A model. In the detection performance analysis section, as shown in Figure 10, the detection performance of the JSRMTL-ALI generally outperforms the other detectors for all the datasets, especially the robustness of the JSRMTL-ALI compared to the rACE and hCEM algorithms. From the separability maps as shown in Figure 11 and detection map as shown in Figure 12, it can be seen that, the proposed JSRMTL-ALI algorithm generally performs well at a distinguishing target from the background. However, the performance of suppressing background for the JSRMTL-ALI algorithm is not as good as rACE, which needs further consideration in the future.

There are three key parameters of the JSRMTL-ALI algorithm, which have been analyzed as depicted in Figures 7–9. As shown in Figure 7, it can be seen that a large detection task number K can affect the detection performance of JSRMTL-ALI. A larger value for detection task number K is recommended for the dataset with more bands, such as 6 for the AVIRIS and Indian datasets and a lower value is recommended for the dataset with fewer bands, such as 3 for the Cri dataset. Then as shown in Figure 8, it can be seen that a too small or too large regularization parameter ρ can decrease the detection performance of JSRMTL-ALI, and a proper value should be set for ρ, such as 0.1. Based on the results as shown in Figure 9, it can be seen that, it is not easy to recommend a regular value for the size of OWR in practical application. Our future research will investigate the construction of a global background dictionary in order to avoid tuning the size of the OWR.

6. Conclusions

In this paper, the adaptive joint sparse representation and multi-task learning detector with locality information (JSRMTL-ALI) algorithm was proposed. Based on the prior class label information of the training samples, this algorithm constructs an adaptive joint sparse representation and multi-task learning (JSRMTL-A) model, where the test pixel (target pixel or background pixel) is separately modeled via the target dictionary or background dictionary. Considering the great difference between the target dictionary and background dictionary, different regularization strategies encoding the task relatedness are employed for the two joint sparse representation and multi-task learning models based on the target dictionary or background dictionary. A locality information descriptor is then introduced to indicate the difference between the central test pixel and neighboring background training samples. A descriptor based weight strategy is applied to reduce the estimation bias caused by ℓ_1/ℓ_2 minimization used in the JSRMTL-A model. The detection decision rules in favor of the target class or the background class with the lowest total reconstruction error difference accumulated over all the tasks.

Experiments in hyperspectral target detection with three datasets confirmed the superior performance of the multiple detection task combination in the proposed JSRMTL-ALI algorithm. With the integration of the JSRMTL-A model and local information descriptor based weight strategy, the JSRMTL-ALI shows its superiority to the traditional JSR-MTL for hyperspectral target detection. In general, the JSR-MTL presents a better detection performance and better separability than the other common detectors.

Acknowledgments: The authors would like to thank the handling editor and anonymous reviewers for their careful reading and helpful remarks. This work was supported in part by the Fundamental Research Funds for the Central Universities, China University of Geosciences (Wuhan) under Grant CUG170617, Grant CUGL140410 and Grant 26420160125; in part by the China Postdoctoral Science Found under Grant 2017M612533; in part by the Natural Science Foundation of Hubei Province, China under Grant 2014CFA052; in part by the National Natural Science Foundation of China under Grant 61471274, Grant 61372153 and Grant 41630317.

Author Contributions: All the authors made significant contributions to the work. Yuxiang Zhang and Bo Du conceived, designed and performed the experiments; Ke Wu and Xiangyun Hu analyzed the data; Liangpei Zhang provided advice for the preparation and revision of the paper.

Conflicts of Interest: The authors declare no conflict of interest.

References

1. Manolakis, D.; Truslow, E.; Pieper, M.; Cooley, T.; Brueggeman, M. Detection Algorithms in Hyperspectral Imaging Systems: An Overview of Practical Algorithms. *IEEE Signal Process. Mag.* **2014**, *31*, 24–33. [CrossRef]
2. Nasrabadi, N.M. Hyperspectral Target Detection: An Overview of Current and Future Challenges. *IEEE Signal Process. Mag.* **2014**, *31*, 34–44. [CrossRef]
3. Kang, X.; Li, S.; Benediktsson, J.A. Feature Extraction of Hyperspectral Images with Image Fusion and Recursive Filtering. *IEEE Trans. Geosci. Remote Sens.* **2014**, *52*, 3742–3752. [CrossRef]
4. Landgrebe, D. Hyperspectral Image Data Analysis. *IEEE Signal Process. Mag.* **2002**, *19*, 17–28. [CrossRef]
5. Yuan, Y.; Ma, D.; Wang, Q. Hyperspectral Anomaly Detection by Graph Pixel Selection. *IEEE Trans. Cybern.* **2016**, *46*, 3123–3134. [CrossRef] [PubMed]
6. Stefanou, M.S.; Kerekes, J.P. Image-derived prediction of spectral image utility for target detection applications. *IEEE Trans. Geosci. Remote Sens.* **2010**, *48*, 1827–1833. [CrossRef]
7. Datt, B.; McVicar, T.R.; Niel, T.G.V.; Jupp, D.L.B.; Pearlman, J.S. Preprocessing EO-1 Hyperion hyperspectral data to support the application of agricultural indexes. *IEEE Trans. Geosci. Remote Sens.* **2003**, *41*, 1246–1259. [CrossRef]
8. Eismann, M.T.; Stocker, A.D.; Nasrabadi, N.M. Automated hyperspectral cueing for civilian search and rescue. *Proc. IEEE* **2009**, *97*, 1031–1055. [CrossRef]
9. Manolakis, D.; Marden, D.; Shaw, G.A. Hyperspectral Image Processing for Automatic Target Detection Applications. *Linc. Lab. J.* **2003**, *14*, 79–116.
10. Wang, T.; Du, B.; Zhang, L. An automatic robust iteratively reweighted unstructured detector for hyperspectral imagery. *IEEE J. Sel. Top. Appl. Earth Obs. Remote Sens.* **2014**, *7*, 2367–2382. [CrossRef]
11. Gao, L.; Yang, B.; Du, Q.; Zhang, B. Adjusted Spectral Matched Filter for Target Detection in Hyperspectral Imagery. *Remote Sens.* **2015**, *7*, 6611–6634. [CrossRef]
12. Liu, Y.; Gao, G.; Gu, Y. Tensor Matched Subspace Detector for Hyperspectral Target Detection. *IEEE Trans. Geosci. Remote Sens.* **2017**, *54*, 1967–1974. [CrossRef]
13. Geng, X.; Ji, L.; Sun, K.; Zhao, Y. CEM: More Bands, Better Performance. *IEEE Geosci. Remote Sens. Lett.* **2014**, *11*, 1876–1880. [CrossRef]
14. Zou, Z.; Shi, Z. Hierarchical Suppression Method for Hyperspectral Target Detection. *IEEE Trans. Geosci. Remote Sens.* **2016**, *54*, 330–342. [CrossRef]
15. Harsanyi, J.C.; Chang, C.I. Hyperspectral Image Classification and Dimensionality Reduction: An Orthogonal Subspace Projection Approach. *IEEE Trans. Geosci. Remote Sens.* **1994**, *32*, 779–785. [CrossRef]
16. Huang, Z.; Shi, Z.; Yang, S. Nonlocal Similarity Regularized Sparsity Model for Hyperspectral Target Detection. *IEEE Geosci. Remote Sens. Lett.* **2013**, *10*, 1532–1536. [CrossRef]
17. Chen, Y.; Nasrabadi, N.M.; Tran, T.D. Sparse representation for target detection in hyperspectral imagery. *IEEE J. Sel. Top. Appl. Earth Obs. Remote Sens.* **2011**, *5*, 629–640. [CrossRef]
18. Zhang, Y.; Du, B.; Zhang, L. A Sparse Representation Based Binary Hypothesis Model for Target Detection in Hyperspectral Imagery. *IEEE Trans. Geosci. Remote Sens.* **2015**, *53*, 1346–1354. [CrossRef]
19. Niu, Y.; Wang, B. Extracting Target Spectrum for Hyperspectral Target Detection: An Adaptive Weighted Learning Method Using a Self-Completed Background Dictionary. *IEEE Trans. Geosci. Remote Sens.* **2017**, *55*, 1604–1617. [CrossRef]
20. Farrell, M.D.; Mersereau, R.M. On the impact of PCA dimension reduction for hyperspectral detection of difficult targets. *IEEE Geosci. Remote Sens. Lett.* **2005**, *2*, 192–195. [CrossRef]
21. Fowler, J.E.; Du, Q. Anomaly Detection and Reconstruction from Random Projections. *IEEE Trans. Image Process.* **2012**, *21*, 184–195. [CrossRef] [PubMed]
22. Wang, Q.; Lin, J.; Yuan, Y. Salient Band Selection for Hyperspectral Image Classification via Manifold Ranking. *IEEE Trans. Neural Netw. Learn. Syst.* **2016**, *27*, 1279–1289. [CrossRef] [PubMed]

23. Binol, H.; Ochilov, S.; Alam, M.S.; BaI, A. Target oriented dimensionality reduction of hyperspectral data by Kernel Fukunaga—Koontz Transform. *Opt. Laser Eng.* **2016**, *89*, 123–130. [CrossRef]

24. Sun, K.; Geng, X.; Ji, L. A New Sparsity-Based Band Selection Method for Target Detection of Hyperspectral Image. *IEEE Geosci. Remote Sens. Lett.* **2015**, *12*, 329–333. [CrossRef]

25. Jalali, A.; Ravikumar, P.; Sanghavi, S.; Ruan, C. A Dirty Model for Multi-task Learning. In Proceedings of the Neural Information Processing Systems Conference, Hyatt Regency, Vancouver, BC, Canada, 6–11 December 2010.

26. Yuan, X.; Liu, X.; Yan, S. Visual classification with multi-task joint sparse representation. *IEEE Trans. Image Process.* **2012**, *21*, 4349–4360. [CrossRef] [PubMed]

27. Yuan, Y.; Lin, J.; Wang, Q. Hyperspectral Image Classification via Multi-Task Joint Sparse Representation and Stepwise MRF Optimization. *IEEE Trans. Cybern.* **2016**, *46*, 2966–2977. [CrossRef] [PubMed]

28. Caruana, R. Multitask learning. *Mach. Learn.* **1997**, *28*, 41–75. [CrossRef]

29. Zhang, Y.; Du, B.; Zhang, L. Joint Sparse Representation with Multitask Learning for Hyperspectral Target Detection. *IEEE Trans. Geosci. Remote Sens.* **2017**, *55*, 894–906. [CrossRef]

30. Zou, H. The adaptive lasso and its oracle properties. *J. Am. Stat. Assoc.* **2006**, *101*, 1418–1429. [CrossRef]

31. Candes, E.J.; Wakin, M.B.; Boyd, S.P. Enhancing sparsity by reweighted ℓ minimization. *J. Fourier Anal. Appl.* **2008**, *14*, 877–905. [CrossRef]

32. Ben-David, S.; Schuller, R. Exploiting task relatedness for multiple task learning. In Proceedings of the Conference on Computational Learning Theory, Washington, DC, USA, 24–27 August 2003.

33. Chen, X.; Pan, W.; Kwok, J.; Garbonell, J. Accelerated gradient method for multi-task sparse learning problem. In Proceedings of the IEEE International Conference on Data Mining, Miami, FL, USA, 6–9 December 2009; pp. 746–751.

34. Tseng, P. On accelerated proximal gradient methods for convex-concave optimization. *SIAM J. Optim.* **2008**, submitted.

35. Kang, X.; Li, S.; Fang, L.; Benediktsson, J.A. Intrinsic Image Decomposition for Feature Extraction of Hyperspectral Images. *IEEE Trans. Geosci. Remote Sens.* **2015**, *53*, 2241–2253. [CrossRef]

 *remote sensing*

Article

Maritime Semantic Labeling of Optical Remote Sensing Images with Multi-Scale Fully Convolutional Network

Haoning Lin [1,2,3], **Zhenwei Shi** [1,2,3,*] **and Zhengxia Zou** [1,2,3]

1   Image Processing Center, School of Astronautics, Beihang University, Beijing 100191, China; harrylin@buaa.edu.cn (H.L.); zhengxiazou@buaa.edu.cn (Z.Z.)
2   Beijing Key Laboratory of Digital Media, Beihang University, Beijing 100191 China
3   State Key Laboratory of Virtual Reality Technology and Systems, School of Astronautics, Beihang University, Beijing 100191, China
*   Correspondence: shizhenwei@buaa.edu.cn; Tel.: +86-10-8233-9520

Academic Editors: Qi Wang, Nicolas H. Younan, Carlos López-Martínez, Xiaofeng Li and Prasad S. Thenkabail
Received: 15 March 2017; Accepted: 10 May 2017; Published: 14 May 2017

Abstract: In current remote sensing literature, the problems of sea-land segmentation and ship detection (including in-dock ships) are investigated separately despite the high correlation between them. This inhibits joint optimization and makes the implementation of the methods highly complicated. In this paper, we propose a novel fully convolutional network to accomplish the two tasks simultaneously, in a semantic labeling fashion, i.e., to label every pixel of the image into 3 classes, sea, land and ships. A multi-scale structure for the network is proposed to address the huge scale gap between different classes of targets, i.e., sea/land and ships. Conventional multi-scale structure utilizes shortcuts to connect low level, fine scale feature maps to high level ones to increase the network's ability to produce finer results. In contrast, our proposed multi-scale structure focuses on increasing the receptive field of the network while maintaining the ability towards fine scale details. The multi-scale convolution network accommodates the huge scale difference between sea-land and ships and provides comprehensive features, and is able to accomplish the tasks in an end-to-end manner that is easy for implementation and feasible for joint optimization. In the network, the input forks into fine-scale and coarse-scale paths, which share the same convolution layers to minimize network parameter increase, and then are joined together to produce the final result. The experiments show that the network tackles the semantic labeling problem with improved performance.

Keywords: semantic labeling; convolution neural network; fully convolutional network; sea-land segmentation; ship detection

1. Introduction

Remote sensing imagery is one important solution to maritime surveillance, because of its wide field of view, satisfying spatial resolution and update frequency. Remote sensing imagery includes various kinds, ranging from hyper-spectral imagery [1], synthetic aperture radar (SAR) imagery [2], to optical imagery. These kinds of imaging technology serve varying purposes according to their different characteristics, and optical imagery is applied widely for its rich presentation and similar reception frequency to that of human eyes.

There has been a considerate amount of research in optical imagery understanding focusing on detection of different types of objects, such as roads [3,4], buildings [5,6], oil tanks [7,8], vehicles [9–11] and airplanes [12–14]. Aside from detecting scattered objects, the classification of scenes also receives a lot of attention recently, such as in [15–17], where the objective is to classify image patches into different classes, such as buildings, forest, harbor, etc.

Two of the most important tasks in understanding remote sensing images that is maritime-related, would be sea-land segmentation and ship detection. Research on ship detection originally focuses on off-shore ships with relatively simple background, majorly on SAR imagery [2,18,19]. In recent literature, both sea-land segmentation [20,21] and ship detection [22–27] tasks are addressed with complex frameworks, which consists of cascaded procedures and have to be designed and fine-tuned with expert knowledge. That is, when the source sensor of the images is changed, the carefully designed framework always has to be re-calibrated or even re-designed by experts. The complex steps that constitute the framework also make the implementation difficult. Furthermore, ship detection, especially when including in-dock ships, are highly dependent of the performance of sea-land segmentation, making it less robust in precarious sea-land situation. Furthermore, to tackle the two problems separately, also inhibits the joint optimization of the designed algorithm.

The recent advancement in the deep learning community motivates us to address these problems with deep neural networks. Deep learning, as a subcategory of soft computing [28–34], is seeing great attention. In our previous work, we focus on the detection of objects instance-wise, i.e., acquiring the location and bounding box of the objects in interest. In this paper, we propose to address the sea-land segmentation and ship detection at the same time, with a deep neural network, in a semantic labeling perspective. The network allows us to cope with these problems in an end-to-end fashion, without complex procedures, and without handcrafted features.

The semantic labeling of everyday images recently receives increasing attention [35–38] and is regarded as a more challenging task compared to object classification and detection of images. Semantic labeling provides a pixel-to-pixel label map corresponding to the input image, as opposed to only a single label in classification task. It also, from another point of view, provides the boundaries of the detected object, as opposed to only bounding boxes in detection task. This is similar to the saliency detection methods [39,40], with the difference that saliency detection is more general and pays less attention to object boundaries. One general approach of semantic labeling is to first process images into over-segmented areas and then classify each area with its extracted features [35]. Yet with the fast-paced development of deep learning, it also proves to be able to achieve state-of-the-art semantic labeling in everyday images [36–38]. Moreover, since recent research shows that neural networks based on everyday object knowledge can have satisfactory performance on remote sensing imagery [41], the application of deep learning in remote sensing imagery is promising.

In both sea-land segmentation and ship detection tasks, semantic labeling using deep networks shows great potential. First, deep network is able to learn high level features, as opposed to that in other methods, features has to be handcrafted and are complex to implement. Second, semantic labeling's pixel-labeling nature allows it to be independent of bounding boxes and are relatively indifference to objects' size and shape. This helps because sea and land are of arbitrary sizes and shapes, and the bounding boxes of in-dock ships are hard to acquire.

However, the deep network, when used to address these remote sensing problems, is faced with one critical problem, to balance between the hardware requirement and the network's efficacy. In remote sensing images, the area of interest can be of arbitrary size. This lead to the need for a network with extra-large receptive field (which will be extensively discussed in Section 3.2), which requires increased amount of weights for the network layers, which then leads to excessive graphics processing unit (GPU) memory requirement from the network and increased computation in training and testing.

To ameliorate the trade-off between the network's receptive field and the GPU memory requirement, we introduce a novel multi-scale structure for the semantic labeling network, which greatly increases the receptive field of the network, with only a small number of parameter increase.

The main idea of our multi-scale structure is different than those of the conventional ones, where shortcuts are created between convolution layers of different levels to utilize the finer feature maps in order to produce finer outputs. Our structure focuses on enlarging the receptive field of the network to incorporate information from larger scale, which is important for understanding remote sensing images.

In the network, the input data is processed in two separate layers, crop layer and resize layer, into different scales of data, fine-scale and coarse-scale, respectively. The fine-scale path with crop layer keeps the fine details in the data, but with small sized receptive field, while the coarse-scale path with resize layer down-samples the data, omitting high-resolution textures in exchange for large sized receptive field. In this paper, the coarse-scale path is more suitable for discriminating between sea and land, for their large proportion in area and usually obscure boundaries (near beaches and other natural shore-lines, for example). The fine-scale path is suitable for ship detection, for exactly the opposite reasons.

The main contribution of the paper is listed as follows,

1. Joint sea-land segmentation & in-dock ship detection. The information extracted by the network is used both for sea-land segmentation and ship detection. The sharing of the information can lead to better performance, especially in in-dock ship detection, since it is no longer dependent on other separated sea-land segmentation methods and can be trained jointly.
2. A different perspective into multi-scale structure for remote sensing images with small parameter number increase. The conventional multi-scale structures connect different feature maps from different layers that represents different level of semantics, aiming to fully utilize fine-scale features. The proposed structure aims to widen the receptive field of the network, designed specifically for remote sensing images. With the multi-scale structure, the network is able to achieve tasks that require different scales, while maintaining relatively small number of parameter and low calculation complexity. An extensive experiment is conducted to compare our proposed structure to several variants to show its superiority in learning speed and performance.

The following content is structured as follows. In Section 2, a brief introduction to fully convolutional network is given. In Section 3, the proposed multi-scale structure is described in detail and the receptive field of the network is analyzed. In Section 4, the given framework and other methods are experimented on two remote sensing datasets. Finally, Section 6 concludes this paper.

2. Fully Convolutional Network

In this section, we will provide a brief introduction to the fully convolutional network (FCN) upon which we construct our semantic labeling framework.

CNN proves to be extremely effective in image related tasks, such as object detection and classification [42,43]. Based on CNN, Fully Convolutional Networks (FCN) are designed to predict a label map rather than a single label for an input image, by replacing fully connected layers in CNN with small sized convolution layers [44]. FCN's pixel-to-pixel label map output naturally suits the need of semantic labeling. Figure 1, modified from in [44], shows a typical FCN structure, when used to semantic label a remote sensing image.

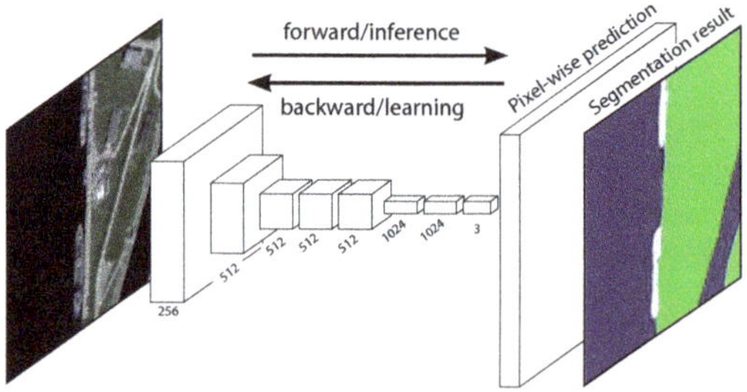

Figure 1. A typical FCN, each cuboid indicating an output matrix of a convolution layer. The numbers indicate the size of the 3rd dimension of each cuboid, or equally, the number of kernels of the corresponding layer.

A typical FCN consists of convolution layers, pooling layers and activation layers [44]. There are also softmax layers for output and loss layers for training. An input data matrix (say, an RGB image $X \in R^{h \times w \times 3}$ or a grayscale image $X \in R^{h \times w \times 1}$) is processed through each layer in sequence in a neural network.

A convolution layer consists of an array of kernel matrices, with which the input data are convoluted. In a convolution layer, the data is processed with the following calculation,

$$Y_l = f_l * X \tag{1}$$

where $*$ is a 3D (3 Dimensional) convolution operator, X is the input matrix of the layer, f_l is the lth kernel of the layer and Y_l is the output matrix correspond to the lth kernel. Here it is mandatory that f_l and X are of the same size in 3rd dimension, so that the size of dimension 3 of Y_l is necessarily 1. Finally, the Y_ls of a layer are concatenated in 3rd dimension, resulting in

$$Y(x, y, l) = Y_l(x, y) \tag{2}$$

where Y is the complete output matrix of the convolution layer. x, y and l are indexes for Y of dimension 1, 2 and 3, respectively. Convolution layers are designed to capture local features and are translation invariant, and the output matrix of a convolution layer is usually called a feature map, since the output represents the extracted features of each single pixels of the input image, with pixel-to-pixel correspondence.

Activate functions are often added after convolution layers to provide non-linear properties for a network to enhance the expressive ability of the features. In an activation function, an element-wise operation is conducted,

$$Y(x, y, z) = f(X(x, y, z)) \tag{3}$$

where x, y, z are indexes of 3 dimensions of a matrix and X, Y are input and output matrices, respectively. f is the function of the layer. In a simple but rather popular activation layer, Relu [45],

$$f(\cdot) = max(0, \cdot) \tag{4}$$

A pooling layer, acting like a down-sampling filter, is often inserted among other layers. It is designed to progressively reduce the size of transferred data to reduce the amount of parameters and enhance the generalization of a network. The most common form of a pooling layer uses max operation to produce results for each local area of the input,

$$Y(x, y, z) = \max_{(i,j) \in \Omega} (X(i, j, z)) \tag{5}$$

where x, y, z, i and j are indexes of their according dimensions of the matrices and X, Y are input and output matrices, respectively. In addition,

$$(i, j) \in \Omega \iff \begin{cases} i \geq x \times step \\ i < x \times step + kernel\_size \\ j \geq y \times step \\ j < y \times step + kernel\_size \end{cases} \tag{6}$$

where $step$ and $kernel\_size$ are the two hyperparameters of the pooling layer, determining the stride of the output according to input and the size of Ω, respectively. For simplicity, the indexes here follow the convention in programming and start from zero.

In an FCN, there are no fully connected layers, which connect all the elements in the input matrix and output results that ignore all spatial information. Convolution layers with kernels of size

1×1 are implemented instead, producing an output matrix of corresponding spatial dimensions [44]. Because some of the convolution layers at the top of the network still act as a role of traditional fully connected layers, in our paper we still distinguish these layers and symbolize them as "fc" layers following the notation in [36].

A softmax layer is a layer for output, it takes in matrices of arbitrary-scaled elements and outputs a matrix of probabilities, with the formula of

$$Y(x,y,j) = \frac{e^{X(x,y,j)}}{\sum_{k=1}^{K} e^{X(x,y,k)}} \tag{7}$$

where X and Y are input and output matrix of the softmax layer, respectively. x, y, j and k are indexes of their corresponding dimensions. K is the size of dimension 3 of X. In a semantic labeling network, the softmax layer outputs the probabilities of every pixel belonging to every category.

A loss layer takes in data both from outputs of previous layers and from ground truth labels. The gradients are firstly calculated from the difference of both sides, and then are back-propagated to previous layers. The kernels of each layer are then updated according to the gradients. This process is gone through iteratively and the network will be trained.

3. Multi-Scale Network for Semantic Labeling

The semantic labeling of maritime scenes calls for multi-scale features because of the tremendous size difference between the sea, land and ships. Sea-land identification demands wide spatial range of input for richer context and comprehensive understanding, whereas small targets, such as ships, demand context of smaller scale but more detailed information from local area. The feature of multi-scale has been extensively utilized in neural networks. Liang et al. connects output of the first few layers to the last layer for attention on fine-resolution layers [36]. Paisitkriangkrai et al. trains several CNNs with different resolution of input images [46]. Eigen et al. concatenates layers that are designed for different scales into a whole [37]. These networks either are trained separately on every scale, resulting in far more parameters to train, or leave the layers trained without the knowledge of its corresponding scale information. Here we present a multi-scale FCN specifically designed for remote sensing imagery. This framework enlarges the receptive field of the network, while preserving the ability to take in fine details, with only a small increase in the number of parameters.

3.1. Network Structure

To implement the multi-scale structure in the network, we introduce two layers, crop layer and resize layer, which is illustrated in Figure 2. In a resize layer, the input is down-sampled, and in the crop layer, the input is center-cropped. The input are separated into what we call fine and coarse scale, respectively, after these two layers.

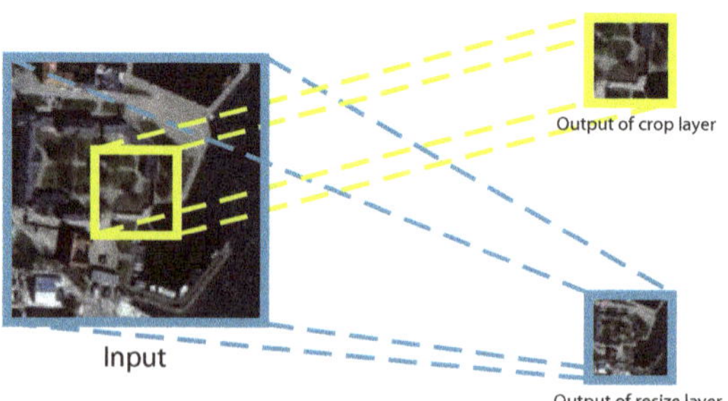

Figure 2. An illustration of the input/output of crop layer and the resize layer.

With the two layers, we have two separate paths of images as well as ground truth labels going through the network at the same time, each representing a different scale.

In Figure 3, the whole network is illustrated. First, an input image patch is duplicated and preprocessed in 2 separate ways, fine-scale and coarse-scale, using aforementioned crop layer and resize layer and are fed into following convolution layers. The outputs of the two preprocessing layers, although cover different areas (Area Yellow vs. Area Blue), are of the same size and thus can be fed into the same layer configuration with the same weights. The convolution layers are configured as DeepLab-LargeFOV [36], with its first 13 convolution layers and are interlaced with Relu and pooling layers. We implement this convolution configuration because it proves to have state-of-the-art semantic labeling performance in everyday images.

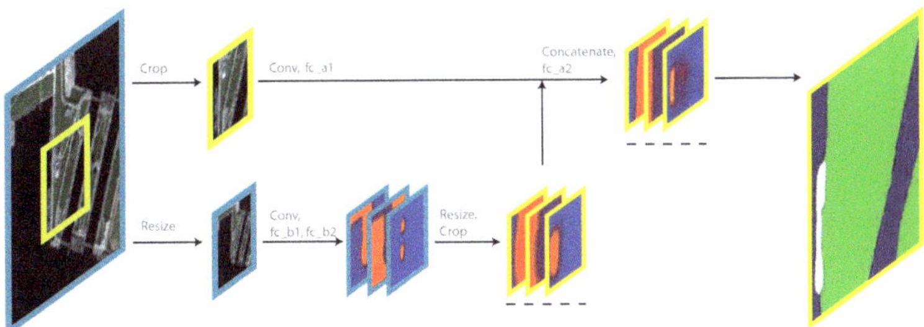

Figure 3. An illustration of the proposed network. The texts on the arrowed lines specify the layers the data go through to produce the displayed results. The color of the outline (blue and yellow) of each result marks the corresponding input area it represents for the sake of clarity. The results that are directly connected to loss layers are underlined with dashed lines.

In Figure 3, some of the results of certain layers are represented as a group of 3 slices, each slice representing the probability map of a corresponding class. We name these groups as score maps for convenience. A score map, in essence, is the same as a feature map, where both maps are the output of a certain convolution layer, but the position and the configuration of the convolution layer define the semantics that the layer is to learn to output the scores of each pixel to belong to a certain category (In fact, a score map is a direct output of a softmax layer, which is placed after a convolution layer. But the function of a softmax layer is relatively trivial compared to the other layers, so the softmax layers are not mentioned either in the figure or in the text).

The network also utilizes two loss layers, each to train the layers in different scales. In Figure 3, the score maps that are connected to a loss layers are underlined with dashed lines. As for the ground truth labels that are needed by the loss layers, they are acquired in the same way as the input patches. The original labels go through crop layer and resize layer separately, and then are fed into loss layers in fine-scale loss layer and coarse-scale loss layer, respectively. With the two loss layers, the convolution layers and fc_** layers learn to produce score maps in accordance. To be specific, the coarse-scale score map is predicted purely from coarse-scale data and then are modified with resize and crop layers, and finally are fed into fine-scale path (Layer fc_a2) to produce fine-scale score map jointly.

Although in Figure 3 the convolution layers are divided into fine-scale and coarse-scale, it is only for clarity. In the practical implementation the fine-scale and coarse-scale data are concatenated first and fed into the same convolution layers, and then separated back to each scale before producing score maps. The weights are shared for convolution layers on the same level and also between fc_*1 layers to minimize the number of parameters. Here the feature extraction mechanism of the convolution layers are not scale specific. The feature maps extracted from different scales may share different semantics, but they are equally effective. We presume that just as deep features can generalize from everyday objects to remote sensing domains [41], deep features can also generalize between different scales of scenes, hence the sharing weights between scales.

The crop layer we design has a simple forward function, which center crops the input with a single parameter, *scale_factor*. The crop function only work on spatial dimensions, which means only the sizes of the first 2 dimension will change. It also has no backward function, meaning no gradient is transferred back through this layer, for simplicity. The simplification is plausible because (a) it is located in special positions in the network, twice after data layers and once after convolution layers and (b) the convolution layers before it have shared weights and can already learn from both scales and (c) coarse-scale layers should focus on sea-land classification and need to take little knowledge from fine-scale losses.

It is also worth mentioning that in [36,47], a 'hole algorithm' is introduced into the deep network for convolution layers, to increase the receptive field of the layers while keeping the number of weights unchanged. A simple explanation would be to put 'holes' in the layer kernels to enlarge the kernels spatially, while maintaining the number of parameters in a kernel,

$$K_{hole}(x,y,z) = \begin{cases} K(x/hole, j/hole, z), \\ \qquad \text{if } x \bmod hole = 0, y \bmod hole = 0 \\ 0, \\ \qquad \text{otherwise} \end{cases} \tag{8}$$

where x, y, z are indexes of their according dimensions of the matrices, **mod** means to calculate the remainder of division and K, K_{hole} are original and modified kernel of the convolution layer with 'hole algorithm', respectively. *hole* is a hyperparameter of the layer, specifying how large the 'hole' you want to insert into the kernels. In this paper, we keep the 'hole algorithm' as is implemented in [36], but with tuned-down size of the hole, in order to acquire more subtle details for the label result.

Table 1 lists the structure setup of the network. The layer names are either self-explanatory or mentioned in the text, so the layer types are omitted. Apart from the Relu layers after each convolution layer, the layers from conv1_1 to pool5b are listed as the exact setup order.

Table 1. The setup of the network.

Layer Name	Kernel Size	Kernel Num.	Remarks
conv1_1, conv1_2		64	-
pool1		-	*step*: 2 *type*: max
conv2_1, conv2_2		128	-
pool2		-	*step*: 2 *type*: max
conv3_1, conv3_2, conv3_3		256	-
pool3		-	*step*: 2 *type*: max
conv4_1, conv4_2, conv4_3	3	512	*hole*: 2
pool4		-	*step*: 1 *type*: max
conv5_1, conv5_2, conv5_3		512	*hole*: 2
pool5a		-	*step*: 1 *type*: max
pool5b		-	*step*: 1 *type*: average
fc_a1, fc_b1		512	*hole*: 2
fc_a2, fc_b2	1	3	-

3.2. Receptive Field Analysis

The receptive field is a vital concept that can affect a network's performance. It is a biologically-inspired term from animals' visual cortex. In a network, it describes the spatial range of input pixels that can contribute to the calculation of a single element in the output. With larger receptive field, each layer can take in more context and represent more abstract meanings. For a network to determine if a pixel belongs to a ship, it is important that the network can determine if the pixel belongs to the forecastle deck or the side of a ship. For ship detection, the receptive field is best to be large enough to cover the space of ship and its context, and for sea-land segmentation, extensively larger receptive field is needed.

The crop layer and the resize layer introduced in the former section is introduced into the network to specifically enlarge the receptive field of one path, while also maintaining the detail feature in another path. The resize layer acts as a downsampling filter, which shrinks the spatial size of the input at the cost of losing detail information, while allowing enlarging the receptive field of the following network path (coarse-scale) without any modification to the existing convolutional layers. The crop layer ensures the input image is cropped to the same spatial area as the desired and maintains the detail information (for the fine-scale). In the training procedure, the parameters of the network is jointly optimized to decrease the loss to the ground truth label. With the different scale of the input data that is given to each path, the network can automatically learn the optimized task for each path, as shown in Section 4.4.

Figure 4 also illustrates the relation between the kernel size and the receptive field of each convolution layer. The kernel size determine the area of the input data to calculate one single element in the output. We can see that with the layers going deeper, or with larger kernel size, the receptive field of the the output layer will increase. Apart from that, the pooling layer also can increase the receptive field, with the possible draw-back of lowering the layer resolution.

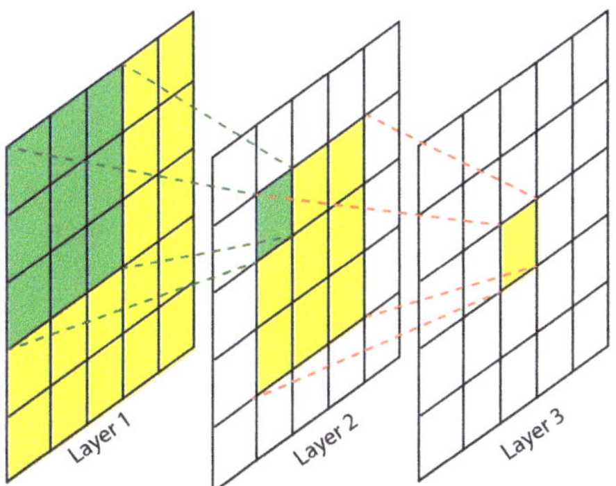

Figure 4. The receptive field of each convolution layer with a 3 × 3 kernel. The green area marks the receptive field of one pixel in Layer 2, and the yellow area marks the receptive field of one pixel in Layer 3.

The whole network's receptive field can calculated by stacking up each layer's receptive radius,

$$R = \sum_L r_l \tag{9}$$

where R is the radius of the network receptive field ($2 \times R + 1 = receptive\_field\_size$), l is the index of the layers and affects receptive field, including pooling layers and convolution layers. L is the total number of the above layers, and r is the radius of the layer's receptive field when considering the subsampling effect of its previous pooling layers. r is defined by

$$r = r_{kernel} \times \prod_N step_n \tag{10}$$

where r_{kernel} is the radius of the kernel of the current layer ($2 \times r_{kernel} + 1 = kernel\_size$), N is the number of pooling layers between the input layer and the current layer, and $step_n$ is the step size of the pooling layer n.

Apart from the crop layers and resize layers, all the layers that affect receptive field are listed in Table 1. All the layers without *hole* hyperparameter have an *r_kernel* of 1, and those with *hole* = 2 have an *r_kernel* of 2. With 13 convolution layers, 5 pooling layers and 2 fc_** layers, our non-multi-scale network has a receptive field of 259×259 pixels. While the ships in our datasets average about 25×150 in size, the receptive field is suitable only for ship detection tasks. To enlarge a network's receptive field for sea-land segmentation, traditional methods such as increasing kernel size or increasing the depth of the network all lead to huge amount of increase in weight number, which in turn leads to harder network training, higher hardware requirement and more computation complexity. The resize layer in the multi-scale structure has a similar effect on receptive fields as the pooling layer, therefore the receptive field of network is enlarged as if a pooling layer is put at the very beginning of the network. With *scale_factor* of both resize layer and crop layer set to 3, the receptive field is roughly scaled up by 9 times in area, into 775×775, with only two additional layers (fc_b1 and fc_b2) with weights. The convolution layers which hold large proportion of the weights stay unchanged, and the network is still able to be fine-tuned from the pre-trained original one.

3.3. Data Preprocessing

Different from most of the previous works that focus on open datasets only containing extracted small image patches, we focus our framework on large, relatively complete images that general remote sensing images are distributed as. The network training and testing on large images brings in new problems, such as how to effectively extract samples or image patches for the network.

Because of the limitation of GPU memory, both training and testing images have to be cut into relatively small patches before being fed into the neural network. For training, we select samples from training images randomly. To be specific, for each original image in the training set, we randomly generate N triplets (x, y, θ), with each symbol indicating pixel coordinate x, coordinate y, and the rotating angle. For each triplet one training sample is selected according to (x, y, θ), with (x, y) being the coordinate of the selected patch in the original image. Finally each sample is rotated by angle θ. For testing samples, the patches are extracted in a sliding-window manner, with a stride the same as the size of the fine-scale input patch, so that the fine-scale inputs has no overlaying on each other. The experiment shows that the network we train performs well on patch borders, especially with the help of the multi-scale scheme. When put back together, the label maps connects to each other well, with no obvious artifacts.

In the literature of semantic labeling, the balancing of samples is barely mentioned, because its application background is mainly on daily images in well-prepared dataset and the problem of unbalanced samples does not exist. In the remote sensing dataset, it is crucial to balance the samples (in this context, to balance the number of pixels of different categories) first for the network to learn equally from different classes. Without the balanced samples, the network will lean towards better performance on sea-land classification, neglecting the accuracy of ship category. In this experiment, firstly, we limit the number of samples that do not contain ships, secondly, we utilize one of the functions of loss layer in DeepLab's Caffe implementation [36], the ability to ignore the loss on the pixels that are labeled to a special class, *ignore.* We randomly set the ground truth label of sea and land pixels to *ignore*, so that when calculating the loss value of the network, the actual functioning ground truth pixels are category-balanced. In our experiment, without balancing the sample, the accuracy of ship detection would decrease dramatically (by 10%).

The samples that contain ships are rotated several times because a ship presented on an remote sensing image can be of arbitrary possible orientation. We also control the number of samples extracted from an image, so that the image is covered roughly twice by the training samples. Although convolution layers have the property of translation invariance, we sample the images more times to counter-act the border effect of the convolution (the borders of a input matrix has to be padded by zero before convolution to maintain output matrix size, thus compromising the effectiveness of features close to the borders).

4. Experiments

This network is implemented with Caffe [48], on Ubuntu 14.04, with one Titan X. The network is trained with mini-batched Stochastic Gradient Descent (SGD) with momentum and step learning rate. The batch size is set to 14, base learning rate 0.001, which drops by a factor of 10 every 2000 iterations. We use momentum 0.9, weight decay 5 and doubled learning rate for biases following the implementation in [36,44]. The network is first initialized with pre-trained weights from ImageNet dataset and then fine-tuned with remote sensing data, to compensate the limited amount of training images. With the pre-trained weights, the network converges to a satisfactory extent at only 4000 iterations.

The selection of the Caffe framework and the training scheme follows the common acknowledgment in the deep learning community [36,49]. Although there are plenty of selection of deep learning framework to use (such as TensorFlow, Torch), the accuracy-wise performance has only a very limited variation [49]. The choice of training scheme has also undergone extensive investigation [50] and we follow [36] because of the similar network architecture. We also experiment other modified version of SGD [50] but yield inferior results.

We experiment our proposed method on two different datasets. The first dataset we use consists of 6 panchromatic (grayscale) images from GaoFen-1 satellite each with above $18,000 \times 18,000$ pixels and a resolution of 2.5 m/pixel. The second dataset has 21 images (RGB) from Google Map, each with above 5000×5000 pixels and a resolution of 1 m/pixel. Both datasets focuses on areas with harbors, where both ships and various types of terrain exist. Although datasets (such as SPOT-4) that has lower resolution can provide competitive results for sea/land segmentation [51], we select the high resolution imagery to meet the requirement for in-shore ship detection, as proposed in [23,25].

Remote sensing datasets from Google Map has received extensive research in the recent days and are recognized as a valid source for remote sensing research [52]. Although imagery from Google Map may be enhanced to different extents, we qualitatively find that the imagery are not too varied to the degree that human cannot distinguish the objects in the imagery in the way on daily life objects, i.e., objects in Google Earth still are faithful to real colors and textures. Nevertheless, we here provide the coordinates and the sensor of the images we use for the experiment. All of the images from Google Map are produced by Digital Mapping Camera (DMC) collected from United States Geological Survey (USGS) High Resolution Orthoimagery and the coordinates of the most north-west pixel of the images are listed in Table 2.

Table 2. Coordinates of maps used in Google Map dataset (excerpt).

Map No.	Longitude	Latitude	Map No.	Longitude	Latitude	Map No.	Longitude	Latitude
1	129.687E	33.122N	2	127.645E	26.214N	3	21.958W	64.132N
4	132.520E	34.199N	5	79.926W	9.233N	6	21.936W	64.140N
7	139.627E	35.267N	8	129.837E	32.702N	9	15.580E	56.128N
10	129.687E	33.122N	11	12.590E	55.662N	12	10.160E	54.293N
13	8.126E	53.504N	14	30.720E	46.450N	15	4.197W	50.355N
16	1.113E	50.774N	17	3.1884E	51.312N	18	27.886E	43.155N
19	4.773E	52.927N	20	8.306W	51.801N	21	12.094E	54.147N

For the Google dataset, we select 7 images as test data and the other 14 as training data. For GaoFen-1 dataset, we find that to augment the training data by including Google images can improve the performance, so we convert the 14 RGB training images to grayscale images and join them to 2 of the GaoFen-1 images as training data, and choose the remaining 4 as test data. Note that the distribution of the ships also varies across the dataset, where the dataset from Google Map has far more in-dock ships. In the test data, Google Map dataset has 55 ships in total, including 50 in-dock ships, while GaoFen-1 dataset has 160 ships in total, including only 20 in-dock ships.

As a novel effort to implement deep learning semantic labeling into the maritime area, we focus our detection target on large navy ships/oil tankers to limit the scale of the target. The length of the target ships vary from 80 m to under 200 m in Google Map dataset and around 300 m in GaoFen-1 dataset. This lead to a similar scale for ships on both datasets because of the different resolution. The ships vary from 80 to 200 pixels in length.

For performance evaluation, we follow the method that is widely used in segmentation/semantic labeling tasks [36,46] . We count the number of pixels that are correctly labeled and those that are not, and compute the confusion matrix and Intersection-Over-Unions (IOU) for each task. Values in a confusion matrix indicate the percentage of the pixels labeled to the column class in the pixels belonging to the row class, meaning a row of a confusion matrix sums to one. Whereas IOU is calculated as

$$IOU = \frac{true\ positives}{true\ positives + false\ positives + false\ negatives} \tag{11}$$

4.1. Benefit of Multi-Class Classification

Previous in-shore ship detection methods rely heavily on the acquirement of shore-line as a 1st step. This step contributes to locating possible areas with in-shore ships and eliminating complex inland areas that could produce huge number of false alarms. Traditionally there are two options to acquire shore-line information, (a) manually labeled shore-line database, which has two problems, the need for constant update and the need for accurate registration between database and image; And (b) a separate algorithm for the detection of shore-line, which is time consuming and requires tedious optimization (possibly hand-tuned) iterated between shore-line and ship detection algorithm.

In our framework the two problems are tackled at the same time and are jointly optimized to achieve better performance. We experiment our network on GaoFen-1 dataset on two different scenarios to show the benefit of multi-class classification of our framework, (1) the network is tasked to classify only 2 classes, Non-ship and Ship and (2) the network is tasked to classify 3 classes, Sea, Land and Ship. Table 3 shows with 3-class task, the network's accuracy on Ship is greatly improved, the network's learning time is also decreased. This is because with the 3-class task, the network in training is given extra information to comprehend the context of the task and by jointly classify multiple classes, the network learns the spatial relationship between the different classes (the Ship have minimal probability to appear in the middle of Land but maximal probability at the brink between Land and Sea). The 3-class problem also provides a more balanced sample pool so the network is easier to train with larger learning rate and faster converging speed.

Table 3. The comparison of Accuracy/Recall on Ship and training time on 2-Class/3-Class problems.

Problem	Accuracy	Recall	Trained Epoch
2-Class	85.3%	83.9%	160
3-Class	94.1%	83.4%	80

Although in the remote sensing imagery the land area features most complex objects, we find the classification of these objects will not contribute to the performance of the task. This is because ship detection is majorly focused at the brink between land and sea. The classification of objects enclosed by land will not provide any additional information for ship-detection, while also unnecessarily taking up the capacity of the network.

4.2. Comparison between Different Realization of Multi-Scale Structure

The multi-scale structure which ensembles paths of different receptive fields has various ways of implementation. In this section we list a few different multi-scale structures and compare the convergent speeds and parameter numbers of the various structures to show the superiority of our choice. Note that although there are already many multi-scale structures proposed in literature, by creating shortcuts between layers to ensemble feature maps of different level of semantics, we here focus on multi-scale structures that use input of different scales.

Figure 5 depicts the some of the common structures feasible for multi-scale implementation that we experiment in the comparison. Network A (Figure 5a) is the most basic multi-scale structure which simply averages the results of different scales. This network is similar to basic scale augmentation of training samples. The network does not learn the relationship between different scales. Network B (Figure 5b) concatenate the results after the convolution layers. Here the fc_** layers start to learn the weights of different paths to classify different objects. In Network C (Figure 5c), the concatenation takes place after the first fc_** layers. The proposed network is similar to Network C except the the network has two loss layers, each on the top of either path. In contrast, Network A, B, C only have one loss layer at the very top of the network.

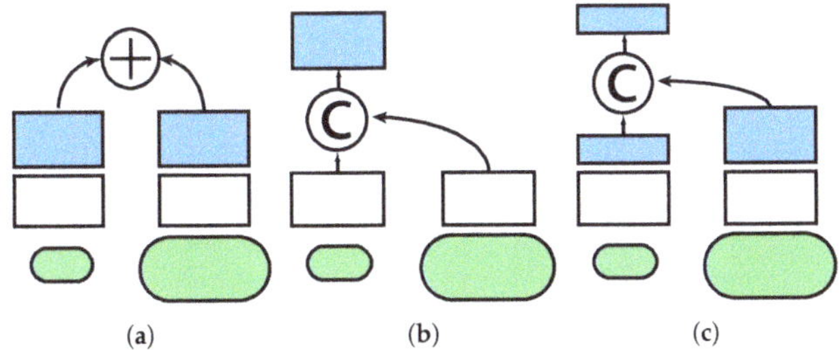

(a)   (b)   (c)

Figure 5. Different multi-scale structures in our experiment, (a) the features are summed up element-wise at the very end, (b) features are concatenated before fc_** layers and (c) features are concatenated between fc_** layers. Here green blocks indicate inputs of different scales, white indicates convolution layers, blue indicates fc_** layers, circle with a plus indicates element-wise addition operation of feature maps, circle with a C indicates concatenation operation. The loss layers are placed on the very top of each network.

We experiment the different networks on Google Map images. Figure 7 shows the training average Accuracy/epoch, Recall/epoch and IOU/epoch curve of these networks. It shows that the proposed method, with 2 loss layers at different path, has overall faster learning speed and higher performance.

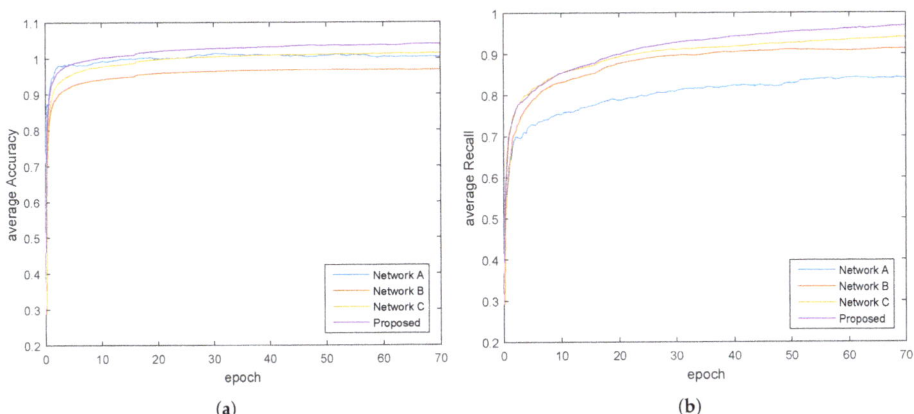

(a)   (b)

Figure 6. *Cont.*

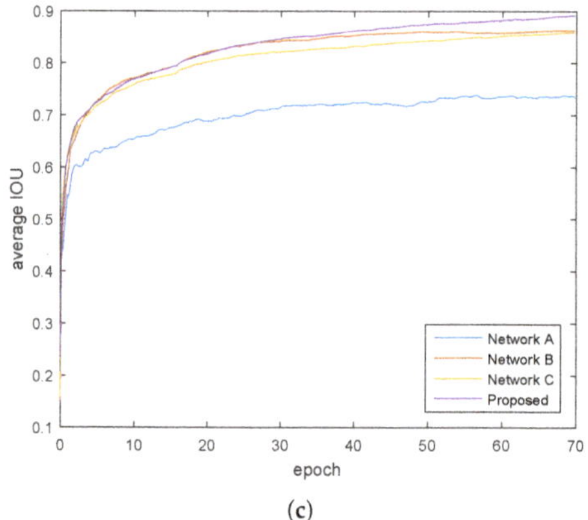

(**c**)

Figure 7. Training average Accuracy/epoch, Recall/epoch and IOU/epoch curve of networks with different multi-scale structure in Figure 5, with (**a-c**) labeled accordingly.

In Table 4 we show the the numbers of parameters and the computation time of a single forward/backward routine on a 961 × 961 training patch of these networks. Since Network C differs from the proposed one only in that it has one fewer loss layer, its data is omitted. The table shows that our proposed multi-scale structure has relatively small number of parameters and considerate fewer computation time compared to Network B.

Table 4. The numbers of parameters of the networks and computation time of a single forward/backward routine per patch.

Results	Network A	Network B	Proposed
# of Parameters	15.2 m	15.7 m	15.2 m
Computation time	0.1525 s	0.2825 s	0.1425 s

We also include an experiment to show the performance comparison between the usage of hole algorithm and different convolution architecture. In one of the experiment we cancel the hole implementation and in the other experiment we use Resnet [53] as the convolution structure. The IOU is shown in Table 5. As shown in the table, the hole implementation and the convolution structure both slightly increase the performance compared to the counterpart. The implementation with Resnet has the worst performance despite it is the more recent architecture. This is because Resnet introduce heavy pooling and the small details are further neglected. This can be seen in the 4% drop IOU in Ship performance.

Table 5. IOUs of the proposed method/without hole/with Resnet.

IOU (%)	Sea	Land	Ship
Proposed	98.2	98.7	68.3
W/O hole	98.0	98.5	68.1
W/Resnet	96.9	97.2	64.4

4.3. Comparison with Other Methods

For a performance baseline, we also experiment the SLIC (Simple Linear Iterative Clustering) method [35] and DenseCRF (Dense Conditional Random Field) [54] two of the most widely used semantic labeling methods other than deep learning networks, to approach the same problem. SLIC is a widely approved way of producing superpixels as a preprocessing step for other process such as object localization and semantic labeling. We first break the large images into small, irregular segments called superpixels and then learn to classify each superpixel into different categories as described in [35], i.e., to extract color, shape and texture info of each superpixel as features and train an adaboost classifier [55] for classification. DenseCRF is a widely used multi-class image segmentation method based on fully connected random field. This model accounts for unary and pairwise potentials among pixels at the same time. The pairwise potential can address the difference between pixels in arbitrary feature spaces and the unary potentials are computed independently on each pixel. The unary potentials are treated as the initial guess of each pixel's category, and the pairwise potentials are to rectify the results. The solution to this model is yielded in an iterative fashion and leads to a refined classification results of each pixel. In this experiment, we follow the implementation in [54], in which the unary potentials are acquired using TextonBoost [56]. Although for the unary potentials there are multiple selection such as convolutional network, we use TextonBoost for the consistency to the original paper.

Table 6 shows the comparison results. We notice that because of the nature of the categories in this problem, pixels that belongs to sea or land takes an extremely great proportion (over 99%), affecting the statistics in the evaluation. So we randomly ignore pixels belonging to sea or land in the evaluation, to ensure the numbers of pixels in different categories are of similar order of magnitude (the ratio between the areas of land, sea and ships is balanced roughly to 4:4:1). We also list the IOUs without the balanced evaluation in Table 7 for completeness, but for future results, we will only show the ones with balanced evaluation.

Table 6. Accuracy of segmentation of different methods. Confusion matrix with percentages row-normalized and IOU of each class.

a SLIC/DenseCRF/proposed network on GaoFen-1 images.

% of Total	Sea	Land	Ship	IOU
Sea	96.1/95.3/**99.5**	3.7/4.6/0.5	0.2/0.1/0.0	93.4/71.9/**99.5**
Land	2.7/8.2/1.4	94.8/91.4/**98.6**	2.4/0.4/0.0	/47.1/**98.6**
Ship	0/27.4/12.8	53.9/61.1/3.8	46.0/11.5/**83.4**	44.8/11.5/**83.4**

b SLIC/DenseCRF/proposed network on Google Map images.

% of Total	Sea	Land	Ship	IOU
Sea	91.4/95.1/**98.2**	8.1/4.8/1.7	0.5/0.1 0.0	78.1/72.0/**98.2**
Land	14.1/8.6/1.2	64.9/91.0/**98.7**	21.1/0.5/0.0	40.4/43.9/**98.7**
Ship	3.1/24.5/6.8	51.9/59.8/24.9	45.0/15.7/**68.3**	37.0/15.6/**68.3**

Table 7. IOUs of the proposed method without balanced evaluation.

IOU (%)	Sea	Land	Ship
GaoFen-1	99.3	95.8	59.0
Google Map	96.9	97.2	40.5

We notice that the SLIC method performs poorly in this problem because a) the superpixels produced are of bad accuracy even with carefully tuned parameters (initial region size and spatial regularizer) and b) at the classification stage, the features extracted are not rich enough to distinguish each category. The DenseCRF's iteration method relies greatly on its initial result, the unary potentials from TextonBoost, which is initially designed for everyday image circumstances. The experiment shows that TextonBoost is, however, not suitable for remote sensing images. We presume the failure of DenseCRF and SLIC is generally due to the fact that remote sensing images have scarce (if any) color information and objects are of much smaller size compared to those in everyday images.

4.4. Experiments on Multi-Scale Structure

Table 8 shows the performance comparison between the network with and without multi-scale structure. The multi-scale structure enhances the network's ability to discriminate categories in different scales, with accuracy on sea and land greatly improved.

Table 8. Accuracy of segmentation with or without multi-scale. Confusion matrix with percentages row-normalized and IOU for each class.

a network without/with multi-scale on GaoFen-1 images.

% of Total	Sea	Land	Ship	IOU
Sea	**99.6**/99.5	0.3/0.5	0.0/0.0	97.7/**99.5**
Land	8.2/1.4	91.8/**98.6**	0.0/0.0	89.2/**98.6**
Ship	14.5/12.8	2.8/3.8	82.7/**83.4**	82.6/**83.4**

b network without/with multi-scale on Google Map images.

% of Total	Sea	Land	Ship	IOU
Sea	97.9 / **98.2**	2.1 / 1.7	0.0 / 0.0	94.9 / **98.2**
Land	2.3 / 1.2	97.6 / **98.7**	0.0 / 0.0	86.4 / **98.7**
Ship	1.3 / 6.8	33.1 / 24.9	65.6 / **68.3**	65.4 / **68.3**

As is shown in Figure 8, after the training of the network, we extracted the weights of Layer fc_a2, which is used to combine the information from fine-scale feature maps and coarse-scale score maps. Only 20 weights of each kernel are shown for clarity. The layer learns that sea and land score maps from coarse-scale have greater weights and ship score map have relatively lesser weight (as it should, intuitively, since coarse-scale network are more reliable for sea-land segmentation).

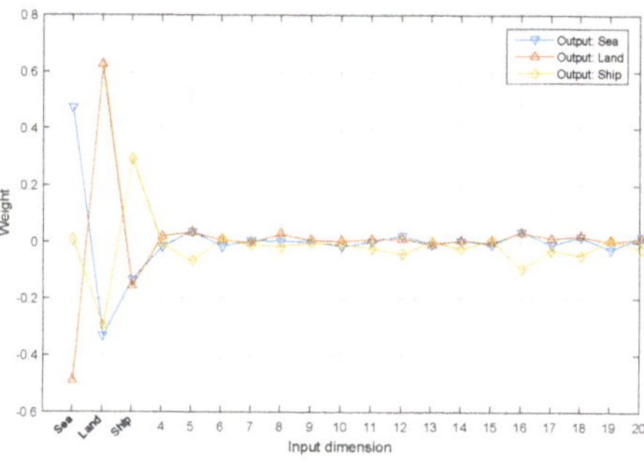

Figure 8. First 20 weights of Layer fc_a2 plotted as lines. Each line represents the weights corresponding to a specific output category (sea, land and ship) as listed in the legend. Each dot on the line represent a weight corresponding to an input dimension. The first 3 input dimensions corresponds to coarse-scale score slices of sea, land and ship, respectively, and the other dimensions corresponds to feature maps from fine-scale Layer fc_a1.

4.5. Qualitative Experiments

The qualitative performance is shown in Figures 9 and 10. Figure 9 features the comparison between our proposed method with and without multi-scale structure. The result with multi-scale structure tends to be more accurate and continuous, especially on GaoFen-1 dataset. Also note that images from GaoFen-1 dataset have more ships off-shore, which can be relatively easy for the network and add to better quantitative performance on GaoFen-1 dataset in Table 6. It is also noticed that the segmentation boundaries are not quite accurate with respect to the original images. This is in accordance with the initial results of DeepLab network [36], which, later implements DenseCRF as a post-process to acquire better segmentation boundaries. However, DenseCRF does not yield satisfactory results in our experiments, due to the fact that the objects in our dataset lack color differentiation and clear boundaries, especially in GaoFen-1 images.

Qualitative comparisons between our proposed method and DenseCRF, SLIC are shown in Figure 11. The compared methods presents inferior results because of two aspects, the classification and the segmentation. DenseCRF and SLIC both have worse performance when compared to our deep network and can not fully identify the ship body. In addition, when the shadows on the ship is evident, these two methods often classify these shadows into sea category.

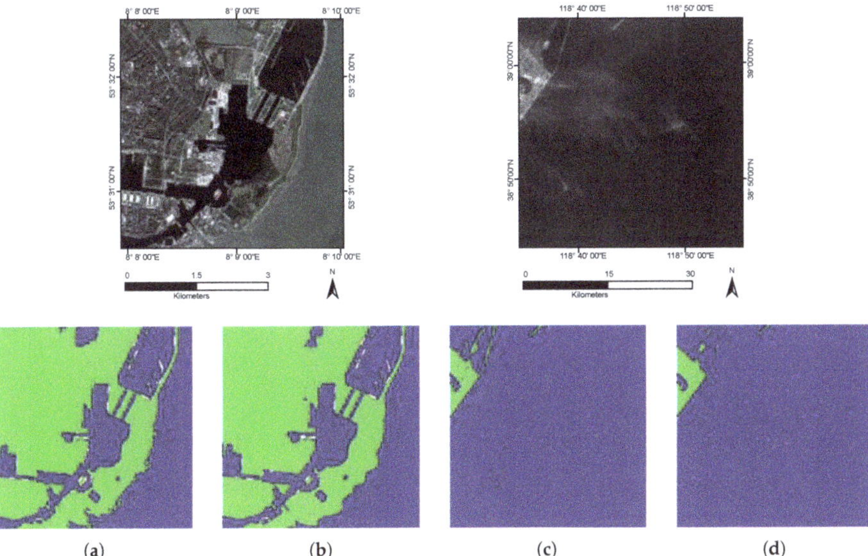

(a)   (b)   (c)   (d)

Figure 9. Semantic labeling results on Google Map images (**a**,**b**) and GaoFen-1 images (**c**,**d**). The images are arranged as original (**top**), proposed method without multi-scale (**a**,**c**) and proposed method with multi-scale (**b**,**d**). Here sea, land and ship are labeled as blue, green and white, respectively.

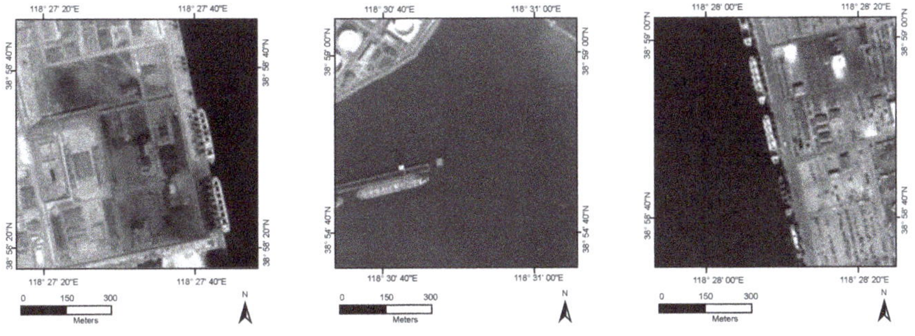

Figure 10. *Cont.*

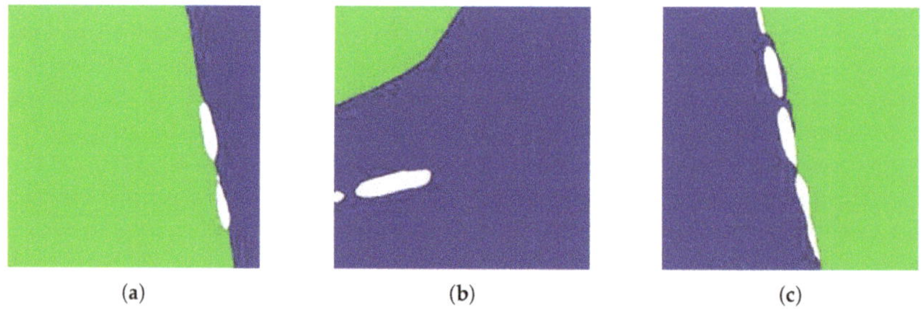

(a)   (b)   (c)

Figure 10. Zoomed in semantic labeling results (**bottom**) on GaoFen-1 images (**a-c**), presented with The original image (**top**). Here sea, land and ship are labeled as blue, green and white, respectively.

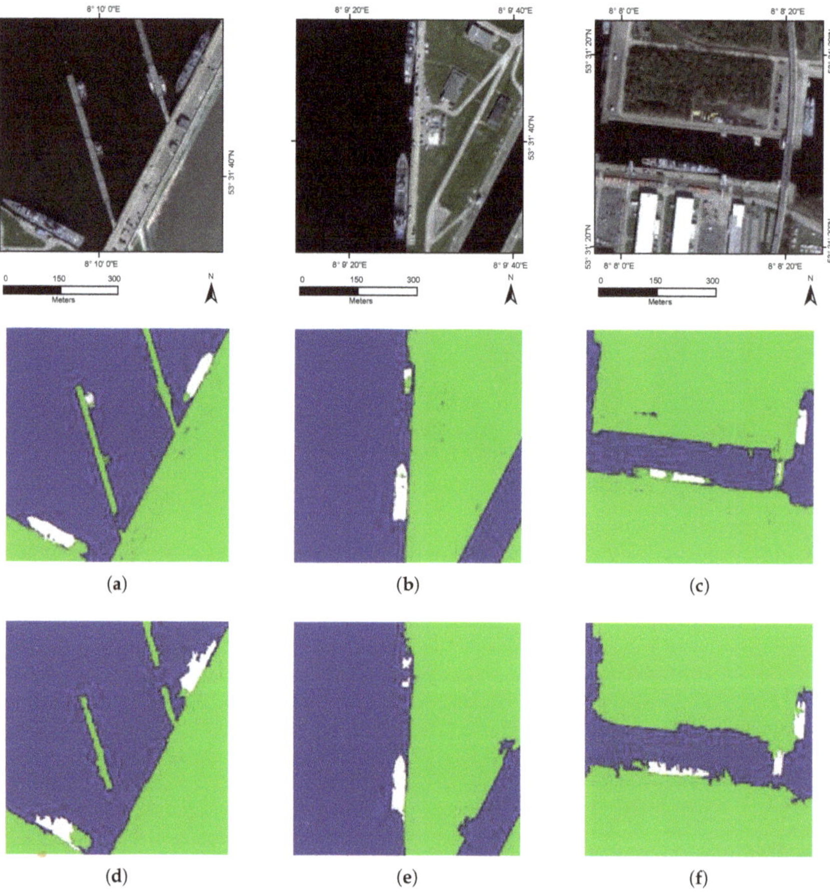

(a)   (b)   (c)

(d)   (e)   (f)

Figure 11. *Cont.*

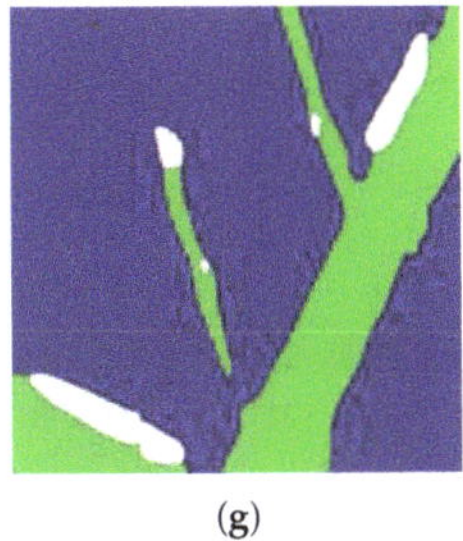 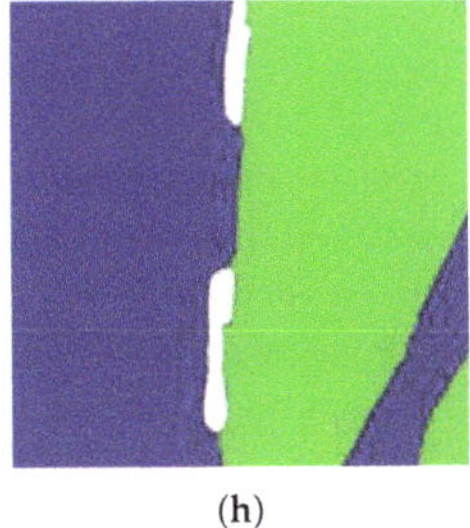 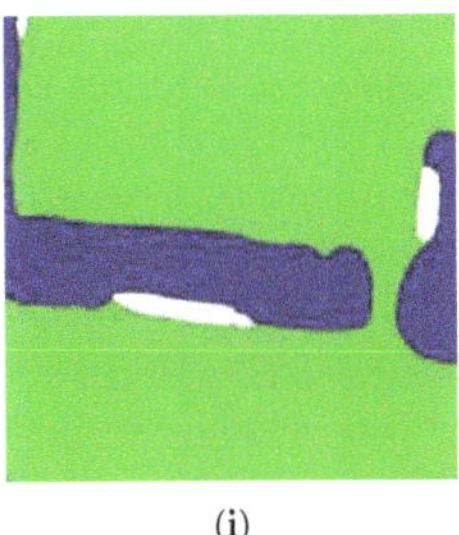

(g)   (h)   (i)

Figure 11. Zoomed in semantic labeling results of DenseCRF (**a-c**), SLIC (**d-f**) and proposed method (**g-i**) with original images (**top**). Here sea, land and ship are labeled as blue, green and white, respectively.

5. Feasibility of Ship Detection via Coastline Detection

Coastline detection has undergone extensive research over the last decades [51,57,58] and it is possible to consider it as an approach towards ship detection to regard dynamic ships as a temporal change in multi-temporal images. The automatic coastline detection can facilitate autonomous navigation, coastal resource management and coastal environmental protection.

Although the accuracy of coastline detection is constantly increasing, it is still not enough for direct implementation for ship detection [59]. Coastline detection methods commonly utilize image segmentation tools such as watershed transformation [59] or graph-based discrimination [60], which are based on the features of textures and intensities and have no knowledge to holistic objects such as ships. As a result, for instance, at the fine scale segmentation stage, shadows on the decks that are cast by ships themselves are often segmented into seas [23]. Besides, a post-validation algorithm is still needed since not all detected changes are ships.

Moreover, single image ship detection, in contrast to multi-image ship detection, has the advantage that it does not need the multiple image registration and the storing of template images. Besides, change detection methods has the disadvantage that it is not accurate when image contrast has severe variation and that it needs constant manual power to update latest coast line.

6. Conclusions

In this paper, we propose a semantic labeling network with unified multi-scale structure which has enlarged receptive field and minimal parameter number increase, which is different from tradition multi-scale schemes that focus on utilizing finer-scale feature maps. The large receptive field is designed specifically for maritime remote sensing images and the experiments show that with the multi-scale semantic labeling scheme, an improved performance is achieved in the problem of sea-land segmentation and ship detection on both GaoFen-1 and Google Map images, under the circumstances that the ship targets are limited to large navy ships and oil tankers. In the future work, we will extend this work for more diversified ship targets such as yachts and fishing boats.

Acknowledgments: The work was supported by the National Natural Science Foundation of China under the Grant 61671037, the Beijing Natural Science Foundation under the Grant 4152031, the funding project of State Key Laboratory of Virtual Reality Technology and Systems, Beihang University under the Grant BUAA-VR-16ZZ-03. *(Corresponding author: Zhenwei Shi)*

Author Contributions: Haoning Lin designed the proposed model and implemented the experiments. Haoning Lin drafted the manuscript. Zhengxia Zou contributed to the improvement of the proposed model and edited the manuscript. Zhenwei Shi provided overall guidance to the project, reviewed and edited the manuscript and obtained funding to support this research.

Conflicts of Interest: The authors declare no conflict of interest.

References

1. Wang, Q.; Lin, J.; Yuan, Y. Salient band selection for hyperspectral image classification via manifold ranking. *IEEE Trans. Neural Netw. Learn. Syst.* **2016**, *27*, 1279–1289.
2. Tello, M.; López-Martínez, C.; Mallorqui, J.J. A novel algorithm for ship detection in SAR imagery based on the wavelet transform. *IEEE Geosci. Remote Sens. Lett.* **2005**, *2*, 201–205.
3. Mnih, V.; Hinton, G.E. Learning to detect roads in high-resolution aerial images. In Proceedings of the European Conference on Computer Vision, Crete, Greece, 5–11 September 2010; pp. 210–223.
4. Wang, J.; Song, J.; Chen, M.; Yang, Z. Road network extraction: A neural-dynamic framework based on deep learning and a finite state machine. *Int. J. Remote Sens.* **2015**, *36*, 3144–3169.
5. Sirmacek, B.; Unsalan, C. A probabilistic framework to detect buildings in aerial and satellite images. *IEEE Trans. Geosci. Remote Sens.* **2011**, *49*, 211–221.
6. Stankov, K.; He, D.C. Detection of buildings in multispectral very high spatial resolution images using the percentage occupancy hit-or-miss transform. *IEEE J. Sel. Top. Appl. Earth Obs. Remote Sens.* **2014**, *7*, 4069–4080.
7. Ok, A.O.; Başeski, E. Circular oil tank detection from panchromatic satellite images: A new automated approach. *IEEE Geosci. Remote Sens. Lett.* **2015**, *12*, 1347–1351.
8. Zhang, L.; Shi, Z.; Wu, J. A Hierarchical Oil Tank Detector with Deep Surrounding Features for High-Resolution Optical Satellite Imagery. *IEEE J. Sel. Top. Appl. Earth Obs. Remote Sens.* **2015**, *8*, 4895–4909.
9. Wen, X.; Shao, L.; Fang, W.; Xue, Y. Efficient feature selection and classification for vehicle detection. *IEEE Trans. Circuits Syst. Video Technol.* **2015**, *25*, 508–517.
10. Yang, L.; Bi, G.; Xing, M.; Zhang, L. Airborne sar moving target signatures and imagery based on LVD. *IEEE Trans. Geosci. Remote Sens.* **2015**, *53*, 5958–5971.
11. Yu, X.; Shi, Z. Vehicle detection in remote sensing imagery based on salient information and local shape feature. *Opt.-Int. J. Light Electron Opt.* **2015**, *126*, 2485–2490.
12. Cai, H.; Su, Y. Airplane detection in remote sensing image with a circle-frequency filter. In Proceedings of the International Conference on Space Information Technology, Beijing, China, 19–20 November 2005; p. 59852T.
13. Bo, S.; Jing, Y. Region-based airplane detection in remotely sensed imagery. In Proceedings of the 2010 3rd International Congress on Image and Signal Processing (CISP), Yantai, China, 16–18 October 2010; Volume 4, pp. 1923–1926.
14. An, Z.; Shi, Z.; Teng, X.; Yu, X.; Tang, W. An automated airplane detection system for large panchromatic image with high spatial resolution. *Opt.-Int. J. Light Electron Opt.* **2014**, *125*, 2768–2775.
15. Cheriyadat, A.M. Unsupervised feature learning for aerial scene classification. *IEEE Trans. Geosci. Remote Sens.* **2014**, *52*, 439–451.
16. Zhang, F.; Du, B.; Zhang, L. Saliency-guided unsupervised feature learning for scene classification. *IEEE Trans. Geosci. Remote Sens.* **2015**, *53*, 2175–2184.
17. Cheng, G.; Han, J.; Zhou, P.; Guo, L. Multi-class geospatial object detection and geographic image classification based on collection of part detectors. *ISPRS J. Photogramm. Remote Sens.* **2014**, *98*, 119–132.
18. Crisp, D.J. *The State-of-the-Art in Ship Detection in Synthetic Aperture Radar Imagery*; Technical Report, DTIC Document; DTIC: Fort Belvoir, VA, USA, 2004.
19. Vachon, P.; Campbell, J.; Bjerkelund, C.; Dobson, F.; Rey, M. Ship detection by the RADARSAT SAR: Validation of detection model predictions. *Can. J. Remote Sens.* **1997**, *23*, 48–59.
20. Zhang, T.; Yang, X.; Hu, S.; Su, F. Extraction of coastline in aquaculture coast from multispectral remote sensing images: Object-based region growing integrating edge detection. *Remote Sens.* **2013**, *5*, 4470–4487.
21. Cheng, D.; Meng, G.; Xiang, S.; Pan, C. Efficient sea–land segmentation using seeds learning and edge directed graph cut. *Neurocomputing* **2016**, *207*, 36–47.
22. Zhu, C.; Zhou, H.; Wang, R.; Guo, J. A novel hierarchical method of ship detection from spaceborne optical image based on shape and texture features. *IEEE Trans. Geosci. Remote Sens.* **2010**, *48*, 3446–3456.
23. Liu, G.; Zhang, Y.; Zheng, X.; Sun, X.; Fu, K.; Wang, H. A new method on inshore ship detection in high-resolution satellite images using shape and context information. *IEEE Geosci. Remote Sens. Lett.* **2014**, *11*, 617–621.

24. Shi, Z.; Yu, X.; Jiang, Z.; Li, B. Ship detection in high-resolution optical imagery based on anomaly detector and local shape feature. *IEEE Trans. Geosci. Remote Sens.* **2014**, *52*, 4511–4523.

25. You, H.M.; Pi, S.H. Ship detection at the dock using a polygon approximation method. In Proceedings of the 2015 IEEE International Conference on Grey Systems and Intelligent Services (GSIS), Leicester, UK, 18–20 August 2015; pp. 500–504.

26. Tang, J.; Deng, C.; Huang, G.B.; Zhao, B. Compressed-domain ship detection on spaceborne optical image using deep neural network and extreme learning machine. *IEEE Trans. Geosci. Remote Sens.* **2015**, *53*, 1174–1185.

27. Zou, Z.; Shi, Z. Ship Detection in Spaceborne Optical Image with SVD Networks. *IEEE Trans. Geosci. Remote Sens.* **2016**, *54*, 5832–5845.

28. Taormina, R.; Chau, K.W. Data-driven input variable selection for rainfall–runoff modeling using binary-coded particle swarm optimization and Extreme Learning Machines. *J. Hydrol.* **2015**, *529*, 1617–1632.

29. Liang, Z.; Shan, S.; Liu, X.; Wen, Y. Fuzzy prediction of AWJ turbulence characteristics by using typical multi-phase flow models. *Eng. Appl. Comput. Fluid Mech.* **2017**, *11*, 225–257.

30. Bellary, S.A.I.; Adhav, R.; Siddique, M.H.; Chon, B.H.; Kenyery, F.; Samad, A. Application of computational fluid dynamics and surrogate-coupled evolutionary computing to enhance centrifugal-pump performance. *Eng. Appl. Comput. Fluid Mech.* **2016**, *10*, 171–181.

31. Zhang, J.; Chau, K.W. Multilayer Ensemble Pruning via Novel Multi-sub-swarm Particle Swarm Optimization. *J. Univ. Comput. Sci.* **2009**, *15*, 840–858.

32. Wang, W.C.; Chau, K.W.; Xu, D.M.; Chen, X.Y. Improving forecasting accuracy of annual runoff time series using ARIMA based on EEMD decomposition. *Water Resour. Manag.* **2015**, *29*, 2655–2675.

33. Zhang, S.; Chau, K.W. Dimension reduction using semi-supervised locally linear embedding for plant leaf classification. *Emerg. Intell. Comput. Technol. Appl.* **2009**, 948–955.

34. Wu, C.; Chau, K.; Fan, C. Prediction of rainfall time series using modular artificial neural networks coupled with data-preprocessing techniques. *J. Hydrol.* **2010**, *389*, 146–167.

35. Achanta, R.; Shaji, A.; Smith, K.; Lucchi, A.; Fua, P.; Süsstrunk, S. SLIC superpixels compared to state-of-the-art superpixel methods. *IEEE Trans. Pattern Anal. Mach. Intell.* **2012**, *34*, 2274–2282.

36. Liang-Chieh, C.; Papandreou, G.; Kokkinos, I.; Murphy, K.; Yuille, A. Semantic Image Segmentation with Deep Convolutional Nets and Fully Connected CRFs. In Proceedings of the International Conference on Learning Representations, San Diego, CA, USA, 7–9 May 2015.

37. Eigen, D.; Fergus, R. Predicting depth, surface normals and semantic labels with a common multi-scale convolutional architecture. In Proceedings of the IEEE International Conference on Computer Vision, Santiago, Chile, 13–16 December 2015; pp. 2650–2658.

38. Noh, H.; Hong, S.; Han, B. Learning deconvolution network for semantic segmentation. In Proceedings of the IEEE International Conference on Computer Vision, Santiago, Chile, 13–16 December 2015; pp. 1520–1528.

39. Wang, Q.; Yuan, Y.; Yan, P.; Li, X. Saliency detection by multiple-instance learning. *IEEE Trans. Cybern.* **2013**, *43*, 660–672.

40. Wang, Q.; Yuan, Y.; Yan, P. Visual saliency by selective contrast. *IEEE Trans. Circuits Syst. Video Technol.* **2013**, *23*, 1150–1155.

41. Penatti, O.A.; Nogueira, K.; dos Santos, J.A. Do deep features generalize from everyday objects to remote sensing and aerial scenes domains? In Proceedings of the IEEE Conference on Computer Vision and Pattern Recognition Workshops, Boston, MA, USA, 7–12 January 2015; pp. 44–51.

42. Krizhevsky, A.; Sutskever, I.; Hinton, G.E. Imagenet classification with deep convolutional neural networks. In Proceedings of the Advances in Neural Information Processing Systems, Stateline, NC, USA, 3–8 December 2012; pp. 1097–1105.

43. Szegedy, C.; Liu, W.; Jia, Y.; Sermanet, P.; Reed, S.; Anguelov, D.; Erhan, D.; Vanhoucke, V.; Rabinovich, A. Going deeper with convolutions. In Proceedings of the IEEE Conference on Computer Vision and Pattern Recognition, Boston, MA, USA, 8–10 June 2015; pp. 1–9.

44. Long, J.; Shelhamer, E.; Darrell, T. Fully convolutional networks for semantic segmentation. In Proceedings of the IEEE Conference on Computer Vision and Pattern Recognition, Boston, MA, USA, 8–10 June 2015; pp. 3431–3440.

45. Nair, V.; Hinton, G.E. Rectified linear units improve restricted boltzmann machines. In Proceedings of the 27th International Conference on Machine Learning (ICML-10), Haifa, Israel, 21–24 June 2010; pp. 807–814.

46. Paisitkriangkrai, S.; Sherrah, J.; Janney, P.; Hengel, V.D. Effective semantic pixel labelling with convolutional networks and conditional random fields. In Proceedings of the IEEE Conference on Computer Vision and Pattern Recognition Workshops, Boston, MA, USA, 7–12 June 2015; pp. 36–43.

47. Papandreou, G.; Kokkinos, I.; Savalle, P.A. Untangling local and global deformations in deep convolutional networks for image classification and sliding window detection. *arXiv preprint* **2014**, arXiv:1412.0296.

48. Jia, Y.; Shelhamer, E.; Donahue, J.; Karayev, S.; Long, J.; Girshick, R.; Guadarrama, S.; Darrell, T. Caffe: Convolutional Architecture for Fast Feature Embedding. *arXiv preprint* **2014**, arXiv:1408.5093.

49. Shi, S.; Wang, Q.; Xu, P.; Chu, X. Benchmarking State-of-the-Art Deep Learning Software Tools. *arXiv preprint* **2016**, arXiv:1608.07249.

50. Zeiler, M. ADADELTA: An Adaptive Learning Rate Method. *arXiv* **2012**, arXiv:1212.5701.

51. Bayram, B.; Bayraktar, H.; Helvaci, C.; Acar, U. Coastline change detection using CORONA, SPOT and IRS 1D images. *Int. Arch. Photogramm. Remote Sens.* **2004**, *35*, 437–441.

52. Hu, Q.; Wu, W.; Xia, T.; Yu, Q.; Yang, P.; Li, Z.; Song, Q. Exploring the use of Google Earth imagery and object-based methods in land use/cover mapping. *Remote Sens.* **2013**, *5*, 6026–6042.

53. He, K.; Zhang, X.; Ren, S.; Sun, J. Deep residual learning for image recognition. In Proceedings of the IEEE Conference on Computer Vision and Pattern Recognition, Las Vegas, NV, USA, 26 June–1 July 2016; pp. 770–778.

54. Koltun, V. Efficient inference in fully connected crfs with gaussian edge potentials. *Adv. Neural Inf. Process. Syst.* **2011**, 109–117.

55. Freund, Y.; Schapire, R.E. A desicion-theoretic generalization of on-line learning and an application to boosting. In Proceedings of the European Conference on Computational Learning Theory, Barcelona, Spain, 13–15 March 1995; Springer: Berlin, Germany; pp. 23–37.

56. Shotton, J.; Winn, J.; Rother, C.; Criminisi, A. Textonboost: Joint appearance, shape and context modeling for multi-class object recognition and segmentation. In Proceedings of the European Conference on Computer Vision, Amsterdam, The Netherlands, 8–16 October 2006; Springer: Berlin, Germany; pp. 1–15.

57. Li, X.; Damen, M.C. Coastline change detection with satellite remote sensing for environmental management of the Pearl River Estuary, China. *J. Mar. Syst.* **2010**, *82*, S54–S61.

58. Ji, R.; Lu, Y.; Zuo, L. Coastline change detection of the Bohai Bay using satellite remote sensing. In Proceedings of the 2011 International Conference on Remote Sensing, Environment and Transportation Engineering (RSETE), Nanjing, China, 24–26 June 2011; pp. 168–171.

59. Sheng, G.; Yang, W.; Deng, X.; He, C.; Cao, Y.; Sun, H. Coastline detection in synthetic aperture radar (SAR) images by integrating watershed transformation and controllable gradient vector flow (GVF) snake model. *IEEE J. Ocean. Eng.* **2012**, *37*, 375–383.

60. Ding, X.; Zou, X.; Yu, T. Coastline detection in SAR images using discriminant cuts segmentation. In Proceedings of the IOP Conference Series: Earth and Environmental Science, Beijing, China, 7–8 July 2016; Volume 46, p. 012035.

Article

A Fuzzy-GA Based Decision Making System for Detecting Damaged Buildings from High-Spatial Resolution Optical Images

Milad Janalipour and Ali Mohammadzadeh *

Faculty of Geodesy & Geomatics Engineering, K. N. Toosi University of Technology, Tehran 1996715433, Iran;
m_janalipour89@yahoo.com
* Correspondence: almoh2@gmail.com; Tel.: +98-218-8888-8445

Academic Editors: Qi Wang, Nicolas H. Younan, Carlos López-Martínez, Soe Myint and Prasad S. Thenkabail
Received: 14 January 2017; Accepted: 1 April 2017; Published: 20 April 2017

Abstract: In this research, a semi-automated building damage detection system is addressed under the umbrella of high-spatial resolution remotely sensed images. The aim of this study was to develop a semi-automated fuzzy decision making system using Genetic Algorithm (GA). Our proposed system contains four main stages. In the first stage, post-event optical images were pre-processed. In the second stage, textural features were extracted from the pre-processed post-event optical images using Haralick texture extraction method. Afterwards, in the third stage, a semi-automated Fuzzy-GA (Fuzzy Genetic Algorithm) decision making system was used to identify damaged buildings from the extracted texture features. In the fourth stage, a comprehensive sensitivity analysis was performed to achieve parameters of GA leading to more accurate results. Finally, the accuracy of results was assessed using check and test samples. The proposed system was tested over the 2010 Haiti earthquake (Area 1 and Area 2) and the 2003 Bam earthquake (Area 3). The proposed system resulted in overall accuracies of 76.88 ± 1.22%, 65.43 ± 0.29%, and 90.96 ± 0.15% over Area 1, Area 2, and Area 3, respectively. On the one hand, based on the concept of the proposed Fuzzy-GA decision making system, the automation level of this system is higher than other existing systems. On the other hand, based on the accuracy of our proposed system and four advanced machine learning techniques, i.e., bagging, boosting, random forests, and support vector machine, in the detection of damaged buildings, it seems that our proposed system is robust and efficient.

Keywords: building damage detection; Fuzzy-GA decision making system; machine learning techniques; optical remotely sensed images; sensitivity analysis; texture analysis

---

1. Introduction

Detecting damaged buildings after a massive disaster in a robust manner is a critical task, because it helps relief and rescue teams to manage related works accurately and precisely and then may reduce losses. Hence, the production of accurate building damage maps after disasters would help relief and rescue teams in emergency situations. Remote sensing (RS) data is one of the sources which can be used for generating building damage maps. Due to specific characteristics of the RS data such as its high temporal frequency and the availability of various sensors with different spatial and spectral resolutions, it plays an important role in producing building damage maps. Satellite optical images, as a source of the RS data, have been frequently used to produce damage maps [1]. In this study, we present a novel semi-automated decision making system based on the fuzzy theory and genetic algorithm (GA) in order to produce the building damage maps. Our proposed system can be used as a knowledge extraction tool in future works. Knowledge extraction is a necessary stage in order to convert a semi-structured problem into a structured one [2].

1.1. Literature Review

The existing damage detection methods can be discussed from viewpoints of data used and methodology. From the perspective of data used, researchers employed different sources of RS data, including Light Detection and Ranging (LiDAR) [3], Synthetic Aperture Radar (SAR) [4–9], and optical imagery [10–12]. Optical satellite imagery is one of the useful sources in building damage detection process. Disasters may damage components of a building. A building's roof is one of these components. Optical satellite sensors usually observe the roof of buildings. The spectral signature is the outcome of an optical satellite sensor. The spectral signature of each phenomenon is unique. Therefore, spectral signatures of a damaged roof and an intact roof are different from each other. For this reason, spectral signatures obtained from optical satellite sensors or their extracted features are suitable for detecting damaged buildings [2,13].

From the viewpoint of the methodology, presenting a comprehensive analysis about existing methods used in damage detection application is a difficult task, because there are many research studies. Therefore, we attempt to mention the related works to our research. In this study, we propose a fuzzy decision making system in order to detect damaged buildings from textural features extracted from post-event optical images. Hence, the literature review is presented in three parts: (1) the use of optical images for detecting damaged areas, (2) the role of textural features for detecting damaged areas, and (3) fuzzy systems used for detecting damaged areas.

Some researchers attempted to specify the role of optical images in damage detection application. Eguchi and Mansouri (2005) focused on investigating and categorizing papers that used RS technology for detecting buildings damaged after the 2003 Bam earthquake. It was concluded that detecting regional damages by RS technology is possible [14]. Voigt et al. (2011) presented results concerning actions of the German Aerospace Center (DLR) after the 2010 Haiti earthquake. It was deduced that extracting building damage maps even with high spatial-resolution optical satellite images is not an easy task and needs several human experts [15]. Lu et al. (2012) implemented a building damage detection method based on mono-temporal very high-spatial resolution optical images. In this paper, integrating manual and automatic interpretations resulted in a robust building damage map [16]. Tiede et al. (2011) used shadow information extracted from pre- and post-event optical images for generating a damage map after the 2010 Haiti earthquake. The proposed method was able to create the damage map of the Carrefour area after 12 h [17]. Lemoine et al. (2013) used aerial optical data for providing a realistic estimate from damaged buildings. Using the aerial optical data instead of satellite data was the key objective of the presented study to obtain more accurate results [18]. Based on the presented research works, it appears that optical data is a suitable source for detecting damaged buildings. However, owing to the complexity of this problem (i.e., damage detection), the role of experts is important and undeniable.

Many researches have benefited from textural features extracted from the RS data for identifying areas damaged after disasters. The ability of textural features in measuring spectral and height variations in the spatial domain over RS data is the main reason for use of them in the damage detection problem. Table 1 briefly depicts researches that used textural features in damage detection applications, especially for building damage detection [1] and road damage detection [19]. The existing researches can be discussed from three viewpoints. The used feature extraction method is the first viewpoint. From this perspective, Laws mask [1], Haralick [20], Multivariate variogram [21], 1st statistical [19], and Gabor filter [22] feature extraction methods were frequently employed to produce textural features in previous research works. Moreover, from the second viewpoint, textural features were extracted from different remotely sensed data including optical images, light detection and ranging (LiDAR) data, and synthetic aperture radar (SAR) data. Based on the literature, textural features extracted from pre- and/or post-event optical images were widely employed for detecting damaged areas. From the third viewpoint, researchers utilized textural features for improving the accuracy of the final damage map. In fact, it seems that textural features positively affect the performance of machine learning techniques and decision making systems in identifying damaged areas.

Table 1. A brief presentation from previous research studies that used textural features in damage detection applications.

Reference	Textural Features Used	Remotely Sensed Data
[1]	Laws mask	Pre- and post-event optical images
[23]	Haralick	Pre- and post-event optical images
[20]	Haralick	Pre- and post-event optical images
[21]	Multivariate variogram	Pre- and post-event optical images and post-event LiDAR data
[22]	Gabor Filter	Pre- and post-event optical images
[19]	1st statistical features, Gabor features and Haralick features	Pre- and post-event optical images
[24]	Multivariate variogram	Pre- and post-event optical images
[25]	Haralick	Pre- and post-event digital elevation models
[26]	Haralick	Post-event SAR data
[27]	1st statistical features, Gabor features and Haralick features	Pre- and post-event optical images
[28]	Haralick	Pre- and post-event optical images

After extracting features, it is necessary to use a classifier or machine learning technique or decision making system for creating a relation between the extracted features and the damage extent of buildings. To this end, some researchers used advanced and non-parametric classifiers. Chesnel et al. (2008) utilized the Support Vector Machine (SVM) classifier to partition the feature space for detecting damaged and undamaged buildings [22]. Li et al. (2010) used the One-Class Support Vector Machine (OCSVM) classifier to obtain damaged areas from high spatial-resolution optical images [21]. Dubois and Lepage (2014) employed a multilayer backpropagation perceptron neural network to detect damaged buildings after the 2010 Haiti earthquake [1]. In addition to advanced classifiers, based on Table 2, some researchers used fuzzy-based decision making systems in the damage detection process [2,13]. The fuzzy-based decision making systems are usually employed in issues where experts want to model their knowledge. Damage detection is one of these issues. Producing damage maps using experts after disasters in a manual manner proves our claim. To the best of our knowledge, in the damage detection application, the fuzzy-based decision making systems can be used for two main procedures including: (1) land use/cover classification [29,30] and (2) modeling the damage extent of buildings from the extracted features [2,13]. Ural et al. (2011) employed a fuzzy classifier in order to map buildings and their rubble after the 2010 Haiti earthquake in a robust manner [30]. Moreover, researches have used Mamdani fuzzy inference systems (MFISs) as a decision making system for modeling the damage extent of buildings [19,27,28]. In these researches, parameters of fuzzy inference systems were manually adjusted in a trial and error manner that is a time consuming task. In these cases, the accuracy of results completely relies on the selected parameters. For this reason, Janalipour, M. et al. [2,13] used semi-automated Sugeno fuzzy decision making systems in order to detect damage and changed areas. The use of these systems was a good solution for improving the automation level of fuzzy systems, but it is a difficult task to extract knowledge from a Sugeno fuzzy system due to the structure of its rules [31]. Knowledge extraction is an important stage for converting a semi-structured problem (i.e., the damage detection) into a structured one. For further study on damage detection methods, we encourage readers to refer to [32–34].

Table 2. A brief presentation from previous research works which used fuzzy inference systems in damage detection application.

Reference	Type of Fuzzy System	Automation Level
[19]	Mamdani	Manually
[28]	Mamdani	Manually
[27]	Mamdani	Manually
[35]	Mamdani	Manually
[13]	Sugeno	Semi-automated
[2]	Sugeno	Semi-automated

1.2. Research Aims

In this study, three important objectives are satisfied. Based on the previous works, researchers widely used Mamdani fuzzy decision making systems for detecting damaged areas whose parameters of these systems were manually chosen in a trial and error basis which is a time consuming task. Moreover, the robustness of outcomes relies on the selected parameters. For this reason, Janalipour, M. et al. [2,13] proposed a semi-automated Sugeno fuzzy decision making system. However, for knowledge extraction, the Sugeno fuzzy system is not appropriate due to the structure of its rules. To this end, it is necessary to employ a semi-automated Mamdani fuzzy system. However, there is no semi-automated Mamdani fuzzy system. Therefore, it is essential to propose a semi-automated (or fully-automated) Mamdani fuzzy decision making system to detect damaged areas. In the first and main objective, we develop a semi-automated Mamdani fuzzy decision making system using Genetic Algorithm (GA). Based on the previous researches [2,13], sensitivity analysis plays an important role in identifying the appropriate parameters of a system leading to more accurate results. In the mentioned researches, a step-by-step sensitivity analysis method was used. However, it is necessary to simultaneously test all parameters of a system, because it permits us to consider the relationship between changes of all the parameters. For this reason, in the second objective, we study the effect of the simultaneous change of all parameters of the system on the final result. To investigate the robustness and effectiveness of our semi-automated Mamdani fuzzy decision making system, we compare results of this system with four advanced machine learning techniques including random forests (RF), bagging, boosting, and support vector machine (SVM)—that is our third objective.

2. Materials and Methods

In this section is included information about study areas and data used and description about our proposed methodology.

2.1. The First Study Area: The 2010 Haiti Earthquake

Port-au-Prince city is the first study area, where an earthquake occurred on 12 January 2010. Port-au-Prince is the capital of Haiti. Two areas including Area 1 and Area 2 were chosen over Port-au-Prince.

The previous research studies proved that ancillary information such as a pre-event vector map improves the accuracy of damage detection methods [36–38]. On the other hand, the use of the pre-event map in our proposed system is necessary, because it is difficult to find the footprint of buildings on post-earthquake optical images. For these reasons, a pre-event building map was injected into our methodology. There are some old-vector maps in the Haiti area such as [39]. To update the old-vector map, pre-event Geoeye-1 and IKONOS-2 images were employed. To this end, the old-vector map was updated as much as possible by an expert. Moreover, in the first study area, an ortho-rectified, pansharpened and georeferenced post-event Geoeye-1 image acquired on 13 January 2010 with a spatial resolution of 50 cm and three spectral bands (blue, green, and red) was employed.

2.2. The Second Study Area: The 2003 Bam Earthquake

Bam city is the second study area, a city located in southwestern Iran, where an earthquake occurred on 26 December 2003. The post- earthquake pansharpened QuickBird image and pre-event digital vector map of the Bam area were used in this study. The post-earthquake image was acquired on 3 January 2004 and also has 61 cm spatial resolution and four spectral bands (red, green, blue, and near infrared). The second study area has about 400 buildings with different damage extent. The pre-event digital vector map with a scale of 1:500 was produced by the National Cartographic Center (NCC) of Iran in 1994, which was updated using an expert according to [13].

2.3. Methodology

Our proposed damage detection system is presented in four main stages according to Figure 1. In stage "1", post-event optical images are pre-processed. In stage "2", Haralick texture features are extracted from the pre-processed optical images using the pre-event map and related equations. In stage "3", a Fuzzy- GA (Genetic Algorithm) based decision making system is developed to estimate the damage extent of buildings from the extracted texture features. In stage "4", a comprehensive sensitivity analysis is performed to achieve the best parameters leading to more accurate results. Finally, the accuracy of results is firstly assessed and then the building damage map is obtained. The aforementioned stages are presented in more detail below.

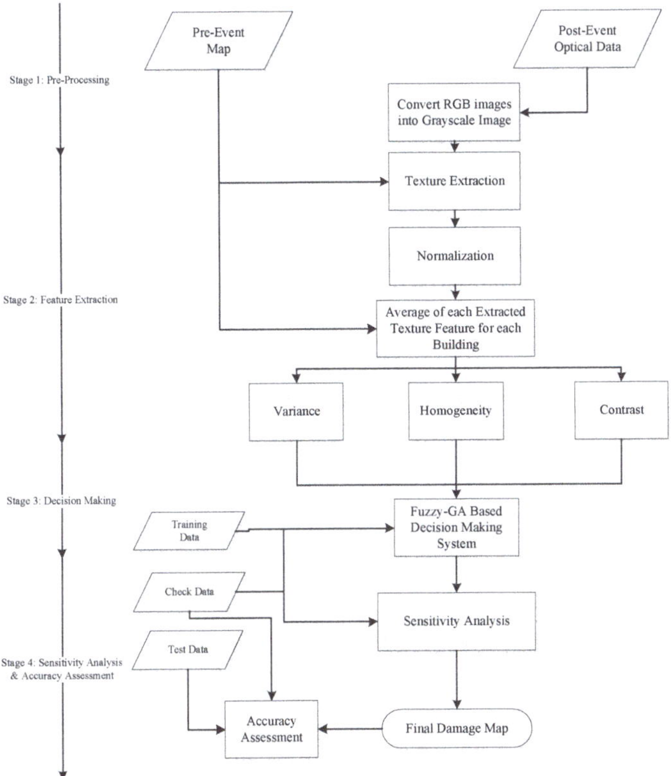

Figure 1. The workflow of our semi-automated damage detection system in this study.

2.3.1. Stage 1: Pre-Processing

Pre-processing is one of the important stages in building damage detection. Geo-rectification and pansharpening are two of the important pre-processes, which should be performed on the post-event optical images. Georeferencing and pansharpening were performed on the post-event optical image of the Haiti earthquake. Moreover, the mentioned pre-processes were performed on the post-event optical image of the Bam earthquake according to [13].

As another pre-process, based on previous research works [2], the correlation between corresponding textural features extracted from spectral bands (i.e., red, blue, and green) is high. Hence, numerous and correlated features result, which increase the computational cost of the proposed method. For this reason, a grayscale image is produced from red, blue, and green bands using

Equation (1) (please see [40] for further study about Equation (1)). Textural features are extracted from the grayscale band.

$$E = 0.2989 \times R_r + 0.5870 \times R_g + 0.1140 \times R_b \tag{1}$$

where, R_r, R_g, R_b, and E are the reflectance value of the red, green, blue, and resulting grayscale bands, respectively.

2.3.2. Stage 2: Feature Extraction

Extracting textural features is the main process of the feature extraction stage. The potential of textural features in measuring variations of digital numbers in the spatial domain enables us to use them in satellite image processing, especially after natural hazards. Natural hazards suddenly cause damage of objects of the earth's surface leading to reflectance changes in the spatial domain. Therefore, the textural features extracted from remotely sensed optical data are widely used for detecting damaged areas. Based on previous works presented in the literature review section, different texture extraction methods have been used in damage detection applications. In most of the previous works [20,23], Haralick features were widely chosen for extracting textural features. For this reason, these features are also used in our study. For further study on the Haralick texture extraction method, please see [41,42].

In this study, in order to detect damaged buildings from textural features, variance, homogeneity, and contrast features were chosen, which can be calculated from Equation (2), Equation (3), and Equation (4), respectively. The selection of these features was based on three reasons. First of all, three texture features with three linguistic terms and Gaussian membership functions (MFs) generate 24 unknown parameters regarding MFs in a Mamdani fuzzy inference system which should be simultaneously set. It seems that the number of unknown parameters is sufficient to test an optimization algorithm and the selection of them by an expert is a difficult task. For the second reason, based on equations of the mentioned features, it appears that correlation among the selected features is low. Finally, the performance of our decision making system and advanced machine learning techniques would be investigated in similar conditions (i.e., with three texture features). Hence, the selection of the mentioned texture features is within the path of objectives of this study.

$$Variance = \sum_{i=0}^{G-1} (i - \mu)^2 P(i,j) \tag{2}$$

$$Homogenity = \sum_{i=0}^{G-1} \sum_{j=0}^{G-1} \frac{P(i,j)}{1 + (i-j)^2} \tag{3}$$

$$Contrast = \sum_{i=0}^{G-1} \sum_{j=0}^{G-1} (i-j)^2 \times P(i,j) \tag{4}$$

where, μ is the mean value of gray-levels in an area selected for producing texture features. Moreover, P and G are the probability matrix and the number of image gray-levels, respectively.

There are two important points about extracting textural features in this study. For the first point, for preserving the negative effects of non-building pixels on extracted textural features, building pixels are specified by the pre-event map and are only used to extract textural features. For the second point, to compare the three mentioned texture features, they should be standardized. Hence, Equation (5) is employed to standardize the extracted textural features.

$$x_i = \frac{D_i - D_i^{\min}}{D_i^{\max} - D_i^{\min}}, \ i = 1 : 3 \tag{5}$$

where, x_i is the ith standardized texture feature; $D_i^{\min}$ and $D_i^{\max}$ are the minimum and maximum values of the ith texture feature; and D_i is an arbitrary value of the ith texture feature.

2.3.3. Stage 3: Decision Making

After extracting textural features, it is necessary to employ a decision making system [43] or a machine learning technique to provide a relation between the extracted features and the damage extent of buildings. In this study, a decision making system based on MFIS and GA is used to provide the mentioned relation. MFIS was firstly proposed by Zadeh [44]. In a MFIS, initially, crisp input values are converted into fuzzy values by input MFs. This is called "fuzzification". In fact, fuzzification is a mapping process that is performed using membership functions. In this process, membership functions act as connectors among crisp and fuzzy spaces. Then, using fuzzy values, the inference system and existing rules in the fuzzy rule base, fuzzy output values are generated. Finally, the fuzzy output values are transformed into crisp output values by a defuzzification method [31].

In general, a MFIS is a function of three main parameters according to Equation (6) including: parameters of membership functions (C_1), rules (C_2), and parameters of the inference system (C_3). Therefore, in designing a MFIS, two essential tasks must be performed by an expert: (1) designing rules of the fuzzy rule base and parameters of the inference system, and (2) designing and selecting type and parameters of input and output MFs. In this study, we focus on the second task, because the number of rules in our study is minor and can be easily selected and also an expert could select the small parameters of the inference system.

$$Mamdani\ Fuzzy\ System = F(C_1, C_2, C_3) \tag{6}$$

For expressing the importance of the second mentioned task, an example is employed here. Please note that this example is also used as a MFIS in our damage detection method. A MFIS with three inputs and one output (its MF type is Gaussian) is presented in Figure 2. Suppose three rules similar to Equations (7) to (9) have been designed by an expert. Based on these equations, we can express that C_1 is a function of some unknown parameters (Equation (10)).

$$If\left(X_1\ is\exp\left(\frac{-(X_1-m_1)^2}{2\sigma_1^2}\right)and\ X_2\ is\exp\left(\frac{-(X_2-m_4)^2}{2\sigma_4^2}\right)and\ X_3\ is\exp\left(\frac{-(X_3-m_7)^2}{2\sigma_7^2}\right)\right)$$
$$Then\ Z\ is\exp\left(\frac{-(Z-m_{10})^2}{2\sigma_{10}^2}\right) \tag{7}$$

$$If\left(X_1\ is\exp\left(\frac{-(X_1-m_2)^2}{2\sigma_2^2}\right)and\ X_2\ is\exp\left(\frac{-(X_2-m_5)^2}{2\sigma_5^2}\right)and\ X_3\ is\exp\left(\frac{-(X_3-m_8)^2}{2\sigma_8^2}\right)\right)$$
$$Then\ Z\ is\exp\left(\frac{-(Z-m_{11})^2}{2\sigma_{11}^2}\right) \tag{8}$$

$$If\left(X_1\ is\exp\left(\frac{-(X_1-m_3)^2}{2\sigma_3^2}\right)and\ X_2\ is\exp\left(\frac{-(X_2-m_6)^2}{2\sigma_6^2}\right)and\ X_3\ is\exp\left(\frac{-(X_3-m_9)^2}{2\sigma_9^2}\right)\right)$$
$$Then\ Z\ is\exp\left(\frac{-(Z-m_{12})^2}{2\sigma_{12}^2}\right) \tag{9}$$

$$C_1 = F(m_1, \sigma_1, \ldots, m_{12}, \sigma_{12}) \tag{10}$$

where, X_1, X_2, and X_3 are input linguistic variables 1 to 3, respectively and Z is the output linguistic variable. Moreover, m_i and σ_i are the mean and standard deviation of a Gaussian membership function.

According to Figure 2 and the designed rules, 24 unknown parameters of MFs (Equation (11)) must be set by an expert. From our viewpoint, the procedure of selection of 24 unknown parameters in a continuous-space is an optimization problem. For this reason, in this study, Genetic Algorithm (GA), as an optimization algorithm, is employed to select unknown parameters [45,46]. The ability of GA in selecting optimum answers was the main reason for the selection of this algorithm. In fact, in this research, MFIS and GA are integrated to select appropriate parameters of MFs leading to the best result. In the following, concepts of GA and its integration with the MFIS are presented.

$$Unknown\ Parameters = \begin{bmatrix} m_1 & \sigma_1 & \cdots & m_{12} & \sigma_{12} \end{bmatrix}_{1\times24} \tag{11}$$

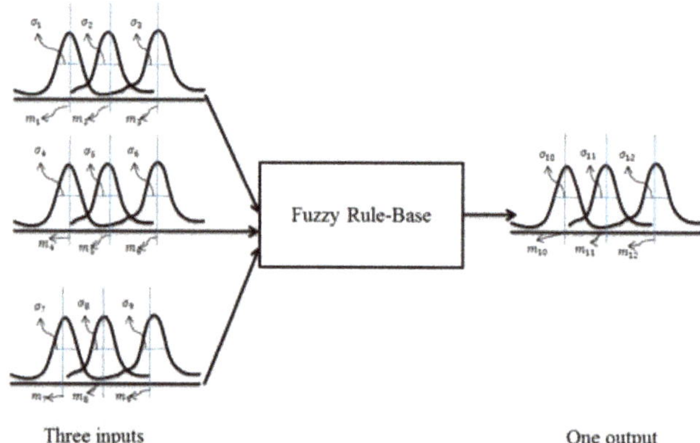

Figure 2. A schematic presentation of a MFIS with three inputs and one output and its MFs.

Genetic Algorithm (GA) is based on the mechanism exhibited by nature incorporating the robustness of biological systems as presented by Charles Darwin [47]. This algorithm is one of the powerful artificial intelligence algorithms, which selects the optimal answer using a random searching method in the search-space.

To find the optimal unknown parameters regarding MFs of a fuzzy inference system using GA, five main steps are employed in GA. The employed steps are presented below:

The first step: initial parameters regarding MFs of the fuzzy system are generated in a random manner. Suppose the number of the population is equal to k and the generated parameters are:

$$positions = \begin{bmatrix} m_1^1 & \sigma_1^1 & \cdots & m_{12}^1 & \sigma_{12}^1 \\ \vdots & \vdots & \ddots & \vdots & \vdots \\ m_1^k & \sigma_1^k & \cdots & m_{12}^k & \sigma_{12}^k \end{bmatrix}_{k \times 24} = \begin{bmatrix} \text{the 1st population} \\ \vdots \\ \text{the kth population} \end{bmatrix} \tag{12}$$

After generating the initial parameters, it is necessary to use a cost function to calculate the efficiency of each population. It should be considered that the fitness function and objective function terms are also used instead of the cost function one. The cost function is at the heart of our proposed system. The integration of the fuzzy system and GA is the main task of this function. Moreover, the cost function is responsible for assessing population. In this study, to obtain the cost of population, some training and check samples according to Equations (13) and (14) are considered. The duty of training samples is to learn the fuzzy-GA system. Furthermore, check samples are employed to prevent an over-learning problem.

$$training\ samples = \begin{bmatrix} x_{t1}^1 & x_{t2}^1 & x_{t3}^1 & z_t{}^1 \\ \vdots & \vdots & \vdots & \vdots \\ x_{t1}^s & x_{t2}^s & x_{t3}^s & z_t{}^s \end{bmatrix}_{s \times 4} = \begin{bmatrix} X_1^{train} & X_2^{train} & X_3^{train} & Z^{train} \end{bmatrix} \tag{13}$$

$$check\ samples = \begin{bmatrix} x_{c1}^1 & x_{c2}^1 & x_{c3}^1 & z_c{}^1 \\ \vdots & \vdots & \vdots & \vdots \\ x_{c1}^u & x_{c2}^u & x_{c3}^u & z_c{}^u \end{bmatrix}_{u \times 4} = \begin{bmatrix} X_1^{check} & X_2^{check} & X_3^{check} & Z^{check} \end{bmatrix} \tag{14}$$

where, x_{t1}^h, x_{t2}^h, x_{t3}^h are values of textural features regarding the hth training sample. Moreover, $z_t{}^h$ is the damage extent of the hth training sample. x_{c1}^h, x_{c2}^h, x_{c3}^h are values of textural features regarding the hth check sample. Moreover, $z_c{}^h$ is the damage extent of the hth check sample. Furthermore, s and u are the number of training samples and the number of check samples, respectively.

To estimate the cost of each population for training samples (Equation (15)), at first, the parameters of the MFs are updated using the population (Equation (16)). For population r, the updated MFIS is represented by Equation (17). Then, using the updated MFIS and Equation (18), the damage extent of training samples is obtained from Equation (19). Finally, the cost of population r ($cost_{train}^r$) obtained from the training samples is calculated from Equation (20). The cost of check samples is also estimated in the same way.

$$Costs_{train} = \begin{bmatrix} cost_{train}^1 \\ \vdots \\ cost_{train}^k \end{bmatrix}_{k \times 1} \tag{15}$$

$$C_1^r = F(m_1^r, \sigma_1^r, \ldots, m_{12}^r, \sigma_{12}^r) \; ; \; 1 \leq r \leq k \tag{16}$$

$$Mamdani\ Fuzzy\ System^r = F(C_1^r, C_2, C_3) \tag{17}$$

$$\hat{Z} = Mamdani\ Fuzzy\ System\ (X_1^{train}, X_2^{train}, X_3^{train}) \tag{18}$$

$$\begin{bmatrix} \hat{Z}^1 \\ \vdots \\ \hat{Z}^s \end{bmatrix} = \begin{bmatrix} Mamdani\ Fuzzy\ System^r\ (x_{t1}^1, x_{t2}^1, x_{t3}^1) \\ \vdots \\ Mamdani\ Fuzzy\ System^r\ (x_{t1}^s, x_{t2}^s, x_{t3}^s) \end{bmatrix}_{s \times 1} \tag{19}$$

$$cost_{train}^r = \frac{1}{s} \times \sqrt{\sum_{i=1}^{s} (z_t^s - \hat{Z}^s)^2}, \; r = 1, \ldots, k \tag{20}$$

where, C_1^r and *Mamdani Fuzzy System*^{r} are parameters of MFs obtained from population r and the fuzzy inference system updated from C_1^r, respectively.

The second step: In this step, new MF parameters are obtained from crossover function and population generated by the previous step. Crossover is one of the important functions in GA, which is responsible for generating new children (parameters of fuzzy systems) from their parents. To generate new children, the number of uses of crossover function ($n_{crossover}$) should be specified. To this end, at first, parameter α is calculated from the crossover rate and the number of population (*population*) using Equation (21). Then, the number of uses of crossover function is obtained from Equation (22). For generating new MF parameters from the crossover function, first, two random parents (like m_i and n_i) are chosen. Afterwards, new children are achieved from Equation (23). Since unknown parameters were defined in specific ranges, there are two conditions according to Equations (24) and (25) for undefined values. Finally, by using Equations (15) to (20), costs of the new children are calculated and inserted into Equation (26) [47].

$$\alpha = \frac{crossover\ rate \times population}{2} \tag{21}$$

$$n_{crossover} = \max\{n \in \mathbb{Z} | n \leq \alpha\} \tag{22}$$

$positions_{crossover}$

$$= \begin{bmatrix} \gamma_1 \times positions(m_1, :) + (1 - \gamma_1) \times positions(n_1, :) \\ \gamma_1 \times positions(n_1, :) + (1 - \gamma_1) \times positions(m_1, :) \\ \vdots \\ \gamma_{n_{crossover}} \times positions(m_{n_{crossover}}, :) + (1 - \gamma_{n_{crossover}}) \times positions(n_{n_{crossover}}, :) \\ \gamma_{n_{crossover}} \times positions(n_{n_{crossover}}, :) + (1 - \gamma_{n_{crossover}}) \times positions(m_{n_{crossover}}, :) \end{bmatrix}_{(2 \times n_{crossover}) \times 24}$$

$$= \begin{bmatrix} \overline{m}_1^1 & \overline{\sigma}_1^1 & \cdots & \overline{m}_{12}^1 & \overline{\sigma}_{12}^1 \\ \overline{m}_1^2 & \overline{\sigma}_1^2 & \cdots & \overline{m}_{12}^2 & \overline{\sigma}_{12}^2 \\ \vdots & \vdots & \ddots & \vdots & \vdots \\ \overline{m}_1^{2 \times n_{crossover} - 1} & \overline{\sigma}_1^{2 \times n_{crossover} - 1} & \cdots & \overline{m}_{12}^{2 \times n_{crossover} - 1} & \overline{\sigma}_{12}^{2 \times n_{crossover} - 1} \\ \overline{m}_1^{2 \times n_{crossover}} & \overline{\sigma}_1^{2 \times n_{crossover}} & \cdots & \overline{m}_{12}^{2 \times n_{crossover}} & \overline{\sigma}_{12}^{2 \times n_{crossover}} \end{bmatrix} \tag{23}$$

$$\overline{\sigma}_i = \begin{cases} 0.01 \ if \ \overline{\sigma}_i < 0 \\ 0.5 \ if \ \overline{\sigma}_i > 0.5 \end{cases} \tag{24}$$

$$\overline{m}_i = \begin{cases} 0 \ if \ \overline{m}_i < 0 \\ 1 \ if \ \overline{m}_i > 1 \end{cases} \tag{25}$$

$$Costs_{crossover} = \begin{bmatrix} cost^1 \\ \vdots \\ cost^{2 \times n_{crossover}} \end{bmatrix}_{(2 \times n_{crossover}) \times 1} \tag{26}$$

where, γ_1 is a random number between -0.1 and 1.1. $\overline{\sigma}_i$ and $\overline{m}_i$ are the variance and mean of the *i*th variable achieved from the crossover function, respectively.

The third step: In this step, one of the parameters of a population is changed using the mutation function. The mutation is another important function in GA. The mutation function has an undeniable role in solving the local minimum problem in GA. To generate new children by the mutation function, the number of uses of the mutation function ($n_{mutation}$) should be specified. To this end, at first, parameter β is calculated from the mutation rate and the number of population using Equation (27). Then, the number of uses of the mutation function is obtained from Equation (28). For each use of the mutation function, one random population is selected. Afterwards, a new child is achieved. Equation (29) depicts all new children achieved from the mutation function. Undefined values of variables are corrected using Equations (24) and (25). Finally, using Equations (15) to (20), costs of the new children are calculated and inserted into Equation (30).

$$\beta = \frac{mutation \ rate \times population}{2} \tag{27}$$

$$n_{mutation} = \max\{n \in \mathbb{Z} | n \leq \beta\} \tag{28}$$

$$positions_{mutation} = \begin{bmatrix} m_1 & \sigma_1 + sigma \times rand_1 & \cdots & m_{12} & \sigma_{12} \\ \vdots & \vdots & \ddots & \vdots & \vdots \\ m_1 + sigma \times rand_{n_{mutation}} & \sigma_1 & \cdots & m_{12} & \sigma_{12} \end{bmatrix}_{n_{mutation} \times 24} \tag{29}$$

$$Costs_{mutation} = \begin{bmatrix} cost^1 \\ \vdots \\ cost^{n_{mutation}} \end{bmatrix}_{(n_{mutation}) \times 1} \tag{30}$$

where, $rand_i$ is a random number. Moreover, $sigma$ is calculated from Equation (31). Variables σ_i and m_i are defined respectively in a range of [0.01–0.5] and [0–1]. Because the range of the variable σ_i is lower than the variable m_i, sigma values of Equation (31) regarding these variables are different:

$$sigma = \begin{cases} 0.049 \ for \ variable \ \sigma_i \\ 0.1 \ for \ variable \ m_i \end{cases} \tag{31}$$

The fourth step: In this step, using elitism operator, GA is able to preserve the best answer of iterations. To this end, at first, all population and costs obtained from the previous steps are inserted in two pools according to Equations (32) and (33). Afterwards, they are sorted in descending order by Equation (34) (i.e., a population with the minimum cost value is the best answer). Finally, we select k population with minimum cost values as the best answers from the sorted population (Equation (35)). With the elitism operator, it is possible to preserve the best solutions and GA can be converged on the best solution. In fact, with deep insight into this step, we can conclude that the artificial intelligence of GA exists in the fourth step.

$$all \ poistions = [positions; positions_{crossover}; positions_{mutation}]_{(n_{mutation} + 2 \times n_{crossover} + k) \times 24} \tag{32}$$

$$Costs = [Costs_{train}, Costs_{crossover}, Costs_{mutation}] \tag{33}$$

$$all\ poistions = sort(all\ poistions, Costs) \tag{34}$$

$$positions = all\ poistions(1 : population, :) \tag{35}$$

The fifth step: The second, third and fourth steps should be repeated to obtain the best solution. The first row of Equation (35) is the best solution with the minimum cost value.

2.3.4. Stage 4: Damage Map and Accuracy Assessment

In order to assess the accuracy of the final damage maps, the confusion matrix and statistical descriptors extracted from this matrix are considered. To generate a confusion matrix, it is necessary to employ training, test, and check samples. To this end, the damage extent of some buildings was specified as training, test, and check samples. More information about these samples is presented in Section 3.2. After generating the confusion matrix, statistical descriptors are employed to specify the accuracy of results. For this purpose, some statistical descriptors, including overall, user, and producer accuracies extracted from the confusion matrix, are used to display the accuracy of the proposed system. Based on a sample confusion matrix presented in Table 3, the overall, user, and producer accuracies are calculated from Equations (36) to (38), respectively.

$$Overall\_Accuracy = \frac{a+d}{a+b+c+d} \tag{36}$$

$$User\_accuracy\_class1 = \frac{a}{a+c} \tag{37}$$

$$Producer\_accuracy\_class1 = \frac{a}{a+b} \tag{38}$$

Table 3. A sample confusion matrix.

	References	
	Class 1	Class 2
Class 1	a	b
Class 2	c	d

Sensitivity Analysis

A sensitivity analysis should be carried out to confirm the stability and the reliability of the proposed system's results with respect to changes of its parameters [48–50]. In this study, the sensitivity of the Fuzzy-GA is assessed against any changes in GA's parameters: (a) the number of iterations; (b) the number of population; (c) the mutation rate; and (d) the crossover rate. In the previous works [2,13], a step-by-step sensitivity analysis method was used. However, step-by-step sensitivity analysis methods are unable to consider simultaneous changes of parameters of a system [51]. For this reason, in this study, a grid-partitioning based sensitivity analysis method was performed to study the effect of change of parameters on the accuracy of the final results [52]. In this method, the mentioned parameters of GA are changed in a limited and meaningful range to achieve accurate results. The range of parameters was adjusted based on experimental results and our knowledge about GA.

3. Results

3.1. Feature Extraction Considerations

In the feature extraction stage, variance, homogeneity, and contrast features were extracted by producing the probability matrix (P) for a distance of 1 pixel, orientation angles of 0, 45, 90, and 135 degrees and a window size of 3 × 3. Our experimental results showed that increasing the window size and the distance parameter negatively affects the accuracy of the building damage detection methods. For this reason, the mentioned parameters were chosen for producing textural features. The textural features were finally calculated from the average of features obtained on all orientation angles.

3.2. The Number of Training, Test and Check Samples Used over Area 1, Area 2, and Area 3

Training, check, and test samples must be used in modeling and validation processes of the Mamdani fuzzy system. To this end, two different sources were employed to extract these samples from the Haiti and Bam areas. The Haiti building damage atlas (the first source) was used to collect the mentioned samples over the Haiti area (Area 1 and Area 2). In this atlas, buildings were classified as undamaged (D1), substantial to heavy damage (D3), very heavy damage (D4), and destruction (D5). Moreover, according to [13], the damage extent of buildings over the Bam area was specified using the visual interpretation of an expert on pre- and post-event high-spatial resolution images (the second source). Table 4 shows the number of training, check, and test samples selected over Area 1, Area 2, and Area 3.

Table 4. The number of training, check and test samples selected over Area 1, Area 2, and Area 3.

	Training Samples				Check Samples				Test Samples			
	D1	D3	D4	D5	D1	D3	D4	D5	D1	D3	D4	D5
Area 1	172	15	30	83	66	5	13	40	185	8	36	100
Area 2	380	22	196	102	118	10	61	35	530	43	268	142
Area 3	25	-	56	115	14	-	30	74	23	-	38	93

3.3. Considerations for Implementing the Fuzzy System

For implementing the fuzzy system, in this study, its parameters were adjusted according to Table 5. Based on the opinion of an expert about the number of linguistic terms and results presented to [2,13], it seems that a number of three MFs for each input or output variable are appropriate for building damage detection. Moreover, according to the previous works [2,13], the Gaussian MF is efficient and robust for damage detection application, therefore this function was also utilized in this study. Furthermore, 12 fuzzy rules were designed by an expert, which were employed over three selected areas. In addition, Min, Max, Min and Max operators were chosen for "and", "or", "aggregation" and "implication" methods, respectively.

Table 5. Parameters of Mamdani fuzzy inference system selected in this study.

Parameter Name	Fuzzy Parameters Selected
Number of MF for each input	3
Number of MF for each output	3
Type of input MF	Gaussian Function
Type of output MF	Gaussian Function
Number of iterations	Flexible
Defuzzification method	Centroid
"and" method	Min
"or" method	Max
Implication method	Min
Aggregation method	Max
Number of Rules	12

3.4. Sensitivity Analysis on Fuzzy-GA Parameters

In order to perform the sensitivity analysis of results with respect to GA parameters, including the number of iteration (it), the number of population (pop), the mutation rate (P_m) and the crossover rate (P_c), these parameters were varied in a limited range. Tables 6–8 depict the overall accuracy of our proposed system obtained from variations of GA parameters over Area 1, Area 2, and Area 3, respectively. The range of values of parameters was selected based on experimental results and our knowledge about GA. Here, our description is presented on the range of the selected values. In general, low mutation rates are selected in GA, because increasing the mutation rate leads GA into a random search method. For this reason, mutation rates 0.1, 0.2, and 0.3 were chosen in this study. In contrast with the mutation rate, the selection of high values for the crossover rate guaranties optimized solutions to be achieved in a speedy manner. Hence, crossover rates 0.7, 0.8, and 0.9 were selected. Furthermore, based on the diagram of convergence of GA (see Section 3.5), it seems that GA is approximately converged after the 100th iteration. Therefore, the sensitivity of results with respect to iterations 100, 200, and 300 was tested. Finally, based on the previous works [53], the effect of population 50, 150, and 250 on the accuracy of the proposed damage detection system was investigated.

Table 6. Overall accuracies achieved from variations of GA parameters over Area 1.

$pop \rightarrow$	50	50	50	150	150	150	250	250	250	$it \downarrow$
0.1	76%	73%	73%	77%	79%	79%	77%	79%	79%	100
0.2	76%	77%	74%	79%	77%	72%	79%	78%	77%	100
0.3	76%	75%	74%	76%	80%	77%	79%	73%	79%	100
0.1	73%	75%	75%	77%	76%	78%	77%	79%	79%	200
0.2	74%	77%	79%	77%	79%	77%	79%	79%	79%	200
0.3	77%	77%	78%	77%	73%	77%	79%	79%	77%	200
0.1	79%	78%	70%	75%	77%	77%	75%	73%	80%	300
0.2	77%	79%	77%	78%	79%	78%	78%	79%	77%	300
0.3	77%	79%	77%	77%	80%	78%	71%	71%	79%	300
$P_m \uparrow$	0.7	0.8	0.9	0.7	0.8	0.9	0.7	0.8	0.9	$\leftarrow P_c$

Table 7. Overall accuracies achieved from variations of GA parameters over Area 2.

$pop \rightarrow$	50	50	50	150	150	150	250	250	250	$it \downarrow$
0.1	65%	65%	65%	64%	66%	66%	64%	64%	64%	100
0.2	64%	67%	66%	64%	66%	66%	66%	66%	64%	100
0.3	65%	67%	66%	66%	66%	66%	66%	66%	66%	100
0.1	65%	65%	66%	65%	67%	66%	65%	65%	63%	200
0.2	65%	64%	67%	65%	65%	66%	66%	65%	66%	200
0.3	63%	65%	64%	67%	66%	66%	65%	66%	65%	200
0.1	66%	67%	66%	66%	65%	64%	66%	66%	65%	300
0.2	65%	67%	67%	65%	65%	65%	64%	65%	66%	300
0.3	65%	65%	66%	67%	67%	65%	66%	65%	65%	300
$P_m \uparrow$	0.7	0.8	0.9	0.7	0.8	0.9	0.7	0.8	0.9	$\leftarrow P_c$

Table 8. Overall accuracies achieved from variations of GA parameters over Area 3.

$pop \rightarrow$	50	50	50	150	150	150	250	250	250	$it \downarrow$
0.1	91%	91%	92%	90%	89%	90%	91%	90%	91%	100
0.2	91%	90%	90%	90%	91%	90%	91%	92%	92%	100
0.3	92%	90%	90%	89%	90%	92%	92%	90%	92%	100
0.1	90%	90%	90%	91%	91%	91%	90%	91%	91%	200
0.2	93%	92%	91%	91%	92%	92%	91%	91%	92%	200
0.3	92%	90%	90%	91%	92%	92%	91%	92%	91%	200
0.1	92%	90%	90%	91%	91%	90%	91%	91%	91%	300
0.2	92%	91%	90%	92%	92%	92%	91%	92%	90%	300
0.3	92%	91%	89%	91%	92%	90%	92%	91%	91%	300
$P_m \uparrow$	0.7	0.8	0.9	0.7	0.8	0.9	0.7	0.8	0.9	$\leftarrow P_c$

3.5. Results of Optimized Fuzzy System

In this section, results of optimized fuzzy systems, including the diagram of convergence of GA and optimized parameters regarding MFs, are presented. Figure 3 depicts the cost value of the best population with the minimum cost at 300 iterations over Area 1 and Area 3. Figure 3 shows that 300 iterations are appropriate for converging GA in this research. Moreover, in order to illustrate the importance of GA in selecting parameters of the fuzzy system, changes of MFs of input "2" and input "3" in an experiment are presented in Figure 4. Based on Figure 4, it is easily observed that vast variations must be applied on MF parameters to achieve optimized results. Therefore, it seems that selecting these parameters by an expert is not an easy task.

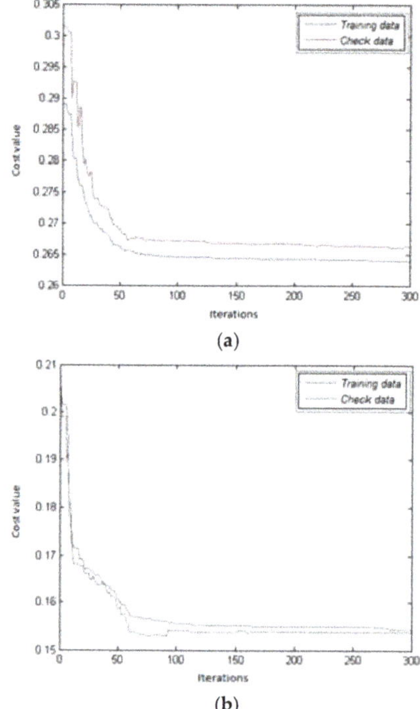

Figure 3. The diagram of convergence of GA over (**a**) Area 1, (**b**) Area 3.

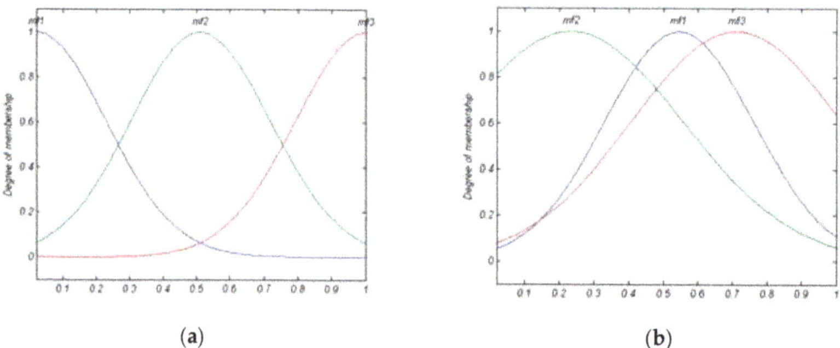

(**a**)   (**b**)

Figure 4. *Cont.*

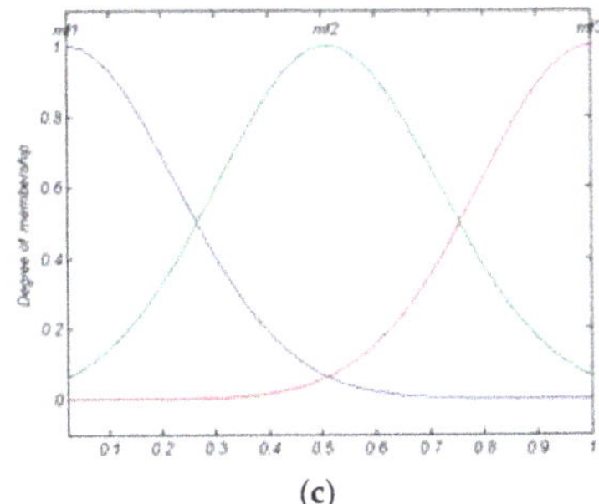

(c)

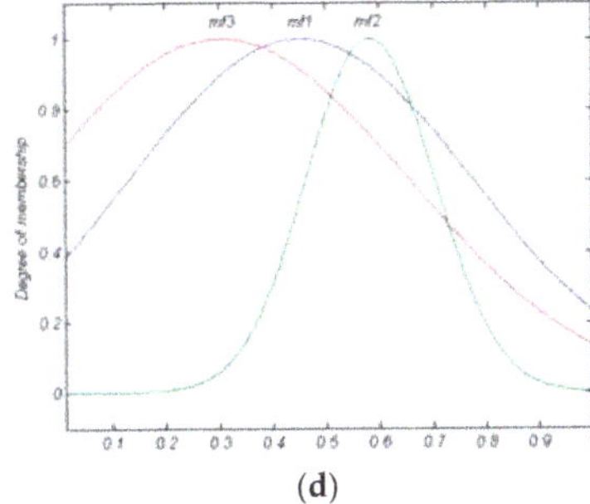

(d)

Figure 4. The presentation of preliminary MFs and optimized MFs in an experiment for input 2 and input 3: (**a**) preliminary MFs for input 2, (**b**) optimized MFs for input 2, (**c**) preliminary MFs for input 3, (**d**) optimized MFs for input 3.

3.6. Accuracy Assessment by Confusion Matrix

According to Section 3.5, to produce a confusion matrix, it is necessary to specify the number of classes and their definitions. In this study, we consider two damage classes including "damaged" and "undamaged" regarding each building. The "damaged" class includes very heavy damage (D4) and destruction (D5) whose definitions of D4 and D5 were presented in European Macroseismic Scale 1998 (EMS 98) [54]. To the best of our knowledge, substantial to heavy damage class (D3) which is related to cracks on the buildings facades would not be detected by our optical data used [54]. Therefore, "undamaged" class includes negligible to slight damage (D1) and D3. The confusion matrix of training, test and check samples as well as some statistical descriptors such as user and producer accuracies are presented to Table 9. Moreover, the range of overall accuracy of the generated damage maps with 90% confidence level is presented in Table 10.

3.7. Damage Map Resulting

In this subsection, final building damage maps regarding Area 1, Area 2, and Area 3 extracted from the proposed method are presented. Figure 5 shows the building damage maps of the mentioned areas.

Table 9. Confusion matrix of training, check, and test samples over Area 1, Area 2, and Area 3.

		Area 1				Area 2				Area 3			
		undamaged	damaged	User acc. (%)	Producer acc. (%)	undamaged	damaged	User acc. (%)	Producer acc. (%)	undamaged	damaged	User acc. (%)	Producer acc. (%)
Test samples	undamaged	153	40	79	79	444	195	77	69	20	9	87	69
	damaged	40	96	70	70	129	215	52	63	3	122	93	98
Check samples	undamaged	51	11	72	82	97	45	76	68	10	7	71	59
	damaged	20	42	79	68	31	51	53	62	4	97	93	96
Training samples	undamaged	142	34	76	81	310	126	77	71	21	4	84	84
	damaged	45	79	70	60	92	172	58	65	4	167	98	98

Table 10. Overall accuracy of the proposed method obtained on Area 1, Area 2, and Area 3.

	Area 1 (with 90% Confidence Level)	Area 2 (with 90% Confidence Level)	Area 3 (with 90% Confidence Level)
Overall accuracy (%)	76.88 ± 1.22	65.43 ± 0.29	90.96 ± 0.15

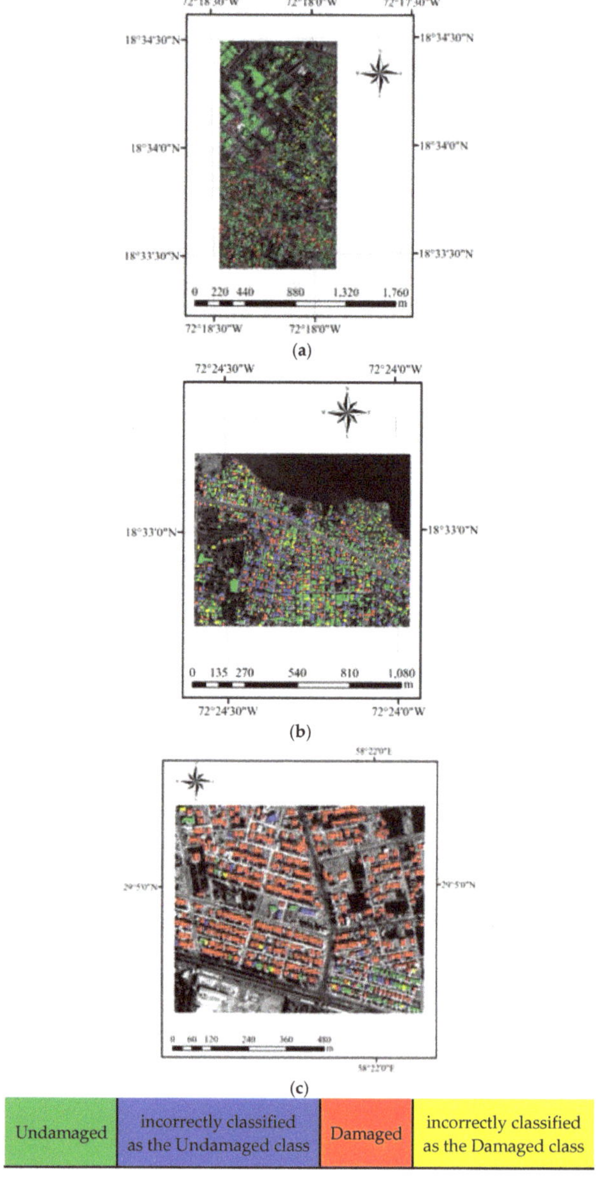

Figure 5. Building damage maps resulting from the proposed method on (**a**) Area 1, (**b**) Area 2, (**c**) Area 3.

4. Discussion

In this section, a comprehensive discussion about the obtained results is presented. Moreover, sources of error of the proposed method are specified. Furthermore, the accuracy and precision of Fuzzy-GA are compared with advanced machine learning techniques.

Based on the convergence diagram of GA presented to Figure 3, it is concluded that GA has been fully converged. Figure 3 shows that the selected parameters regarding GA were appropriate for providing a robust fuzzy system. Moreover, based on Figure 3, Fuzzy-GA succeeded in decreasing the cost value of training and check samples over the selected areas. It should be considered that the reduction of cost value directly improves the accuracy of the final results. These results show that the change of parameters of MFs in a fuzzy system is very important in obtaining an accurate result. Furthermore, based on Figure 4, in order to obtain more accurate results, vast variations should be performed on parameters of MFs (i.e., mean (m_i) and variance (σ_i) of Gaussian MF). Owing to employing an optimization algorithm (i.e., GA) in our study, the selection of the optimized parameters was carried out in a semi-automated way. However, it seems that adjusting these parameters in a manual way is not an easy task.

In this part, conclusions obtained from the sensitivity analysis stage are presented. Based on sensitivity analysis results (i.e., Tables 6–8), it was found that the selected parameters are appropriate for extracting an accurate damage map. Moreover, based on the outcomes, the accuracy of the final damage maps varies over a specific range. For example, overall accuracies of 90%, 91%, and 92% were achieved a lot over Area 3. In fact, in this study, it seems that the optimum answer is defined for a limited continuous range of variables. For this reason, increasing or decreasing the parameters of GA in the defined ranges does not follow a predictable procedure. Hence, based on these results, it appears that step-by-step sensitivity analysis methods presented to [2,13] are not proper for performing the sensitivity analysis in optimization-based decision making systems.

Based on the description presented in the previous paragraph on the range of optimum answers, it is better to present the overall accuracy of the obtained damaged maps in a $(a \pm b)\%$ form. In this form, a is the most probable overall accuracy and $[a - b, a + b]$ is the most probable range of overall accuracy. Based on Table 10, overall accuracies obtained on Area 1, Area 2, and Area 3 were equal to $76.88 \pm 1.22\%$, $65.43 \pm 0.29\%$ and $90.96 \pm 0.15\%$, respectively. Based on these results, the study area and its characteristics completely affect the accuracy of the damage detection method. For example, Area 2 is a complex urban region. In this area, different types of buildings, including buildings connected with trees, buildings with small area, and gabled roof buildings, are observed. It should be considered that a complex area could spread many uncertainties and errors over the final damage maps (we will present the source of errors in the following). For this reason, the overall accuracy of the proposed system over Area 2 was lower than the other areas. In general, based on our visual observations from high-spatial resolution satellite images, Area 1 and Area 2 are more complex than Area 3. For this reason, the accuracy of our proposed system over Area 3 was higher than Area 1 and Area 2.

There have been many damage detection methods implemented in the Haiti and Bam areas [4,13,55,56]. However, it is a difficult issue to present a fair and comprehensive judgment between the existing methods over study areas and our proposed method, because based on our experimental results, study area and its characteristics affect the accuracy of damage detection methods. Results achieved on Area 1, Area 2, and Area 3 completely confirm our claim. In this part, we compare our achieved results with the outcomes of [13], because Area 3 of our study is similar to the selected area of the mentioned paper. Janalipour and Mohammadzadeh (2016) employed a Nuero-fuzzy decision making system in order to create a relation between geometrical features obtained from post-event satellite image and the damage extent of buildings [13]. They reported an overall accuracy of 76% for detecting damaged buildings. While, in our study, the use of Fuzzy-GA and Haralick textural features resulted in an overall accuracy of $90.96 \pm 0.15\%$. Therefore, as a result, Fuzzy-GA and Haralick textural features outperformed Nuero-fuzzy and the geometrical features in detecting damaged buildings.

In this part, outcomes of Fuzzy-GA decision making system are compared with four advanced machine learning techniques, including bagging, boosting, random forests (RF) [57] and support vector machine (SVM), from viewpoints of accuracy and precision. It should be considered that results of the mentioned techniques and our decision making system were achieved with similar textural features. Hence, we can compare them with respect to each other. Based on [58], precision measures the degree of consistency among overall accuracies obtained in the selected areas (Tables 6–8) and accuracy shows the degree of closeness of measurements to true value. Based on the presented definitions and the form of presentation of overall accuracy (i.e., $(a \pm b)\%$), a and b can be used respectively as an accuracy measure and a precision creation. Based on Table 11, from the perspective of the accuracy, the Fuzzy-GA decision making system was more successful than bagging, boosting, and RF and SVM machine learning techniques. For example, over Area 3, overall accuracies of Fuzzy-GA, bagging, boosting, RF and SVM were respectively equal to 90.96%, 89.05%, 87.47%, 88.03% and 89.03%. To compare results of machine learning techniques with our proposed system from the viewpoint of precision, it should be considered that b is a function of precision. A machine learning technique with the lowest b is more precise than other ones. Because values of b for our proposed system are lower than the corresponding values for the advanced machine learning techniques, it appears that Fuzzy-GA decision making system is more precise than bagging, boosting, RF and SVM machine learning techniques.

Table 11. Overall accuracies of Fuzzy-GA, bagging, boosting, RF, and SVM machine learning techniques obtained on Area 1, Area 2, and Area 3.

	Area 1 (%)	Area 2 (%)	Area 3 (%)
Fuzzy-GA	76.88 ± 1.22	65.43 ± 0.29	90.96 ± 0.15
Bagging	74.5 ± 2.0	56.03 ± 1.2	89.05 ± 0.6
Boosting	71.33 ± 2.2	62.79 ± 2.9	87.47 ± 1.0
RF	73.07 ± 1.4	55.92 ± 1.4	88.03 ± 0.5
SVM with a radial basis function (RBF) kernel	72.53 ± 1.6	60.52 ± 1.2	89.03 ± 0.6

As mentioned, an urban area with a complex structure could spread many uncertainties and errors on outcomes. In this part, reasons of some misclassifications that occurred in the study areas are discussed. Table 12 depicts post-event optical image, variance feature, and damage map of nine miss-classified buildings. Building No. 1 is connected to a tall building. According to Table 12, parts from building No. 1 were covered with the shadow of the tall building. This is sufficient for texture extraction methods to produce high texture values in the roof of building No. 1. For this reason, this building was incorrectly classified as damaged class. The root of error of building No. 2 is similar to building No. 1 but with the difference that the overlapped shadow with this building resulted from a tall tree. This type error was frequently observed over Area 2 which is a complex urban area. Moreover, based on the Haiti building damage atlas, building No. 3 was classified as undamaged class by experts. While our visual interpretation showed that this is a damaged building. Hence, the proposed method correctly performed its task. Building No. 4 is an inclined damaged one. Based on the definition of inclined buildings [59] and Table 12, textural features are unable to detect these damage types. Therefore, the class of this building was incorrectly assigned as unchanged category. The use of LiDAR data may be an appropriate solution for detecting inclined damaged buildings.

Table 12. The presentation of pre-event image, variance feature, and damage map of nine mis-classified buildings.

No.	Post-Event Image	Variance Feature	Damage Map
1			
2			
3			
4			
5			
6			
7			
8			
9			

The high spectral variation of pixels of undamaged building roofs over satellite optical images is a critical issue for texture-based damage detection methods, because the behavior of texture features of these buildings is similar to damaged ones. This issue was the main reason for classifying building No. 5 as a damaged one. Building No. 6 is a gabled roof one, in which parts of the roof of this building were destroyed. The texture extraction method correctly identified the damaged parts. However, it seems that the Fuzzy-GA decision making system was the main reason for classifying this building as undamaged category incorrectly. The class of building No. 7 is undamaged. The spectral variation of pixels of building No. 7 is very high. For this reason, our proposed system classified building No. 7 as damaged category. Based on our interpretation, the texture extraction method and Fuzzy-GA decision making system are two sources of error for the misclassification of building No. 8. Finally, the damage extent of building No. 9 is totally pancaked. The proposed system was unsuitable in the detection of the damage class of this building, because the variation of the digital numbers of the building roof was not high enough for assigning it to the damaged class. The use of a normalized digital surface model may be an appropriate way for identifying totally pancaked damaged buildings.

5. Conclusions

In this study, a semi-automated Mamdani based fuzzy decision making system was developed in order to identify damaged buildings using their textural features. For improving the automation level of the Mamdani fuzzy system, a genetic algorithm was used to find its optimized parameters concerning membership functions. The proposed system was tested over two areas of the 2010 Haiti earthquake and one area of the 2003 Bam earthquake. Based on the concept of our proposed system, its automation level is higher than other existing decision making systems [19,27,28]. Moreover, based on the statistical descriptors and results of bagging, boosting, RF, and SVM machine learning techniques, it seems that Fuzzy-GA decision making system is more accurate and precise than the mentioned techniques for building damage detection. Furthermore, based on outcomes of the sensitivity analysis stage, it seems that results of our proposed system are robust enough for building damage detection. Based on the results of the sensitivity analysis stage, the overall accuracy of $76.88 \pm 1.22\%$, $65.43 \pm 0.29\%$ and $90.96 \pm 0.15\%$ was obtained on Area 1 (the Haiti earthquake), Area 2 (the Haiti earthquake), and Area 3 (the Bam earthquake), respectively. According to these results, the study area and its characteristics directly affect the accuracy achieved from the proposed method.

Based on the presented discussions, there are some major error sources: (1) high spectral variation of digital numbers over the roofs of undamaged buildings, (2) the shadow of tall buildings and trees connected with undamaged buildings, (3) inability of optical data in detecting inclined and pancaked damaged buildings.

As a future work, based on limitations of this study, it will be necessary to propose a damage detection method for integrating optical and LiDAR data. Moreover, due to the importance of the automation level of the damage detection method, it is important to present an automatic and accurate fuzzy decision making system in these future works. As another future work, the robustness of the Fuzzy-GA decision making system can be assessed over SAR data for detecting damaged areas. Moreover, the Fuzzy-GA decision making system can be adapted for applications that use hyperspectral bands. Because we are dealing with a high dimensional feature space, it is very important to select the appropriate bands using efficient feature selection methods such as [60,61]. Finally, owing to our proposed method which depends on a pre-event updated map, proposing an efficient building extraction method such as [62,63] for obtaining building footprints from pre-event optical images is very important to consider as a research study.

Acknowledgments: We would like to express our sincere thanks to the National Cartographic Center of Iran (NCC) who provided the pre-event map of BAM city. The author thanks DigitalGlobe for providing the pre- and post-event high spatial resolution images of the study area. The Haiti building damage atlas was produced by the United Nations' Institute for Training and Research (UNITAR) Operational Satellite Applications Programme (UNOSAT), the European Commission's Joint Research Centre (JRC), and the World Bank in support to the Post Disaster Needs Assessment (PDNA) process led by the Government of Haiti. The authors are grateful to the anonymous reviewers for their time and effort spent in reviewing the paper and for their constructive comments. We also like to thank Qi Wang, Nicolas H. Younan, and Carlos López-Martínez for the rapid peer reviewing process.

Author Contributions: Milad Janalipour proposed and implemented the method, also wrote the manuscript. Ali Mohammadzadeh supervised the research and also reviewed and revised the manuscript.

Conflicts of Interest: The authors declare no conflict of interest.

Abbreviations

The following abbreviations are used in this manuscript:

LiDAR	Light Detection and Ranging
SAR	Synthetic Aperture Radar
OA	Overall Accuracy
EMS 98	European Macroseismic Scale 1998
GA	Genetic Algorithm
Fuzzy-GA	Fuzzy Genetic Algorithm
RS	Remote Sensing
SVM	Support Vector Machine
RF	Rnadom Forests
OCSVM	One-Class Support Vector Machine
MF	Membership Function
MFIS	Mamdani Fuzzy Inference System

References

1. Dubois, D.; Lepage, R. Fast and efficient evaluation of building damage from very high resolution optical satellite images. *IEEE J. Sel. Top. Appl. Earth Obs. Remote Sens.* **2014**, *7*, 4167–4176. [CrossRef]
2. Janalipour, M.; Taleai, M. Building change detection after earthquake using multi-criteria decision analysis based on extracted information from high spatial resolution satellite images. *Int. J. Remote Sens.* **2017**, *38*, 82–99. [CrossRef]
3. Khoshelham, K.; Oude Elberink, S. Role of dimensionality reduction in segment-based classification of damaged building roofs in airborne laser scanning data. In Proceedings of the International Conference on Geographic Object Based Image Analysis, Rio de Janeiro, Brazil, 7–9 May 2012; pp. 372–377.
4. Dell'Acqua, F.; Gamba, P.; Polli, D.A. Earthquake damage assessment from post-event VHR radar data: From Sichuan, 2008 to Haiti, 2010. In Proceedings of the IEEE 2011 Joint Urban Remote Sensing Event, Munich, Germany, 11–13 April 2011; pp. 201–204.
5. Balz, T.; Liao, M. Building-damage detection using post-seismic high-resolution SAR satellite data. *Int. J. Remote Sens.* **2010**, *31*, 3369–3391. [CrossRef]
6. Matsuoka, M.; Yamazaki, F. Use of satellite SAR intensity imagery for detecting building areas damaged due to earthquakes. *Earthq. Spectra* **2004**, *20*, 975–994. [CrossRef]
7. Matsuoka, M.; Yamazaki, F. Building damage mapping of the 2003 bam, Iran, earthquake using ENVISAT/ASAR intensity imagery. *Earthq. Spectra* **2005**, *21*, 285–294. [CrossRef]
8. Matsuoka, M.; Yamazaki, F. Comparative analysis for detecting areas with building damage from several destructive earthquakes using satellite synthetic aperture radar images. *J. Appl. Remote Sens.* **2010**, *4*. [CrossRef]
9. Dell'Acqua, F.; Polli, D.A. Post-event only VHR radar satellite data for automated damage assessment. *Photogramm. Eng. Remote Sens.* **2011**, *77*, 1037–1043. [CrossRef]
10. Sirmacek, B.; Unsalan, C. Damaged building detection in aerial images using shadow information. In Proceedings of the IEEE 2009 4th International Conference on Recent Advances in Space Technologies, Istanbul, Turkey, 11–13 June 2009; pp. 249–252.
11. Geiß, C.; Pelizari, P.A.; Marconcini, M.; Sengara, W.; Edwards, M.; Lakes, T.; Taubenböck, H. Estimation of seismic building structural types using multi-sensor remote sensing and machine learning techniques. *ISPRS J. Photogramm. Remote Sens.* **2015**, *104*, 175–188. [CrossRef]

12. Geiß, C.; Taubenböck, H.; Tyagunov, S.; Tisch, A.; Post, J.; Lakes, T. Assessment of seismic building vulnerability from space. *Earthq. Spectra* **2014**, *30*, 1553–1583. [CrossRef]
13. Janalipour, M.; Mohammadzadeh, A. Building damage detection using object-based image analysis and anfis from high-resolution image (case study: Bam earthquake, Iran). *IEEE J. Sel. Top. Appl. Earth Obs. Remote Sens.* **2016**, *9*, 1937–1945. [CrossRef]
14. Eguchi, R.T.; Mansouri, B. Use of remote sensing technologies for building damage assessment after the 2003 Bam, Iran, earthquake—Preface to remote sensing papers. *Earthq. Spectra* **2005**, *21*, 207–212. [CrossRef]
15. Voigt, S.; Schneiderhan, T.; Twele, A.; Gähler, M.; Stein, E.; Mehl, H. Rapid damage assessment and situation mapping: Learning from the 2010 Haiti earthquake. *Photogramm. Eng. Remote Sens.* **2011**, *77*, 923–931. [CrossRef]
16. Lu, L.; Guo, H.; Corbane, C.; Pesaresi, M.; Ehrlich, D. Rapid damage assessment of buildings with VHR optical airborne images in Yushu earthquake. In Proceedings of the 2012 2nd International Conference on Remote Sensing, Environment and Transportation Engineering, Nanjing, China, 1–3 June 2012.
17. Tiede, D.; Lang, S.; Füreder, P.; Hölbling, D.; Hoffmann, C.; Zeil, P. Automated damage indication for rapid geospatial reporting. *Photogramm. Eng. Remote Sens.* **2011**, *77*, 933–942. [CrossRef]
18. Lemoine, G.; Corbane, C.; Louvrier, C.; Kauffmann, M. Intercomparison and validation of building damage assessments based on post-Haiti 2010 earthquake imagery using multi-source reference data. *Nat. Hazards Earth Syst. Sci. Discuss.* **2013**, *1*, 1445–1486. [CrossRef]
19. Haghighattalab, A.; JAVAD Valadan zoej, M.; Mohammadzadeh, A.; Taleai, M.; Kalantari, M. Détection de dommages et évaluation des dégâts du réseau routier après un séisme, en utilisant des images quickbird haute résolution. *XYZ J.* **2010**, *32*, 41–47.
20. Vu, T.T.; Matsuoka, M.; Yamazaki, F. Multilevel detection of damaged buildings from high-resolution optical satellite images. In Proceedings of the 2006 International Society for Optics and Photonics Asia-Pacific Remote Sensing Symposium, Goa, India, 13 November 2006.
21. Wang, X.; Li, P. Urban building collapse detection using very high resolution imagery and airborne Lidar data. *ISPRS Int. Arch. Photogramm. Remote Sens. Spat. Inf. Sci.* **2013**, *40*, 127–132. [CrossRef]
22. Chesnel, A.-L.; Binet, R.; Wald, L. Urban damage assessment using multimodal Quickbird images and ancillary data: The Bam and the Boumerdes earthquakes. In Proceedings of the 6th International Workshop on Remote Sensing for Disaster Management Applications, Pavia, Italy, 11–12 September 2008.
23. Miura, H.; Modorikawa, S.; Chen, S.H. Texture characteristics of high-resolution satellite images in damaged areas of the 2010 Haiti earthquake. In Proceedings of the 9th International Workshop on Remote Sensing for Disaster Response, Stanford, CA, USA, 15–16 September 2011.
24. Li, P.; Xu, H.; Guo, J. Urban building damage detection from very high resolution imagery using OCSVM and spatial features. *Int. J. Remote Sens.* **2010**, *31*, 3393–3409. [CrossRef]
25. Tian, J.; Nielsen, A.A.; Reinartz, P. Building damage assessment after the earthquake in Haiti using two post-event satellite stereo imagery and DSMS. *Int. J. Image Data Fusion* **2015**, *6*, 155–169. [CrossRef]
26. Polli, D.; Dell'Acqua, F.; Gamba, P.; Lisini, G. Earthquake damage assessment from post-event only radar satellite data. In Proceedings of the Eighth International Workshop on Remote Sensing for Disaster Response, Tokyo, Japan, 1 October 2010.
27. Samadzadegan, F.; Rastiveisi, H. Automatic detection and classification of damaged buildings, using high resolution satellite imagery and vector data. *ISPRS Int. Arch. Photogramm. Remote Sens. Spat. Inf. Sci.* **2008**, *37*, 415–420.
28. Mansouri, B.; Hamednia, Y. A soft computing method for damage mapping using VHR optical satellite imagery. *IEEE J. Sel. Top. Appl. Earth Obs. Remote Sens.* **2015**, *8*, 4935–4941. [CrossRef]
29. Chen, P.; Wu, J.; Liu, Y.; Wang, J. Extraction method for earthquake-collapsed building information based on high-resolution remote sensing. In Proceedings of the IOP Conference Series: Earth and Environmental Science, Beijing, China, 22–26 April 2014; p. 012096.
30. Ural, S.; Hussain, E.; Kim, K.; Fu, C.-S.; Shan, J. Building extraction and rubble mapping for city port-au-prince post-2010 earthquake with GeoEye-1 imagery and Lidar data. *Photogramm. Eng. Remote Sens.* **2011**, *77*, 1011–1023. [CrossRef]
31. Jang, J.-S.R.; Sun, C.-T.; Mizutani, E. Neuro-fuzzy and soft computing; a computational approach to learning and machine intelligence. *IEEE Trans. Autom. Control* **1997**, *42*, 1482–1484. [CrossRef]

32. Dong, L.; Shan, J. A comprehensive review of earthquake-induced building damage detection with remote sensing techniques. *ISPRS J. Photogramm. Remote Sens.* **2013**, *84*, 85–99. [CrossRef]

33. Dell'Acqua, F.; Gamba, P. Remote sensing and earthquake damage assessment: Experiences, limits, and perspectives. *IEEE Proc.* **2012**, *100*, 2876–2890. [CrossRef]

34. Geiß, C.; Taubenböck, H. Remote sensing contributing to assess earthquake risk: From a literature review towards a roadmap. *Nat. Hazards* **2013**, *68*, 7–48. [CrossRef]

35. Rehor, M.; Bähr, H.P.; Tarsha-Kurdi, F.; Landes, T.; Grussenmeyer, P. Contribution of two plane detection algorithms to recognition of intact and damaged buildings in Lidar data. *Photogramm. Rec.* **2008**, *23*, 441–456. [CrossRef]

36. Gamba, P.; Dell'Acqua, F.; Trianni, G. Rapid damage detection in the Bam area using multitemporal SAR and exploiting ancillary data. *IEEE Trans. Geosci. Remote Sens.* **2007**, *45*, 1582–1589. [CrossRef]

37. Dell'Acqua, F.; Lisini, G.; Gamba, P. Experiences in optical and SAR imagery analysis for damage assessment in the Wuhan, May 2008 Earthquake. *IEEE Int. Geosci. Remote Sens. Symp.* **2009**, *4*, 37–40.

38. Trianni, G.; Gamba, P. Fast damage mapping in case of earthquakes using multitemporal SAR data. *J. Real-Time Image Process.* **2009**, *4*, 195–203. [CrossRef]

39. Berman, L. Haiti Earthquake Data (Vectors). *Harv. Dataverse* **2015**. [CrossRef]

40. Pascale, D. *A Review of RGB Color Spaces*; Technical Report; The Babel Color Company: Montreal, QC, Canada, 2003.

41. Theodoridis, S.; Koutroumbas, K. Chapter 7–feature generation II. In *Pattern Recognition*; Academic Press: San Diego, CA, USA, 2009; pp. 411–479.

42. Haralick, R.M.; Shanmugam, K.; Dinstein, I.H. Textural features for image classification. *IEEE Trans. Syst. Man Cybern.* **1973**, *3*, 610–621. [CrossRef]

43. Mollalo, A.; Khodabandehloo, E. Zoonotic cutaneous leishmaniasis in northeastern Iran: A GIS-based spatio-temporal multi-criteria decision-making approach. *Epidemiol. Infect.* **2016**, *144*, 2217–2229. [CrossRef] [PubMed]

44. Zadeh, L.A. The role of fuzzy logic in the management of uncertainty in expert systems. *Fuzzy Sets Syst.* **1983**, *11*, 199–227. [CrossRef]

45. Homaifar, A.; McCormick, E. Simultaneous design of membership functions and rule sets for fuzzy controllers using genetic algorithms. *IEEE Trans. Fuzzy Syst.* **1995**, *3*, 129–139. [CrossRef]

46. Lee, M.A.; Takagi, H. Integrating design stage of fuzzy systems using genetic algorithms. In Proceedings of the 2nd IEEE International Conference on Fuzzy Systems, San Francisco, CA, USA, 18 March–1 April 1993; pp. 612–617.

47. Haupt, R.L.; Haupt, S.E. *Practical Genetic Algorithms*; Wiley-Interscience: Hoboken, NJ, USA, 2004.

48. Hwang, D.; Karimi, H.A.; Byun, D.W. Uncertainty analysis of environmental models within GIS environments. *Comput. Geosci.* **1998**, *24*, 119–130. [CrossRef]

49. Lodwick, W.A. Developing confidence limits on errors of suitability analyses in geographical information systems. *Accuracy Spat. Databases* **1989**, 69–80.

50. Tarantola, S.; Giglioli, N.; Jesinghaus, J.; Saltelli, A. Can global sensitivity analysis steer the implementation of models for environmental assessments and decision-making? *Stoch. Environ. Res. Risk Assess.* **2002**, *16*, 63–76. [CrossRef]

51. Iooss, B.; Lemaître, P. A review on global sensitivity analysis methods. In *Uncertainty Management in Simulation-Optimization of Complex Systems*; Springer: New York, NY, USA, 2015; pp. 101–122.

52. Srinivas, C.; Reddy, B.R.; Ramji, K.; Naveen, R. Sensitivity analysis to determine the parameters of genetic algorithm for machine layout. *Procedia Mater. Sci.* **2014**, *6*, 866–876. [CrossRef]

53. Roeva, O.; Fidanova, S.; Paprzycki, M. Influence of the population size on the genetic algorithm performance in case of cultivation process modelling. In Proceedings of the 2013 Federated Conference on Computer Science and Information Systems, Krakow, Poland, 8–11 September 2013; pp. 371–376.

54. Grünthal, G. *European Macroseismic Scale 1998*; European Seismological Commission, Subcommission on Engineering Seismology, Working Group Macroseismic Scales: Luxembourg, 1998.

55. Labiak, R.C.; Van Aardt, J.A.; Bespalov, D.; Eychner, D.; Wirch, E.; Bischof, H.-P. Automated method for detection and quantification of building damage and debris using post-disaster Lidar data. *Proc. SPIE* **2011**. [CrossRef]

56. Pham, T.-T.-H.; Apparicio, P.; Gomez, C.; Weber, C.; Mathon, D. Towards a rapid automatic detection of building damage using remote sensing for disaster management: The 2010 Haiti earthquake. *Disaster Prev. Manag.* **2014**, *23*, 53–66. [CrossRef]
57. Kuncheva, L.I. *Combining Pattern Classifiers: Methods and Algorithms*; John Wiley & Sons: Hoboken, NJ, USA, 2004.
58. Wolf, P.R.; Ghilani, C.D. *Adjustment Computations: Statistics and Least Squares in Surveying and GIS*; Wiley-Interscience: Hoboken, NJ, USA, 1997.
59. Schweier, C.; Markus, M. Classification of collapsed buildings for fast damage and loss assessment. *Bull. Earthq. Eng.* **2006**, *4*, 177–192. [CrossRef]
60. Yuan, Y.; Lin, J.; Wang, Q. Dual-clustering-based hyperspectral band selection by contextual analysis. *IEEE Trans. Geosci. Remote Sens.* **2016**, *54*, 1431–1445. [CrossRef]
61. Yuan, Y.; Zhu, G.; Wang, Q. Hyperspectral band selection by multitask sparsity pursuit. *IEEE Trans. Geosci. Remote Sens.* **2015**, *53*, 631–644. [CrossRef]
62. Sirmacek, B.; Unsalan, C. Urban-area and building detection using sift keypoints and graph theory. *IEEE Trans. Geosci. Remote Sens.* **2009**, *47*, 1156–1167. [CrossRef]
63. Sirmacek, B.; Unsalan, C. Building detection from aerial images using invariant color features and shadow information. In Proceedings of the 23rd International Symposium on Computer and Information Sciences, Istanbul, Turkey, 27–29 October 2008; pp. 1–5.

MDPI
St. Alban-Anlage 66
4052 Basel
Switzerland
Tel. +41 61 683 77 34
Fax +41 61 302 89 18
www.mdpi.com

Remote Sensing Editorial Office
E-mail: remotesensing@mdpi.com
www.mdpi.com/journal/remotesensing

9 783038 976844